Emanuel Feuermann

Emanuel Feuermann

Annette Morreau

Yale University Press
New Haven and London

For information about this and other Yale University Press publications, please contact:
U.S. Office: sales.press@yale.edu   www.yalebooks.com
Europe Office: sales@yaleup.co.uk   www.yaleup.co.uk

Set in Minion by Northern Phototypesetting Co. Ltd, Bolton, Lancs
Printed in Great Britain by Biddles Ltd, Guildford and King's Lynn

Library of Congress Cataloging-in-Publication Data

Morreau, Annette.
   Emanuel Feuermann / Annette Morreau.
      p. cm.
Includes bibliographical references (p.   ) and index.
Discography: p.
   ISBN 0–300–09684–4 (cloth)
      1. Feuermann, Emanuel, 1902–1942. 2. Violoncellists—Biography.
I. Title.
   ML418.F49 M66 2002
   787.4′092—dc21   2002002004

A catalogue record for this book is available from the British Library

10   9   8   7   6   5   4   3   2   1

To the memory of my mother
Beryl Scawen Blunt (1911–1987)

*Even if music and some of its great performers are still a mystery to me, the possibilities and probabilities in doing the most impossible and most improbable things on a cello or any other instrument never will surprise me.**

Emanuel Feuermann

*Emanuel Feuermann MS, 'My dear friend', p.2.

Contents

Preface and Acknowledgements

I place him as the most important figure for 20th-century cello playing because he was the one who proceeded to carry cello playing as such to a higher level. If he had lived longer he would literally have taken the place of Casals.

János Starker*

The subtlety of phrasing which is so unobtrusive and so uniquely shapes the music of which he was very, very conscious in every detail. Yet when you hear a performance everything falls into place and you never have the feeling that anything is studied. It is the complete equipment in the service of the artistic purpose as it should be.

George Szell†

A talent like Feuermann's comes around once in a hundred years.

Jascha Heifetz‡

He became for me the greatest cellist of all time because I did hear Casals at his best. He had everything in the world, but he never reached the musicianship of Emanuel Feuermann. And this is a declaration.

Artur Rubinstein°

* Janos Starker interview with the author, April 1994, Manchester.
† George Szell interview with Monica Feuermann, 1967.
‡ George Neikrug interview with the author, April 1994, Concord, MA.
° Artur Rubinstein interview with Monica Feuermann, 1966.

It is a paradox of modern life that despite means to conserve everything, memories are so short. To cellists, Emanuel Feuermann remains a legend; but more widely his name is virtually unknown. And yet his death in America nearly 60 years ago was as shocking to the wider public as the tragic silencing through debilitating illness of Jacqueline du Pré. Like du Pré's, Feuermann's career came to an untimely end. At the age of 39 he died in New York, as a result of the failure of an operation for a trivial complaint. Death has claimed the young lives of many great musicians – Ginette Neveu, William Kapell and Guido Cantelli all died violently in air crashes; George Gershwin, Dinu Lipatti and Emanuel Feuermann died as a result of illness and medical negligence.

The story of Emanuel Feuermann is not an unfamiliar one: a prodigy from humble Jewish origins who through his uncommon talent crossed boundaries of wealth and class. Less familiar is the track he took: many great cellists at the beginning of their careers were obliged to play in cafés or orchestras, but Feuermann, at the age of 16, became a professor at one of Germany's most prestigious conservatories. By the time of his tragically premature death 23 years later, he had revolutionized cello playing.

Like all prodigies, Feuermann enjoyed no normal childhood. Born in 1902, in some real sense he remained always young, for his main European colleagues – Arturo Toscanini (b.1867), Bruno Walter (b.1876), Artur Schnabel (b.1882), Bronisław Huberman (b.1882) and Otto Klemperer (b.1885) – were a generation or more older. As were most of the cellists active during his time, all of them born in the 19th century: Pablo Casals (1876–1973), Paul Grümmer (1879–1965), Arnold Földesy (1882–1940), Guilhermina Suggia (1888–1950), Felix Salmond (1888–1952), Maurice Maréchal (1892–1964), Beatrice Harrison (1892–1965), Gaspar Cassadó (1897–1966) and Enrico Mainardi (1897–1976).

Pablo Casals's contribution to the modernizing of cello technique is unarguable. We are fortunate today in having available recordings of the same works by both Casals and Feuermann. Feuermann was very much younger than Casals and on this ground alone it may be inequitable to compare the playing of these two artists. Feuermann, however, had the technique of a virtuoso who never had to struggle even if he died before any final maturing could take place. His recorded performances from the 1930s and early 1940s come as a revelation, a testament to what might have been. To those who know Feuermann's playing, it would seem some ghastly aberration that an artist of this calibre can so quickly be forgotten; many cellists and string players revere his name above all others. But in an age where even the name Heifetz produces a blank stare among young violinists, what hope for a cellist (whose instrument was never as popular as that of a violinist) who died during the Second World War?

Feuermann kept no official diary. Copious personal letters surviving from his tours form something of a diary, but their contents are mainly of a personal nature, and correspondence with professional colleagues remains relatively slight. However, his own quite extensive writings about cello playing and general aspects of music are invaluable – probably intended for publication in his lifetime, the bulk nevertheless remained unpublished. Time and two world wars have destroyed much. Those who knew Feuermann are now elderly, with necessarily dimmed memories; facts are not easily checked. And as in most families, antagonisms remain to colour the story. Little writing exists about Feuermann; a single biography was published in 1979 by Seymour Itzkoff. There is little secondary material and primary source material is hard to find.

I have tried to let Feuermann tell his own story through his letters. In his own colourful and often unusual language, they convey his thoughts and actions more accurately than I could ever guess. Reviews, as well as conveying contemporary opinion, add interesting historical colour, while interviews with family, colleagues, students and contemporaries help to bind the various strands.

The book is divided into two sections: life and legacy. The first section covers chronologically the duration of his life from 1902 to 1942. Recordings are noted but generally not discussed in order to preserve the flow of the chronology. The second section, the legacy, considers Feuermann's writings and his students' views on his performing, his teaching and on being taught. It also considers in greater detail his recordings.

My own interest in Feuermann came about somewhat unexpectedly. I trained as a musicologist and cellist – my mother was a professional viola player, a member of the Macnaghten String Quartet – but gave up playing when a year at the University of Indiana, Bloomington, in the 1960s convinced me that a career as a cellist was unlikely. Nevertheless, a certain ground was laid. Thirty years later I was asked to review Pearl's newly issued series *History of the Cello on Record* for *BBC Music Magazine*. Feuermann was one of the 70 or so featured cellists; I believed that I had never heard such great playing. The redoubtable Keith Harvey, cellist and collector extraordinary, had supplied the precious 78s to Pearl for transcription to CD. On meeting him, I suggested we make some radio programmes, and two sets emerged: a seven-part series of 15-minute programmes for the BBC World Service based on the Pearl CDs (broadcast in 1993) and a four-part series of two-hour programmes for BBC Radio 3 (broadcast in 1994 and 1996). This latter series was devoted solely to Feuermann.

In the course of the research, I read Itzkoff's book to discover that Feuermann at the age of 16 became professor of cello at the Cologne Conservatory. I also discovered that he was looked after, or taken in, by a family called Reifenberg. The name rang a dim bell; were they not relatives of mine? My memory served me right. When I met Feuermann's widow, Eva (née Reifenberg), she gave me copies of his letters including one written on the headed notepaper of my grandmother, Alice Morreau, which contained a postscript written by my grandmother, whose handwriting I recognized.

The writing of my book was not triggered by the family connection, though knowledge of it has been both helpful and bizarre. I was born after Feuermann's death but cousins of mine remain cousins-by-marriage of his and I am enormously grateful for the help, guidance and encouragement that so many various cousins have given.

Coincidences. What are we to make of them? A chance meeting at a London art gallery led to the daughter (resident in Israel) of Feuermann's first love, Lily (Hofmann, née Mayer). Daniela Cohn-Hofmann had kept not only quantities of Feuermann's letters to her mother but also the land in Ascona on which the original house (now replaced by a new one) that Feuermann so frequently visited once stood.

Feuermann's mother tongue was German. The occasional Yiddish and English words crop up and towards the end of his life he began to write in English. I am enormously indebted to many translators, but the principal ones are Daniela Cohn-Hofmann and Hede Stadlen. Where Feuermann writes in English, the quoted material is in italics.

Books of this nature can only be collaborative affairs; they depend greatly on the generosity of individuals for their time and on organizations for their money. The chief sources of financial support for which I am deeply grateful are: The Society of Authors; the Hinrichsen Foundation; the Leverhulme Trust; the Ludwig Sievers Stiftung; the Juneberry Trust; and the Bunting Fellowship Program from the Mary Ingraham Bunting Institute of Radcliffe College, Cambridge, MA. Among the many individuals who have guided me over several years, there are two without whose help this book could not have been written: Feuermann's widow, Eva Feuermann Lehnsen, and Feuermann's sister, Sophie Feuermann Brown [Braun]. And there are five people without whose help the book would not have been written: Keith Harvey, Daniela Cohn-Hofmann, Hede Stadlen, Jon Samuels and Milard Irion.

In attempting to list all the individuals and institutions to whom I am deeply indebted, I fear that some may inadvertently have slipped my net. To them I can only offer my sincerest apologies.

Of members of Feuermann's family I would like most sincerely to thank the following: Katya Andy (Aschaffenburg), Meta Cordy, Bea Parry (née Reifenberg), Kurt Reifenberg (deceased), Eva Nizan, Marvin Hughes, Marika

Hughes, Werner Vorster, Marianne Pentmann, Harold Hönigsberg, Maurice Zimbler, Robin Firman, Michael and Christopher Freudenberg, Frank Law and Françoise Weinmann.

Of Feuermann's students, colleagues and admirers, I would like to thank the following: George Neikrug, Marian Davies, Shirley Trepel, Bernard Greenhouse, Mosa Havivi, George Sopkin, Zara Nelsova, Suzette Forgues Halasz, David Soyer, Bernard Richards (deceased), Leon Barzin (deceased), Albert Hirsch, Edmund Kurtz, William Pleeth (deceased), Carl F. Flesch, Eleanor Saidenberg (deceased), Elinor Lipper, Wolfgang (Z'ev) Steinberg, Daniela Cohn-Hofmann, Peter Emanuel Gradenwitz, Erich Toeplitz, Lady Barbirolli, Charles Beare, Peter Diamand (deceased), Max Salpeter, Seymour Itzkoff, Janos Starker, Yo Yo Ma, Laurence Lesser, Aldo Parisot, Jack Pfeiffer (deceased), Witico Adler, Wolfgang Stresemann (deceased) and Seiji Osawa, who all willingly succumbed to the tape recorder.

I am indebted to Lotte Klemperer, Wolfgang Boettcher, Peter Mann, Albrecht Dümling, Dr Hans Mayer (deceased), Mauricio Kagel, Thomas Bösche, Elmar Weingarten, Hans-Joachim Leetz, Karlheinz Weber, Sylvana Sentov, Raimund Trenkler, Harvey Sachs, Walfredo Toscanini, David Geringas, Steven Isserlis, Ralph Kirshbaum, Guy Fallot, Martha Babcock, Miklos Perenyi, Leonid Gorokhov, Dr Leo Morgenstein, Saul Jarcho, Barbara Rosenkrantz, Paul Olefsky, Tsuyoshi Tsutsumi, Christopher Nozawa, Sumio Okahashi, Yoshio Iwama, Anne Harvard, Peter Hawley, Raphael Wallfisch, Galina Solodchin, John Underwood, Julian Futter, John Lucas, Norman Lebrecht, Debbie Stones, Joanna Kelly, John Willett, Christopher Fifield, Rebecca Walsh, Rob Cowan, Tully Potter, Maeve Auer, Humphrey Burton, Jason Osborn, Woijciech Michniewski, Yan Pascal Tortelier, M.A. de Valmalète, Michael Rainer, Andrew Hill, Ed Smith, Judith Salpeter, Ronald Wilford, Gary Stucka, Dorothy Crawford, Ellen Harris, Lewis Lockwood, Reinhold Brinkmann, Mark Obert-Thorn, Frank Mortimer, Jacques Français, René Morel, Harriet Feinberg, Steven Beller, Ruchama Marton, Tzvi Avni, Leo Birnbaum, Teddy Birnberg, Shumuel Hacohen, Terry King, Selma Gokcen, David Spelz, Jeffrey Solow, Blair Chotzinoff, Anne 'Cookie' Grossman, Jesse Levy, Avner Offer, Carmit Gai and David S. Josephson for supplying valuable information and leads.

I am also grateful for all the help given by the following archivists and archives: Österreichische National Bibliothek; Wienerkonzerthausgesellschaft Archive; Dr Otto Biba, archive director, Gesellschaft der Musikfreunde; Dr Lynne Heller, Hochschule für Musik und Darstellende Kunst, Vienna; Françoise Granges, Bibliothèque Nationale de France; Dr Kleinertz, Historisches Archiv der Stadt Köln; Dr Giselher Schubert, Paul Hindemith

Institute, Frankfurt; Akademie der Künste, Berlin; Die Deutsche Bibliothek, Frankfurt; Deutsches Musikarchiv, Berlin; Dietmar Schenk, Berlin Hochschule der Künste; Helge Grünwald, Berlin Philharmonic Orchestra Archive; Jurgen Wetzel, Landesarchiv Berlin; Musikinstrumenten Museum, Berlin; Dr Hell, Staatsbibliothek Preussicher Kulturbesitz, Berlin; Claudius Böhm, Leipzig Gewandhausarchiv; Leipzig Universitätsbibliothek der Karl-Marx-Universität; Christiane Schafferhans, Deutsches Rundfunkarchiv, Frankfurt am Main; Herman Weiss, Institute für Zeitgeschichte, Munich. Ephraim Mittelman, Israel Philharmonic Orchestra Archive; Erit Schönhorn, The Felicija Blumental Music Center and Library, Tel Aviv; Prof. Jehoash Hirshberg, Department of Musicology, Hebrew University, Jerusalem; Gila Flam, director of music department, Hebrew University, Jerusalem; Lazlo Somfai, Institute of Musicology, Bartok Archive, Budapest; Mercedes Guarro, Fundació Pau Casals, Barcelona; Anna Pia Maissen, Stadtarchiv Zürich; Trygve Nordwall, Tonhalle Orchester Zürich; Johan Giskes, Concertgebouw Archives; Frits Zwart, Haags Gemeentemuseum; Don McCormick, curator Rogers & Hammerstein Archives of Recorded Sound, New York Public Library for the Performing Arts, Lincoln Center; Linda Fairtile, New York Public Library for the Performing Arts, Lincoln Center; John Newsome, head of music division, Library of Congress; Virginia Danielson and Robert Dennis, Eda Kuhn Loeb Music Library, Harvard University; Ernst Toch Archive, UCLA Music Library; Edwin A. Fleisher Collection of Orchestral Music, Free Library of Philadelphia; Richard Boursy, Yale University Music Library; Institute for Jewish Research, New York; New York Academy of Medicine; Bridget P. Carr, Boston Symphony Archive; Carol S. Jacobs, Archive of the Cleveland Orchestra; JoAnne E. Barry, Philadelphia Orchestra Archive; Brenda Nelson-Strauss, Rosenthal Archives, Chicago Symphony Orchestra; Barbara Haws, New York Philharmonic Archive; Teri A. McKibben, Cincinnati Orchestra Archive; Gayle M. Morton, Indianapolis Symphony Orchestra Archive; Steve Lacoste, Los Angeles Philharmonic Archive; Joel F. Reid Jr., Pittsburgh Symphony Archive; Larry Rohe, San Francisco Symphony Archive; Richard S. Warren, Toronto Symphony Orchestra Archive; Ruth Edge, EMI Music Archives; British Library: Hugh Cobbe, Sandra Tuppin, Steve Cork, Tim Day (National Sound Archive), John Rattigan (Newspaper Library); and Neil Somerville, BBC Written Archives, Caversham.

In addition, my sincere gratitude to translators Daniela Cohn-Hofmann, Monica Bloxham, Anita Lasker, Brigitte Loesser, Elgin Ronayne, Christoph Niedermayer, Becky Smith and Takash Koto; to Heini Schneebeli for painstakingly making negatives of original Feuermann photos; to my Radcliffe College research assistants Jennifer Lee, Cathy Bauer and Trica Manoni; and to many colleagues at the Bunting Institute of Radcliffe College, Harvard University; Quincy House, Harvard University; and St Cross College, Oxford University; to Robert Baldock and his colleagues at Yale University Press; to John Cruft for so painstakingly reading the proofs. And lastly to my friends, who kept up my spirits and provided distractions during so long a period of time: Ursula Oppens, Sandy Solomon, Maria Bremmers, Dave King, Sue Lubbock, Jackie and Patrick Morreau, Paul Driver and Neill Aitkenhead.

Abbreviations

AWmk   Archive of the Hochschule für Musik und Darstellende Kunst, Vienna.
Bhm   Archive of the Hochschule der Künste Berlin, Bundesallee.
DC-H   Daniela Cohn-Hofmann archive
EF   Emanuel Feuermann
ET   Ernst Toch Archive, UCLA Music Library
FA   Feuermann papers belonging to Eva Feuermann Lehnsen
HA   Huberman Archive, Felicija Blumental Music Centre and Library, Tel Aviv
HI   Paul Hindemith Institute, Frankfurt
IPO   Israel Philharmonic Orchestra Archive
KfdK   *Kampfbund für deutscher Kultur* (Combat League for German Culture)
LEu   Leipzig Universitätsbibliotek der Karl-Marx-Universität
N   Eva Nizan archive
N&A   Emanuel Feuermann, 'Notes and some Anecdotes about Feuermann written by himself'
NOA   National Orchestral Association
NYp   New York Public Library at Lincoln Center, Library and Museum of Performing Arts
OAI   Organisation Artistique Internationale, Paris
SE   Schnabel Estate

Illustrations

Plates

Figures

Unless otherwise acknowledged, illustrations are from the Feuermann papers in the possession of Eva Feuermann Lehnsen [FA].

Chapter 1
The Beginning
1902–17

Emanuel Feuermann was born on 22 November 1902 in the town of Kolomea in Galicia, eastern Europe. Kolomea (or Kolomyja), situated roughly 300 km south east of L'vov, has suffered a chequered history: in 1902 it was part of the Austro-Hungarian empire; after World War I, in 1918, the whole of Galicia was claimed by Poland; today Kolomea is situated just inside the border of Ukraine. In 1900, 'It was an enclave for very poor, very miserable Jewish people',[1] with a population of just over 34,000, of which approximately half were Jewish.

Feuermann's parents, Meier Feuermann and Rachel Hönigsberg, were married in 1897 and had five children: Gusta (b.1898), Sigmund (b.1900), Emanuel (b.1902), Rosa (b.1904) and Sophie (b.1908). They were 'stettl' Jews. A *Geburtszeugnis*, a printed form filled out by hand, gives the name of 'Emanuel' to a child born on 22 November 1902 who was circumcised on 29 November 1902, but this document is dated 23 June 1912, nearly ten years after Feuermann's birth. Sophie Feuermann maintains that her brother did not acquire the name Emanuel 'until after he became famous'.[2] Throughout his life Feuermann was known to his friends and family as 'Munio', a name derived not from 'Emanuel' but from 'Mendel', the name of Rachel Feuermann's father. Just six weeks before Feuermann was born, his mother's father, Mendel Hönigsberg, had died. The custom in families of religious Jews was to name a baby after a recently deceased relative. Sophie maintains that Mendel was the name given to the child. We have her word alone to support this; no documentary evidence survives to prove it.

Like many great performers, Feuermann was born into an intensely musical family. His father was the 'Klezmer of Kolomea', and his mother also came from a musical family – the six children of her brother Schmuel Hersh Hönigsberg all became musicians. The Hönigsberg Orchestra, a light music orchestra, was well enough established for Columbia to record it commercially.[3] Within the family there was intermarriage: Adolf, Schmuel's eldest boy, married Feuermann's sister Rosa. At the insistence of Toscanini, he became principal trumpet of the Palestine Symphony Orchestra. Two of Meier Feuermann's five children – Sigmund and Emanuel – were widely acclaimed as child prodigies. Sophie, the youngest child, became not only an accomplished pianist but also one of Emanuel Feuermann's favourite accompanists. In the words of Sophie, their father Meier Feuermann was principally a cellist but in effect a jack of all trades. He taught most instruments with the exception of the piano – few people in the impoverished circles of the ghetto Jews of Kolomea owned pianos. She maintains that he never really knew what he was teaching.[4] This was no impediment, however.

Meier Feuermann seems to have been an exuberant wheeler-dealer. Sophie tells how he fiddled tickets for his two boys by trying to pay half instead of full fares on the tram. The age limit was ten. When the conductor challenged him, Meier pronounced, undaunted: 'You want to tell me how old my boys are? This one is nine and a half and the other is going to be ten'. No doubt this was a useful characteristic for a man faced with bringing up five children on very slim pickings.

As the family was so poor, Meier was obliged to teach from early morning until late at night. According to Sophie, the two boys, Sigmund and Emanuel, were woken as early as five in the morning and Sigmund would be given a violin lesson while Emanuel watched. The children had no toys, but when Meier disappeared, off came the pegs of their violins, through the scrolls went the strings, and at a stroke violins became little toy carts with which they raced around – like normal children.

There was little doubt, however, that Sigmund was far from normal. At the age of three and a half he had shown unusual aptitude for the violin and Meier had begun to teach him. Meier's attention became obsessively centred on his son's abilities. At five and a half years old, Sigmund performed the Mendelssohn Violin Concerto with full orchestra in the city of Lemberg (L'vov).[5] It was not long before Meier decided that a child of such gift needed special tuition. The violin pedagogue, Otakar Ševčík (1852–1934) had recently been appointed to teach at the Vienna Akademie für Musik und Darstellende Kunst, and so it was to Vienna that Meier and the family, or part of the family, moved in 1909.

No address is listed in Vienna for Meier (sometimes known as Max) Feuermann in 1909, so it seems likely that he stayed with friends or relatives. A Simon Feuermann is listed as living in the 16th district at Hippgasse, moving in 1910 to Koppstrasse, also in the 16th district. It is only in 1912 that an independent address is given for Max Feuermann, Musiker, Obere Augartnerstrasse in Leopoldstadt, the 2nd district.[6] Although this area of Vienna was associated with poorer, lower-class Jews, the apartment faced the green spaces of the Augarten.

In 1909 Ševčík began a masterclass at the Vienna Akademie with the aim of '*Advancing players of the violin of both sexes, who show outstanding musical talent and have achieved an advance level of technical ability . . . to the highest level of technical perfection*'. It is said that Sigmund enrolled in this class and that Emanuel went with him to these lessons.[7] From an early age Sigmund's practising would have been in Emanuel's ear, and under Ševčík's guidance this practice would have been intensive: he required between eight and ten hours daily of his students. But if Feuermann did attend his brother's lessons in 1909/10, it was not at Ševčík's masterclass; Sigmund is not listed in the *Jahresbericht*.[8] Puzzlingly, however, Sigmund is listed as enrolling for the 1916/17 masterclass (which included Erica Morini and Walter Schneiderhan), but according to the 'Schüler Index' for 1917 he attended no sessions.[9]

The lifelong importance to Feuermann of hearing at a young age his brother's violin playing cannot be stressed too highly. At the age of seven, Feuermann would have been deeply susceptible to Ševčík's teaching, absorbing, perhaps intimidated by, the rigorous approach and exacting standards demanded. But by the age of 14 it would have been an entirely different matter. Besides, in 1916 both brothers were launched on concert careers. The discrepancy in the dates of Sigmund's lessons with Ševčík is critical. Would the academy have accepted so young a child into the masterclass in 1909? Could Sigmund have met the entrance requirements? Although there was no statutory age limit, the entrance exam would have been stiff even for a gifted eight year old: students were obliged to play a Bach sonata, a Paganini study, a Classical concerto or concerto movement, and a modern concerto or concerto movement, all by heart. However, Sophie Feuermann insists that Sigmund attended the 1909 masterclass, proved, she says, by the existence of a class photograph. Her word is all we have, for, as she poignantly puts it, 'Hitler has it.'[10] Since Sigmund was engaged in a busy concert career in 1916, the only possible explanation is that in 1909 Ševčík taught him privately and that it was to these lessons that Feuermann was taken.

Sigmund's 1916/17 appearance in the academy ledgers nevertheless remains odd. He took an entrance exam (apparently his first at the academy) for the

1916/17 masterclass on 7 March 1917, was excused from attending lectures on violin literature on 21 March and announced his departure on 6 August. He received no marks for the summer semester of 1917 and is not mentioned in the annual report, which normally included students who had left during the year. On the other hand, an application from Sigmund for permission to give concerts, a stipulation of the school, is noted. If Sigmund enrolled merely to obtain an official record of study in Vienna, it was neither granted nor withheld.[11]

In 1909 Emanuel Feuermann began to have cello lessons with his father. His hands were now large enough to begin. Significantly, this coincides with the time Sigmund began private lessons with Ševčík. One of Meier's young pupil's had left his cello at the house overnight and Feuermann had tried it. Immediately drawn to it, he begged his father to get him an instrument. Up to this time Feuermann is said to have fooled around with Sigmund's violin, playing it between his knees like a cello.[12] An early photograph shows Feuermann fingering a cello the same height as himself, no doubt his father's instrument (see Plate 1). The provenance of Feuermann's first cello is not clear. Sophie maintains that he was given a ⅞-size cello that was half French, half Italian, 'the best instrument Munio ever had'.[13] A cello of this size would be large for a seven year old, in effect a small full-size instrument; however, an instrument that does appear to have been Feuermann's first cello has come to light, and it is in fact ½-size. This instrument, probably Italian, is of exceptional quality with a sound as large as that of a full-size instrument. It may be a late violoncello piccolo.[14] If this was Feuermann's cello, how could the Feuermann family have afforded it?[15]

With the move to Vienna, Meier Feuermann needed a job. His chutzpah and *joie de vivre*, qualities Emanuel was to inherit, came to the fore. As Sophie Feuermann recalls:

> There was an opening in what you would call the Volksoper. He knew he would never get it. So on the morning when he had the audition he said 'Sigmund, pack your violin and come.' My mother said 'You have the audition, you can't take the child.' He went to the audition, the man opened the door and when he saw the child he said 'you can't have the child in here.' He pushed Sigmund in and said 'unpack your violin and play!' He played. My father never unpacked his cello and he got the position![16]

It seems likely that it was Ševčík who noticed Emanuel's gift, urging that the boy should be taught by someone other than his father, and it was probably through Ševčík that a *mäzen* (sponsor) appeared. Wilhelm Kux, a Czech Jew and wealthy banker living in Vienna, was well known for his patronage of gifted musicians, in particular string players (Sigmund Feuermann and Erica Morini were also sponsored by him). He owned a fine collection of stringed instruments, at least one of which was loaned to Emanuel and another to Sigmund.[17] Kux supported not only the children's basic needs but provided valuable advice. Kux, who never married, came to regard Emanuel as a surrogate son. Throughout his life Feuermann kept in touch with Kux, reporting his progress to him, but most of these letters are lost. Kux lived to a great age, dying in Chur, Switzerland, at the age of 102.

After Meier Feuermann, Emanuel's first teacher was the cellist Anton Walter, who later became a member of the distinguished Rosé Quartet.[18] Whether it was Ševčík or Kux who recommended him is not clear, but only months after beginning lessons with his father Feuermann began to study with Walter. Little more than anecdotal tales remain about Walter's teaching, but the relationship seems to have been a good one. Evidence of Feuermann's early confidence is suggested by a story in which Feuermann is reported to have said to Walter that he played an adagio movement too fast. In a letter from Walter to Meier Feuermann, which reported that Emanuel had played a work with only five notes out of tune, Emanuel added in his child's handwriting: 'No. There were many more than that.'[19]

As a child prodigy, Sigmund Feuermann's early concerts were extraordinary and invitations to play came pouring in. In February 1912 the periodical *Die Musik* reviewed a concert from London in November 1911 with the Philharmonic Society conducted by Sir Charles Stanford: 'The 10-year-old violinist Sigmund Feuermann caused a sensation with the Brahms Concerto that was fully justified; one rarely hears the work performed so perfectly by adults.'[20] It so happens that another violinist wunderkind of the same age was also causing a sensation: Jascha Heifetz. Sigmund Feuermann and Heifetz's debuts in Vienna and Berlin interestingly intertwine. Sigmund made his Vienna debut in 1910, Heifetz in 1914.[21] Sigmund's debut in Berlin took place in early 1912, Heifetz's in September 1912. In the light of Emanuel's later involvement with Heifetz, one wonders whether there was any mutual awareness at this time. By November 1912 comments on Sigmund's playing were already less kind.

> A young violinist, Sigmund Feuermann, attempted to deceive the public by his lack of years. Technically he succeeded very well because what he played was clean and secure; but with regard to interpretation and spirituality the childishness showed itself everywhere. Beethoven's 'Kreutzer' Sonata! Why drag an immature child, who has learnt so much in spite of his youth and has worked so assiduously, onto the stage before he is ready? Who must bear responsibility?[22]

It is said, somewhat in contradiction, that initially Feuermann was not seriously interested in the cello. He regarded it more as a plaything, something with which he could compete with Sigmund. It is also said that a concert in Vienna given by Casals changed his attitude completely.[23] But which concert was this? Feuermann's biographer, Seymour Itzkoff, points vaguely to a concert in 'late 1912 or 1913' in the large hall of the Musikverein, in which Casals played Boccherini's Concerto in B♭ and Haydn's Concerto in D.[24] Margaret Campbell suggests that Feuermann heard Casals's Viennese debut in 1912, also in Boccherini and Haydn.[25] (Casals's Viennese debut actually took place in January 1910, when he played a concerto by Emanuel Móor.) Casals performed frequently in Vienna and frequently played the Haydn. But at this time he never played a programme that included the Boccherini and Haydn concertos together.[26]

Feuermann would have had ample opportunity to hear Casals in all the standard repertoire of the time – Brahms's Double Concerto, both Saint-Saëns concertos, and the d'Albert, Schumann and Dvořák concertos – and also in less standard works; for example, the Móor Concerto for solo cello and Móor's Concerto for two cellos, which Casals performed with Guilhermina Suggia on 11 December 1911. He could also have heard Casals play Bach's unaccompanied suites; as was the custom, a solo work was often included in an orchestral programme: between January 1910 and November 1913 Casals played Bach's G major, C major and D major suites in Vienna. If it is not possible to determine exactly the Casals concerts that Feuermann heard at this time, the breadth of programming combined with the talent of the greatest living cellist would, doubtless, have made a very strong impression on a very musical child.

Feuermann's own debut is said to have occurred at around this time, although precise details are uncertain. Much incorrect information has been published and Feuermann himself contributes to the uncertainty. *'His first concert was in Vienna in Febr. 1914 at the age of 11'* is what Feuermann 'wrote' in his own *'Notes and some Anecdotes about Feuermann'*, a seven-page typed document with the words 'written by himself' handwritten in his wife's hand. This undated document is puzzling. It is written in the third person, in simple English, and has many grammatical mistakes. That Feuermann wrote all of it seems unlikely, since towards the end of it there is the sentence: 'two weeks later, May 25, 1942, he passed away.' The last sentence, however, suggests a clue: 'I am enclosing a tribute to his memory which was written by the Cellist, Joseph Schuster, at the time, I think, first cellist of the New York Philharmonic. It speaks for itself.' A tribute to Feuermann by Joseph Schuster published on his death is not this seven-page document. A possible explanation is that Feuermann put some notes and anecdotes together at some time, and Eva Feuermann, on his death, forwarded them to those concerned as the basis for an obituary. Whatever the explanation, of greater concern is the general vagueness of the document with regard to specific dates in his youth, suggesting that it was written long after his early days, and indeed from memory.

His sister Sophie maintains that Feuermann's recital debut took place when he was nine, which suggests some time between November 1911 and November 1912. Sophie herself would have been three or four years old, so her knowledge about such a concert can only have come from her family. Seymour Itzkoff wrote: 'It was decided that the inaugural [*sic*] would be only a modest affair in a small hall in Leopoldstadt.'²⁷ Such a concert might have taken place; Leopold-stadt at the time was known for its small halls often attached to restaurants. Such a gathering would have involved family and friends. No documentary evidence, however, has come to light. Hearsay from Sophie records that Munio had a serious memory lapse at his first recital, which caused Meier to rush on stage with the music. (Sophie maintains that Emanuel never possessed a photographic memory whereas Sigmund did.) According to Feuermann's own words about his 'first concert':

> *The greatest critics of the time 'pre-world-war 1' attended the concert. [Julius] Korngold and [Max] Kalbeck praise [sic] him as the most unusual Cellotalent. The morning after the debut, friends came to the house to congratulate the parents and they wanted to see the 'prodigy'. They found him in front of the house on the street, playing soldiers with the boys of the neighbourhood.*²⁸

It seems unlikely that Korngold and Kalbeck would have attended a recital in Leopoldstadt, and so here Feuermann must have been referring to a concert held elsewhere.

A more likely candidate for a debut is a concert that took place on 28 February 1914 in the large hall of the Musikverein announced in the series Die Jugend für die Jugend as 'Ausserordentliches Jugendkonzert', in other words, an exceptional concert. Feuermann took part with Sigmund, Maria Kogan (piano), Trude Zerner (piano) and the 'Chor der Kinder-Singschule' of Professor Hans Wagner. Feuermann played a concerto in D major by Tartini with piano accompaniment – Otto Schulhof, a regular accompanist of Casals, was the pianist. But this concert does not appear to have been reviewed by Korngold or Kalbeck.

A 'J.K' attended a recital by Feuermann on Saturday 21 March 1914 in the small hall of the Musikverein, billed as a concert by the ten and a half-year-old 'cellovirtuosen'. (A customary liberty had been taken with his age. He was not ten and a half years old but eleven and a half.) The pianist was again Otto Schulhof, who was frequently to accompany both Feuermann children. From the tone of

Konzert-Direktion Gutmann (Hugo Knepler).

Samstag, den 21. März 1914, abends halb 8 Uhr

im Kleinen Musikvereins-Saale:

KONZERT

Emanuel Feuermann

Mitwirkend: **Otto Schulhof** (Klavier).

PROGRAMM:

Brahms	Sonate E-moll, op. 38 für Cello und Klavier. Allegro non troppo. Allegretto quasi Menuetto. Allegro.
2. Saint-Saëns	Cellokonzert A-moll (in einem Satze).
3. Beethoven	Sieben Variationen über das Duett „Bei Männern welche Liebe fühlen" aus der Oper „Die Zauberflöte" von Mozart.
Tschaikowsky	Variationen über ein Rokokothema op. 33.

Klavier: **Bösendorfer.**

=== **Preis 20 Heller.** ===

the review, this concert was the first time 'J.K.' had come across the boy. Without doubt 'J.K.' was Julius Korngold, the distinguished critic who wrote for Austria's most influential paper *Neue Freie Presse* at this time. He was amazed:

> Again a little Feuermann. An even smaller and younger Feuermann, but not a smaller miracle, rather an even bigger one. Emanuel, the brother of the violinist Sigmund, has devoted himself to the cello; and at the age of ten, most recently educated by our excellent Viennese cellist, Walter, this little boy masters his instrument, which reaches over his head, like an adult artist and also very musically, a virtuoso talent. Technique, purity, as well as richness and warmth of the sound in the cantilena are quite extraordinary. Even more extraordinary, the phenomenal effortlessness and naturalness of the phrasing and the openness of musical feeling. Brahms's Sonata in E minor, Saint Saens's A minor Concerto, a Casals piece, after which the ten year old grasps and, wonderfully enough, is permitted to grasp, variations by Beethoven and Tchaikovsky ['Rococo'], the latter a technically demanding piece for virtuoso. All this the little boy masters, without leaving anything unwished for. Through an extraordinary talent, from the first to

the last note of every piece, he grabbed attention. An unexpectedly inspiring evening at the tail-end of the season, for which we hurry to give an immediate report, to recommend to the attention of readers the quite unbelievable talent of the little prodigy cellist.[29]

This seems to be Feuermann's official recital debut, a major solo recital, for up to this time he had been presented only in the context of other musicians. Before this March recital, it seems likely that he was gently introduced to the public without facing the glare, for instance, of a subscription audience.

Over the years, vagueness about the precise nature of Feuermann's debut remained. Press material issued by his managers in America, NBC Artists Service, for the 1940/41 season asserted: 'Feuermann has been playing publicly since he was eleven years old . . . He made his debut as guest artist with one of Europe's finest orchestras,— the Vienna Symphony, under Felix Weingartner. He was at that time eleven years old.' Feuermann did indeed perform in 1914 with Weingartner but, as stated by Itzkoff[30] and Campbell,[31] this performance did not take place in February 1914, nor did he play Haydn's Concerto in D major. Feuermann's first concert with Weingartner took place on 12 December

---

Konzert-Direktion GUTMANN (Hugo Knepler)

Unter dem Protektorat Ihrer kaiserl. und königl. Hoheit der Durchlauchtigsten Frau Erzherzogin Zita

Samstag, den 12. Dezember 1914, abends halb 8 Uhr

im Großen Musikvereins-Saale:

KONZERT

Zugunsten der Kriegshilfsaktion der „Wiener Freiwilligen Rettungsgesellschaft"

Ausführende: **Lucille Weingartner-Marcel,** Hofschauspielerin **Lili Marberg, Felix Weingartner, Sigmund Feuermann** (Violine), **Emanuel Feuermann** (Cello) und das **Wiener Tonkünstler-Orchester.**

PROGRAMM:

1. Mozart	Ouverture zur „Zauberflöte".	Das Orchester.
2. Hans Müller	Die verwandelte Welt.	Lili Marberg
3. Mozart	Arie des Cherubin aus „Die Hochzeit des Figaro".	
Schubert	Ständchen. (Instrumentiert von Felix Weingartner).	Lucille Weingartner-Marcel.
4. Brahms	Konzert op. 102 für Violine und Cello mit Orchester. Allegro. Andante. Vivace non troppo.	Sigmund und Emanuel Feuermann.
5. Schubert	Hymne an die Jungfrau.	
F. Weingartner	Im Moose. (Zum ersten Mal.) Ritterliche Werbung. Liebesfeier.	Lucille Weingartner-Marcel. Am Klavier: Felix Weingartner.
6. Dvořák	Zwei romantische Stücke für Violine und Klavier. Allegro moderato. Allegro maestoso.	
Paganini	La clochette.	Sigmund Feuermann. Am Klavier: Otto Schulhof.
7. Wagner	Vorspiel zu „Die Meistersinger von Nürnberg".	Das Orchester.

Klavier: **Bösendorfer.**

=== Preis 20 Heller ===

1914 in the large hall of the Musikverein. He and Sigmund took part in a
benefit concert to raise money for the voluntary ambulance service in Vienna
(Zugunsten der Kriegshilfsaktion der 'Wiener Freiwilligen Rettungsgesellschaft'). The First World War had begun that summer. This concert,
conducted by Weingartner, was with the Wiener Tonkünstler-Orchester. Also
taking part was the singer Lucille Weingartner-Marcel, Weingartner's third
wife. Feuermann and Sigmund played the Brahms Double Concerto. Next day
there was a review in the *Neue Freie Presse*:

> Sigmund and Emanuel Feuermann's performances always cause a small
> sensation, and tonight was no exception, as the tiny boys courageously
> tackled the Double Concerto for violin and cello by Brahms. They played
> this difficult piece with complete signs of spiritual penetration and with
> almost complete technical mastery – that is, as far as the strength of their
> fingers and arms would allow. The pronounced wish a year ago that the
> extraordinary talent of the boys may find a more understanding impresario
> seems to have been realized. The little firefighters have advanced artistically,
> they have good instruments at their disposal and they look well fed. We do
> not want to investigate which one of the two is better.[32]

It seems likely that this is the concert referred to by NBC Artists Service
although the later name 'Vienna Symphony' is used for the Wiener Tonkünstler-Orchester. The name 'Wiener Symphoniker' ('Vienna Symphony')
was adopted only in 1933.

Coincidentally, the Italian cellist Enrico Mainardi made his orchestral debut
in Vienna in the large hall of the Musikverein in an astonishing programme on
7 February 1914 with the Wiener Tonkünstler-Orchester. Mainardi, who was
five years older than Feuermann, played three concertos – Haydn D major,
Dvořák and Saint-Saëns A minor – as well as *Träumerei* for cello and orchestra
by Lio Hans.[33] Before the year was out, he had performed a further four times
in Vienna. Mainardi was to become a serious competitor.

So within a very short time there was not just one Feuermann wunderkind,
but two. Soon the two children, like the little Mozarts, were playing in concert
halls all over Europe, meeting kings and queens and receiving velvet suits with
lace collars (see Plate 2). Was this exploitation on Meier's part? Sophie
Feuermann would deny it: 'There was never any idea of exploitation. The
children were so gifted that everyone came to us. And I don't mean that in an
arrogant or conceited way.'[34]

The First World War may have hampered Meier's wider plans for his two
children, but between 1914 and 1917 Sigmund and Emanuel gave many concerts
together in Europe. Emanuel, in his own problematic 'Notes and Anecdotes'

wrote: '*World War 1 came and made it impossible for Emanuel to fulfil his contracts for America, England and Russia.*' Evidence of such plans does not survive. *Die Musik* in May and July 1914, however, notes concerts in Berlin and Halberstadt. In Halberstadt the two brothers played in one of their earliest performances of the Brahms Double Concerto, which was to become a party piece. 'To the first Schimmelburg concert, the 12-year-old Sigmund Feuermann, known from the previous year, brought his younger brother Emanuel. The Brahms Double Concerto created a justified sensation.'[35] Again, a slight adjustment of age: Emanuel would have been 11 years old, his brother 13.

In 1915, Feuermann appeared in January, February and March at the Konzerthaus in Vienna. He played twice with Sigmund and Otto Schulhof in a mixed programme with other soloists and as a trio in the Mendelssohn D minor and Schubert B♭ trios. In 1916 he again appeared at the Konzerthaus during the first three months. A concert on 29 January with Sigmund and Oskar Nedbal conducting the Wiener Tonkünstler-Orchester, was particularly remarkable. It consisted entirely of concertos – Feuermann played Haydn's D major Concerto and Sigmund the Brahms and Mendelssohn violin concertos. On 24 February he and Sigmund again played the Brahms Double with Nedbal

and the Tonkünstler-Orchester in the large hall of the Musikverein. It may have been at this concert that Sophie recalled the following incident:

> My mother was sitting on the left side and I was sitting with her and she always had a mirror so that I shouldn't fall asleep. All of a sudden my mother jumps up and says 'Oish!' The whole hall looked at her. Nedbal had thrown [hit] Sigmund's Guarneri . . . out of his hand; it was like paper. My mother jumped up. But he [Sigmund] grabbed it and played on.[36]

A 'Jugendkonzert' in April in the large hall of the Musikverein again presented a programme of concertos: Emanuel played the Haydn, Sigmund played the Viotti Concerto in A minor no.22, and Rudolf Serkin played Mendelssohn's G minor Piano Concerto. This appears to be the earliest incidence of Feuermann and Serkin playing together, a professional relationship that would last for years. There were more performances of the Brahms Double: with the Vienna Philharmonic conducted by Weingartner, and on 9 November in Leipzig with one of Europe's most prestigious orchestras, the Gewandhaus, conducted by Artur Nikisch. The latter seems to have been Feuermann's debut with the Leipzig orchestra. A review leaves little doubt of the sensation the two young boys created. But there is a salutary sting in the tail: 'The public appearance of children (one is about 12, the other about 16) should be forbidden in their own interests, however talented they are.'[37]

There was no bar mitzvah for either child, a highly significant omission for a Jewish family. The Feuermanns kept high holidays but it was not a Kosher household, suggesting that the family was observant rather than orthodox. According to Sophie Feuermann, the two boys' concert activities were so demanding that no time was available for the necessary preparation. Schooling too, in terms of traditional education, was largely incompatible with the touring activities of the two boys. Both attended Volkschule, but in 1912/13, Emanuel's first year at the Erzherzog Rainer Real Gymnasium, he received such appalling marks that his formal education came to an end.[38] Education, however, did not cease. As Sophie remembers, 'in our house there was always learning'.[39] A tutor, Professor Knepfelmacher, was engaged to teach the two boys at home when time permitted. Feuermann's wife was later to recall: 'He went to school a little bit in Leipzig but he was the most avid reader. As far as his own education is concerned he got it from life.'[40] Many recall his excellent understanding of business, his awareness of history, his uncanny ability to predict political fortunes, his fluency in many languages, and his penetrating intelligence.

Chapter 2

Prodigy

1917–23

As long as they are under the influence of teachers or their often profit-seeking parents, they are treated as machines.

Emanuel Feuermann

Feuermann's concert career was so active so quickly that the temptation to let it continue must have been tremendous; such is the dilemma posed by the prodigy. Feuermann, later in life, influenced no doubt by the circumstances of Sigmund, commented tellingly: 'I am even of the opinion that a prodigy is not always destined for music . . . Certainly, it is a fact that most prodigies do not develop into artists, but just when their own personality should make its appearance, they fail completely. . . . as long as they are under the influence of teachers or their often profit-seeking parents, they are treated as machines.'[1]

It was probably Wilhelm Kux who advised a halt to Feuermann's public performing. Feuermann's facility was beyond question, but careful guidance through the critical transition from prodigy to mature artist was needed. The choice of Julius Klengel as teacher was inspired. Klengel, born in 1859 into a musical family in Leipzig, had himself been a prodigy, but of more modest dimension. At the age of 15 he had joined the Gewandhaus Orchestra, becoming principal cellist at the age of 22. Klengel's technical facility was legendary. One of his last students was William Pleeth: 'He was known as the Paganini of the cello. To him it was the same as a fiddle running around. He must have had a phenomenal technique because even when I knew him – he died a few months after I left him – he could still get around. It was incredible.'[2]

Klengel was principal cellist of the Gewandhaus Orchestra when Feuermann made his debut in November 1916. He was also Royal Professor of Cello at the Leipzig Conservatory. The German school of cello-playing with Klengel in Leipzig and Hugo Becker in Berlin predominated at this time. It seems likely that Kux, an amateur cellist, influenced the choice of Klengel over Becker. Klengel was a gentle, kind man, 'a walking angel',[3] ideal for the teaching of a child. By contrast, Becker was more authoritarian, less pliable, and often criticized by his students for being pedantic. Klengel, who was also prolific as a composer, is principally remembered as the teacher of many of the greatest cellists of the twentieth century: Guilhermina Suggia, Paul Grümmer, Gregor Piatigorsky, Alfred Wallenstein, Joseph Schuster, Mischa Schneider, Benar Heifetz, Edmund Kurtz, William Pleeth and Feuermann.

Klengel was 58 when in 1917 Feuermann went to study with him. Feuermann was 14. Like Sigmund in Vienna, Emanuel was not enrolled officially at the Leipzig Conservatory – he was too young.[4] As he was leaving for Leipzig a well-wisher made a remark that Feuermann was to return to almost ten years later: 'As a small child I replied to a lady who said to me that I might well become a second Casals, "No, I hope to become a first Feuermann."'[5] At Kux's expense, evidently as a private student, Feuermann studied with Klengel at his house in Kaiser Wilhelmstrasse while living in a pension (perhaps the Hartung boarding-house where many of Klengel's students stayed, including Piatigorsky). Klengel's approach to teaching was to praise his students individually, encouraging a natural sense of competition and rivalry between them. As Piatigorsky recalled:

> He would remark, '[Mischa] Schneider's vibrato is marvellous.' Everyone would come to 'spy' on Schneider's vibrato. To Schneider he would say, 'Auber's trill is the best.' The students, though jealous, learned from each other. I marvelled at Klengel's art of teaching by really not teaching. At lessons one seldom heard suggestions or discourses on music from him. He let a student play a piece to the end and said 'Fine' or in a severe case, 'Watch your left arm, young man.'[6]

As William Pleeth recalled, perhaps Klengel's greatest gift was to allow his students to develop in their own way: 'You were you.'[7]

As we can hear from archive recordings, Klengel's own technique reflected the practice of his era with prominent slides, or *portamenti*. For several years after leaving Klengel's tuition Feuermann used slides in this old-fashioned way, and this can be heard on his early recordings. But as Feuermann was later to write, during these years with Klengel he was already experimenting with different fingerings so as to shape a phrase without drawing attention to the physical problems associated with shifting to another position. Klengel, however, believed that Feuermann had adopted different fingerings on account of his long fingers.

Klengel was an exceptionally well-rounded musician, his knowledge of the repertoire formidable. Any work his students chose, whether from the solo, chamber or symphonic repertoire, he could accompany from memory at the piano. As far back as 1880 he was teaching Bach's unaccompanied cello suites to his students.[8] Although no documentation has survived from Feuermann's period of study with Klengel, we can surmise that he must have been an ideal teacher for Feuermann. He would not have wanted to change Feuermann's precocious technique, but would have been able to open the child's eyes and ears to the widest possible repertoire. Throughout his career Feuermann was known, sometimes notoriously, for hardly practising. He had an extraordinary intuitive ability, but it would not be accurate to suggest he never worked for it. He later maintained that during his two years between 1917 and 1919 with Klengel he worked hard, for instance mastering all six Bach suites by heart in one week.[9] An example of Feuermann's astonishing gift was recalled by Klengel in conversation with Joseph Schuster. A new book of difficult studies had been put before Feuermann: 'Before he [Klengel] had the chance to point out the problems of one, Feuermann was playing away at sight with the greatest finish and ease. The whole book was run through in that manner in that one lesson.'[10]

The instrument Feuermann used while studying with Klengel was probably a Nicolo Amati on loan from Kux.[11] He would have outgrown his ½-size cello by this time, but the Amati must have presented quite a challenge. Nicolo Amati (1596–1684), son of Andrea Amati from Cremona, was one of the earliest makers of the instrument recognized today as a cello. Andrea's instruments were considerably larger than the standard modern cello and Nicolo's instruments could be even larger. Feuermann was not physically small but this instrument after the ½-size must have felt very different. It is a feature of Feuermann's cellos that they varied so greatly in size.

Ravages of war and time have claimed all correspondence between Feuermann and his immediate family. No first-hand evidence exists about those years in Leipzig and how he managed as a small boy on his own. Clearly as one of Europe's most important cultural centres, Leipzig must have had a profound influence on him, particularly as he was at such an impressionable age. At the same time, the seeds of separation from his family were sown, which in due course would lead to estrangement, in particular from his father. Feuermann's father, deeply immersed in the activities of Sigmund, seemed reluctant or unable to recognize that his second son was as talented as, indeed even more talented than, the older boy. There seems little doubt that from an early age Feuermann was wounded by his father's attitude towards him.

In July 1919, Friedrich Grützmacher, professor of cello at the Cologne Conservatory, died suddenly at the age of 54. The Cologne Conservatory was one of Germany's principal music conservatories. The position of professor of cello carried with it not only a teaching responsibility but membership of the Gürzenich Quartet and occasional duties as principal cellist of the city orchestra, the Gürzenich Orchestra. Grützmacher came from a long line of distinguished string players. His uncle was the Dresden Friedrich Grützmacher (1832–1903), infamous arranger of Boccherini's concertos and Bach's solo suites. Klengel, a close friend of Grützmacher, was contacted to recommend a candidate who might make an appropriate successor. The Cologne authorities, however, were astonished by Klengel's suggestion: they had not anticipated the recommendation of a 16-year-old boy. Klengel's views on Feuermann's talent were certain. The previous year he had written to Feuermann's sponsor, Kux: 'It is necessary that I reiterate, in all sincerity, that of all those who have ever been entrusted to my guardianship, there has never been such a talent as this gifted one, Munio.'[12] Appointing a 16-year-old boy, however, to so important a position at one of Germany's leading conservatories seemed to the authorities unthinkable. When further pressed by the Cologne Conservatory, Klengel merely insisted that it would be misleading even to suggest that there could be a second or third choice.[13] Feuermann was auditioned but not without incident: '*When he went to Cologne for an interview, he had to wait for a while in a teacher's room. A secretary saw the young boy there, and furiously told him that this was a room for the teachers and not for pupils.*' (see Plate 6)[14] Hermann Abendroth (1883–1956), chief conductor of the Gürzenich Orchestra and director of the Cologne Conservatory declared: 'the faculty [Board] has had a unique experience. It has witnessed in the playing of the young cellist, Emanuel Feuermann, abilities of unimaginable scope. He is truly a talent of the utmost rarity. In spite of his age we have agreed to appoint him to the faculty. Feuermann will be a brilliant jewel in our crown.'[15] Feuermann was offered the job. For legal reasons, or on account of his age, the title of professor was withheld. 'Officially he told everybody that he was 18, and there was a big "HelloH" when it was found out that he had just turned 17.'[16] In fact, when Feuermann was appointed he was still only 16 years old. In all but title, Feuermann went from student to professor in one bound.

Feuermann's position changed from the supported to the supporter: he was glad that he would now be able to send money to his parents.[17] But his appointment posed a dilemma; Feuermann had spent two years away from the family in Leipzig but he was still a child. In Leipzig, he had been in the company of fellow students, now he would be expected to act as a responsible 'professor'. Someone needed to look after him. Gusta, his elder sister, was the solution. She would accompany him to Cologne, acting as surrogate mother, chaperone and guide. Satisfactory cook and housekeeper she may have been, but it seems unlikely that Gusta, aged 21, having lived a secluded life with the family in Vienna, was more worldly than the widely travelled Munio.

As a musical centre in 1919 Cologne was outstanding. Otto Klemperer, then aged 32, was established at the opera house with the young William Steinberg, his assistant. The Gürzenich Orchestra, the city orchestra conducted by Hermann Abendroth, was also remarkable. Numbering 60 players, it played for the theatre and for the Cologne Concert Society. The relationship between the orchestra and the Cologne Conservatory was a close one; Abendroth was director of both. When larger forces were required, players from the Cologne Conservatory were brought in. Bram Eldering, professor of violin at the conservatory, was both leader of the Gürzenich Orchestra (he had previously led the Berlin Philharmonic, 1891–4) and leader of the Gürzenich Quartet. The orchestra's concert programming was largely conservative. New work was occasionally programmed by such composers as Lothar Windsperger, Franz Schreker, Rudolf Siegel, Franz Schmidt, Volkmar Andreae, Joseph Haas, Walter Braunfels and Otto Klemperer (his Mass in C). In 1926 Béla Bartók was soloist in his own piano concerto. Cologne's musical life was enlivened by competition between Abendroth and Klemperer. Beginning in 1919, Klemperer had secured the right to give a series of concerts at the opera house in direct competition with Abendroth at the Gürzenich concert hall. In addition to the two concert series and the opera, chamber music was prominently presented by the concerts of the Gürzenich Quartet.

A first priority for Feuermann was to find accommodation. Writing to Klengel soon after his arrival in Cologne, he described his searches: 'We only found a flat yesterday after having tried for two weeks and it is with relatives of a person I know. Several times I had gone to the office of the Stadtanzeiger (the local newspaper) at 7 o'clock in the morning without having found anything suitable.'[18] The rooms they found were with Joseph Steinberg and his wife, Emmy, who lived at Venloerstrasse 24, first floor on the Friesenplatz. It was a very large apartment where two rooms were rented out, frequently to musicians. Feuermann kept his rooms there for seven years, and at various times Sigmund and Sophie also lived there.

Joseph Steinberg was William Steinberg's uncle.[19] His son, a violinist, was studying at the Cologne Conservatory with Bram Eldering. Joseph was an agent of Reifenberg & Cie, one of Cologne's largest and best-known industrial concerns.

Feuermann's pupils, with one exception, were all considerably older than him, but an early letter to Klengel rings with confidence.

> In the conservatory I have already given a few lessons and I hear from my pupils (only 11) that I am very strict. The reason is that from the beginning I have made them change the position of both hands and I don't let a single mistake go by. One of them didn't want to do everything the way I wanted it, so I told him quite bluntly that if he wanted to study with me he would have to do <u>everything</u> that I told him, and he should consider once again whether he really wants to continue with me and give me an answer in the next lesson. Is that right?[20]

Perhaps this was youthful confidence and youthful inexperience. In any case it was very different from Klengel's approach, but Feuermann had had no experience as a teacher:

> *Most of them had just returned from the war and I began teaching them entirely according to my own ideas for I had never been at a conservatory. When I first began teaching, as I knew music from the platform only, I assumed as a matter of course that no one should study music who did not hope to become a concert artist. It is no wonder that I was soundly scolded by the board of directors of the Hochschule when they discovered that after I had heard all 16 [sic] of my cello students in auditions I had asked them: 'What is the reason for you playing cello?' I had never thought of orchestral music and other fields of endeavour.*[21]

And indeed, Feuermann himself never played as a regular orchestral member. Feuermann was immediately very active : 'With the quartet I have already been on a short tour to five cities (Iserlohn and surroundings). We have already become well adjusted to each other (Haydn, Schumann, Beethoven). On the 28th I am playing the Dvořák Concerto in the Gürzenich. Isn't that great?' After these engagements, as he reported to Klengel, he had little work for the next period and the reason for this was significant.

> I am not prepared to go low enough in my [financial] demands. I already have two private pupils, one of them is only just beginning. I have hopes for a few more [students] including an Englishman from the London Opera. If only everything wasn't so cursedly expensive, much more expensive than in Leipzig, then I would be even more satisfied than I am.

Feuermann, however, was well aware of how fortunate he was: 'What would I have done in Vienna? Here I have a position, lessons, engagements even if only a few, everything that my heart desires – everything only not enough money.

And to whom do I owe all that? Do you know? Shall I say it to you again?'[22] Aged 16, Feuermann was well aware of his financial worth and in a hurry to escape the poverty of his background.

A memorial concert to Friedrich Grützmacher was given by the Gürzenich Quartet on 21 October 1919. The programme included Schumann's A minor Quartet and Haydn's op.20 in C major. A review makes clear that the Gürzenich Quartet was fielding not just one new player, but two.

> Mozart's E♭ Divertimento for violin, viola and cello must have been chosen deliberately to show the two new members in an exposed manner. Apart from Herr Emanuel Feuermann who has taken the heritage of Grütz-macher, M. Joseph Schwarz, the longstanding member of the quartet, has been replaced by Hermann Zitzmann [a pupil of Bram Eldering]. Feuermann, whose acquaintance as a soloist we will make in the next Gürzenich concert, commands a sweet, subtle cantilena, the perfect musical equipment of a musician and a technique that is capable of dealing with all problems. Whether in the matter of the size of the tone, which seemed a little soft, he offered all that there is, we will only be able to judge on another occasion.[23]

That other occasion occurred a few days later on the 28 October, in the second concert of the 1919/20 Gürzenich Orchestra season. The 16-year-old Feuermann triumphed: 'The oh so terribly young Emanuel Feuermann, successor of the deceased Grützmacher, stepped on to the podium to play Dvořák's Concerto. The young Feuermann is a cellist endowed with genius who offered a perfectly mature effort and was, according to his merit, stormily celebrated.'[24] The ability of a child to transcend its youth in the profound communication of a musical work remains the mystery of the prodigy. Feuermann not only triumphed but became a celebrity:

> *One day, when he was on the way to the conservatory with his cello, a man started a conversation with him. Feuermann said that he was a pupil of the conservatory, whereupon the man praised the new teacher Feuermann of whom he had heard a great deal and he spoke of his own love of the cello. When Feuermann asked him whether he had ever heard someone play the cello really beautifully, he replied quite angrily: Young man I have heard great cellists when you were not even born. You go ahead and practise a great deal and try to be at least a good cellist.*[25]

Concerts of the Gürzenich Orchestra, a focal point of Cologne's musical life, usually took place fortnightly. The audience was on the whole middle-aged and well established, with most seats taken by subscribers. One pair of subscribers was Paul and Emma Reifenberg. Paul Reifenberg employed Joseph Steinberg with whom Feuermann was lodging. The Reifenbergs were friends of the conductor, Hermann Abendroth, and, overwhelmed by Feuermann's performance, they went round to the green room to offer congratulations and meet the young boy. This seems to have been the beginning for Feuermann of a pivotal relationship that was to influence him in innumerable ways for the rest of his life.

If the Reifenbergs had been overwhelmed by Feuermann, it is hard to imagine the impression the Reifenbergs must have made on him. Paul Reifenberg was an austere man, a textile merchant. The firm manufactured the fabric, with trimmings, for ladies' clothing, particularly evening dresses. Paul's father had founded the firm in the 19th century. Reifenberg & Cie had offices in Cologne, Annaberg, Berlin and Paris and was a well-known company with representatives in many countries of the world. 'They had no shops, just the factory in a very good location. The factory made the material – silks, satins, with pearls and other decorations added. You could buy it by the metre.'[26] A silk factory in Viersen, not far from Cologne, was also owned by the family. The Reifenbergs lived at 376 Alteburgerstrasse in the affluent Bayenthal area not far from the river, in one of the largest houses in Cologne. It had 32 rooms (see Plate 7). Paul Reifenberg had built it at the beginning of the century. Their lifestyle was that of the *haute bourgeoisie*, who at meal times would have many servants on hand. They were wealthy and known to be hospitable and very supportive of the arts. Paul, it is said, was less interested in classical music than his wife, preferring military music. His brother Hugo, who ran the Paris office, was the more musical, a violinist. Wolfgang Steinberg, grandson of Joseph, gave his view of the Reifenberg family:

> Like most educated Jewish families in Cologne, they were reticent. They were not showy. The showiness was inside their houses, not outside. They had beautiful paintings. In the garden they had objects by great sculptors. They had a library that even by today's standards would make many German intellectuals envious. But they were not ostentatious. That was too deep in the Jewish blood of that time. They were liberated, assimilated [. . .] They dressed like other businessmen, not differently, not better, although they could have, had they wanted to. They wanted to be the same, so they took special care to be the same.[27]

A glance at the guest book kept by the Reifenbergs suggests, however, that this family was far from 'the same'. Indeed, the guest book covering the period December 1917 to October 1932 reads like a who's who, with messages, fragments of music, pictures and signatures (often on a number of occasions) contributed by Reifenberg guests.[28] 'Everyone who had a name was pleased to be invited to the Reifenbergs. Everyone who had concerts stayed with them, sometimes remaining in Cologne for as long as a week. There were always musicians staying with them.' It is no wonder that the cellist Mischa Schneider auditioned for the Budapest String Quartet in the Reifenberg drawing room. Politicians were attracted to the house too: 'Conrad Adenauer was there constantly. He was a really close friend.'[29] Adenauer was mayor of Cologne at that time and as Paul Reifenberg played a major social role they met frequently. A cousin of the Reifenbergs, Katya Aschaffenburg,[30] who herself was a music student in Cologne, recalled that the Reifenbergs gave frequent house concerts. 'Whenever a quartet like the Rosé Quartet visited the town, they would stay at the Reifenbergs' and give a concert for them.' Furtwängler was a house guest too.

It is possible that Paul Reifenberg was already aware of the Feuermann family before Emanuel's remarkable debut. In 1912, at the home of his brother Hugo Reifenberg in Paris, Sigmund Feuermann had played for Casals.[31] Hugo was described by Sigmund in 1949 as 'tremendously rich and leading in the society of Paris, and France. Even if he was a great businessman, he played for his enjoyment sometimes chamber music and had also a Stradivarius violin

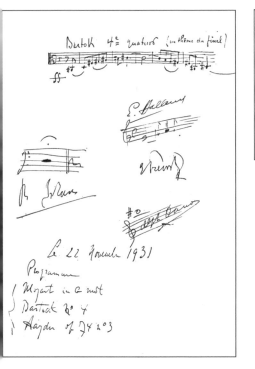

Bartók's fourth quartet (left) and Pablo Casals's inscription (above) in the Reifenberg visitors' book.

which Huberman planned to buy. Pablo Casals was a very good friend of Mr Reifenberg.'[32] Reifenberg owned not only one Stradivarius but a complete quartet of instruments. When Casals passed through Paris there were frequent chamber music sessions with Reifenberg, Jacques Thibaud, Casals and other friends.

The Feuermann family – poor, eastern ghetto Jews from Galicia – could not have contrasted more strongly with the Reifenbergs. Like the Feuermann family, the Reifenbergs had five children,[33] but, unlike the Feuermann children, all five Reifenbergs were baptized. In the matter of language, the two families were also very different. The Reifenbergs spoke flawless 'Hoch-Deutsch', but the German of the Feuermanns – new arrivals – was riddled with Yiddish expressions and intonation. Such language was unacceptable to the educated, assimilated Jew who did not want to be associated with lower-class Jews, and Feuermann was careful not to speak like that with the Reifenbergs; it would have been inappropriate.[34] He never denied his Jewishness nor his Galician origins, but he wanted to be accepted in the world of the assimilated Jew and that was not always easy for him.[35]

Many were overwhelmed by the activities of the young Feuermann. Katya Aschaffenburg's father, the distinguished neurologist Gustav Aschaffenburg, went to Cologne to hear a concert in which Eugen d'Albert was playing the Brahms B♭ Concerto. She waited up for him to hear how the concert had gone. When he came home, instead of talking about D'Albert, her father could only talk about the new solo cellist in the orchestra – a 16-year-old boy with the most gorgeous tone he had ever heard in his life. At the end of the second movement, d'Albert had been so moved by the cello solo that he had jumped up from the piano stool and embraced the child.

Wolfgang Steinberg was another eyewitness to Feuermann's early days in Cologne. He was 16 years younger than Feuermann: 'My grandmother usually called me "bubi" so when Munio came I was the "kleiner bubi" he was the "grosser bubi". At that time he was always there for a big joke. He fooled around with anyone and everyone. Sometimes we would have a competition in potato-pancake eating and of course, Munio usually won.'[36]

Feuermann had a lively and exuberant personality. His sense of humour – ironic, witty and playful – was a marked feature of his personality, but in its clever ambiguity it was often misunderstood. He did not tolerate fools and never tolerated pomposity: 'Munio was invited in Berlin to some big salon and the hostess kept talking about Prof. Feuermann from Vienna and Berlin etc. Finally Feuermann could stand it no longer and said in a loud voice "I am Prof. Feuermann but I am from Kolomea in Galicia".'[37] Not what his hostess had wanted to hear.

Feuermann's schedule was a heavy one. As well as teaching and his solo career, the Gürzenich Quartet gave regular concerts that often included new work requiring extensive rehearsal. There are anecdotal stories of Feuermann falling asleep during a performance and having to be kicked to wake up. Katya Aschaffenburg recalled, nevertheless, that young as he was, Feuermann kept his own end up. 'He was not shy. He was extroverted. It did him no harm that he was the youngest. He would give his opinion to Bram Eldering and the others that played with him. It was not easy for them!' (see Plate 8).[38] A charity concert in early February 1920 – in which Feuermann played the Haydn Concerto in D – caused one reviewer to remark: 'Feuermann brought new proof of his tremendous achievement', but also 'occasionally the temperament of this young virtuoso could have been less forward'.[39] But a few days later, Feuermann stepped in to replace an indisposed lady violinist. Dr Eugen Schmitz in an unnamed paper wrote: 'Emanuel Feuermann is one of the few cellists of genuine world reputation.' He was still only 17.

The 1920/1 season with the Gürzenich Quartet brought an entire cycle of Beethoven quartets, eight concerts in all, to mark the Beethoven anniversary. The extent of Feuermann's phenomenal gift can be seen from a handwritten summary of some striking reviews: 'Fabulous technique, and a refined musical sensibility, seldom encountered these days, in virtuoso playing in the classical style' (*Danziger Allgemeine Zeitung*, 11 October 1920); 'Out of this world' (*Casseler Allgemeine Zeitung*, 16 October 1920); 'Harmonics extraordinarily effortless, his cantilena soft but not flabby. Magic which only he can play and which everybody can recognize immediately' (*Kölner Zeitung*, 12 November 1920); 'Emanuel Feuermann plays with that natural virtuosity that cannot be learnt. With this technique one is not astonished by anything and one takes for granted his noble tone, with its absolute purity in the most fearsome positions and passages' (*Essener Allgemeine Zeitung*, 18 January 1921).

In February 1921 Feuermann and Gustav Havemann were soloists in the Brahms Double Concerto with the Berlin Philharmonic under Nikisch. Havemann, regarded as one of the most prominent German violinists of his generation, had been a pupil of Joseph Joachim and succeeded Adolf Busch at the Berlin Hochschule. He had been a guest at the Reifenberg house. Scarcely more than ten years later, he was to become one of the most active agents of the National Socialist Party. In 1921 the reviewer merely noted that 'the two masters made a persuasive case for the somewhat difficult work with such success that one forgot the brittleness of this music and honoured the artists by recalling them several times.'[40]

The leading concert agency in Berlin, the all-powerful Wolff & Sachs, now began to show interest. On 3 November 1920 Feuermann gave a recital in the Beethovensaal, under their auspices.[41] Wolff & Sachs represented and presented the greatest artists of the time – Schnabel, Casals, Elman, Heifetz, Nikisch, Bruno Walter, Klemperer and Furtwängler. In that same week of Feuermann's Berlin recital other Wolff & Sachs artists billed to give concerts included Edwin Fischer, Fritz Busch, Carl Flesch, Eugen d'Albert and the Klingler Quartet.[42]

Concert flyers and reviews reveal the repertoire that Feuermann was playing in these early years to 1921: Haydn's D major Concerto, Schumann's Cello Concerto, Dvořák's Cello Concerto, d'Albert's Cello Concerto, Tartini's Andante, Dvořák's Rondo, a Chopin nocturne, Brahms's F major Sonata and Tchaikovsky's 'Rococo' Variations. There were also the virtuoso salon works that Feuermann tossed off with such ease and which the public adored: Paganini's *I palpiti* (in Feuermann's own arrangement, no doubt fired up by competition with Sigmund, who played the original violin version) and David Popper's *Elfentanz*. Not four years earlier, when Feuermann went to study in Leipzig, Klengel had observed that his repertoire barely extended beyond Brahms's Double Concerto, and the piece certainly occurs more frequently than any other in his programmes. With Sigmund, Emanuel had a built-in partner, and the Brahms was a wonderful vehicle for the two of them. As early as 1921 Reger's unaccompanied Suite in G Major, a work written for Klengel in 1914, occurred in Feuermann's programmes. Klengel and Reger were colleagues in Leipzig, Reger being professor of composition at the university. Feuermann was also playing Bach's unaccompanied suites.

Feuermann established a phenomenal reputation very quickly, which can be measured by the invitation to make gramophone records. It must be remembered that the industry was in its infancy, the cello was not well suited to the new medium, and the cello as an instrument was by no means established as popular with the public.

The earliest recording of Feuermann to have come to light dates from 1921, scarcely five years after Casals had made his first recordings. Whereas Casals was 39 and in his prime, Feuermann was just 19.[43] These early recordings are of immense importance, since over a period of little more than five years the vast distance Feuermann travelled in terms of technique and musicianship can actually be heard. This development may simply have been a process of maturing; on the other hand, there may have been an external influence, for instance, perhaps another player who showed Feuermann another way. Or had there been a player in Feuermann's life who had held him to the routines of 'old-fashioned' playing, which by 1924 he was able to slough off? Bram Eldering, for instance. In Cologne, Feuermann was heavily committed to the Gürzenich Quartet. Eldering, the leader, a student of Hubay and Joachim, was in his late fifties. If Eldering used prominent slides, Feuermann, within the context of the string quartet, would have been obliged to follow. Contemporary reviews do not touch specifically on this matter, but the general amazement about Feuermann's ability suggests that his technique was new and very different from that expected of a cellist. A review in March 1922 of a performance of the Brahms Double Concerto with Eldering and Feuermann as soloists is tantalizingly unclear: 'Prof. Eldering, who was brought up in the Brahms tradition, and the young cellist, Emanuel Feuermann ... were excellent in their ensemble playing, although in the matter of tone they diverged in the cantabile passages.'[44] Might this suggest that there was a divergence of views in the cantabile passages relating to the use of slides? With Feuermann freed from a partner in a performance a month earlier of the Dvořák Concerto the reviewer remarked: 'in the creation of a musical line, Feuermann scarcely has a rival'.[45] In Richard Strauss's *Don Quixote* with the Berlin Philharmonic in September 1922 the *Allgemeine Muzik-Zeitung* mentioned the 'supple cantilena, played with such beauty right up to the highest of registers'. One wonders whether 'scooping' would have engendered 'such spirituality of playing encountered with very few representatives of this instrument'.[46]

The pianist and conductor George Szell, five years Feuermann's senior, might have been another influence. In November 1922 Feuermann gave a recital with him in Berlin. The programme included a Brahms sonata, an unaccompanied suite by Reger, Tchaikovsky, Dvořák and Sarasate. Could Szell, never a musician to favour schmaltz, have had some input into Feuermann's playing? Szell had first met Feuermann under unusual circumstances. He had just become Music Director of the Municipal Opera House in Düsseldorf. There was a fine music society devoted mainly to chamber music, and the two Feuermanns announced to the president of the society, who was responsible for planning the programmes, that Szell would be happy to participate in trio concerts with them. Needless to say, Szell had not been informed. When he arrived in Düsseldorf he saw posters and prospectuses for concerts in which he was supposed to appear. He was furious. His initial fury was directed at the president of the society, but when Szell met Feuermann he was so disarmed by his playing that from then on they remained close friends.[47]

Feuermann had the courage, the intelligence and the will to keep developing his playing throughout his life. In 1940 he wrote:

A teacher is not a lifeless thing, but a human being who has to grow and change himself, and he should not try to conceal that fact. .... I, for example, do not hesitate to play old recordings of mine with new ones for my students, to show

*how my playing has changed and developed. Not only do I feel unashamed to
let them see how differently, and to be frank, less well, I may have played a work
before; I do not mind opening their eyes, even at my own expense.*[48]

The music community in Cologne was close-knit and a call to Feuermann
to deputize in a concert would not have been unusual. More unusual was the
work: Schönberg's *Pierrot Lunaire*. At very short notice Feuermann took over
the cello part in a performance conducted by Klemperer on 12 May 1922; Marie
Gutheil-Schoder (one of the great Elektras) was soloist.[49]

The reviews for Feuermann's 1922/3 season reflect astonishment. Cello
playing like his was unknown:

> It is rare in a concert occupying a whole evening to encounter a famous
> cellist as the only soloist. That is caused by the peculiarity of the instrument
> that plays so vital a role in the orchestra and in chamber music. It lacks the
> fluency of the violin and a performance on the cello alone without accom-
> paniment even of a piano can easily seem heavy handed and tiring unless it
> is an exemplary master of the instrument who performs. Such a master is
> Emanuel Feuermann, who will soon be regarded as the best cellist of
> contemporary times.[50]

As well as four recitals in Berlin, Feuermann appeared twice with the Berlin
Philharmonic – in September 1922 playing *Don Quixote* with Volkmar Andreae
and in February 1923 playing the Haydn Concerto in D with Furtwängler,
Feuermann's first (and only) concert with this conductor. For a solo cellist to
perform twice within the same season was highly unusual. A review in the
Berliner Tageblatt of the Furtwängler concert compared his sound favourably
with that of Casals. It also noted that the cadenza of the first movement was a
technical masterpiece. Feuermann was to write a flamboyant cadenza for the
Haydn Concerto (which can be heard on his Columbia recording of 1935), but
at this time the cadenza was probably by Klengel, who had published an
edition based on an early printing of the original manuscript. Feuermann was
now so busy as a soloist that conflicts with his duties at the Cologne Conservatory were inevitable. He wrote to Klengel:

> Now listen and be amazed. I have given notice here for the autumn. I cannot
> stand this position. Apart from the fact that I have a disinclination
> amounting to a revulsion against this 'regular' position, it is in my opinion
> my moral duty to give notice. I have played only half (five) of the Gürzenich
> concerts, only some of my pupils had lessons, namely between Christmas
> and Easter, seven times. The quartet played chiefly with Hesse.[51] Where I
> shall go from here, whether I shall remain in Cologne I do not know. I have

Konzert-Direktion Hermann Wolff und Jules Sachs, Berlin W 9.

PHILHARMONIE

Montag, den 19..Februar 1923, abends 7½ Uhr pünktlich:

VIII. Philharmonisches Konzert

Dirigent: **Wilhelm Furtwängler**

Solist: **Emanuel Feuermann**

Vortragsfolge:

1. **Ouvertüre** zu „Das Käthchen
   von Heilbronn" . . . . *Hans Pfitzner*
2. **Violoncell-Konzert D-dur** . . . . . . *J. Haydn*
   Allegro moderato
   Adagio
   Finale
   (Vorgetragen von Emanuel Feuermann)
3. **Symphonie Nr. 4, c-moll** . . . . . *J. Brahms*
   Allegro non troppo
   Andante moderato
   Allegro giocoso
   Allegro energico e passionato

IX. Philharmonisches Konzert: Montag den 5. März 1923
Dirigent: **Wilhelm Furtwängler**
Solist: **Maurits van den Berg**
(Violine)
Auf dem PROGRAMM: Ouvertüre zu „Benvenuto Cellini" von Berlioz –
Symphonie Nr. 5, c-moll von Tschaïkowsky

X. Philharmonisches Konzert: Montag den 19. März 1923
Dirigent: **Wilhelm Furtwängler**
Auf dem PROGRAMM: Symphonie h-moll von Schubert – Symphonie
Nr. 5, c-moll von Beethoven – Brandenburgisches Konzert von Bach

played a great deal, partly with very great success. In the middle of April I'm going to London. Dir. Kux puts money at my disposal for a concert and a stay in London of several weeks. Have you got anyone there to whom you could give me a recommendation? I would be very grateful indeed. You would have to send it to me very quickly since I will be leaving very soon.[52]

Since Klengel had recommended Feuermann to Cologne, he was among the first to hear of his departure.

Chapter 3
Nomad
1923–8

Technical difficulties do not seem to exist for him.
Allgemeine Muzik-Zeitung (16 March 1923)

After less than four years, Feuermann wanted to free himself from his duties at
the Cologne Conservatory. With management from Wolff & Sachs, the
prospect of recording opportunities and the knowledge that his playing was
received 'partly with very great success',[1] Feuermann believed he could go it
alone. It says something of his courage and confidence, qualities that would
remain always in his playing. The notion of a solo cellist attracting large
crowds on a level with a singer, pianist or violinist was barely established.
Casals alone occupied this position with any confidence. And it was the period
of hyper-inflation in Germany – something to which Feuermann never refers.
However, a review in the *Allgemeine Musik-Zeitung* for a recital in Berlin on 6
March 1923, just four days after Feuermann had written to Klengel announcing
his departure, must have encouraged him: 'Technical difficulties do not seem
to exist for him. With amazing security he jumps the most difficult hurdles. At
the same time, there is musical blood in the veins of this young, God-gifted
artist.'[2]

Feuermann had written to Klengel that he would spend time in London and
indeed his first concert took place on 21 June 1923 at the Aeolian Hall. The
programme was designed to astonish: Boccherini's A major Sonata, Valentini's
E major Sonata, Bach's Sixth Suite, Saint-Saëns's Concerto in A minor,
Chopin's Nocturne in E♭ op.9 no.2 and Paganini's *I palpiti*, the last two works

```
AEOLIAN HALL                          THURSDAY   EVENING
NEW BOND STREET :: W.                 JUNE 21, 1923 at 8.15
```

EMANUEL FEUERMANN

PROGRAMME

1. (a) SONATA in A major   ....   L. BOCCHERINI
         Adagio
         Allegro moderato

   (b) SONATA in E major   ....   G. VALENTINI
         Largo—Allegro
         Gavotta—Adagio
         Vivace

2. SUITE, No. 6 in D major   ....   J. S. BACH
         Præludium—Allemande
         Courante—Sarabande
         Gavotte—Gigue

3. CONCERTO in A minor, Op. 33   ....   C. SAINT-SAËNS
         (In one movement)

4. (a) NOCTURNE, No. 2   ....   F. CHOPIN—FEUERMANN
   (b) I. PALPITI   ....   V. PAGANINI—FEUERMANN

At the Piano   ....   **SERGE KRISH**

BLÜTHNER GRAND PIANOFORTE

LIONEL POWELL & HOLT   Vail & Co., Ogle Street, W.1
5. Cork Street, London, W.1

arranged by Feuermann. A review in the *Daily Telegraph* is somewhat whimsical: 'To make old music the chief test of a recital – this is a new and a good notion. After all, no modern writer for the cello gives the player as good opportunities for the display of bowing as Valentini. As for elegance and distinction of style, surely Boccherini in this respect has never been surpassed.' But the unnamed reviewer had good ears: 'Mr Feuermann is a past master of bowing technique – he performs all the tricks of the virtuoso of the bow with unerring skill and with the ease of a violinist.' The review, however, is not without reservation: 'Strangely enough, as is the case of some modern violinists also experts in the art of bowing, this facility and dexterity goes hand in hand with a sweet but far from powerful tone.' This was not the first reference to a smallish sound and quite sharp similar comments were reserved for Feuermann's Bach: '[It] was in many ways a highly creditable performance, but we felt at times the need for a little more "body" in the tone, and one of its movements – the Allemande – was distinctly lacking in virility. Bach may mean various things to various men, but it will never do to treat him as a composer of "pretty" music.'[3] But Feuermann's concert did astonish sufficiently for him to make a re-appearance in London only four months later in two further recitals at the Aeolian Hall.[4]

Feuermann took leave of Cologne in a concert on 30 June 1923 at the Opera House conducted by Klemperer. He played the Dvořák Concerto: 'Emanuel Feuermann surpassed himself as if he wanted to make his farewell from Cologne particularly hard to bear. Who is the virtuoso who could play this concerto equally wonderfully, technically and musically?'[5] For the next six years, Feuermann led the nomadic life of a soloist, not accepting another paid position at an institution until 1929.

In his known concerts during the 1923/4 season Feuermann presented a wide repertoire: duo works included Valentini's E major Sonata, Beethoven op.69, the two Brahms sonatas, Grieg's Sonata, Rubinstein's Sonata op.18, and there was Reger's unaccompanied Suite in G major and Bach's C major, C minor and D major unaccompanied suites; the concertos were Saint-Saëns A minor, Haydn D major, d'Albert C major and Tchaikovsky 'Rococo' Variations; and the salon works were Nardini's Larghetto, Fauré's *Sicilienne*, Chopin's Nocturne in E♭, Piatti's Tarantella, Dvořák's Rondo and Sarasate's *Zigeunerweisen* in Feuermann's scintillating arrangement. On the whole, Feuermann's recital programmes conform to a general pattern: three or more substantial works – often a concerto and an unaccompanied Bach suite – followed by a group of lighter, virtuoso pieces. These last were designed to function like a Rossini crescendo, raising the tension and the blood pressure, as Feuermann played with a brilliance never previously associated with the cello, and audiences adored it.

Feuermann began his first season 'alone' in Poland in September. Although playing the same programme, he was obliged to use different pianists: Artur Müller, Stanisław Lipski and Teodor Ryder. It would be a long time before he worked with a regular partner. In Warsaw he performed with the Philharmonic Orchestra, playing two works, the Saint-Saëns and Tchaikovsky's 'Rococo' Variations, but he was as likely to play this repertoire with piano. Travelling, finding the hall, finding the accommodation, rehearsing each day with a new accompanist and performing must have been stressful – although stress to Feuermann at this age, or any other, may not have meant much.

Reviews show that in October and November Feuermann played in Switzerland with the Swiss pianist Walter Frey in La Chaux-de-Fonds, and with Hermann Scherchen in Winterthur (the Haydn D major Concerto). In December Feuermann returned to Vienna, where he joined the Rosé Quartet and friends to play a house-concert of Schubert's String Quintet and the 'Trout' Quintet for the Reifenbergs. In March 1924 the reviewer for the *Allgemeine Musik-Zeitung* wrote revealingly that he 'left the Furtwängler concert to go to the Singakademie to hear Emanuel Feuermann. A perfect beauty of tone even in the course of the most highly developed virtuosity, and accuracy of intonation in those glacial regions where only the chosen can dare to move without being punished.'[6] His accompanist was Michael Taube, a colleague from Cologne who had become a close associate as both pianist and conductor.

The new season, 1924/5, brought further trios. In the autumn of 1924, Emanuel and Sigmund teamed up with Bruno Walter (as pianist). Sophie Feuermann maintains that they never enjoyed playing with Walter, firstly because he talked too much and secondly because his playing was too loud (he liked to play with the piano open on full stick). But they were a 'star attraction'[7] and had many engagements. A review appears to confirm Sophie's comments on Walter: 'His piano playing . . . was rough and crude, nearly always covering the string instruments.' Comments on Sigmund were no more flattering: 'The violinist Feuermann, far inferior to the excellent cellist, has a rather feeble, sweetish tone, not at all suitable for chamber music. The whole ensemble between these three gives the impression of improvisation as if they might have met at a party rather than being carefully prepared.' The same review mentions a rival trio: 'Kreutzer/Wolfsthal/Piatigorsky are of a totally different calibre. It is a sheer joy to listen to the playing of these splendid artists full of genuine musicianship performing with understanding and love.'[8] Competition was tough.

But the same journal was ecstatic about a performance days later of the Brahms Double Concerto with the Feuermann brothers and Bruno Walter conducting the Berlin Philharmonic: 'One doesn't often come across this work in programmes because solo partners who are completely adjusted to each other are not easily found. Sigmund and Emanuel Feuermann complement each other wonderfully. It is music making without reserve, without ugliness of sound, without any inhibitions. . . . Under the hands of such master players, even this somewhat cool work comes alive.'[9] Berlin was a dazzling centre for classical music, as a page of advertising that week in the *Berliner Tageblatt* reveals: Carl Flesch, Eugen d'Albert, Szigeti, Gaspar Cassadó, Kreisler, Gieseking, Furtwängler (with Stravinsky as soloist) were all jostling for audiences and on the day of Walter and the Feuermanns' performance of the Brahms concerto Thomas Mann was reading from his new novel, *The Magic Mountain*.

Apart from a few reviews, detailed information about Feuermann in this 'freelance' period is scarce. A few letters to Lilli, the eldest Reifenberg daughter, with whom Feuermann had a flirtatious friendship, provide some clues. Sophie Feuermann has described the Reifenberg family as cold and without

heart and she came bitterly to resent the fact that Feuermann so enjoyed his life in Cologne. She believed he had been taken over. And perhaps he had, wisely assessing that the Reifenbergs could offer him so much more than his own family, not least in relation to his father, whose obsession with Sigmund so hurt him. The warmth towards the Reifenbergs is unmistakable in this extract from a letter from Feuermann to Lilli:

> You are quite right to be very, very cross with me. I am a terrible fellow. But for the silver wedding I'm coming all the same, only you mustn't tell your parents or anyone. I'm looking forward to it tremendously and I think your mother will enjoy the surprise very much. You will make sure that I will get two portions of ice-cream.[10]

The ease with which he writes, cracking jokes, making puns, in particular mixing and playing with languages ('verstandez-vous'), and poking fun indicate that he felt a fully-fledged member of the family, sending news and gossip about Reifenberg relatives from wherever he was. Paul and Emma Reifenberg had 'adopted' Feuermann; he enjoyed the status of favourite son, some felt to the exclusion of the Reifenbergs' own three boys who were around the same age as Feuermann. 'Mrs Reifenberg protected him enormously. He was the prince of the family, very difficult for the other boys. It would have been unlikely for the Reifenbergs to take in an Ost Jew but then there was enormous prestige attached to being a 16-year-old professor.'[11]

An example of the closeness with which Feuermann communicated with the Reifenbergs at this time concerns the purchase of a cello. Feuermann had found an instrument that he very much wanted to buy and appears to have been trying out. In December 1924 he wrote to Lilli Reifenberg: 'I'm pre-occupied with buying a cello to such an extent that I can't think of anything else. The cello is here [Vienna] but I have to negotiate with Stuttgart which is where the cello comes from. It has a beautiful tone but it has a few flaws through which its value is reduced; we haven't agreed a price yet.'[12] Enigmatically, Feuermann referred to someone who was very much against him acquiring the cello. Perhaps it was his father, who might well have wondered how Emanuel would pay for it. Feuermann continued in his letter to Lilli: 'it is so congenial to me that I will do everything in order to get it. Let's hope for the best, dear reader.' What he did not write was that he had sent a telegram to her mother: 'Please make a telegraphic transfer to the Bank Kellers, Söhne, Stuttgart of 14,000. Receiving cello only after the money has been paid. Very urgent. Fabulous cello. Happy Christmas.'[13] The nonchalance of the telegram, demanding that money be deposited forthwith, says much about the relationship. Perhaps Paul Reifenberg was merely bank-rolling the young star, but according to one of Paul's sons, Kurt, it seems more likely that his father paid for it.

What instrument had Feuermann bought? Before leaving to study with Klengel in Leipzig, Feuermann, aged 14, had graduated to a full-size instrument by Nicolo Amati, which had come from Kux's important collection of stringed instruments. Sophie Feuermann maintains that, of all the instruments Feuermann played, this was his favourite one. It has been said that the Amati suffered severe damage on a Cologne bus and that Kux came to the rescue by loaning Feuermann a Pietro Guarneri.[14] Just when the Amati came to grief is not specified. If there was a loan of a Pietro Guarneri, the period of time that Feuermann played it was short. More probably, there was no loan, the Pietro Guarneri confused for another instrument. In a letter dated August 1935 from Feuermann to persons unknown he wrote: 'I played on the Josef Guarneri cello, which Mr Josef Schuster purchased from me four years ago, in all my concerts for a period of seven years.'[15] This suggests that Feuermann acquired the Josef [Giuseppe] Guarneri 11 years previously, in 1924. A letter from the Stuttgart dealer Hamma & Co., presumably to Joseph Schuster, reads: 'In answer to your letter, we are very pleased to confirm to you that the cello in your possession is a genuine masterwork of Josef Guarnerius Fils Andrea Cremona and that until 1931 it was in the possession of Prof. Em. Feuermann who secured it from us through Georg Rauer in Vienna.'[16] There seems little doubt that this is the cello that Feuermann acquired in December 1924 with the help of Reifenberg's money; a Giuseppe (not a Pietro) Guarneri.

As well as having a thriving solo career, Feuermann delighted in playing chamber music. Unusually for a soloist, he was to prove to be just as great a chamber music player. Soon after the trios with Bruno Walter and Sigmund, Feuermann returned to Cologne in December 1924 to play with Eldering and Uzielli (cheekily referred to by Feuermann as 'the old masters'[17]) in the Cologne Trio. And in February 1925 Feuermann played in yet another trio with the violinist Boris Kroyt and the pianist Karol Szreter at the Singakademie and the Blüthnersaal in Berlin. A review of this trio highlights familiar problems: 'The somewhat narrow and thin tone of the violinist cannot compete with the voluptuous fullness of Emanuel Feuermann's cello tone and moreover is easily drowned by the colourful, rhythmically sharply defined piano playing of Karol Szreter.'[18] Kroyt joined the Budapest String Quartet in 1936 as their viola player.

In March, Feuermann began his first tour to the Soviet Union, a country he was to visit frequently. 'I'm very successful here [Leningrad]. Today Klemperer has arrived with his wife. On 8 April, Szigeti is expected. I am well but it is sad to be all alone without being able to communicate.'[19] A review of a sonata programme suggests that Feuermann's youthful exuberance may well have taken over, his playing accused of being somewhat reckless, the ensemble with his accompanist, Ignaz Zadora, leaving something to be desired.[20] But *Izvestia* thought differently: 'Emanuel Feuermann is a great artist. His technique is remarkable and his tone is beautiful.'[21] Feuermann was taking part in an international season of concerts promoted by the Leningrad Philharmonic Orchestra to which, as well as Klemperer and Szigeti, a number of foreign conductors and instrumentalists were invited, including Artur Schnabel, Hermann Abendroth and the pianist Egon Petri.[22] It has been asserted that Feuermann was the first foreign artist to visit the Soviet Union.[23] This is incorrect; Casals performed in St Petersburg in 1905.[24] Feuermann however, may well have been the youngest foreign cellist to perform in the Soviet Union.

In April, Feuermann was back in Berlin giving a recital with Michael Raucheisen at the Singakademie in an adventurous programme that included not only Bach's Sixth Suite but the first Berlin performance of Arthur Honegger's Cello Sonata, a work by Florent Schmitt and the Lalo Concerto (with piano accompaniment). In May, following more trios with Bruno Walter in Vienna, Feuermann travelled to Spain: 'Today is the first day without the train and without a concert (what one here calls a concert). For the whole morning and afternoon I have been fooling around on the beach. Tomorrow is the last concert. I had great success everywhere but they don't understand anything.'[25]

An important work which entered Feuermann's repertoire at this time was the Cello Concerto op.35 by the Austrian composer Ernst Toch. Toch, who became active in Berlin, was to remain a close colleague, particularly in California, during Feuermann's final years. Feuermann gave the world premiere of Toch's concerto on 17 June 1925 at the Kiel German Music Festival, to which it was considered by Hugo Leichtentritt to be the most important contribution.[26] In the *Berliner Tageblatt* Alfred Einstein referred to it as an 'enchanting and felicitous work in which the solo instrument is the *primus inter pares*, yet dominates, is new in expression and old in form.'[27] During the next seven years Feuermann performed the concerto more than 60 times in Europe and it remained a work that he played throughout his life. Regrettably there is no surviving broadcast and he never recorded it.[28]

Feuermann's touring between 1923 and 1929 was relentless. In his own writings he mentioned playing in 167 different German towns and 132 towns in other parts of Europe.[29] From the summer of 1926 to December 1927 alone, Feuermann performed in Scheveningen, Paris ('Played here twice, of course quite unsuccessfully and very badly'[30]), Kissingen, Vienna, Poland, Zürich (giving the first Zürich performance of Walter Schulthess's Variations op.14 for cello and orchestra), Cologne, Magdeburg, Kiel and Bremen (where he played a concerto by Kurt Atterberg).

Joseph Schuster recalled that 'unlike us ordinary mortals, he practically did not even have to practise.'[31] Indeed, in a letter to Lilli Reifenberg, Feuermann gaily recounted: 'For the last months that I am here, I hardly play the cello but all the more tennis so for instance 4½ hours on Sunday, yesterday 2½, today 1½, that's enough for modest demands, isn't it? In my second profession, I transcribe things written for the organ for cello.'[32] Schuster and Feuermann spent a vacation in Baden-bei-Wien in the summer of 1926. Schuster claimed that during five or six weeks he never saw Feuermann touch the cello.

> I don't think he even had one with him. Yet when he received a telegram to come to Budapest to substitute for Arnold Földesy, on two days notice, he was as fit as if he had practised every day. A few of us went along to hear him, and I can well remember that the performance which he gave that day of the Dvořák Cello Concerto was almost unbelievable for its perfection and beauty.[33]

Between April 1925 and February 1928 there was one city in which Feuermann did not perform: Berlin.[34] Feuermann's gap in performing there is puzzling. It may be explained by his busy concert schedule elsewhere – but Berlin was Europe's musical centre and Feuermann's reputation was high. No correspondence from him is identified as sent from Berlin during this period, though a letter from Emma Reifenberg in September 1927 indicates a visit, if not a longer stay: 'Go ahead and go to Berlin, I am glad to hear you finally overcame your doubts and made that decision.'[35] One explanation is shortage of money. In 1926 Feuermann had visited the mother of the cellist Edmund

Kurtz, telling her that he was going back to Berlin but could not decide whether to buy a suit or give a recital. She was puzzled by his remark, believing that if Feuermann gave only one recital he would be able to buy several suits. But at this period in his career Feuermann may well have paid for some of his recitals. And there was competition: many cellists were giving concerts in Berlin, including Gregor Piatigorsky, Francesco von Mendelssohn, Hans Hagen, Raya Garbousova, Edmund Kurtz and Beatrice Harrison. Perhaps the market was saturated. It seems unlikely that Feuermann had fallen out with Wolff & Sachs, since a letter to Lilli Reifenberg suggests that she could contact him at Wolff & Sachs Berlin W9 Linkerstrasse 42.[36] Louise Wolff, however, was a formidable woman. After the death of her husband, Hermann, she took over the running of the agency with a partner, Jules Sachs. As Piatigorsky recalled:

> Her knowledge of music was not above the level of other managers but her judgement had great weight and her influence reached every corner of the globe where tickets were sold for concerts. Many feared her sharp tongue; many sought her favour; everyone admired her wit. Her nickname, 'Queen Louise', stuck to her solidly, and a queen in her field she was indeed.'

Piatigorsky recounted the story of a young pianist trying to get taken on by the agency who had presented Louise Wolff with a sheaf of good reviews: 'Hm, it's too bad. I am afraid you must look for another manager. You see, young man, in my long experience I have never met a poor artist who wasn't in possession of glowing reviews, as I have yet to meet a great one who has escaped unfavourable ones.'[37]

Another twist to Feuermann's absence from Berlin concerns Furtwängler. Louise Wolff had clinched Furtwängler's position at the Berlin Philharmonic following Nikisch's death in 1922. Feuermann's only appearance with Furtwängler was in 1923. If Feuermann was on the Wolff & Sachs books, it seems odd that he didn't work with Furtwängler again. Unfortunately, no documentation has survived the forced disbandment of Wolff & Sachs following the rise to power of the National Socialists.[38] Whatever the explanation for the gap in concert-giving, Feuermann's first recital in Berlin after nearly three years on 4 February 1928 in the Bachsaal was presented by another management, the Internationales Impresariat, and a recital in Berlin eight months later was presented by Konzertdirektion Leonard GmbH. (A recital in April 1929 in the Beethovensaal with Otto Schulhof, however, was presented by Konzertdirektion Hermann Wolff und Jules Sachs.) The February recital may, however, never have taken place. On 17 February 1928 Feuermann wrote cheerfully to the Mayers from the Public Hospital in Mainz:

Losing a concert is expensive! Even a 'Kaik' must be pitied. When it takes him so long to recuperate! But, when it's all over, he'll be fresh and cheerful and as you can see from the above my illness has moved upwards and has finally landed on the brain! Otherwise I'm fine, I just have to keep lying down and all my plans have taken a dive. Today I should have been travelling from Freiburg via Cernobbio to Milan to Monte Carlo then to Marseilles; it's all collapsed. But we still go ahead with the 1st March in Paris. Berlin could have been made up on the 17th March, but Casals will be playing on that date so that's no good either.[39]

Feuermann was being treated for a sciatica attack.

If Feuermann's concert-giving appears limited in Berlin, his recording schedule was active. Between December 1921 and April 1927 he took part in five sessions, recording not only movements of the Haydn, Boccherini and Dvořák concertos but also numerous salon works, including Sarasate's *Zigeunerweisen*. *Zigeunerweisen*, a virtuoso showpiece for violin, had a particular Berlin connection. The Berlin Philharmonic had a tradition whereby, as a kind of rite of passage, the first cello of the orchestra had to play *Zigeunerweisen* in his own arrangement to colleagues. While Feuermann never held the position of first cello, there seems little doubt from his 1927 recording that he would have passed the test.

In late 1927, as well as performing in Poland and Sweden, Feuermann again visited the Soviet Union. In Riga alone between 25 December and 5 January he played eight concerts 'with unusually sensational success'.[40] A typewritten set of extracts in German of reviews from the 1927/8 season includes an undated criticism from the evening paper *Rote Abendzeitung* by Musalevsky, entitled 'Feuermann and Schnabel'. The extract does not mention Schnabel's playing, but they played together on 3 January in the Leningrad Philharmonic Hall. Strangely, no mention of concerts with Schnabel is made by Feuermann in his surviving letters. However, Sophie Feuermann recalled that Feuermann 'liked the ensemble very much. He wrote me that they had hardly time to rehearse and it worked very fine.'[41] Schnabel in his autobiography fails to mention playing with Feuermann at this time, but his biographer Cesar Saerchinger writes that in 1928 Schnabel played Beethoven's cello sonatas with 'the young and greatly gifted Emanuel Feuermann, whom he first met early that year in Leningrad, and whose talent and musicianship he greatly admired'.[42] Feuermann was again in Riga and Leningrad in November and December 1928. In Leningrad he performed twice with the Philharmonic Orchestra conducted by Alexander Gauk. A *Rote Abendzeitung* extract dated 15 December 1928 refers to performances of Toch and Haydn.

A critical turning-point took place in April 1928; Feuermann began to make the first commercial recording in its entirety of Dvořák's Concerto – Casals was not to record it until April 1937, nine years later. With his friend Michael Taube conducting members of the Berlin State Opera Orchestra, Feuermann began recording on 30 April. But the work was not completed. Indeed, the third movement was to wait until September 1929, with further retakes in January 1930 conducted not by Taube but Frieder S. Weissmann, with Feuermann possibly playing another cello.

It was during the 1927/8 season that Feuermann began to work extensively with his sister Sophie, the youngest in the family (see Plate 9). An undoubtedly talented child, it must have been some struggle for her to compete with her two brothers. And she was a girl. She had lived with the Aschaffenburg family, cousins of the Reifenbergs, in Mönchengladbach, a textile town near Cologne. Following the First World War, when children were starving in Vienna, the Aschaffenburgs had invited her to stay with them until economic conditions improved. As a sister of Munio, she was readily accepted. Katya Aschaffenburg was about the same age and also a pianist. Sophie studied in Cologne with Michail Wittels, an assistant of Edwin Fischer, and in Vienna with Richard Robert (who taught Rudolf Serkin, George Szell and Clara Haskil among others). In 1924, both Katya and Sophie were in Berlin. 'Long live competition' as Munio put it in a letter to Lilli Reifenberg.[43]

Feuermann was very close to Sophie and loved performing with her. According to Wolfgang Steinberg: 'Not even looking at each other, they were together. They played nearly by heart the entire standard repertoire for cello – Beethoven sonatas, gamba sonatas by Bach, the Brahms sonatas.'[44] There was an innate, musical empathy between them and for a few years she was one of his favourite pianists. Already in December 1927 Feuermann proudly wrote that out of 14 concerts with Sophie in the current season six had gone well, even indicating a preference for her over Walter Lang (a pupil of Busoni) for a recital in Zürich. But as so often happens between siblings, Feuermann could find her immensely irritating: 'During the drive here [Berlin] I was furious with her. She just sat there with a face like doom and with 2000 years of Jewish suffering on her shoulder. In the evening at the hotel I just let rip. She cried and now she's charming.'[45]

Despite the rigours of touring, Feuermann still found time for letter writing and romantic attachments. He was clearly attractive to women of all ages. Reifenberg cousins in Lemberg and Leverkusen were all said to have been in love with him. Elinor Lipper, a cousin of Lily Mayer, first came across him when she was a young girl.

Sonntag, den 21. April 1928, 5 Uhr nachm.

II. SEMINARKONZERT

In der Aula der Aufbauschule in Olpe.

Emanuel Feuermann-Wien (Cello)

Sofie Feuermann-Wien (Klavier)

I. a) **Beethoven:** Variationen über: „Bei Männern, welche Liebe fühlen"
aus der Zauberflöte von
Mozart

b) **Locatelli:** Sonate D-dur
Allegro vivare — Adagio —
Tempo de Minuetto

II. **Chopin:** Sonate G-moll für Klavier und
Cello

III. **Chopin:** a) Impromptu As-dur
b) Ballade   G-moll } f. Piano solo

VI. **Schubert:** Sonate A-moll für Klavier und
Cello. Allegro moderato —
Adagio — Rondo

Whenever Feuermann made an appearance everybody became crazy because there wasn't a woman who didn't react to him. Old or young, it didn't matter because he had very big charm. I was about 13. He came to Holland where I lived with my mother and stepfather and he stayed with us and I had a very nice room with the piano. When he came to us he had my room and I went to the guest room. After he left I went back to my room. Since he always had trouble with his hair – he lost his hair very early – he used to use all sorts of brilliantine and when I came back to my bed it smelt still of his brilliantine. So for weeks on end I sniffed this beautiful perfume.[46]

Later in Berlin, where Elinor was a medical student, a relationship developed. But the young Feuermann also encouraged mothering: 'During a whole year he had one of the lenses of his glasses loose and it kept falling out. I don't know why he didn't get it mended. I must have told him 50 times but you couldn't tell him anything.'[47]

His first fairly serious flirtation was with Lilli, the Reifenbergs' eldest daughter, who was four years younger than him. The attachment was not intense: 'This month I've been to Berlin for about two weeks and played with Sigmund and Bruno Walter twice, the trio and the Double Concerto by Brahms. I have to confess that at the moment I am fairly unfaithful to you. The unfortunate one is Gretl, the daughter of Walter . . . It will probably pass pretty soon.'[48] Lilli later married Ernst Lucas from Mönchengladbach, 'a good Jewish man',[49] a doctor, whom Feuermann greatly liked. When they moved to London, Feuermann often stayed with 'Look-Look' in Hampstead. A notable characteristic of Feuermann emerges from this early romantic attachment: his loyalty to friends. He continued to correspond with the women to whom he was romantically attached, often writing hilariously and flirtatiously, despite their moving on to new friendships: 'Every morning you clean the noses of 35 little children or is your service even more strenuous? The experience of nose cleaning you could use for Eva I think.'[50]

The life of a touring musician was a lonely one and Feuermann's intense interest in minute family details – particularly those of the Reifenbergs – was his way of keeping in touch. There are good grounds for believing that Feuermann needed a substitute family, but the lack of preserved correspondence with his own family may unduly emphasize this impression: 'He had difficulties with his family but somehow there was a big attachment. It was his background and he felt very strongly about it.'[51]

Following Lilli Reifenberg, Lily Mayer became Feuermann's next serious romantic interest. She was Swiss, a few months older than him, the second child of Bernhard and Guste Mayer. They met probably through the Steinbergs in Cologne to whom the Mayers were distantly related. Bernhard Mayer was a remarkable man: Jewish, self-made, a very successful fur merchant and widely travelled in Europe and the United States. Mayer & Co. had branches in Paris, Berlin, Amsterdam and Zürich. Even if in terms of money and social standing there was common ground, the difference between the far from conventional Swiss Mayers and the formal Cologne Reifenbergs must have been profound. Mayer, a year younger than the formidable Paul Reifenberg, remained a socialist throughout his life, actively supporting the cause. If the greatest musicians passed through the Reifenbergs' doors, Bernhard Mayer sought intellectuals and visual artists, patronizing them by lending or giving money, buying works, and inviting them to his houses in Zürich and Ascona. As his granddaughter has said, Mayer 'collected' people – Peter Kropotkin, Martin Buber, Fernand Crommelynck, Albert Ehrenstein, Ignaz Silone, Alexey van Jawlensky, Marianne von Werefkin, Arthur Segal and his son Walter were all close friends. The family was an exceptionally warm and easy-going one into which Feuermann was welcomed, becoming a frequent visitor at Russenweg no.8, in Zurich, or Villa

Bernardo in Ascona. 'They always had guests from all sorts of places. In the summer they all came to Ascona, sometimes staying for months or even years.'[52] In 1908 Mayer had bought a plot of land, marvellously situated overlooking Lake Maggiore, on which in 1926 he built a large house. Ascona had been an abode for nature worshippers and vegetarians who lived in wooden huts and went round with not much on. Soon it became a popular place to stay 'especially for artists, anthroposophists, astrologers and other eccentrics'.[53]

The Mayers provided yet another alternative home for Feuermann, even if he did simultaneously remain firmly established with the Reifenbergs. His characteristic exuberance and closeness to the Mayer family comes out in his fulsome letters to Lily. After a stay in Ascona, he wrote:

> Your mother has kindly released me from an official thank you letter and I just want to say again that the weeks with you were unbelievably wonderful. By the way, the day after tomorrow I'm travelling to Scheveningen. I've been practising every day and have noticed that cello playing isn't all that easy, but it's still a lot easier than dancing, riding a bicycle, etc.[54]

Lifetime passions – smoking and cars – were well established by this time: 'It's just after breakfast and I'm smoking one of those . . . fabulous cigarettes and the aroma conjures up Ascona for me.'[55] Feuermann remained a heavy smoker throughout his life; rare is the photo of him without a cigarette. The ash would fall into his cello without causing him concern. Later, in the United States, he even posed for a cigarette advertisement. Cars were the other abiding passion. The cars and chauffeurs of the Reifenbergs and the Mayers were doubtless a strong influence. And a car was a practical way of transporting a cello. Just after his 22nd birthday in November 1924, he wrote to Lilli Reifenberg notifying her that he was considering buying a little car (an 'autochen') so that he could 'race round properly this summer'.[56] The fact that he was not yet able to drive was of no importance – he was truly his father's son! Three months later he proudly wrote: 'I have learnt to drive. Really! 10 days ago I went from Bern to Freibourg. The most beautiful experience was yesterday, a tour round the Thunersee. 1000 times more beautiful than in summer. Wonderful sun, clearest view, much snow up above. I drove from Bern to Thun and back at up to 55km per hour.' Almost as an afterthought he added: 'By the way I was called out seven times after the Bach.'[57]

The romantic attachment to Lily Mayer lasted about three years. Feuermann in 1927 was barely 25 and testing his wings whereas Lily was ready for marriage. When she became engaged to Leo Hofmann in May 1927, Feuermann's reaction was boisterously good-humoured:

'Dear Lily, Bride of Another; Amen!!

Thrilled to pieces, down in the dumps.[58] That is what the oh so formal announcement of your engagement has done to me. So you won't be left on the shelf then, you won't become an old maid; and now I won't have to marry you out of love for your mother. What joy, what a relief for me. Now my biggest worry is that I'm no longer going to be the cock of the walk. All gone, bye bye, over!!! But don't suddenly turn all horrid to me! Compris? How much longer are you actually going to be staying in that dreadful place Ascona, where I'm hoping you have the most dreadful weather!? I suppose I'll never see it again. Warmest regards to your fiancé! But if he's not nice to you I shall challenge him to a duel with cello bows!!!! Le violoncelle est mort, Viva la cravate![59]

But for all the humour, Lily Hofmann's daughter maintains that Feuermann had not really entertained the idea that Lily might marry somebody else. While he was perhaps sorry and surprised that Lily had decided to take her affections elsewhere, Feuermann was possibly more concerned about losing his 'homes' in Zurich and Ascona.[60] Elinor Lipper claims that Feuermann, while interested in the Mayer money, would never have married Lily: 'She was in love with him but she was a very plump, fat girl and I think this made a difference'.[61] Lily married in September 1927. A letter from Feuermann in December seems to laugh it off: 'I hope to find the woman who will be my Mrs Right in some 15 to 20 years.'[62]

Chapter 4
Berlin
1928–30

The greatest cellist of our time.
Hamburgischer Correspondent (9 October 1928)

In the first years of the Weimar Republic following the brutal suppression of the KPD (German Communist Party), the left-wing SDP (Social Democrats) dominated German national politics, the Prussian state and Berlin's municipal government. For the arts this was to be of significance. At the Prussian Cultural Ministry, an institution long in need of reform, now renamed the Prussian Ministry for Science, Art and Public Education, Leo Kestenberg, a Hungarian Jew, in December 1918 was put in charge of music. As a trained musician, a student of Busoni, Kestenberg had taught at the Stern and Klindworth-Scharwenka conservatories in Berlin and had for some time been associated with the educational work of the Social Democrats. Up to this time the Prussian Cultural Ministry had been run by bureaucrats with little experience in the arts who relied on the advice of elected members of the Prussian Academy of Arts whose interests were usually vested. Kestenberg was a new broom. His combination of musical expertise and political knowledge made him powerful. His tenure was of the utmost significance to Berlin's musical, educational and operatic life, a significance that would be felt through the years to 1932, when he was dismissed from his position by the National Socialists.

The Berlin Akademische Hochschule für Musik was Germany's leading educational establishment for music. Founded in 1869, Joseph Joachim was its first director; he remained at the Hochschule until his death in 1907. Joachim established the main strengths of the school as string playing and chamber music, but by the time his successor, Hermann Kretzschmar (1848–1924), retired in 1918, little had changed. It was a highly conservative institution badly in need of rejuvenation. One of Kestenberg's first tasks was to appoint a new director to the Hochschule able to entice leading musicians to the institution and so attract the most talented students to study. As Kestenberg was to find, the task was far from easy: Max von Schillings turned it down, as his eyes were on the position of intendant at the Berlin State Opera; the Austrian theorist Ernst Kurth preferred to remain with his professorship in Bern; Hugo Becker, professor of cello at the Hochschule, also declined his offer. The most controversial candidate Kestenberg approached was the composer Franz Schreker. As the Hochschule's main strengths were associated with string playing and chamber music, composition was a weak area, so the invitation to Schreker was daring. Schreker, at the age of 42, was experiencing considerable success with his operas throughout Germany, but he was regarded as belonging to music's left wing; nevertheless, in the early months of 1920 the appointment went ahead. As a condition of acceptance Schreker insisted that he must have sufficient free time to compose. He was more public figurehead than active administrator, his teaching duties light, his vacations long. All final decisions on staff appointments and Hochschule policy were, however, his. Georg Schünemann (1884–1945), vice-director, had the day-to-day task of running the school.

Schreker considered a galaxy of stars for appointment to the Hochschule, including Ferruccio Busoni, Béla Bartók, Artur Schnabel, Edwin Fischer, Fritz Kreisler, Bronisław Huberman, Bram Eldering, Adolf and Fritz Busch and Wilhelm Furtwängler. Within a few months Schreker had appointed the violinists Gustav Havemann and Carl Flesch (part-time), the pianist Max Trapp and Hermann Scherchen, conductor and authority on contemporary music who in the same year founded *Melos*, an influential journal promoting the latest German and international contemporary music. Plans for new departments – schools for opera, opera chorus, preparatory orchestra, conducting – were soon realized. A recording archive was set up, an acting school, and, under the personal guidance of Schünemann, a music education seminar. In a stroke, the hidebound Hochschule had become a progressive, lively organization, 'a contemporary synthesis of old and new'.[1]

The cello department of the Hochschule had since 1909 been under the directorship of Hugo Becker. Becker, born in 1864, was a son of the well-known violinist Jean Becker, founder of the Florentine String Quartet. In his teens Hugo had toured with the 'Jean Becker Family Quartet', later forming a permanent trio with his sister and brother. He held the position of principal cello at the Frankfurt Opera for two years (1884–86), but it was as a chamber musician that he was most skilled; he became a member of the distinguished trio with Artur Schnabel and Carl Flesch, colleagues at the Hochschule. Becker and the slightly older Klengel were Germany's two principal teachers of the cello. Becker's students included Paul Grümmer, (1879–1965), Arnold Földesy (1882–1940), Beatrice Harrison (1892–1965) and Enrico Mainardi (1897–1976). In July 1925 Becker's retirement and replacement was under discussion. Becker himself suggested Mainardi as successor. Schünemann, however, had other plans: 'I am going to make the suggestion in a few days which has already been made quite frequently that a new position for cello should be created. If we were to get this permission, we could engage two replacements for Becker in which case the departure of Prof. Becker would not be so painful.'[2] Handwritten over the words 'two replacements' are the names Mainardi and Földesy. This second, full-time appointment would, at a stroke, double the teaching capacity for cello at the Hochschule. But the economic situation was worsening and Schünemann held out little hope of a positive reply.

At this point there is no mention in any correspondence at the Hochschule of Feuermann. When and how his name occurred as a candidate is not clear. It is said that he was invited to apply.[3] His achievements in Cologne and throughout Europe performing with the finest orchestras, conductors and accompanists, all widely reported in the press and periodicals, were doubtless well known. Despite the gap in his concert-giving in Berlin between 1925 and 1928, he had been in the city for recording sessions. In his letters to Lily over the summer of 1928 he made no mention of any approach by the Berlin Hochschule, but he did show obtuseness and indecision:

> For the past few days I've been like 'a reed in the wind' and didn't know till now what I ought to do. I had the following plan: to go to Mittenwald in Bavaria with my few cellists and not to honour you with my presence before next month. As I only let the boys know what the fee was at the last minute, only one of them has remained. I obviously didn't want to go to Mittenwald just with him. And I felt a bit embarrassed about foisting myself upon you. Well, I would absolutely adore to come to you. In fact I will be there next week. Will you be picking me up with your Willi[4] at Bellinzona? When I think about being there so soon I feel quite blissfully happy![5]

'There' is the beautiful house on the lake in Ascona. Just ten days later he wrote again:

> I've been behaving abominably with you. I just couldn't fight all the good 'Eizes' [advice] that's been thrown at me and so I agreed to go to the

mountains first. It's probably the right thing to do, but I don't like doing it. Of course it's appalling manners of me not to have let you know sooner, but I was wavering up until the last moment. I'm not asking you to forgive me because it will only make matters worse, but I am counting on you not being angry with me and 'throwing out' a few kind words in my direction (Munio the Keilef!). If I am not wrong, you might write and let me know whether I could come in mid August. There's nothing to beat chuzpe!

The letter also refers to a few days spent with the Reifenbergs in Badgastein, and wryly makes mention of an ailment of Mrs Reifenberg's: 'Unfortunately Mrs. R. is in bed with a terrible tooth problem, had dreadful pains. You know the old joke where the nurse – says: "Dear Doctor, my life, have I had a night." I could say the same.'[6] By mid-August Feuermann had again decided not to visit Ascona.

Feuermann's letters to Lily Hofmann, like those to Lilli Reifenberg, do not, by and large, touch significantly on musical events. Neither of the women was a musician, but they were friends in whom he could confide. References made lightly to musical activities occasionally mask events of considerable importance. In a quite mundane letter of 4 October 1928 he wrote about domestic arrangements for a meeting in Zürich where he would be playing with Sophie on the 10th. He was to arrive from Hamburg following a concert on 8 October.[7] What he did not spell out was that he was in Hamburg for a performance with Carl Flesch (1873–1944), one of the greatest living violinists who since 1921 had been teaching at the Berlin Hochschule. The fact that the name might mean nothing to Lily and that it was once again the Brahms Double might account for Feuermann failing to indicate that this concert was of any significance. But it also reveals his boundless confidence at this age, appearing never to need support nor suffering nerves. Somewhat surprisingly, since Feuermann had played the Brahms so often, a letter to Flesch indicates that for the first time he would play it by heart.[8] The performance in Hamburg conducted by Dr Karl Muck was reviewed ecstatically: 'It is impossible to imagine this wonderful work performed more perfectly.'[9] Feuermann was hailed as 'the greatest cellist of our time'.

In his biography Seymour Itzkoff gave this performance particular significance in relation to Feuermann's success in securing the position at the Hochschule of professor of cello. The implication is that Flesch had this appointment within his gift: 'Flesch, having limited facility, needed all kinds of performing concessions from his partner. Feuermann obliged so unobtrusively as to make it seem natural; thus the ensemble was flawless. Two weeks later, Feuermann was notified of his appointment as professor of cello at the Berlin Hochschule.'[10] Carl F. Flesch, Carl Flesch's son, took issue with Itzkoff bluntly: 'In other words, out of gratitude to Feuermann for helping him with a concerto that was really beyond his technical capacity, my father made sure he got the Hochschule position. Whatever criticisms one might have of Carl Flesch's playing, a "limited technique" was definitely not one of them. He certainly did not need the forbearance of any duo partner.'[11] Carl F. Flesch also pointed out that the ensemble was far from faultless: 'As it happened, my father reported laughingly on his return from that particular engagement that he had lost concentration for a moment and missed an entry. Feuermann, "with mischievous sang froid", as he put it, played it for him.'[12] In fact it was not for many months that Feuermann was officially confirmed in his appointment – on 10 April 1929.[13]

Feuermann, however, was not the only cellist appointed: 'Under the stated circumstances I have no objection to negotiations with the cellists Feuermann and Mainardi regarding the professorship which has become necessary because of the retirement of Prof. Becker.'[14] The ministry had given the go-ahead. Schünemann had got his way. But Feuermann's name rather than Földesy's was under consideration. Conditions were attached: it was to be an experiment for one year; the title of 'professor' was not to be promised;[15] Becker's monthly salary of 1300RM would not be available to pay the joint salaries; the appointments had to be made on the lowest level of entry for the grade.

With negotiations still incomplete, Schünemann announced Feuermann's appointment to the press. Feuermann, however, refused Schünemann's offer of 775.75RM per month, an improvement on the basic salary of 625RM but far short of a professor's salary. He was holding out for 800RM.[16] As in Cologne when still a teenager, Feuermann was determined that his worth should be recognized financially. Mainardi was offered only 500RM, significantly less than the monthly minimum. For another month, negotiations twisted and turned. Finally the ministry caved in, agreeing to a one-off sum for one year only, making it clear that such a payment of a full salary for a temporary appointment – Feuermann's – was a definite exception.[17] Meanwhile, Feuermann had received the names of his students: Helmut Auer, Elisabeth Gros, Hans-Joachim Kittke, Herbert Lehmann, Theodor Schürgers, Bruno Sesselberg, Ernst Zimmermann and Walter Jäkel. The first lesson was fixed for 15 April at 9.00am in Room 10.[18]

The politics of the Feuermann/Mainardi appointment now took a colourful turn, as Schünemann wrote to Becker in an exceptionally long letter:

The appointment of Mainardi has led to a shocking article in the newspaper called 'Das kleine Journal' under the heading 'Cinema Cellist is Appointed

Academy Teacher Evidently because he's a Foreigner'. The article has the further heading 'Connections Replace Ability' and it speaks about the fact that Becker has been responsible for this support. Further there is talk in the most vile manner about this 'cinema cellist' and the undeserved backing for his being a foreigner and it appears that the writer 'Audivi' is knowledgeable about the division of the position and the salary. The essay itself is too contemptible to be answered but it could be that via the Landtag[19] there might be a question addressed to the minister. I would therefore be very grateful if you, revered Professor, could supply us with a testimony about Mainardi's artistic and teaching capacities in order that I might add it to the documents about the appointment. It is rather important for me to have this testimony straightaway in case something should happen.

Schünemann smelt a rat: 'In the same article, Feuermann is mentioned with praise so that I think that the author must be suspected to be among cello playing colleagues.'[20] The attack on Mainardi as a foreigner is intriguing. He was indeed Italian, but was not Feuermann Austrian? Perhaps for 'foreign', one must read non-German-speaking.

Despite the intrigues, Feuermann appeared remarkably unruffled. A letter to Lily is brimming with news: 'If you haven't already heard it, listen and be astonished: I have been teaching here at the university since the 15th. Everything's perfect: 6–8 pupils, lots of holiday, freedom to choose my teaching days etc., everything wonderful except that I haven't got the title of professor yet.'[21] As in Cologne ten years before, Feuermann wasted no time in making his presence felt: 'It's going quite well with my students, I've thrown two of them out. No one believes that I could have done such a thing. The famous Prof. Becker has left the people here in such a sloppy, physically and spiritually undernourished condition, that what I would really like to do is have him arrested. A real Augean stable!' Frank comments from a 26-year-old about one of Europe's most respected pedagogues. Feuermann's confidence seems unshakeable; however, the following passage from the same letter reveals a mixture of confidence and modesty: 'The day before yesterday I had my second evening here.[22] I played quite well. Casals should have played two evenings in March – I wasn't there – but apparently he was indisposed for both evenings. You know what musicians are like; they're already beginning to say that I play better. It's nonsense of course, I play much too quickly.'

Feuermann now had a much wanted home:

You remember my permanent complaint, especially in the spring, that I didn't know what to do with myself and where to go. Now I know that I have to stay here, just imagine: 3 months, with practically no break, in one and the same town! When was the last time I stayed so long in one place?! . . . Now that people know where I am they're coming up with the strangest offers. Yesterday someone approached me and asked me whether I could play principal cello at the State Opera in the summer, especially during the Festival. However, I don't know if I'll do that.[23]

In Feuermann's first year at the Hochschule he had many distinguished colleagues: George Szell, Carl Flesch, Karl Klingler, Josef Wolfsthal, Hindemith, Schnabel, Curt Sachs, Oskar Daniel and, of course, Franz Schreker. One of Feuermann's students in Berlin was the Palestinian cellist Mosa Havivi.[24] He had heard about Feuermann through his sister, a pianist who was studying at the Hochschule and from whom he received letters raving about a fantastic cellist:

> The greatest thing about him was that he didn't theorize and didn't lecture. He just took the cello and played it in any position, even side-saddle. It didn't matter because he'd produce this sound and that's all any student needs to see and hear how it's being done. He was a man full of ability. No problems. His physical ability towards the instrument was unique. Big cellos, small cellos, he picked up any cello and the playing was faultless.[25]

In his teaching at that time, Havivi remembers that rather than explaining shifts, vibrato and trills, Feuermann just demonstrated: 'These were all higher trained cellists that came to him and if you had to explain it was a little too late. Whenever he touched the cello it was demonstrative. If you missed it you didn't belong there.' From an early age Feuermann had played music of all kinds, including new music, an area in which he encouraged his cello students to be involved. Havivi recalls an amusing incident:

> I played chamber music as a young boy. There was a quartet in my family. In those days the most modern composer for me was Debussy. At the Hochschule they assigned me to a string quartet. They said that I would play in a class where Hindemith was involved. Of course, I had never heard of Hindemith. So we went in there and behold it was his composition class and we were supposed to perform all the works of his pupils, handwritten on manuscript. First of all it was difficult to read. Second the new language – the harmonies were so devastating. The first rehearsal I went to lasted about three and a half hours. I walked out of that room. I was numb! I was confused! I was hurt! Hindemith's style was so new and the more dissonant it was the better – it was experimental composition. So as a result I had a very bad evening and a restless night. In the morning I decided to be smart and talk to Prof Feuermann. So I told him how difficult it was for me. I liked

playing chamber music but not this kind of music. So he looked at me with a smile and raised his finger. 'Du Dummkopf! You are stupid! You go there and you learn something about music!'

Havivi recalled Feuermann's sharp tongue, something forcefully remembered by many who came into contact with him. 'The sharp tongue was full of humour. To him if someone had difficulties – it was funny – he had to giggle and, if you didn't like it, you thought he was making fun of you. For him if someone had difficulties on the cello it was funny.' Many remark on Feuermann's sarcasm. But in so many of his letters he is so boisterously good-humoured, exuberant and self-deprecating, that it is hard to believe that he set out consciously to wound. On the other hand, there were occasions when his remarks were open to conflicting interpretation. One example, witnessed by Havivi, concerned the cellist Joseph Schuster.

Schuster and Feuermann had been friends since their Leipzig days together. Schuster also knew the Reifenbergs well. Following the departure of Piatigorsky in 1928, Schuster became first cello of the Berlin Philharmonic and soon gave a recital that Feuermann and his class attended.

> We went in late and sat at the back with Feuermann – no one went to sit in their proper seats. The concert hall wasn't very crowded. Feuermann was like a leader with about a dozen pupils around him. Feuermann couldn't sit still! Everything was funny to him. . . . After the concert he said 'let's go to congratulate him'. We went upstairs and of course everybody else in the green room moved away so that Feuermann and his gang could proceed. He shook hands with Schuster and said 'Oh, Joseph, you were terrific.' I knew he had complimented him in a funny way. The moment Schuster heard these compliments he said 'Oh yes. You know, this time I really had time to practise and I worked really hard.' Feuermann turned to look at his pupils – 'He really believes that I meant it!'[26]

Havivi was devastated. How should Feuermann's remark be interpreted? If Feuermann meant Schuster to hear it, it must surely have been said as a joke, albeit in bad taste. Had Feuermann made the remark behind Schuster's back, a very different interpretation might be made. Piatigorsky too was not untouched by Feuermann in tongue or spirit. Sophie recalls that Piatigorsky came to perform in Cologne: 'Munio and I were a little late. During the intermission we went to say hello. He said 'Sophie and Munio. I give you my fee but leave!'[27]

If Schuster was hurt by Feuermann, his tribute on Feuermann's death does not reveal it: 'As a man, Feuermann was the kindest, most magnanimous person I have ever known.' But he did refer to Feuermann's humour: 'When he met someone, he often couldn't help making some witty remark or pointed quip. Many people took it as sarcasm or malice. But it was no more than a protection against his deep and inner warmth and an expression of his great exuberance.'[28] Artur Rubinstein thought similarly: 'He was very witty and very malicious. He had the sharpest tongue I could remember. God help the person who got on his tongue, but it was very funny, never really vindictive or bad, never a "malice" or something that was evil. It was always just for the humour's sake. . . . If a man has a sense of humour it's a divine gift.'[29]

Despite his commitment to the Hochschule, Feuermann's concert schedule was as hectic as ever. Appearances took place throughout Europe – Leningrad, Paris, Scheveningen, Budapest, Prague, Amsterdam, Riga and, of course, Berlin. At a house concert in Cologne, Feuermann wielded his inveterate wiles:

> They provided me with a Stradivarius belonging to some I.G. Farben director; probably the second most beautiful instrument in existence. Of course I was mad with delight and explained to the gentleman quite firmly that I had met him before and that there was no way I could play on my own cello in Berlin two days later. I would have to have the cello there. I would pay the necessary expenses to have someone accompany the cello etc. To cut a long story short: his beloved better half travelled to Berlin on Sunday evening, I played on the cello and could only offer two encores, because she had to take the cello back to Cologne on Monday evening.[30]

Feuermann's first Berlin address was Uhlandstrasse 32, Wittenberg, Berlin W 15, but within a year he was giving Rudolf Vedder, Hubertusbaderstrasse 12, Berlin-Grunewald as his address.[31] Vedder, who had worked as a secretary to Edwin Fischer and Georg Kulenkampff, both Wolff & Sachs artists, was an unsavoury character who later became a concert agent. In what capacity Feuermann knew him, as secretary or agent, is unclear, as is whether Feuermann actually lived at this address or was merely giving it as a postal address. What is clear is that a few years later, it was probably Vedder, an associate of Hermann Goering and commercial director of the Reichskammer, who set his sights on the destruction of Wolff & Sachs, blackmailing Louise Wolff into yielding her company to him.[32]

Feuermann may, perhaps, have wanted a different address because of an unpleasant incident that had occurred at the Hochschule. Feuermann, who was without doubt attractive to women, believed that he had been set up: 'At the medical examination, it turned out that the claim made by the Goldberg family was a lie. Miss G. is *not* pregnant. I am anxious to tell you that immediately'.[33] Three months later, in a letter to the now married Lily Hofmann, Feuermann commented on a woman, although probably a different woman:

My 'beloved' keeps trying, but gently: first she came up to me, I threw her out. Then a few love letters, a birthday present and then the day before yesterday I played with Klemperer, flowers. I'm returning everything. She's a mad girl. However it is making me become a little bit conceited about my irresistible looks. I can't help noticing that the fair sex reacts rather powerfully in my presence and sometimes I find it difficult to remain faithful to you. Isn't it lucky that I've got so little time?[34]

In May 1931 he wrote: 'I still have a flock of virgins around me, they're very nice, but I'm bored.'[35] Elinor Lipper believes he was not a womanizer: 'He charmed everyone but he was not necessarily charmed by the women. He was always at arm's length. Maybe he wasn't so terribly interested in women. All right he liked to be cuddled and spoilt by everyone, but he wasn't someone who fell in love and suffered from women.'[36] When asked whether she thought he was a womanizer Marianne Pentmann, a cousin of the Reifenbergs, answered 'yein' – half yes, half no.[37]

If Feuermann really found women boring, what he certainly enjoyed in his scarce free time were movies and fast cars. He adored the cinema and Berlin was the right place to be. A cousin of the Reifenbergs, Meta Cordy, sometimes went with him to a film: 'During his concert tours at that time, he had to travel by train and it was very tiring. In the movies he went to sleep. After a while when the movie was finished, I felt I had to wake him up. "Have we arrived already?"'[38] Years later, the pianist Franz Rupp, who became Feuermann's recital partner, recalled that in the afternoon of a concert he would always try to go to 'a very cheap movie. ... I went once with him and I was so scared because I had to play in the evening but he went to the movie for two hours – a whole film, a Western.'[39] Rupp wondered whether it was to quieten his nerves.

Feuermann had difficulty in Berlin finding and remaining in suitable accommodation.

The whole matter of the apartment is crazy: I left the Hohenzollerdamm[40] because of too much noise, the Reichskanzlerplatz where I lived for 2 months was just as noisy, but instead in the mornings, when I would have rather slept a little longer, there was a drop of sunshine. Now and until the holidays I'm staying at a very nice pension[41] and would like to get myself an apartment from the autumn.[42]

He was lucky. Two months later he wrote: 'Some friends of mine have a beautiful studio on the Lützow-Ufer, they've just moved to a house of their own and I'm moving into the studio, they're leaving the furniture, sheets, etc.

This means I won't have to buy any furniture, which I was so worried about.'[43] Feuermann's first surviving letter from Berlin W, Lützow-Ufer 23, Bavaria 2300, is dated 29 September 1931; he could now afford a maid: '"My Margot" cooks excellently. I haven't had any meat for the past 4 days. She prepares wonderful things and is extremely respectful. She's taken out a subscription to the title "Herr Professor".'[44] But by July 1932 he was at yet another address: Berlin-Westend.

Back in November 1924, although unable to drive, Feuermann had stated that he wanted an 'autochen'. Now, in May 1929, with driving under his belt, he was torn between the desire to buy a car and the need to buy a cello. He decided to ask the Mayers and the Reifenbergs for help. To Lily he wrote: 'I've been offered a cello for 45,000 marks, and I also want to buy myself a car. Ask your mother whether and what she wants to "contribute" to me.'[45] Feuermann shows the same kind of nonchalance that he had directed towards the Reifenbergs in 1924 when acquiring the Guarneri. Elinor Lipper believes that Bernhard Mayer refused to 'contribute' to the cello. The austere Prussian Paul Reifenberg also felt that Feuermann needed bringing to heel, delivering him a stern sermon:

> I would like to remind you that I am decidedly a person committed to doing his duty [*Pflichtmensch*] who regards the carrying out of his duties as the most important task of all, particularly the duties with regard to other members of the family, towards our profession and our other activities. As far as your family is concerned, you carry out your duties in exemplary manner so it seems to me. However, you seem to have your own views on what your duties are towards your own profession. You point to a '*Gottesgnadentum*' ['Grace of God'], which placed the 'Staccato' in your cradle. You even mention proudly that you practise for two hours. This, in my view, is incompatible. I think that an artist who has been blessed by God must toil assiduously in order to develop the gifts he has been endowed with to a perfect height. Of course I understand that sometimes one prefers to do anything rather than practise. To conquer such moods and wishes there is the awareness of duty. I think that if one has done one's duty everyone has enough leisure time. Your duty towards your profession seems to me also to consist of the need to consider your financial circumstances carefully with regard to the future and there it seems to me your main concern should be directed towards acquiring a perfect instrument and that you should regard this as your most important duty for the immediate future. If other wishes should come up in your consciousness, then the awareness of your duty should guard you against wrong actions particularly when you say yourself

that after fulfilling a current wish – buying a car – another wish might crop up. If you utter such views then given that you are a mature, moral human being, your awareness of duty should put a brake on this.

Reifenberg must have been well aware of how hot-headed Feuermann could be:

Quite apart from all such moral and financial concerns, I would advise you for practical reasons against the purchase of a car. Do use cars. There are very nice ones for hire as often as you want to but don't drive yourself, particularly without a chauffeur. Your whole capital is in your two hands and arms and you expose them to extremely violent dangers apart from accidents or breakdowns etc. where you have to handle heavy keys and instruments. I have absolutely no right to tell you these things but I do from a heartfelt interest in you.[46]

Paul Reifenberg's fatherly interest may have been reinforced by the fact that Feuermann was not only hot-headed but colour-blind, something well recalled by frightened passengers! By September 1929, however, Feuermann was the possessor of a blue convertible Itala, and all Paul Reifenberg's worst fears seemed confirmed. In September, Feuermann wrote to Lily:

I wanted to try and get to Vienna in 2 days and in the afternoon between Innsbruck and Hall, on an unbelievably beautiful asphalt road, I ran over a cyclist. He was riding in front of me in the middle of the road, I drove in the middle. I hooted, he doesn't move, I decide to overtake on the left, he steers left at the same time, I drive into him at about [?]o km per hour, he is thrown sideways between 2 trees into a soft bit of earth, bicycle ruined, he gets away with grazes. One of my lights is totally destroyed etc. but we were both very lucky.

If this one incident was not enough, Feuermann continues: 'Yesterday, I ran over and killed the poor dachshund which was his own fault. Runs straight into my car on an open road. Braking was impossible. In short, I'm selling the car, even if I get nothing for it. It's a shame about all that money.'[47] A letter in May, however, suggests Feuermann changed his mind: 'I've exchanged my car for a 10/50 Wanderer. I just can't give up this idiotic driving and I want to continue treating myself to this extravagance for as long as I can.'[48] But by June he had no car. 'For 6 weeks I haven't had a car, financially a relief but not for "the soul".'[49]

Feuermann experienced all sorts of adventures with cars, but what had happened to the purchase of a cello? Although his correspondence does not specifically mention it, the cello offered to him was most probably an instrument made by David Tecchler.[50] His colleague Hindemith played a Tecchler viola, which may have encouraged Feuermann's interest. Papers referring to a sale do not survive. If indeed he acquired this cello after May 1929 but before September 1929, he may have used two different instruments for his ground-breaking recording of the Dvořák Cello Concerto. In view, however, of the recording session on 27 September, he may perhaps have delayed playing on the Tecchler. But on which cello did he play for the retakes in January 1930? If the point of acquisition is unclear, the sale of the Tecchler in May 1932 to Thelma Yellin is confirmed in a letter from Eva Feuermann to Yellin dated 27 January 1948. Another possibility is that Feuermann recorded the Dvořák Concerto on the Josef Guarneri, since we know that he played on the Guarneri for seven years from 1924.[51] Feuermann appears to have acquired the Tecchler while still keeping the Guarneri.

In October 1929 Feuermann was finally given the title of professor and hailed in the press as the youngest professor of music in the whole of Germany. As in Cologne, his position caused him as much amusement as pride: 'I still think it's a little funny and have to laugh when I see how difficult some people find it when they feel obliged to address me as such.'[52] A few months before, Mainardi had departed from the Hochschule to become principal cello at the Berlin State Opera – a position Feuermann had declined. A letter from Schünemann to Becker suggests, however, that Feuermann's age was problematic for the august Hochschule: 'We are lacking a commanding personality in the cello class.'[53]. Notwithstanding Feuermann's age, with Mainardi's departure and Feuermann's constant travelling, a vacuum may well have developed. In a letter to Lily, Feuermann wrote:

> The Hochschule is taking up a lot of time, despite the relatively few hours. Sometimes I'm in Berlin just for a day and then I teach for 8–9 hours. I have a lot of playing to do. Unfortunately the concerts aren't well placed so I have to travel a great deal. And in between I keep having to return to Berlin. It's a lot of work, costs an absolute fortune! as I have stopped travelling third class ... The car is still costing a lot of money and isn't as much fun any more. I spend almost less time in Berlin than last year. There's no chance of settling down. I haven't danced for months, I don't get to a theatre.'[54]

And in a letter to Klengel's wife he wrote: 'I am emerging from a colossally strenuous concert schedule ... The greatest success I had was in Amsterdam in the Concertgebouw under Monteux with the Toch and Schumann. It was the greatest thrill for me to play with this orchestra.'[55]

Feuermann's comment about not getting to the theatre is significant. At a time when Berlin was Europe's artistic centre, it is striking that in his surviving letters he never wrote about or made reference to events of even an outstanding musical kind. Apart from the occasional reference to his own concerts, no mention is made of Klemperer at the Kroll Opera or new work by Schönberg, Hindemith, Stravinsky, Krenek or Weill. It is hard to believe that he was not interested, but perhaps the recipients of his letters were not. In any case he had little time to attend events other than his own. He was also, at times, hard up.

Feuermann, nevertheless, did perform in a Kroll Opera concert on 5 December 1929 under Klemperer. It was a typically adventurous programme: the world premiere of Kurt Weill's cantata *Der Lindberghflug*, Stravinsky's *Les Noces*, and Hindemith's Cello Concerto op.36 no.2. He was rewarded by a review from the distinguished Berlin critic Alfred Einstein, who noted Feuermann's 'strong, virile, nearly Casals-like tone as the primus amongst the elite chamber orchestra of Klemperer.'[56]

As well as his appearances as a soloist, Feuermann had now formed a string trio with Hindemith and Josef Wolfsthal. In the mid-1920s, Wolfsthal had established a piano trio with Leonid Kreutzer and Gregor Piatigorsky with which the Feuermann brothers and Bruno Walter had been unfavourably compared.[57] Feuermann replaced Piatigorsky when in 1928 the latter went to America. At about the same time, Hindemith succeeded Kreutzer (Feuermann had found that he could not work with the 'emotionally wild Russian') and the piano trio became a string trio (see Plate 10). Wolfsthal, born in Lemberg in 1899 and a fellow Galician Jew, was regarded by many as the most gifted of Carl Flesch's students. In a letter to a concert promoter in 1916 Flesch, recommending Wolfsthal to take his place, wrote: 'In my opinion he is altogether the best violinist of the younger generation.'[58] In 1921, at the age of 21, Wolfsthal became leader of the Berlin State Opera Orchestra. It seems possible that he would have encountered Feuermann during the recording session in 1921 when Feuermann recorded with members of the Berlin State Opera, and perhaps also in 1922 – although the recording orchestra is not named.

Recordings of the trio do not exist, but recordings of Wolfsthal reveal a strong focused sound, with sensitive phrasing and minimal slides. He may have had the reputation of 'burning the candle at both ends – and in the middle',[59] but his death in February 1931 from a chill caught at a friend's funeral was not expected. Sophie Feuermann maintains that Wolfsthal's young widow, Olga (previously the wife of George Szell), was so interested in Feuermann that Mrs Reifenberg arranged for her to go to Switzerland with her young baby; Mrs Reifenberg had plans for her own daughter Eva to become Feuermann's wife. Whatever the romantic intrigues, the Berlin music community was profoundly shocked by Wolfsthal's death. The trio's forthcoming engagements, however, had to be fulfilled, and Szymon Goldberg was the obvious candidate to replace Wolfsthal. At the age of 20 he had been appointed leader of the Berlin Philharmonic Orchestra. Born in Włocławek, Poland, in 1909, he became a student of Carl Flesch at the age of ten, continuing his studies at the Hochschule. Flesch wrote: 'Amongst my other pupils, the sixteen-year-old Max Rostal and the thirteen-year-old Szymon Goldberg were by far the most outstanding.'[60] The chemistry between Feuermann, Hindemith and Goldberg seemed to work well and for the next few years this trio held together (see Plate 11). In an interview with Feuermann's daughter, Goldberg vividly described the working of the trio:

We rehearsed quite a lot. We played through the works very often and we of course interrupted each other very often. Whenever we discussed tempi or phrasing it was your father [Feuermann] mostly who was first to come to a satisfactory solution. Not because he was so sure of himself. Sure of themselves are only those who know very little. But his quick mind came quickest to a solution and his arguments were convincing enough to accept his suggestions. The illustrations on his cello were also so amazing that we just accepted his suggestion.

Goldberg encapsulated Feuermann's gift when he said: 'He was, to start with, a great musician. It means he had the instinct for what cannot be learned and the ability and the will to learn what can be learned.'[61]

So what was the quality of this trio? No recordings exist before 1934 when it was recorded by Columbia in London; the trio by that time could no longer work in Germany, proscribed by the National Socialists. The trio was uneven: Hindemith's playing was adequate but not technically on a level with that of Feuermann and Goldberg, but he was one of Germany's most distinguished composers.

Feuermann was now living at yet another address: Berlin-Wilmersdorf, Hohenzollerdamm 27. He was pleased to have his own apartment where he could receive friends, having felt himself more often to have been received, but in June 1930 he was not feeling cheerful. He wrote to Lily:

I feel rotten. It all concerns myself: 1.) Fear that I will have fewer concerts in the next season. 2.) I don't at all feel at home here in Berlin. 3.) I have problems with boils. On top of this, the illness of Gusta, the hordes of money this costs me, the uncertainty about her marriage, the unhappy nature of Sophie, the intention of Rosa to marry a cousin [Adolf Hönigsberg] (our parents absolutely don't want it and he doesn't earn anything) who has the sick nature of father. And finally Sigmund has been

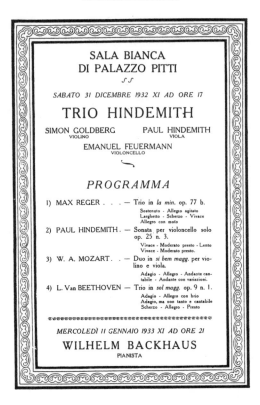

SALA BIANCA
DI PALAZZO PITTI
♪♪

SABATO 31 DICEMBRE 1932 XI AD ORE 17

TRIO HINDEMITH

SIMON GOLDBERG   PAUL HINDEMITH
VIOLINO   VIOLA

EMANUEL FEUERMANN
VIOLONCELLO

PROGRAMMA

1) MAX REGER . . . — Trio in *la min.* op. 77 b.

Sostenuto - Allegro agitato
Larghetto - Scherzo - Vivace
Allegro con moto

2) PAUL HINDEMITH . — Sonata per violoncello solo
op. 25 n. 3.

Vivace - Moderato presto - Lento
Vivace - Moderato presto.

3) W. A. MOZART . . — Duo in *si bem magg.* per violino e viola.

Adagio - Allegro - Andante cantabile - Andante con variazioni.

4) L. Van BEETHOVEN — Trio in *sol magg.* op. 9 n. 1.

Adagio - Allegro con brio
Adagio, ma non tanto e cantabile
Scherzo - Allegro - Presto

MERCOLEDÌ 11 GENNAIO 1933 XI AD ORE 21

WILHELM BACKHAUS
PIANISTA

back two weeks. He hasn't (strictest discretion, even towards your parents) achieved a thing in America and now stands 'naked'. It has come to this that I am feeling a bit better only because I have no news from home. It is terrible not to know of a way out.[62]

Feuermann sought a cure for his boils in Bad Schinznach. The situations of Sigmund and Gusta were more serious. Sigmund had gone to the United States in 1925, having been invited to tour and to teach at the New York College of Music. Little was heard from him over the five years and the letters received were uninformative. When he returned to Vienna it quickly became clear that he had collapsed as a player, withdrawing into himself, a prodigy unable to make the psychological development to mature artist.[63] The case of Gusta was stranger. Through contact with a dog she had developed a water cyst on the brain. Feuermann had written of her pitiful condition in January 1930. In September he wrote to Lily Hofmann: 'You have probably already heard from Sophie that Gusta is no more. Be happy, be happy and grateful as long as you are all together. The idea that from now on there is a part of us that's missing is neither dreadful nor terrible. For the moment it's just unthinkable.'[64]

Chapter 5
'Intolerable Jew'
1931–4

It's all over with Germany; all over with Europe.

Emanuel Feuermann[1]

After his initial outburst at the state in which Becker had left the cello department of the Hochschule, Feuermann made rapid progress. He enjoyed teaching:

> Last week I had a students' evening. Four of them played, difficult pieces, for example Hindemith Sonata, Brahms Sonata, etc. And apparently it was a gigantic success for me as a teacher. People were quite surprised, the directors thanked me etc., etc. I'm not conceited about it just content that I have done good work. The class was at a very low level and now I have five–six who are worth listening to.

The four students taking part in the evening of 10 July 1931 were Kurt Reher, Jonel Fotino, Helmut Reimann and Bruno Sesselberg. Feuermann was now beginning to feel more comfortable in himself: 'You know my *meschuggas* [neuroses] about not feeling at home anywhere; now I know I belong in Berlin where I have my work.[2]

In November, Feuermann travelled again to the Soviet Union. He informed Lily Hofmann that he would be in Leningrad from the 11th to the 18th (of November), staying at the Hotel Europeiski. He was not looking forward to it: 'Am not very curious, know that it can only be worse than it was before. And

I don't yet know what I should do about money.'³ He was again at the Leningrad Philharmonic with his friend William Steinberg conducting. Their method of payment was a Guadanini violin and large quantities of caviar.⁴

Feuermann's touring so far had been confined to Europe. In 1925, there may have been plans for him to visit the United States as Bronisław Huberman, passing through Cologne and visiting the Reifenbergs, had suggested that Feuermann play chamber music with him in America.⁵ Sigmund would have been there at that time too. Now Feuermann's agents were working on another American tour:

> Just imagine, I have to go to Berlin today. There's something about America in the pipeline, the impresario is in Berlin for 3 days and I have been summoned there by telegram. I am very excited because I don't have a lot of confidence in my business acumen and I'm worried that I'm going to do something terribly stupid. We're talking about 1932–33; and even if it doesn't work out it's good that the contact has already been made.⁶

He was represented in America by Siegfried Hearst of NBC Artists Service at 711 Fifth Avenue, New York, an agency set up in 1928 and soon in serious competition with Columbia Concerts Corporation. Both NBC and Columbia ran national touring schemes: NBC offered 'Civic' town touring while Columbia offered Community Concerts. Feuermann's tour proposed for November and December 1932 came to nothing. He had wired: 'Impossible because of too low fee and because everything is changing here.'⁷ (This gnomic remark is not explained.) Hearst's response to the cable was anguished; he pointed out that in relation to prevailing economic conditions, the offer for this introductory tour was good and future years would build on it. If Feuermann was now to decide not to come to the United States those organizations that had already engaged him would be far less keen to re-engage him in the future:

> Is not America worth a tour of 8 guaranteed concerts @ $400 a total of $3200 – or 1650 Gold Marks, bearing in mind the worst times we have ever known and the fact that in Europe you wouldn't get half that amount? For that reason, it is a great pity that you have come to the decision that your fee is too low. We wouldn't have made any money out of your tour because we have already spent a lot of money on advertising in musical journals and various circulars. If, after receiving this letter, you are able to change your mind and accept our offer, please cable me HEARST NATBROCAST NEWYORK.⁸

NBC had already issued publicity material including an enthusiastic but somewhat inaccurate press release: 'Cellists. First American Tour. One of the great cellists of the present generation. Though not yet thirty years old, Emanuel Feuermann holds the post once occupied by Joseph Joachim [*sic*] – that of director of the cello department of the Berlin Hochschule Für Musik.'[9] Feuermann did not change his mind. More cryptically, in a letter to Lily he wrote: 'By the way I'm not going to America, it's been postponed by a year. Funnily enough I'm not upset about that.'[10] Feuermann must have rejected the tour because the fee was too low.

As in the previous year he was in Leningrad, in December 1932 for six days: 'looks as though it will be very relaxing again for me. The people really seem to like me. One lady said she felt as though I'd never gone away – I've also been lucky to get a stunning "apartment" in the hotel, so everything falls into place and allows me to feel really relaxed here after such restless days in Berlin.'[11] But apart from radio programmes where recordings were played, known performances by Feuermann in Germany at that time are few. An important premiere did take place on 3 October, in Dortmund, where Feuermann, with Wilhelm Sieben, played Glazunov's *Concerto ballata*, a work dedicated to Casals but never performed by him.[12] And in December he included only one major concert (also broadcast), with Eugen Jochum and the Berlin Philharmonic.[13]

Feuermann's career on the concert platform and at the Hochschule was flourishing and after a break of two years, in September 1932 he made one new gramophone record: Popper's *Hungarian Rhapsody* with Paul Kletzki conducting the Berlin Philharmonic. For unknown reasons, this recording was made for Telefunken. But this was a period of change; storm clouds had been gathering for some time. The Wall Street crash of 1929 had wrought severe economic decline worldwide, and by 1930 4.4 million Germans were unemployed. In his surviving correspondence Feuermann hardly refers to the worsening political climate, although he was with Bruno Walter listening to the radio during the night of 14 September 1930 as the results of elections were announced. Walter recalled:

> Every few minutes, the triumphant voice of the announcer would tell of the progress of the election. We knew at about three in the morning that Hitler had polled about 6,500,000 votes and that the Nazis would be the new Reichstag's largest party. Feuermann, usually so gay, left us with the words: 'It's all over with Germany; all over with Europe'.[14]

The Berlin Hochschule, as a government-funded institution, was particularly vulnerable to the changing circumstances. One edict after another arrived from the ministry. 'Special economic measures' were demanded: contracts should not be renewed; promotions should be frozen; vacant positions should remain vacant; salaries should be cut by as much as 20%.[15] In

September 1930 the Hochschule tried to plead its special status, declaring that it could not reject talents 'that come to us in large numbers and exclude them from professional teaching'.[16] On the other hand, the Hochschule was aware that with the impossibly poor conditions of the job market the number of students accepted into the school would have to be curtailed. The advent of sound cinema in the late 1920s had alone thrown approximately 12,000 musicians out of work.[17]

But if the Hochschule was suffering the difficulties of the economic climate, the racial and foreign make-up of the teaching staff was even more problematic. Anti-Semitism and right-wing anti-internationalist sentiments were rife. Envy was inspired in those who felt that the numbers of Jews and foreigners at the school were not only too high but occupied a disproportionately large number of positions. (In Germany as a whole, Jews occupied a higher percentage of 'intellectual' positions than the proportion of Jews in the population.) Within the Hochschule, tensions were evident. Artur Schnabel gave his forthcoming tours as his official reason for not renewing his contract in 1931. Later he admitted that the real reason was the constant friction and conflict he experienced among his colleagues.[18] Carl Flesch's publication in 1931 of a brochure *Das Klangproblem im Geigenspiel* ('The Problem of Sound in Violin Playing'), suggesting that Jews, rather than German, Slavic or Romance races, produced the finest violin sound, did nothing to help the general atmosphere.[19] Flesch left himself vulnerable to attack, which came from his colleague and rival at the Hochschule, the violinist Gustav Havemann, to whom Flesch had expressly sent the document. Havemann's own study of violin technique, *Die Violintechnik bis zur Vollendung* ('Violin Technique to Perfection'), had been published in the same year (1928) as Flesch's two-volume *Kunst des Violinspiels* ('The Art of Violin Playing'). In the *Allgemeine Musik-Zeitung* Havemann accused Flesch of 'deliberately wanting to impose on the far more numerous musical works of our race, the Jewish tonal sense which we reject as too sweet and sensual'.[20] As a prominent member of the National Socialist Party and the *Kampfbund für deutscher Kultur* (Combat League for German Culture, or KfdK), Havemann was soon to become one of the most effective ringleaders in the 'cleansing' of the Hochschule. In March 1933 he led a vociferous public campaign against the Berlin Philharmonic, demanding that all Jews should be removed from membership and management.

For a time, Feuermann remained unaffected at the Hochschule. He was as active as ever on the concert platform and could be heard frequently on the radio.[21] His contract was renewed in February 1932 for the period 1 April to March 1934.[22] Right away he purchased a new car, the first of many Buicks, at a princely sum of 9412RM.[23] And he purchased a cello. He had written excitedly

EDUARD WINTER A. G. BERLIN					1519 ✷	
Buick–		IIEL ABTEILUNG				

Wagen-Rechnung
(Original)

Com. 4108

Datum 23. April 193 2

Verkauft an Herrn Prof. Emanuel Feuermann,

Verkäufer Habermann.   Adresse Berlin W., Lützow Ufer 23

Fabrikat	Modell	Neu oder Gebr.	Chassis No.	Motor No.	Bezeichnung	RM	RM
					Lt. Bestellschein vom: 28. 10. 1931		
					ab General–Motors G.m.b.H.		
					New York – Berlin		
Buick	14/	neu	2620678		Cabriolet,		
	80			2769634	6fach bereift,		9.400.—
	PS						
					Zulassung		
					Fahrschule		
					Fracht ab Werk und Ablieferung		
					Versicherung		
					Finanzierungsgebühr		
					°/₀ Zinsen Diskontspesen		10.—
					Steuer		
					Typenbescheinigung		
					Wechselstempel ················		2.—
					Vertragsstempel		
					Gesamt Verkauf		9.412.—
					Abrechnung:		
					Bar bei Lieferung	1.843.—	
					Anzahlung		
					Gebrauchter Wagen 14/80 PS Buick	5.625.—	
					Modell		
					Chassis No.		
					Motor No.		
					1 Wechsel p.7.5.32	1.944.—	
					Gesamt	9.412.—	

to Lily that 'the cello will be in Berlin. I had to play on a different cello every few weeks.'[24] Quite why is unclear. He had sold his Guarneri in 1931 to Joseph Schuster. In March 1932, Feuermann had lent his Tecchler to the cellist Thelma Yellin (née Bentwich), who was on a visit to Berlin from Palestine. She fell in love with the instrument and hoped Feuermann might sell it. In April, he offered it to her for 10,000 marks, a sum she considered enormous but in May she bought it.[25] It seems likely that he asked so large a sum to pay for the car – at almost the same figure. The sale of the Guarneri should have provided sufficient funds for the next cello he was to buy: a Montagnana from Hill in London. Hill wrote:

> I personally am very pleased to see the Montagnana cello pass into your hands for I am perfectly convinced of the tonal possibilities of the instrument and wish once more to impress upon you that you cannot judge of its merits in a few weeks, but must continue to play on it for 2–3 months and then only will you be in a position to discover its *real merits* and *its faults*, if any! Had I not every confidence in the former, I should not have

been disposed to give you a year's option on the instrument, but should have sold it to you outright![26]

Conditions for Feuermann, however, were changing. By July 1932 he was uneasy: 'I can't talk from my own experience just yet, but it's pretty dreadful here, all sorts of things are happening at the Hochschule; of all people I'm the one they say has German culture, apparently I'm different etc. etc.'[27] This suggests that already there were discussions about which of the Jewish teachers might have to go, but in recognizing Feuermann's importance to the Hochschule, they attributed to him a commitment to German cultural values.

In January 1933 Hitler was appointed chancellor, and measures to curb the activities of Jews were swiftly and harshly enacted. In March, Bruno Walter was barred from conducting concerts in Berlin and Leipzig with the Gewandhaus Orchestra, of which he was principal conductor (Richard Strauss took over these concerts), and broadcasts of Schnabel's series of Beethoven concerts in Berlin were cancelled. Schnabel never played another note in Germany. On 5 April, Klemperer abruptly departed for Zürich.

In March 1933 Feuermann received a letter from Schünemann advising him that his new contract would be terminated on 1 July 1933 and remarking: 'I presume you are familiar with the reasons for the termination of the contract.'[28] A further letter of April 8 states: 'Being empowered by the Herr Reichskommisar for the Prussian Ministry for Science, Art and Public Education, with immediate effect you are given leave of absence from now to the end of your contract.' The previous day the 'Law for the Restoration of the Civil Service' had come into effect, enabling the Nazis to dismiss any state-employed Jew from his position. Feuermann had been summarily sacked. The purification of Jewish influence had begun.

The 'cleaning up operation' at the Hochschule was both disgraceful and distasteful. At the instigation of the KfdK, Schünemann (acting director since the dismissal of Schreker in 1932) was dismissed and Fritz Stein installed, a trumped-up appointment engineered by Havemann. Havemann intended Stein's appointment to be a temporary one. Stein would carry out the task of 'sanitizing' the Hochschule, after which Havemann would become the 'elected' director. As Havemann cravenly wrote to Hans Hinkel, director of the KfdK and State Commissioner in the Prussian Ministry: 'Were the choice of rector to be decided by the teachers, I can surely say without arrogance that the majority of the teaching staff would nominate me.'[29] Using the letterhead of the Berlin section of the KfdK, Stein put forward the wishes of the department of music for the reformation of the Hochschule für Musik. Against the Jewish names 'reasons' were appended for their dismissal:

Staatl. akad. Hochschule
für Musik in Berlin
Der Direktor

Charlottenburg, den 8. April 19³³
Fasanenstraße 1

Sehr geehrter Herr Professor!
    Durch Ermächtigung des Herrn Reichs-
kommissar für das Preussische Ministerium
für Wissenschaft, Kunst und Volksbildung
beurlaube ich Sie mit sofortiger Wirkung
bis zum Ablauf des Vertrages.

            Mit vorzüglichster Hochachtung

Herrn
Prof. Emanuel Feuermann

Oskar Daniel: 'Polish Jew, not fully in command of the German language'
Franz Ludwig Hoerth: 'Jew holding two jobs'
Frieda Loebenstein: 'Kestenberg follower, cultural bolshevist, Jewess'
Leonid Kreutzer: '12 Professors petitioned against his renewal of contract "because of various occurrences"'
Charlotte Pfeffer: 'protégée of Kestenberg'
Dr Hugo Strelitzer: 'shabby character'
Emanuel Feuermann: 'intolerable Jew'
Stefan Jeidals: 'incapable'
Siegfried Borris: 'carried out Kestenbergian policies in tuition'[30]
Proposals for 'acceptable' replacements are made in the document too, entered without comment. Paul Grümmer was Feuermann's suggested replacement.

These were not the only dismissals: Alexander Zemlinsky, Fanny Warburg, Hugo Rüdel, Bruno Eisner, Professor Dr Curt Sachs and Charlotte Schlesinger were all dismissed. During the 1932/3 academic year 33 teachers at the Berlin Hochschule lost their jobs. A number of Feuermann's students left as a mark of solidarity. A photograph was taken in Munich of Feuermann with these students, among them Reimann, Sesselberg and Georg Ulrich von Bülow, although the others are not identified. Documents show that during the winter months of 1932/3 there were 24 cello students at the Hochschule, but by the summer that figure had reduced to 12.[31] Some are shown to have left at Easter, but whether this relates directly to Feuermann's dismissal cannot be assumed.

Little was certain. Many, including Paul Hindemith, believed that a democratically elected government would have to be tolerated until the next elections; many Germans (and Jews) gave this government only months to remain in power. 'There wasn't a unified view even among the intelligentsia. It was very difficult to imagine that the whole nation had gone totally crazy with this blatant idiot.'[32] Feuermann's letter to the violinist Bronisław Huberman, just days after he had been dismissed, is very mixed. Feuermann had seen Furtwängler's open letter to Dr Goebbels pleading the neutrality of art, and still believed that there might be some hope of remaining in Germany. Yet he commented: 'It is easy for him because he is not acting on his own behalf. He is however the first who has dared to say a free word.'[33] Furtwängler was not a Jew.

Feuermann understood the situation sufficiently to realize that he must look to other countries for work. He hoped that Huberman might be able to arrange work for him in London: 'That way you would open a new country for me which is more than necessary. The most wonderful thing would be if I could play in May/June and the most wonderful thing would be [to play] once with you and once alone.' But Feuermann's apparent breeziness later in the same letter seems oddly misplaced:

> We – Mrs Reifenberg and her daughter Eva with me as chauffeur – are doing a wonderful journey. If one thinks one has reached the highest point, there is always another surprise that puts what one has seen before into the shade (Lago Maggiore, Bergamo – Verona – Vicenza – Venice – Padua – Bologna – Ravenna – Urbino, now Perugia and Assisi and as the final point Rome). Wonderful! You should make a journey too.[34]

Hardly the words of someone sacked not ten days before. Huberman's reply was prompt and practical. London would make a promising base for Feuermann, particularly as in recent years arts institutions and concert organisations were flourishing, and public interest in music both in quality and quantity was encouraging. Huberman believed that Feuermann would find little competition from local cellists. Obtaining permanent domicile might, however, prove more difficult. There was the issue of passports: Huberman was uncertain as to whether it would be more advantageous for Feuermann to have an Austrian or a German one. Had Feuermann retained his Austrian citizenship? Regarding playing together, Huberman hinted that he had some special idea, but for the moment any discussion was premature. Huberman was remarkable not only for his gifts as a distinguished performer and organizer but also as a man of unusual vision. There were not many who predicted with such accuracy the cultural outcome of a policy designed to expel Jews from their jobs:

> I think in principle it quite right that you should not impose yourself on Germany. In the end every medal has two sides. In the case of German artists and academics, in my opinion it is more a matter of the Germans losing a great part of those representatives of culture that have made them seem great in the eyes of the world, than about the Jews losing their positions. And if the Jews are going to be expelled from their positions, the German people will not be saved from that loss of culture by a sentimental insistence by Jews to remain in Germany.[35]

Huberman worked hard for Feuermann:

> I have just received a letter from Warsaw where I am told that – after several interventions on my part – you're going to be asked to play the Brahms Double Concerto on 7 May. I can reveal to you that somebody else was intended (although not firmly engaged) but I made the point that you, as a victim of anti-Semitic activities, deserved to be preferred, apart from any artistic considerations.[36]

Huberman had also discussed Feuermann's situation with Harold Holt, one of the most influential artists' managements in Britain, and intended contacting the BBC. One wonders how exasperated he must have been by Feuermann's eventual refusal to play in Warsaw because he believed he was worth more than the payment of expenses only. Feuermann seems seriously to have been misjudging the times. Yet a letter to Lily shows that he was now seriously affected by events:

> I try not to bother anyone with my affairs, I even think of myself as totally unimportant, but now even I've got to the stage that people think of me as "nervous". It's really not very nice just sitting here so idly. Don't take what I say too literally, because I am busy with pupils and would be even busier practising: but that feeling of expectation for the forthcoming season, the Hochschule, the rehearsals, which usually sets in about now, is missing. Not to mention what's going on inside of me. I don't even know if it's right for me to stay on here. But I feel that, particularly now, I would feel lost and useless in another town.[37]

Eva Reifenberg wrote to him about her various ideas for training for work outside Germany. His reply is a chilling reaction to the dreadful impact of the new government on the Jews. 'You are a 100% example for the cruelty of the new regime not only to punish children like yourself for the intelligence and creativity of their ancestors but also, through the new regime's viciousness, to attack everything that the old society encouraged.'[38] Feuermann reminded her, however, of her considerable advantage over most Jews: the Reifenbergs had money.

It is difficult to assess the dislocation that Reifenberg & Cie in Cologne suffered at this time. No correspondence survives to indicate how severely the company was hit by the national boycott of Jewish businesses and no living relative remembers what happened. Mrs Reifenberg, however, had become very dependent on Feuermann. Following the sudden death in September 1929 of Paul Reifenberg, Emma had turned to Feuermann, as Eva Reifenberg recalled: 'When my father died my mother broke down completely. 100%. I mean, really, awful. The only one who understood her right and was sweet with her was Feuermann. We children didn't know how to deal with a broken-down mother.'[39]

Many letters from Emma to Feuermann survive – although none from the period October 1929 to June 1935. Deductions only can be made about the content of Feuermann's letters to her, since none survive. From as early as 1920, only one year after Feuermann had stormed Cologne, Emma was writing to him like a son, her letters full of family news and gossip. She, the more musical of the Reifenberg couple, followed Feuermann's activities assiduously and was able to report to him on concerts she attended, the musician friends she met (Furtwängler, Klemperer, Abendroth), programmes she heard on the radio, and records of his and others that she bought. Her expression of closeness and warmth towards him might suggest that this was something she missed from her husband Paul, to whom she frequently refered as 'the Almighty'. Paul led the life of a successful businessman travelling between the Reifenberg offices, picked up by company chauffeurs, even flying by plane. Her gratitude to Feuermann could be an indication of her isolation: 'These lines should only tell you how eternally grateful I am to you for all the love and loving that you give to my children. Please be still[40]for such a feeling of genuine friendship occurs so rarely that one cannot be thankful enough when it is present.'[41] She also wrote to him more intimately in apparent response to his anxiety: 'If only you knew how often you pervade my thoughts amongst all the other things that surround me you would be satisfied, and the feeling that this romantic love of the 20th century has lost intensity would never occur to you.'[42]

Just how far Feuermann's relationship with Emma Reifenberg developed is impossible to know. She was 15 years his senior. Her feelings certainly appear more than motherly, but given the conventions of the period it seems unlikely that the relationship developed further. What does seem clear is that Mrs Reifenberg's involvement suited Feuermann well. As a child he had spent so little time with his own family and had lived away from home so much that a pattern of seeking closeness with 'adopted' families had formed. About his own family in Vienna he had written in 1931 in some desperation:

> The situation must be dreadful at home: father being an unbearable hypochondriac making my mother's life hell, Sigmund practising all day, quite hopelessly, Rosa does after all want to marry our cousin, parents are against it – and over it all the pain of Gusta. And – I cannot do a thing. It is wretched. I think if things were different at home I would be a lot calmer too.'[43]

Feuermann's letter of 22 May 1933 to Eva, however, marks a turning-point both in his relationship with Mrs Reifenberg and in his relationship with Eva. With Paul Reifenberg now deceased, Feuermann's relationship with Mrs Reifenberg had changed. Eva, Emma's youngest child, was just approaching her 19th birthday:

> Eva, think when and wherever you can of your mother who must be in a terrible state. I am afraid that I am not completely innocent about this. We spoke yesterday on the phone, she again made arrangements for me, and I again had the feeling that I am not my own master ... Do be kind and considerate towards her. But you must never go so far as to give up your own personality out of love and pity for your mother as I have done. . . . How I envy you Eva, that you have real friends. Now, since Franz [Osborn?] has left I, a 30-year-old man, who has been living for years in Berlin, have no one to whom I can say I feel friendly (excluding Lily). And to a certain degree I blame your mother because despite my apartment and work, I was here only as a guest and was at your mother's disposal whenever I had time.

His feelings towards Eva had changed: 'I think I would be very happy if you would look upon me as your friend and not as something burdensome. I am afraid that I am the teeniest bit in love with you. Nevertheless you don't have the obligation to answer me nor explain that the love remains unrequited.'[44] Eva was to complain that Feuermann seemed like a fourth brother to her whose lecturing she much resented. And indeed, just a few weeks later he showed her his lecturing side, venting his anger and frustration over her attitude to her mother:

> Is it possible that you don't want to be together with your mother in the summer? If that is true then you are the most heartless creature that I can

imagine. Your mother who hasn't got over the death of your father, who
with the business problems and other things is just half a person, you want
to abandon her? . . . My God, are you Reifenbergs really such fantastic
egoists? Don't you have any love, if you like, Christian love in your heart? . . .
You will be angry about this letter. But I feel justified in saying this. Half of
my life I live together with you, I love you, your worries, your friends, I don't
experience them superficially; . . . I don't expect an answer because I assume
that after this letter you will be angry with me. But it would be wonderful if
I could contribute to your becoming clearer about yourself and becoming a
human being, and not remaining the creature you seemingly are.[45]

Feuermann could not believe that a Jewish girl, however assimilated, could put
her life before that of her mother.

Feuermann was now reluctantly realizing that he would have to leave Berlin.
He had decided that London was his choice, although he had received a letter
from his agent, Dr Paul Schiff, saying that the BBC was not willing to offer
work. Feuermann knew that he needed a major introduction and was still
hoping that he could play with Huberman, to whom he wrote: 'How could one
draw their attention to the apparently existing vitamins and calories in my
playing? I have great confidence in you but of course I don't want to be a
nuisance. Unfortunately I am quite convinced that England can manage quite
well without me and I don't think that with such feelings one can conquer a
country.'[46] Ibbs and Tillett, the other foremost London concert agency did,
however, offer him management.

'Round-up' reviews of concerts in early 1933 appear in the periodicals
Zeitschrift für Musik and *Die Musik*, but Feuermann could no longer perform
in Germany, except under the auspices of the Jüdischer Kulturbund. This
organization was the somewhat paradoxical attempt by the Prussian Ministry
of Education to provide work for the thousands of Jewish artists still living in
Germany but thrown out of work by the April 1933 legislation; it was feared
that a disestablished minority without work could cause political instability.
With this organization, the Nazis hoped to convince the outside world that
Germany was not really treating its Jews badly. The Kulturbund's headquarters
were in Berlin, but local associations were established in other cities where
there was a significant Jewish population. Events were open only to Jews, who
had to be registered members of the Kulturbund. The German press was
forbidden to report on its activities or even acknowledge its existence – an odd
response to the need to publicize it in the outside world.

In October 1933 Feuermann visited Paris, where his colleague Arnold
Schönberg, dismissed from the Akademie der Künste, had taken refuge.

Schönberg was at this time exploring the possibilities of performance and publication of his new work for cello and orchestra based on a concerto for harpsichord by the 18th-century composer Georg Monn. He fervently hoped that this work would be given its first performances by Casals, to whom he had dedicated it. Casals, however, had written: 'I have never worked so assiduously, which testifies to my admiration for you. The difficulties will be overcome, which is saying a lot. Impossible however to say *when* the work will be ready to be given in public.'[47] During his visit to Paris, Feuermann performed the concerto privately for Schönberg with the conductor Walter Goehr at the piano.[48] The composer confirmed that Feuermann played it fabulously, while 'Casals is not quite ready for it.'[49] An American newspaper article a year later declared: 'When Mr Feuermann worked on it with the composer last summer in Paris, he found him "tolerance itself", amiably agreeing to all the suggestions made by the cellist.'[50]

It was during this time in Paris that Feuermann received a letter from the Jüdischer Kulturbund Rhein-Ruhr outlining a tour between 15 and 19 October to include concerts in the Cologne and Essen synagogues, as well as in Krefeld, Aachen and Bochum. This was a decidedly risky venture. Quite what was meant by the veiled words of a letter to Feuermann is unclear: 'It is understood that knowledge of your conditions will not go beyond the circle of our committee.'[51] But evening dress and a cover for the head (Yamacha) were required.

Feuermann badly needed work. Even Eva Reifenberg thought that he could do more to help himself:

> Please stop only helping others for a while, you HAVE to take better care of yourself and use your fists to fight for yourself. Don't rely on managers and other such people; you yourself should negotiate, insist, persist for every single pathetic little concert whether you get paid or not. Go ahead and impose your name on people. You have to put your own money into advertising, first recitals and so on. It will be worth it later on. Do you understand me? Please do not smile because although I am still an inexperienced little sheep that doesn't mean that I am wrong.'[52]

Despite his misgivings about London, in December Feuermann began an extended stay which, on and off, was to last until the beginning of February 1934. He was not alone – Mrs Reifenberg and Eva were both in London, where Eva was studying. There had been discussion about renting an apartment, but as this would have required Feuermann to have a visa he stayed in South Kensington at the Hotel Rembrandt. Eva was reluctant to believe that her mother could not continue living in Cologne. She wrote to Feuermann:

'Assuming all goes well, why should we not let her stay there as long as the house should remain the way it is and since she truly (which I can understand quite well) likes it BEST there, why not? We could always visit her.'[53] Despite the dangers, Feuermann was still travelling monthly to Berlin to teach private pupils.

Feuermann had few concerts. His earnings had collapsed, with no salary from the Hochschule nor income from concerts in Germany. But work was finally offered by the BBC, a broadcast concert on 19 January 1934, as indeed were recordings for the Columbia Graphophone Company. Both engagements were with his colleagues Goldberg and Hindemith, and both involved performing Hindemith's new string trio, his second, which he had written for them in the previous year. Feuermann had made no gramophone recordings since 1932. These London sessions were the first for Columbia and his first outside Germany. Hindemith's Second Trio and Beethoven's Serenade op.8 were recorded on 21 and 22 January. But when the Beethoven session came to an end there was a problem: a blank side remained. With no obvious four-minute trio to fill the side, Hindemith volunteered to write a piece overnight. As Goldberg had to leave, the piece, a Scherzo, was written for viola and cello only. Hindemith, in a letter to his publisher, wrote that the piece was composed between five and eight o'clock in the morning. Goldberg recalls that he came back to the studio at about ten o'clock to say goodbye to his colleagues and could hear them already listening to the first playback. He maintains that Feuermann 'could have had little more than half an hour to learn this extraordinarily difficult little piece and record it'.[54] Feuermann's sight-reading ability was legendary, but this must surely have stretched him (and indeed Hindemith!) as can be heard to this day on the recording. Hindemith, in the same letter to his publisher, was candid about their sessions: 'The recordings were an awful sweat. I played my fingers to blood-blisters and even exposed the nerve on one finger, which makes playing particularly pleasant.'[55] A few days later Feuermann recorded Hindemith's Solo Sonata op.25 no.3 – a work deemed unsaleable in the United Kingdom and released only in the USA.

During his stay in London, Feuermann made good contact with Miss Bass, his British manager (she was later to become Mrs Tillett). In February he listed his concerto repertoire, of which a high percentage was by living composers; he was already offering the Schönberg for performance.

In 1932 Feuermann had felt able to turn down an American tour. Now, however, Germany was lost as a concert base, although he was able to continue performing in other European countries – Austria, Switzerland, Holland and Italy. But the landscape had changed completely and for him touring on a far wider scale was about to begin: 'I'm playing in Palestine from 20th to 28th

April. I'm so looking forward to it. I'm going to Japan and Java in August – I'll be playing there in September and October. And at Christmas it's off to America for 2 months.' Feuermann was clearly delighted with his schedule, so much so that he wickedly adds in this letter to Lily: 'If I'm successful in all these places I could almost turn into a Nazi out of gratitude for the kick up the . . . .'[56]

Palestine was important to Feuermann, but not only because he was a Jew. His friend and colleague Huberman had embarked on a visionary project to set up an orchestra there. It would provide a lifeline for Jewish musicians in Europe, and Huberman worked tirelessly: 'Can you imagine a pro-Jewish and pro-Zionist propaganda more effective than a concert tour of the Palestine Orchestra, undertaken in a couple of years throughout the civilised world and acclaimed both by Jews and Gentiles as amongst the best in existence?'[57] In March 1934 Feuermann contacted Huberman about Michael Taube who was then working for the Jüdischer Kulturbund in Berlin:

> Taube is in his late 30s, from Łodz. I got to know him recently in Cologne. He was conductor in Godesberg and Bonn and for some years he gave subscription concerts in Cologne, and was at the State Opera in Berlin and had a chamber orchestra for years whose concerts were described by the critics as musical events and he is now, together with Rosenstock, conductor of the Jüdischer Kulturbund. I have the greatest admiration for him. Above all I want to tell you that it is not a question of charity even though Taube is in need of it . . . it's a question of conducting.

As musician to musician, Feuermann could not resist telling Huberman: 'Just imagine, he accompanied me with a full orchestra, we played sonata evenings together, quartets privately – he plays the viola, and as a joke he once played the Saint Saens concerto on the cello. . . . If you will help him, you will do a great service to the musical life of Palestine.'[58] Taube did indeed become involved with Huberman's orchestra.

The previous year Feuermann had declared that he was 'the teeniest bit' in love with Eva Reifenberg, but now he was uncertain and discussing that uncertainty with others. In the following Feuermann the teacher is confused with Feuermann the suitor:

> I see too much in you and have too high expectations of you. You were a charming girl but if a person like me would marry you, it would be quite wrong. You are lacking, etc. etc. I'm afraid that this opinion of Dr. Schmid's wife comes as a surprise, but I am sure that you don't look upon this as gossip and most of all I think that you are in the process of changing for the

better so I hope that you understand why I am writing this to you: to open
your eyes about yourself and also about your fellow men.

The blow is somewhat softened by Feuermann's suggestion that her life had
been 'damaged' by her father's resolve to have all his children baptized with no
alternative idealistic basis. In somewhat awkward German he wrote: 'You all
had the most wonderful home. As an appendage, I am happy to have found
that home too. But it was a home of wealth, of respect for the parents, not a
home where the children were shown love for other people or that they should
not put their own interests first, what one calls simply heart, soul and feeling.'[59]
Somehow the storm was weathered.

Feuermann travelled to Palestine with Eva, Mrs Reifenberg and several other
relatives. Sophie was his pianist. The organization was shambolic – a young
impresario in charge had arranged no concerts. The excuse was that
Huberman had given several concerts and now the public had no money for
tickets. A potential disaster was averted by Feuermann's Palestinian student
Mosa Havivi, who was acquainted with Haim Friedmann, the organizer of
Cultural Activities of the Histradut (or workers' union), which financed
concerts. Havivi was convinced that a concert could be organized overnight; all
that was needed was a big announcement: 'Feuermann is playing the Haydn
Concerto.' Havivi brought Friedmann and Feuermann together, and no money
was discussed: the orchestra agreed to waive its fee because of the highly
unusual circumstances. A concert was arranged to take place at the Beit Ha'am
(the House of the People – a large cinema) in Tel Aviv. Havivi believes that
Feuermann had not touched his cello in weeks. At the first rehearsal he opened
the cello case: '"Good! All strings are on the cello." And right away he began
playing with the orchestra. It was tremendous. It was stunning. It was a
miracle.' The concert was sold out. Feuermann played both the Haydn and the
Saint-Saëns concertos, followed by many encores with Sophie at the piano.
After the concert, Havivi recalls going to the box office and finding the receipts
in a suitcase: 'The money was brought up to Feuermann – he didn't even count
it. He just put it on the table. He was so amused. It was real amateur emergency
stuff.'[60]

A further recital and a concert in the kibbutz Ein Harodt was arranged. Ein
Harodt, situated to the north of Tel Aviv, was one of the largest kibbutzim in
Palestine. It was a good choice. In the first years of Nazi rule it had accepted a
large number of German Jews aged between 20 and 35 and there was a high
intellectual level. Wolfgang Steinberg, a grandson of Joseph and Emmy
Steinberg, with whom Feuermann had lived in Cologne, lived in this kibbutz
and attended the concert:

They played a regular programme including one of the Beethoven op.5 sonatas, then he played a lot of the virtuoso pieces – everything with Sophie. After the concert was over, near midnight, a small circle of people, the real aficionados, begged him to play some Bach. He played the whole C minor Suite and I remember writing to my parents about it. Good artists would come and after there would be a reception, chocolate, cakes, tea and we always asked them to play some more because both the Polish and the German immigrants were missing concerts and theatres a lot more than the good food or the good beds that we had in Germany. We only had cold water but the culture shock was enormous – we were cut off. We even had trouble getting books – German books because we couldn't read Hebrew yet.[61]

Sophie Feuermann also recalled the experience of Ein Harodt: 'There was a big dining room with the stone floor and table where you ate. Afterwards everything was cleared, the windows were opened and, believe it or not, they came from all over. There were a thousand people there. I had a piano – upright – the keys didn't work but I never played better!'[62] The experience for Feuermann was also profound, as revealed in a letter to Bernhard Mayer, Lily Hofmann's father, whom he colourfully addresses as Honorary Chaluz ('Pioneer') Mayer: 'I'm several days into my return trip and it has been wonderful, of course quite a different atmosphere and yet, despite my ability to assimilate, as you keep stressing, I cannot forget the days in Palestine. . . . this trip leaves one with a great feeling of regret: the regret that one is not a part of it all.'[63]

Feuermann was doubtless moved by his experience in Palestine, but he did have an ulterior motive in writing to Bernhard: he wanted help for Havivi.

Now let's turn to *Tachles* [get to the point], dear Herr Mayer. My pupil Chavivi[64] is coming from Tel Aviv to study with me in Ascona. He is the nicest person I know, but of course he hasn't got two pennies to rub together. He could teach Hebrew very well and I have promised him that the 'Mayers' would look after him. If anyone deserves to be helped then it's this boy. Would you???[65]

This was not the first time Feuermann had contacted the Mayers about Havivi. Twice in 1931 he had written to Lily to try to organize money for him. He was Feuermann's first student in Berlin whom he felt to be a major talent.

Feuermann returned to Europe aboard the Lloyd Triestino *Conte Rosso*. May was spent mainly in London, where there was further work from the BBC. Adrian Boult and Bruno Walter were sharing the conducting of the BBC

Symphony Orchestra in six concerts between 4 and 16 May, the London Music
Festival organized by the BBC. Held in the Queen's Hall, these concerts were a
distinguished series: Carl Flesch played Beethoven's Violin Concerto; Vladimir
Horowitz Tchaikovsky's B♭ minor Concerto; Wilhelm Backhaus Brahms's B♭
Concerto; Feuermann was the soloist in Strauss's *Don Quixote*; and there were
performances of Hindemith's *Das Unaufhörliche*, Bruckner's Te Deum with
Isobel Baillie and Heddle Nash, and Mozart's D minor Piano Concerto K.466
with Walter as soloist and conductor. A publicity card proudly pronounced the
strength of the orchestra as 119 players. 'Analytical programmes' were for sale
at a price of 3s. for all six concerts. Perhaps it was misinformation in the
programme notes that gave some critics the wrong idea: 'The soloists in this
work were the leader of the Berlin Philharmonic Orchestra, Emanuel
Feuermann, who came a long way for a short stay, and Bernard Shore.'[66]
Feuermann was never leader of the Berlin Philharmonic Orchestra.

A few days later, on 25 May, Feuermann gave a recital in the Wigmore Hall.
It was a typical programme – Brahms's F major Sonata, Schubert's 'Arpeggione', the Valentini Sonata in E major and a group of small, virtuoso works.
The pianist was Ivor Newton. Feuermann frequently complained about the
coldness of reviews he received in London. Gerald Moore, who later accompanied him, also believed that British critics were slow to recognize
Feuermann. But on this occasion he could have had no complaint: 'To those
who did not already know it Mr Emanuel Feuermann proved at his recital at
the Wigmore Hall on Friday that he is in the front rank of violoncellists.'[67] And
in another paper the reviewer wrote tellingly: 'He has the real gift of changing
his style in accordance with the character of the music played. . . . Indeed, Mr
Feuermann can claim the great honour of giving us the same impression of
inevitability as does Casals: here, we feel, is the music exactly as Brahms or
Schubert would have liked to have heard it played.'[68]

Feuermann was in London again in July, recording at Abbey Road. These
recordings were made at the request of Nipponophone, the Japanese
subsidiary of Columbia, in canny expectation of Feuermann's forthcoming
visit to Japan that autumn.[69] Havivi attended these sessions. Just as in
January, one blank side remained to be filled. Havivi suggested the Mélodie
from Gluck's opera *Orphée*, which Feuermann had never played. Havivi
brought the music to the session the next day and, without reading it
through, Feuermann recorded it. Here there is an intense luminosity, a sound
quite different from the Brahms E minor Sonata recorded at the same time.
Havivi maintains that Feuermann used a different instrument from his
Montagnana.[70] Was it the Stradivarius he later owned? It seems unlikely, for a
letter written more than a year later suggests that Hill showed him a

Stradivarius that he had not seen before, the 'De Munck' that he was eventually to buy.

For his first major tour outside Europe, Feuermann took the Montagnana he had purchased from Hill. His journey to the Far East began in August on board the MS *Terukuni Maru*, which took him through the Suez Canal. For nine days he would see no land and almost immediately he was lonely. In a long and convoluted letter to Eva he wrote:

> It is very difficult for me, because for a long time I have a question on the tip of my tongue, whose fulfilment through you will bring me pain but at the same time clarity. Namely: write to me that it is impossible that we should ever marry. I assume it is impossible that this thought has ever occurred to you, but for me it has been going through my head for more than 2 years. If I imagine my future life, it is always in connection with you; whether regarding where I could live or when generally thinking of marriage. Always I imagine that you are the woman. I have to rid myself of this 'complex'. Even if you don't utter the 'no' that I demand of you, there is so much against the idea, so very much that I am forced to request this 'no' from you. I am a bit strange, the times are crazy, so I find that such a negative proposal of marriage fits rather well . . . I hope that you are aware that this is not the act of a moonstruck youth and that is how you must look upon it in this request for a negative answer.

Feuermann seems to be willing rejection. His mood is confused; on the one hand he is in love with her but on the other hand he is only too aware that she may not be a suitable partner for an artist and all that an artist's life entails. And, even if by now he was acknowledged as one of the world's greatest performing artists, he was still a Galician Jew. How could he hope that the daughter of the Reifenbergs, a very young woman, coming from a family so far removed from his own background, could see him as a potential spouse? Paradoxically, the National Socialists may have helped his cause; with the arrival of this regime a certain social levelling had occurred. Such differences were now less relevant. But he still felt insecure. Insecurity apart, Feuermann was also engaged in emotional gambling; he hoped to win the daughter without losing the mother. In his letter he admits that he has discussed his thoughts with her mother but suggests, even requests, that she should discuss it no further. If the letter was convoluted so were the relationships. On his journey Feuermann was lonely, but he was not alone, for with him was his accompanist, Fritz Kitzinger – but he was no substitute for Eva or her mother: 'I must scold you and your mother – I can't fully enjoy anything without you.'[71]

The boat arrived in Singapore on 23 August; that night Feuermann gave his first concert. The Far Eastern leg of the tour was arranged by Mr A. Strok, described by Feuermann as 'an old, very clever Russian Jew'.[72] He was a well-known impresario operating out of Shanghai who had established a circuit for Western musicians. After Singapore, the tour took Feuermann and Kitzinger to Batavia and Java, with performances taking place under the auspices of various *Kunstringe*. Feuermann's programmes embraced a wide repertoire – it was not a case of repeating one or two standard programmes – although the shape of them remained the same as before: serious works followed by a group of smaller pieces, ending invariably with virtuoso fireworks.[73] The single contemporary work he performed was Berthold Goldschmidt's Sonata for piano and cello op.23, a work dedicated to Feuermann. Years later, Goldschmidt, almost an exact contemporary of Feuermann and a student at the Hochschule in Berlin, recalled the circumstances under which this sonata came to be written:

> Whereas I was still a student, he already had an international reputation as an outstanding cellist. After a triumphant concert in Berlin we met at a party. Feuermann retired to a corner, protecting his instrument like a bodyguard. 'Please be careful not to knock against my precious cello' he said when I went to congratulate him, and he added with a smile, 'rather, compose something for it!' That, however, came ten years later in 1932, as a result of which I was able to present him with a composition for cello and piano.[74]

Feuermann was impressed by Java, but he found the heat and humidity troublesome: 'Even in the evening it drips down you (scusi!). It's terribly trying to play in that, and my playing wasn't even 90%, not even <u>once</u>. But it was a success, the people terribly nice.' Feuermann, who travelled by car to some of his concerts, vividly described what he saw:

> West–East is full of mountains, some over 3,000 metres high, wonderful large formations, not at all "frightening", and then the tropical vegetation, all the villages hidden under palm trees, a country road <u>never</u> without people, the roads up to 1400 metres are generally not wide, but excellent, the difference in temperature between the coast and the mountains wonderful. The most beautiful thing of all though was the excavated Borobudur Temple of Buddha, enormous and very symmetrical in its structure, with <u>2,000</u> reliefs, tapering upwards to four levels. From the plateau there is a <u>panorama</u> over the tropical plain, easily 60–80 kilometres in diameter, surrounded by the beautiful high mountains. In translations from the Latin this would be called 'sublime'.[75]

Feuermann was a keen photographer, but a log of his photographs alone is all that has survived from his trips.

On 15 September, he and Kitzinger left Singapore again on an English ship bound for Japan: 'I'm curious to see what the food will be like.'[76] On these long journeys letters were of considerable importance; Feuermann wrote a great deal but was often frustrated by lack of replies. In Batavia he missed an air mail delivery and realized with dismay that for one month he would have no news. A surviving letter to Hindemith's wife Gertrud reveals many anxieties. The trio was no longer working together because, as Jews, Feuermann and Goldberg's movements were proscribed, and so they were unable to meet frequently. But there appears to have been some more specific estrangement, not fully articulated:

After all, as far as I am concerned, we were friends for years. I cannot imagine that you only pretended to be. The business about the trio we explained to one another and I don't know what would be in the way for Goldberg, Hindemith and myself to play trios again if we felt like it – I certainly will continue to think of you in friendship. I can't excise you from my thoughts about the Berlin days but I must know, obviously, what your attitude to me is. . . . I beg you to write to me there [San Francisco], should you not do it I have to assume we are divorced, which I would feel very, very sad about.

Feuermann's thoughts were also of his future: 'Naturally I would be much happier if I knew where to go when I return to Europe. I don't feel so young any more . . . And my longing for a home base has perhaps grown ever greater.'[77]

Feuermann appeared to have received no reply from Eva to his convoluted marriage proposal. Marriage was on his mind; both Lily and his sister Sophie were about to marry.

Eva, have we become closer through my perfidious attack or have we drifted apart? Done is done; the effect which I had hoped to achieve from my letter didn't occur 100%. I can't exactly declare that you don't exist for me any more, I simply am very fond of you and harbour the one wish that you trust me and look upon me as your friend. Can you and do you want to be?[78]

Feuermann's first concert in Japan took place in Tokyo on 4 October at the Gunjin Kaikan. Four further recitals were announced for the 5th, 6th, 8th and 9th October in the same hall, with Feuermann playing a different programme at each recital. Japan's interest in Western classical music was remarkable. Since 1915, many Russian Jews escaping the pogroms had arrived in Japan and some

Japanese had studied in the West. By 1930 many distinguished Western artists had visited Japan, including the violinists Efrem Zimbalist, Kreisler, Thibaud and Heifetz and the pianists Godowsky and Levitzki. Advertisements in Feuermann's programmes show that Artur Rubinstein was touring hard on Feuermann's heels. A big surprise awaited Feuermann at his first recital: there was no audience. What had happened to Nipponophone's recordings? Of the nine people attending the concert one was a music critic who was ecstatic:[79]

> I had heard the name of Emanuel Feuermann before but only on 4 October did I, at last, hear him play and was truly amazed. . . . Emanuel Feuermann's music is like the power of the unending sea, the shining of a glittering diamond. I have in earlier years heard the famous cellist, Casals, but my memory of him has somewhat faded. Now that I have heard Emanuel Feuermann, I can say with certainty that Feuermann is greater than Casals. . . . Those who have an interest in European music must hear Emanuel Feuermann.[80]

Word soon spread: the next four recitals were sold out,[81] one review reporting blocked roads as crowds stood in front of radio shops listening to Feuermann's broadcast.[82]

Feuermann was a sensation and Nipponophone again went into action. The earlier recordings made in London may not have been released in time, or perhaps they had failed to make an impact; none the less Nipponophone were now inviting Feuermann to record four short pieces by two Japanese composers for release just ten days later. Three of the works were by Kōsaku Yamada (1886–1965), the fourth by Rentarō Taki (1879–1903). Feuermann's student Hideo Saito had introduced Feuermann to the Yamada arrangements. Saito's own student Seiji Osawa later commented: 'Obviously, Feuermann had never heard these tunes before. He took them home and next day he played them and phrased them better than any Japanese folk singer.'[83] On 17 October Feuermann's first orchestral concert in Japan took place in Tokyo's main concert hall, the Hibiya Public Hall. A review read: 'It is difficult to remember having seen the Hibiya Public Hall so crowded on the occasion of an ordinary subscription concert of the Japan Philharmonic Society. . . . His rendition of the Dvořák concerto effected the deepest impression and stood out as the feature of this season's musical events so far. It transported the large audience to a seeming ecstasy of enthusiasm.'[84] Viscount Hidemaro Konoye conducted the New Symphony Orchestra. Konoye, a brother of the Japanese prime minister, had studied at the Berlin Hochschule and had made his European debut conducting the Berlin Philharmonic in January 1928. Feuermann may perhaps have come across him in Berlin.

Feuermann's first two weeks in Japan were strenuous, with performances in Tokyo, Osaka, Kyoto and Kobe. He was also teaching. Apart from the rain, which was almost continuous, Feuermann was deeply affected by Japan:

Do you know that until 75 years ago Japan was completely untouched by white culture? Now after a relatively unbelievably short period it is in many ways just as modern as America and has retained in private life the forms, dress, social life and views as reigned before the 'European' time. I am extremely grateful to chance, or whatever, that just at the right time I could escape the desolation of Europe and see the world.[85]

From Japan, Feuermann moved on to China – Dairen, Tientsin and Peking. In Tientsin his recitals took place at the Astor House Hotel. A review published on 30 October reported: 'Commencing slightly melancholy, the Beethoven Sonata in A Sharp [*sic*] awakened a variety of divergent emotions upon progressing, and at the finale became teasing and tantalizing.'[86] A misunderstanding of the German 'dur' led to a clutch of delightful mistakes: as well as this unusual Beethoven sonata Feuermann played Valentini's sonata in E# and Breval's sonata in G#. On leaving Tientsin, Feuermann boarded the Shanghai Express for a journey to Shanghai of 40 hours. Letters and a caricaturist, in Japan a popular public relations tool, awaited him. Perhaps affected by the journey, or by the receipt of letters, Feuermann now wrote one of his lengthiest and weightiest missives. With all the seriousness of a lecture, he addressed Eva

with an analysis, an intense exploration, of the meaning of German or Jew. She was in London, which may have permitted him to write freely, reflecting openly on the turmoil in Germany.

> I remember that you said: I am a German, I cannot suddenly become a Jewess, etc. Did you ever think what it means to be a German or a Jew? Is one only a Jew if one keeps the religion? <u>Is one</u> German just because the parents at the birth of a child believe that through baptism and education 100% of the Jewish heritage can be lost while 100% of that which is called German can be acquired? Is it the race or the religion? Jews now wanting to be German begin to argue: Germans are mixed with many races, Jews as well, so Jews can also become German; and also, after all, the Jews have been living for so many centuries in Germany. Shall I try to say a few things in answer?'

Feuermann's 'answers' are of profound significance. Nowhere does he signal more comprehensibly his deepest feelings and how these affect his sense of identity as a Jew:

> A German is one whose ancestors have lived for centuries in Germany as a Christian, in <u>German</u> surroundings, in German tradition. If one or other of these factors is absent, i.e. as in an immigrant Frenchman or Slav, the remaining factors are still strong enough to ensure that after one or two generations the adjustment is complete. A Jew is someone whose ancestors have lived as Jews. You cannot become German of your own free will, the tradition within you lives on too strongly. Being a Jew does not only have to do with religion, it has to do with inherited perceptions, thoughts, feelings. . . . compare yourself with your Christian girl friends and you will see more clearly that you are a Jew through education, religious tuition, and school, but long to feel as a German. What way out is there for you? <u>I</u> only know of one: to reject that longing; to feel as a Jew; to realize that you cannot be a German; to try to <u>understand</u> that Jewish heritage is just as honourable as German heritage. As a résumé: [one should endeavour] to become a good person from Jewish descent with German culture, a human being such as the great men of our time, Goethe, Heine, Beethoven, who longed to be citizens of this earth, and not become a person who corresponds to the wishes of chauvinists who have gone mad, whether in the German or the Jewish camp. Can you be proud of what is now happening in Germany and can you be proud of the ancestors of these Germans who murdered our ancestors, mishandled, exploited and treated them as dogs? Can you do that? As children we were given books about knights and instructed to

worship the German burghers and emperors and counts of the middle ages as the rulers of our ancestors. This is a lie; this is deception. For these people we were a piece of dirt, different only from other manure, in that out of Jews one could extort money. But who says that we who speak German and have a German culture shouldn't have a part in some really great deeds of Germans? Is German feeling, German music, German poetry so different from that of other European countries? Don't Germans take the greatest delight in Shakespeare and the French in Wagner? Europeans we may be, not in the political sense of a Pan-Europe, but as carriers and supporters of a culture that is foremost in those men who think of themselves as a person rather than a Saxon, a Swiss or a Jew.

Few of Feuermann's letters to Eva are more intense, and it is of no surprise that in the same letter he soon lowers the tension: 'I am shocked by all this scribbling, but it is not stupid. While writing, it just dawned on me properly how much more complicated the questions are and that I am not yet finished with them. Take my answers as an attempt to become clearer myself.'[87]

In Shanghai on 6 and 9 November, Feuermann gave two recitals in the Lyceum Theatre; both were enthusiastically received. But on his return to Japan there was once again a shock in store. A 'Farewell Recital' in Osaka had been announced with the Takaradzuka Symphony Orchestra conducted by Jos. Laska, but no tickets had been sold. Quite why is unclear. Sophie has suggested that because Feuermann had performed scarcely a month before in Osaka, the audience had stayed away – an artist appearing twice in one season was unknown.[88] In Tokyo, however, the farewell recital of 14 November with the New Symphony Orchestra at the Hibiya Hall produced very different results. Unusually, it was Kitzinger who conducted the orchestra as well as accompanying at the piano. Feuermann played two concertos (Haydn D major and Schumann), concluding with a virtuoso set of pieces with Sarasate's *Zigeunerweisen* placed tactically at the end. As usual, the reviews were ecstatic.

Feuermann's first Far Eastern tour had been a resounding success. On board the American mail line *President Jackson*, bound for Victoria, Canada, he wrote to Lily: 'Japan was a triumph!! It was the greatest success for years, the last concert had ten times the takings of the first one. I'm going there again at the beginning of March 1936.'[89] He had spent three and a half months abroad and would be away from Europe for a further three months, returning in February 1935. His ship was to arrive in Victoria on 27 November. Feuermann's entourage had increased; as well as Kitzinger, the 22-year-old Japanese student Shoji Asabuki was now travelling to Europe in order to study with Feuermann. The boat was virtually empty, with a mere 34 other people on board, but

Feuermann found the journey very pleasant, and it was his birthday, an occasion about which he was remarkably sentimental. Invariably in his letters written around his birth date (22 November) he would make it clear how special this day was to him. On this occasion he was thrilled, for he could celebrate his birthday twice: on 22 November the ship passed over the international date line, gaining another day and another birthday! He wrote to Eva: 'Ghastly, I will be 32 years old. All the more I would like to be with you and convince myself that the time hasn't passed, that I am still the little Munio and not a "man" with a bald head – or rather, not really a man, and with a bald head.'[90]

Much as he delighted in his birthday, he was anxious about his forthcoming debut in New York: 'Now I have to tighten my belt when I think of New York. I am a bit afraid and I hope it will be okay. It's terrible how much depends on one evening. I am somewhat spoiled by these last weeks. I come to America as a small cellist where there are so many famous people.'[91]

Chapter 6

North America and Europe
November 1934 to June 1935

Difficulties do not exist for Mr Feuermann.
New York Times (14 January 1935)

On 27 November 1934 the *President Jackson* arrived in Victoria, British Columbia. For two days Feuermann and Kitzinger rested, staying at the Empress Hotel, before setting out on a 50-hour trip via Canadian National Railways to Winnipeg. Feuermann regarded the journey as passing through a 'Super-Switzerland' as the route travelled through the highest mountains in North America. His first concert was an afternoon event for the Winnipeg Women's Musical Club. It was a private concert for members only, the third in which outstanding musicians of Feuermann's generation were presented, the two previous performers being Egon Petri and Joseph Szigeti. Feuermann's programme included the Strauss Sonata, Schubert's 'Arpeggione' Sonata and the Valentini E major Sonata. The *Winnipeg Free Press* expressed its enthusiasm:

> Monday afternoon was a time of extraordinary happenings at the Women's Musical Club ... one might imagine that the cello was the easiest sort of instrument to play, so free and supple was the bowing, so agile his left hand and clear the notes.... While the technical resources caused amazement, for here was a cello being made to behave as though it were a fine violin in the hands of a master, one was always conscious of the great musical sensibility in reserve, and of the emotional expressiveness wherever there was substance in the music to bring it.

The reviewer had little time for Strauss's Sonata, but with the arrival of Schubert's 'Arpeggione', the recital took on a different air: 'The cello sang its way through the work and the beauty, variety and meaning of the tone were heart stirring.'[1]

Feuermann's first modest steps on North American soil had gone well. Now came Chicago. Between 5 and 12 December he played three times with the Chicago Symphony Orchestra under its Music Director, Frederick Stock. He also appeared at the Winnetka Music Club, a name Feuermann found particularly amusing, but less amusing the fact that his recital on 10 December was a shared one with the soprano Ninon Vallin. Nathan Milstein and Myra Hess, who appeared later in the season, were offered full recitals. Feuermann hated shared recitals, but was obliged to take part in many. No doubt it was the implicit undervaluing of cellists that caused him to dislike them so much.

His first appearance with the Chicago Symphony Orchestra, on 6 December, was in the evening, with a repeat performance of the same programme the following afternoon. The work Feuermann performed was the Lalo Concerto, an appealing, popular choice for his most significant concert in America so far. The programme was an adventurous one: Rezniček's overture to *Donna Diana*, Sibelius's Symphony no.4, Stravinsky's Symphony no.1, followed after the interval by the Lalo. The reviews were mixed. The *Herald and Examiner* implies that in the first concert Feuermann had trouble with his strings that led to difficulties of intonation; the *Chicago Daily Tribune* reported coolly: 'He would seem entirely able to cope with the physical problems of the instrument, and he would seem to have no exaggerations of any kind. Wherefore with his sustained melody in the slower passages, his rapid and accurate bravura, and his well shaped phrasing, he made a success.'[2] Only Edward Barry in the *Chicago Tribune* was unequivocally enthusiastic: 'We shall all be a lot older before we hear anything surpassing the tone which Emanuel Feuermann drew from his cello in the first theme of the second movement of the Lalo concerto yesterday.' A few days later, Feuermann performed the Dvořák Concerto, which caused Eugene Stinson in the *Chicago Daily News* to make not just significant but highly perceptive comments: 'The young Austrian cellist's approach to music is a curious mixture of the subjective and the objective. . . . At the moment of performance, [however,] he seems pre-eminently concerned in observing, as if from the outside, all that is put into a performance, not merely by himself but by those he joins in ensemble playing of the finest sort.' (Feuermann advised his students always to listen as intently to their playing as any listener might do.) Stinson also lighted on a characteristic gesture: 'I fancy the pleasure Mr Feuermann freely expressed in a recurrent smile during yesterday's Dvořák had something in it of the interest golfers might experience in watching the course of a ball, once it had been driven and was proceeding upon an impetus that could no longer affect its movement.'[3] A nice metaphor, although the smile was probably more a fish-face caused by a puckering of the cheeks; Feuermann invariably sucked in his cheeks when playing.

After Chicago, Feuermann appeared on 13 December in Montreal at an afternoon concert held in the Ritz-Carlton Hotel. The Strauss Sonata and Schubert's 'Arpeggione' were again the main works, preceded by Frescobaldi and Valentini with a group of 'salon' pieces ending with Sarasate's *Zigeuner-weisen*.

On 16 December in the *Sunday New York Herald Tribune* NBC Artist Service announced its concert plans for January. Heading the list was Feuermann's New York debut: two orchestral appearances on 2 and 4 January at Carnegie Hall with the New York Philharmonic-Symphony Orchestra conducted by Bruno Walter and on 13 January a recital in New York's Town Hall. Around the same time Schnabel also was to play with Bruno Walter and the New York Philharmonic-Symphony and give a recital in Carnegie Hall. Feuermann was both fearful and terribly excited by the prospect of his New York debut:

> I am seriously crazy until I have played, I'm at my wit's end with all the goings on, you can't imagine. And even for next year, concerts are already fixed, also an evening with Schnabel. I am terribly stupid, I'll yet have a stroke – I am so happy about it all. You know, maybe things will really go a step higher for me now.'[4]

But from the date of this letter he still had the two weeks of Christmas to wait. A train trip to Boston in order to play for the Harvard Musical Association on 21 December allowed him time to write at length to Eva; his descriptions of New York are particularly vivid:

> The skyscrapers are so impressive, especially in the evening when the lighted windows on top look like candles, so small. Moreover, this is the first original style of building for many centuries that people have developed. Roads are very wide, so it doesn't even make an impression when cars <u>speed</u> by 4 in a row in each direction. Car driving is fantastic; I think with horror how I would fare if I sat behind the wheel looking for a street. The sea of lights on Broadway I saw for only a moment. I'm doing far too much.

He was surrounded by well-wishers:

> The people are so awfully nice, really caring for me. They want to introduce me to important people. Cellists are also here, concerts and some 'family' too. I can't even take a bath in peace. I think it is like this for everyone but

for me, in contrast to London, it is also that all the musicians here and their circle know me. . . . Feelings of inferiority don't surface here. Wherever I played I had fantastic reviews and I am supposed to come back next year to New York. I am approached here as a well-known man, not like in London. 'Businesswise' I am in the best hands. It will amuse you that I already have concerts for next year and that there is talk – about this prospect I am elated – that I should play sonatas with Schnabel, and also trios with him and Huberman.

But Feuermann was not unaware of how cruel the place could be:

I have never yet read such awful reviews and heard such impertinent opinions for instance about Huberman and yesterday Walter played the Mozart concerto and afterwards there was a really heavenly performance of 'Das Lied von der Erde' (Mahler). Kitzinger has just showed me an abominable review. Just keep your fingers crossed, if only I will have a good day here. Everybody is terribly afraid of New York. Szigeti says that every concert is like a debut. . . . You can't imagine how dead these people like Walter, Huberman, Szigeti and so many others look. It is really awful and yet they are of course terribly friendly, but in my view too taxed to show much interest in anything else.

He could see below the surface: 'I don't think that I would want to live here, people are terribly superficial. Under the charming exterior, there lies a craving for showing off and self-interest. But it doesn't bother me in the least as long as I am here on a professional basis, though it would bother me if I would wish to live here.'[5]

A spectacular concert-cum-social event took place in Washington, on the Wednesday of Christmas, at the Mayflower Hotel Ballroom under the auspices of Mrs Lawrence Townsend's morning musicales. The concert, a shared recital with the Metropolitan Opera prima donna Grete Stueckgold, was attended by Mrs Roosevelt, Mrs James Roosevelt (mother of the President), and a host of dignitaries including the German ambassador, the Austrian minister, the counsellor of the German Embassy, and members of the British Embassy staff.[6] The review in the *Washington Star* was not as fulsome as Feuermann might have liked: 'Mr Feuermann has been likened to Casals, and in many respects the comparison is correct. However, the beauty of Casals' tone, which is as remarkable as his mechanical proficiency, is not quite matched by that of Mr Feuermann.'[7] (Casals had last played in the United States six years before.) The *Washington Post*, however, characterized Feuermann very differently: 'As a master of the violoncello, he is a worthy colleague of Pablo Casals and Felix

Salmond, and one is tempted to call the trio, in allusion to a famous triumvirate of romance, the Three 'Celloteers.'[8]

The following day, Thursday 27 December, Feuermann was back in New York performing at another concert-cum-social event, this time at the Waldorf-Astoria in Mr Bagby's 377th Musical Morning.

> Founded by Albert M. Bagby in his former studio at 152 W. 57th in 1891, Bagby's Musical Mornings became so popular that in 1893 he moved to the former Waldorf-Astoria Hotel at Fifth Ave. and 34th Street where Nellie Melba was the first artist to appear. When this hotel was closed in 1929, the concerts were moved to the Hotel Astor for two seasons and then to the new Waldorf-Astoria. The subscription list closed except for those removed by death, 30 years ago.[9]

Bagby, who once studied with Franz Liszt in Weimar, is described as '5 feet 2 inches tall, his white moustache waxed to excruciating fine points'.[10] An average Bagby audience consisted of 1800 women and 50 men. These gatherings had considerable social importance:

> Nearly every society woman and music lover in Manhattan is looking forward to November 21 which brings the first of Albert Morris Bagby's 'musical mornings'- a social 'must' for the last 40 years or more. Every deb. and dowager will don her newest hat and her best fur coat to appear in the grand Ballroom at the Waldorf-Astoria . . . to make sure that every detail of his musicales run smoothly, he imports scores of men from the Metropolitan Opera House who are familiar with every aristocratic music lover in the Golden Horseshoe. The floor of the Grand Ballroom is especially transformed by a series of elevations into a real theatre about which stalls and loges are created directly under the double tier of boxes that run around three sides of the room.[11]

As is the custom of social gatherings, the audience was mostly concerned with itself. Greta Garbo attended the 16th annual concert 'wearing mink, low heeled brown suede shoes, and a brown felt umbrella hat'. Her presence 'caused hardly a ripple. . . . A group of tardy dowagers chatted nearby, unaware, as was most of Mr Bagby's audience of the screen star's presence.'[12] Mr Bagby did, however, engage heavyweight soloists: Erica Morini, Lauritz Melchior, Emanuel List, Ezio Pinza, Raya Garbousova, Rudolf Serkin, Efrem Zimbalist, Lotte Lehmann, Artur Rubinstein, Zinka Milanov and Feuermann. That morning Feuermann shared the bill with Madame Elisabeth Rethberg and Mr Richard Bonelli. In between arias by Handel, Bizet, Wagner and Verdi, Feuermann wove works by Frescobaldi, Bach, Popper and the show-stopping *Zigeunerweisen* of Sarasate.

As the day of the New York debut approached, various newspapers flagged Feuermann's concerts along with other forthcoming events. In the first few days of January 1935 Lotte Lehmann was appearing as the Marschallin at the Metropolitan Opera while the violinist Viola Mitchell was billed to play an afternoon concert with the Boston Symphony Orchestra on a visit to New York. The *Sunday New York Herald Tribune* of 30 December displays prominent photographs of all three artists. The same, somewhat deathly, picture of Feuermann appeared also in the *New York Sun*. Apart from announcing Feuermann's debut playing Haydn's Cello Concerto in D major, several newspapers concentrated on the fact that Feuermann was bringing with him to the United States Schönberg's new Cello Concerto based on Georg Monn: 'Negotiations are now pending for performance of the Schönberg by two major symphony orchestras during the current season.'[13] These negotiations came to naught, although one newspaper made the unlikely suggestion that Feuermann had considered playing the Schönberg in place of the Haydn at his debut.[14]

Feuermann's choice of the Haydn concerto for his New York debut rather than the more expansive Dvořák Concerto does seem unusual, although Casals also had made his New York debut (1904) playing the Haydn. George Sopkin, a student of Feuermann, maintains that Feuermann indeed wanted to perform the Dvořák but that Walter wanted to perform Dvořák's 'New World' Symphony in the same programme.[15] Clearly too much Dvořák for one concert. But the programme performed on 2 and 4 January at Carnegie Hall included neither Dvořák's Cello Concerto nor his 'New World' Symphony. Whatever the explanation, the choice of pieces was not a conventional one. The concert began with the Philharmonic-Symphony's first performance of Roussel's Symphony in G minor op.42, a work completed in 1930: 'Just why Mr Walter saw fit to revive it is by no means clear to the writer. It is a work of little inspiration, whose only interest lies in its manner'.[16] Then followed the Haydn Concerto and, after the interval, Berlioz's *Harold in Italy*, with Mishel Piastro, concert master, as viola solo. Feuermann had been fearful about his debut in New York and his fears proved partially correct. Samuel Chotzinoff in the *New York Post* was cool and cutting:

> The concert served to introduce to New York the celebrated Russian violoncellist, Mr Emanuel Feuermann, who played Haydn's Concerto in D major. Mr Feuermann's European reputation had preceded him here, and many of our local cellists were on hand to judge for themselves. I liked Mr Feuermann very much for his cool and accomplished technique, his firm but not extraordinary tone, his musicianly but not imaginative phrasing. He

---

The Philharmonic-Symphony Society of New York
1842-1878
CONSOLIDATED 1928

1934 · · NINETY-THIRD SEASON · · 1935

CARNEGIE HALL

Wednesday Evening, January 2, 1935*
AT EIGHT FORTY-FIVE

Friday Afternoon, January 4, 1935
AT TWO-THIRTY

3051ST AND 3052ND CONCERTS

Under the Direction of
BRUNO WALTER

Assisting Artists:
EMANUEL FEUERMANN, *Violoncellist*
MISHEL PIASTRO, *Violist*

1. ROUSSEL...Symphony in G minor, Op. 42
   I. Allegro vivo   II. Adagio   III. Vivace   IV. Allegro con spirito
   (First time by the Society)

2. HAYDN...................................Concerto for Violoncello and Orchestra,
   in D major, Op. 101
   I. Allegro moderato   II. Adagio   III. Finale: Allegro
   EMANUEL FEUERMANN, *Violoncellist*

INTERMISSION

3. BERLIOZ................"Harold in Italy": Symphony in Four Movements,
   with viola solo, Op. 16
   I. Harold in the Mountains, Scenes of Melancholy, Happiness and Joy
      (Adagio; Allegro)
   II. March of Pilgrims Singing their Evening Hymn
      (Allegretto)
   III. Serenade of a Mountaineer of the Abruzzi to his Mistress
      (Allegro assai; Allegretto)
   IV. Orgy of Brigands; Recollections of the Preceding Scenes
      (Allegro frenetico)
   Viola Solo: Mishel Piastro

Instead of Thursday Evening

ARTHUR JUDSON, Manager   BRUNO ZIRATO, Assistant Manager
THE STEINWAY is the Official Piano of The Philharmonic-Symphony Society

ORCHESTRA PENSION FUND
It is requested that subscribers who are unable to use their tickets kindly return them to the Philharmonic-Symphony Offices, 113 West 57th Street, or to the Box Office, Carnegie Hall, to be sold for the benefit of the Orchestra Pension Fund. All tickets received will be acknowledged.

---

is a distinct addition to our already large circle of good cellists. But he is, as yet, no Feuermann [a sarcastic play on the English translation of the word 'Feuermann': 'man of fire'].[17]

In the *New York Times*, Olin Downes wrote similarly:

Mr Feuermann played the Haydn Concerto in D major with a sonorous tone, with amply sufficient technique, but not in distinguished style, not with the grace, the transparency, the classic proportion that the music implies. It would be interesting to hear Mr Feuermann in other works. His reputation justifies expectation of more distinctive qualities than he displayed last night, though the audience greeted him cordially and called him back repeatedly after he had played.[18]

It is tempting to presume that Chotzinoff and Downes were responding to an off night. Other critics, however, felt very differently.

. . . a cellist of exceptional talent and musicianship. His tone was remarkably warm and mellow in texture; not, indeed, massive, but full and far carrying

and observing an unusually consistent standard in a quality eminently satisfactory to the ear. . . . his tasteful interpretation resulted in marked enthusiasm on the part of the audience and many recalls.[19]

How do we interpret this mixed critical response? Perhaps it relates to the
place of the cello as a solo instrument at that time. Leonard Liebling, in the
New York American, hints at that: 'If anything is helping to restore the
dwindled popularity of the cello as a solo attraction, it is the appearance of
some new and gifted interpreters and virtuosi of the instrument. A couple of
seasons ago, Gregor Piatigorsky started a cello renaissance hereabouts; early
this Winter came a follow up with the amazingly talented young Raya
Garbousova.'[20] Casals was the only cellist with a worldwide career but he had
not played in the United States for several years. Or perhaps there was
competition in New York: not two weeks after Feuermann's debut, Piatigorsky
performed Castelnuovo-Tedesco's Cello Concerto with Toscanini.

Feuermann, who had given this debut with none of his closest family
around, seems to have been satisfied with the response, but success had not
gone to his head: 'Yesterday there were two bad notices about the concert. I am
glad that in one of them it was only the impertinent Jewish tone that annoyed
me.' Here he was no doubt referring to Chotzinoff's review. But he had found
Carnegie Hall very exciting: 'It stimulates even the most routine player.'
However, in this letter to Eva a sense of isolation is, as ever, omnipresent:

> I am again and again astounded about myself, even though I shouldn't have
> to be any more, how foreign it all remains to me, how I live my life only with
> you and Sophie. People with whom I meet frequently tell me they can't
> make me out. But I think it is fine this way. I think it is wonderful to feel so
> close to you all. This support does me good.

Significantly, Feuermann then wrote to Eva about Schnabel, who had no
doubt attended his concert: 'In many things he is strange, but he radiates such
an acceptance of himself that it does one good to be together with him.'[21] Days
later, he and Schnabel played chamber music: 'Yesterday evening I played trios
with Schnabel and Huberman. It again was very funny. The greatest themes
were deliberated, colossal conversations held, the result was a colossal banging
and scratching: and I was so violently involved that I actually snapped my C
string. We had a good time.' Despite enjoying the company, Feuermann was
less sure about New York City: 'I wouldn't want to live here for anything but
would like to come frequently.'[22]

Between the orchestral concerts and recital in New York, Feuermann went
again to Canada, this time to Quebec City, 20 hours away. In the imposing

Château Frontenac, where the Quebec Ladies' Musical Club held their concerts, he tried out his New York Town Hall recital programme: Brahms's F major Sonata, Schubert's 'Arpeggione', Valentini, and a group of small pieces ending with Frescobaldi's Toccata. Kitzinger was at the piano, as usual. In summing up the occasion, Feuermann chose to write to Eva in English:

> What do you say to my wonderful *English? Home spun- English? ...* *Yesterday I played badly but nevertheless it was a great success. After the concert there was a reception which I enjoyed very much. Quite simple people, not rich, no Jews, they sang and played the piano. I was impressed to find here such a musical atmosphere, I didn't expect it.*

The calm before the storm, he feared: '*To-morrow morning I shall be back in New York with all its trouble. I am afraid I am not the right type for N.Y.*'[23]

Despite mixed reviews for his orchestral debut, and before his New York Town Hall recital, Feuermann was contracted for the following year. The programme billed for the Town Hall concert was the same as in Quebec; however, it was not the programme played. The reviews note the inclusion of Bach's Third Suite. There was only a small audience, but it included some of the most illustrious instrumentalists of the day.[24] The impact of Feuermann's playing was sensational. He gave six or seven encores: 'if you please, the Sarasate "Zapateado" for violin, transposed for cello';[25] 'Emanuel Feuermann, German [*sic*] cellist, created a furore'.[26] Even the feared Samuel Chotzinoff and Olin Downes reacted with contrition: 'There are pleasanter things for a reviewer to do than to eat his own words. Yet, what else can I do but say that as a virtuoso on his instrument, Mr Feuermann seems to me to be miles ahead of his colleagues. . . . I feel better, now that this report is off my chest.'[27] And: 'Difficulties do not exist for Mr Feuermann, even difficulties that would give celebrated virtuosi pause. It would be hard to imagine a cleaner or more substantial technique, which can place every resource of the instrument at the interpreter's command.'[28] Downes was well aware of the make-up of the audience:

> It is safe to say that no cellist who was at large last night in New York failed to attend Emanuel Feuermann's recital in the Town Hall. There they sat, some with folded arms and beetling brows. They listened; they cogitated; earnest conversations were held in corners of the foyer during the intermission. Mr Feuermann had met and survived the ordeal of fire – not merely the judgement of newspaper reviewers but the more severe examination of his colleagues.[29]

In a single month Feuermann had succeeded in winning over New York, his colleagues and North America. NBC hastily issued a press release with a collection of the juiciest phrases drawn from his reviews covering the period 13 December 1934 to 14 January 1935: 'Feuermann: "a sensation"; "absolutely phenomenal"; "the audience belonged to him"; "his qualities will ensure him success"; "the concert stage is the richer for his proved capacities".'[30] 'Miles ahead of his colleagues. He plays the cello like a great violinist.'[31] 'One of the greatest cellists of all times.'[32] 'Something beyond brilliance. Something more important than excitement.'[33] 'The performance approached perfection. No better cello playing has been heard here.'[34]

Feuermann was touchingly proud of his success and yet modest – in a letter to Eva he wrote:

> A man who these last days is very 'famous' in New York writes you this. Are you proud? I walk around like a peacock, because I had such a colossal success the day before yesterday. It came completely unexpectedly. . . . I didn't expect any more in my old age that I would be a small sensation in N.Y. The people from N.B.C. absolutely insisted that I give a second evening but couldn't find a day. Just now when I wanted to leave, they telephoned very excitedly that February 15 was free – the night I steam off to Europe. I'm sure they threw out someone else so that I could play. . . . Unbelievable what praises I receive, beginning with Schnabel, from people who don't even know me. Now I am somewhat more happy.'[35]

If he was happy about the outcome of his initiation into New York, he was even more happy that Eva would be there for his second recital. He had found the pressure of New York hard to handle on his own but as usual had made light of it:

> What about you, Eva? Still not pleased with your studies? . . . How about lying down to sleep and waiting until the prince will come who will wake you with a sweet kiss. It seems that for some girls this dream has come true with the result that most of the time they would wish that the prince had let them snore [sleep].'[36]

But before Eva's visit many more long journeys had to be made – to Indianapolis, Baltimore, Chicago and Cleveland. On 2 February, Feuermann was back in New York where he sought out a concert conducted by Serge Koussevitzky. However, although he performed a number of times with the Boston Symphony Orchestra it was never under Koussevitzky. It is not even certain that they met. While staying once again at the Dorset Hotel, 30 West 54th Street, he wrote to Koussevitzky:

> After the concert on Saturday, there were so many people trying to come to the artists' room and you must have been very tired. Therefore I prefer to tell

you in this form that it was wonderful. I now know what the 'Pathétique' is really like. Please allow me to tell you that. In veneration, I am your Emanuel Feuermann.[37]

At the Arts Club, Chicago, on 10 February, Feuermann shared a programme with the Mischakoff String Quartet, who gave the first Chicago performance of John Alden Carpenter's Quintet for piano and strings, with Carpenter on the piano. Daniel Saidenberg, cellist of the quartet and principal cellist of the Chicago Symphony Orchestra, had met Feuermann at his debut with the Chicago orchestra a few weeks before – they were to become close friends. Two days later, Feuermann was in Cleveland in a recital with the Polish pianist Ignaz Friedman. It was the final concert of a series presented by the Cleveland Museum of Art in which Rachmaninov, the Monte Carlo Ballet Russe, Heifetz and Melchior had appeared.

Feuermann arrived back in New York on 13 February, two days before the hastily arranged second recital. Eva had arrived from Europe. Much as he

30 WEST 54TH STREET
NEW YORK

THE DORSET

3. Februar 1935

Sehr verehrter Herr Kuznitzky,

am Sonntag nach dem Konzert drängten so viele Menschen zum Künstlerzimmer, außerdem waren Sie gewiß sehr müde. Ich gebe es daher vor, Ihnen auf diesem Wege zu sagen, daß es wunderbar war. Ich weiß jetzt, wie die Pathétique in Wirklichkeit aussschaut. Das, bitte, erlauben Sie mir Ihnen zu schreiben.

In Verehrung bin ich

Ihr

Emanuel Feuermann

wanted to see her, the energetic Feuermann also wanted to take in a movie, a concert of Toscanini, Harlem, the Rainbow Room (he was an expert social dancer) and jazz. '*He always was fascinated with Jazz music and could listen to a good band again and again.*'[38] The second recital at New York's Town Hall, billed as his 'Farewell', and as always with Kitzinger, was very successful, the audience once again filled with musicians. Handel and Tartini were followed by Beethoven's A major Sonata op.69, Reger's G major Suite for unaccompanied cello (inserted to please Eva[39]) and the usual salon works – Ravel, Dvořák and Piatti. Feuermann's first American tour, a whirlwind six weeks and a day, ended as he and his entourage stepped aboard the steamship that night, bound for England. He had conquered New York.

London was a very different matter. Eva was no longer with him. After six months away the return to Europe, as Feuermann had feared, was a disappointment: 'Here in London, I have to slowly build up and I have to be resigned to the fact that it will be a long time before I stand at first place.'[40] By mid-March he had given concerts in London and Paris and was teaching his English pupils Peggy Sampson and Hilda Jamieson. He had been touched that on a visit to the violin dealers Hill and Sons, the whole firm had turned out to greet him. Quite why he was there is not explained but a courtesy call would have been normal.

While his letter to Eva from the Hotel Rembrandt on 11 March begins warmly – he comments jovially on the condition of her wisdom teeth – it soon becomes much more serious; once again it is the tone of Feuermann the mentor:

This division of humanity is not by chance and cannot be looked upon by mankind as chance, despite equality, right to vote, etc. Man and woman have different duties and different joys, and this outcry from women for freedom, which is justified for many, is surely not a desire by women to give up their particularity. You, in any case, are so feminine that you will only find satisfaction as a woman. What lies beyond will be only half-hearted and therefore unsatisfactory. But now enough, you will find the right path on your own. I firmly believe that you are quite clear about this but look on it as dishonourable to admit. Right??[41]

Eva was approaching 21 years of age and Feuermann was trying to clarify his feelings about her. As the youngest daughter, the favourite child of her father, her attempts to find herself are those of someone privileged, confused, naïve and demoralized. Two years earlier she had written to him:

I should educate myself enough so that I would be able to enter a publisher or shop which collects antique music and first editions and be able to judge them, help collect or something similar. I should study in France and Italy, always learning the language first. If it turns out that I am altogether unsuitable for this profession and there are difficulties that are impossible to overcome, I would still have the languages. I am aware of the vastness of this area, of the difficulties and of my naïveté and lack of talent, and still I do want to try it. My mother told me your opinion in short and opaque hints, that it was the most difficult thing to choose and so on. In short, I distilled from it that you are violently opposed to this idea. Please write me what you think about it, I would be GLAD to hear it. You cannot discourage me any more, and you cannot destroy anything either – there is almost nothing left. All the small sky palaces, escape routes, possibilities that I saw again and again, have disappeared or have shrunk to a minimum.[42]

Even if Feuermann did not encourage her, it was in response to this letter that he had admitted to being 'the teeniest bit in love'. Now, several years into Nazi rule, if his feelings were still unclear about Eva, his sense of responsibility towards Mrs Reifenberg had not dimmed. He wrote to Eva: 'You are right, it is best to let Oma[43] go, she can't be helped. But still I can't put her out of my head. It is terrible for me to know and feel how she suffers.'[44] His attitude to Eva's mother is, as always, complicated. He saw her as a widow, a woman used to being in control, trying to understand the changing times, deeply dependent on him and deeply fond of him: 'If she would only let herself be convinced that I should be out of this near slavery, it would only heighten my love for her.'[45] However, his own habits can only have encouraged her dependence on him; after every significant concert he would write to her about it.[46]

London concert life in the 1930s echoed that in Berlin in the 1920s. The roll-call of artists was spectacular. A concerts announcement for 9 March 1935 in *The Times* lists Heifetz, Richard Tauber, Kreisler, Rudolf Serkin, Solomon, Cortot, the Lener Quartet and the Busch Quartet. An advertisement in *The Times* on 11 March bills Feuermann to perform Bloch's *Schelomo* in the Queen's Hall on 18 March with the London Symphony Orchestra conducted by Sir Hamilton Harty. By 13 March, however, circumstances had changed: 'I had an exciting day because Sir Harty, the conductor, became sick for Monday and I really hoped that the replacement would not want to conduct that damned "Schelomo". I arranged with Miss Bass a conspiracy to that effect – and now she has just called me to say that "Schelomo" stays.' Feuermann seems really to have disliked *Schelomo*: 'If only it will go all right, it is such a Jewish lament, without rhyme or reason, and, by the way, it is the first piece which doesn't want to go into my head.'[47] His antipathy to this piece is notable for the complex feelings it undoubtedly stirred up in him. As early as 1922 – only six years after it was written – he had enquired about the whereabouts of a score in order to programme it.[48] But although he played it incomparably, he never liked it. The reason for his dislike seemed to be revealed at a lesson when he interrupted a student playing the work, saying: 'Do you have to show the whole world that you're a Jew?'[49]

Sir Landon Ronald replaced the indisposed Sir Hamilton Harty and Feuermann continued to work on *Schelomo*. When the Schumann Concerto was eventually substituted, Feuermann wrote: 'Now I am almost upset by it, for to have done all that work for nothing is stupid.'[50] But the concert went well:

> It was a fantastic success. The people screamed, I partly played very well, but in both concertos [Boccherini and Schumann] it wasn't quite right at the beginning. That is because of this damned climate. In the artists' room my fingers froze and only while playing they warmed up! But it was quite a decent Halloh, it again managed to surprise me. I am curious to see the reviews.[51]

The review in *The Times* was bland and matter-of-fact:

> This programme . . . was one of the kind which might have been called everybody's taste but for the fact that very few people came to hear it. It was played throughout with the air of easy efficiency which Sir Landon Ronald knows so well how to impart to his orchestra, and which is also character-istic of the performance of Mr Emanuel Feuermann.[52]

While in London, Feuermann was writing to Eva almost daily. He also began to mix English in with his German. Following a concert given by the Busch Quartet, he wrote:

> *I for my person as a professional was* horrified *about* such mediocrity. *I must be right for I know how much I am enchanted by real perfect performances or pictures or sceneries, but I get furious to hear* a performance *like that. I even didn't go back stage, I felt insulted. I would say all right if that would be a Quartett playing in at homes or in Bielefeld,*[53] *but as a quartet with such a reputation,* this is too bad.[54]

He had gone to this concert with Eva's brother Kurt and 'Look', the husband of Eva's sister, Lily. There he had met Heinz Simon (former editor of the *Frank-furter Zeitung*), Robert Mayer and John Christie as well as '*three girl pupils of mine*'. He did not find London appealing:

I can imagine what a bad time you had here in the autumn. If on top of that one isn't altogether in high spirits it must be just terrible here. I have just noticed now that it is pitch dark, cold, simply awful. I think this country isn't for us – I mean each one of us. When someone has a profession which holds him here and keeps him busy 8 hours a day, it may be different. But for someone like me, with a "free" profession it is awful. . . . Even though I imagine it as very nice to be here for shorter periods (but also not <u>completely</u> alone), the idea of living here permanently doesn't attract me. Besides, I love to be in a city that isn't so big that one <u>has</u> to feel lost. Since I've been here, Zürich has sat in my head and stomach. *I shall think it over, it is no hurry at all, but next week I have got to pass Zürich and I have the intention to talk about it to Leo Hofmann.*[55]

A few days later Feuermann was in Luxembourg and Schaffhausen with the Schumann and Boccherini concertos again. Writing to Eva from Luxembourg, the first hint of a medical problem is mentioned, although Feuermann had not felt well in the final days in New York:

I really believe that I will let Rosenau do this operation. In the days from the 15th to the 28th of April I am free and I don't want to be hindered by the worry that something could happen. Already during the trip I had some pain, but am so reluctant to go to strange doctors and I didn't think it was anything serious.[56]

The exact nature of the problem is not disclosed, but a hernia was suspected. Eva recalled: 'I was a little perturbed because Feuermann wasn't feeling well. I went to meet him at his agents. I had a bottle of castor oil in my hand.'[57]

He continued to tour, however, believing his condition was not serious. On 30 March in the Grand Hall of the Liszt Academy he gave a 'Sonata evening' with Béla Bartók at the piano. On the programme was Beethoven's Sonata in A major op.69, Kodály's op.4, Debussy's Sonata and the Brahms F major Sonata. Just as Feuermann as a young child had attended a catalytic concert given by Casals, so another very young and gifted cellist, János Starker, heard Feuermann for the first time on this occasion:

I must have been approximately nine years old when I walked into a hall of the Franz Liszt Academy in Budapest and was exposed to a memorable concert of Béla Bartók playing with, for me, a not very well-known cellist, Feuermann. It didn't take very long to understand that there was something different about this man's cello playing because up until then the one we truly admired was Casals. Then, and since then, I have always felt that Casals was responsible for establishing cello playing of the modern age at that time and Feuermann was the one who showed us the way to the next development where the cello was no longer an instrument to be excused because of its difficulty. He overcame all the difficulties pretty much which up until his time were considered almost invincible obstacles.[58]

Feuermann returned to Vienna via Cologne:

The flight to Cologne was very agreeable. Before Cologne I had fallen asleep. When the motors were turned off, I thought that it meant an emergency landing, had for a moment a queer feeling – but we already were in Cologne. The meeting with the Buick was very exciting. I had also forgotten my passport at the controls. The reunion with the Alteburgerstrasse was 'moving', I really was terribly, terribly happy.

He had not been at the Reifenberg home for six months and the welcome from all the family was a royal one; Eva, however, was now in England. His medical problem was to be dealt with by Dr Rosenau in Cologne: 'I "ordered" the operation for Monday the 15th in the morning. . . . The operation will probably not be very painful and I'm looking forward to the restful time afterwards.' But as usual Feuermann's schedule before then was hectic: 'I will travel quickly to Cannes, then to Milano, Cremona, Padua and Bologna . . . and hope to be back in Cologne on the evening of the 14th.'[59] Although acknowledging that he would have to be a convalescent, he still expected to be in London on 28 April and to see Eva there.

At the beginning of April, Feuermann visited his own family in Vienna: 'the deadest city I know.' Sophie had married Harry Braun in December 1934 and Feuermann was now seeing her for the first time as 'my Mrs sister Sophie'.

The two are lovely together, the mother-in-law as nice as can be – it is almost too good to be true. My God, Sophie has had such a difficult life, heightened by injustice and stupidity; and now she is together with Harry, who is delicate, witty and seemingly very smart. They, of course, have to be very thrifty and Sophie has to rush around with her lessons.

Feuermann himself was still unmarried:

I feel like a high-school pupil and not at all like an already-ex-professor with advancing baldness. Have you noticed that so many longings are in me that don't fit my age at all? I never thought about marriage because I connected marriage with the idea of dignity etc. etc. And still when I look at myself I must say that I am far removed from it. But now I add: Thank God! Terrible the people who know everything exactly and have firm opinions.'[60]

Eva had still not made her feelings known to Feuermann but his own desire for a settled life was clear:

> I'm afraid that I demand, respectively long for, too much from you or from 'woman' in general. Through the profession and these unfortunate times there is for me just one home and that is the woman. I don't want an affair, I want a human being with whom I am one. I wish for warmth. I want a woman who will give me so much that I won't feel a stranger in this world, be it together in Botokuden [Timbuktu] or separated by 15,000 kilometres. The woman must present the countercheck and if she thinks, which I can accept absolutely, that I can not give her the same or generally what she wants from a marriage, then she should say: dear little Uncle Munio, be a good friend to me, continue to be fond of me – but what cannot be cannot be. Here is something for you to think about if you please, it is far from me to press you, to impose on you. ... This 'conquering a girl' I find meaningless. How long can 'schmoose' go on for? I don't want this and I am even wondering if I could do it. This mutual throwing of sand before marriage into one another's eyes can only lead, after the eyes are opened, to one thing: disappointment. This making a girl fall in love only makes sense if one intends a short relationship like a summer spent together or a ski trip. On the other hand, I respect <u>time</u> immensely. It is not a change in feelings that destroys most marriages; it is mostly the effect of time, the duration, the disillusion itself, because feelings limited in time or quasi feelings cannot last a lifetime.'

What was Feuermann saying? On the one hand he longed for marriage; on the other hand his doubts about love's durability are plain to see. And his remarks become ever more pointed:

> This letter is again becoming something like a lecture, it's terrible with me. I would welcome it <u>if you</u> would for once give me a lecture. I actually don't know much about you at all. So much so that I am incapable of telling you about my small and bigger troubles in a natural way, as it should be. You are a very spoilt and demanding girl but I don't know if that is by nature or habit. May I say something else quite freely? I don't think you like me for marriage, otherwise you couldn't say certain things and think them. Instead of being anxious to be with me (and that after all is the most direct sign of love), and knowing that I visit only briefly, you continue to get on with your semester and examination madness, dream of a trip to the north with two children and long for a prince. .... All these wishes that are in you are not very honourable for your husband-to-be but maybe also not for you

because what it shows is that you want to 'have a fling' before. What remains is good enough for the husband. Right?'

If these forthright remarks suggest Feuermann's insecurity with Eva, his insecurities with himself were just as crippling:

> I am not very taken with myself. I believe I try to be good and know that I have a comparatively good character. Lying, bluff, everything shabby, acting, I hate. But if I look at myself with the eyes of a girl expecting a lot from life, I must admit that I don't stand very tall. This is not a criticism of such a girl, absolutely not. But I believe that you are such a girl. And my wife will be forced to see the good or even better things in me and will have to convince me of this again and again. But for that she has to see it, feel it and appreciate it. You are still so young Eva, why do you want to be involved with such an exacting, difficult person? Not to speak of the real difficulties. Oh, Eva, am I very bad?[61]

His next letter, two days later from Milan, is softer in tone.

> This is starting out to be really good! Each reproaching the other. You don't write to me. I don't write to you. I think my things don't interest you, you believe your things don't interest me – well, if that isn't love then what is? . . . As Austrian war reports said for a time: the situation is hopeless but not serious. What I mean: serious but not tragic. In certain respects I am 'unknowing', I have been until now a 'lone wolf'.

However Feuermann may have felt, he rarely lost his sense of humour: 'By the way, I am walking around for the first time yesterday, the first nice day, with a parting, and I think I am beautiful, stand whenever possible before the mirror – for years this has been happening in spring, this is the !!eruption!! of my spring feelings.'[62] He suffered premature balding, so what hair there was to part leaves much to the imagination.

Feuermann was still unsure that Eva would marry him and in planning his next few months this uncertainty is clear. He wondered where he should go in August and September: 'Maybe I will play in Biarritz; I would also like to pay my respects to Casals – somewhere near Barcelona. That is where the Pyrénées are. Wouldn't that be a *rather* pretty idea? I will probably have given lessons till I'm fed up in those 3 months till the end of July.'[63] No visit to Casals took place.

On 8 April, Feuermann gave a recital with Marino Beraldi as accompanist for the Società del Quartetto di Milano. This was already Feuermann's third visit – he had performed in 1926 and in 1934 visited with the Goldberg and Hindemith trio. The following concert for the society was to be given by

Heifetz. Feuermann's programme was the usual mix of flashy virtuoso works and more substantial pieces – Reger's Suite in G major and Schubert's 'Arpeggione'. He returned to Cologne for the hernia operation to be performed by Dr Rosenau on 15 April. Documentary proof in the form of letters from Feuermann about his operation do not exist, but it is said that serious complications occurred. Sophie received a postcard from him in which he wrote that during the course of the operation he suffered an allergic reaction, with the result that his intestines became paralysed. Eva recalled: 'I only know from doctors – his intestines did not function and they were thinking and thinking and then they came to the idea that he didn't smoke. We had to give him a nicotine injection which they did and then it functioned! So he was pretty poisoned.'[64] The administration of a nicotine enema was recommended, a treatment apparently responsible for saving his life. He was advised not to smoke or drink coffee, but took little notice. It is not clear whether this incident coloured Eva's decision to marry him, but at the beginning of June their engagement was announced.

Chapter 7

Commitments
June 1935 to April 1936

You must have realized that for a long time now I've been thinking of getting married. And I do believe that you had an inkling that it was Eva, because you did 'warn me' not to marry anyone too young. I'm very sorry, Lily, that I couldn't take your advice. It was quite clear for me: Eva or not at all.[1]

So the die was cast. On 29 May 1935 Feuermann and Eva became engaged in London. A few days later he wrote to Lily: 'The family at home seem to be overjoyed. My good mother will have been worried by now that neither Sigmund nor I would get married. After all, now that the girls are married and I'm settled professionally I could think about myself. And that meant marrying Eva.'[2] Eva maintains that her decision to marry Feuermann was not taken easily – he had been present in her life like an older brother or uncle. Although their letters to one another show that they were in love, some believe that there were other reasons behind their marriage: 'He was controlled by Mrs Reifenberg. She made the marriage since she couldn't have him herself. It wasn't something that would have happened otherwise.'[3] What truth there may be in this is hard to determine. Mrs Reifenberg's letters to Feuermann reflect joy that the marriage was to take place.

Warm letters of congratulation were received from Edwin Fischer, Bruno Walter and Schnabel. Schnabel, writing from his home in Tremezzo, indulged in familiar wordplay: 'The symbols fire, man, maturity [Reife], wheels [Reifen], and mountains [berg], are a promising conglomeration. But do experience them as an obligation!'[4] He had heard rumours of Feuermann's illness and assumed that his plans 'to educate "Kniegeige"' on the shores of Lake Como had come to nothing as a result. Trusting that the rumours were false, Schnabel spelled out his summer plans; he hoped they might meet.

The marriage did not take place until October. During the summer Feuermann was based mainly in the Semmering and at St Gilgen. To reach the Semmering, a resort area in the mountains outside Vienna, he took the train. As he described in a letter to Eva, he was about to board when on the platform he saw the conductor Hans Knappertsbusch, whom he affectionately called 'Knappi'. Knappertsbusch at the time was Generalmusikdirektor of the Bavarian State Opera in Munich, a position that implied collaboration with the regime. Feuermann's instinct was to avoid him. 'I wanted to sneak away but when I noticed that we would be the only ones in the sleeper-car I approached him courageously and then we gossiped for hours and he unburdened himself properly.' Knappertsbusch was delighted to see him, then and there wanting to fix a concert in Vienna and saying to Feuermann that nobody approached him in terms of his playing. Feuermann was shaken by the conversation, memories of his past world as a free citizen in Germany painfully aroused:

> He was the first one to whom I spoke again, everything loomed up, a submerged world, my world and then this nagging, that I can't offer that world to you anymore. Yes, Eva, I am carrying a certain past on my back but I prefer to think of the present and the future. There is no going back anyway and really I mustn't complain.[5]

In the Semmering, Feuermann was installed in the Pension Sonnhof, where he undertook his teaching. Eva missed him but believed it better for his pupils that she was not around. But as usual he was surrounded by many members of the extended Reifenberg family and he also received visits from his own family. He wrote to Eva: 'I have even found some favour in the eyes of my father. He is at the moment keen on Zionism, but it did give him a shock when he heard that you wanted to become Jewish.'[6] His mother, somewhat to Feuermann's surprise, paid him a visit during his stay:

> This morning at 9:30 there is a knock on my door. And who enters? My mother. . . . I can't remember ever having been together for such a long time with my mother. She told me about Sigmund and father, about Sophie who doesn't eat anything and still rushes about too much, about Rosa who is so modest but feels good with this, about the family and acquaintances in Kolomea, old Jewish names, familiar and yet so strange. . . . It is unbelievable how hard this woman has worked all her life. Isn't it a great pity that I can't help her in the slightest way? The obduracy of father and

Sigmund weigh on her, and yet she couldn't live without this weight, at least not far from it.

Feuermann always remained close to his mother. The reality of marrying into the Reifenbergs was beginning to dawn on him: 'I the son and brother <u>am going</u> to marry a rich girl, that is <u>marry into</u> a rich family. How does that affect <u>my</u> family?' His mother had arrived by train third class and he had been unable to persuade her to take a fast train back, and Sophie, urged by her mother to spend a few days with Feuermann, would only visit for <u>one</u> day for fear of it being too expensive for him. He found it touching but troubling. He was still dazed at the idea of being married:

> I feel quite peculiar when I think that <u>I</u> will be married and, on top of it, with <u>you</u>. I still don't have to accept it passively. For a long time you are no more a child and the last two years have certainly turned you into a grown-up and lucid person. That you trust yourself to me for the rest of your life, I can still neither grasp nor take in.[7]

Away from Eva for many weeks, he was glad of a visit by Daniel and Eleanor Saidenberg from Chicago. Eleanor recalled:

> We had adjoining rooms. My husband had brought his cello and was practising. Feuermann came in and said 'how can you do this?' And my husband said 'do I do everything wrong?' To which Feuermann retorted 'you do more right than any American cellist I've ever met.' He was a little critical. But we spent all our time together, going for little rides. He talked a lot about Eva. They were engaged at that time. And he was always making some kind of a joke. He loved jokes. But talked seriously about the cello.[8]

While in the Semmering, Feuermann worked on his forthcoming performance schedule. His agent Paul Schiff had moved from Berlin in 1934 to the Organisation Artistique Internationale: Marcel de Valmalète, on Rue de la Boëtie (Maison Gaveau) in Paris, following the Nazis' enforced closure of Wolff & Sachs. Schiff now wrote to Feuermann outlining a tour from December 1935 to December 1936, in effect an entire year away from Europe: December to March, America; to mid-May, Japan; to mid-June, Java; to September, South America; October, Mexico; and until the middle of December, North America. Feuermann did not expect to make much money, but in terms of his career it would establish his presence for the future and consolidate his reputation in those places where he had previously performed. With the collapse of Germany as a centre for his performing career, he had to accept concerts from wherever they were offered. He was well aware of the 'childish fees' that Italy and England could pay, but at this point the choice was not his – a reaction so different from two years previously when he had turned down work because expenses only were offered.

The prospect of this year-long tour beginning in December 1935 presented Feuermann with a new situation. For the first time he would be travelling with a wife. He wrote to Eva: 'I am already very curious what you will say to the plan of staying away for a whole year. It's a bit long. Alone I wouldn't have had the strength to say yes but together it could actually be very nice. Or do you think that it will be beyond your strength?'[9] Eva was intrigued by the prospect: 'Munio, I have such unlimited faith in you, I believe in your protection so much, and I am so incredibly sure of the fact that I belong with you that it is simply self-evident that I should be travelling with you.'[10] But to Feuermann's surprise, she raised certain issues about his long-term strategy. How did the importance of this journey relate to the importance of a season in Europe? Was 'getting known' in America more important for the future than building up in Europe? Should he really let Europe go? Wouldn't other artists occupy his patch? Might he be forgotten? Were the managers honest? Were their commissions too high? Her concerns were real enough, but it seems that she – rich and bourgeoise, having had an immensely privileged and protected upbringing – was not entirely aware of whom she was marrying. He was after all 'Uncle Munio'. Feuermann's comments confirm this view:

> What I most feared was that my concerns would seem too unimportant to you, but that isn't at all the case. I am so happy about the way you think everything through and want to know. I will try to explain some things: You have the feeling 'why wander to foreign fields etc.', and here you are very wrong. Europe without Germany is only worth a third, and if one plays a lot in England and Italy it increases maybe to 60%. As the fees are substantially reduced and distant trips are necessary, the results are even poorer. If for instance I play for a whole year in Europe, and play a lot, I can maybe make a bare living, but not much more. Now I am going to South America for the first time and can maybe cover the costs, but if I am successful and go back after a few years then quite a different result will emerge. Compris? That is what is happening in North America: the first time I just covered the costs, but if I'm not mistaken I will have a surplus this year.

Feuermann's strategy was one of future investment. Eva's fears that another cellist might encroach on his territory were put to rest by her future husband's resolute self-confidence: 'That in the meantime another will be able to establish himself seems unlikely because there isn't anyone and because I don't miss out a single season.' And on the honesty of agents: 'In South America the conditions are 50/50, it depends whether I will be successful. The impresario is Quesada. He has been active there for decades and will probably not cheat me any more than all the others. Even Kreisler, on whom Quesada can be absolutely certain, receives only 55%.'[11]

In July, Feuermann moved to the Hotel Excelsior in St Gilgen near Salzburg in the Salzkammergut, where many pupils arrived to study with him: 'Peggy, Mary, Goodchild, Miss Butler, Lustgarten, Jane, Tusa and Sturzenegger.'[12] He found his hands full with each student playing twice a week. His expectations of his students were high, but then so were the parents' expectations: 'There was a great tragedy: the parents of Lustgarten are here, are very ambitious and thus not satisfied with him. After the last lesson there was a row and they were really afraid that he might harm himself. So he had to sleep with his father!' The Salzburg Festival was in full swing and Feuermann attended various events including Toscanini's legendary *Falstaff* and the dress rehearsal of *Fidelio*: 'Even if the singers except [Lotte] Lehmann, who sang mostly half voice, were not first class, what the old T. got out of the orchestra, how clear the music becomes through him, is great, fabulous.'[13] Feuermann also went to Thomas Mann's lecture on Wagner: 'Am curious, have never seen him, much less heard him.'[14] In 1933 Mann had given a famous series of lectures outside Germany, pleading that Wagner should be saved from the contamination of the Nazis. Feuermann was not impressed:

> Of course a lot of what he says is very intelligent but where is the great thought? The most interesting thing in Wagner is this contrast of larger than life and extreme weakness of character, which for him maybe isn't even a contrast, or this admiration for the German myth that he injected into the German people. About all this not one word. He didn't even touch on Wagner's clear-cut attitude towards the Jews – to take advantage of them and then to throw them away like squeezed lemons.[15]

Feuermann was as usual happily gregarious. Salzburg offered the opportunity to see family and friends and make new acquaintances. He gave an account of a particularly enjoyable day in a letter to Eva:

> Yesterday I had a fantastic day in Salzburg. I picked up Rosa and Adolf early and brought them to Salzburg. I drove with Strok to the Gaisberg [an inn] for lunch where a real thunderstorm erupted. Afterwards, great meeting in the Bazar (the coffee house where the in-people meet, of course mostly hangers-on), got to know Stabile (he gave Falstaff most beautifully . . .) and the daughter of Chaliapin (he has 10 children!). I drove R. & A. to the station, actually they wanted to go to Ischl, but with this rain they chose

correctly. I had dinner with Strok and the daughter Cha[aliapin], who is very beautiful, a living figure out of the Blue Bird. I diligently looked at my ring and talked a lot about you.[16]

Wilhelm Kux was also in Salzburg. He had tried to arrange for Feuermann to conduct a masterclass (similar to that run by Huberman) at the Akademie in Vienna by speaking to its president. In view particularly of the strong anti-Semitism in Vienna, Feuermann was doubtful that anything would come of this. He was right.

In the weeks leading up to his marriage, Feuermann performed for the Jüdischer Kulturbund in Cologne and Frankfurt, with his old friend Wilhelm Steinberg conducting. At the beginning of October he was in Vienna, where he had not performed for some time. In this concert, on 9 October with the Vienna Symphony Orchestra for the Gesellschaft der Musikfreunde and Austrian Radio conducted by Oswald Kabasta (head of music, Austrian Radio), Feuermann was about to re-establish the original version of one of the most important works in cello literature: Haydn's D major Concerto (Hob.VIIb:2). In a feature article in the Viennese newspaper the *Wiener Tag* he wrote:

> For the first time I will play the famous cello concerto by Haydn in the original version, which I have reconstructed in accordance with the autograph in the Prussian State Library, which I photographed page by page. It is mainly a matter of important changes in the solo part to which were added in the course of time certain virtuoso decorations that are stylistically alien to the character of the original but which were included in later Haydn editions such as that by Gevaert in Brussels.[17]

In another Viennese newspaper, the *Neues Wiener Tageblatt*, dated 9 October, it is revealed that Feuermann found the autograph in 1934.

What had Feuermann found? Haydn's autograph manuscript for the D major Concerto – written in 1783 in Esterházy – was thought lost and for many years the authenticity of the Concerto was disputed, its author believed to have been Haydn's student and principal cellist at Esterházy, Anton Kraft. In his 1984 edition, H.C. Robbins Landon noted that the autograph manuscript reappeared after the Second World War, rediscovered in the vaults of the Austrian National Library.[18] This may well be the case. What appears unrecognized, however, is that in 1934, more than ten years before, Feuermann was in possession of a manuscript copy of a full score and had performed from it. This score, still held in the Berlin Staatsbibliothek, consists of 20 pages with title page.[19] Written in the top right-hand corner of the first page is: 'Jos. Haydn

Concert für Violoncell. (Offenbach. Op.101. pr.2½ fl. No 1862. 1962).' This manuscript is a copy of the André first edition, plate numbers 1862 (orchestral parts) and 1962 (violoncello principale), published in 1804, which comprises parts only. In painstakingly neat handwriting, the unknown copyist put together perhaps the earliest full score. This Berlin manuscript for 'Oboi', 'Corni in D' and strings carries the solo part on the line above the 'Basso e Violoncello'. From a letter of 7 February 1940 from Feuermann to Harold Spivacke at the Library of Congress it is clear that Feuermann was using the André score: '*The old edition of the Haydn concerto in D major which I use bears the number 1962 of André in Offenbach. Do you think the numbers can help you to find out in which year the concerto was printed?*'[20] Listening alone will establish that it is from this Berlin score that Feuermann recorded the concerto in 1935, shunning the standard 1890 edition by François-Auguste Gevaert used at the time.

Feuermann's contribution to modern scholarship remained and remains unsung. An edition edited by Kurt Soldan purportedly using the Berlin manuscript copy was published in 1934 by Peters Edition, but this was not the music Feuermann used. Georg Prachner Verlag, Vienna, published an edition in 1962 in the Museion series for the Austrian National Library, edited by Leopold Nowak, claiming to be the first based on the original manuscript (despite the André first edition referring specifically to the work as by Haydn, adding the words: 'Edition d'après le manuscrit original de l'auteur'). What is erroneous in the Nowak edition is the apparent implication that the concerto had not been performed in its original form before 1957: 'The first performance of the work in its present form was given by Enrico Mainardi in the Vienna Konzerthaus (Mozart Saal) on May 1957.' Mainardi may have given the first performance of this edition but this should not be understood as the first performance in modern times of the original version.

In relation to Feuermann's great interest in Haydn's Concerto, it is interesting to speculate as to whether as a child studying with Klengel in Leipzig he may have come across the original version. C.F. Peters in Leipzig published a piano reduction by Klengel based on the André edition in 1906.[21]

In anticipation of Feuermann's second tour to Japan, Columbia offered to record him in London for the Japanese market, as before. Nipponophone intended recording him in Japan playing solo works or sonatas, but they were also interested in the possibility of a recording in London of the Haydn Concerto. Rex Palmer, manager of the International Artistes' Department, replied dispiritingly: 'We regret we cannot justify making the Haydn Cello Concerto with Feuermann from our own account.'[22] The cost, estimated at £200 for orchestra and conductor plus a royalty to Feuermann, was deemed too high. Schiff might have anticipated this reply since at a meeting it had been made abundantly clear that 'with an artist like Feuermann, who plays only the cello, the cost of an orchestra for a big concerto work places such records outside commercial possibilities at present.'[23] London was making clear its commercial views: cellists did not pay.

An engagement party was held in Vienna at Feuermann's parents' house. Eva recalled: 'I must have been pretty and he really was in love with me . . . he had this great longing to belong, to be bourgeois . . . he wanted to be like the others. He was so eager to have the regularity of a normal person's life who had

a business from 8 to 5 and then was free on Sunday.' The desire for regularity
is understandable in a person never still, but Feuermann's interest in making
Sunday special was almost comic: 'He had very little hair, so he had a parting
to recognize this as a special day.'[24]

Feuermann, having virtually grown up with the Reifenberg family, was
particularly close to Eva's brother Kurt, who was two years younger than him.
But it was Kurt, quite unexpectedly, who declared that Eva should not marry a
Galician Jew. The issue of intermarriage between Jews and Aryans was at the
top of Hitler's agenda, and the Nuremberg laws forbidding racial intermarriage were promulgated only months after Eva's engagement. But this was not
about racial intermarriage (an assimilated Jew was nevertheless a Jew), it was
about the traditional contempt of assimilated Jews towards non-assimilated
Jews. Kurt was incensed that he had not been consulted on the engagement
and had not been party to it. In his eyes (those of a rich assimilated Jew) his
younger sister should marry an Aryan blonde to rid the family of its
Jewishness. He could not have been more hurtful. Not only was Eva being
judged for marrying a Jew but she was also being judged for marrying a
socially inferior Jew beneath her assimilated Jewish class. And Feuermann was
deeply hurt, as expressed in an extract from a letter to Eva of June 1935:

> I am trying to recuperate from the shock I had through Kurt. It is wretched
> to have to admit that everything could have been different if I had been a
> better psychologist. . . . It was too much as you said. There <u>had</u> to be a
> setback. Well, it came, but something less serious would have quite sufficed.
> . . . At the moment my pity for Kurt is almost stronger than my feeling of
> hurt. I have you. I have an easy profession – what does he have? In addition
> to all the negative attitudes he has or believes, he must accept, if only as a
> minor evil, that he has lost me as a friend. And both my hands are tied. I
> can't come to him.[25]

Despite the distressing hurt, the other Reifenbergs attempted to behave as
normal. The traditional *Polterabend*, an excuse for high jinks, was held as usual
the evening before the marriage. Tante Nelli, Emma Reifenberg's sister, dressed
up as Toscanini to conduct a selection of relatives in Leopold Mozart's 'Toy'
Symphony. Plans were made for the distinguished architect and close family
friend Paul Bonatz to give Eva away, but these plans came to nothing. Bonatz
felt that his presence might compromise the feelings of the guests as he was
officially employed by the Nazi government.[26]

The wedding ceremony on 21 October, a civic one, was held at the fine old
Rathaus in Cologne (see Plate 13). As Eva remembers, the judge sat below a
wall plastered with pages of the virulently anti-Semitic newspaper *Der*

Stürmer. Eva attempted to embrace Kurt who was smoking a cigar that burnt her wedding veil.[27] According to Eva, her parents and Feuermann's parents never met, not even at the engagement party in Vienna. Even on the occasion of the wedding she does not remember Feuermann making any attempt to bring them together. Although the social, economic and class differences between the two families were wide, Emma Reifenberg's letters to Feuermann invariably display interest and concern about his family; and the children mixed (Sophie was in regular contact with the Reifenbergs).

The ten-day honeymoon was spent on Lake Como, at the Hotel San Giorgio in Lenno. Feuermann had expressed doubts about the wisdom of honey-mooning in a country at war; Mussolini's invasion of Abyssinia had begun not three weeks before. During the honeymoon, Feuermann continued work on the new Cello Concerto by Schönberg; and they were able to visit the Schnabels.[28] It was from Lenno that Feuermann wrote to Columbia's influential artistic director, Fred Gaisberg.[29] Unaware of internal correspondence at Columbia, Feuermann was at a loss to understand why Schiff, who he believed had successfully negotiated new recordings, had received no news. He planned to be in England only between 4 and 21 November, giving ten concerts, so time was limited. And there would be no other convenient time for recording, as after the 21st he was playing in Holland, Switzerland and Italy and leaving for America on 16 December. Feuermann added lightly: 'You might be interested to hear that I have a tour of 30 concerts planned in the States, and am going on to Japan, China, South America and Mexico.'[30] On 4 November Gaisberg replied to Feuermann, who had just arrived at the Hyde Park Hotel:

> I have not definitely decided on any recording here because I have been advised that the Nipponophone Company hope to record you in solos on your visit to that country. We have not had a communication from them to do any further recording [and] for this reason and at this time of the year, we are so booked up with urgent recording which has been arranged for many months, that we have no free time in our studios to undertake more recording.[31]

Two days later, Hans A. Straus from Nipponophone, Rex Palmer's opposite number in Japan, contacted Columbia to say that Nipponophone could afford £200 plus Feuermann's royalty for a recording of the Haydn Concerto. Columbia started to process a contract. Rex Palmer, Gaisberg's boss, had earlier commented that he would not like to guarantee that the work could be recorded in less than two sessions, six hours. Nevertheless he wrote to Feuermann saying that he thought there would be no difficulty in completing it in three hours, but that the session could be extended if necessary.[32] An orchestra was fixed, Malcolm Sargent was engaged to conduct, and a single session of three hours on 25 November was booked at the Abbey Road Studios. The recording was to be squeezed in after Feuermann's dates in Holland.

In the days before the recording session Feuermann had several important concerts, including one of the most significant of his entire career: the world premiere of Schönberg's Cello Concerto. The history of this concerto's first performance is a chequered one. Schönberg had written the piece for Pablo Casals, whom he had first met during the period late 1931 to early 1932, when a guest of the Catalan composer Roberto Gerhard. At Casals's instigation Schönberg enthusiastically began writing a work for cello. Feuermann had played the concerto for Schönberg in 1933, when he was in Paris.[33] In 1934 Feuermann, in an interview for an American newspaper, said of the work:

> It is wholly Schönberg but a different Schönberg from the one the world generally knows and is somewhat afraid of. It is modern without having any harsh dissonances. In fact it is quite melodious – a delightful mixture of the old and new idioms. When I worked with him I was pleasantly surprised to find him tolerance itself, allowing the artist all the freedom in the world. He amiably agreed to all the suggestions I made in regard to the cello portion, which at the start was so tremendously difficult that it appalled me. It is still the most technically complicated composition for cello that has ever been written, producing entirely new effects and for that reason is to me extremely interesting.[34]

In the *Wiener Tag* he again described the piece:

> It is interesting that this new work by Schönberg is not written in accordance with the 12-tone system but is built on themes from a pre-Classical Viennese composer, J.G. Monn. Schönberg already years ago edited a work of this little-known master who was stylistically influential with the Classical school for the Denkmaeler der Tonkunst in Oestereich. The new cello concerto after motivs by Monn is not an edition but a thoroughly new work and shows Schönberg at the height of his mastery. Schönberg, who was himself a cellist, opened up for the cello new technical paths. Incredibly difficult are the technical problems that the player has to master here, particularly a double flageolet [harmonics] on the cello that in combination with the orchestra yields hitherto unknown sound effects.[35]

Casals had been enthusiastic about performing the piece until early in 1933 when he received the score. Some technical difficulties he regarded as 'out of the question, if one considers the figurations and the cellistic writing'.[36] In

September 1933 Schönberg, just dismissed from the Akademie der Künste in Berlin, again pressed Casals to give the first performance in London, where the BBC had offered him an opportunity for a concert in November that he was desperate not to lose. Casals's response was regretful:

> I regret very much what you say about your situation after the decision of the German government regarding you, and I understand your desire for an artistic activity that would help you face the present difficulties. I am doubly frustrated by not being able to accept your proposition – first of all because even though I am well along, I still cannot perform in public and even less on the radio the concerto you did the honour of dedicating to me.[37]

Early in 1935 Casals was on the verge of performing the concerto when the publisher, Schirmer of New York, informed him that he would have to pay $100 for each performance. Casals later recalled: 'I said I did not agree, and on hearing my answer they reduced it to fifty dollars. This haggling made me feel so sick that I said I would have nothing to do with it.'[38]

In February 1934 Schönberg, now in America, was again in touch with Feuermann:

> Recently in Chicago, I happened to meet Piatigorsky, whom I did not know, and who introduced himself to me and asked me about my cello concerto. He did not know anything about our rehearsals and I did not tell him anything about them, but only about Casals. However, he presented me, it seems to me, a rather practical proposition: I should not grant the performance rights to one, but to several (4, 5, 8, 10), then nobody can be insulted.'[39]

It seems unlikely that Piatigorsky had seen the score. When he did look at it on board a liner returning to Europe with Nathan Milstein his comments were none too encouraging: '[I] had to sacrifice playing bridge with Nathan and even promenading with an attractive Italian lady for the morbid company of music by Schönberg and Schnabel.'[40] Schönberg's agent in America also saw complications for Feuermann as sole cellist – Feuermann as yet had not made his American debut. Schönberg wrote to Feuermann: 'He considers it improbable that, at present, he could find a sufficient number of orchestra engagements for a young cellist, even though he considers you as the foremost among the generation of the younger cellists. . . . Thus I do not see any prospect of bringing you to America as I would have liked to for my own sake.' Schönberg then came up with an even more convoluted suggestion for Feuermann to consider:

> I would grant you <u>tacitly</u> the premiere performance and possibly an option for 4–5 more concerts in Europe under the following conditions: tacitly

means that we shall deal with it thus: if within six weeks plus twice ten postal days, that is until 30th April as the absolute deadline, you come up with five engagements, which would include the provision to pay to me as a fee for the material about $30-50, or at least $200 or so altogether, I would be willing to have the material produced for you and to leave it with you for the time necessary. . . . Perhaps make me a proposition which is acceptable to me. . . . I am sorry that for the present nothing can be done here, but I believe that the local agents are already degenerating; I do find them just as narrow-minded as the European ones.[41]

Needless to say, nothing came of this Talmudic plan.

It was therefore not until 7 November 1935, under the auspices of the august Royal Philharmonic Society, that the Schönberg Cello Concerto was finally given its premiere with Feuermann and the London Philharmonic Orchestra under the unlikely baton of Sir Thomas Beecham. The reviews were excoriating:

There are always some things that nobody can understand, and now there is one more. Why did Schönberg write the Cello Concerto produced for the first time at Queen's Hall last night? Why did such an admirable musician as Emanuel Feuermann elect to play it? Above all, why did the Royal Philharmonic Society aid and abet them in this nefarious undertaking? It is a long time since I heard music that I am ready to pronounce with such complete conviction after one hearing to be not only bad but silly.[42]

In the *Sunday Times*, Ernest Newman wrote:

We were regaled with the first performance of what is called a cello concerto by Schönberg, but what turns out to be an elaborate embroidery of his upon a claviecembalo concerto by one Georg Matthias Monn, who died some six years before Mozart was born. One could hardly see the baby for the outrageous clothes in which Schönberg has dressed it up and the big clumsy perambulator in which he carts it about. . . . Only a man completely lacking in the [*sic*] sense of humour could have done with it the ludicrous things Schönberg does. . . . One's conclusion when it was all over was that Schönberg is no better hand at writing other people's music than he is at writing his own. Mr Emanuel Feuermann was the soloist.[43]

After so much work over so many years – including precious time during his honeymoon – these reviews must have irked Feuermann. But in his surviving letters the event is not even mentioned.

A few days after the performance, Feuermann visited the instrument dealer Hill and Sons with his student Mosa Havivi: 'Hill showed me a Stradivarius, *much more brilliant than my Montagnana.* He says that it isn't much more expensive than mine. Maybe I'll try it out on Wednesday with Fischer.'[44] For the next few months, while still in Britain, he played the 'De Munck' Stradivarius 'on loan'.

Edwin Fischer, another colleague from Berlin, had succeeded Schnabel at the Hochschule in 1931. Feuermann's recital with him took place at the London Museum, in St James's, on 20 November. From Feuermann's remarks it appears that Fischer was uncertain and unsettled by the troubled times.

> I had a rehearsal with Fischer at Makowers. I didn't tell him anything, but he inquired earnestly about America and Japan – and I couldn't stop myself from making it clear to him <u>how</u> advantageous it might be if he would travel widely so that his horizon would become wider. From time to time I also mentioned here and there, not without intended effect, the name Schnabel. He is no worse than the others, only <u>too</u> cautious, and outside [Germany] he hardly earns the butter on his bread.[45]

Fischer was Aryan and not obliged to look elsewhere for work; Feuermann was teasing him perhaps about the necessity for wider horizons, a condition imposed on Jews.

Feuermann remained in close contact with Lily Hofmann. Writing to her from Edinburgh, he quipped:

> Do you still want to welcome a married Munio? I played here yesterday, tonight it's Glasgow, tomorrow London, Thursday Manchester, Friday birthday in Amsterdam where I'm meeting up with Eva. Saturday Hilversum Radio, Sunday Concertgebouw Amsterdam, Monday Columbia Haydn concerto in London again (I'm terribly excited) and from there to you in Switzerland. . . . I would be so happy if I could be with you on Tuesday afternoon so that we can have a nice quiet heart-to-heart. Wednesday it's Winterthur, Thursday, St Gallen and Friday I'm free!! Can I come to you then? Saturday I'm playing in Luxembourg. I hope I'll have enough time if I leave Zurich in the morning. That is how agitated my life has been since the 4th, so you can imagine how much I'm looking forward to quiet days and even just hours.

But marriage had changed him. The letter contains a rare admission that his personal life could affect his playing: 'A characteristic example of our first few weeks together: Eva has actually become more beautiful thanks to the happy expression she has and I am much calmer on the podium. It may seem very odd for me but it does prove to me that I feel happy and calm.'[46]

The recording of the Haydn Cello Concerto had been set for Monday 25 November at Abbey Road in London. Four days before this, he played the Concerto in Manchester with the Hallé Orchestra under Sir Thomas Beecham; in the same concert, he played Strauss's *Don Quixote*. From an article in a Manchester paper written by Carl Fuchs, cellist of the former Brodsky Quartet, it is clear that at the last moment the Haydn Concerto was substituted for Schönberg's new concerto – 'to the regret of many'. Fuchs, however, was delighted to hear the original, unabridged version of the Haydn Concerto. One can only speculate on what prompted the change in Manchester: the Schönberg had received very poor reviews; the orchestra might not have had time to learn the new work; Feuermann wanted an opportunity to use his newly acquired Stradivarius in a performance of the Haydn before the recording. Indeed, Fuchs comments: 'He played on a magnificent Stradivarius lent him the day before by a London firm of dealers, and the fact that he seemed quite at home on a strange cello speaks volumes for his technical gifts.'

Feuermann, delighted to be recording the Haydn, informed Gaisberg: '*I am very happy about playing just the Haydn Concert* [*sic*] *and shall try to do my best.*'[47] Final financial terms, however, were not settled and haggling continued:

THE HALLÉ CONCERTS SOCIETY
SEASON 1935-1936.

〜

FIFTH CONCERT
Thursday Evening, November 21st, 1935, at 7-30.

Artist :
Violoncellist - EMANUEL FEUERMANN

〜

PROGRAMME
Part I.

SYMPHONY No. 4, IN B FLAT (Op. 60) - - - *Beethoven.*

CONCERTO FOR VIOLONCELLO AND ORCHESTRA,
IN D MAJOR - - - - - - - - - - - *Haydn.*
EMANUEL FEUERMANN

INTERVAL OF FIFTEEN MINUTES.

Part II.

FANTASTIC VARIATIONS ON A THEME OF A KNIGHTLY
CHARACTER—"Don Quixote" (Op. 35) - - - - *Strauss.*
Solo Violoncello - EMANUEL FEUERMANN
Solo Viola - - - - - - - FRANK S. PARK

Conductor:
Sir THOMAS BEECHAM, Bart.

With regard to payment on account of royalties, I am afraid we can only give you a nominal advance, as the orchestral fees involved make this recording very expensive. However, we are willing to advance you £25 on account of royalties to be earned on this work. The rate of royalty will be 5% on the retail price, payable on 85% of the sales.[48]

An internal document at Columbia however, indicates exasperation: 'We are sorry to report that there is a change in the Emanuel Feuermann terms. After accepting a royalty only, he now insists on an advance of £25 for the whole work.'[49] Indeed, Feuermann was far from happy. In a letter to Gaisberg he wrote (in English):

I am a little disappointed about your letter. At first I find £25 a very small amount for the Haydn Concerto. For my first Columbia records I received 5% royalties. Colleagues of mine told me that their royalties are much higher and I really cannot understand why it should remain at 5%. Please be so nice to think it over and we can talk about it when I am recording on Monday. I do not think about me as about a lesser class artist.[50]

He felt undervalued. Columbia had made plain that it did not regard Feuermann as a star and worse was to come.

The decision to use Sargent was not unreasonable, but the use of a freelance group of players booked for one day only was questionable. It is possible that at this relatively short notice no named London orchestra was available, but the solution was not a happy one. Anecdotal reports of this recording session continue to circulate. Feuermann, having played this concerto with the finest orchestras and conductors worldwide, was horrified by what he found. It is said that at the morning rehearsal, after the long opening tutti of the first movement, he repeatedly failed to come in. When asked what the problem was he suggested to Sargent that the orchestra should tune. The orchestra was affronted, but eventually a flute (*sic* – there is no flute in the orchestration of the original concerto) is said to have begun a D major scale, which was reluctantly followed by the rest of the orchestra. Students of Feuermann attending the session, it is said, tried to point out to him that his behaviour towards Sargent was unacceptable and might prove counter-productive, whereupon Feuermann mischievously suggested: 'Lunch?'

Although the orchestral playing is undeniably poor, rhythmically ragged and lacking in energy, the above account of the recording session has proved to be unreliable. But, acknowledging Feuermann's exuberant personality, there is a ring of truth. On the other hand, the violinist Max Salpeter, a member of this freelance band, has given a very different account. Salpeter had just joined the London Symphony Orchestra and five years later became joint leader of the Philharmonia. He maintains that the freelance group booked to record with Feuermann also worked with Heifetz and Casals on recordings made just prior to Feuermann's. Salpeter could recall no instance of Heifetz or Casals registering any disapproval at the standard of the orchestra nor, in the case of Feuermann, did he have any memory of the orchestra being specifically asked to tune.

> At the coffee break, we crowded around him and there he was as right as rain, happy. He had his cello. Instead of putting his cello down he was standing slightly bent laughing and played the first bars of the first movement of the Mendelssohn Concerto. He was in a marvellous mood. If he had been disappointed he would not have wanted to do this. He might have sulked, perhaps, or something like that. But I don't remember consciously being asked to tune. We just thought what a nice man and of course what a marvellous player.[51]

Salpeter was in his nineties when he recalled this occasion. Heifetz recorded the Sibelius Violin Concerto with Beecham and the London Symphony Orchestra in November 1935[52] but there are no Casals recordings.

The total cost of the recording was £135 including Feuermann's advance of £25. Nipponophone had hoped to pay £110, believing that the work could be accommodated on two double sides or, at the most, three double sides for £165. It took four double sides. This recording was achieved wilfully on the cheap. However, nothing can detract from the brilliance of Feuermann's performance and to this day his playing remains astonishing. It was the first time the Haydn Concerto in its original version had been recorded, and it remained the only commercial recording Feuermann made of this work in his maturity. It is one of music's greatest losses that he was never to record it with a great orchestra. Purported plans made with the Philadelphia Orchestra and Ormandy came to nothing, thwarted by Feuermann's tragic early death.

Columbia was satisfied with the recording: 'We were very pleased with the records and think you will agree that they do you justice,'[53] to which Feuermann replied, possibly tactfully; 'I think the Haydn Concerto came out very well.'[54] Straus at Nipponophone, having encouraged a hard bargain, now belatedly enquired about which orchestra had performed; the information sheets gave only the name of Sargent: 'May we assume that it is the London Philharmonic Orchestra?'[55] A not unreasonable assumption since Sargent had been associated with that orchestra since its beginning in 1932. It was not, of course. It was only several months later that Straus made his views clear: 'We were not entirely satisfied with Mr Sargent who conducted the Haydn concerto. By the way, the Haydn concerto was not a success in this country and we did not sell more than 1000 sets. We would like to hear from you how the sales of this work in Europe have been.' A handwritten note in the margin of the letter, presumably by Francis Brand Duncan, reads 'almost 500 sets.'[56] Japan's record market was advanced, but for Japan to sell double the quantity of Europe and regard it as a poor sale is both surprising and telling.

After recording the Haydn Concerto, Feuermann returned the Stradivarius to Hill. A letter from Alfred Hill indicates, however, that Feuermann had asked to continue 'trying out' the cello on his forthcoming tour, leaving his Montagnana instrument in exchange. Hill had held this Stradivarius for eight years without a sale; these were hard times economically. A few more months – or years, as would be the case – on loan to Feuermann was not likely significantly to affect any sale. Alfred Hill's response was generous: 'I see no reason why we should not comply with your request more especially as I am desirous of proving to you that we are your friends.'[57] Hill obligingly shipped the Stradivarius to Paris, where Feuermann and Eva were staying, retrieving the Montagnana but without its fine oak case, a subject to which Hill was later to return.[58] Hill, however, was trying to negotiate a deal: 'We have invariably asked £5000 for this "Stradivari", at which figure, we should not be making a profit.' Despite making no profit, Hill offered Feuermann the Strad for £4500. Hill valued the Montagnana at £3500 and asked Feuermann to pay the balance of £1000 if he should finally decide to purchase the cello. Hill described the Stradivarius as in 'a thoroughly healthy state'. It had never been seriously repaired. It had come to Hill from a pupil of De Munck. De Munck, 'a cellist of repute', had bought it from the family of the great French cellist Franchomme. Franchomme had originally purchased the instrument for his only son, who had shown great talent but had died at an early age. (Had Feuermann been a superstitious person, the omens were not good.) In the opinion of Hill, it dated from about 1730, its dimensions suggesting that it was made for the use of 'lady-players'. As an aside in his letter to Feuermann, Hill added: 'Remember my advice, not to have your strings too thin, for this detracts from the volume of the tone.'[59]

A few days later, Feuermann and Eva, with the pianist Wolfgang Rebner, left Europe for the United States on the *Ile de France*. It was the beginning of Feuermann's second world tour. The first four months would be spent in the United States, where he was to give about 35 concerts. His arrival was widely noticed in the press, as was the simultaneous arrival in New York of Heifetz, Milstein and Efrem Zimbalist.[60] Much was made of the fact that he was bringing this 'last cello' of Stradivarius; less accurate was the reporting that he would be playing this instrument for the first time.

Feuermann's first world tour had ended in New York, and now he began in New York with two performances on 26 and 27 December in Carnegie Hall of the Schumann Concerto with the New York Philharmonic-Symphony and Klemperer. It was Klemperer's farewell for the season in a programme that included the string orchestra arrangement of Schönberg's *Verklärte Nacht* and Beethoven's 'Eroica' Symphony. Feuermann's choice of Schumann's Concerto was not universally welcomed: 'Mr Feuermann elected to play a concerto which is weak in invention and which, for the average 'cellist, seldom repays the labour of preparation.'[61] Similar views were expressed in the *New York Sun*, *New York Evening Post* and the *New York Herald Tribune*. Olin Downes, who the previous year had initially written so negatively, now wrote: 'All was done that could be done with the piece, which clearly shows the weakening of Schumann's creative power. Few had expected that so much could be accomplished. Mr Feuermann's prowess won the heartiest recognition.'[62] Feuermann, several months later in a letter to Hindemith, was to comment humorously on this concert:

> The first concert was with the tall Otto Klerper [*sic*]: Schumann. Last year I had the impression that he – I don't mean Schumann! – changed very much to his advantage. I also considered him to be THE promising star. This winter he destroyed everything through bad programming, through being offensive etc., well, you know him! His farewell interview was only a slightly dampened down invitation from the Gods to the audience.'[63]

As in the previous year, Feuermann was booked to give two recitals in New York's Town Hall, but before his first recital on 19 January he travelled once again to Winnetka, where this time he was given the entire programme: 'That was one of my nicest concerts. And do you know why? Because I really had a most crazy success with: Bach, Beethoven and Debussy. That gave me such a satisfaction that I am almost reconciled to playing the cello.' Feuermann's satisfaction relates significantly to playing 'substantial' works, for he adds: 'When I am back we will talk very seriously about my programmes. . . . Of course I also have to play "virtuosi" pieces, but the programmes must be constructed in such a way that I feel a musician, not as competition to music halls.'[64] Feuermann did not want to feel like a circus animal. This was a common complaint; Schnabel famously eschewed playing trivial show pieces, but his situation was somewhat different from Feuermann's, for he had neither the required virtuoso technique nor the type of personality to bring them off. Feuermann wanted to be valued for the great music he played rather than for virtuoso 'bons-bons'.

In St Louis, however, where Feuermann was playing for the first time, he was still obliged to play these 'bons-bons' and the recital was a shared one. There was an audience of about 3,000 at the Municipal Auditorium Opera House for his concert with the Russian pianist Mischa Levitzki, which, according to a local paper, was not an unusual attendance. Together they played Beethoven's A major Sonata op.69 – wrongly described by the *St Louis Globe Democrat* as the well-known 'Kreutzer' Sonata[65] – and Grieg's A minor Sonata op.36. With Rebner, Feuermann played his salon pieces.

Feuermann was fascinated by America. A local St Louis paper strapped a feature article: 'Noted Artists Here for Recital predict New U.S. Music Era' in which Feuermann was quoted:

> It's so different from what they say about America in Europe. They still have the old Wild West ideas there. The most remarkable and unique things in American musical life are the concert series being presented in schools and colleges throughout the country. I have seen nothing like it anywhere else, but it's wonderful and should create a great audience for the future.[66]

For many years, however, a career in New York depended on being European, as the list of performers in January and early February 1936 in New York's Town Hall shows: Schnabel (playing the complete Beethoven sonatas over six evenings), Pinza, Lotte Lehmann, Segovia, Robert Casadesus, Egon Petri and Myra Hess.

Feuermann's Town Hall recital on 19 January coincided with particularly bad weather, but as the *New York Times* headline blazed: 'Feuermann gives brilliant Recital. The Storm Fails to Keep Away Admirers of Noted Master of Violoncello.'[67] Once again Feuermann triumphed: 'In a day that is glutted with instrumental executants of high technical and interpretative accomplishments, Emanuel Feuermann must still be considered a *rara avis* among virtuosi. This little, spectacled, poker-faced Viennese gave such an exhibition of musical and mechanical gifts that no ears, howsoever jaded by a lifetime of concert going, could but marvel.' The reviewer was Gama Gilbert in the *New York Post*:

> It is difficult to speak with restraint of such matters as Mr Feuermann's breathtaking ease of execution. For the truth of the matter is that not only does it encompass with surpassing facility those technical problems indigenous to the cello but it tosses off feats – as for example in the cellist's own arrangement of Sarasate's 'Gipsy Airs' – that must hitherto have been considered beyond the potentialities of the instrument.[68]

The programme included Bach's G minor Viola de Gamba Sonata, Stravinsky's *Suite italienne* and Brahms's E minor Sonata, and was a success despite what Feuermann had written in a letter a few days earlier: 'the Stravinsky wants to enter neither my head nor my fingers. If only this won't be a flop.'[69]

On 30 January and 1 February, Feuermann was in Cleveland for his first appearances with the Cleveland Orchestra. Artur Rodzinski conducted works by Beethoven and Ravel, but it was left to the associate conductor, Rudolf Ringwall, to direct Boccherini's B♭ Cello Concerto. The local critic described Feuermann's playing: 'With the utmost simplicity, with none of the see-sawing so typical of cellists, he set forth the music in a tone not large, but vibrant and clear in texture.'[70] Standard contracts were issued by the Cleveland Orchestra, but one clause in the contract is particularly mystifying: all soloists were expected to provide a score and complete orchestral parts for the 'numbers' to be performed: 'It is understood and agreed that this means NOT A PIANO SCORE but A COMPLETE ORCHESTRA SCORE of EACH AND EVERY NUMBER.'[71] The notion of a soloist being responsible for providing parts seems today very startling, but these were relatively early days for the Cleveland Orchestra – the 1935/6 season was its 18th – and so its library may have been small. Singers, it seems, did not carry this obligation: in Emanuel List's contract for the same season this clause is struck out. However, in contracts for Heifetz and Mischa Levitzki the responsibility for providing parts remained. It is worth noting the disparity in fees paid by the Cleveland Orchestra in that season: Heifetz and List both received $1500 whereas Feuermann was paid only $550.

As in the previous season, Feuermann appeared in Boston – this time under the auspices of the Boston Morning Musicale at the Statler Hotel – in another joint recital, on this occasion with the tenor Giovanni Martinelli. It was a morning concert, and so Feuermann's programme was suitably lightweight. However, the critic, noting the slight content, observes one of Feuermann's greatest gifts – that of turning works of no particular musical significance into pieces worthy of attention: 'Even in a display piece of the type of Sarasate's "Zigeunerweisen" he is always the musician, first and last, integrating the composer's thoughts, rather than dividing them into sweet morsels. . . . it did not take the listener long to discover that those who rank this young man of thirty-one with Casals have every reason for their enthusiasm.'[72]

A very different 'shared' concert took place days later: 'Three renowned virtuosi pooled their talents last night for the greater glory of chamber music', began Samuel Chotzinoff's review in the *New York Evening Post* of 8 February 1936. It was the sixth event in the New York Town Hall Endowment Series. A capacity audience had gathered to hear Schnabel, Huberman and Feuermann perform Beethoven's D major Trio op.70 no.1, Brahms's op. 8 and Schubert's op.99. Although these three musicians had previously played together on an informal basis, this was their first public appearance as a trio. Only months before, Fred Gaisberg had floated the idea with Feuermann of recording trios, naming Schnabel and a violinist 'of international fame'. This first outing was not, however, an unqualified success, as Chotzinoff comments:

> It is commonplace that the temporary conjunction of celebrated players does not always produce that ensemble on which chamber music is based. Individually [*sic*], which is the essential in solo performance, cannot be countenanced when the players are many. . . . It would be, then, unfair to expect Messrs Feuermann, Huberman and Schnabel to bring to their performance the unified approach of players who are more used to acting in concert. That they acquitted themselves as well as they did last night is a tribute to their sound and serious musicianship. Or have they secretly practised together for years?

Practising together would not have solved the problem of distinctively different styles of playing: 'Generally, my ears favoured Mr Feuermann, whose impeccable artistry was as much in evidence as it is in his own concerts.' Chotzinoff's comments (and those of several of his colleagues) on Huberman were not as kind: 'Mr Huberman often forced his tone, and was much addicted to sliding. The emotion he expressed was either inflated or precious, while he succeeded [*sic*] the regulation amount of off-pitch playing.'[73] There can be little doubt that Huberman's playing was idiosyncratic. While he could be exquisitely expressive, evidence from his solo recordings indicates that his slides would have been more excessive than Feuermann's. He might also have been the most wilful player of the three. In a letter to the Hindemiths, Feuermann later commented: ' . . . books would not suffice to tell the tale, these few days were indescribable', adding, 'By the way, Schnabel played wonderfully'. Schnabel was the butt of a hilarious story recounted by Feuermann in this same letter to the Hindemiths, involving mischievous wordplay on 'piece' and 'piss'. Feuermann wrote partly in German and partly in English.

> Once I slipped up with big success. In Cleveland after a concert – I played the next evening – we were together in a private house. Schnabel talked and talked and talked, he became very agitated resulting in the comment: 'You know that in London I played in 9 seasons 109 different big pieces.' In response I said in a very low voice into the solemn silence of admiration '*Yes Mr Schnabel you are a big "piecer"*'. After one moment of deathly silence, a

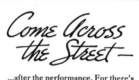
neighing started in which Schnabel joined enthusiastically and which wouldn't stop.[74]

Feuermann's stamina was legendary, and the next few days brought back-to-back concerts. On 9 February he even took part in two concerts on the same day, the first in New York's Town Hall, the second as guest soloist in the *General Motors Concert Hour* broadcast. The first concert, in the late afternoon, was a series of lecture-recitals for the International Music Guild, in which the critic Leonard Liebling was billed as commentator. Feuermann played Beethoven's A major Sonata op.69 and Saint-Saëns's A minor Concerto. So full was New York's musical life that one reviewer of this concert noted that barely 150 minutes earlier Piatigorsky had played the same Saint-Saëns concerto in Carnegie Hall.[75] The General Motors Concerts was a distinguished series broadcast widely over NBC Red affiliates.[76] Among those listed to take part between January and March 1936 were Erica Morini, Stokowski, Melchior,

Bonelli, Toscanini, Josef Hofmann, Grace Moore and Yehudi Menuhin. It must
have been a tired Feuermann who performed Popper's *Hungarian Rhapsody*,
Granados's *Danse espagnole*, Dvořák's Rondo and some Saint-Saëns between
10.00 p.m. and 11.00 p.m. on 9 February. But to the car-loving, Buick-driving
cellist this series must have seemed particularly appropriate. One hopes he
received a complimentary copy of *We Drivers* as advertised in the programme,
described as 'a little book containing discussions dealing with Night Driving,
Driving in Mist and Fog, Hill Driving, Slippery Weather Driving, Curves and
Turns, City Traffic, and similar subjects of interest to us all'.[77]

Feuermann was back in the Town Hall the next evening for the Beethoven
Association where he played op.102 no.2 with the pianist Frank Sheridan. Of
the sublime Adagio the *New York Times* commented: 'One seldom hears as
stirring a distillation of the materials of music-making – tone, phrasing, style,
emotion – as Mr Feuermann's playing of this movement.'[78] Other performers
taking part included the celebrated Danish tenor Lauritz Melchior with his
accompanist Ignace Strassfogel, and Mishel Piastro, concertmaster of the
Philharmonic-Symphony.

After such a concentration of appearances in New York, Feuermann now left
with his accompanist Wolfgang Rebner to give recitals across the States: Grand
Rapids, Michigan, Chicago, Lafayette, Pittsburgh, East Lansing, Denver,
Colorado Springs and, eventually, California. As usual, there were the joint
recitals that he so hated: 'Yesterday the concert was terrible. I will let Levine
know that I can do without such pleasures. Three of us in the same program,
that reminds one of the circus!'[79] This he wrote to Eva, who for the moment
was not travelling with him. In Los Angeles, as he humorously described to the
Hindemiths, he tasted real show business for the first time:

> I played jazz for the radio with Bing Crosby, the film star, and with two little
> street girls who had become starlets and animal mimics etc. for 'American
> Kraft Cheese', and this probably caused great upset to those listeners with
> better taste. On the other hand, to the popular audience it was bad enough
> to be presented with the cello; and you cannot force a free American to listen
> to a movement by Schubert . . . I saw the disappointed faces before my eyes
> and could imagine so well how thankful they were at this moment for the
> possibility of turning off the radio. And now imagine Huberman in this
> environment who played the previous week the first movement of the César
> Franck sonata. You must have a vivid imagination!!![80]

From Los Angeles, Feuermann rented a Studebaker for two weeks in which he
drove to his various concerts with Eva, who had now rejoined him. He found
California 'really cold and windy in the north and in the south, warm only

during the day'.[81] In San Francisco on 24 March he performed for the first and only time with the San Francisco Symphony Orchestra and Pierre Monteux. It was a 'Viennese Evening', essentially 'pops', although Feuermann played the Haydn Concerto.

Feuermann's final concerts in America before embarking for the second time to the Far East took place in Los Angeles, with the Philharmonic Orchestra and Klemperer; he had also begun the American tour with Klemperer. Klemperer had become music director of the Los Angeles Philharmonic Orchestra in 1933, when the large-scale emigration of Jews to the West Coast of America had begun. Schönberg, initially based in Boston at the Malkin Conservatory, moved to California in 1935, accepting a professorship at the University of California in Los Angeles in 1936. 'Before the emigrés began arriving in the early thirties, Los Angeles musicians were isolated, and largely unaware of modernity in music beyond the works of Debussy. The indigenous musical culture was conservative.'[82] Feuermann and Klemperer had a surprise. These concerts on 2 and 3 April 1936 were the penultimate pair of concerts that season. As usual, there was an evening performance followed the next day by a repeat in the afternoon. The American premiere of Schönberg's Cello Concerto, only its second performance, was included in the programme, and the composer was in the audience. His views are not recorded, but the audience was described as 'almost capacity and warmly appreciative',[83] a very different reaction from that in London. Klemperer's views were recorded in a letter to Schnabel: 'He (Schönberg) was very happy with the performance which we prepared in five very careful rehearsals (the piece is also orchestrally very difficult). I think that no living cellist can play this piece like Feuermann.'[84] Feuermann also commented on Schönberg's presence in a letter to the Hindemiths: 'Schönberg was touching in his appreciation of me, annoying the Americans in their holiest feelings, when he declared that I am the best player, even better than Heifetz.'[85] As well as the Schönberg, Feuermann played the Haydn Concerto, which Klemperer referred to in his letter to Schnabel: 'Feuermann played astonishingly beautifully, much better than in New York, the Haydn was perfection.' An error on the concert flyer suggested that the Haydn rather than the Schönberg was receiving its American premiere. A local paper, the *Herald Express*, believed this to be true.

After 35 concerts, Feuermann's second American tour was over. In a long letter to Lily he gave a blow-by-blow account:

> The success has been even greater than it was last year. I think you can be quite pleased with me. The new Stradivarius cello is the tops. The first two months were full of work for me and much too much socializing for Eva.

Seventeenth Season—*1935-36*

THE PHILHARMONIC ORCHESTRA

WILLIAM ANDREWS CLARK, JR., *Founder*

OTTO KLEMPERER, *Conductor and Musical Director*

Sponsored by Southern California Symphony Association

THURSDAY EVENING April 2, at 8:30	1348th and 1249th CONCERTS	FRIDAY AFTERNOON April 3, at 2:30

✦ ✦

PROGRAM—*Eleventh Pair of Concerts*

OTTO KLEMPERER, Conductor

Soloist: EMANUEL FEUERMANN, Violoncellist

✦

BERLIOZ

"Harold in Italy," Symphony in Four Movements with
Viola Solo, Op. 16

- I.   Harold in the Mountains; Scenes of Melancholy,
  Happiness and Joy, (Adagio - Allegro)
- II.   March of the Pilgrims Singing their Evening
  Hymn (Allegretto)
- III. Serenade of a Mountaineer of the Abruzzi to His
  Mistress (Allegro assai - allegretto)
- VI. Orgy of Brigands; Recollections of the preceding
  scenes (Allegretto Frenetico)
  Solo Viola: Emile Ferir

✦

HAYDN

*Concerto for Violoncello and Orchestra in D-major. Op. 101

- I.   Allegro moderato
- II. Adagio
- III. Allegro

Intermission
Fifteen Minutes

SCHOENBERG

✗ Concerto for Violoncello and Orchestra from the Concerto for
Clavicembalo After Georg Matthias Monn in a Free
Version by Arnold Schoenberg

- I.   Allegro moderato
- II. Adagio (alla marcia)
- III. Tempo di menuetto

✦

ROSSINI

Overture: "Semiramide"

✗

*First Time in America

But from 28 February it was wonderful: Niagara Falls, Ford factory, Eva skiing at 3,700 metres, a few days in a charming hotel in the desert, the GRAND CANYON, 14 days in California driving ourselves from Los Angeles and back, half days in the film studios, etc., etc. – that gives you an idea of all the wonderful and new things that we're experiencing. We're only staying for six weeks in Japan, then it's South-central America and Mexico and October to December back in North America – and, God willing, back in Europe for Christmas!

In the same letter he gave an indication of how Eva was surviving the rigours of touring and married life:

I can safely say that Eva and I make a lovely married couple. It is unbelievable how Eva has settled into her role of wife to [an artist],[86] how she stands out with her charming character, her looks, her unspoilt nature compared to most other women. She's not in the least bit gossipy, arrogant or affected, she's so lovely and natural – and she keeps out of the way, has nothing to do with her husband's profession. It was so sweet, for example, I played the new Schönberg concerto in Los Angeles under Klemperer; they were so excited by the fact that Eva didn't come to a single one of my rehearsals. She much preferred to wander around town.

Feuermann's letter to Lily also shows that he was now anxious to indulge a lifelong passion:

> If I have enough money I do want to buy myself a car in America. I can get an eight-cylinder Buick or Chrysler for about 1,000 dollars (convertible). Would it be possible for Leo to find out certain details at his club or at a relevant place? What I would like to know is: how high the duty is, how it is calculated, whether it is different for new or used cars; how long I may drive in Switzerland with an American number plate; if I have the car in Switzerland with an American number plate, whether I can have that changed to a Swiss one by paying the necessary duty; how high the tax is for a car with 100 hp and how much the insurance is; how much a similar convertible would cost in Zürich. It would be so kind of Leo if he could find all this out for me.

Lily and Leo Hofmann were to remain Feuermann's close friends in every way.

Chapter 8

Full Sail
April to December 1936

In these days of Casals's old age, there is no equal to Feuermann under the sun.

Motoo Ohtaguro[1]

'This week holds unusual riches in store for the musically inclined of Tokyo residents, for it offers an unusual array of concerts by excellent visiting artists. The few who complain that there is nothing worth hearing in Japan must be blind or deaf, perhaps both.'[2] The *Japan Advertiser's* chiding of the musical public is striking. Striking, too, is the diet of musicians visiting Japan in April 1936 from the West: the celebrated Hungarian pianist Lili Kraus with Feuermann's colleague Szymon Goldberg performing a series of Beethoven concerts; the German pianist Wilhelm Kempff performing concertos by Bach, Brahms and Beethoven with the New Symphony Orchestra; and Feuermann with his accompanist Wolfgang Rebner. Once again, Strok was responsible for managing the Far East tour. After a brief stay and concert in Honolulu, Feuermann arrived in Japan.

Strok had established a pattern in Tokyo whereby visiting artists would give up to five concerts in the main concert hall, the Hibiya Public Hall. Feuermann gave three recitals on 23, 24 and 27 April[3] with Wolfgang Rebner, followed by orchestral concerts on 30 April and 1 May with the Chûô Symphony Orchestra conducted by Hidemaro Konoye.[4] He had previously played with Konoye in 1934, but in the intervening 18 months Japan's musical life had changed considerably and Feuermann found himself caught up in the chaos:

There is a big mess in Tokyo. Konoye had a fight with the orchestra.[5] Konoye
has founded a new orchestra.[6] Now everybody is screened by everybody to
establish their loyalty according to the following principle: whoever is not
for me is against me. I was in a very tricky situation because Strok, the
manager, was loyal to Konoye and I played under his baton. On the other
hand, the two principal cellists, Saito and Ohmura, are the two most
important people in the old orchestra. They were my pupils at the
Hochschule and we are now old friends. For that reason, I also played with
their orchestra. This is characteristic of the inexplicable character of the
Japanese. Konoye and his orchestra have declared war against each other,
especially the orchestra against Konoye. One would think that they wouldn't
even greet each other. Wrong. Not only do they talk to each other at
gatherings, Konoye even conducted a part of the orchestra for a recording
of mine!![7]

Since his previous visit, Feuermann's impact on cellists had been profound. He
told his British student Bernard Richards that on his second tour he had been
astonished to find that his two Japanese students had taught all the other
cellists in the orchestra to bow in the same way that they had been taught by
Feuermann.

The response to Feuermann was, as usual, extraordinary: 'In the allegro of
Locatelli's sonata, the notes jumped around like many little fish, the bow
vividly and finely carving out the notes like a kind of magic. In these days of
Casals's old age, there is no equal to Feuermann under the sun.'[8] To another
reviewer, Feuermann had improved since his previous visit: 'When I see his
hands, I am almost hypnotised. I can't believe that the five fingers of his left
hand press four strings.' But the orchestra, as so often, was not up to
Feuermann's level. Ignoring the inclusion of an unusual work (Glazunov's
Chant du Ménéstrel), the same critic found that the orchestra played so quietly
that the music became 'less energetic' – perhaps a reflection of Konoye's
conducting.[9]

Financially the visit to Japan was not as successful. As Feuermann cheerfully
put it: 'The people had had enough of me.'[10] A gap of 18 months between visits
was insufficient time for the public to turn out again to hear him. And,
unusually, within one year Maréchal, Piatigorsky and Feuermann all appeared
there.

Nipponophone, however, was convinced that recordings should be made.
Feuermann was willing to sign a contract on condition that 'England releases
ten doubles within three years'.[11] London's reply was as usual cautious: 'Cannot
guarantee issue Feuermann records but will give them preferential consider-

ation.'[12] Nipponophone replied: 'The artist was pretty disappointed as he is very much interested that his records are released and advertised in England and other European countries.'[13] Following the loss of Germany as a concert base, dissemination of recordings was vital to Feuermann. Significantly, Columbia's Export Department now alerted their agents in New York, Brussels, Bucharest, Copenhagen, Milan and Paris to performances he would be giving in Chile, Peru, Argentina, Mexico, North America and Europe:[14] 'We give you this information since we feel sure you would like to take the opportunity of his visit to push his records, and you will probably wish to prepare some advertising material in order to take full advantage of his tour.'[15]

Feuermann agreed a contract with Nipponophone and proceeded to record fifteen sides: ten 10-inch sides, and five 12-inch sides of salon pieces. That Nipponophone was more enterprising than Columbia in London is noticeable. Solo cellists in the concert hall or on disc were not as popular as solo singers, violinists or pianists, but Nipponophone had no doubt about Feuermann's exceptional gift. Having completed the recording of these minor works, they then wanted Feuermann to record more substantial pieces: Schubert's 'Arpeggione' Sonata and Beethoven's A major Sonata op.69. Nipponophone asked Columbia to record them in London following the completion of Feuermann's tour to South America:

> We are aware that the Schubert Sonata in A minor has been recorded by Cassadó some years ago in an arrangement for orchestra but we heard Feuermann playing this sonata on the stage and the comparison with Cassadó's version rather overwhelmed us. Feuermann has, in our opinion, become an artist of such outstanding qualities that he may safely be compared with Casals; especially his version of the Schubert Sonata is far superior to that of Cassadó.

The Spanish cellist Gaspar Cassadó, five years older than Feuermann and a pupil of Casals, was well established, pursuing the same international circuit as Feuermann. Nipponophone suggested that Schubert's Sonata be recorded with Feuermann's 'usual accompanist' but that the Beethoven be recorded with the better-known English pianist Myra Hess.

Nipponophone recognized Feuermann's importance but, like Columbia in London, they still seemed reluctant to offer him the financial conditions he believed his right:

> Apart from the question of a guarantee for releases in Europe, we had great difficulty in negotiating with Feuermann about the rate of royalty because Strok, his manager, told him that we have paid rather a considerable flat fee

to Zimbalist [the violinist] a year ago and Huberman has told him that he receives 10% of the retail price. Our argument was that cello records do not sell as well as violin records and furthermore the royalty paid to Huberman is an exceptional one and that we would not be willing to pay similar royalties in the future.[16]

Gieseking, another Nipponophone artist, also received 10%.[17] Feuermann had argued the same case in the previous year with Columbia when for the Haydn Concerto he was offered 5% on the retail price, payable on 85% of sales.[18] In his contract dated 4 June 1936, four rates of royalty payments were established: 7½% , 6%, 5% and 3⅓ of the retail price on 75% of manufacture. Various conditions determined the levels: the type of piece (solo, with piano or orchestra), whether he worked with his 'usual' accompanist, whether it was a work already recorded by Parlophon, or whether Feuermann was a member of a trio. Nipponophone's exclusive contract with Feuermann required that he record 15 double-sided records to be made in the period to 31 December 1938. He was restricted to Nipponophone and its associated company, Columbia Graphophone Company Ltd.

One particular project that was to drag on futilely for several years was now raised: recording trios with Schnabel and Huberman. In January 1935, in New York, just after his debut, Feuermann had got together with Schnabel and Huberman in his hotel and had had a marvellous time playing chamber music. Schnabel, however, was an HMV artist. Another pianist would be required. In somewhat awkward English, Straus wrote to Francis Brand Duncan at Columbia:

> The only artist who would be suitable, in our opinion, is Gieseking. It is doubtful whether Gieseking will play with Huberman and Feuermann after the experience Hindemith has made [*sic*] with the Nazis after having played with Goldberg and Feuermann, but after all Gieseking has already played under the baton of Bruno Walter who is Jewish and that should solve the question.[19]

Nipponophone was weighing up the chances of Gieseking risking his skin to perform with Huberman and Feuermann, who were both Jews. Any reply has been lost, but it seems unlikely that Feuermann and Huberman would have been keen to collaborate with Gieseking; and no trios were recorded with him.

Feuermann continued to Shanghai, where he gave two recitals in the Lyceum Theatre, returning on 3 June to Tokyo's Hibiya Public Hall for an orchestral concert and broadcast with the New Symphony Orchestra. Wolfgang Rebner heroically took the place of the indisposed Walter Herbert;

Feuermann played the Dvořák Concerto and C.P.E. Bach's Cello Concerto no.3.[20] A long boat trip to South America now awaited Feuermann, his wife and Wolfgang Rebner. On board the SS *Santa Rita*, Feuermann had time to waste: 'yesterday I discovered when I unpacked the cello after three weeks that 3 strings had broken and that the soundpost had fallen down and so I can't practise.'[21] He took to the typewriter, writing long letters to Hindemith and Huberman. To Huberman he revealed: 'I am not writing with the typewriter to save time, on the contrary, it takes ages but it is fun.' Then he outlined his trip:

> On the 15th [July] we will arrive in Valparaiso, and stay in Santiago, Buenos Aires and Rio de Janeiro for 3–4 weeks. I will then play from the end of October to the middle of December in North America and for Christmas we will be in Europe and then we will settle in Zürich. Then you must come and stay with us!! Do you prefer veal *nature* or wiener schnitzel? C minor? The Harp quartet?

Huberman had been negotiating with Feuermann's brother-in-law, Adolf Hönigsberg, who wished to join the Palestine Symphony Orchestra; Huberman was unaware that Adolf belonged to Feuermann's family. In the same letter to Huberman, Feuerman wrote:

> You and your orchestra are the topic of conversation throughout the whole world, which shows that you will achieve your purpose to create, if I under-stand you rightly, a Jewish propaganda machine in the noblest sense of the word. . . . We both have a really bad conscience because, touch wood, we are so well off because we are so far away from all the terrible and horrific things to which those closest to us are subject. . . . A propos: has Dr Schiff contacted you about the concerts in Palestine? To be invited would mean an enormous amount to me. I thought it would be wonderful to play in November 1937 in your concerts. Perhaps one could combine this with Athens and Egypt.[22]

The trio recordings with Schnabel were also concerning him. Despite contractual difficulties, time had been put aside to record at the end of the year. It has been said that Feuermann had artistic misgivings about the stylistic match between Schnabel, Huberman and himself.[23] If this was so, it is not revealed in this letter: 'I am tremendously interested in these trio recordings from every point of view.'[24]

Nipponophone continued negotiations with Columbia, London, over the availability of Myra Hess to record Beethoven's A major Sonata. And a new idea was floated: Feuermann suggested re-recording the Dvořák Concerto. It had been several years since his Berlin recording and contractually Nippono-phone had the right to re-record and pay a mere 5% royalty with no advance payment. Nipponophone, however, hoped that Columbia would pay the recording costs: 'If you are not prepared to do so, we would like to hear from you what the approximate expenses for the orchestra and conductor would be.' London quoted £500, to which the Japanese replied, 'We are sorry to say that an expense of £500 for the Dvořák concerto is definitely prohibitive. We would like you to consider whether you could share in those expenses.'[25] No response has survived and no further commercial recording was ever made.

Matching the availabilities of Myra Hess and Feuermann proved exasperating, so much so that Columbia suggested Harriet Cohen as an alternative pianist, adding: 'Alternatively, Feuermann could do this work with his regular accompanist.'[26] Sophie Feuermann maintains that she was engaged to make the recording.[27] No correspondence survives to support this.

Despite eight months on the road, Feuermann greatly enjoyed his South American tour. From Santiago he wrote (on the typewriter) to Schnabel: 'The journey through America, then Honolulu, Japan, a bit of China, the voyages by sea, the Panama Canal and now the wonderful Andes – we enjoy all this very much and we are very much aware of our undeserved advantage compared to other human beings.' Once again, his infectious enthusiasm for life bubbles over: 'Today, we should have been flying over the Andes to Buenos Aires but Eva has a bit of a cold. This exciting event – one climbs up to a height of 6000 metres and the airplane is equipped with oxygen – will only take place on Saturday.' Feuermann found Santiago incomparably beautiful with its mimosas, magnolias and camelias, but he commented wryly: 'above all, what flowers is the dirt, the chaos, and the factions. What isn't flourishing is music. (I'm not merely talking as a cellist.) However, we have met here the nicest people of our whole journey.'[28]

Between 22 August and 9 September, Feuermann gave five recitals at the Teatro Colón, Buenos Aires, in which he played duo works. Only in his concert on 6 September did he include piano arrangements of orchestral pieces, as was the custom: Haydn's D major Concerto and Tchaikovsky's 'Rococo' Variations. For some unexplained reason, his final recital on 9 September was with the pianist Sofia Knoll, rather than Rebner.

The South American tour ended in late September in Rio de Janeiro, from where he wrote to Lily Hofmann: 'This Rio is really indescribably beautiful. We did also manage to catch the best weather – it's not like our March, but it's like a warm, beautiful summer. This hotel is on the beach, we put on our swim suits in our rooms! We're so thrilled to have "granny-in-law", she's really enjoying the trip.' Mrs Reifenberg had joined them in Buenos Aires. Feuermann also had reason to be pleased about something very different:

I've been in a good mood for the past few days because the Swiss franc has dropped so beautifully – something I've been awaiting for a year. Now it's evened out and I don't have to feel guilty that I moved to foreign parts. I can imagine there are people who are not quite <u>so</u> thrilled about the devaluation (!), I hope that doesn't include you.

But returning to Europe and finding somewhere to live were pressing issues:

So the trip is coming to an end. Really rather sad. Who knows when we will experience such fabulous things again. Eva feels the same way and is even more keen than I am to stay away. She's so afraid of Europe. Do keep your ears and eyes open, you might hear of a little house that might seem right for us. Eva and her mother will be in Cologne again from 15th November and could come to Zürich to have a look at anything. I'm afraid though that it's not going to work without an agent. I would like to live up high (less fog) with a little garden and with <u>one</u> large room.[29]

It seems odd that in his correspondence concerning the Reifenbergs Feuerman did not comment on their situation as Jews in Germany at the time. Either it was too dangerous to put anything on paper, or the Reifenbergs were somehow insulated from public life. It is surprising that they were still living in Cologne at that time; with their financial resources and contacts, the Reifenbergs could have emigrated far sooner.

By mid-October, Feuermann was back again in America. It had been six months since he had left California after his concerts with Klemperer in Los Angeles. Eva and her mother had returned to New York and would return to Europe ahead of him. More touring was ahead: 'Rebner was very curious about the night life of New Orleans – I imagined something like an American Marseilles – and we were quite disappointed, it was surprisingly similar to the harbour district of Trinidad and Panama, but otherwise nothing.' However, the circumstances in Galveston, Texas, were more unexpected: 'It turns out that the president of the Civic Concerts, Mr Springer, an American from "Dieringen" [play on "Thüringen", a province in Germany], is looked upon by the Jewish clique as a Nazi. This mutual snooping is bad enough – but that it happens in Galveston on the Gulf of Mexico!'[30] Feuermann had survived European anti-Semitism only to find a virulent breed of the very same thing in America. But he was impressed at what could be done in such a small community: 'I was interrupted by the Rabbi who came to show us the synagogue and his community house. For his 40-year anniversary of service they wanted to give him $50,000, but he wanted this house and it was built for

$100,000. And the community has only around 250 families.' Feuermann's concert was the first to take place in the town.

Feuermann proceeded to Houston: 'I read a few "*items*" about Texas and am again completely dumbfounded by these Americans. 100 years ago Texas had 50,000 inhabitants – now it has 1½ million cars!!!'[31] But he was missing Eva and writing to her almost every day:

> I am again travelling through the same landscapes as in March – it makes me quite melancholy. It is beautiful outside, desert, mountains, sunset; but a refined married man who travelled with his wife for one year is spoiled, and can't get along with himself alone. Now I realize that our travelling has stopped. That belongs to the past. Too bad, but wasn't it just wonderful???[32]

At the end of October, Feuermann was again in Los Angeles performing on a radio show, the 'Kraft-Phoenix Cheese Corporation' (later 'Kraft Music Hall'), the 'Cheesey Hour' as he put it, and visiting friends. Although Klemperer was away, Feuermann's agent Paul Schiff and his family, the Tochs and the Schönbergs were all in the vicinity. While visiting Schönberg, an attractive suggestion was put to him by the composer:

> He is still full of love towards me, very nice and somehow the grand old man who sees to it that the younger deserves recognition. Now comes something very funny: we spoke about all sorts of things, one thing led to another and then he told me that the president of the Music Department of the University wants to really build it up and maybe I could come in the near future to California. Give Schönberg his due, but is he a reliable organizer?? I don't believe in it. I was very careful, [and] only told him that it was my dream to have besides the cello [department] the whole string department in a large school. Everything is still very vague, the president told him he could have everything only no money. So how would it be Oeff,[33] would you like to be Mrs Professor of the University of Southern California?[34]

Feuermann's instinct was right. It came to nothing. Feuermann was playing in tiny communities:

> Visalia *was* an agreeable surprise. The town itself doesn't have a station; you have to get out in Sashen Junction. A young man with a Buick was there [and] besides this Buick and the *station house* building nothing! I had terrible premonitions, but it turns out that this God-forsaken place Visalia, with 7000 inhabitants, has 1000 *members* in the *Civic Concerts!* They come with their cars from the whole *county!* After me, Pinza and then Marian Anderson will come! Isn't that fantastic?[35]

Even more unexpected was the appearance of a member of the audience in the green room with an old concert programme from a performance by Sophie and Feuermann in Vienna. And even more thrilling was a newly built house belonging to a Mrs Doffelmeier, which Feuermann was shown around: 'So many new and unknown things which can be found there: the whole house is *air-conditioned*, the office of the husband *soundproof* – that is, protected against noise – and in the kitchen an electrically run dish washer!'[36] And of course Feuermann was delighted to indulge his passion for cars:

> Before dinner I went in Visalia to the Buick agency and let them show me the new cars. Just enchanting! But all this publicity regarding prices is nonsense. The 4-seater cabriolet of the 'smallest' Buick (100 horse-power that goes up to 150 kph) costs in New York with the discount surely between 1100–1200 dollars. Please tell Dagmar Godowsky[37] that I would like to have an *appointment* for the 7th with her and her Buick friend. The car is heavenly![38]

Feuermann continued to travel: to New Mexico and then to Canada again. At the Canadian border he ran into unexpected trouble: 'Canada's national policy is protectionist, but the Canadian customs authorities at Windsor should be informed that it is the government's aim to administer the Customs Act without being idiotic.' The Windsor officials had refused Feuermann permission to bring in his cello, the Stradivarius valued at $25,000, without paying a deposit of $12,000. Of course, Feuermann was not carrying $12,000. The customs authorities compromised by allowing him to return to Detroit, from where the cello could be sent to Ottawa in bond. 'So this precious instrument entered Canada in the baggage car, while the celebrated owner spent a sleepless night travelling in the Pullman. Thanks to the care of the railway baggage handlers, Feuermann's irreplaceable cello arrived undamaged. He was able to claim it in time to appear before the Morning Music Club audience.'[39]

Back in New York at the beginning of November, Feuermann enjoyed many social moments, meeting friends (the Wallensteins and Brascha and Mischa Schneider), lunching with Rachmaninov, checking out the Buick, going to movies, teaching, and visiting the instrument 'doctor' Sacconi, when the cello needed three and a half hours of attention.[40] Feuermann's carefree attitude to cello maintenance is recorded by Havivi, who went with Feuermann, possibly on this occasion. Feuermann's bridge needed adjustment:

> Sacconi said that the easiest way is to cut the bridge down, which means you ruin the vibration, especially on the A – it was a mistake. Sacconi was

probably so busy that he made a shortcut. It took 10, 15 minutes and the cello sounded horrible so Sacconi said 'OK, we make a new bridge.' He didn't have to ruin this bridge, but Feuermann didn't care one way or the other. Bridge, hair, bow, he could play well with anything.[41]

Feuermann had admitted to feeling tired after the long tour and on 13 November he noted that he weighed only 74 kilos (162lb), 3 kilos (7lb) less than his heaviest weight. His height was 5 feet 11 inches (1.8m). He wrote to Eva: 'In the restaurants I don't order the menu any more and instead only eat light things. This tour now is very easy, don't have to travel days between the concerts but only hours, the hotels are good and I even practise.'[42] In the course of 17 days he was able to spend only 7 nights in a hotel.

A few days earlier he had heard the Philadelphia Orchestra:

> I am still in raptures over Stokowski and his orchestra. It was a Russian programme and on the surface he looks like a clown. I don't know how or if a Beethoven symphony could stand up to the soaring fantasy of a Stokowski, but what I do know is that there has never been such an orchestra and that I never believed a person could wrest THIS from the passive resistance of an orchestra. How it sings and rejoices and dances and . . . well, I am getting poetic, terrible. But after all it is my profession and I'm allowed to be happy when I hear what until now I have only dreamt of.[43]

Feuermann was soon to have his most important orchestral and recording relationship with this orchestra.

Feuermann's touring continued relentlessly:

> On the evening of my birthday [22 November] I will travel to New York, will be there early on the 23rd and continue that same evening on to Raleigh (lies behind Charlottesville), will play there on the 24th; am in New York noon the 25th, evening at Elsie's; on the evening of the 26th *Thanksgiving turkey dinner* at Mrs Goldmann's; on the afternoon of the 27th in Baltimore (leave at 11 o'clock, the concert at 4 and back in New York at 10 o'clock, like last time!); on the 29th is the stupid concert in New York and on the 30th I leave again.[44]

This 'stupid concert' (with the Kolisch Quartet) was an all-Beethoven programme for the New Friends of Music, an organization newly founded by Ira Hirschmann, an amateur pianist. He had studied with Schnabel but became a vice-president of Bloomingdales department store. Hirschmann had been present at that memorable evening in January 1935 when Schnabel, Huberman and Feuermann had played chamber music in Feuermann's hotel, resulting in the broken C string:

The music was overwhelming in its impact and quality. It was a privilege to hear them in a small room where all their personalities and their profundity in approaching the music one could hear at such close range. It was as a result of hearing the several Beethoven trios in this room that the idea came to me that this chamber music should be heard by many people.[45]

According to Hirschmann, there was scarcely any knowledge of chamber music in America at that time. He had set up the New Friends with impressive and idealistic aims:

1) To offer the best in the literature of chamber music and Lieder.
2) To embrace complete cycles of composers' works rather than 'little pieces', wherever possible.
3) To conceive the music in the season's programs as a unit divided into 16 concerts with a view to offering the subscribers as complete a representation of the literature of individual composers as feasible.
4) To perform neglected music in unusual instrumental and voice combinations along with the better-known chamber music works.
5) To make the music available at very low prices on a subscription basis; in all cases under $1.00 and student tickets at 25c.
6) To build the programmes first and choose the artists on the basis of the programmes.
7) To eliminate all elements foreign to the music itself, such as exploitation of artists' personality, display pieces, encores, flowers, interruptions between movements, intermissions, etc.
8) To offer no free passes with a hope of helping to curb this practice, so unfair to artists and managers.
9) To attempt to demonstrate that there is a large public for the best music and that even at low prices, under careful management, the best music can be self-supporting without patrons or patronesses.[46]

This first season of 16 concerts was devoted to Beethoven and Brahms, with many of Feuermann's friends taking part: Artur Schnabel, Karl-Ulrich Schnabel, Elisabeth Schumann, Mischa Levitzki, Egon Petri, the Budapest Quartet, the Pro Arte Quartet and the Pasquier Trio.

It was while touring in America that Feuermann's dilemma about where to live was finally resolved. A document dated 27 October 1936, 'Zusicherung der Erteilung einer Aufenthaltsbewilligung', gave him official permission to establish residence in Switzerland. But conditions were attached, according to which he was not allowed to: engage in private tuition, except for occasional masterclasses; open a private institute for musical tuition; or take up a teaching position as the director of a cello masterclass in a public or private conservatory. That he received a residence permit relatively quickly was a surprise, as was the permission to teach, albeit only a masterclass. As a neutral country, Switzerland did not wish to provoke the Nazis by offering displaced Jews favourable opportunities. The permission seemed to have been granted for a bizarre reason: in Berlin, Feuermann had taught a student whose father was an official in the Swiss government. The student was not gifted and Feuermann had asked him to leave the class. The student, eternally grateful to Feuermann for showing him that he could never be a cellist, prevailed on his father to speed up the process for obtaining the residency permit.

Feuermann wrote from Santiago of his permission to live in Switzerland to Wilhelm Kux. This letter has not survived, but Kux's undated reply has. He regretted that Feuermann had not chosen Vienna as a domicile, but from Feuermann's letters it seems that Vienna was never a consideration. And it is not hard to see why: his relations with his father were dreadful and he was convinced that Austria's independence was threatened by the Nazis. Only time would tell how wise this decision was, although his parents continued to live in the Weimarerstrasse until the *Anschluss*. In this same letter Feuermann must have indicated to Kux that Eva was pregnant, for Kux wrote: 'I may assume from your remark that you may soon be a father. I say bravo to that. About how we will educate your son and what profession we will allow him to choose, we will talk presently. But one thing I will say is that I am hoping even now that he will be more like his mother than his father.'[47] Eva, however, suffered a miscarriage, the first of many.

It was not until November that Feuermann received Huberman's letter of 18 October. As usual, it concerned the twin subjects of the Palestine Symphony Orchestra and the trios. Huberman was working strenuously towards the formation of the orchestra and sincerely hoped that Feuermann would perform in the first season – Toscanini was to conduct the opening concert; Adolf Busch would also appear in the first season. But Huberman was troubled by Feuermann's agent, finding Paul Schiff and his office 'torturous' in their thought and attitudes:

> I am quite pleased to negotiate this matter directly with you, all the more so because this is primarily not a business excursion, nor an ordinary elevated cultural matter, but a Jewish renaissance of the greatest importance. Secondly, because it is also a matter between two friends. Not that I want to exploit this friendship as such in order to offer you a smaller fee, but only to render these negotiations more pleasant.

Huberman proposed that Feuermann should play a single concerto in an orchestral concert that would be presented in Tel Aviv, Haifa and Jerusalem; additional 'workers" concerts would be held in Tel Aviv, Haifa and possibly in a kibbutz. He wrote: 'The fee you would have to envisage is a kind of fiction, namely one performance and 3 public rehearsals! You see, when it comes to the orchestra, there's nothing I will not do, even fairy stories.' As for the trio recordings, Huberman could do little to rescue them. As Feuermann had feared, Nipponophone would not allow him or Huberman to record with Schnabel, an HMV artist. The tireless Huberman, however, was not going to let the project drop; he wondered whether HMV could take it on. It also emerged that Huberman was no longer free in the December period: the opening concerts of the Palestine Symphony Orchestra had been postponed until December and so he was obliged to cancel many of his own engagements 'because I cannot let Toscanini down after all he has done for us.'[48]

Feuermann was also reluctant to let the trio idea pass, and suggested that they at least play together at the Salzburg Festival. He was sure there was nothing better 'on the market'. But the tone of his reply to Huberman about the Palestine Symphony Orchestra was mixed. He was flattered to be invited to perform but oddly confused about his feelings: 'As far as I know, I make a rather confident impression which on my part is a principle – a certain "*keep smiling*". In spite of my success, however, I have considerable doubts about myself and so it does me a great deal of good that a man like you seems to like me both in my profession and as a human being.' But over fees he was more confident:

> I am very keen on coming to Palestine for several obvious reasons: the country and your work attract me and I am enchanted by what is being created there. However, in spite of that I must agree with Dr Schiff that I must ask for a certain fee for my concerts and that I have after all proved that I am doing everything possible to help us.[49] I find it rather hard to write to you of all people about business, but I can see it has to be. . . . May I suggest the following: 8 concerts, orchestra and recitals, at a fee of £50 each. I would forgo bringing my own pianist in order to make it possible. And I would like to do two concerts without fee; that would in fact amount to 10 concerts.

But there was another obstacle: if he were to start in Palestine on 5 May 1937 after his European concert season had ended, he would have been on the road since October 1935, for 19 months, without a break. His letter ends in higher spirits, but still there are hints of uncertainty: 'Once again I have quite a lot of success here in America and I am daring (on 11 December) to have a recital at

Carnegie Hall.' But his hopes for Huberman's enterprise are heartfelt: 'The day
on which your spiritual child will see the dark-light[50] of this world comes ever
closer and I hope from the bottom of my heart that you and your orchestra
will be able to realize your wonderful idea completely.'[51]

Feuermann appears to have been somewhat parsimonious over his fees,
surprisingly so, given the exceptional nature of the Palestine Symphony
Orchestra. But his attitude to money was complex. While always sensitive to
any hint of injustice in the area of fees and royalties, this sensitivity seems less
to do with poverty than self-worth. The fact that the cello as a solo instrument
held a comparatively low status, something that Feuermann detested, no
doubt contributed to his hard line.

On stage Feuermann was a performer without a hint of the showman, but
off-stage expensive cars were an indulgent hobby. He wrote to Eva: 'It's not
working out so well with the Buick. Mr Bierman cabled me that they can't
deliver a convertible that quickly. General Motors were swamped with
demands. But I believe that it isn't so bad. I'll arrange everything here and will
let the car follow with a later ship of the Cunard Line.' He had the means not
only to afford a car but also to ship it to Europe. By contrast, his accompanist,
Wolfgang Rebner, was desperate for work and money: 'Rebner did something
incredible yesterday: just like that he went into one of the better music schools
of Pittsburgh and asked if they had a position for him.' Feuermann was taken
aback because Rebner's circumstances were of great concern and Feuermann
talked constantly to people about him:

> Really on the one side [Rebner is] Chuzpish and pretentious and then again
> he grovels, profiting to the full from his difficult situation. But he gave me a
> nice birthday gift, a cigarette lighter. It was necessary, because yesterday he
> spoilt the beautiful Adagio from the Beethoven sonata . . . doing exactly the
> opposite of what we had decided during the rehearsal. But I'm not angry at
> him any more, I only pity him.[52]

Feuermann again travelled to Canada. Yet again he encountered trouble at
the border. In a letter of 20 November he wrote:

> Now imagine, in the afternoon in Fort Erie, on the river, a few minutes from
> Buffalo, the Canadian *immigration officer* took me out of the train. Reason?
> My American visa had expired and the Canadians are obliged to retain those
> travellers to whom the American consulate in Toronto or wherever have
> declined visas. The officials have the strictest instructions. He was very
> friendly. I explained to him my situation, showing him all my papers, and I
> was able to take the next train.

In Toronto he was able to indulge his other great passion – the movies. 'I again had time in the evening and went of course to the movies. A charming new Mickey Mouse movie and afterwards "Libelled Lady". A great movie? Our love of Great Ziegfeld, William Powell again incomparable. Had a great time, was unfortunately alone.'[53]

Feuermann began to think about his summer plans. One project was to find and arrange music for the cello. He was keenly aware of the relative paucity of the cello repertoire and was hoping to take little-known works by composers such as Haydn, Mozart, Schubert and Weber written for other instruments and arrange suites: 'I think that I will succeed and am looking forward to good music.'[54]

The question of accompanists was also occupying his thoughts. The fees and expenses of accompanists (as distinct from named pianists) were normally paid for by the principal artist. Except on foreign tours, accompanists were usually found locally. In Europe, Feuermann wanted to work with Sophie, but with concerts in Rome, Florence, Bucharest, Riga and Kovno he suspected that the cost of bringing her from Vienna would be too high.

But however worried he was about the cost of accompanists, purchase of the Buick had to be sorted out:

> I gave a down payment of 100 dollars and made the contract. At the car show in Montreal I saw a convertible that would be far too beautiful for me alone, but will look nice on you, Oefchen: black, grey leather inside, a lot of chrome and a heater for your poor toes. I let it be delivered to Emil Stern; his chauffeur can drive it a bit and tune it. I think it will leave with the *Berengaria* on 5 January and then will be in Cherbourg on the 11th or 12th. Maybe Aunt Clara will lend us Rolland and then we can drive (without him of course) with the little car to Brussels and Liège and *finally* to Cologne. Will that be nice???[55]

Surely the words of a confident, prosperous man, content with life and not overwhelmed by the political and economic circumstances in Europe.

In New York, arriving from Montreal, he went to visit some friends with the pianist Jan Smeterlin. When Feuermann was asked to play the cello, he declined: 'He would not spontaneously pick up the cello and play. He stayed in the house at one of the Reifenbergs, in Düsseldorf perhaps, who made money with silk. The Reifenberg brother asked him to play in order to show off. Munio said, "No. I won't play. Do you give away silk?"'[56] However, he did borrow a violin from Sacconi to visit the violinist Remo Bolognini, with whom he indulged in playing Beethoven and Mozart sonatas.[57] Feuermann probably played the violin between his knees as he had as a child, competing with

Sigmund. Sophie remembers that as far as was possible Sigmund played the whole cello literature on the violin while Feuermann played the whole violin literature not only on the cello but also on the violin, holding it like a cello. Feuermann's violin 'performances' were phenomenal. George Szell, conductor and long-time friend, remembered: 'He used to pick up a fiddle, hold it like a cello and play the last movement of the Mendelssohn Violin Concerto from the first to the last note so impeccably that it couldn't be matched by many violinists!'[58] This was a regular party trick.

Touring in North America continued until 16 December, with concerts in Chicago, Winnipeg, Cincinnati, Bloomington (Indiana) and New York. Feuermann was tired: 'Sometimes I think my head is going to explode and I must admit that for the first time in my (long?) life I have difficulty in falling asleep, my head just continues to work.' But his concern for Eva is touching:

> Oefchen, your letter worried me somewhat and I thought a greeting would please you and show you that I will do anything so that you may look gladly into our future. I'm prepared to work as much as I only can. For what? So that life is good for you and thus me too. Oefchen, dear, don't make it harder than necessary. I also won't let YOU have the responsibility alone. That's stupid. We are married and I won't evade things in perhaps the most important question. Even Schopenhauer, the pessimist par excellence, who talks again and again of foresight and that one shouldn't follow too much the momentary mood, says that one cannot see into the future and that one shouldn't exaggerate in being too careful. I believe that it will be calm these next years and to look further makes no sense. And don't believe that this is meant as a sedative. I speak also in my own interest;;;;;;!!!!!!![59]

Feuermann's concert on 29 November was in New York, again for the New Friends of Music. In this fourth concert of the season the Kolisch Quartet played Beethoven's C# minor Quartet op.131 and Sextet op.81b, while Feuermann played Beethoven's Cello Sonata in D op.102 no.2.[60] He felt that 'the encounter with the Kolischs was very warm; they played the C sharp minor Beethoven Quartet, very quickly, not cleanly, but it was well liked. My Beethoven sonata was, thanks to M. Rebner, very good, only he is not secure in holding the tempi.' Feuermann again played chamber music with friends during his stay in New York, this time at the house of cellist and conductor Alfred Wallenstein:

> I didn't feel at all well, felt a cold coming up, provided myself with aspirin from Elsie and tried to cancel Wallenstein for the evening, which of course I didn't succeed in doing – they had already invited musicians for me etc. So

I went there and didn't regret it. I think that I laughed myself healthy, feeling dead tired at the end like after a children's party 25 years ago. We played quintets by Brahms and Mozart and the first Brahms sextet, among the loudest works there are. We made a racket like a whole orchestra and we answered the *mistakes* of the respective players with all sorts of things, only not with grace and reserve.[61]

Feuermann, like Heifetz, was notorious for immaculately mimicking and 'correcting' others' mistakes on his cello, at whatever pitch, something particularly galling for 'victims'.

Once more in Chicago, Feuermann stayed in the Standard Club, a Jewish club 12 storeys high with 60 rooms for rent. He visited his friends the Saidenbergs and was amazed again by the American way of life: 'They live fantastically, have many large rooms on the 4th floor and on top of that on the *roof*, a real hall where 120 people can be seated, where they teach and work, with a boudoir and bathroom. Altogether 4 bathrooms! And it only costs $200 a month.'[62] But Feuermann reports this without envy; he was well aware of his good fortune. Responding to Lily Hofmann's birthday wishes, he wrote:

We have to be grateful each and every day, each and every hour that fate, touch wood, has treated us well. But I don't take anything for granted and am grateful. . . . I myself am tired and exhausted, but very cheerful. It is dreadful being married to a girl like Eva and being apart from her for so long. Still, I do not regret having 'ordered her home', she was overtired and as I'm only in New York for a few days and am rushing from town to town, in dreadful weather conditions, it is better for her to rest and look after herself.

He also had a secret: 'I'm sailing at noon [on 16 December] with the Queen Simpson, pardon me, Queen Mary![63] And what's going to be travelling with me on the ship? A 1937 Buick Convertible! With loads of chrome, radio, heater, etc. It's supposed to be a surprise for Eva. She thought the car would be coming on a later ship, so please don't tell her!' So he had closed the deal! More seriously, he again asked Lily to keep her eyes open for a little house in Zürich with enough room to house another couple 'so that there is a man in the house when I am away, which just <u>might</u> happen'. But he was still not completely convinced about Zürich:

There's been a lot of excitement around here because the notion was being discussed that it might be safer and wiser – looking ahead to the future – for us to move to New York rather than to Zürich. We just can't decide, and Eva has suffered a lot over this. It's dreadful when you look at the papers. How is it possible for the world to look quite like that??[64]

After more than a year of touring in the Far East, South America and North America, Feuermann's final concerts took place in New York. The most important was his recital debut on 11 December in Carnegie Hall, where almost two years before his New York orchestral debut had taken place. Using RMS *Queen Mary* stationery provided in his cabin on his return journey to Europe, Feuermann wrote out the verdicts of the *New York Evening Post* and the *New York Times*: 'Solo cello recitals in Carnegie Hall are infrequent enough; such a one as Emanuel Feuermann gave us last night comes once in a blue moon, or – to put it less exorbitantly – will probably come as often as Mr Feuermann comes.'[65] The recital with Rebner had included not only standard works but also Hindemith's Solo Sonata (its first New York performance) and Feuermann's astonishing arrangement of Chopin's Introduction and Polonaise.[66] In New York that week, performances were given by three other cellists: Joseph Schuster, Ernst Silberstein and Gaspar Cassadó. But Feuermann's recital was in a different league: applause and encores lasted 40 minutes. Feuermann sent a wry telegram to Cologne: 'OVERWHELMING SUCCESS SIX ENCORES DOWNES SATISFIED ME TOO PITTY [*sic*] ALONE.'[67] Olin Downes had heaped praise on him:

> To speak of technic [*sic*], indeed, where this artist is concerned is almost beside the mark. Virtuosity, almost unlimited, is with him a foregone conclusion. Mr Feuermann can afford to forget virtuosity and, what is still better, to cause his listeners largely to forget it with him. . . . The familiar piece of Sarasate provided in itself sufficient provocation for the remark that Mr. Feuermann can play the cello as a Heifetz his fiddle.[68]

Could there be any higher praise than for a cellist to be compared with the greatest virtuoso violinist alive?

Chapter 9

Europe
1937

*You probably realise that he is somewhat of a dilatory nature,
particularly now that he is married to a wealthy wife and does not take
his career very seriously.*

Columbia to Nipponophone, 14 September 1937

RMS *Queen Mary* arrived at Southampton docks on the morning of 22
December 1936. Feuermann, in his new Buick Convertible, drove straight to
the Abbey Road Recording Studios in London. He was supposed to record
Schubert's 'Arpeggione' Sonata and Beethoven's op.69 for Nipponophone, but
clearly arrangements had not been completed and instead that afternoon he
recorded the Andantino and Variations from Weber's *Konzertstück* op.20. He
was paid £50.[1] His accompanist was Gerald Moore, whom he was meeting for
the first time. Moore recalled the occasion:

> He recorded with me and then about 7 o'clock in the evening he got in his
> car, and it was a filthy, foggy night and he was off to the coast to catch the
> night boat to go to Amsterdam. He took the car to Harwich. A very difficult
> drive, right across London in the fog. I said 'you're afraid you'll miss the
> boat?' 'Not at all. Oh no'.[2]

Not an unusual response from the high-spirited, energetic Feuermann who
now had a new toy (see Plate 14).

Gerald Moore was to accompany many recitals in Britain and make further
recordings with Feuermann:

I never sat down and played one phrase without learning something from him because he had a mind. And he had an extraordinary flair for all the music that he played. I said to him once 'you must work for hours and hours a day, because on top of all your feeling and temperament and musicianship there is such a perfection about your playing which is uncanny.' To which Feuermann said, 'I never practise for more than 2 hours a day!'

This was not entirely true, but more importantly Feuermann knew how to practise. As Moore remarked: 'Others might take 4 hours at their instrument, an hour and a half of that would be wasted effort, wasted thought through lack of concentration, but Feuermann would know exactly what he wanted to do and what he wanted to concentrate on. He wouldn't be exhausted because he was a man of tremendous resilience.' Moore also noted perhaps Feuermann's most outstanding characteristic:

> He was not introspective about his playing and this was a wonderful thing. So many of us when we play in public if we are a little bit off-colour it worries the life out of us and we are not able to sleep after it. . . . I remember one occasion, one of the big cities, I think it was in Glasgow or Manchester or Liverpool, he came up to me after the concert and laughing said 'I was in bad form tonight.' I said 'Well, I didn't know you were.' And he said 'Oh, I was!' But you see he laughed. He wasn't happy that he hadn't been in what he called his very best form but it didn't worry him. He accepted it. Even a great artist like Feuermann cannot be 100% every time and I suppose on this occasion he was what, 95/96%?[3]

Moore always felt that the British music critics were slow to recognize Feuermann's gift, but after a recital at the Wigmore Hall on 8 February 1937 an unattributed review in the *Observer* was unflattering to them both: 'There is rather less colour and character in Mr Feuermann's playing than in that of the two or three really supreme living cellists, but otherwise he is unsurpassed. . . . Beethoven's sonata Op.102 No.1 sounded unexciting partly because the quality of tone Mr Gerald Moore produced did not suggest imaginative and intellectual alertness on his part; he seemed merely to "accompany".'[4]

The year of 1937 was the last extended period Feuermann was to spend in Europe. As usual, the pace of touring was relentless. In the first two months he appeared in Amsterdam, Monte Carlo, Brussels, Liège, Copenhagen, Paris, Göteborg, Zürich, London, Manchester, Bradford and Burnley. In Manchester and Bradford he played once again with the Hallé Orchestra conducted by Sir Thomas Beecham. It was just over two years since his last appearance, when he had played the Haydn D major. This time he played the Dvořák Concerto. An

WIGMORE HALL
WIGMORE STREET, W.1

EMANUEL
FEUERMANN

*Violoncello
Recital*

MONDAY,
FEBRUARY 8th
at 8.30

Pianoforte :

GERALD MOORE
BÖSENDORFER PIANOFORTE

TICKETS (Including Tax) : Reserved, 9/- and 6/-   Admission, 3/-

May be obtained from the BOX OFFICE, WIGMORE HALL ; usual Ticket Offices ; and

IBBS & TILLETT, 124, Wigmore Street, W.1

Telephone: Welbeck 4323 (5 lines)   Ticket Office : Welbeck 8411
Telegrams : " Organed, Wesdo, London "   Hours, 10—5   Sats. 10—12

For Programme P.T.O.

amusing account of the Beecham experience can be found in one of his letters to Eva:

> The day before yesterday the concert in Bradford was again a hit. That they printed <u>Emil</u> F. is already not bad. But Sir Thomas is unsurpassable. He was very gracious and would like to make a tour with me. But that doesn't pay; he talks a lot. After the concert there was a special train back to Manchester. Beecham had a bottle of whisky. He gave it to the musicians and the 1st horn player *got so drunk* that he had to be helped by 2 other men to get out of the train. In his stupor he kept singing the beginning of the Dvořák concerto.[5]

Earlier Feuermann had noted the care that Beecham had taken at rehearsal: *'I had a lovely rehearsal with Sir Thomas; the rehearsing of the Dvořák concerto took 2 hours and you know how much I appreciate carefulness in rehearsals. I played extraordinarily happily and I think Sir Thomas felt the same way.'*[6] Humphrey Procter-Gregg, Reader in Music at Manchester University, attended that Manchester performance:

After a magnificent reading with Feuermann of the Dvořák cello concerto (in which the orchestra has an unusually big part to play), and cellist and orchestra had excelled themselves in fire and poetry, and warm, glorious sound, the genial Feuermann, who had smiled contentedly throughout the piece, refused to take any calls till he could drag on the reluctant Beecham every time, and the orchestra were as delighted as the audience. Afterwards I got nothing out of Sir Thomas in his room in response to my enthusiasm but a querulous recital of all the difficulties of balance and phrasing in that particular work, and how insufficient had been its rehearsal. I asked had he ever heard a better performance, and he just changed the subject: he <u>hadn't</u>, of course, and knew it.[7]

For part of the time, Feuermann stayed with cousins of the Reifenbergs in the affluent Jewish neighbourhood of Didsbury in Manchester. Rudolf, brother of Katya Aschaffenburg, Eva's cousin and old friend from Feuermann's Cologne days, had also fled the regime in Germany and was staying there too:

I had a very happy day yesterday. Mrs Morreau is just a little too nice and attentive to be perfect. . . . But I feel very comfortable here and Rudolf shows how happy he is with being here. . . . I am staying until Sunday as I have to play today in Bradford – the same programme we did yesterday – and on Sunday in Burnley, where I am going with Rudolf by car – and I am going to drive myself. It will be great fun.[8]

Feuermann found the arrangements in Burnley highly amusing: 'The hotel is, of course, like 300 years ago, here a room, there a room, and of course penny heating. . . . The concert is organized by the city, but the soloist doesn't play [rehearse?] with the orchestra, but with piano!! And the rehearsal doesn't start until 4:30, because the orchestra is already screeching and the piano is on stage.'[9]

Since November 1935 Feuermann had been playing the 'De Munck' Stradivarius on approval from Hill in London. On returning in December 1936 from his world tour he took the Stradivarius back to Hill and retrieved his Montagnana, which they had kept in their care. Needless to say, it was not long before Feuermann contacted Hill from Paris to ask for the Stradivarius to be returned to him, and a further extended loan of the instrument ensued. After these concerts in the north of England, Feuermann took the cello back to Hill for 'a beauty treatment'.[10] A couple of letters from Hill to Feuermann reveal that the Hill brothers really wanted to conclude a deal proposed to Feuermann long before in December 1935. Alfred Hill once again confirmed that the 'De Munck' Stradivarius would be sold to Feuermann for £1000 with the

Montagnana in part exchange. Payment in stages and the transfer of the oak cello case were agreed.

Feuermann lightheartedly reported his feelings about London to Eva, who was skiing in Switzerland: 'Two impressions predominate: how many people from Berlin are here who call me; and how many girls want to have lessons. I already have 5 requests; am very curious. I believe they can't imagine how disagreeable it is to study with me, and besides, they will be repelled by the price.'[11] He was always in demand as a teacher. Wherever he played, cellists would arrive to play for him or teachers would ask that he hear their students.

As always, if the chance was offered, Feuermann would play chamber music. This time it was with Carl Flesch. As well as Flesch, other Berliners in London included Alexander and Mischa Schneider and Franz and Tamara Osborn. The pianist Franz Osborn had studied with Leonid Kreutzer and Schnabel at the Berlin Hochschule when Feuermann was teaching there and was a close friend of the Reifenbergs. Feuermann and Mrs Reifenberg both helped the Osborns get out of Germany.

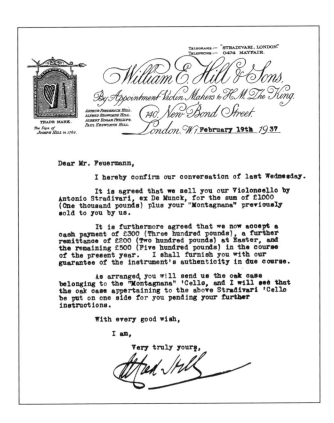

During this period, Feuermann received an invitation from the Vienna Academy to participate in the jury of a competition for voice, violin and cello that was to take place between 7 and 19 June. Feeling that it would take up too much time, he declined.

Feuermann now took up residence in Switzerland. A house had been found at 31 Goldauerstrasse in Zürich-berg, an affluent neighbourhood of Zürich, and Feuermann acquired it for rent. It was on two floors and substantial in size: Feuermann had his own music room, there was a dining room that could seat six people, a maid's room, and accommodation for guests. Following the long tour, Eva was exhausted, and Mrs Reifenberg felt that Feuermann was putting too much pressure on her with all the arrangements for their accommodation. So in February 1937 it was Mrs Reifenberg who supervised the renovation and furnishing, including the purchase of a piano. It seems likely that Reifenberg money paid for it all; it was still possible to take money out of Germany. Eva recalled her first 'official dinner' there: 'It was with Thomas Mann and Bruno Walter. They must all have thought "what kind of ridiculous person did this Feuermann marry? Must have been a money marriage."'[12] Feuermann looked forward to having a permanent home: 'I am now terribly looking forward to the little house. It is time that I remain AT HOME a bit longer.'[13] A vain hope indeed.

His April touring alone took him to Vienna, Warsaw and Kovno. In Warsaw he played two concertos (C.P.E. Bach and Haydn), with Edward van Beinum conducting the Warsaw Philharmonic. While Feuermann was relentlessly touring, Eva was 'recovering', enjoying a full social life, a life of considerable ease, in which she took holidays with friends and visited relatives. Her letters to Feuermann are deeply affectionate but the gap in age and experience and her lack of musical knowledge – although she was not slow to give an opinion – point to something of a mismatch, even if Feuermann at this time was clearly in love with her. But the long periods of separation were hard on the marriage, even though the couple wrote to each other almost daily. The tone of Feuermann's letters at this time to Eva is frequently that of mentor and protector, although often seeking reassurance of her love, whereas Eva writes as a young, carefree 23 year old, missing him perhaps, but certainly not unduly put out by his absence. Mrs Reifenberg, no doubt, engineered a kind of stability; she was always on hand to guide Eva both emotionally and practically and to offer Feuermann the support and interest he needed from a more worldly person.

Feuermann's extended stay in Europe allowed the record companies to follow up on delayed projects. In January 1937, a merger between Nipponophone and RCA was proposed. In view of the link with RCA, perhaps

Nipponophone might now not object to the trio recordings being issued on HMV. Nipponophone also had a new idea. An article in *Gramophone* had suggested that a recording of Beethoven's Triple Concerto would be greatly appreciated by the public. H.A. Straus at Nipponophone wrote to Duncan at Columbia: 'It would surely have a tremendous success in Japan. We still think that Bruno Walter would be the most preferable conductor. As to soloists we would like to have either a combination of Szigeti, Feuermann and Gieseking or Szigeti, Feuermann and Friedman, but if Bruno Walter conducts even less known soloists chosen by the conductor would do.'[14]

Feuermann invited Rex Palmer to his Wigmore Hall recital in February. Palmer was unable to attend but suggested a meeting with Feuermann to discuss recordings at Abbey Road: 'I shall look forward with pleasure to seeing you next week and in case you feel disposed to record either of the two sonatas, I am holding the studio on Wednesday morning.'[15] Feuermann was taken aback: '*I am sorry that I shall not be able to do any recording on Wednesday morning as I am not prepared for it at all and besides – I wouldn't know with whom.*'[16] Not only was the identity of the accompanist unclear but also that of the works to be recorded. Nipponophone wanted Feuermann to record all the Beethoven sonatas but refused to pay his travel expenses to record in Japan 'as we do not need these recordings urgently and we are willing to wait until he comes to London'.[17] By April, however, only Beethoven's A major Sonata op.69 was under discussion, but negotiations over this recording and that of Schubert's 'Arpeggione' had been going on for some time. Myra Hess was not available before June, and Feuermann was now being asked if he would like to record one of the other sonatas with another pianist. He was confused, and wrote to Columbia:

> *I am rather astonished about your last letter. I am still waiting to hear from you if Miss Myra Hess has definitely given you her decision to record the Beethoven sonata with me? Besides, it is up to you to let me know when Miss Hess will be back in Europe and which part of June would suit her best. . . . I would like to record the last days of June. Of course I prefer to record at your studios in London. But if you think that the Paris engineers are as good as the London ones I would go to Paris. Besides the Beethoven sonata I have to record the Schubert Sonata (that is with <u>accompaniment</u>) and perhaps some small pieces. I do not quite sense what Tokyo wants.*[18]

Nipponophone wished to extend Feuermann's contract for a further three years, and Columbia in London was asked to take on the negotiations. In a letter to Palmer, Feuermann hedged:

When I was in London I wanted so much to talk to you about all the questions concerning my recording but I could not because Mr Szigeti was present at our lunch. Even being aware of the limits for a cellist I am not satisfied with Columbia. I do not feel any interest for [in] me. I want very much to record all the Beethoven sonatas, but before I am going to decide that and the extension of the contract I have to get in touch with you seriously.[19]

Palmer brushed aside Szigeti's presence as an obstacle: 'I fully appreciate your wishing to discuss the question of your contract and am quite at your disposal. We could easily have found time to discuss this on your last visit, apart from the lunch at which Szigeti was present.'[20] Again he asked Feuermann to suggest a pianist, to which Feuermann, bewildered, replied: '*I have no idea who the Columbia pianists are and thus I cannot make any suggestions for the case that Miss Hess would not play with me. The only one from whom I know that he is under contract with Columbia is* <u>Rubinstein</u>.' Relations were very uneasy. Feuermann suggested that if Myra Hess was not available then a pianist of equal international reputation be used: '*or I would suggest to play with my sister Sophie. She plays with me very often and for the recording with her I would guarantee an absolutely perfect ensemble. Of course for the sale and for my own pleasure as an artist I prefer Miss Hess. But when will you know whether or not?*'[21] Two days later, Palmer wrote: 'I feel pretty sure that Miss Hess will be free and happy to play the Beethoven Sonata with you on June 28. I am engaging the studio for this date and have written Miss Hess to fix this.'[22]

Plans were finally agreed, and on 28 June, with a rehearsal the day before, Feuermann began to record the op.69 Sonata with Myra Hess. It was the only Beethoven sonata he was to record commercially. He was booked the following day to record Schubert's 'Arpeggione' Sonata with Gerald Moore, but the Beethoven did not go well. Eva recalls that the morning session on 28 June with Myra Hess went badly, with Feuermann uncharacteristically in poor shape; only the first movement was recorded, and Hess sent him home. The next day, however, all was well and the Beethoven was completed, along with the first two movements of the 'Arpeggione'. The third movement of the Schubert was recorded on 30 June, one day later than intended. It is worth noting Nipponophone's parsimonious attitude to Gerald Moore: 'We have no objection against making the Schubert Sonata with Gerald Moore provided that his fee is a reasonable one but we would have been satisfied if Feuermann would record the Schubert Sonata with his usual accompanist as in this case we would have to pay only a fee of 7½% of retail price to Feuermann without paying the accompanist separately.'[23]

While in the recording studio, Feuermann again raised the subject of his contract with Palmer without success: *'Our talk in your studio, on the occasion of my recording, did not seem to me very satisfactory. Either you do not understand me or, may I be permitted to say, you do not quite want to understand me.'*[24] If proof of Feuermann being 'misunderstood' by Columbia is required, Palmer's letter to Nipponophone of 14 September amply provides it:

> We have so far done our utmost to induce Mr Feuermann to continue his contract and carry out the recording you require. Needless to say, we shall be only too pleased to continue with our efforts. You probably realise that he is somewhat of a dilatory nature, particularly now that he is married to a wealthy wife and does not take his career very seriously. We had endless trouble to arrange the recent recordings with him last June.

The suggestion that Feuermann did not take his career seriously was as mischievous as it was extraordinary. Could Palmer see no further than Feuermann's exuberant exterior? It was a shameful slur and Palmer was deeply disingenuous: the problem of arranging dates for the June recording lay largely with Myra Hess. Behind these remarks, however, lurked Palmer's real thoughts: 'In view of the very small demand for cello records in our territories, we do not think Feuermann will have the chance of signing up with another company, if he does not accept your offer.'[25] Nipponophone was not so sure: 'We still think that the Decca people in England perhaps under the advice of Japan Polydor would like to get Feuermann.'[26] The warning signs were there but still Nipponophone turned down the Dvořák Concerto: 'We note that you do not wish the expense of the Dvořák concerto as he suggests and no doubt you are aware that this has recently been recorded by Casals for HMV.'[27]

Plans for recording the remaining Beethoven sonatas and also Tchaikovsky's 'Rococo' Variations came to nothing. A letter in August (now lost) indicated that Nipponophone had supplied a list of works they wished Feuermann to record, 'however without any advance payment or guarantee as foreseen in his contract'. The list has not come to light but would seem to have referred to recordings eventually made in 1939. Nipponophone's miserliness may be explained by the wider context of Japan's war with China – business in Japan was in a parlous state. 'As we do not have to make any investment on those recordings except paying the pianist for the popular solos and the waxes, we think that those recordings could still be made.'[28]

Over the summer of 1937 in Switzerland, Feuermann took part in the Musikalischer Ferienkurs Braunwald 1937: Die Romantik in der Musik. The Swiss authorities had given him permission to teach a masterclass and about 15 students came from all parts of the world to study with him, but there was always danger.[29] 'There came a detective – a little boy – who wanted to take lessons and Munio very soon found out what that was all about.'[30] He may have had to be on his guard, but that his stay in Switzerland was marred by the interference of the Frontische, an organization making anti-immigrant propaganda paid for by Goebbels, is not recalled by Eva.[31] One of his students in Switzerland was British cellist Bernard Richards, who vividly described his experience with Feuermann:

> He was the exact opposite of the popular idea of an international star who was so full of his own importance that he did not pay much attention to others. On the contrary, he seemed to delight in meeting people and especially his pupils and he took great interest in their activities. He spoke English well and his lively personality endeared him to all his pupils. . . . When I looked back after those six lessons I thought to myself how much I had learned from him, especially just watching and hearing him at close quarters. He frequently illustrated any point he wished to make and this was done so fantastically well technically and musically. . . . One morning I needed help with changing position efficiently and produced a study by Grützmacher, the one in C major from book 2. In this study the left hand has to move every second note starting on middle C going up to high G on the A string. Feuermann did not know this study. This was rather a surprise to me, actually; I thought he'd know all Grützmacher, but he read it at top speed and so efficiently that I could not tell when he needed to change position and when not. It was unbelievably good. Quite magical![32]

During the summer Feuermann received an 'Express' letter from the Guest Bureau of the Committee for Cultural Affairs, Moscow. His agent, Paul Schiff, had informed them that a tour planned for the beginning of the forthcoming season now could not take place. Messrs Kramer and Kolscher, the authors of the letter, unable to rearrange their dates, hoped that Feuermann could visit in the second half of the season: 'The earlier your arrival the better. We hope that you will deal with this question as soon as possible and that we will soon be able to welcome you to Moscow.'[33] Feuermann had not performed in Russia since 1932. He did not visit.

Negotiations with the Palestine Symphony Orchestra were faring little better. Feuermann, frustrated by lack of precise information and the slowness of correspondence with the orchestra, had been obliged to withdraw from concerts with them in November because of an option taken out three years before, long before the orchestra had been founded, by a Mrs Hakim. There was stress and misunderstanding between him and Huberman's personal representative, Dr Heinrich Simon, a former anti-Nazi editor and co-proprietor of the *Frankfurter Zeitung* who had fled Germany in 1934:

> It was strange that there was a certain tension between you and me, despite or maybe because we hardly knew each other. I would very much like it to be different between us . . . I am the greatest admirer of Huberman's deed, the creation of the orchestra. Hardly anyone can appreciate this super-human achievement as I can. I have several times witnessed the intensity of his exertions. It is all the more strange that I should not play with the orchestra. Long before the founding of the orchestra Huberman spoke to me about his idea and also that I certainly must play with the orchestra when it is a possibility. . . . For my part I am prepared as far as possible to prove my good will towards the orchestra . . . Should it be already too late for this year you can maybe fix a date for the coming season? I have to assume that I will be successful in the spring in Palestine and I imagine that this could be advantageous for future participation with the orchestra. I have worked together with Dr Schiff for maybe 16 years and we have always got on well together during this time. I would be sorry if you could not accept aspects of his behaviour towards you. By the way, it is perhaps not necessary for you to pity my financial situation.

Schiff had apparently written advising the orchestra that Feuermann was in dire financial straits – Feuermann wrote: 'It is incomprehensible to me what could have caused him to make this remark.'[34]

On 5 October, Feuermann played at the opening concert of the Tonhalle-Gesellschaft 1937/8 subscription season in Zürich. This was a distinguished series of ten concerts in which Schnabel, Milstein, Casals and Cortot all appeared as soloists. Feuermann's concert included not only Strauss's *Don Quixote* but also Beethoven's Triple Concerto – with Stefi Geyer (violin) and Paul Baumgartner (piano) – conducted by Volkmar Andreae. A month earlier, Columbia in Austria had been in touch with Columbia in London to see if plans could be made to record the Triple Concerto in Vienna. (Such a recording had been suggested by Nipponophone in December 1936.) Palmer was as usual cautious: 'You do not say in your letter what three soloists are finally agreed upon. If Feuermann is in Vienna and will agree to do it for a flat fee, well and good, but he has a royalty contract with the Nipponophone Company of Japan and he must clearly understand that this recording will be quite outside the terms of that contract.' He added: 'the cost of this ambitious recording is bound to be high and unless we can do it within our limits, we shall have to abandon the idea of making it in Vienna and arrange to do it elsewhere, as we do not require it as urgently as all that.'[35] No recording of the Triple Concerto was made.

Soon after the Tonhalle concert, Feuermann was in Prague performing with Sophie in a concert and broadcast. In a letter to Eva, he wrote:

> Today I had lunch with Szell; it was very good and nice. Afterwards he played for me the first movement of the Dvořák concerto which he had done <u>here</u> with the Czech Philharmonic. He only has a portable phonograph, but I could hear how everything came off well. Casals is astoundingly good. A lot was different from what I regard as beautiful but most of it enviably beautiful. And so superior! Tomorrow morning I will hear the 2nd and 3rd movements and I am already looking forward to it. I actually think I play just as well but Casals has more refinement and as I said is calmer, so that less can go wrong with him. . . . Casals definitely isn't as sloppy as I am! . . . The moment I'm on stage I think that everything <u>must</u> go wrong, and that is an impossible state. The tiniest thing is enough to make me blunder.

Earlier in his letter he had described his concert with Sophie: 'It was too silly that I let myself be affected by Sophie to such an extent that as soon as she made a mistake I answered with out of tune notes. That I find extremely bad, it shows that I am nervous.'[36]

The autumn continued with Feuermann performing in Winterthur, Basel, on 29 October, with Paul Sacher conducting his chamber orchestra in an all-Haydn programme. Sacher is generally known for his patronage of new music and the Baroque, but he was keenly interested in Haydn, whose music at that time was as unfamiliar as any new work. The chance of having Feuermann play the original version of Haydn's D major Concerto in his programme that included the Basel 'premiere' of Haydn's Symphony no. 44 (*Trauersinfonie*) and a Notturno in F must have appealed greatly to the ambitious Sacher. Feuermann's own programming was enterprising too: a concert in Zürich on 31 October with the organist Heinrich Funk[37] included a Tartini sonata with organ accompaniment – an early understanding of Baroque performance practice? – together with Bach's sixth unaccompanied suite; and in Schaffhausen, after the Haydn Concerto, he gave the Schaffhausen premiere of Hindemith's Solo Sonata.

He was again in London in November for a recital in the Aeolian Hall, New Bond Street, with Sophie now billed under her married name, Braun. The programme comprised Beethoven's Variations on a theme from Handel's *Judas Maccabaeus*, a Bréval sonata, the Brahms E minor Sonata, Schubert's 'Arpeggione' and Tchaikovsky's 'Rococo' Variations. Feuermann considered a review in the *Daily Telegraph* to be 'very good for local conditions', and Carl Flesch had telephoned to say that it was the first cello recital he had ever enjoyed.[38] Schnabel was also staying at Feuermann's usual hotel, the Hyde Park, and plans were made to play chamber music at Flesch's house.

With the endless periods of touring and isolation, Eva did provide something of an anchor:

> You have no idea how the thought of you, what will come, and also our home supports me. I know now what I'm living for. The foul thought that one shouldn't bring children into this world must not arise. We are here to reproduce; children make life rich; to have children is God's wish and with this everything is said. I can't in all honesty say that my worries these last years have become less but how small they are in comparison to other people's. It is terrible that I am away so much, but that is my profession and must be borne.[39]

Eva was expecting a child. Feuermann wanted to name the child after Wilhelm Kux: 'Maybe you don't yet see that directly and indirectly I have him to thank for almost everything: the years of instruction with Klengel in Leipzig and also afterwards he was like a father to me.' Kux was nicknamed 'Willo', a sound Feuermann liked. The second name would have to be Paul, after Eva's deceased father (in accordance with the Jewish custom of naming a child after a deceased relative): 'If, God willing, it is a boy he would be called Willo Paul Feuermann. What do you think of this? You know that I am very much for reverence and besides I think it sounds good. Will you not say <u>no</u> right away this time? Or rather, first say no and then try to get used to the name.'[40] Where the child should be born preoccupied both Eva and Feuermann, since he would be away at the time of the birth. Eva's sister Lilli, married to a doctor, was advocating London. But Feuermann looked gloomily into the future:

> One could imagine that there might be a war between Austria and England, in which case my son would have an English passport; such a situation is not worth imagining. . . . Since she is so happy in Zürich and has immense trust in the doctor and the environment, she should stay in Zürich. If Eva was not so delicate I would have made a different decision. But I don't think I am acting like this because of giving in but because I think I know her, and regard it to be the most important thing that she and therefore the child as well before and after the event should live under the most agreeable circumstances. Added to that it's not at all impossible that one day we may end up in America. For the moment there's no sign yet of that but it's always possible. However, should we remain in Switzerland and should we have a

son, who will grow up, he will surely become Swiss. It is rather uncanny to be so far ahead of fate or rather help fate forward.[41]

In December, Feuermann was in Copenhagen and Stockholm: 'Isn't that utterly stupid: now we are married instead of living together, we have to write each other letters a great part of the year. If only I had something interesting to write to you. But I hardly see anyone here and pass my days with writing letters, practising, reading and, in the evenings, the movies.'[42] But only days before, he had reported:

> The concert yesterday was very good. Did you listen? [It] would please me. Slipped only rarely. Afterwards there were a few gentlemen from the radio and by the way an excellent Danish conductor, for a change, a former cellist. They were with me in a restaurant where we ate very well and I drank much too much. I suggested they engage Heifetz and myself for the Brahms Double concerto. They have a lot of money and could do something like that. Probably nothing will come of it.[43]

This seems to be the first direct reference by Feuermann to working with Jascha Heifetz, who was soon to become an important colleague.

While Feuermann was in Scandinavia, Eva and her mother went to some of Casals's rehearsals in Zürich. Casals had been a visitor to the Reifenberg home in Cologne. His signature in their guest book appears only once, in 1931, without month or day, but since Casals was an acquaintance of Hugo Reifenberg, with whom he played chamber music in Paris on occasion, there was a connection with the family. Eva wrote of the rehearsal to Feuermann: 'The Schumann concerto rehearsal this morning wasn't a pure pleasure, a lot of the technique was superb, but as a whole your version was much more beautiful and richer in terms of sound. If you could take over another few fine points of fingering from him (exactly what you are lacking for the Bach), you would be an Über-Casals.' She also wrote of Casals's appearance:

> He looks horrifying, like a wreck, old, yellow, fat, he only arrived in the morning and was almost dying with pain. He was very happy with mother and me in the Artists' room. He was so lonely with two Catalan priests as his only company with whom he had a very agitated conversation. I sent him a little heated pillow to the Baur au Lac because he was so longing for a little warmth on his little potbelly. Horrible. A man aged 64 should a) not have to play any more and b) never travel alone; especially from Bucharest to here! We felt so sorry for him. . . . He makes a lot of things much easier for himself but perhaps only in the rehearsal; some of the tempi are slower than yours and he doesn't hold them evenly either, he just does it differently;

much of it perfection, but – it is sad to say, 64 years and —— 35! The evil course of time! Amen.[44]

Feuermann was amused by Eva's observations:

Your descriptions of the Casals rehearsal are very funny. But Casals isn't 64, only 61, and you don't have to pity him quite so much – or maybe yes! One shouldn't praise the day before the evening but why do almost none of these people have an aura of human contentment, of family relationships about them? Are all soloists like that?! Maybe that's why they play so well! What a pity! Did Casals receive my short letter? I admire him immensely, for me he is a very great man, but he seems to be just as strange as great. Did you really send him a hot water bottle?'[45]

The tone of this letter suggests that Feuermann had not met Casals at the home of the Reifenbergs. But Sophie Feuermann and Katya Aschaffenburg both recall that Feuermann and Casals met, though details of when and where are no longer remembered.[46]

After Scandinavia, Feuermann travelled to Italy, where he wrote to Eva: 'Why didn't I take you here together with Baruch or Baruchina?[47] Italy is so beautiful and we would enjoy it together. It rains, hails, thunders alternately and not much sun, but still this country is so wonderful, the cities for me unbelievably attractive and I also like the people. I am terribly hot with the heavy Canadian coat.' In Naples he experienced audience resistance to a contemporary work: 'After the interval, during the Hindemith sonata, I sensed already a certain disquiet and when I had finished they whistled! Do you know what I did? I stood up with a little smile and shrugged my shoulders. Thereupon the whistling stopped and we were even called out again.'[48] Feuermann was performing with Paul Baumgartner:

I told Baumgartner in Napoli before the Rococo Variations of T'kowski that he should make the accompaniment a bit richer. Whereupon he did nothing but arpeggi, crescendi, decrescendi, filling in the notes. It was very funny and while I was schmalzing on the cello, I was grinning so much that I had to be careful not to burst out laughing. I then told him that in Rome he shouldn't do so much, but he forgot and did even worse things. Quite a fellow.[49]

Feuermann had considerable success in Rome:

Molinari is screamingly funny. I went to him today at 5.30; we played the things through – Schumann and Weber with piano. . . . He only has 1 concert a week but 5 hours daily of rehearsal and those he has to fill out with something. Well, this is OK with me; the orchestra is excellent and he too seems brilliant. Sacconi apparently always reproached him that he had never played with me!⁵⁰

The next day he reported: 'Today in the rehearsal they were practising my slides, violinists and cellists, it was very funny, one was always hearing A–D with a glissando in between.'⁵¹

In the past Eva had expressed her views quite forcefully about Feuermann's playing, but surely nothing could have prepared him for the outburst following a broadcast she heard just after Casals's concert in Zürich:

> You terrible person! We are infuriated, i-n-f-u-r-i-a-t-e-d! You started so nicely and decently and then you finished with that Bach encore; that was more than terrible, absolutely below you and indecent! You must not play any more Bach solos because you just can't play them. To your misfortune we had just heard Casals who played the D major Suite in a more than perfect way . . . after that one cannot hear any other string player play Bach no matter whether it's the violin or the cello. But besides that (I become ambitious for you because I had just heard Casals) how could you play that Bach in this undisputedly bad manner. I thought it really impertinent; it was terrible in interpretation (please excuse the word) as well as technically. Go ahead and play it out of tune, scratch here and there, these are mere slips. But to play without rhythm, tight, clumsy, stiff in your left hand, that was just too much. Please stop playing Bach. You just can't do it. You ruin the whole impression of a concert.

She did not reveal which work by Bach so offended her and she continued with an assessment of the rest of the programme, ending with: 'The Haydn Rondo was charming, "almost" as beautiful as the Casals recording. Now let's forget the end [the Bach encore]. After all, I am only a dumb girl but still you should think whether you should still play Bach; you do want to give your best, after all, and you can't do that when you play Bach. I should leave it at that.' But she didn't, and offered more 'advice': 'If you have the summer off, go to Casals and listen to how he plays it again, then you will learn more than through practising.'⁵² Feuermann's reaction was mild: 'I was very proud of my temperamental wife and how right she is. But you know that I don't feel comfortable with Bach and that it has always been my intention to look up Casals. Should we take that into consideration for the coming autumn? You must have been very nice for him to have phoned <u>and</u> written.'⁵³ Casals had telephoned Mrs Reifenberg the day after his concert. He had been very grateful for the heated pillow and the flowers sent as well as a letter he had received from Feuermann.

Feuermann's concert with Molinari was also broadcast. He asked Eva what she thought of that one:

How were you satisfied yesterday? I was terribly cross with myself for I was in top form. Molinari and the orchestra accompanied delightfully, but in spite of this I was afraid on and off. But I believe that on the whole I played well and in any case this was not a success but a real triumph! The good Camûs [another agent of Feuermann's] was beside herself with sheer enthusiasm and satisfaction. Too bad that Oma and you couldn't be here; these concerts are on the whole very beautiful.

Feuermann was writing from Rome: 'walked alone around the Forum and the Therms of Caracalla and I became quite philosophical about the greatness of the past. A wonderful city this Rome! Tomorrow morning at 7:45 I leave for Torino and will be there only at 6:30 in the evening, horribly long trip.' In Turin another cellist would be waiting: 'Imagine, the day after tomorrow Piatigorsky is also playing in Torino, both of us on the same evening. I am looking forward to seeing him and am curious what he has to tell.'[54]

Chapter 10

Momentous Year
1938

By the way, Mr. F., in which business are you in?

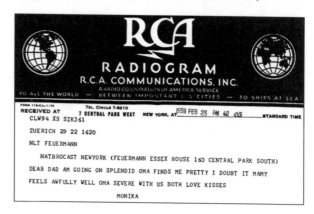

The year 1938 began in Paris, but Feuermann was soon on the move to the United States. In a letter to Eva he mimicked her complaints: 'Does Munio really have to turn away from me for so long in order to play to other Jews with his two clumsy hands in America while I, his Eva, have to stay in Zürich in order to bring his child into our world, and am I not even allowed to grumble properly[?].' But he also wrote:

> Do you know what gallows humour is, Oefchen? How ever tremendously happy I was a little while ago with your voice on the telephone, it was terrible for me to hear you cry. Only at the moment of my departure did it become clear to me that I would not see you for such a long time. And all the things that are going to happen to you in these months! When I come back you, my little Oeff, yourself still a child, will with God's help be a mother. And I a father.[1]

On 12 January he sailed for New York on the MS *Lafayette*. The boat was relatively small and completely empty. It had been newly renovated: 'of course tastelessly modern, like the French always do.' Feuermann's large and comfortable cabin was on A deck, in a quite central location: 'I find that a good cabin on a good ship awakens in one "embassy" feelings, everything so well groomed and high class.' The trip, however, was full of adventures: 'Before dinner I unpacked like a good boy and made war on the cockroaches, which meant for them a lot of casualties.[2] And a couple of days later:

> As I was sitting in my cabin and writing, a huge swell of water with a colossal noise came through the porthole and the whole cabin was wet from 'top to bottom', including myself. The evening suit was laid out already and was wringing wet, and water entered the drawers. When I emptied the drawers small waterfalls cascaded down, the paper, music, books, everything wet. But now imagine how lucky I was: 10 minutes earlier I was still practising![3]

And worse still:

> Yesterday evening I had a terrible shock. I was already in bed, had turned out the light, and suddenly it occurred to me that when I was going to bed I had not seen the cello that was supposed to be lying on the second bed. I never got out of bed faster, but all the searching didn't help. The cello wasn't in the cabin. Quickly I put on my dressing gown and went to the office. We searched some more and at last the cello was found in the next-door cabin where the good steward had put it without telling me. After the initial shock I had been quite calm because the cello couldn't have gone, but it was nevertheless very embarrassing. A cherry brandy helped get over the situation and I slept very well.

When not reading novels or passing longingly by a couple of deserted ping-pong tables – like so many musicians Feuermann was addicted to the game, although only a modest player – he indulged his great love, the cinema. This, too, was not without incident: 'Today in the afternoon there was a magnificent film, but at the most exciting spot the sound faded away. Once it was the other way round; we heard quite well but couldn't see anything. A colossal mess. On a Swiss ship such a thing would never happen.'[4] Somehow Feuermann found time to practise – about four hours daily, which he felt to be quite a triumph.

Owing to very bad weather, the ship arrived in New York one day late, on 21 January.

> My first outing tomorrow will be to Sacconi. I didn't bring any <u>strings</u>. Otherwise the cello is OK. Am beginning to be agitated; the immigration officer always frightens me, and I have decided to be very cheerful towards NBC, despite the tour being so paltry.[5] I have to play well and behave properly. Have the best intentions for both – I hope I'll do both.[6]

But on arrival there were more problems: 'I have been here only one day and I'm already quite distraught. On top of this, the weather is awfully dreary rain-snow, and in the houses it is so hot that one can't breathe. Please send me immediately a few short summer underpants!!!! And please write mother that she should make another half dozen. (How do you like such orders??)'[7]

At the Essex House Hotel ('1200 Rooms of Sunlight Overlooking Central Park'), 160 Central Park South, Feuermann found that his room was not ready but his student Edgar Lustgarten had come to meet him. They went to the cafeteria, where they saw sitting not far away from them the cellist Gaspar Cassadó. The prankster Feuermann got a waitress to deliver a note to him saying that someone wanted to interview him. Naturally, the egotistical Cassadó agreed. Up crept Feuermann, a handkerchief over his face, and it was not long before hilarious laughter erupted. Cassadó was also staying at the Essex House Hotel. They could each hear the other practising. And in the thin-walled hotel another musician could hear them too: Segovia. He was furious. Cassadó was blamed for keeping him awake, although the culprit was actually Feuermann.[8]

Feuermann found that Sacconi had a new shop: '<u>Frightfully</u> chic. We chose strings and his heart bled when he saw that I was now playing a metal A string.'[9] Two years before, Feuermann had come back from America with a steel string. As Havivi remembered: 'We thought this was the end of every-thing, because nobody ever played with metal strings. We all played with gut strings.'[10] Feuermann was one of the first, if not the first, to use a metal A string. On his first trip to the Far East he had complained vigorously about the heat and humidity. A plain gut A string might have lasted little more than a day in the various climate changes. A metal string, however, would both keep its pitch and allow him to move faster and with greater clarity in this sticky climate. Hill had advised him not to play on thin strings, believing it would affect the volume of the sound; but had he ever imagined that Feuermann would choose steel?

In his first few days in New York, Feuermann caught up with all the gossip, particularly at meals with his agent, Siegfried Hearst:

> The food at their place was excellent. He talked an awful lot, and is very disappointed because the business with good artists is getting so difficult. He insists that Schnabel has only 7 concerts, that Rubinstein will take away everything from Serkin because Hurok out of revenge will do everything to harm Serkin, that Morini has great success but also only 7 concerts but will get on, that the Menuhins spent $50,000 for publicity this year [Menuhin was playing the newly discovered Schumann Concerto], that the Heifetzes live in the country (Connecticut) and that he will at the most get $40,000 for his film, etc. etc. Then we played old gramophone records from the time of the war by Kreisler etc. and also of Casals playing two things by

Bach. I was enthused, but <u>like this</u> I cannot play Bach because I believe it is wrong.

Feuermann did not amplify this last statement. In the same letter to Eva he wrote about an amusing call he had received from the press: *'he was so sorry, he missed me on the boat and we <u>had</u> to fix a date for taking photographs and so on and on. Saying good by [sic] he all of a sudden asked: By the way, Mr. F., in which business are you in?* Isn't that wonderful??'[11] Steinways organised a lunch where Schnabel was also a guest. Surprised to see Feuermann, he gave him a big kiss. 'Schnabel has very few concerts, joked about this the whole time, but you could see that he was a little bit sad about it too.'[12]

Feuermann could be so delightfully indiscreet: 'I had lunch with: Kolisch, Luka [wife of Jenö Léner] and husband, Heifetz [Benar], Milstein and his terrible wife and the Sarburn who is very nice and witty. We sat at a big table in the Russian tea-room, there was <u>no one</u> else there!!' In the afternoon he visited the Wallensteins: 'he is supposed to earn a lot of money; has besides his position as a radio director another few commercial radios [sic] at the NBC. God, he must be a shrewd fellow! Virginia is looking pretty but rather wilted. But they are both funny and very kind towards me.'[13] Later the same day, Feuermann was obliged to accept another invitation:

Mrs Rosenwald[14] had invited me to dinner between bridge playing. I called and let her be told that I wasn't feeling well. She then called again and I went there anyway and it was a *waste of time*. She is very nice, but the Milsteins were also there, and the Milsteins twice in one day is a bit too much. On top of that I had to listen to 2 hours of Milstein's political views; also Mittmann, his accompanist, knows everything exactly. I was home early, but I would have preferred to practise a bit and write to you in peace.[15]

Feuermann's social engagements also took in 'the old Godowski', with whom he went to a Toscanini radio concert: 'Tomorrow T'nini has a benefit concert, there a box costs <u>200</u> dollars, about 900 Franks! Colossal!'[16] He also met the conductor Alexander Smallens and the Elmans; Mischa Elman regaled him with stories about their Far Eastern agent, Strok.

Feuermann was now with NBC Management: 'I was put on the list as the only cellist, and unanimously, which suggests I'm rated very highly.' But there was no 'house' pianist with whom he could be paired: 'Schnabel is too expensive and <u>only</u> wants sonatas, which wouldn't work, and Serkin has his father-in-law [Adolf Busch].' Feuermann noticed, however, that his agent, Marks Levine, was depressed. The United States, in particular New York, was awash with European musicians escaping Hitler. NBC had many more artists than concerts. Feuermann's colleague Szymon Goldberg was experiencing considerable difficulties: he was waiting for the arrival of Lili Kraus, with whom he was supposed to play, but because of visa problems he had to endure Ellis Island for five days. Feuermann wrote:

> While I try to continue to practise, the little Goldberg phones me. I right away went to him, as he was alone, we ate together in the Russian tea-room. . . . The little fellow impresses me, he is even enthused about Ellis Island, even though the recital costs him <u>1700 dollars.</u> If he knew what Elsie [at NBC] told me! Namely that he can't be put on her list for next year; only if he has an <u>extraordinary</u> success can it be. This is terrible.[17]

Feuermann, at the top of his tree professionally, was never obliged to pass through Ellis Island as a port of entry. He could afford to be confident, but he knew his good fortune, surrounded as he was by old friends from Europe, some managing well, some in desperate need:

> *I had lunch with Käthe and Kitzinger who has his birthday today. He really has a marvellous studio and he still has tears in his eyes thinking of Germany. His mother in Munich has no passport anymore and besides he lost just half his money in stocks. Käthe is a sweet girl and it is striking how wonderfully she and Meta are in their spirits and behaviour considering their most awful situation. They have to fight so hard.*[18]

In the same letter he wrote:

> This afternoon Milstein is playing, before that I am eating with Alexanian, who apparently has enough to live on. For dinner I am at Wallensteins and afterwards, from 10–11 with Dijane [Hearst, wife of his agent] at the Toscanini radio broadcast. Imagine, the hall holds only 1400 people and 120,000 people have applied for tickets, that is approx. 100 persons per seat. Crazy.

It has been suggested by Claus Adam and David Soyer that Feuermann studied with Diran Alexanian (1881–1954), who himself studied with Grütz-macher before settling in Paris, where from 1921 he was Casals's assistant at the Ecole Normale de Musique. In 1937 he moved to the United States, teaching at the Peabody Institute in Baltimore and the Manhattan School of Music in New York City. Several of Feuermann's American students, including Bernard Greenhouse, George Neikrug and David Soyer, studied with Alexanian before studying with Feuermann. Sophie Feuermann maintains that Feuermann himself never studied with him and has suggested that Alexanian may have taken over Feuermann's pupils when he was unable to teach.[19] Eva Feuermann contends, however, that Alexanian was the only person that Feuermann heeded: 'He was able to criticize Munio and he would take it.'[20] This accords with a recollection by David Soyer:

> I remember once going to a concert with Alexanian of Feuermann's where he played the C major Bach Suite and we went backstage after the concert. I'm tagging along, and Alexanian said 'Oh Munio, you know you played that first scale out of tune' and Feuermann said 'that's ridiculous. What are you talking about? C major! You're crazy!' 'No, no, you played that out of tune.' And then we had a class the next day with Alexanian. The telephone rang and it was Feuermann who said 'Yes, you're right, I did play it out of tune. I was going to go to the movies and I stayed home and practised instead!'[21]

As usual, in his spare time Feuermann played chamber music: 'in the evening at Mrs Rosenwald a quartet with Milstein; extremely *unsatisfactory*; we played only a little, but at the end a Beethoven trio with Mrs Rosenwald at the piano. Milstein <u>cello</u> and me violin; it was very funny.'[22] Despite his irritation with Milstein's political views, Feuermann enjoyed his playing: 'The Milstein concert on Saturday afternoon was interesting: if you had left the concert after 2/3 of the program you would have had a sad impression; it was boring, thin and unmusical. But towards the end, the virtuoso things he played fantastically, unbelievably well.'[23]

Feuermann once again played for Bagby, in a gala concert for the Bagby Music Lovers' Foundation held in the Grand Ballroom of the Waldorf-Astoria. It was a benefit concert to raise money for pensions to artists who had given distinguished service in music but were without adequate means. Taking place in the afternoon of 31 January, the concert was given by a galaxy of stars: Kirsten Flagstad, Grete Stueckgold, Erica Morini, Maurice Maréchal, Giovanni Martinelli, Richard Bonelli, Emanuel List and Feuermann. He enjoyed himself immensely:

> I don't think I ever laughed so much in my life. We were 10 'artists' and 8 accompanists. . . . The old Bagby clatters with his teeth and eats noisily, sometimes even in rhythm; the old Martinelli spitting and 'mi-mi-mi'; the fat List, pompous and stuttering; as for MacArthur, Flagstad's accompanist, the only thing he didn't do was carry her chamber pot after her etc. etc. I was completely exhausted when we had finished.[24]

Despite his apparent gaiety, it was a difficult time for Feuermann to be in New York. Eva, who remained in Zürich, was about to give birth to their first child. The mail was very slow and he missed her dreadfully: '*I am longing for you, but I know that I have to try to make some money and that you will try with much more success to have a nice Baruch.*'[25] But he had to be in America, for he had received an invitation he could not refuse; even the birth of his first child had to take second place. America's National Orchestral Association (NOA) had invited him to play virtually the entire known repertoire for solo cello and orchestra: 'For the first time in New York, a comprehensive cycle of 'cello literature is offered. The National Orchestral Association presents Emanuel Feuermann in a distinguished series of four membership concerts.'[26] In four concerts, Feuermann would play 13 works. No cellist had attempted such a feat; it would be nearly 30 years before another cellist, Rostropovich, emulated him.[27]

The NOA was not a professional orchestra but a training orchestra, founded in 1930. It was the brain-child of the Belgian viola player Leon Barzin. Born in 1900 in Brussels, Barzin had been taught as a child by Eugène Ysaÿe. In 1919 he joined the New York Philharmonic and was later for ten years Toscanini's principal viola. He became intensely aware that the make-up of the orchestra was almost entirely European; out of 104 musicians only 4 were American-born. However, this was not unusual in American orchestras at that time. The NOA's goal was to give young American-born players the opportunity to learn the orchestral repertoire in a professional atmosphere with a view to increasing their prospects of finding permanent employment with major symphony orchestras. The ages of the players ranged from 18 to 29 and competition to be accepted, always by audition, was fierce. The organization's aims were well realized: many of America's finest musicians soon occupied important positions in all the major American orchestras, having trained with the NOA.

Soloists brought in to play with the NOA were always of the highest distinction. Between 1935 and 1940, Shura Cherkassky, Mischa Elman, Rudolf Serkin, Myra Hess, Mischa Levitzki, Rosalyn Tureck, Joseph Schuster, Schnabel, Elisabeth Schumann and Nathan Milstein all played as soloists. Concerts and rehearsals were held in Carnegie Hall. Each season a special series was held in the spring for which tickets were sold only on subscription: 'Positively No Tickets Available for Single Concerts.' In 1936 Mischa Elman played 15 concertos in four concerts; in 1937 Myra Hess and Rudolf Serkin shared 5 concerts, playing Mozart and Beethoven. Although the NOA was a training orchestra, graduates would return to play for these special concerts so that the student body was 'strengthened' by young professionals. No matter who the soloist was, these concerts were an important event.

It was Leon Barzin who suggested that Feuermann play the marathon. Feuermann, although undaunted himself, was sceptical that any orchestra could cope with so many pieces in so short a time. But the orchestra was not

1. Emanuel playing his father's cello, August 1912.

2. Sigmund (*left*) and Emanuel as children.

3. The Feuermann children ?1914:
(*back row, from left to right*)
Emanuel, Gusta and Sigmund;
(*front row, from left to right*) Rosa
and Sophie.

4. Emanuel with his mother, Rachel
Feuermann, 1917.

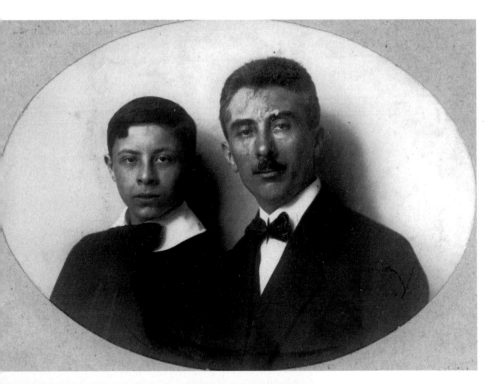

5. Emanuel with his father,
Meier Feuermann, 1917.

6. Feuermann, Cologne, 1919.

7. The Reifenberg home, 376 Alteburgerstrasse, Cologne.

8. The Gürzenich Quartet (*from left to right*): Bram Eldering and Karl Körner (violins), Feuermann (cello) and Hermann Zitzmann (viola).

9. Sophie Feuermann.

10. (*from left to right*) Feuermann, Paul Hindemith and Josef Wolfsthal.

11. (*from left to right*) Feuermann, Paul Hindemith and Szymon Goldberg.

(*facing page*)12 and 13. Eva Reifenberg and (*below*) at her marriage to Feuermann, October 1935.

14. Feuermann with his
Buick convertible, 1937.

15. Feuermann, the
inveterate smoker: an
advertisement for
Chesterfield cigarettes.

16. Jascha Heifetz (*left*) and Feuermann, 1939.

17. Feuermann serenading his young daughter, Monica, Scarsdale, 1941.

18. Feuermann with Albert Hirsch, 1942.

19. (*from left to right*) Artur Rubinstein, Jascha Heifetz and Feuermann, California, 1941.

20. Feuermann (*left*) and Daniel Saidenberg, New York, December 1941.

21. Feuermann at Fort Riley, Kansas, April 1942.

22. Feuermann with 'Corporal Bolo', a Boston puppy, Fort Riley, Kansas, April 1942.

23. 'I am an American' Day, 16 May 1942.

24. Feuermann, 1939.

25. Feuermann's tombstone, Kensico Cemetery, Valhalla, New York.

HALTUNG DES INSTRUMENTS / TENUE DE L'INSTRUMENT

26. 'Holding the instrument'.

Illustrations from Sebastian Lee's *Praktische Violoncello-Schule* which was revised and enlarged by Feuermann and Dr J. Sakom and published in 1929.

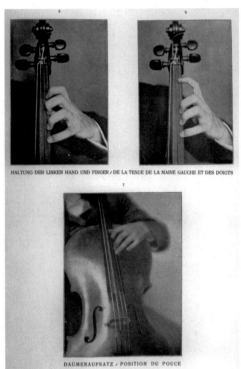

HALTUNG DER LINKEN HAND UND FINGER / DE LA TENUE DE LA MAINE GAUCHE ET DES DOIGTS

DAUMENAUFSATZ / POSITION DU POUCE

27. 'The left hand'.

HALTUNG DES BOGENS
TENUE DE L'ARCHET

HALTUNG DES BOGENS AM FROSCH
TENUE DE L'ARCHET AU TALON

HALTUNG DES BOGENS AN DER SPITZE / TENUE DE L'ARCHET À LA POINTE

8. 'The bow'.

29. The 'Feuermann' Stradivarius.

unionized; Barzin could have eight to ten rehearsals per concert. Feuermann's concerts took place on Saturday afternoons. The programmes played, however, were not entirely those announced. Saint-Saëns's D minor Concerto, Ibert's Concerto and Hindemith's *Kammermusik* no.3 gave way to Saint-Saëns's A minor Concerto, Tchaikovsky's 'Rococo' Variations, the Schönberg Concerto and Toch's Concerto. Of the 13 works performed, three had not been heard in New York before: Toch's Concerto, the Schönberg Concerto and Weber's *Konzertstück* op.20, the manuscript of which Feuermann had found in the Dresden Library.[28] Presenting these works was an exceptional opportunity. For financial reasons alone, no commercial orchestra could or would have entertained the idea of such a series. After the first concert on 5 February, the *Sunday New York Times* chimed:

> Yesterday's performances strengthened the conviction that as far as the cello and cello-playing are concerned, Mr Feuermann is a one-man revolution. He has pushed the capacities of the instrument to almost incredible limits, and wholly in the interests of its expressiveness. While his virtuosity is the peer of any, in whatsoever instrument, it is rigorously disciplined by a native musicianship that makes no easy compromises for the favour of the crowd. His is a technique that could storm the concert halls by its sheerly unbelievable ease and brilliance; wedded to the musical ideals of a mature and perceptive mind, its product, utterly removed from mere sensation, is something for the heart and mind to cherish.[29]

Feuermann also recorded his views on this concert, which had comprised C.P.E. Bach's Concerto in A minor, Bloch's *Schelomo* and Haydn's D major Concerto:

> I am enthused about myself, never played as well. Before I went on stage I again thought I wouldn't be able to play a note. But the first note – in the Bach concerto – sounded so well that I enjoyed myself and was able to play well. But also Barzin is brilliant, not <u>one</u> phrase where he disturbed me, on the contrary, he feels exactly as I do. And the boys played brilliantly. Barzin says quite correctly that they only make an effort when they have a public *to show off* to. Even before 'Schelomo' I wasn't afraid, but I just can't stand the piece. In the Haydn everything also went well. <u>Nothing</u> happened to me where it might have, but in the slow parts there was sometimes an out-of-tune note. I was simply tired and had to pull myself together again and again. At the end I was called out 6 times.

The reviews amazed him: 'They are all here very *excited.* They were a bit asleep but this concert has woken them up. . . . This concert consolidated my reputation and, even if it sounds funny, it does me good to write to you optimistically particularly now. And how happy I am that my child, at least at birth, can be proud of me.'[30]

As the NOA series was spread over a number of weeks, Feuermann also gave recitals elsewhere, including St Louis, Missouri; Richmond, Virginia; and Texas. Later he was in Utica, NY, as part of a joint recital with the pianist Josef Lhevinne (9 March), Rochester, Minnesota (11 March), Lawrence, Kansas (14 March), Omaha, Nebraska (16 March), and Indianapolis, with the Indianapolis Symphony conducted by Fabien Sevitzky (18 and 19 March). While he was away at NOA rehearsals, one of his students covered for him; Suzette Forgues, Mosa Havivi and Edgar Lustgarten were all playing in the orchestra. Feuermann's stamina was phenomenal, but the distances he travelled were huge, suggesting that the main motive was to make money: 'I am terribly thrifty. I haven't told you until now that I have only <u>one</u> room here in the Essex House. I don't need an apartment and thus I pay only 35 Dol. a week. I earn so little, that is so little remains, that I must look out and be careful.'[31] His fee per NOA concert, before 10% commission, was only $250. Recitals paid better, between $450 and $650, though out of this figure was drawn an exorbitant 25% agent's commission, Wolfgang Rebner's fee and all their travel expenses.[32]

On 19 February, Feuermann was back in New York for the second NOA concert. In the *New York Sun*, Irving Kolodin commented wryly:

> One would not be surprised to hear almost any day of a meeting of cellists, gathered in protest against the recent activities of Emanuel Feuermann. Certainly the kind of playing he offered on Saturday was an unending joy to the listener, but it was obvious that his standards are hardly a pleasure for other cellists to contemplate. Plainly this is unfair competition, restraint of trade or something equally uncomradely.[33]

Feuermann described the programme – Boccherini, Schönberg and Schumann concertos as well as the Tchaikovsky 'Rococo' Variations – as 'hellish':

> at the end in the 'Rococo Variations' I was so tired that I could hardly hold the bow. This time the cello is just wonderful! I believe even <u>you</u> would have been satisfied with me, at least most of the time. But I did have to take myself in hand again and again when it went through my head that maybe just at this moment you will be ready. Fantastic! Moldernu said afterwards: *for an expecting father he played very well.*[34]

But unwittingly Feuermann had given himself extra difficulties: 'In the second half I felt so restricted, although I didn't pay much attention to it. Yesterday I noticed that I had put on Barzin's waistcoat. Barzin is, of course, much thinner than me.' But even this did not detract from his success: 'Many people are quite crazy about me and I believe that these concerts have helped me very much.'[35] This was the boost he had hoped for. After the first concert, many additional subscriptions were sold for the remaining three; no single tickets were available.

Now Feuermann was frantic for news of his child. The baby had been due while he was in Texas playing concerts in Corpus Christi and Longview, but by 20 February, having returned to New York, he had still heard nothing:

> It is just crazy that I am sitting here in New York and don't know anything. What a misery! I am also tired of New York. I'd just as soon not see anyone. . . . What do I care about these people. Some I like, but [not] the many others with whom I also have to be. Today the NBC is closed and maybe, just today, there will be a telegram. Unimaginable, but still, God willing when you receive this letter you are, Oefchen, a mother, and I, Munio, a father. Oefchen, why am I here?

The following day, he went to the NBC office with Szymon Goldberg, whom he was still trying to help in establishing a foothold in the United States. Goldberg had given a recital, his American debut at Carnegie Hall, but it was not the stunning success necessary for him to be taken on by NBC. News, however, had arrived from Zürich: 'Miss Mobert rushes towards me with something in her hand and says: *Mr. F. you have a daughter.* Just at that moment 2 telegrams had arrived. I looked at them for a moment completely without any understanding and rushed to a corner because I, the father, suddenly had a crying fit. Schnuck, loved one, I am delirious.' Monica was born on 19 February: 'I worked out that you must have had the child towards 11 o'clock at night. Do you know that you had birth pains while I played in Carnegie Hall? Isn't that fantastic!'[36] He was ecstatic, though very frustrated by the thought of having to remain in America until after his final concert on 26 March.

Feuermann's concerts were very successful, but if proof were needed that cellists did not command the status of violinists, pianists or singers, his agent from NBC, Marks Levine, provided it: he did not attend the first NOA concert. Feuermann angrily sent a letter and Levine dutifully turned up for the second concert, having warned Feuermann that he could only stay for the first half. Acutely embarrassed, Levine admitted he had never heard such playing. NBC's problems were twofold: too many artists to promote; and little confidence in, or idea of, how to elevate a cellist. Levine had admitted to Siegfried Hearst that Feuermann's status in relation to his playing did not correlate. Feuermann wrote of their remarks: 'they <u>must</u> find a way to elevate me; the way I stand today does not correspond to my playing.' He felt triumphant: 'because it is what I am saying all the time; they must make an artist out of a cellist, *beyond the instrument.* Only they don't yet know <u>how</u> they should go about it.'[37] He wondered whether he should engage someone to do public relations: 'That probably wouldn't cost more than [advertising in] the *Musical Courier* and maybe one should try it to see what the effect would be,'[38]

The NOA concerts were packed out and Feuermann was enjoying enormous publicity. Many old friends were at the concerts, including the violinist Mischa Elman. Feuermann at this time also met Jascha Heifetz: 'Yesterday there was a huge benefit affair, to which Mrs Heifetz had invited me. In all, 20 people played, including Heifetz and Cassadó! I could punch him on the nose, because he is fabulously talented, knows a lot, plays like a swine and is coifed like a street girl.' The next day, Feuermann was at Heifetz's concert: 'I was very excited because in the afternoon Heifetz played in the Philharmonic, unfortunately the Elgar concerto. It was exciting how he played, he is a colossal violinist. I am proud because I am being compared to him.'[39] No documentary evidence exists to confirm when he first met or heard Heifetz, and the precise date that they first played together is also not known. However, one thing is certain – if circumstances had allowed, the two musicians would have played together in New York around this time: 'Am furious that this very day I am away from N.Y. because tomorrow Heifetz sails for Europe and he wanted to play quartets today before leaving.'[40]

The day after his 19 February NOA concert in Carnegie Hall, Feuermann was in the Town Hall playing Schubert's 'Arpeggione' in an all-Schubert concert for the New Friends of Music. 'Another great and neglected master-piece of chamber music received one of its infrequent hearings.' The piece? Schubert's Octet. 'If the Octet contained the most memorable music in this programme, the finest interpretation was given to the sonata.'[41] Feuermann felt differently about his playing: 'I wasn't quite satisfied, but it again was a huge success and there seems to be a quiet understanding among people to tell me that they had never heard anything like it.' And tensions between him and Wolfgang Rebner, which had begun to develop in Texas, were showing: 'He makes me nervous; he is immodest; he irritated me before the concert [by saying] that I may not make "ps ps" towards him on the stage; and besides he began too slowly because he wanted to play <u>too</u> beautifully.'[42]

Feuermann loathed the 'political' socializing of New York's concert life but had to endure it and was often very amusing about it. He reported on a tea party given by the singer Hulda Lashankska following Heifetz's performance of the Elgar Concerto: 'Very noble, a better-looking class of Jewish ladies. I best liked Mrs Muschenheim [owner of the Astor Hotel on Broadway]. Mrs Metz, who has a turned-up nose, was asked publicly by a lady with a huge hooked nose: did you have your nose operated on here or in Europe[?] How do you like that???'[43] About another gathering he wrote: 'The whole time they gossiped about Mischa, Jascha, Sasha, Toscha.' And he was incensed by the injustice of the times:

> we went together (with Virginia Wallenstein) to a piano recital, where I again got so mad I could have burst. A Russian pianist (Anya Dorfmann) from Paris, who is friends with everyone and the devil (Toscanini, Horowitz), is a protégée of Sarnoff (NBC president), so a certain circle around these people makes a big noise – and she plays so badly, like a machine. At least the public has better taste, it was quite empty. I always think of the fact that so many who have talent don't get a chance to show it, but such a person because she is clever can give recitals in New York.[44]

These were unusual times; Europeans swarmed New York:

> Yesterday I had a charming evening at Mrs Muschenheim's with Tommy [Mann] and wife and daughter Erika and the Toscanini family; Mrs Bodanski (wife of the conductor) and Mrs Mann were my neighbours at table whom I had to charm. I liked the evening very much. T'nini of course remembers Zürich very well, and he had a fit of laughter because I still think about it. The Manns are partly very enthusiastic about America and it seems that he is negotiating with Yale University, so as to spend the greater part of the year here. Today I lunch with Hindemith and I'll tell him this. For these creative people who need the masses and who are needed by the masses, America is the country.[45]

It seems likely that the reference to Toscanini 'remembering Zürich' relates to an amusing incident in 1927, when Feuermann played a C.P.E. Bach concerto at a concert in the Tonhalle. A friend of Feuermann's sitting beside Toscanini in the audience became aware of him sighing and groaning all through the concerto, mumbling something like 'O, il porco, il porco!' Years later, in the safety of Mrs Muschenheim's social occasion, Feuermann decided to unburden himself: 'Maestro, I am very much ashamed. Eleven years ago, I played miserably in your presence.' 'Nonsense, nonsense. I never heard you play except on the radio.' 'Yes, you did, Maestro. It was in Switzerland.' Toscanini laughed: 'You mean to say that you are that rotten cellist I heard in Zürich?'[46]

The NOA concerts proceeded, but with more programme changes, and as Feuermann had predicted, the orchestra was finding it difficult to rehearse all the works. On 5 March the Dvořák Concerto was substituted for Strauss's *Don*

Quixote and the rest of the programme consisted of the Saint-Saëns A minor Concerto and Weber's *Konzertstück*:

> It is altogether crazy what a reputation I have. Toscanini's pales next to mine. It is really a pity that you aren't experiencing this, it would give you pleasure. . . . The orchestra was bad, we didn't have enough rehearsals. But again – surprisingly – I played well and Al Blume[47] insists that even for Heifetz they don't shout as much (I would prefer a little less shouting and more dollars).[48]

On 12 March, Hitler marched into Austria. Feuermann was frantic, isolated as he was in middle America: 'I am too bewildered about the goings-on in Austria. In what a bad state you must be with your fear of war! If only I could be with you! I am worried about you, Oeff, you shouldn't excite yourself too much in your condition. Think of Monica and of me. One must not let oneself go to pieces in such times.'[49] And his own family was in Vienna – he wrote to Eva's mother: 'To imagine that my parents should be living in Nazi Germany!! Unthinkable! But where should they go? Will Sigmund wake up? And if he wakes up he will need money! What is Kux doing? And all our friends? Don't forget that these ***[50] in 5 days are showing in Vienna what they learned in Germany in 5 years!' He never imagined that events could move at such speed.

> My head is fit to burst, am thinking, calculating, making plans but can't get ahead. Again and again the questions: what will happen to my parents; where will Rosa and Adolf get money to emigrate? I already received a cable from Sophie that I should get affidavits, but how can she do all this when she is going to have a baby? That is the first thing. The second regards us: can we continue to live in Zürich with a good conscience? If we go to America, where and how will we live and will I earn enough?[51]

Feuermann had always supported his family in Vienna, but now the need was desperate. 'If only I had some money to be of real help to my people in Vienna. I still have this colossal feeling of responsibility towards my family, but can only help now through my connections.'[52]

Feuermann's life had turned upside-down. On the one hand, he was overjoyed by the birth of his child and his success in America; on the other, Eva was in Zürich, panic-stricken, and his family was stranded in Vienna. In a letter to his old friend Sashinska, a cousin of the cellist Joseph Schuster and friend of the Reifenbergs who was now living in America, Feuermann's thoughts were very gloomy: 'I know, Sascha, that you don't feel 100% happy in your position and I wish you all the best, but maybe you don't know how happy you should be to have an American passport.'[53] Indeed, Feuermann was desperately concerned about his own passport: 'What will be with our passports, heaven only knows, I only have two pages left.'[54] He was not as worried about his passport being removed as about what would become of his status as an Austrian citizen: 'I am just reading that there are no Austrian consulates any more, only German ones. . . . Can I enter Austria, excuse me, in this part of the German Reich any more?'[55] His thoughts were centred on urgent practical considerations: the necessity of opening a bank account ('the older the account, the easier it is to emigrate'[56]) and the need for affidavits of financial support to permit entry to the United States. His friends in Chicago, the Saidenbergs, and three relatives already based in America were willing to provide affidavits and Feuermann was to ask many for their help. But to whom should they be offered? 'I thought of Rosa and Sophie because Americans prefer poor, close relatives to rich friends.'[57] Rosa, Sophie and their respective husbands would be able to work but Feuermann was aware that his parents, 'the old people', and Sigmund might not find work. Indeed, Feuermann had written to his mother to suggest that Sophie should work with him in the autumn which, if the tour was good, might pay her $1000. 'I most prefer to play with Sophie, it would help her – but it won't be possible if she has a baby in September.'[58]

It was Gerald Warburg who produced the precious affidavits most rapidly. Gerald, a descendant of one of the wealthiest banking families in Germany, had been a family friend in Vienna. He came regularly to the house to study in his modest way with Feuermann. Within 48 hours of Sophie contacting him, Warburg deposited $100,000 for an affidavit. Vast as this sum was, Sophie still passed through Ellis Island, but not for financial reasons:

> When I landed here, I went First Class; the Third Class was completely Warburg's charity – philanthropists. I was without a husband and my address was of Fritz Kitzinger. Munio had written to me 'if you arrive Kitzinger won't be in New York so you can have his apartment there and very cheaply.' And so I wrote the address as c/o Mr Fritz Kitzinger. So when I arrived and showed it to the immigration, they said 'What? Mr Kitzinger is the father of your baby and your husband threw you out. We don't want such people in this country.'[59]

Money was a permanent worry. Feuermann considered an offer from the Mannes School in New York to give lectures.[60] He also considered returning to Cologne (absurdly dangerous for a Jew) in order to transfer money to his family in Vienna; Austria was now dealing in German currency.

Despite all the difficulties, his playing remained unaffected:

There seems to be something in my playing at the moment that convinces people more than before. . . . Is it because I enjoy my scratching more and therefore play more freely and am more secure? This series with Barzin was a great chance . . . it has changed my position from that of one of three cellists to first cellist. It would be a misfortune if Casals would come here.[61] But I don't want to think about this, I have to be an optimist.[62]

Which were the other two cellists Feuermann had in mind? By implication Casals, the other perhaps Gregor Piatigorsky or Gaspar Cassadó. George Neikrug, who later became a student of Feuermann, was in New York at the time:

I used to go to all the rehearsals and the concerts [NOA], and the way he played a piece like the Philipp Emanuel Bach Concerto – it was a totally different style. The way he used his bow. It was like listening to somebody of the stature of Heifetz or Kreisler and to me there hasn't been anyone on the cello before or since like that.[63]

The final concert of the NOA series took place on 26 March. On the programme was Strauss's *Don Quixote*, the Toch Concerto and a concerto by Tartini; Feuermann played his own cadenzas in the Tartini.[64] Feuermann had fun: 'It was brilliant, the orchestra played excellently and I played the end of "Don Quixote" in so sentimental a manner that I was even moved myself. But it was very touching when the orchestra and the public stood up as one man when I came out for the "Don Quixote". Something like that happens only very rarely, with Toscanini and similar people.'[65] Mosa Havivi, who was leading the cello section, witnessed in the Tartini a string player's nightmare:

I was sitting there and Feuermann's A string busted. It busted just before the end of the first movement. I gave him my cello and took his cello and walked off the stage to the left of Carnegie Hall. His case was standing there. I reached for a string, pulled it up fast and tuned it up, straightened out the bridge and walked back. They'd just finished the first movement. It was so beautiful, the audience applauded. It was lucky for me, because it gave me more time. He knew exactly what I was going to do. He counted on it! I give him back his cello and took my seat and the audience quietened down and he started playing the second movement.[66]

Feuermann delighted in playing with this orchestra: 'The second piece was the Toch concerto, which no orchestra has yet played like these young fellows. Even after that I was called out 4 times. I am very happy with this series, I really believe that I am now *on top*.'[67] As *Time* magazine put it:

Ten years ago the undisputed title of No. 1 living cellist was held by a stocky, bald-headed Spaniard named Pablo Casals. . . . Last week cellist Feuermann finished the most ambitious cellistic venture ever witnessed in Manhattan concert halls. . . . Critics and public were agreed that if 61-year-old Casals's crown could be claimed by anyone, most impressive claimant was 35-year-old Feuermann.[68]

After the concert, tea was served by one of the socialite Jewish ladies. Feuermann had invited a number of guests, including Russell Kingman, 'a real American Industrialist from Orange, New Jersey, who also plays the cello and who is pretty crazy about me. And imagine, when I came down yesterday for my meal on the table – with the compliments of Mr Kingman there is standing a bottle of champagne.'[69] Kingman was to crop up again later in Feuermann's story.

NBC Artists was so thrilled by Feuermann's success that his manager, Siegfried Hearst, came up with a novel idea: a trio, the 'Feuermann Trio', with Szymon Goldberg and possibly Sophie. The programming formula was simple: two trios sandwiching Feuermann as soloist in the middle. Feuermann was unimpressed:

I screamed at him in the NBC that he was mad. Then I went to their house for dinner. And now I am no less against it. He insists that for this combination he could easily get 10 concerts, one after the other. So I told him that he should send out two dozen telegrams and the answers will show us if one could count on engagements. In Europe this idea would be ridiculous, but here it is something else. Siegfried says that every known violinist forms a trio or quartet, and after all as I am a cellist one had to find something new. Maybe he is right.[70]

Feuermann believed that if NBC did not slacken its efforts, the next season (1938/9) would be very successful; eight concerts were already booked. But oddly, he wrote that eight concerts next season would be equivalent to the number of concerts in the current season. Can this be correct? In a schedule from NBC giving Feuermann's income from 24 January to 26 March 1938, 18 concerts, including those with the NOA and his recitals, are listed.[71] The income from these concerts was $6950 less $1562.50 commission fee, which in 2002 value is just over $68,500. Not much for a superstar. Meanwhile, elsewhere a change of management was in the air:

After my last 'success' in London I had more or less given up on England, on the other hand Simon and Schiff are negotiating with Holt, but I wanted to go to him only if he would give me the celebrity tour, but he didn't want that as a condition – so I stayed like a good boy with Miss Bass. Maybe I'll also get on in England. With luck![72]

Feuermann had been away from Europe for three months. So much had happened: his daughter had been born, the *Anschluss* had occurred, and his reputation in the United States was assured. He now left for Europe on the SS *Normandie*. To his regret, Zürich was not the first stop: concerts and broadcasts in London, Paris and Monte Carlo had to be given – in spite of his success, he felt obliged to accept every engagement, so insecure was he feeling financially. The boat left on 31 March, a day late, and it was then delayed 17 hours by fog; consequently he lost his first radio broadcast in England. Nevertheless, he enjoyed the *Normandie*:

> Imagine who's on the boat: Mr Horwitz [his French agent] from Paris, Piatigorsky and wife, Ria Ginster,[73] Prokofieff, and the old art dealer Hirsch . . . I have a nice cabin with bath and it is a pity that you aren't with me. You would enjoy it! There are also 5 ping-pong tables on deck and every day there is a movie. The food is excellent – and I even convinced myself to play for the crew. As you know, I hate doing it.[74]

He finally arrived in Zürich in mid-April. Eva met him at the station, an Eva very different from the one that had taken him to the station three months before. At last he was to meet his daughter:

> I was ravished. I had imagined something much worse. In fact she's anything but terrible. She's an immaculate little creature with a pretty face that has changed to its advantage within the last 4 days. . . . When she's asleep in the garden I stand next to her quietly and enjoy her calm sleep and the little person altogether. May God grant that things will continue to go so well for her.[75]

At this point, Columbia in London again raised an old topic. Rex Palmer wrote to Feuermann:

> We are considering the possibility of making a series of new recordings by a celebrity trio, as this repertoire has never been adequately covered since the days of the Cortot–Thibaud–Casals combination. If you are interested, would you let us know your movements during the next two or three months . . . Your collaborators would probably be Artur Schnabel and Bronisław Huberman and we should hope to commence the recording in London or Paris, if we can find a time that equally suits the convenience of all three.[76]

Less than two years previously, nothing had come of the same idea, the record companies refusing to release their 'exclusive' artists. Feuermann's reply now, in English, was straightforward: '*Your idea of recording Trios with Schnabel, Huberman and myself is very touching. I would love to do it.*' However, he did let slip that should Nipponophone make any objections to a release on HMV his contract with them would end in January 1939, and he referred to conversations he had had in New York on his recent trip: '*You know my point of view regarding my situation. I am not satisfied and my complaints are certainly not without any reason and so I refused any recording right now. I don't think that I have to be in a hurry as my success in America is increasing quite amazingly and there are symptoms even for a success in England.*'[77]

His success in New York in Strauss's *Don Quixote* with the NOA had been immense and a possible result was a performance of the same work with Toscanini and the BBC Symphony Orchestra on 23 May in the Queen's Hall, broadcast live as part of the BBC's London Music Festival. This was Feuermann's first concert with Toscanini. The pianist Gerald Moore recalled this performance:

> For years, musicians everywhere looked up to this great man's art with something more than admiration, with something that was akin to awe. We English are slow to take people to our hearts, but when we <u>are</u> won over, we're staunch for ever. I used to tell Feuermann this, because he paid many visits to this country without getting the recognition from the general public that was due to him, and he'd get a little discouraged sometimes, and perhaps that was natural; after the acclamations of the American public and of Europe, it <u>was</u> hard to come to England and literally struggle for recognition. Nevertheless he persevered, and at his last appearance in London playing the cello part of *Don Quixote* conducted by Toscanini, he created such a sensation that the Queen's Hall audience – Toscanini leading the applause – went wild with enthusiasm. On that night was born promise of future brilliant successes in <u>this</u> country such as Feuermann had had abroad.[78]

(Moore's assertion that this performance in London was Feuermann's last is incorrect, rather it was his last performance of *Don Quixote* in London.) The press indeed raved:

> More is needed to present a faithful reading of the score than the mere ability to rush up and down the 'cello fingerboard with the agility of a monkey. The artist's vision is needed; that vision that comprehends all in a flash of intuitive understanding, and is capable of presenting that vision

clearly to the public – a comprehensive whole, an organised unity, untram-
melled by considerations of technical expediency. It is this artist's vision that
Feuermann possessed, despite the fact that his technique is so fascinating
and so tremendous that it is inclined to blind the listener to the artistic
ability that lies behind it, conditioning and controlling it.[79]

Like Heifetz, Feuermann was in danger of dazzling less well-informed listeners
with the sheer brilliance of his technique.

Eva recalled Feuermann's regard for Toscanini: 'Feuermann was flat on his
stomach in admiration of Toscanini. He loved this way of conducting, he loved
this exacting conducting. He was a soloist so he didn't meet him many times.
Of course, Toscanini was surrounded by beautiful blondes and that was a blow
to me, he didn't like my looks.'[80] Toscanini was well known for intimidating
performers, but Feuermann experienced no such problems, as Mosa Havivi
recalled: 'Toscanini was Toscanini. You always had to watch out in case he
exploded from friend to enemy. I never heard any derogatory remark [from
Feuermann himself].'[81] According to Sophie, on one occasion Feuermann said
of Toscanini 'I'm so nervous I won't take it if he's rough on them or on me.' On
his return from the concert that had been conducted by Toscanini, he said to
Sophie: 'I want to tell you. He didn't interrupt once and he didn't say one
word.'[82] Toscanini, indeed, reported to Ada Mainardi that the concert had gone
very well.[83] It is of little surprise that he and Toscanini got on so well; their
attitudes to the performance of music were similar. Feuermann was a
Classicist. Any Romantic licence or excess would have been alien to them both.

In June, following concerts in Lisbon, Feuermann was once again in contact
with the Palestine Symphony Orchestra, trying to finalize details for a visit
later that year. Heinrich Simon wanted a programme that Feuermann
described as both too long and unrepresentative of the cello. Feuermann
wanted to play the Dvořák Concerto, failing that, the Haydn D major Concerto
and Tchaikovsky 'Rococo' Variations: 'the latter very suitable with the many
Russian listeners in your concerts.'[84]

Feuermann also turned again to Huberman over the plight of his family in
Vienna. Sigmund and his parents were supposed to go to Palestine, but
financial arrangements had still to be made. Feuermann could act as guarantor,
paying a monthly sum of £4 per person at the Swiss Palestine office in Basel,
but he doubted his ability to convince the Swiss officials. In his letter to
Huberman of 25 July he wrote: 'If I go to the office without any recommendation, I fear that given my not terribly imposing manner I will not be
successful. I take it as evident that a line from you or a telephone call would
work wonders. Could you do that for me??' New York may have been at

Feuermann's feet, but as a Jew in Switzerland he knew the power of petty officials. And this was not all. Sigmund needed a job:

> I dare to address the following questions to you: 1) In the dire straits in which my brother finds himself, he would be very happy to be leader or one of the 1st violins in your orchestra. 2) In case this is not possible, could you nonetheless send him a contract so that he can enter Palestine? 3) Do you know the relevant person at the Vienna/English consulate and would you give a recommendation for my brother? . . . Please don't be cross. As I said in the beginning, I would be only too glad not to bother you with my problems but it's not possible. My brother has already been forced to sweep the road, my family has to leave their flat very soon, every day something even worse may happen, and so it is obviously my duty to take steps to find out how these three people can be got out of Vienna as soon as possible. Now it is certainly not your duty to help me. It is only in the belief that you have a friendship for my 'married' family and for me and after conquering a natural inhibition that I have brought myself to ask you for help. Please answer me as quickly as possible. It is very urgent.[85]

Huberman did react quickly with a phone call to the office in Basel, and Feuermann was graciously received. The passage to Palestine for Sigmund and his parents would be arranged soon. The question of Feuermann's own travel status was also being resolved; he was now in possession of a Swiss identity document that allowed him to obtain a visa from another country: 'It's great that I was able to get the better of the Germans in that way. Moreover I today received the American quota visas and we are breathing a sigh of relief. It is mad the kind of worries one has these days.'[86]

On 2 August, Feuermann performed in Lucerne at the 'alternative' Salzburg. He wrote to Huberman: 'I wanted to write to you immediately after my visit to the Palestine office in Basel but I didn't get down to it because in addition to all the running around, I had to practise for Lucerne. Yesterday I played there, it was really very amusing and hot. Certainly today I'm not going to touch my cello.'[87] Following the *Anschluss* of Austria, the mayor of Lucerne with other notable city figures had decided to mount a small music festival to which performers no longer able or willing to perform at the Salzburg Festival could come. Eight concerts were arranged during August, with appearances by Cortot, Ansermet, Serkin, Fritz and Adolf Busch, Bruno Walter, Mengelberg and Feuermann. A 'Swiss Festival Orchestra' made up of five Swiss string quartets, led by the Busch Quartet, was conducted by Toscanini.[88]

It has been said that Feuermann, so as to secure a regular income, broached with Toscanini the possibility of becoming principal cello of the newly formed

NBC Symphony Orchestra, of which Toscanini was music director.[89] Sophie has denied this: 'I doubt it very much. He didn't need it. I'm sure Toscanini would have said yes!'[90] Eva recalls some misunderstanding whereby Feuermann's agent may have approached NBC, but she maintains that there was never any serious consideration of such a position. Feuermann never referred to it in any letters.

Feuermann's 1937/8 season ended in London with a Promenade concert (and broadcast) from the Queen's Hall on 31 August, in which he performed Bach's Suite in E♭ and the Brahms Double Concerto with violinist Antonio Brosa and the BBC Symphony Orchestra under Sir Henry Wood. He was impressed by Sir Henry, and the rehearsals for the Brahms went well; however, in performance the Brahms did not go well: 'The good Brosa failed. I held on to Wood otherwise the whole thing would have fallen apart. He was so excited he could neither see nor hear.'[91] But Ernest Newman, reviewing for *The Times*, failed to notice any difficulties: 'Antonio Brosa and Emanuel Feuermann were an ideally matched pair of soloists.'[92] Feuermann was, however, pleased with his Bach:

> I was quite satisfied. It must have sounded very voluminous in the large hall. I hardly got tired and felt secure so that my fingers didn't run away. It was the first time that I played a Bach suite according to <u>my</u> idea and I wasn't disappointed <u>in myself</u>. The success was enormous. After I had gone out 5 times the people were still clapping and eventually the conductor just went out instead of me to put an end to it. By the way such a promenade concert is something fabulous, sold out, and at least a dozen women faint.[93]

Reid Stewart in *The Strad* was even more emphatic: 'I do not think that there can any longer be any doubt that Feuermann is the greatest living cellist, Casals alone excepted. . . . His facility is only one facet of a musicianly equipage that amounts to genius; it is allied to a powerful rich tone and a sweeping type of phrasing that is Titanic in conception.'[94]

Chapter 11

Breaks
October 1938 to February 1939

America is the last frontier of freedom for artists. Here, the idea that a musician or composer would be barred because of his racial background would be as ridiculous as it would be for me to destroy my Stradivarius cello because it was made by an Italian.

Emanuel Feuermann[1]

'A dark brown costume, very distinguished for nice luncheons in New York, warm with brown Nutria fur; a little short afternoon dress, plum colour; a white <u>very</u> simple, <u>beautiful</u> evening dress.'[2] While Feuermann was performing in London, his wife was in Paris buying clothes for an October arrival in New York. A decision had been taken to leave Europe and settle in the United States. Eva later recalled: 'It was terrible in Switzerland especially. That is why we had to leave. It [talk of war] was all around. There was no possibility to play any more.'[3] Eva was also attempting to obtain a visa for her mother. A friend had fixed an appointment at the US Embassy with the head of the passport department, but things were not good: 'I will go there on Thursday morning. I don't know what we will do if everywhere they refuse the visa.'[4] Feuermann was still planning to go to Palestine, which Eva in the current political circumstances considered senseless: 'Schiff says that if the situation in October is still the same as it is now, it would be obvious that you could not go because everybody thinks there will be war. . . . Please see to it that it is settled amicably with Simon that you do not go.'[5] A letter in early September suggests that

Feuermann had already cancelled his visit: 'I asked young Flesch[6] to send me a written declaration that Lloyds wouldn't cover any damage to myself and my cello under the present circumstances. This written declaration I will receive this afternoon. Thus I won't be a breaker of contracts.'[7] And a week earlier Feuermann had written to Schnabel: 'I have been engaged to play with the orchestra in Palestine, in the middle of October, but I fear that because of the prevailing conditions I will not be able to go.'[8] Feuermann was no longer in possession of a passport, only a Swiss travel document; in another letter to Schnabel he wrote:

> You cannot imagine the fear in which we live at the moment. On 26 October I am supposed to go to America with Eva and our little Monica. I've just been standing at the French Consulate for hours to get a transit visa only to be told that I could only have a visa for a specific boat and would have to show the tickets. It is horrendous to be deprived of one's freedom of movement.'[9]

Towards the end of August, Feuermann asked Schnabel to take part in a benefit concert to raise money for Jewish refugees from Germany:

> I feel very positive towards such an idea and I think that if you, Huberman and I would give such a concert in Zürich, a lot of money would be raised and apart from that it would be fun for us. What do you think? Personally, I obviously feel an obligation to do everything I possibly can for my fellow sufferers – and I hope that you feel the same.[10]

He must have regretted Schnabel's reply, but a second letter from Feuermann reveals that he himself had had second thoughts: 'I am sorry that on principle you are against charity concerts. In this specific case of playing in Switzerland for the Jews, i.e. to give big concerts, I have also changed my mind . . . because one should not bother the public with our worries and because there are sufficient rich Jews who will offer help.'[11]

Feuermann was anxious to see Schnabel, but Schnabel was living on Lake Como in Italy and Feuermann could no longer enter Italy:

> Assuming that you continue to have freedom of movement, will you come to Switzerland in the near future? Surely you will be going to London soon. Will you then not go by Switzerland? Will you come through Zürich? If not, would it be possible for you to make a stop in Lucerne or Basel if you don't travel by car? I would so much like to meet you since I want to ask you many things, including an important point about the trio recordings which one cannot very easily discuss in writing.[12]

By a week later, however, everything had changed: '*I couldn't stand it any more so I suddenly decided yesterday that we shall sail as soon as possible instead of waiting here whether there will be war or not. So we are sailing on Saturday on the SS* Statendam.'[13] Feuermann was now in possession of Affidavit of Identity no.498, issued by the chief of police in Bern and granted on 27 July 1938, as well as US Quota Immigration Visa no.981, which had been issued by the American Consul in Zürich on 3 August. 'Mr and Mrs Emanuel Feuermann and Miss Monica Feuermann' are listed as Cabin Class passengers on the twin screw turbine steamer *Statendam* leaving Rotterdam on 1 October 1938 for New York. The *Statendam* carried 1139 passengers, 350 of them refugees from central Europe. Misha Elman's sister was among the passengers who took care of a very seasick Eva Feuermann. The boat arrived late, storms and gales causing severe damage.

For the first few days after their arrival, the Feuermanns stayed in the Dorset Hotel, after which they took an apartment at 100 Pelham Road in New Rochelle, north-east of New York City, overlooking the Sound. Feuermann is said to have had little work at this time, but a schedule of engagements issued by NBC Artists for the period 22 October 1938 to 24 January 1939 lists 27 concerts, an average of almost 10 a month. For the time and for a cellist, this was plenty of work. His first engagement took place on 22 October. Less than a month earlier, Feuermann had still had the intention of visiting Palestine at this time, so this date appears to have been very hastily arranged. And yet it was an extremely prestigious concert: a live performance and broadcast over NBC's Blue Network from Radio City in New York with the NBC Orchestra and Toscanini. The *New York Herald Tribune* noted: 'He will be the first soloist to be heard in one of Mr Toscanini's radio concerts with this orchestra.'[14] Once again, Feuermann repeated his triumph in Strauss's *Don Quixote* with Toscanini: 'No such performance of this music had ever before been achieved in New York', wrote Chotzinoff.[15]

Feuermann had become not only a star but also a personality recruited to endorse products such as Chesterfield cigarettes and the *New York Post*'s special offer of symphonic masterpieces (see Plate 15). The *New York Post* was using records as bait to increase its circulation:

> Anyone who plays these wonderful recordings over a few times – be he tone-deaf or jazz mad – could not fail to be stirred sufficiently to delve further into music's wonderful realm. . . . It has been my observation that the first step in teaching people to appreciate good music is to overpower them completely by sheer majesty. You cannot acquire a love of music by listening to simple pieces first and gradually working up to more complex ones. The

THE NATIONAL BROADCASTING COMPANY

Presents

ARTURO TOSCANINI

Conducting the

NBC SYMPHONY ORCHESTRA

EMANUEL FEUERMANN, SOLOIST

SATURDAY, OCTOBER 22, 1938
10:00 to 11:30 P.M., EST.
In NBC Studio 8-H, Radio City

Program

Overture to "Cenerentola, Ossia la bontà in trionfo"
("Cinderella, or Virtue Triumphant") . . . *Gioacchino Rossini*

* * *

"Don Quixote", Fantastic Variations on a Theme of
Knightly Character, Opus 35 . . . . *Richard Strauss*
Emanuel Feuermann, Solo Cellist
Carlton Cooley, Solo Violist

Introduction: Don Quixote and the Snapping of His
Overstretched Imagination

Theme: Don Quixote, the Knight of Sorrowful
Countenance, and Sancho Panza

Variation I:	The Battle with the Windmills
Variation II:	The Battle with the Sheep
Variation III:	Dialogues of the Knight and the Esquire
Variation IV:	Attack of the Penitent Pilgrims
Variation V:	The Knight's Vigil
Variation VI:	The False Dulcinea
Variation VII:	The Ride through the Air
Variation VIII:	The Voyage in the Enchanted Boat
Variation IX:	The Combat with the Two Magicians
Variation X:	The Defeat of Don Quixote
Finale:	Don Quixote's Peaceful End

Symphony No. 5, in C minor, Opus 67 . . . *Ludwig van Beethoven*
I. Allegro con brio
II. Andante con moto
III. Scherzo: Allegro
IV. Allegro

(over)

best way to give people a love of music is to make them listen to music so overpowering in its beauty and force that they are stunned into listening.

In this same article, Feuermann, who since 1934 had toured the USA every year, recorded his observations on music in America:

> I am amazed at the growing interest in music here. There is nothing like it in Europe, which seems to be resting on a musical tradition of centuries. But the United States is doing something about music. I have never seen so many schools with such fine music departments – so many clubs that exist just for music. Every child appears to be studying music in some form.

The article reveals that Feuermann had decided to take the first steps towards becoming an American citizen: 'America is the last frontier of freedom for artists. Here, the idea that a musician or composer would be barred because of his racial background would be as ridiculous as it would be for me to destroy my Stradivarius cello because it was made by an Italian.'[16]

On Monday 7 November, Feuermann performed not only in New York's Town Hall for the New Friends of Music with their newly established orchestra under Fritz Stiedry, a fellow European exile, but also at the Brooklyn Academy of Music with John Barbirolli and the Philharmonic-Symphony Chamber Orchestra. 'Europe's loss is America's gain in the case of Emanuel Feuermann', signalled the *Brooklyn Eagle*: 'It is no exaggeration to compare him favourably with Pablo Casals, Catalonia's great cellist whose achievements on this difficult instrument have long been considered unequalled.'[17] Feuermann had played C.P.E. Bach in New York and the Haydn D major Concerto in Brooklyn. During the rehearsal, Barbirolli had asked Feuermann about his fiendishly difficult first-movement cadenza: 'Now in your solo passage how do you end?' Not hesitating for a moment, Feuermann replied: 'Out of tune!'[18]

Touring then began: Bloomington, Indiana; Davenport, Iowa; Lincoln, Nebraska; Oberlin, Ohio; and Duluth, Minnesota. Eva remained in New Rochelle with the baby. Whether it was the effect of precipitously leaving Europe, the absence of Mrs Reifenberg's support or simply the wide intellectual gap between Emanuel and Eva, strains in the marriage were beginning to show in Eva's letters:

> What a pest I was, poor you – always this business of repenting, what's the use of it, so foolish. I *could* be so nice and I do want to be nice. I don't know what makes me that way, some nasty evil has gotten hold of me, I guess. . . . If only I could relax for one minute when you are with me how perfectly lovely it would be.[19]

But her *naïveté* towards the man she had married was clear: '*For the first time since 3 years, I thought today: I am the wife of a famous artist and even he loves me. I start to become proud, I am already proud after your Brooklyn concert.*'[20]

For the moment, they had escaped Europe, but Feuermann was only too aware of how quickly politics could change, even in America:

> I follow the newspapers *very* carefully. The elections seem to show that America is distant from Hitler and Mussolini. But we gradually understand how easily a people can be converted. For the moment, I do not think this is the case in America although there is a concealed campaign, particularly against the Jews. One can only hope.[21]

Feuermann had played in Bloomington two years earlier, and now the university employed a number of people connected with him: 'The cello teacher is from Weggberg, an old Finn, the piano teacher from Cologne, the dean a friend of the Saidenbergs.' Acquaintances came to his concert: 'From Indianapolis came the Strausens – she is a pupil of Alexanian – Miss Essex, Mrs Sevitzky whom you met in Gstaad, a critic, etc. Four cellists also came in the car from I[ndiana]polis. On the way they ruined their car and went to the next gas station——where a fifth cellist on his way to the concert passed by and took them along.'[22]

Feuermann was using a number of different pianists: in Davenport he played with John Gurney, in Bloomington with his long-term partner, Fritz Kitzinger, and in Oberlin with Franz Rupp. This appears to have been Feuermann's first engagement with Rupp (born in Bavaria in 1901), who from 1930 to 1938 was Fritz Kreisler's partner; it was with him that Kreisler recorded all the Beethoven sonatas in 1936. Rupp, whose wife was Jewish, followed Kreisler to the United States in 1938; however, they ceased playing together and Carl Lamson became Kreisler's exclusive partner in the United States. Rupp had met Feuermann in Germany but they had not performed together. Rupp, also with NBC Artists, now became Feuermann's principal recital partner, a relationship that was to continue until February 1941. Rupp later said: 'Emanuel Feuermann was the most accomplished instrumentalist I ever played with. In the same way that Heifetz set new standards in violin playing, Feuermann's mastery of the cello was unparalleled.' But their relationship was not a close one. 'He did not tolerate mistakes, and was often bothered by the most trivial matters. Feuermann's cynical and sarcastic manner could occasionally be off-putting, but his artistry was always sublime.' They rehearsed at Rupp's studio in New York. 'Unlike Kreisler, Feuermann loved to rehearse. He constantly strove for perfection, and worked everything out to the last detail.'[23] Feuermann may have needed to practise little, but rehearsing was another matter.

Feuermann's status as an entertainer is testified by the fact that on 20 November he was back in New York playing for the *Magic Key of RCA*, a radio programme from Radio City Music Hall with Milton Cross as host and Clifton Fadiman as master of ceremonies. In a programme of light music, including *Follies of 1919*, *A Pretty Girl is like a Melody* and *Farmer in the Dell*, Feuermann, somewhat incongruously, played the slow movement of Dvořák's Cello Concerto with the Magic Key Orchestra conducted by Dr Frank Black.[24] His fee of $600 for this appearance was significantly larger than the fee of $350 paid to him for his concert broadcast of *Don Quixote* with Toscanini and the NBC.

Soon after that, Feuermann gave his first concerts in Philadelphia. In a life and career so short, his relationship with the Philadelphia Orchestra was to be his most significant with any professional orchestra. Under Leopold Stokowski, this orchestra had become the finest in America, and from this point until his death Feuermann appeared with them in every season; the recordings that he began making in December 1939 provide one of his greatest legacies. His first appearances, on 25 and 26 November, took place within the framework of a four-concert cycle devoted to Brahms. Eugene Ormandy had recently become music director after a period as co-conductor to Leopold Stokowski, and it was under his direction that Feuermann and Erica Morini opened the Brahms cycle with the Double Concerto. Morini had been a childhood friend of the Feuermanns in Vienna and had also been sponsored by Wilhelm Kux. Like Sigmund, she had studied with Otakar Ševčík. Now, aged 27, she was widely regarded as one of the finest women violinists. Henry Pleasants, in reviewing this concert, could not help noting: 'Miss Morini and Mr Feuermann are not members of the same family, but the quality of their ensemble suggested both a long association and exceptional musicianship. . . . It would be hard to find another cellist and another violinist so perfectly qualified to give a just account of this particular work.'[25] Their shared musical background in Europe was doubtless a strong contribution. Once again, a critic observed of Feuermann: 'playing like his has not been heard in Philadelphia since the last appearance of Pablo Casals'.[26] In this 1938/9 season, Feuermann was the only solo cellist to be engaged by the Philadelphia, whereas ten pianists (including Gieseking, Rachmaninov and Rubinstein), six violinists (including Mischa Elman, Fritz Kreisler and Jascha Heifetz) and eight singers (including Kirsten Flagstad, Lotte Lehmann and Marian Anderson) all made appearances. As the critic Irving Kolodin once remarked, a gathering of cellists in protest at Feuermann's success might well have been expected.

With scarcely time to draw breath, two days after the Philadelphia concerts, Feuermann gave what was to become his annual November recital in Carnegie Hall. Assisted by Franz Rupp, the structure of the programme was his usual one: Handel, Tartini's variations on Corelli, the Bach Suite in E♭, Chopin's Cello Sonata op.65, and a group of salon pieces by Mozart, Senaillé, Dvořák and Lalo. *Cue* magazine believed the performance of the Chopin to be its American premiere.[27] Kolodin doubted it, but could not recall another performance in half a dozen years: 'When the performance was over, one reason for avoidance of the Chopin by many cellists was evident: few soloists are blessed by the collaboration of such a pianist as Franz Rupp to play the difficult and closely woven piano part.'[28] Another critic was particularly impressed by the Bach suite.

For a player of Feuermann's musical intuition, it is striking that as he matured he became not more but less certain about how to play Bach's suites. During the Cologne years, Reger's unaccompanied suites turned up more frequently in his programmes than those of Bach, but Feuermann's playing of Bach was nevertheless praised. Only after 1923, having left Cologne, do Bach's suites, in particular the sixth, appear regularly in his programmes. It is tempting to speculate that the unaccompanied suites – with the exception of the sixth – did not provide a technical challenge. But for the acutely intelligent

Feuermann, his unease seems to have been more to do with a state of temperament. He had written that he did not feel comfortable playing the suites. He also found Casals's recordings of Bach 'wrong', although he never spelt out clearly what he meant by this remark. As Feuermann disliked Casals's interpretation, the fact that Casals enjoyed such success with the suites must have caused Feuermann to be less certain about his own approach. The E♭ Suite, however, was the one he had just played at the Proms in London, a performance with which he had been pleased. American critics were also impressed by his performance of this piece on 28 November: 'Only a player of Mr Feuermann's abilities could impart to Bach's E♭ cello suite an interest not implicit in the music itself. Anyone who has heard a mediocre cellist perform this suite knows how endless and sapless it can sound.' The Bach Suites were to remain unapproachable to many for a very long time; the same reviewer regarded the works by Handel and Tartini in the programme as of far greater intrinsic value than the Bach or the Chopin.[29] Once again, Feuermann's musicianship was celebrated: 'little doubt that he belongs at the head of the class among cellists. One might put it more strongly and say that Mr Feuermann belongs in the front rank of musical interpreters, whatever the instrument.'[30] It had taken him little more than three years to achieve this accolade in perhaps the world's toughest musical environment.

Days after the Carnegie Hall recital, Feuermann applied for American citizenship. A newspaper read: 'Two leading exponents of German art and German music who left Nazi Germany as exiles, adopted the United States yesterday as their homeland.'[31] The artist was the painter and caricaturist George Grosz. Feuermann's request was widely reported in the press. Mrs Reifenberg, in London at the time, had been unaware that the family would not be returning to live in Switzerland and was very upset.

For some time Emma Reifenberg and other members of the family had been locked in difficult negotiations with Kurt (who had assumed business control of the Reifenberg company) over complicated arrangements to move Reifenberg money out of Germany. Feuermann had tried with relative success to mediate. Exactly how large Mrs Reifenberg's fortune was is unclear (Reifenberg & Cie was sold), but certainly it was substantial. An indication of how poor her relationship with Sophie had become and how strong her influence was within the family, is evident from Mrs Reifenberg's Christmas plans for 1938. She wanted to give money to those in need and instructed Feuermann to give $10 each to various friends and relatives. But to Sophie, now living in the United States with her husband, Harry, she would cheerfully have given money to rid Feuermann of her: 'with those people you have to be absolutely finished. I will not rest until then. Damn it, such an ungrateful pack.

It must be the last time you play with her, <u>that</u> I gladly take upon myself.'[32] Why Mrs Reifenberg was so angry is not clear.

Despite Emma Reifenberg's views, Feuermann continued to perform with Sophie. Following concerts with the Pittsburgh Symphony Orchestra and their new music director, Fritz Reiner, he travelled to San Juan and Ponce in Puerto Rico, where in December he gave two recitals with Sophie as pianist: 'Rehearsed this morning with Sophie, who seems to be very nervous. Fortunately we are playing the same programme each evening.'[33] The programme was a demanding one for the pianist: a transcription of the Lalo Concerto in D minor, Schubert's 'Arpeggione', and pieces from Feuermann's usual repertoire, by Handel, Tartini, Senaillé and Dvořák, recently performed at Carnegie Hall with Franz Rupp. We have only Sophie's account of what happened between them in Puerto Rico:

> We were close, but I was proud. I went with him to Puerto Rico and I played with him because I had to play. I had to make a few pennies. I knew all the repertoire. He had no way of getting rid of me, breaking with me, but that's what the family wanted – the Reifenbergs. So what did he do with his phenomenal talent on the stage? At the concert he changed everything; the tempi, everything and he got infuriated because I jumped with him. He couldn't say I'm not good enough. I jumped with him because I knew him. It is psychological. Everything was different. I didn't say a word. I wrote a letter. He flew home to New York and we were supposed to play at a big club. He didn't pay me to fly. He didn't pay me anything when I played with him so I took the boat. But I took my last few pennies, had a pageboy go to the airport with the letter that I wrote to him to make sure that it arrived with him. And I wrote in this letter 'I will not play with you any more. I want to make music. I cannot play like this. It is impossible.' That is when I broke.[34]

Sophie always believed that Mrs Reifenberg was responsible for ruining her career. She maintains that Feuermann offered her a contract to play 60 concerts and that it was rescinded on the advice and pressure of Mrs Reifenberg. Apparently the Reifenbergs 'took over' Feuermann, who was weak-willed, and as a result he abandoned his own family. But there is no trace of this contract. What seems more likely is that Feuermann's American management ruled against Sophie. NBC acknowledged difficulty in selling a cellist and may have advised Feuermann against playing with a female relative. Yehudi Menuhin may have been successfully touring at this time with his pianist sister, Hephzibah, but the case was not parallel; however great an artist, Feuermann was a cellist, not a violinist. From that moment in December 1938 until May 1942, Sophie never met her brother again. The professional consequences of this break may not, for Feuermann, have been serious, but the personal consequences were arguably fatal: if the quarrel had not occurred, Sophie might perhaps have been able to intervene positively in his medical treatment three years later.

Feuermann's surviving letters do not mention the break with Sophie. She was closer to him than any of his other siblings and had seen and shared aspects of his life with the Reifenbergs, indeed frequently benefiting from them. He genuinely enjoyed working with her and had tried to help her career. Many have testified to the musical closeness they enjoyed with each other. He was touchingly sympathetic at the time of her realization that she would never be the artist she had hoped to become. She was a perfectionist, hard on herself and hard on others, making demands that appeared relentless. As the youngest child, a girl within a family that had produced not one but two prodigies, both boys, there was little room for her and doubtless she had to fight. Many of her concerts with Feuermann were well reviewed, but there were no recordings and no broadcasts of hers have survived. Feuermann may have been difficult at those two concerts in Puerto Rico and Sophie may have been right in her reaction, but the professional consequences for her were disastrous.

The 'big club' to which Sophie referred was no doubt Mr Bagby's 40th Musical Morning, held at the Waldorf Astoria on 26 December. 'Mrs Sophie Braun' is listed in the programme as 'at the piano', as well as Rainaldo Zamboni and Celius Dougherty. It is not known who actually accompanied Feuermann, but it was certainly not Sophie. He played Tartini, Schumann and Klengel alongside vocal contributions from Dusolina Giannini and Beniamino Gigli. That evening he performed again, this time in Carnegie Hall in a benefit concert for German and Austrian refugees, with Mischa Elman, Rudolf Serkin and Hulda Lashanska; Governor Lehmann made the opening remarks. While Feuermann had been in Puerto Rico, Mischa Schneider had sat in for him at rehearsals. Commenting on the rehearsals, Rudolf Serkin observed that Elman played Tchaikovsky convincingly but with loads of schmaltz – not a style that Feuermann would have favoured; whereas in the Mendelssohn he was somewhat restrained. The concert was a sell out, with 'a special Jewish audience', as Serkin remarked.[35] The programme comprised the Mendelssohn D minor and Tchaikovsky A minor trios, and an arrangement by Halvorsen of a Handel passacaglia, played by Elman and Feuermann; the trio then accompanied Lashanska in Schubert's *Litanei*, Brahms's *Die Mainacht* and Ochs's *Dank sei dir, Herr*.[36] Just over two weeks later Feuermann recorded the Ochs aria and the Schubert with his colleagues for RCA Victor. This would result in serious consequences for his relationship with Columbia.

Feuermann's recording situation was still not resolved. His contract was to expire on 31 December and Columbia in London were supposed to have been negotiating an extension on Nipponophone's behalf. By 24 December, with only seven days of the contract to run, Hans Straus was desperate and wrote to Rex Palmer:

> We would be indebted if you would approach Feuermann (100 Pelham Road, New Rochelle, N.Y.) and suggest to him renewal of the contract either in our name or your name. We would appreciate if you will do your best to keep Feuermann on the Columbia list, who is in our opinion the No.1 cellist of today, superior to Piatigorsky, and not taking into consideration Casals, whose latest recordings, in our opinion, do not show his old vigor.[37]

To make matters more confused, Feuermann had lost his copy of the contract and was uncertain whether under the original terms he owed more discs to Nipponophone. In January he had been assured that with what he had recorded in June 1936 in Japan and with the Haydn D major Concerto, Beethoven A major Sonata, Schubert 'Arpeggione' and Weber Andantino, and variations from the *Konzertstück*, the requirement to record a minimum of 15 double-sides had been met. By January 1939, however, Nipponophone was demanding four more sides of *'dirty little pieces'*, as Feuermann put it. He could choose the pieces. He wrote: '*I think I shall have the opportunity to play at least two good ones*', and proceeded to recommend the Reger unaccompanied Suite in G major (which had never been recorded) and two movements from Bach's E♭ Suite.[38] A month later in England, Feuermann learnt that far from there being four sides to be recorded, seven sides were owed, since the Haydn Concerto and the Weber Andantino recordings had been made under an arrangement drawn up before the current contract. Well after the expiry of the contract, Palmer coolly wrote:

> I was going to suggest that you agreed to the extension of this contract for another year, during which we would take these 7 titles and say another 7, to include a Beethoven Sonata, one or two popular pieces and possibly the Unaccompanied Reger Suite which you propose, although I must warn you that the latter will not be welcomed by our Branch Managers as they consider that the sales of such a work will be very small indeed.[39]

And he continued: 'The position, however, is complicated by the fact that you recorded for the Victor Company last month. Did you make any solos in addition to the record with Lashanska, Elman and Serkin and have you engaged in a period contract with Victor?' Was Palmer berating Feuermann or was he, belatedly, finally seeing the light? Feuermann did indeed honour his contract. The Reger was recorded but not the Bach. In its place were the 'dirty little pieces': Drigo's 'Les Millions d'Arlequin', Cui's *Orientale* op.50 no.9, 'Chant Hindou' from Rimsky-Korsakov's *Sadko* and Albéniz's *Tango* op.165 no.2. But the course of events could have been of little surprise to Palmer, who wrote: 'I saw Feuermann immediately on his arrival in this country and regret to inform you that he has signed a contract with the Victor Company in America to begin 1 April 1939.'[40]

Feuermann left the United States on 28 January 1939 with Eva and his daughter, for concerts (and recording) in various countries: England, the Netherlands, Switzerland and Bulgaria. As he put it: 'the only ones left us in Europe, except for Scandinavia'.[41] His last weeks in North America were hectic. Before leaving he had performed in New York (Bach's Sixth Suite in a concert given by the Budapest Quartet for the New Friends of Music); Toronto, with the Toronto Symphony and Sir Ernest MacMillan (Dvořák Concerto); Montreal, at the Ladies Morning Club with Franz Rupp; Orange, New Jersey; Lubbock, Texas; Hollywood; Manitowoc, Wisconsin; and finally, on 24 January, in Chicago with Daniel Saidenberg's Sinfonietta. The pace was relentless and some travel arrangements he concealed from his wife: 'Do you notice something? I am already writing today from Los Angeles! I have to own up to you that I came by train today from Lubbock to Amarillo and from there flew here. I always knew that I would have to fly again but didn't want to worry you. Is that very bad??? My first real fib since we are married!'[42] A year before he had assured Eva that he would never fly, even if it meant missing a good concert.[43] Despite the fact that aeroplane accidents were daily reported, Feuermann was exhilarated:

> A cloudless sky, but a few times it did bump. We flew all along the Grand Canyon, which was in the truest sense of the word indescribably magnificent and beautiful. I would never have imagined that I would see this once from above. It was a great experience and I had to think of the wonderful day that we spent there. Then we flew over the Boulder Dam – not bad either. . . . The flight was wonderful, but I was glad nevertheless when we arrived here – and I had and still have a very bad conscience towards you.[44]

He had taken the flight to Los Angeles in order to take part in the *Kraft Music Hall* radio broadcast from Hollywood with Bing Crosby and Bob Burns as hosts. He found that he had to practise his dialogue with Bing Crosby: 'It was again terribly funny, Anita Louise plucked the harp a little bit etc. etc., Bob Burns really very funny – but I was pretty bad, unfortunately, don't know why.' While in Los Angeles, Feuermann slipped into one of Klemperer's rehearsals. The Los Angeles Philharmonic Orchestra was preparing for a concert with

Artur Rubinstein; but, to Feuermann's irritation, the rehearsal for *Kraft Music Hall* forced him to leave before the Tchaikovsky Concerto. He did, however, manage to see Arnold Schönberg at the University of California: 'I was very sad to see this man with his pupils. My God, that gave me a blow. We were only able to talk a short time.'[45] What did they talk about? It seems likely that they discussed Schönberg's latest ideas for works for cello. In December, Schönberg had written to Feuermann about his intention to arrange 'one or several of the cello sonatas by Bach (from the "Ninth Jahrgang" of the *Bach-Gesellschaft* by Breitkopf and Haertel) for cello and orchestra.' He intended taking the sonatas for viola da gamba, leaving the solo voice unchanged but adding a 'more brilliant version (at least in part) besides the original part'. He also contemplated 'interspersing one or several cadenzas (ad libitum, of course)'. He wrote: 'You are the first person I ask, even though you do not perform my Monn any more, because you played it really extraordinarily well.'[46] Once again he offered a range of options on the performance rights. Feuermann replied:

I am enthusiastic about your idea to create a Bach concerto for us cellists. I find your idea wonderful and I will be grateful when it becomes a reality. Unfortunately, I cannot consider your proposals concerning performance rights, etc. The reason is purely financial; due to my various commitments it is really impossible at present. The other reason is that because of the availability no longer of Germany, the number of orchestral concerts is quite reduced and with it the possibility of performing such a concerto. What I believe I can promise is a considerable number of performances in America, England and Holland. It would be very unfortunate if in this case, too, wretched money were to throw a wrench in the works.'[47]

Feuermann was clearly recalling Schönberg's proposal to him in 1934, with a similar range of options on the Monn concerto that had led nowhere. Schönberg, anticipating a favourable reply from Feuermann, began work on a concerto based on Bach's Sonata for viola da gamba in G major (BWV 1027). Although he sketched a few bars, the project went no further.

The contrast between life in America and life in Europe at this time was extreme. Mrs Reifenberg wrote to Feuermann in January 1939: 'What you write about concerts sounds like a fairy-tale of bygone days, for that's how it was for us in Germany. I am thinking about my childhood and youth that is prehistoric!!'[48] Mrs Reifenberg, who was now in London, seems never to have been under direct threat, and received Feuermann's letters with equanimity. She was active, helping friends and relatives who were in a much less favourable position, still able to travel between Cologne, Paris, Zürich and London with little hindrance. Money was no problem. Feuermann's parents were grateful for the help they received from her and Lily Mayer's husband, Leo Hofmann. Finally they escaped to Palestine. Of Feuermann's mother Mrs Reifenberg wrote: 'She is completely helpless regarding her sea voyage. I will relieve her of her fear. I am altogether very strong with her and repeatedly have to tell her that she isn't the worst off which is what she is saying all the time.'[49]

Feuermann, too, having had to cancel his visit to Palestine the previous October, was now planning to go there in April and May, this time for concerts with Malcolm Sargent. Before that, however, he had a couple of engagements with Sargent in London. The two had last worked together on the ill-fated recording of the Haydn Cello Concerto in November 1935; now, in February 1939, Feuermann took part in the tenth series of the Courtauld-Sargent Concerts.

Schnabel had been influential in setting up the Courtauld-Sargent Concerts:

One day Mrs Courtauld told me she was a little tired of supporting Covent Garden Opera, which she had done continuously since the First World War, and asked me whether I knew of something else they could do on behalf of music. So I devised the plan of the Courtauld-Sargent concerts, which soon became a regular institution, were extremely successful and should be imitated everywhere.'[50]

Schnabel's plan was an enlightened one. A series of symphony concerts was presented for those music lovers unable to pay the high price of tickets to regular symphony concerts. Membership was restricted to employees of department stores, smaller stores, shops, banks and other firms, with each firm obliged to take at least six subscriptions. Six concerts were presented per year, each concert given twice. The series was named the Courtauld-Sargent Concerts because Sargent became its regular conductor. The concerts were very successful, always fully subscribed with a particularly appreciative audience. By the tenth series, the Courtauld-Sargent Concerts had expanded. Nine concerts alone were scheduled at the Queen's Hall and Royal Opera House between 30 January and 11 February, with the London Symphony Orchestra, the BBC Symphony Orchestra and the London Philharmonic Orchestra, and Weingartner, Adrian Boult, Charles Hambourg, Beecham and Sargent as conductors. On 6 and 7 February, Feuermann played the Dvořák Concerto with the London Philharmonic. These concerts also included a rarity: Haydn's Concertante in B♭ for violin, oboe, cello and bassoon performed by section principals John Alexandra, Leon Goosens, David McCallum and Anthony Pini. Feuermann was well known for his pranks backstage and it seems likely that it was at one of these concerts that, minutes before going on to play, to Sargent's fury, he was seen calmly walking round balancing his bow on his nose.[51] Nevertheless, Ernest Newman found Feuermann's Dvořák 'burnished with ineffable virtuosity'.[52] Earlier in the day on 7 February, Feuermann had recorded the Reger Suite.

A short tour of England included a recital at the Holmsdale Fine Arts Club in Redhill in which Feuermann was accompanied by Gerald Moore (a concert shared with the pianist Eileen Joyce and the singer Ivor John) and a 'Grand Concert' on 12 February in the Palace Theatre, Burnley, in which, despite the presence of the Municipal Symphony Orchestra, Feuermann played solo works. The orchestra accompanied Isobel Baillie in 'Dove sono', the Countess's aria from Mozart's *Marriage of Figaro*. The following day, Feuermann was in Ireland for the Royal Dublin Society where he again gave two recitals on the same day (at 3.00 p.m. and at 8.15 p.m.), with the pianist Ernest Lush. Apart from Stravinsky's *Suite italienne*, the repertoire was standard: the Lalo Concerto, Schubert's 'Arpeggione', Beethoven's A major Sonata op.69 and Valentini's E major Sonata, with the customary 'salon' pieces to end the programme.

Feuermann's schedule was heavy. Eva believed it was too heavy.[53] Three days later, he was in Amsterdam playing the Schumann Concerto with the Concertgebouw and Eduard van Beinum. Eva heard this concert on the radio and was full of praise, addressing him in her letter as 'Engelsbild' ('image of an angel').[54] She and the baby had returned from America with Feuermann perhaps hoping that the situation in Europe could yet allow them to stay. She was reluctant to leave Europe, but it did not take long for her to realize that they would have to move permanently to the United States. She would cope. They were fortunate to have visas, but she was concerned for other relatives and friends unable either to get visas to the USA or to leave Germany. For her, the prospect of meeting Sophie cast a shadow on proceedings, for relations between them, never easy, had deteriorated completely following the events in Puerto Rico.

On 19 February, still in Holland, Feuermann once again caught up with the pianist Theo van der Pas, with whom he had recorded Brahms and smaller works for distribution in Japan before his first tour in 1934. Now in the Hague they played Locatelli, the Chopin Sonata and Stravinsky, to which Feuermann added Bach's Sixth Suite. This programme was repeated on 27 February, but before then Feuermann returned to England, where in Liverpool the local critic was grudging and vehemently anti-Bach:

I should have supposed that a Philharmonic audience would be superior to the silly, and greedy habit of demanding an encore after so fine a performance he gave us of the Tchaikovsky variations. It must have been a piece by that 'dreadful bore', Bach, which he played unaccompanied, as his unnecessary encore, but Bach is only a bore in the wrong place and this was the wrong place. Nevertheless, Feuermann's playing was the outstanding event of this concert. I wish I could compliment the orchestra.[55]

The next day Feuermann was in Leeds with Gerald Moore where the programme book carried an illuminating gloss on his career: 'In 1929 he was appointed to the Faculty of the Berlin Hochschule, but his concert engagements throughout the world prevented his continuing in this position.' He rounded off his tour in England on 23 February with another concert for the Hallé Concerts Society in Manchester. Once again Sargent was the conductor, and once again Feuermann was playing the Dvořák Concerto. Neville Cardus reviewed the event for the *Manchester Guardian*: 'Dr Sargent conducted watchfully and well, so that Feuermann was free to go his ways untroubled. And so we were momentarily enabled to forget the world outside, the wretched night, and what not. These are the divine visitations which, though they come but rarely in the concert hall, make the public dissemination of music a blessing to mankind.'[56]

Chapter 12

Trios
March to November 1939

I am thrilled that the recordings will really happen. I am looking forward to it and I will try my best that my 33⅓% will turn out beautifully.[1]

It was almost three years since Fred Gaisberg had first mooted the idea of Schnabel, Huberman and Feuermann recording together. In July 1938, the trios finally looked like going ahead. Nipponophone had merged with the Japanese Victor Company. But although the difficulties caused by the exclusivity of the three artists to different recording companies had now been resolved, sorting out the availability of each musician to record was to prove a nightmare. Added to the expected difficulties of matching the free time of three exceptionally busy musicians, Huberman had been involved in an air crash and, although he was lucky to have escaped alive, suffered injuries to his hands and arms. As Feuermann wrote to Schnabel in July 1938:

> Huberman, understandably, is not quite on top form either emotionally or psychologically. . . . He has not regained the necessary confidence in himself and in order to give him a little push we have arranged to play trios at our place. I'm not sure that it will really happen, I really fear that the accident and current events have not made Huberman any stronger. I presume that you have direct news of him. Since you are sympathetic to the idea of a trio and since I would be very happy to join you, any difficulties if there are any would be with Huberman.[2]

This was to prove correct. By February 1939 not much progress had been made. A 'Celebrity tour' for the trio in England organized by Harold Holt, around which the recordings were planned, would not take place. Despite the fact that Feuermann had signed a contract with RCA Victor to begin in April, certain Columbia projects were still in the pipeline. On 10 March, Feuermann wrote to Palmer setting out his activities as far as he could see: June 1939 in America for summer concerts and teaching; Europe at the beginning of September for the trio recordings; October in the USA; Europe for a tour in February 1940. In this same letter, he asked:

1) *Will You arrange with Victor [the record company] to 'ok' the Trio recordings?;*

2) *Will there be a recording of the Brahms Double concerto? I am afraid there will not be time for it as I shall not be able to be here before round Sept. 10th;*

3) *As I told You when I had the pleasure to have tea with You and Mr Gaisberg there is the question of the fare New York–Europe–New York in the case the Celebrity tour will not take place. The expenses will amount to 100 Pound. When Mr. Gaisberg over the telephone mentioned the sacrifices the HMV were ready to make I quite naturally thought of the expenses in question and I am almost sure that You will understand my point of view.*

He had been counting on Holt to pay these expenses.

Feuermann also added a fourth point: '*will You send me a letter in which You confirm all the details, as up to now I do not have in my hands anything written about the whole affaire.*' But his final sentence seemed to sum up the whole project: '*As I wrote to Huberman the other day: we need a dictator because it looks hopeless to get things settled between us three.*'[3]

Huberman, indeed, understood the dates very differently and he wanted to 'run in' the trios with public performances. Far from the recordings taking place in September, he envisaged a rehearsal period from mid-September to the beginning of October; public concerts from then until mid-October in Holland and Belgium; and recording to 25 October. His letter of 17 March to Feuermann was curt:

I can't conceal my disappointment about the way you are dealing with the trio business. Either you want to do the gramophone recordings or not. In the latter case you can say so openly to me and Schnabel, but it is not acceptable that 6 months ago we had come to an agreement about the date of the recordings and then, without telling us, you accept American engagements for the same time which apparently you are able to postpone only with difficulties or reluctantly. Even less tolerable is it that after innumerable consultations with me, you accept the period up to 25 October for concerts and recordings and then, in a way as if nothing of the kind had been agreed, you speak of your departure date as 10 October. I must tell you that I cannot accept this way of dealing with such serious matters between serious colleagues with mutual respect and respect for themselves. Nonetheless, I will ask you in a friendly way but for the last time, to say definitively whether you are in agreement with my *marschrouten* [military term for planing a route].[4]

This letter crossed with Feuermann's next one, in which his exasperation is clear:

As far as I can see, I am not being engaged by you for the trio recordings but every one of the three of us should do as much as possible to ensure that the recordings come off. However disagreeable it is for me, it seems necessary for me to have to tell you how far I have departed from fixed plans in order to make the recordings possible. Apart from the fact that my summer classes over there [USA] should have been extended into September, we decided six months ago that we want to rent a house near New York in September and make it habitable. With a wife and a baby, I am not very mobile and not very independent and I still can't see when, if not as planned in September, we can organize a change of our living quarters and all that that involves. You really mustn't overlook the extent to which my personal circumstances have changed and that I have to be responsible for the well-being of a family, however small. That I am doing the small round-trip America–Europe–America specifically for these recordings is surely not a sign that I am uninterested in it.

Huberman had asked Feuermann to postpone the beginning of his American tour until 1 November, and Feuermann had cancelled a number of proposed concerts. But a new opportunity now arose: a concert on 31 October in Boston with Sergey Koussevitzky. 'This is my first concert with Koussevitzky who up until now wasn't interested in having me and so this is a very important event for me.' The letter continues: 'I take it for granted that no one who understands the importance of individual concerts can reproach me for not wanting to cancel this concert simply because it is ONE day before the date you and I agreed. So if I accept my first concert in America as 31 October rather than 1 November, I am doing so in the knowledge that I am doing nothing which in the slightest way could endanger the trio recordings.'

But there was still another matter of fundamental disagreement:

> Perhaps I shouldn't leave it unmentioned that only now, in London, is there talk of the necessity of playing in public before the recordings. Of course, for artistic and financial reasons I am very much in favour of these concerts. But that they are of basic importance for ensemble, I cannot agree. Of course, it is not up to me to judge whether you personally find it necessary to play each trio in public before the recording, but with your permission, I am not of this opinion.[5]

This is a somewhat disingenuous remark from Feuermann. Days earlier he had written:

> I am very happy in the thought that a man like you evidently regards me quite highly as a musician. However, since we are of fairly different opinions in such matters, it will be necessary that we make compromises in order to achieve, as far as possible, a united sound between the two instruments. I am still rather reticent although I think I have successfully shed my earlier, somewhat dry, style.[6]

Here Feuermann appears to have been acknowledging that differences in stylistic approach would need to be ironed out.

If Feuermann was to play in Boston on 31 October, he would need to leave Europe between the 20th and 22nd. Therefore he would be available from about 10 September for six weeks, which was roughly the same period of time that had been initially agreed.

> I am very sorry that our anticipated joy is a little tarnished through this silly question of dates. I can't judge to what extent the dates clash with other arrangements of yours and Schnabel's. I, at any rate, have the pleasant feeling that I have done what I can to solve these difficulties which, without intention, have arisen on my side with regard to the recordings. I tried to explain to you in this letter my position, and I hope that I have expressed myself in such a way that you understand me correctly. Since I am interested in the trio recordings, you must not imply an opposite meaning to my words; nor have I ever thought of placing the responsibility of the failure of this project on you or on Herr Schnabel.[7]

Huberman's reference to *marschrouten* caused Feuermann to explode:

> You are a great and famous artist, the Palestine Orchestra is a unique deed, your activity is admirable and inimitable, a model for others. Nonetheless, your relation to me is not a matter of *marschrouten* or anything like it, in

dates or artistic matters. The idea of playing trios with Schnabel and you is wonderful and makes me very happy. I am conscious that I am much younger and have a natural respect for Schnabel and yourself, but between respect and the remark of organized *marschrouten* lies a whole world. I grant you that this word may merely have escaped from your mouth, but what will a trio be like where one of the partners may have an attitude, even in musical matters, towards his partner that could lead to, forgive me the word, 'derailment'.

Strong words, the jousting of egos characteristic of great soloists attempting to play chamber music together, but not of friends. Feuermann firmly believed that Huberman's achievements had gone to his head:

Since you are very spoiled [Feuermann used the aggressive word *verwöhnt*] and perhaps still see me as the little boy, I anticipated something like this. For that reason in my recent letter, I suggested that we must come to terms with each other musically so as to achieve the best ensemble playing. I am even convinced that you have the same opinion. Nonetheless, I can understand that it is easier said than done. Perhaps it is quite a good thing that we are discussing a number of things at this early point.[8]

Huberman was furious: 'I think your letter was neither altogether proper nor altogether factual, but there is no point in continuing this discussion any further. The ensemble will not improve and that is what matters to all of us.'[9]

Despite this acrimonious negotiation with Huberman, Feuermann continued to try to arrange an appearance with the Palestine Symphony Orchestra. These discussions were almost as protracted as those regarding the trios: in 1937 Feuermann had declined an invitation since it would have meant touring without a break for 19 months; and in October 1938 fear of war put paid to a visit. Now Feuermann was negotiating with the orchestra's new director, Leo Kestenberg, whom Feuermann remembered well from his days at the Berlin Hochschule: '[It] ... will always remain for me the most exemplary institute, to which I was attached with such love that I will mourn it until the day I die. The orchestra deserves and needs a man like you. With all my heart, I wish you the greatest success for your work and equivalent personal satisfaction.' Feuermann was hoping that plans for Palestine would work out this time: 'It seems that I will finally be able to come to Palestine, even though daily something could get in the way. However monstrous this latest criminal deed of Hitler's, there is one good thing: it has finally opened the eyes of those who were deluded or who didn't WISH to open them. I see the danger of war drawing ever closer.'[10] Hitler had seized the non-German areas of Czechoslovakia.

Feuermann planned to take the boat in April from Marseilles and travel via Cairo to Palestine. He was concerned, once again, about obtaining visas for Palestine and Egypt, but he had no qualms about working with Malcolm Sargent: 'Just now in February I played the Dvořák Concerto in London and Manchester with Sargent. He did it excellently, we were heart and soul. If it can't be arranged otherwise, it would even go well in rehearsals WITHOUT me. Any worries about playing together are superfluous, really!!!'[11] However, Feuermann was anxious in these uncertain times to be leaving Eva and the baby for a whole month, but 'if circumstances make it at all possible I will accept some personal difficulties in order not to embarrass the orchestra with a renewed cancellation.'[12]

Huberman knew about the negotiations with Kestenberg. Angry as he was with Feuermann over the trios, he was sympathetic to Feuermann's fears about leaving his family. On 5 April, from Paris, Huberman suggested: 'I could enquire by way of a telegram, whether they could give up your collaboration without damage to the orchestra and also without damage to your name. In reality, it is almost a sacrifice to make such a huge journey there and back just for Palestine.'[13] Schiff had failed to arrange further concerts in the region to link with Feuermann's Palestinian dates. Huberman's words were prophetic. One week later, it all fell through. Feuermann wrote to Kestenberg:

> Rarely has a letter been more difficult for me to write. And rarely have I had days of such desperate thoughts as these recent days. In March, when the Germans entered Bohemia, friends advised me to cancel the concerts in Palestine as they could foresee that the political situation would not settle quickly but could only get worse. I was not able to decide to take this step. But as the situation is now, with the Italian entry into Albania, I see myself forced to cable you that I cannot come.

The 'danger zone', as Feuermann put it, had moved to the Mediterranean. The Italian shipping lines and airlines were closed to him. He had no state protection, travelling merely on an identity paper. He wrote: 'I am supposed to be away four weeks. This is an eternity in these times in which atrocities can happen. With a heavy heart, I have had to come to the conclusion that I may not take such a risk.' This was a severe embarrassment for Feuermann: 'Since the founding of your orchestra, I have wanted to give my service to this organization but fate wishes, for the second time, that my voyage falls into a time of the greatest political confusions and tensions, which makes it impossible for me.'[14] Since the forced cancellation in October 1938, he had wanted to 'make good' his intentions towards the orchestra, but he also wanted to see those members of his family now living in Tel Aviv, in particular his mother. Even

Eva, who had been so against the visit the previous year, did not on this occasion try to influence him against going. The best that Feuermann could offer was his services in the event of a benefit concert being organized in America.

But the orchestra would not accept his reasons for cancellation; Sargent had arrived without difficulty. Feuermann, in desperation, contacted Huberman, advising him of the telegram he had sent to the orchestra: 'Sargent, Englishman. Myself stateless without a passport therefore unprotected in a dangerous situation. Cancellation decided after very considerable consideration. I am myself sad.' He regretted greatly that he had not been in direct touch with Huberman:

> I am extremely sorry that I did not establish contact directly with you. That the gentleman in Tel Aviv should compare my situation with Sargent is incomprehensible to me. Mr Sargent could rely at any time on aeroplanes, perhaps even battle ships, whereas last September I explained to the gentlemen Simon and Levertoff what my situation would be if I was overtaken by war or similar circumstances. I hope that the gentlemen after this telegram and my letter, which they should get soon, will be able to summon the necessary understanding. I have NEVER cancelled a concert willingly and I have certainly not cancelled, of all places, Palestine twice without weighty reasons. I am sincerely unhappy that I have been obliged to do this by *force majeure.*[15]

Events in Europe were now so dangerous that Feuermann, having thought that Eva and Monica should stay in Switzerland during his summer in America, began to have doubts. He had planned to leave Europe for the United States on 3 June, but in a letter to Hulda Lashanska dated 26 April all was changed. They would now take the SS *Champlain* on 16 May: '*This time we are coming for good, inspite of me going back to Europe as soon as September 1st. The situation here in Europe is too horrible for words and we shall only be too glad to be in America again. . . . the war scare we suffer from is absolutely killing.*'[16]

However, Dr Schiff continued blithely to organize European dates for Feuermann: 'Ibbs and Tillett have a few requests that they couldn't accommodate in February but probably could do in October. I assume that Huberman and Schnabel will not create difficulties if you're absent for a day once or twice during the recordings. There is at this moment an offer for Belfast.'[17] Was Schiff completely unaware of the heated exchanges between Feuermann and Huberman? A week later, Schiff wrote: 'Huberman told me yesterday that he had cancelled all engagements in the period in which he will be recording, including engagements at a very high fee. According to Huberman, it is impossible that in this short time each one of the three partners should give separate concerts.[18] Schiff could only agree. Nevertheless, a tour planned in Europe for the spring of 1940 looked promising: 20 concerts between early February and mid-March in England, Belgium, France, Denmark, Switzerland and Holland, with the pianists Paul Baumgartner, Gerald Moore, Theo van der Pas, Miklos Schwalb and Geza Fried. An engagement in Paris in February involved an appearance within a conference organized by Nadia Boulanger, a fervent admirer of Feuermann. She had requested that she should accompany him: 'Since Madame Boulanger is a very influential lady in America I would advise you to accept this proposal.'[19] A shrewd recommendation.

For some time, a possible tour to Australia had been mooted. Strok in 1934 had recommended it and a certain amount of preparatory work had been done. But by May 1939 the Australian Broadcasting Corporation had ruled it out. Any tour in 1940 could not be organized in time, but a later period was promised.[20] This never materialized. Correspondence from Feuermann's European agents, Organisation Artistique Internationale (OAI), suggests that he (quite understandably) was trying to ease himself out of working in Europe and out of paying commission to OAI on his American work. OAI failed to understand his wish to cut short European work in favour of concerts with Leon Barzin. They asked: 'Are the Barzin concerts really worth it?'[21]

When Feuermann arrived in America with Eva and the baby, he was lent a small cottage on the estate of some friends in Mamaroneck, Westchester, not far from where they had previously lived in New Rochelle. But by July they had a new home. As Feuermann proudly pointed out (in English) to Ibbs and Tillett's Miss Bass:

> *not only in our own house but even in our own furniture from Switzerland! We are happy not to be in Europe in these hectic months, people over here treat us very nicely, the house is situated in the most charming neighbourhood. Eva likes it here very much – to her own surprise. Monica is sweeter than ever, I myself had a few outdoor concerts with unbelievably big success – altogether we are grateful and very satisfied.*[22]

He was writing from 7 Chedworth Road in Scarsdale, which he found to be the prettiest suburb of the entire area and only 40 minutes from New York.[23]

One of the outdoor concerts referred to in the above was a performance at the Newark High School Stadium in June; 10,000 people attended. Amplification had to be used, which to Irving Kolodin's ears 'minimised many of the subtleties of his playing, coarsened the texture of his tone'.[24] With Alexander

Smallens conducting, Feuermann played Bloch's *Schelomo* and the Saint-Saëns A minor Concerto. Another outdoor concert took place in July, when Feuermann appeared for the first time at Ravinia as part of Music Under the Stars, the Chicago Symphony Orchestra's summer festival in the park.[25] Yet another outdoor concert in which he participated was held on 16 August, in New York at the Lewisohn Stadium, the summer home of the New York Philharmonic-Symphony Orchestra. The Lewisohn Stadium concerts, begun in 1918 by the philanthropist Mrs Charles S. ('Minnie') Guggenheimer, started with two specific aims: to bring good music to people at low prices and to provide the New York Philharmonic-Symphony with a summer income. Generally only the orchestra got paid, while soloists and conductors donated their fees. Performing at the Lewisohn Stadium was a prestigious engagement; only the Hollywood Bowl ranked higher in importance. Big names – Reiner, Stokowski, Rubinstein – were persuaded to perform, and during the 1930s the concerts became immensely popular; 21,000 people crammed in for a Heifetz concert. Tables for eight could be reserved for $12; single tickets ranged from $1.50 to 50¢; mats could be rented for 50¢. Smallens and Feuermann repeated the Newark programme of Saint-Saëns and Bloch, and the concert was broadcast over WABC and the CBS Network. Much of this broadcast has been located, including, most importantly, the Sarabande and Bourrées from Bach's C major Suite, which Feuermann played as an encore. Announcing the encore himself, this is the sole aural record of Feuermann playing unaccompanied Bach.

During the summer, Feuermann made his first recordings in New York under his new contract with RCA Victor: three sessions took place – on 31 July, and 1 and 8 August. Between the two August sessions he made a lightning trip to California to take part, once again, in the *Kraft Music Hall* radio show broadcast nationwide on 3 August. Under 'Outstanding events on all stations' the *New York Times* announced: 'Bob Burns, Comedian; Emanuel Feuermann, Cellist; Pat Friday, Music Maids, Songs – WEAF'.[26] Other guests included Melvyn Douglas and Fay Holm, stars from the screen. It was probably in this programme that Feuermann played Sarasate's *Zapateado* and Fauré's *Après un rêve*, accompanied by Theodore Saidenberg, Daniel's brother; a recording of a concert including these two works survives (this is the only surviving recording of Feuermann playing *Zapateado*).[27] To have reached California from New York by 3 August, despite Eva's anxieties, Feuermann must have flown. Not impossible – American Airlines ran a three-stop service taking 17½ hours from New York to Los Angeles.

Feuermann's summer spent mainly in New York was hot and hectic: '*I never had a busier summer than this one playing, recording, teaching, driving*

THE BRITISH BROADCASTING CORPORATION

Broadcasting House, London, W. 1

TELEPHONE: WELBECK 4468   TELEGRAMS: BROADCASTS, LONDON

ADMINISTRATION DIVISION

Reference: AP/WLS   13th September, 1939

Emanuel Feuerman Esq.,
c/o Ibbs and Tillett

Dear Mr. Feuerman,

This is to inform you with regret

that owing to the state of war your broadcasts

on   26th September, 1939, and on   are
    28th September, 1939
necessarily cancelled.

Yours faithfully,

W. L. STREETON

Programme Contracts Executive

GP

around etc.' But the dates with Huberman and Schnabel were unravelling once again:

> *Everything was settled that Schnabel, Huberman and I should meet at H's place in Switzerland on Sept. 8 – what does good Mr Schnabel do. He changed his plans and shall go directly to London, but about 10 days later. I very gladly am following his footsteps and shall also come to London right round the 10th of Sept. Mr Huberman will feel like Napoleon after Waterloo.*[28]

Feuermann had intended sailing to Europe on 29 August, but on 11 September he was still in New York, at a recording session with Franz Rupp; in the intervening days Hitler had invaded Poland and Britain had declared war. The BBC spelt out the situation bluntly: 'This is to inform you with regret that owing to the state of war, your broadcasts on 26 and 28 September are necessarily cancelled.'[29] So too were the trio recordings. After years of trying to negotiate dates with Schnabel, Huberman and Feuermann, war finally scuppered the project. Columbia was hugely disappointed. Gaisberg wrote to Charles O'Connell at RCA:

One of the most cherished projects of our programme this autumn, was to carry out a series of Trio recordings by the above artists. After months of correspondence we had actually negotiated terms with the artists and reserved ten dates at our Abbey Road Studios. The repertoire was to have been: Beethoven Trio in G major, Beethoven E Flat Major Op.70 No.2, Beethoven in B Flat Major Op. 97, Schubert Trio in B Flat, Brahms Trio in B major, Brahms in C major and if time permitted, the Beethoven Triple Concerto. The war forces us to cancel such International recording and we wonder whether you would be interested in taking over the idea for your own account. Schnabel and Feuermann are now in New York and Huberman will arrive shortly.[30]

Columbia could only recommend the project with no material support, but permission was given to contract the artists. If circumstances permitted, Columbia would look favourably on issuing the recordings in their territories. These trio recordings never went ahead. The project was abandoned.

Feuermann remained in the USA for the rest of his life. He became something of a household name, the butt, even, of cartoons: 'This is America's greatest cellist **Emanuel Feuermann** who habitually buys an extra Pullman berth to bed down his $30,000 Stradivarius for the night.'[31] Gossipy feature articles concentrate on his domestic ordinariness: 'he's living the life of a true American family man. He has a house in Scarsdale, he mows the lawn, he pushes Monica about in the pram. He'd even like to help Mrs Feuermann with the dishes, only she won't let him.' The *New York Post*'s journalist Michel Mok wove elaborately embroidered 'Feuermann stories' into his copy:

> Last Fall, I was travelling through the Middle West. I was riding in a Pullman chair and, as usual, I had reserved a seat for my cello. When I got out at Des Moines, I handed the instrument to a coloured porter and told him to be very careful of it. 'What's so wonderful about it?' he asked. 'Last week I handled Kreisler's violin. Is this thing any better than Kreisler's Strad?'[32]

That Feuermann was fully regarded, and indeed regarded himself, as an American musician can be seen from his money-raising activities for fellow musicians. On 27 November in Madison Square Garden he took part in a benefit for Local 802's Musicians' Fund to provide medical services for 5000 unemployed musicians and their families. A 150-piece orchestra conducted by Frank Black was made up of members of the NBC Symphony, Metropolitan Opera and New York Philharmonic-Symphony orchestras. The 11-year-old pianist prodigy Teresa Sterne took part, as did jazz performers Ella Fitzgerald, Glen Gray, Russ Morgan and Blue Barron.[33] Earlier in the month, Feuermann's long-awaited debut with the Boston Symphony Orchestra, the last remaining major American orchestra with which he had not performed, took place. In view of his international standing, it is surprising that he had not performed before with this orchestra. But there is a probable explanation: Gregor Piatigorsky. If Feuermann was acknowledged to be the greatest living cellist in the USA at that time, Piatigorsky was not far behind. The Boston Symphony Orchestra's music director, Serge Koussevitzky, was Russian, and so was Piatigorsky. They had met at the Bolshoi in Piatigorsky's youth and a close friendship had developed between them, almost like father and son. Whenever Piatigorsky appeared in Boston, he stayed at Koussevitzky's house. Piatigorsky was Koussevitzky's cellist.

This engagement with the Boston Symphony Orchestra meant a great deal to Feuermann, and he had assumed that Koussevitzky would conduct. But in Feuermann's performances on 3 and 4 November of the Haydn Concerto in D major, Richard Burgin, the concertmaster, took the baton. Was this a snub? The *Boston Evening Transcript* reported: 'Yesterday, for the first time this season, Dr Koussevitzky took a well-earned rest from the regular subscription series.'[34] In the 1939/40 season 24 pairs of concerts were presented in which all but five were conducted by Koussevitzky; Stravinsky conducted twice. Koussevitzky did, however, conduct for Piatigorsky later in the season (Strauss *Don Quixote*). And Feuermann was not the only soloist to play under Burgin: the pianist Josef Hofmann was conducted by Burgin too. But even if Koussevitzky did prefer working with Piatigorsky, Feuermann was better paid.

Feuermann's autumn tour continued in the usual way. A critic noted thoughtfully that had Feuermann been a violinist, there might have been fewer vacant seats for a concert of the New Friends.[35] On the other hand, another writer reported:

His modesty gives one no conception of the active life he leads professionally. Although many people think the cello is rather limited in its appeal, Mr Feuermann is booked for more appearances in New York City this season than any other artist in any other field. He will be heard eleven times in Greater New York between 8 November and 22 April.[36]

In Cleveland, Arthur Loesser opined: 'It would be easy to defend the thesis that Mr Feuermann is the world's leading artist upon his instrument today.'[37] About the same concert Feuermann commented: '*I played the Dvořák concerto with Rodzinski. He accompanied marvellously and the success was quite extraordinary.*'[38] The leader of the cello section was Leonard Rose.

The music world was at Feuermann's feet but still he felt the need for help in his career and support for his family within this 'new' country. Colleagues were generous. Hulda Lashanska, with whom he had recorded at the beginning of the year, arranged an evening.

> *I think I even didn't tell you how much I enjoyed the party you gave for Eva and me. Besides I am afraid I also didn't thank you for your generosity and your thoughtfulness towards my 'career'. You had arranged everything so beautifully, I met nice people and I felt so happy that I forgot entirely that there was also a certain purpose 'behind the curtains'.*[39]

The tone of this letter reveals Feuermann's feelings that competition was tremendous and memories were short. He was so grateful to have escaped Europe:

> For the moment it seems that God is smiling upon me, despite the terrible times, despite one's own worries and the worries of our families, which I partly have to bear. I can be grateful for Eva, for Monica and for being able to play well – not forgetting that we were not too late in coming here. The nightmare of being caught in Switzerland could have been reality if we hadn't left Zürich in time. . . . Heaven knows when and where we'll see each other again, but if things don't become even crazier in this world I hope it will be before we're both grandparents!'[40]

The Feuermann family was separated. Feuermann's parents and Sigmund had joined his sister Rosa and her husband Adolf in Palestine. Feuermann was no longer in direct contact with Sophie following their split in Puerto Rico, but news of her did get through. Feuermann wrote to Lily: 'Little sister Sophie apparently weighs only 40 kilos. Harry, who's got something to do with imports, doesn't earn a penny. Things must be awful for them.' Sigmund had married a woman who owned a shop selling corsets: 'so he's become a Corset Captain!' Feuermann gaily quipped. But Sigmund had argued with his parents and a rift had developed. Feuermann, despite his own feelings of neglect, recognized how hurt his father would now be: 'I feel so sorry for *Tate* [dad], who only lived for Sigmund.'[41]

Sigmund's story is a sad one. He did not fulfil his early promise. Sophie Feuermann maintains that the source of his problems was physical: 'When he died they examined the brain. His veins, these tiny little veins hardened and because they hardened he developed into something entirely different.'[42] She insists that he was a genius. Aged 11, he had played the Brahms Violin Concerto in London with Sir Charles Stanford; aged 13, he had played three concertos in the Salle Gaveau. As child prodigies, Sigmund and Feuermann performed widely together. In the mid-1920s, he visited America, where his concerts were said to have been successful and where he lectured at 'the Institute in New

York'.[43] In October 1934 he performed in Barcelona with Casals conducting.[44] In July 1938 Emil Hauser, original first violin of the Budapest String Quartet and later Director of the Palestine Conservatory of Music and Dramatic Art in Jerusalem, attempted to gain work for him in the Palestine Symphony Orchestra:

> In Vienna I spoke to the violinist Siegmund [*sic*] Feuermann, who has been more than enough tormented there, among other things he was made to wash streets with caustic solution. According to authoritative people he is a good violinist, and expressed to me the wish to have any kind of place in your orchestra. May I ask you to take this kindly into consideration and if possible to help him. To be able to help an Austrian in these days is truly a 'Mizwah' ['good deed'].[45]

Sigmund appeared as soloist in August 1939 at the Cinema Esther with the Palestine Symphony Orchestra. In April 1940 he reported to Feuermann that he was with the radio orchestra in Jerusalem. 'I hope for longer than a week,' Feuermann rued.[46] In 1941 he began teaching at the American University of Beirut.

In July 1946 Sigmund was again a soloist with the Palestine Symphony Orchestra. A letter from the orchestra in August 1946, however, suggests that this appearance did not go well: 'As we have already told you orally, we confirm that we are unfortunately not able to accept you as a member in our orchestra. The committee discussed thoroughly your request but we had also to take into consideration the opinion of the principal and the group of viola players who decided in the negative.'[47] Both the violin and viola sections rejected him. Three years later he again attempted to get work with the orchestra, setting out in a letter pathetically his achievements as a youth. He wanted to play for Paul Paray: '*I hope to appear as a soloist under his baton, and when he will be very generous, will he find a way to make me a member of your orchestra. I play also viola, if it should be necessary, as every violinist should also know the viola.*'[48] Yet another plea was addressed to the orchestra in 1950, this time by Erna Catak, an 80-year-old woman who had dedicated her life to social work:

> In memory of this great Jewish human being [Huberman had died in 1947] I wish to address these lines to you and ask of you to help a worthy musician who is apparently not capable of managing here. The name should not be unknown to you – it is the violinist Sigmund Feuermann – the brother of the deceased cellist. Sigmund Feuermann is in great depression and has lost all courage. Please call him to you and try to be of help so that he can again find courage. As I am an old acquaintance of his family and cannot bear to

see how he and his old tired mother torment themselves – I allow myself to approach you – because I see a possibility to be of help. 'Where there is a will there is also a way' is a saying and I ask you to make these words come true and add to your great artistic achievements also a simple human deed.'[49]

It seems that nothing came of this.

Sigmund died in Tel Aviv in 1952. No recordings of his exist; no commercial companies appear to have approached him. Reviews of his playing as a child are astonishing, but it seems that, whether for physical or psychological reasons, he was never able to complete the transition from prodigy to mature artist.

Chapter 13

Cellist at Large
November 1939 to February 1941

*'Emanuel Feuermann was at Carnegie Hall again last night, playing cello in
a way that would start our grandfathers on a witch hunt.'*[1]

In what had now become an annual November appearance at Carnegie Hall,
critics appeared to give up on superlatives to describe Feuermann's playing. On
23 November Howard Taubman wrote: 'Emanuel Feuermann was at Carnegie
Hall again last night, playing cello in a way that would start our grandfathers on
a witch hunt. . . . for all but a handful of other professional cellists, he is simply
unfair competition.' The programme had included Mendelssohn's D major
Sonata op.58, a work 'rarely taken off the shelves of the studio'.[2] Irving Kolodin,
in the *New York Sun*, pointed to the racial association of Mendelssohn and
Feuermann, both proscribed in Germany. Franz Rupp was again Feuermann's
partner, and 22 November 1939 was Feuermann's 37th birthday.

The age of full-blown public relations had not yet dawned, but Feuermann
and his agents were not above grasping publicity moments of a somewhat
dubious nature. A story was widely publicized in the press in December: 20-
month-old Monica had 'adopted' a three-year-old Spanish refugee, Antonia
Cara, whose parents were killed in the flight over the snow-covered Pyrenees
from Barcelona to France. Monica had become the youngest 'foster parent' on
record. It seems hard to recognize this action as any more than a stunt, and Eva
Feuermann remembers no further contact with the refugee.

The impact of the war in Europe was palpable in the United States and from
now on Feuermann was to take part in numerous activities that had some

bearing on events. A concert in observance of Finland Day was given on 17 December by the New York Philharmonic-Symphony Orchestra with John Barbirolli at Carnegie Hall. As in his previous concert with Barbirolli the year before, Feuermann played the Haydn Concerto in D major. Cheers were reserved not only for him but also for the former President, Herbert Hoover, who was in the audience. As one critic noted, Hoover stood in response to the ovation but did not speak: 'It was a moving demonstration of sympathy for a distressed nation and recognition of Hoover's efforts on its behalf.' Feuermann played the original version of the Haydn, to which the *New York Times* critic responded: 'If purists thank Mr Feuermann for restoring the real Haydn ... what will they say to the cadenzas used by the cellist, presumably his own?' Feuermann's first movement cadenza is stylistically flamboyant but not inconsistent with the spirit of the piece. Gama Gilbert continued: 'It is difficult to maintain the purist's attitude toward Mr Feuermann when he plays as he did yesterday. Never has his performance been more amazing in its combination of vital musicianship and consummate technique. The audience was his from the moment he put bow to strings.'[3]

Days before this concert, Feuermann had been in the recording studio: from 12 to 14 December he and his partner Franz Rupp had completed recordings of the Mendelssohn Sonata in D major plus a series of other works that they had begun in August. Days after it, he made one of his greatest recordings, not in New York but in Philadelphia. It was the first in a series of recordings with the Philadelphia Orchestra. On 21 December, with Heifetz as violinist and Eugene Ormandy conducting, Feuermann recorded the Brahms Double Concerto. The entire recording was completed in just over two and a half hours. It was only the second recording of the piece; the first, by Jacques Thibaud and Casals with Alfred Cortot conducting, was made ten years before in 1929. The musical match between Heifetz and Feuermann was extraordinary. Feuermann's technique, intense sound, focus and brilliance were frequently compared to that of Heifetz. There was no string player Feuermann regarded more highly (see Plate 16).

It is said that Feuermann was much influenced by Heifetz, but it seems just as likely that he came to his own way of playing as a result of competition with his violinist brother Sigmund. Feuermann's brilliant, focused sound is evident from his earliest recordings, as is his propensity to play fast. It is not clear when or where Feuermann first met Heifetz. From the tone of a letter written from New York in February 1938,[4] it might have been as late as then that they met, although in 1935 Heifetz had suggested to Gaisberg the idea of recording trios with Feuermann.[5] Eva recalls two New Year's Eve gatherings (but not the years) at Heifetz's house in Connecticut. Katya Aschaffenburg recalled a house concert in Scarsdale with Heifetz and Adolf Busch at which quartets had been played 'unconventionally': Adolf Busch played the viola, Feuermann second violin, and Heifetz first violin. She could not remember who played the cello.[6] Without being specific about dates, Feuermann wrote (in English) in his 'Notes and Anecdotes': '*Whenever Feuermann had a free moment, he would call up friends to play chamber music with him for recreation. One of the typical afternoons in his house in the suburbs of New York was: Heifetz and Busch taking turns playing first violin, [William] Primrose viola and Feuermann himself cello.*'[7] In the late 1930s in America, Feuermann was a star and Heifetz could not have failed to be aware of him. And he would have known a lot about him through his brother-in-law, Samuel Chotzinoff, who was enormously influential in New York's music circles. In 1919 Chotzinoff became Heifetz's permanent accompanist and in 1925 he married Heifetz's sister. He gave up his career as a pianist in favour of journalism, music criticism and management. He was music critic on the *New York Post* from 1934 to 1941 and in 1936 was appointed music consultant for NBC Radio. It was Chotzinoff who persuaded Toscanini to accept the invitation from David Sarnoff, president of RCA, to form the NBC Symphony Orchestra. NBC was a giant subsidiary company of RCA. It was Chotzinoff who initially gave Feuermann such a poor review at his debut in New York.

Feuermann and Heifetz shared not only a common European background, ethnicity and musical values but also other significant interests: cars and ping-pong. Feuermann's long-held ambition to beat him at ping-pong, it seems, was realized (and in one set!)[8] but whether Feuermann shared Heifetz's views on the necessary attributes of a great concert artist – 'the nerves of a bullfighter, the vitality of a night-club hostess, the concentration of a Buddhist monk'[9] – is not recorded. Eva Feuermann recalls that he adored Heifetz. Although Heifetz was generally viewed as a cold man 'in private he was a warm, charming, lively person and an excellent host to his friends. He enjoyed being the life and soul of the party.'[10]

One such party, indeed an hilarious romp, took place on 29 December, days after their Brahms recording: a benefit concert for the Chatham Square Music School on New York's Lower East Side. The Chatham School had been set up by an idealistic Chotzinoff with the aim of allowing students free study with first-class teachers. As always, financial support was needed. The evening, solemnly presented with a printed programme, gave a running order of 12 items. In 'An Audition at the Chatham Square Music School' the applicants were Feuermann, Heifetz, Horowitz and L. Tibbett.[11] Horowitz had one line: 'I play the piano.' Toscanini conducted 'The Chatham Square Music School Orchestra', known as 'Toscanini's Children' – a veritable galaxy of stars! In the string section alone there was Heifetz, Adolf Busch, Joseph Gingold, Milstein, Oscar Shumsky, William Primrose, Feuermann, Frank Miller and Alfred Wallenstein. Other players were drawn from the front desks of the NBC Symphony and New York Philharmonic-Symphony orchestras. Toscanini's grandson, Walfredo, was not allowed to attend the event (he was aged ten and a half), but a silent, black-and-white 'home' movie was made:

> Toscanini was dressed in a long black frock coat like an old school teacher with a large red handkerchief sticking out of his pocket to wipe away the sweat. Many of the players were in short pants and other 'appropriate' outfits. When the orchestra played a crescendo, they would all rise out of their chairs slowly and then sit down abruptly.

Walfredo Toscanini believes that they played Leopold Mozart's 'Toy' Symphony: 'If they had started to play as a lark, they soon found out that grandfather was serious about the music and rehearsed them vigorously.'[12] 'L'apres midi d'un phoney' was followed by 'Say Ah!' (music by Frank Black) with a chorus that included Heifetz and Feuermann. Feuermann wheeled his cello around on a roller skate. Wanda Horowitz (Toscanini's daughter) played the Maestro in 'The Maestro Comes to Dinner', with Heifetz's sister Pauline (Chotzinoff) and his mother, Annie, in supporting roles. Even the 'ads' were spoofed up: 'Guarnerius – The Instrument of the Immortals. Jascha Heifetz says 'I use the Guarnerius exclusively – it satisfies.' – advertisement placed by 'Joseph Guarnerius & Co. Cremona'. 'Antonius Stradivarius Inc. Cremona' had also posted an ad: 'Jascha Heifetz says: "I use the Stradivarius exclusively – It's real mild." Every Strad contains 25% more notes than any other comparably priced instrument.' On the back of the play bill an advertisement for the 'Corny Change Bank Trust Co (Established 1939)' with 'A Bank Statement that any Moron can understand' is placed:

Due Individuals, Firms, Banks and Simpson's	$300,000,000.17
To meet this indebtedness we have:	
Cash in Vault and Due from Banks	$36.02
Austrian-Hungarian Empire Bonds at Cost	$50,000,000.00
Albanian Government Securities	$40,000,000.00
Loans Unsecured	$80,000,000.00
Less Reserves	$79,999,999.83

A positive balance of 17¢ is recorded.

The new year of 1940 began for Feuermann with concerts in Illinois, Ohio and New Jersey. Musical life in America impressed him – in a newspaper article he wrote: 'Full orchestras in the U.S. just a few years ago could be counted on both hands, while today they are being organized and developed in hundreds of cities.' But he was well aware how different Europe and America were in the matter of support for musical institutions. In this feature article he pointed out what he regarded to be a little-publicised fact: in Europe, governments through public taxation funded these organizations. 'That the people accept such taxation with little protest is an indication of the appreciation the European public has for music.' He could not fail to mention current circumstances in Germany, in particular the ironic fact that the Reich had maintained subsidies to opera companies, theatres and orchestras even if Germany, that 'country of orchestras', had lost much of its spirit. 'His [Hitler's] decrees have sent many skilled artists from the countries [Germany and Austria] in the role of the refugee and his complete control of the various music organizations has removed much of the inspiration and quality from music.'[13]

War in Europe wrought havoc on performing schedules in America. In January 1940 the cellist Hermann Busch was unable to reach the United States from Europe to perform with his brother Adolf and Rudolf Serkin. One of their concerts was in Cincinnati. Feuermann, already performing with the Cincinnati Symphony Orchestra under Eugene Goossens, stepped in. The Matinée Musicale Club concert was rapturously received: 'Joy of Ensemble Playing Apparent as Three Outstanding Artists Provide Perfect Concert.'[14] Feuermann again deputized for Busch in New York for the New Friends of Music in the Town Hall on 21 January. This concert, which was also broadcast, included the 'Ghost' Trio by Beethoven, Mozart's Trio in C K.548 and Brahms's C major Trio op.87. In a letter to Hermann, Adolf wrote:

> Yesterday was 'our' second trio concert. Feuermann played for you – also in Cincinnati. I am sending along the programme from N.Y., so that you can see that they explained the situation to the audience in a nice way (this was also done in Cincinnati). From the enclosed reviews you will also be able to see that Feuermann has only 'temporarily' taken your 'regular' place. We played very well, but everyone – Feuermann too – was very sorry that you couldn't be there.

Adolf was trying to persuade Hermann to come to the States: 'You <u>must</u> come over (with family) and stay here (for heaven knows what will happen to Europe and concert life there).' Significantly he continued 'and we will have to lower our fees and play, if at all, for only a little more than other quartets.' Adolf was desperately trying to keep the Busch Quartet together; Hermann was based in Switzerland and Gösta Andreasson, second violin, was considering setting up in Sweden. Adolf described the scene vividly:

Now we are trying to find, and hope to find, directly and through friends, some kind of position for each of you in a college (university or conservatory), even a modest one, with the expectation that your living here (in a modest form) would be taken care of, so that the quartet playing and other possible concerts could pay for a better life. We and these friends are trying everything, but the difficulty is that they are no longer allowing artists to come over here, as they are under the impression that all of them are already here. And it is true that the most competent musicians, conductors with great names, soloists, and *x* number of quartets etc. are running around here with nothing or virtually nothing to do.'[15]

Another artist affected by war was the pianist Myra Hess. The NOA in its usual spring concerts, the Gabrilowitsch Memorial Series, had in 1940 planned to present a season featuring three performers: Myra Hess, Mischa Elman and Feuermann. Myra Hess, involved with the concerts at the National Gallery in London, chose to remain in England; Rudolf Serkin took her place. Mischa Elman was also unable to fulfil his engagement and was replaced by Nathan Milstein. Only Feuermann was able to honour the engagement as planned.

The NOA was a valuable tool for Feuermann. Not only did it substantially increase his reputation through the 'marathon' in 1938, but also it allowed him to play a wider, non-standard repertoire. On 27 January, the first concert of the NOA's 1940 season, Feuermann played the Dvořák Concerto and introduced another Bohemian work, a 'new' concerto for cello and orchestra by the Czech composer Josef Reicha (1752–1795), uncle of the prolific Antoine. Reicha's A major Concerto op.4 no.1 is in three movements, closely following the standard 18th-century model, and is reminiscent particularly of Haydn's C major Concerto – a work not discovered until after Feuermann's death. Throughout his life, Feuermann scoured libraries for works: that the cello repertoire was so limited can be seen by his endless repetition of a few works. As reported in the *New York Times*, he found the Reicha Concerto in the Edwin A. Fleischer[16] Collection in Philadelphia, where he also found concertos by Massenet and Victor Herbert.[17] He felt the Reicha to be unjustly neglected in the interests of a narrow reverence for the great names of the period, in particular Haydn and Mozart. And parrot-fashion, the *New York Times* critic reflected: 'Reicha had no great personal voice . . . he merely helped himself to the tasteful eighteenth-century clichés that were accessible to all his contemporaries. . . . It would be as hard to distinguish it from other works of the time as one Tin Pan Alley song from another.'[18] This work may be of no great profundity but it does have great charm. As *Musical America* observed: 'It's high time that the work was added to the repertoire familiar to listeners on this side of the ocean, for it is delightfully fresh and vivaciously written.'[19] One of Feuermann's greatest skills was his ability through sheer musicianship to transform a piece of little significance into one of some consequence. Little wonder that he was able to so capture his audiences in the performance of salon works, lifting them to realms of utter charm.

This concert, and a number of others, were recorded in Carnegie Hall for the NOA's president, Mary Flagler Cary, daughter of a wealthy oil associate of John D. Rockefeller. The Carnegie Hall Recording Corporation at this time could be commissioned to record performances. Feuermann is said to have been unaware of this. Leon Barzin recalled: 'People who were there never forgot the occasion because it wasn't a soloist coming to us, it was a great musician. And he talked to them [the players] as though he was playing in the orchestra. . . . there was a relationship because of the educational side.'[20] Feuermann did indeed enjoy playing with this orchestra, as recordings and letters amply testify.

Following the recording of the Brahms Double Concerto in December 1939, Feuermann recorded two more works with the Philadelphia Orchestra: Strauss's *Don Quixote* and Bloch's *Schelomo*. On 24 February, in just under two and a half hours, the recording of *Don Quixote* was completed – remarkable speed for a work of such complexity.[21] Ormandy conducted, while the leader of the orchestra, Alexander Hilsberg, and principal viola, Samuel Lifschey, were the other soloists. Feuermann was in Philadelphia again on 27 March to record *Schelomo*, this time with Stokowski. A few days before, he and Stokowski performed the piece in a benefit concert for the China Aid Council. The concert was a remarkable affair, notwithstanding a row between the sponsors of this gala in Philadelphia and the Theater Authority who, on behalf of its affiliated unions, felt that 15% of the take should be theirs. An orchestra of 162, made up of players from the Philadelphia Orchestra and the Philadelphia-based Curtis Institute, was conducted by Stokowski, Ormandy, Saul Caston and Charles O'Connell, with the singers Alexander Kipnis and Rose Bampton, and the instrumental soloists Szigeti and Feuermann. 'The Academy's regular staff of ushers was augmented by personable Chinese usherettes and the stage adorned with appropriate flags.' Feuermann's performance was described as 'memorably moving and absorbing'.[22]

Between the Philadelphia recordings, Feuermann, back in New York on 25 February, appeared playing the slow movement of the Dvořák Concerto in a broadcast with the NBC Symphony Orchestra conducted by Dr Frank Black. This broadcast was a 'Special hour program presented by NBC saluting America's Civic Music Association from coast to coast, in commemoration of

NBC's ten years' affiliation with the Civic Concert Service'. The *NBC Civic Concert* was a regular radio programme with Milton Cross as presenter. Other guests on the programme that day included Erica Morini, Ezio Pinza and Kirsten Flagstad.[23]

Feuermann's trips to Philadelphia allowed him to scour the Fleischer Collection and visit the Library of Congress in Washington, where he found four concertos by Boccherini and a concerto by Arthur Sullivan.[24] But Feuermann needed help, as he pointed out in a letter to Harold Spivacke, director of the music department of the Library of Congress: '*All my friends, conductors as well as pianists have abandoned me. Everybody is busy and nobody can spare 2–3 days to go with me to Washington. If I should come by myself is one of your assistance [sic] or some young musician there willing and able to go through the music with me on the piano?*'[25]

Events in Europe were becoming increasingly ominous, as illustrated in one of Feuermann's letters to Mrs Reifenberg:

> I am sure that you, too, are deeply affected, as we are, by the invasion of Denmark and Norway by the Germans. My fears in Zürich that one goes to bed in Switzerland and wakes up next morning to German domination, have become reality for the poor people of Copenhagen. It is terrible and I still think that we have not, as yet, reached the end.

The letter was sharp: 'I do not know one of your family or acquaintances who recognized the situation at an early stage. It is sad to see that most of them continue to be blinkered and are still unconvinced.'[26] A letter written a few days later contains news of a concert he had attended – he had been to hear Horowitz: 'Such an ability on the piano with this art of differentiating his touch on the one hand and the craziest feats on the other. This to me is just as puzzling as, for instance, radio. I found that some things he played too fast.' But the same letter continued more pessimistically, the effects of war never far from Feuermann's mind:

> Even though I hate to write this, I fear that for a time it is possible that many articles of food will be difficult to acquire in England. But surely only for a short time because other countries will be happy to sell their surplus food. What is happening in the North Sea one can't yet foresee. One has to wait and drink tea. In any case, the '*wishful thinking*' of the Jews and Democrats was, once again, no good. Unfortunately I seem to have been right in my assumption that the Germans will survive for a long time. Very long. If only, God willing, I should be wrong.'[27]

Despite the recording, Heifetz and Feuermann never publicly played the

Brahms Double Concerto. Indeed they never publicly performed together at all. In terms of orchestral repertoire, the Brahms Double was the only substantial work that the two might have performed together. The reason they did not play the Brahms may lie in the simple fact that Feuermann's life ended less than two and a half years after the recording was made, only eight months after its release. In his letters, apart from his slightly tongue-in-cheek suggestion in December 1937 that he and Heifetz should play together in Copenhagen,[28] Feuermann never mentioned plans for any public performance. Had Feuermann lived longer, however, it seems impossible that given the extraordinary reviews of the recording and their individual reputations, these two artists would not have performed the Brahms. For a performance in May with the Philadelphia Orchestra at the University of Michigan, Ann Arbor, Szigeti was booked as solo violinist. The rehearsals took place in April: 'Szigeti played well in the rehearsal today; between the quick Ormandy and myself he wasn't able to play the dignified elderly man with a slow tempo.'[29]

On 22 April, Feuermann was again soloist with the NOA. This time, the novelty was the Cello Concerto op.20 by Eugen d'Albert (1864–1932). Feuermann was obviously fond of this work, playing it frequently (with piano or orchestra) in the early 1920s and taking it to the Far East on his 1934 tour. But the critics in New York were dismissive: 'The sad fact is that the concerto did not come alive even under such expert ministration. It is a music that seems to have faded and wilted. Its cantilena themes which are meant to be sung ardently, have a distant nostalgic fragrance; they sound like diluted romanticism.' Howard Taubman's words damn the work, but thanks to the foresight of Mrs Cary it was recorded during the concert and remains a great curio in the recorded legacy of Feuermann. Taubman also commented on Feuermann's research: 'One cannot blame Mr. Feuermann for looking for different scores where he can. But perhaps he could induce some talented contemporaries to compose several concertos for him.'[30]

Feuermann appears to have commissioned no work specifically, but his commitment to new work and lesser-known work was substantial. (He had severely admonished his student, Mosa Havivi, in Berlin for his lack of interest in new music, in particular that of Hindemith.) In the years to 1933, apart from new chamber music played with the Gürzenich Quartet, Feuermann performed new work by Gottfried Rüdinger, Emil Bohnke, Arthur Honegger, Jacques Hert, André Caplet, Walter Schulthess, Kurt Atterberg, Hans Chemin-Petit, Glazunov, Hindemith, Goldschmidt and Toch, and 'recent' work by Debussy, Reger, Stravinsky and Bloch. After 1933, except for Hindemith's Second Trio and the Scherzo, the most important work he premiered was

Schönberg's Cello Concerto. As discussed, Schönberg's plans to arrange Bach's viola da gamba sonatas for obbligato cello and orchestra came to nothing, but at the time of Feuermann's death Toch was working on a new concerto for him. It seems that little of this new work, not least Schönberg's Concerto, has successfully entered the repertoire. Even Hindemith's solo sonata (op.25 no.3), a work Feuermann performed so frequently, is rarely heard.

It was with Hindemith that a major split occurred at some time in the summer of 1940, a split that was to remain unresolved at Feuermann's death. It now appears, tragically, that a mere misunderstanding may have been its cause. Although no correspondence at the time from Feuermann has survived, a letter to Toch in March 1941 seems to explain the situation: 'Between Hindemith and me it was understood that he would write a second cello concerto that I should play. You can imagine my disappointment in him as a person and, as I thought, a friend, when I read that Koussevitsky and Piatigorsky would play the second concerto.'[31] This concerto, written in the summer of 1940 in Tanglewood, was the first piece Hindemith composed in the United States following his emigration. He had been invited to Tanglewood by Serge Koussevitzky to give composition lessons; for the first time, an academy for advanced musicians had been organized at the Boston Symphony Orchestra's summer residence. In a letter to his wife, Gertrud, Hindemith wrote:

> The cello concerto is not quite finished as yet. In the past 10 days, I have had too much other work so I could not write. Furthermore, the heat was such that even moving a pen caused continual perspiration. I did not exactly think of Munio while writing it, actually about no one in particular. I was only interested, after the violin concerto, in trying out something similar for the cello. Besides, Munio could have shown interest and contacted me after I had met his wife in a concert in New York and told her I would be beginning a cello concerto soon.

It seems that Feuermann never heard about this conversation, and Eva has no recollection of meeting Hindemith on that occasion. What appears to have happened is explained precisely in Hindemith's letter:

> After I had finished the first few pages, Koussevitzky saw them and immediately commandeered the piece. By chance, Piatigorsky was also passing through and the piece was assigned to one of the Boston programmes [concerts] with further performances in New York and elsewhere. In any case, Koussevitzky has been very nice and friendly towards me and performed everything of mine that he could (<u>Symphonic Dances</u> 5 times, <u>Mathias Symphony</u> 10 times!) so I am happy to give him the new piece. He

does not have enough with that [the concerto] and wants to perform the 'Nobilissima Suite' in the same concert. The only thing I heard relating to Munio was in a letter from Stiedry where he writes that should I have a concerto he would like Munio to play it in his 'New Friends of Music'. This is a decidedly second-rate group, like the ensembles we had in Europe. I definitely prefer the Boston Symphony.[32]

Only one of Feuermann's letters from the summer of 1940 remains: a lengthy but incomplete communication to his Viennese sponsor, Wilhelm Kux, now resident in Switzerland. In touch with several European musicians, he gave news of the exceedingly hard times so many were suffering:

> I sit here in America and although I don't earn very much at least I can keep alive. Even a clever man such as Huberman made a miscalculation, and I've heard from Walter[33] that he has at least managed to get Huberman a position, probably a performer affair, in Cincinnati so that he can enter America on a non-quota visa. Flesch was caught up in Holland, but as he's got a Hungarian passport he was immediately engaged by the Curtis Institute in Philadelphia and that will enable him too to come over here. Bruno Walter is here. We visit one another. Both of them are very down – the loss of Gretel[34] is terrible. He is conducting the day after tomorrow. About a year ago, Klemperer had a terrible operation for a tumour but he has actually overcome it quite well; but his strange nature is much more apparent than it used to be and I'm afraid they're going to prefer Walter as a permanent conductor. Your friend Elman performed here not long ago. It was terrible. He plays like an old man – he puts too much pressure on the strings – and since he makes his living with the so-called 'Elman sound' . . .[35]

Life for Feuermann, now in California, was by any comparison favourable. He was to spend the whole summer there. True to form, he had driven from the East Coast, taking four days. Mrs Reifenberg, who had left Europe some time before and was now in California, was charged with finding a house to rent. Feuermann wrote: 'Didn't you understand from my letter that I am not for hearing months on end, day and night, the rushing of the sea?' Even more emphatic was another demand: 'I am utterly against living so near to Heifetz.'[36] Feuermann's apparently sour remark suggests not so much dislike but more probably a lack of enthusiasm for living cheek by jowl with another artist. Mrs Reifenberg found a house in the Hollywood area, in Chautauqua Boulevard, Pacific Palisades, situated quite high so that there was some breeze against the oppressive heat. As Feuermann explained to Kux, he had become intensely involved with her affairs, having to take decisions about 'vast sums of money':

In the winter I often had hours of discussions with bankers, brokers and lawyers and that was far more exciting than any concerts. When I went into town my programme looked something like this: lawyer concerning Mrs R's domicile in the USA; working with Szell on the Mozart concerto; consultation about shares; and a rehearsal with a pianist for a concert. Very interesting for me but also very exciting.'[37]

The Mozart concerto he referred to was planned for performance in January 1941 with Klemperer and the New York City Symphony Orchestra. Its first performance, however, was delayed until December 1941, and was not with the New York City Symphony and Klemperer.

About 15 students followed Feuermann to California, which made him assure Kux: 'it makes it impossible for me ONLY to be lazy'. And humorously he reported: '*She (Eva) is a great success in English and I call myself the prince-consort.*' His warmth towards and interest in the children of friends and family is a feature in many of his letters. His own daughter, Monica, now two years old, was naturally the apple of his eye:

> Monica I'm glad to say is just how one would want her. I just cannot believe that you and my own mother cannot see her. She is a naughty little thing and I'm told she's very similar to me – and very pretty. It's very funny; she only speaks English and refuses to speak German. The child is sweet. If I have to practise some time – heaven help me – she bursts in and says 'must help Papi'. She stands in front of me and we both hold the bow and play 'Haenschen klein, Oh Tannenbaum' (children's songs). I have to be very careful because she seems to be in love with music or sound.[38] (See Plate 17.)

Another displaced friend and protégée of Kux was Erica Morini. Feuermann wrote to Kux:

> We have lots of fun with Erika [*sic*]. She is very nice – and very fat – and her husband seems to be charming. Through sheer chance I was able to give her good advice last autumn, and since I had given her acceptable advice on other occasions she seems to trust me. But that does not alter the fact that she finds it difficult to accept facts in the profession and therefore puts quite a few people off. But it does look as though she might get to the top again. She is a brilliant violinist.

Feuermann was a very great artist, but his modesty and sense of awe towards his career is both striking and touching. As striking is his frequent self-mocking: 'It's lucky I am not satisfied with myself and I don't earn a lot of money. Without these restraining factors, I would now be very conceited, seduced by the really great reputation I have here. Even if I know I play well, or perhaps just because of it, I could slap myself every time I step down from the podium.'[39]

Kux's reply in September tantalizingly suggests topics that Feuermann must have written about in the missing section of his letter: the influence of Paganini in the development of violin playing; an indication that some of his writings were about to be published (in September 1940, an article, 'The Contralto of the String Family', was published in *Etude Music Magazine*). His difficult relations with Sophie were surely touched on; months earlier Feuermann had admitted to Kux that he continued to be a red rag to her. Kux's response now was sanguine:

> It is a well-known fact that quarrels and contradictions between blood relations are usually far more violent than would be the case with regard to strangers. In the interest of Sophie, I can only plead mitigating circumstances because people having a hard time are unable to be just and . . . fight with each other.[40] I could write pages about observations that I've made since the eruption of the Nazi gang. To what extent the character of the wretched victims becomes depraved, how they themselves, the persecuted, have lost a feeling for justice and decency. Therefore, forget all that has happened and try to normalize your relationship because you are on a level today able to gloss over trivial things.[41]

Alas, Feuermann's relationship with Sophie was never 'normalized'.

Kux was writing from Switzerland, where Feuermann's recordings continued to be broadcast, unlike in the rest of Nazi-occupied Europe. Within one week alone, the Haydn Concerto and the Brahms E minor Sonata were transmitted, while plans to broadcast the trio with Goldberg and Hindemith were also announced. Meanwhile, in Hollywood, almost exactly a year after the previous broadcast, Feuermann was again on the *Kraft Music Hall* radio programme. With host Bob Burns and Theodore Saidenberg at the piano, Feuermann performed Chopin's Nocturne in E♭ and Falla's *Jota*. Much of this broadcast has survived and includes both speech and performance from Feuermann. Bob Burns referred to 'my pal Emanuel Feuermann', saying: 'When we get in the mood for some real cello playing around the hall, we look for Emanuel Feuermann'. He praised Feuermann's playing: 'I don't know of a more beautiful sound than when you're playing that cello', and, with much banter, asked 'When a lady plays the cello, does she use a side-saddle?' Feuermann good-humouredly replied: 'I don't know, Bob, but I use knee

action. I have used it ever since a cellist-friend of mine developed bow-legs.'
Feuermann played 'Jota' by Manuel 'de Filla', as announced by Burns. This
broadcast reveals not only Feuermann's apparent ease within the context of
show business but also his enthusiasm for popular music. The next act was
Marie Green and her Merry Men. Bob Burns mentioned that 'some fine
musicians don't care for swing'. 'Who says I don't like swing?' retorted
Feuermann, asking what Marie Green was going to sing. 'Just a little piece of
jazz called "Caro nome".'[42] '"Cara nome" a little piece of jazz?' chimed
Feuermann. 'Why. That's opera.' 'Mr Feuermann is right,' Marie Green joined
in. 'It is opera. The Merry Men and I just gag it up a bit.'[43]

From the outbreak of war in September 1939, touring in Europe was finished
for Feuermann and the amount of work he received declined substantially. In
September 1940, however, he was able to visit Mexico, where he performed the
Dvořák Concerto with the Mexican Symphony Orchestra under its distinguished director Carlos Chávez; but substantial foreign touring had come to a
halt, and so, to an extent, had substantial touring in America. The beginning
of Feuermann's 1940/41 season was disastrous. Apart from the Mexican tour,
only two known concerts took place, both in New York. He may have given
more concerts, but the fact that there are no personal letters to Eva from him
in the months up to Christmas 1940 suggests that he was not touring – no
touring meant, of course, that there was no necessity to write. In fact, no
personal letters at all have survived from the period 23 January 1939 to 6
December 1941. And there is very little surviving professional correspondence.
RCA has not kept papers from this period and papers pertaining to
Feuermann from NBC Artists, in the course of various takeovers, have also
disappeared.

Piecing together events in Feuermann's life at this time is hampered by the
non-existence of his correspondence, but letters from others throw some light
on his activities. An interesting proposal survives from the great patron of the
arts Elizabeth Sprague Coolidge in a letter of late September 1940 to Adolf
Busch. In the summer of 1940 she had presented two series with great success
at the universities of Stanford and California in which Beethoven's cello and
violin sonatas as well as the trios had been performed. She now proposed a
similar series under the auspices of the Coolidge Foundation at the Library of
Congress. She wrote: 'Do you think that you could interest Mr Feuermann to
play 'cello sonatas and trios with you and Rudolf . . .?' She had in mind four
concerts, which would include the five cello sonatas and seven trios. The
foundation would pay $750 apiece, which, she wrote, 'I know is less than your
usual price, but which might be compressed into a short consecutive period in
Washington.'[44] Her letter must have caused some embarrassment, since she

seemed unaware that Adolf had an established trio with his brother, Hermann, as cellist. Perhaps she had assumed that Feuermann had replaced Hermann when he had deputized for him in January. Coolidge further proposed a fee of $4000 apiece to four musicians for four concerts – a generous fee compared to a string quartet. Her comments on the most suitable time of day for concerts are both canny and amusing: 'if we had them at a quarter before five in the afternoon quite promptly, and finished as promptly at a quarter past six, we should probably not interfere with so many diplomatic dinners, which I think still interest many Washingtonians more than chamber music does.'[45] The series was proposed for February 1941. It did not take place. Adolf Busch suffered a heart attack and all his engagements were cancelled.

Feuermann's next major event in the autumn of 1940 was his regular November recital at Carnegie Hall, which took place with Franz Rupp on the 19th. Howard Taubman noted the predominantly sober nature of the programme: what emerged was 'a central unity – that of the dignity and aspiration of man and art. . . . There were no fireworks . . . there was only music making of a lofty and distinguished order. . . . It was as if Mr Feuermann, mindful of the weight and sorrow of the times, deliberately eschewed the gaudy and the frivolous.'[46] The programme comprised the Brahms E minor sonata, Bach's Suite no.1 in G major, Strauss's Sonata in F op.6 and a final group that included Schumann's Adagio and Allegro, a Mendelssohn 'Song without Words' and Chopin's Introduction and Polonaise op.3 in Feuermann's own sensational transcription. Many musicians attended the concert – Feuermann was always a musicians' musician. As Taubman continued: 'The race of stormy, mane-tossing virtuosos has thinned in recent years, but Mr Feuermann is the kind of musician who never would have bothered to build an act to go with his virtuosity.'[45] A veiled reference to Piatigorsky, perhaps?

On 22 December, a huge audience of over 2000 attended the concert in Carnegie Hall given by the Orchestra of the New Friends of Music conducted by Dr Fritz Stiedry. This was the organization that Hindemith had been so dismissive about a few months before, an attitude not entirely reflected in the *New York Times* review: 'The concert was a charming one. . . . The orchestra played with freshness, purity and delicacy and Mr Feuermann, showing evident signs of enjoyment to be playing with such friendly, alert young instrumentalists, played with technical brilliance and a fine singing tone.'[47] The programme had included an unusual work, Jacques Ibert's Concerto for cello and ten wind instruments, as well as Tchaikovsky's 'Rococo' Variations. This concert was broadcast and a part has been located.[48]

Feuermann was again in Carnegie Hall on 5 January 1941. Klemperer conducted the New York City Symphony Orchestra, formed under Roosevelt's Works Project Administration scheme. A reviewer noticed that:

The depression has made deeper marks on their faces, they are perhaps a little older, there are four or five women among them, and they don't wear formal clothes when they give concerts but otherwise the ninety men of the New York City Symphony Orchestra look like the members of any of the country's major orchestras when they are assembled on stage. Under Otto Klemperer and Sir Thomas Beecham they have sounded like one of the country's top-flight orchestras, too. But here similarities with privately supported orchestras end. In administration, financing and working conditions the orchestra is unlike anything that ever was on sea or land before the coming of the WPA.[49]

The orchestra was indeed different. Giving its first concert in December 1939, 95 per cent of its members were required to be drawn from the registered unemployed; for 30 hours a week, they were paid a weekly wage of $23.60. The concert that day included Haydn's 95th Symphony and D major Cello Concerto and Beethoven's 7th Symphony.

On 9, 10 and 14 January, Feuermann was in Chicago as soloist with the Chicago Symphony Orchestra. Apart from performances with the orchestra in their summer season at Ravinia in 1939 and 1940, this was his first appearance in the main season since he had made his debut in December 1934. Oddly enough, he performed the same two concertos – the Lalo and the Dvořák. Dvořák's Concerto on the 9th was broadcast live over WGN; this broadcast has survived and been reissued on CD by the Chicago Symphony Orchestra.

In February 1941, he played once again for the New Friends of Music in New York's Town Hall. Elizabeth Sprague Coolidge's proposed Beethoven series with Adolf Busch had not taken place, but the New Friends, whose aims had been to offer complete cycles of composers' works, announced a very similar series. In two recitals – on 9 and 16 February – Feuermann performed Beethoven's complete works for cello and piano. This 1940/41 season was an enterprising and exciting one for the New Friends; plans included Bartók and his wife performing his Sonata for two pianos and percussion (it was a new departure for the New Friends to embrace contemporary work), Lotte Lehmann singing *Winterreise*, and performances by Adolf Busch, Rudolf Serkin, Edward Steuermann and the Budapest, Busch, Primrose, Kolisch and Gordon string quartets – almost a clean sweep of exiled Europeans, most of them Jewish. Franz Rupp, who should have partnered Feuermann, had been removed by NBC Artists as Feuermann's principal partner in order to work with the American contralto Marian Anderson. Feuermann's new partner for these recitals was Albert Hirsch, a young pianist born in Chicago in 1915 who had been a student of Dijane Lavois. Lavois 'ran a "salon" in New York and knew everyone'.[50] She was married to Siegfried Hearst, a manager with NBC Artists and close personal friend of Feuermann. Hirsch had been taken on by NBC Artists as a promising young soloist. These Beethoven concerts were the first that Feuermann and Hirsch gave together. The rehearsals took place at the apartment of Hirsch's wife's parents in New York (see Plate 18). Hirsch, in his early twenties, was more than 12 years younger than Feuermann and had never before worked as an accompanist. He recalled: 'I learned them [the pieces] very quickly and I think I had it all memorized – I always did in those days, every-thing I played with anybody'.[51] Mildred, Hirsch's wife, recalls Feuermann shouting at Hirsch and that, at least initially, Feuermann was very cruel to him. Perhaps Feuermann was upset about NBC taking away his marvellous regular pianist, Franz Rupp. But an incident reported by Mildred in the green room following the first of the two Beethoven recitals reveals the familiar streak of sarcasm in Feuermann's character: 'After the first Beethoven concert for the New Friends of Music, Dijane in the green room said to Feuermann: "Didn't Albert play beautifully?" Feuermann replied: "Why yes. He never played before." Dijane slapped his face.'[52]

Hirsch, like Gerald Moore, acknowledged the great teacher in Feuermann: 'He was very fussy about details, but after the first few rehearsals things went smoothly and we didn't waste time. Rehearsing was as concentrated as Feuermann's practising. I'm sure what he did in making me aware of details was wonderful and without thinking I've applied them for the rest of my life.' Hirsch described Feuermann's approach: 'He was very direct and very simple. He immersed himself in the music he was performing. He didn't practise much. He would leave his cello at our apartment for a few days between rehearsals.' In recitals with Hirsch, Feuermann did not use music for the salon works. 'He never was unwilling to play encores – we would play a few. He very much enjoyed playing.' Hirsch was never aware of Feuermann being nervous, but instead noticed him fooling around backstage. Even if Feuermann was as hard on Hirsch as he was on so many other colleagues, Hirsch was overwhelmed by his playing: 'He was absolutely the tops as far as I was concerned. There will never be a cellist of his stature.'[53]

Hirsch was Feuermann's last regular accompanist, but they made no commercial recordings together. NBC did, however, broadcast the two Beethoven recitals, though not the two op.5 sonatas. Feuermann's student Suzette Forgues heard the first recital: 'Feuermann was playing the Beethoven/Mozart Variations, which I happened to be studying at the time, and the next day was my lesson. I had noticed that in one of the variations

Feuermann didn't play a few bars, so at the end of that variation I did exactly what he did.' Feuermann asked: 'What's the matter with you? Can't you read? You didn't play this.' To which Forgues replied: 'But Mr Feuermann, I listened to your performance yesterday and you didn't play it either.' As she recalled, Feuermann burst into laughter, getting everybody off the sofa and throwing himself on it. 'He is rolling with laughter and I think what's so funny? Then he says "Well, yesterday I was so taken by Hirsch, he played so beautifully that I turned around and I watched him."' Nevertheless, Feuermann was forthright with Forgues: 'Why must you do the things I don't do right? Just do the things I do do right!'[54]

Feuermann's Beethoven appears to have been revelatory. A critic wrote: 'Rarely have performances of these numbers revealed so searchingly the essential nature of their contents.'[55] Reviewing the second recital, F.D.P. in the *New York Herald Tribune* suggested that there was a new maturity in Feuermann's playing: 'The assets of his tone are well known, but its lyric spaciousness, consistent clarity and luminous warmth were particularly in evidence on this occasion, with continuity of musical curve and line, while his technical and interpretative mastery, as before, were constantly and objectively at the service of the music.'[56]

Chapter 14

Difficult Times
February 1941 to 10 May 1942

After all I am only a cellist[1]

'Feuermann, Serkin Astonish; Feuermann Stuns, Amazes' shrieked the oldest college newspaper in the United States, *The Dartmouth*. In February 1941, Feuermann and Rudolf Serkin gave a joint recital at Dartmouth College, where they played Schubert's 'Arpeggione' and Beethoven's A major Sonata op.69. The newspaper's unattributed reviewer summed up Feuermann's performance simply: 'The music that he played, the things he did. Don't try to imagine them. They are impossible.'[2]

Feuermann had just over a year to live. Little correspondence has survived from this period and so merely a patchwork of his life emerges. What does seem evident, however, is that his concert schedule for the 1940/41 season continued to be dramatically reduced. A month after Dartmouth, he was in Montreal playing in the final concert of the Concerts Symphoniques season under Désiré Defauw and a few days later he was with the University Orchestra of Miami. (A local Miami paper referred to him as 'an Austrian who was born in Spain'[3] – the familiar confusion between Galicia in Poland and Galicia in Spain.) A week later, he was in Cuba, with Massimo Freccia directing the Philharmonic Orchestra of Havana. On all three occasions, he played the Dvořák concerto. As in the previous year, he was to spend from June until the end of September in California. Once again, he drove, this time taking a leisurely ten days from Scarsdale to Pacific Palisades. Suzette Forgues recalled:

'When I saw him there he had a very red arm because he said proudly "I came with the car open and had my arm like this. You see what happened!"'[4]

As dreadful as the war in Europe was, there were some unexpected dividends. 'Chaos and mass slaughter have driven out nearly all of that which is beautiful to a refuge within the historically hospitable shores of the United States.'[5] Hollywood and the area around the Hollywood Bowl had become a magnet to exiled Europeans, especially Jews. By 1941 the roll-call of artists drawn to live there was extraordinary: as well as Schönberg, Stravinsky, Toch, Erich Korngold, Hanns Eisler, Klemperer, Lotte Lehmann, Heifetz and Rubinstein, Aldous Huxley, Christopher Isherwood, Thomas Mann, Max Reinhardt, Rudolf Schindler and Franz Werfel were all 'exiles in paradise'. In the previous year, Mrs Reifenberg had busied herself with finding a house for Feuermann at 444 Chautauqua Boulevard, Pacific Palisades. Toch now recommended another house, which he described as 'more 100% for you than Chautauqua'. It was evidently a vast property with lawns and fruit trees, ample room for servants and views of the sea and mountains on Adelaide Drive. Toch wrote: 'It is situated in such a way that one doesn't hear or feel the fact that one has neighbours anywhere in the whole house and yard.'[6] The fact that Toch recommended such a place gives an idea of how others expected Feuermann to live, even if Feuermann himself chose to remain in the house that they had rented the previous summer:

> We love it here and from the very first day we have had that 'sad farewell feeling', because we can hardly imagine that we will be going so far away in the next summers. Our place is not only not too warm, but often almost too cool, we're on the ocean on a hill, always a breeze and have our couple with us, so that we feel totally at home.[7]

Yet again, students followed Feuermann to California. He wrote to Kux: 'I had about 20 pupils from all over the country, not only cellists, but also violinists and viola players.'[8] Among the students known to have been there were the cellists Claus Adam, Suzette Forgues, Robert LaMachina, Daniel Saidenberg and Marion Davies and the viola player Milton Katims. During the summer, the beach and playing ping-pong were as important to Feuermann as lessons. Claus Adam recalled: 'He used to enjoy ping-pong tournaments after a long day of teaching in California and I must say that he got so anxious about beating his students that he would tense up and do all the wrong things that he would criticize us for.' As usual, Feuermann appeared to practise very little:

> He never touched the cello except sometimes to demonstrate for his students. And one day I remember looking, his nails were so long that the

average cellist couldn't even play with his nails, and he played with almost flat fingers and he could demonstrate. A week later he had to make the recordings – the famous trio recordings with Heifetz and Rubinstein. I could never understand how any person could come back to complete playing shape in one week.[9]

Playing chamber music was an essential part of life in California. With so many musicians living close to each other – Heifetz in Newport Beach, Rubinstein in Brentwood, Feuermann in Pacific Palisades – music was habitually played in one or other's house. In interview with Monica Feuermann, Rubinstein recalled one occasion most colourfully:

> There were about nine bigger chamber music works being played and I implored them to play for me for my benefit the two-cello Quintet of Schubert in C major. Heifetz wasn't very willing because he hadn't played it that much before. He always liked to right away give a concert performance, but that was not at all my idea. I wanted them just to read it for me. Well, they did it for me, just to give me that pleasure and they did it so divinely that I was absolutely out of bounds, out of my head. I never heard such a performance in my life before, and again the biggest element in it was your father. He played so divinely the cello and it was always standing out, inspired the others. It made Heifetz, who was rather cold, just as warm as you could imagine. . . . I heard many performances but never such a one, never! And I love that work so much, you wouldn't believe it, I wanted to pay for it. So I sent all the money I had in my pocket to the Musicians Emergency Fund in honour of that. It was not too much. I think I had $80 in my pocket. Fortunately not $5000! But I did send all this money to the tremendous astonishment of my colleague Heifetz![10]

Another chamber music participant was Daniel Saidenberg: 'We played chamber music almost every Sunday at the home of Heifetz and it was quite an experience to hear the two of them [Heifetz and Feuermann] play at each other.'[11]

Charles O'Connell from RCA got wind of these chamber music sessions. The Budapest Quartet had recently left RCA in circumstances not dissimilar to those behind Feuermann's casting off of Nipponophone and Columbia; RCA had dawdled over renegotiating their contract and the quartet, dissatisfied both financially and artistically, had left the company. The Victor company was stunned; they stood to lose leadership in the recording of chamber music. The gap in the market for a first-class piano trio still remained to be filled. O'Connell, aware of Columbia's failure to record Schnabel, Huberman and

Feuermann, realized that California, particularly in the summer, provided an ideal opportunity for the matching of performing schedules – so many musicians were based there. He turned to Heifetz, artistic and commercial star of RCA, to recommend musicians for a series of chamber music concerts to be recorded on disc. O'Connell viewed the project as a long-term investment, with recording taking place over many years. At this stage, however, only duos and trios were the suggested repertoire. Predictably Heifetz had no hesitation about the choice of cellist, and in the Scottish William Primrose (described by Feuermann as 'the fabulous viola player'[12]) he could rely on viola playing at its highest level. It was the choice of pianist that proved more problematic. Serkin was first considered, but it seemed unlikely that he would play 'outside' the Busch circle. That left Rubinstein, whose main problem for Heifetz and Feuermann was his casual attitude to rehearsing. They were both also concerned that he might not fit in. Rubinstein was 'notorious at the time for neglecting the rigours of an exact, correct playing in favour of deliveries of pathos and élan'. A Heifetz biographer observed: 'Right from the beginning of the recording sessions, there was a certain tension between Heifetz and Rubinstein. . . . Heifetz complained that Rubinstein liked to linger over romantic passages. The pianist found the violinist too aggressive, always thrusting ahead. The violinist felt the pianist to be superficial. The other felt the former to be too cold.'[13]

These were Feuermann's final commercial recordings. The sessions began on 29 August in the Hollywood Recording Studio. Feuermann and Primrose recorded Beethoven's Duet in E♭ 'with two *obbligato* eyeglasses' WoO 32 (1796). On 8 and 9 September, Feuermann and Primrose were joined by Heifetz to record works for string trio: Dohnányi Serenade in C op.10 and Mozart's great Divertimento K.563. The piano trio recordings with Rubinstein took place on 11, 12 and 13 September, with the Brahms op.8, Beethoven's 'Archduke' op.97 and Schubert's Trio B♭, op.99 (see Plate 19).

Years later, in an interview with Monica Feuermann, Rubinstein's recollections on how the trio worked together uncannily echoed the words of Szymon Goldberg on their string trio in Europe: 'At our sessions at the actual working on the records, Feuermann without knowing it became the leading light. He was really the leader of the three of us. The pianist usually leads but he had such an enthusiasm and he had such a lot to say about phrases and so on that his influence was the important one.' Nevertheless, moments of disagreement were inevitable, as one would expect from the coming together of three very strong egos:

We had many little quarrels. . . . Don't forget that trios or quartets or quintets don't have a conductor. . . . Heifetz was going always for the success. He wanted to shine out to give a great violin performance. I'd like to say, and I don't like to brag, but I would sacrifice anything the pianist would say for the work's sake. But I had also my private conceptions about how the work should sound. But Feuermann had a very, very strong conception about it and he fought for his ideas and mostly he was the winner.

As always, tension between Rubinstein and Heifetz was evident, albeit lightly expressed: 'I tell you Heifetz was always a little egoistic – he always was, even artistically, even when he played the violin. When Feuermann looked away he tried to get the mike a little nearer to the violin, but inevitably Feuermann spotted it! So back the mike went where it should be!'[14] But from O'Connell's view as producer of these records, Rubinstein was no angel either:

One of these recordings provided the only occasion I ever had to practise any deception on Rubinstein and, incidentally, the only moment throughout these sessions when Rubinstein refused a concession to a colleague. We were recording the 'Archduke' trio and at a certain point a low note in the cello is doubled in the piano part. Both are marked 'fortissimo'. In this particular range the timbre of the cello and of the piano are not very dissimilar, but the piano tone is, of course, much more powerful. Rubinstein's *fortissimo* is a mighty sound, and here it completely blotted out Feuermann's corresponding *fortissimo*. 'Munio' complained of this, and in the most comradely way endeavoured to persuade Rubinstein to deliver a somewhat smaller volume of tone. Rubinstein refused, pointing out that his part said *fortissimo*, and *fortissimo* it was going to be. I did my best to compose the difficulty, but I had no success except in provoking the resentment of both men. We made record after record, and invariably at this particular point both artists would detonate their biggest explosions; and on hearing the record played back would turn away in anger and disgust. Finally, during a little intermission, I took Feuermann aside and asked him, as a friend to stop arguing with Rubinstein; if they would try just once more I would see to it that his cello would be heard together with the piano in their proper relationship. It happened that we recorded this group with several microphones simultaneously in order that we could more easily adjust such discrepancies in balance as might develop because of the varying power of piano, violin and cello. On the next attempt to make the record, when we came to the danger spot I simply had the engineer suppress the piano to a point where it was just possible to hear the cello tone cut through. Rubinstein knew nothing of this, and probably would not have permitted it, but when he heard the playback he said gleefully, 'You see,

Feuermann, I was right; you can be heard no matter how loudly I play if you just bear down a little harder and give a real *fortissimo*.' Feuermann was satisfied.[15]

Feuermann's own views on the enterprise are contained in a letter to Wilhelm Kux: 'First two or more weeks of colossal practising and then for one week, every day from the morning till night in front of the microphone, the last day 11 hours!'[16] Charles O'Connell admitted:

> I think it is extraordinary that a group of virtuosos, men of such extraordinary individuality, force, and diverse temperaments could come together, even in music, and so completely submit themselves to ensemble. . . . Making these records, though it represented extremely taxing labours on the part of the artists, was really a joy. There were difficulties, to be sure, but somehow the spirit of this ensemble made itself felt so strongly that all difficulties, personal and other, were resolved quickly and amicably. There was no haste, there was no compulsion, there was no thought of anything but making music, making it beautiful, and making it permanent. I think everybody sensed that an extraordinary achievement was being accomplished, though, like big-league ball players when a pitcher is trying for a no-hit game, we kept our mouths shut and our fingers crossed until it was all over.[17]

If melding of temperaments, musical and psychological, proved demanding on the three virtuosi during the recording process, agreement on the choice of takes was yet another challenge. On 24 October, Feuermann, who had clearly not yet heard the pressings, wrote to Rubinstein: 'Just now Dr Schiff told me over the telephone that you spoke with such enthusiasm to him about our trio recordings. . . . From Heifetz and Florence [Heifetz's wife] I had 'raving wires' about the trios. You can imagine that we are dying to hear the records. Since you also seem in agreement, I'm already looking forward to the pleasure of hearing them.'[18] By mid-November, Feuermann had heard the pressings over and over again and while he reported finding certain passages wonderful, he had reservations about others: 'I found my own playing at most good (no more) [but] was enchanted by your and Heifetz's playing.' Interestingly, Feuermann had checked out the competition:

> By chance, I was in town this afternoon and I had a little time and listened in the gramophone shop to the Beethoven trio with Cortot, Thibaud, Casals. Now I am without any reservation enchanted with us. I regard our trios in details and ensemble perfect, beautifully phrased – apart from the fact that sometimes something is perhaps a little bit fast. I cannot imagine

anything more beautiful. I was compelled to convey this to you and if you are here and have a little time, do have the Beethoven Trio played to you. Since my experience of today I know <u>how</u> good our trio is.[19]

But a few days later, Feuermann wrote to Rubinstein that Heifetz had still not told him which takes had been chosen. Feuermann had sent Heifetz a telegram with three particular choices in the Brahms, Beethoven and Schubert but: 'It seems that these three numbers deviate from those you selected. There seems to be more of a hurry than I thought.' Feuermann had been hoping to see Rubinstein – he was giving a recital – but a sciatica attack prevented him from getting to Rubinstein's concert: 'I was rather badly in pain but hoped that the doctor, in spite of it, would allow me to go to your concert. I still didn't want to give in even when he said I had to stay in bed, but my wife sent you a telegram without asking me. Since I have never heard you in recital, it is like a blow of fate.'[20] It seems that Feuermann never did hear Rubinstein in a recital.

The choice of takes finally agreed were Feuermann's.[21] But problems still remained. On 15 December 1941, Feuermann, just back from touring, wrote to Rubinstein: 'You in a personal row with Victor and our trio question again or rather perpetually not settled. I assume that your controversy with Victor has meanwhile been settled and naturally in the way you wanted it. And now what about the trios?'[22] Rubinstein's 'personal row' with Victor concerned, in particular, his recording of the Tchaikovsky Piano Concerto no.1 with Barbirolli; the company favoured its new Horowitz–Toscanini recording. Rubinstein also had no liking for O'Connell, whom he found bossy – as did other Victor artists, including Toscanini.

The only commercial film made of Feuermann playing probably dates from this time. Two works occupy the seven-minute black-and-white film: Dvořák's Rondo (with slight cuts) and Popper's *Spinning Song*. The accompanist is Theodore Saidenberg. Despite the loss of a few frames at the beginning, this film is an extraordinary document, even if the camera work is poor, with little synchronization of sound and picture. Feuermann's appearance is one of complete disengagement, with no energy. He is not even seen displaying his usual mannerism of sucking in his cheeks. The explanation is clear: Feuermann was filmed (at least in part) to playback and quite probably the soundtrack had been laid down long before. So poor is the editing that in one passage he is shown 'playing' high on the D string while the sound is clearly that of the A string; several moments show the bow sounding on one string but 'playing' on another. Nevertheless, the chance to see him – to take in the size of his hands, the stretch, the flying staccato, his thumb position – makes this film invaluable.[23] It seems likely that this film formed part of *Music of the*

Masters, a film in six sections, each of which consisted of a performance 'by an outstanding musical attraction'. Performers included José Iturbi, the harpist Mildred Dilling and baritone Igor Gorin.[24] What fee Feuermann received (if any) is not known. Had it approached the $60,000 fee Hurok negotiated for Rubinstein a few years later for his part in dubbing what Rubinstein regarded as 'a ridiculous picture', no doubt the fee would be known.

Feuermann returned to the East Coast in late September 1941. Despite the excitement of the chamber music recordings the summer had not been entirely happy. He and Eva badly wanted a second child and Eva had had a miscarriage. Feuermann wrote to Kux in December: 'I myself was very depressed.'[25] But he did have projects to keep him busy. He had been asked to write a book on cello playing, although, as he wrote to his friend Lily: 'I don't think that I'm going to have the courage or the tenacity to do so.'[26] And that autumn he took up an appointment as 'instructor in cello' at the Curtis Institute in Philadelphia.[27] The violinist and composer Efrem Zimbalist was the newly appointed director there, following the resignation of Randall Thompson. Various other appointments were made as well as Feuermann's, including Richard Bonelli (voice), Carl Flesch (violin), Gian Carlo Menotti and Samuel Barber (composition, instrumentation, orchestration). But the new appointments, particularly Feuermann's, were not well handled: 'Zimbalist hired Feuermann without telling [Felix] Salmond who was so angry and incensed that he resigned.'[28] However, Salmond did not leave immediately, and so there was considerable tension as both cellists were active. Eva recalled: 'All the cellists who studied with Salmond minded that Feuermann got this position because I think – this is guess work – that it was done very badly, that Salmond was deposed from the position at Curtis, so there were bitter feelings about that.'[29] Suzette Forgues, however, has suggested that Feuermann himself was quite pleased to have 'dethroned' Salmond.[30]

Even if he had only a few students and his salary was not large – he was teaching only one afternoon a week – Feuermann liked the Institute. He was glad to be back in a teaching institution (he referred to the Curtis as 'noble') and saw great potential for developing his position. His Curtis students included some of those who had been in California with him: Shirley Trepel, Robert LaMachina, Rowany Coomara and Marion Davies. Marion Davies recalled Feuermann's teaching:

> Lessons at Curtis were about an hour. He could be very sarcastic but when he liked something he could be equally complimentary. I was 16 when I started with Feuermann and 18 when I had my last lesson. At Curtis I worked on the Boccherini and Schumann concertos and also the Brahms

F major, which I played on a recital – I was the only one of his students to play on a recital. . . . When Feuermann died Zimbalist hired Piatigorsky. So I studied for three years with Piatigorsky. The difference was so great you wouldn't imagine it. For one thing, Feuermann rarely played for us – he could explain very well. Sometimes he would grab the cello when he was standing up, any student's cello, and he always sounded great. Piatigorsky would play at length, performing to show how things should go rather than explaining. They were entirely different personalities. Piatigorsky was so loose and friendly and outgoing, telling stories – a great raconteur. Feuermann was not like that. He was introverted.'[31]

Yet on disc the flamboyant Piatigorsky comes over as the more introverted whereas the less demonstrative Feuermann sounds spontaneous and free.

Another project occupying Feuermann at this time was the building of a house, of which he wrote to Lily:

We thought about it a long time, I've certainly told myself how peculiar it is for me, an emigrant of all things, to build a house etc. etc. and yet we are daring to do it. We're building it together with Granny [Mrs Reifenberg], who will have her own self-contained apartment in the house with kitchen, porch etc. The house will be very simple, but I can't get rid of the feeling that I'm turning into a fraud.[32]

But, as he revealed to Kux on 31 December 1941, the financial obligations of the house were enormous, far greater than he had anticipated:

Building began August 1 and we are hoping to begin to furnish it in January/February. I am not building because I feel I have made it but, on the contrary, because in the long run it is cheaper and more convenient than having to pay rent for Mrs R. and ourselves separately. Mrs R. is giving the cash and I took a mortgage as I don't have any money. Everything would have been all right if I hadn't noticed too late that it's not enough to buy the land and build the house, but that you need lots of money for the garden, the road, electric connection, carpets, curtains. Now the headache begins. On the whole I guess I didn't make a mistake, as rents are rising a lot, but I did take on a bit too much. But it will be ideal and beautiful, much too nice for myself. We will live far out on a hill. Mrs R. has her own wing and will also have her own maid etc., etc.. We are looking forward to the day when we will leave here and get in there, although I know that I will still have a lot of worries and headaches with the house.'[33]

The house was indeed grand. As described in a feature article in the *New York Times*, the 12-room mansion designed by Wells, Merrill & Merrill was to occupy two and a half acres of slightly sloping land at Rockledge Road in Rye near Harrison, Westchester County: 'When musicals [*sic*] are to be given, the living room, dining room, library and the hall can be thrown together to act as one large space. The musicians would then use the library, which, being several steps higher than the living room, would form a small stage. Concealed lighting troughs in the library ceiling enhance this stage effect.'[34] A studio was to be built over the garage, well away from the main part of the house, where rehearsals could take place, students could stay and children could play. A separate wing was designed for Mrs Reifenberg. Feuermann was attempting to build a dwelling comparable to the vast Reifenberg mansion in Cologne. While waiting for the house to be finished, the Feuermanns lived in a small hotel, the Scarsdale Lodge.

That autumn, Feuermann continued discussions with Toch about a cello concerto. It appears that Toch, in something of a depressed state, was considering writing a work for Feuermann, but without the idea of a specific commission. But while Toch was willing to write a concerto for Feuermann, he was not willing for Feuermann to reject it. Feuermann had written to Toch in March, somewhat amazed:

> I didn't argue with you when you told me that you couldn't compose something for me while giving me the right to play it only if I liked it. I would never have dared to think and speak of it in this manner and I have to admit that I was so quiet because I thought it such an absurd idea. Would you be in the right mood now and in the summer to write something for the cello and to let me play it? I think I'll have the possibility of playing such a new piece, primarily in my 4 concerts with the Philadelphia Orchestra. I have been working on the programme with Ormandy for quite a while now, and I have already 'threatened' to play something of yours.

Feuermann had a good reason for wanting Toch to write him a piece – he wanted to wreak 'The revenge of the good old Jewish god', as he described in his letter to Toch:

> Between Hindemith [and me] it was sort of understood that he would write a second cello concerto that I would play. You can imagine my disappointment in him as a person and, as I thought, a friend, when I read that Koussevitzky and Piatigorsky will play his second concerto. It is supposed to be a weaker piece, rather dull, and had no success.[35]

Ormandy's initial response was favourable and Toch went on to indicate to Feuermann the costs involved:

The price for the performances would be the cost of production of the material (score and parts), which would have to be returned to me after the concert. Since the piece would be about equivalent to the first cello concerto (this answers the 'timing' question), but would be played by a normal-sized orchestra, it would cost about $150 to $200. I would gladly guarantee that these figures are the upper limit. If the piece were to be printed, no publisher would sell the premiere for less, let alone for four concerts. I would be very grateful if you could let me know Mr Ormandy's definitive decision as soon as possible, since I'm really writing the piece for you (that is, I'd be writing something else otherwise), and such a state of suspense doesn't inspire me. I could send you the piece, movement by movement so that you can begin to occupy yourself with it in a leisurely way.[36]

Three weeks later, Feuermann was able to respond:

I have now received a letter from Ormandy, which as far as I could tell agrees to a cost of $150 to $200, but he assumes that the concerto would last no more than 20 minutes. I hope that this time limit accords with your idea of the duration for the concerto. (You're probably already used to tailoring your pieces to the wishes of others!)

He signed the letter in English: '*Eva's husband, Monica's daddy, Toch's first performer, Oma's business manager.*'[37]

But the project was to have a tangled and unhappy ending. Ormandy was impatient: would Toch accept the sum of $50 as an honorarium? Could Feuermann <u>guarantee</u> that the work would be no longer than 20 minutes? Feuermann was desperately embarrassed. In December he wrote to Toch: 'I was so ashamed at this offer that I didn't dare tell you about it but tried to find a way out. After TWO days I got a letter from O., saying that since I hadn't replied to his previous letter, he'd made a decision and I should play Mozart.'[38] The 'Mozart' was the delayed project with George Szell, whose arrangement of a Mozart concerto Feuermann was supposed to have played the previous January with Klemperer and the New York City Symphony Orchestra. When the Klemperer performance fell through, Feuermann hunted round for other opportunities to play the piece. When Ira Hirschmann of the New Friends declined it, saying 'You would Szell Mozart short',[39] Feuermann promised it to Daniel Saidenberg and his Little Symphony. He wrote to Toch: 'I should have played that Mozart concerto now, on the 22nd of December, here in N.Y. with Saidenberg, who already had put advertisements in the papers.' The trouble worsened and Feuermann suddenly faced breach of contract. Feuermann, while trying to insist on the Toch concerto, was promptly informed by the

Philadelphia management that his contract expressly forbade him from playing the Mozart in New York before any Philadelphia date. (Even NBC had to admit that this was true and that they had agreed to it.) Ormandy, it seems, behaved very badly. Feuermann went on: 'After I had exchanged a few more letters with him, all of a sudden [he] insisted that he had never definitely accepted your concerto and would never accept it. I would HAVE to play Mozart.' Saidenberg, a close friend, agreed to allow Philadelphia the Mozart. But as soon as this agreement was made, McDonald, manager of the Philadelphia Orchestra, was on the phone to NBC saying that Ormandy now insisted on Feuermann playing Haydn. Feuermann was furious and angrily wrote to Toch:

> If you consider the fact that I, generously, wanted to free Ormandy from the Mozart concerto, which he doesn't like; that I was absolutely enthusiastic about playing your concerto in such a framework, and of course, was of the opinion that O. would be more than happy to have a new piece instead of the same old tune again (by which I mean no slight with this comment) – then you'll understand how upset and confused I was when it turned out that everything I did was taken the wrong way and was turned upside down in its meaning.[40]

It was not until January 1942 that Toch replied:

> I wanted to let a little time pass but not this much, over my annoyance with the Philadelphia issue; I cannot deny that I am very sorry about the time I spent over the cello concerto. So let's forget about it now. I know that you didn't have any bad intentions. But with this experience behind me I will never start work on a composition unless performances are guaranteed by directors and managers of the New York Philharmonic or the Boston Symphony.[41]

The concerto was never completed. According to George Neikrug, Toch continued working on it but on Feuermann's death revised it to become a symphony.

By comparison to the 1940/41 season, with its dismal number of known concert appearances, autumn 1941 was far healthier. On 16 October, Feuermann gave a joint recital in Washington's vast Constitution Hall with the Scottish-Canadian pianist Reginald Stewart. This recital was the first of C.C. Cappel's new Concert Guild series. Stewart, better known as a conductor but recently appointed director of the Peabody Conservatory in neighbouring Baltimore, was making his piano debut in the capital. Despite low ticket prices, only 1800 people filled the cavernous 5000-seat Constitution Hall. Franz Rupp was once again partnering Feuermann, but by the end of the month at Ann Arbor, Michigan, Albert Hirsch was his pianist.

The war in Europe brought conflicting demands and honours for Feuermann. *America Preferred* was the name of the United States Treasury Department's bond-boosting radio show, a regular feature with Alfred Wallenstein conducting and Deems Taylor as host. As guest soloist on 6 November in Tchaikovsky's 'Rococo' Variations, Feuermann received a signed citation from the United States Treasury Department 'in recognition of distinguished and patriotic services to our Country, rendered in [*sic*] behalf of National Defence on a nation-wide radio broadcast'. But at about the same time Feuermann himself signed a very different document at the British Consulate General in New York, which stated: 'I solemnly declare that I have no intention of travelling or returning to enemy or enemy-occupied territory for the duration of the war, and that no part of the above mentioned security, bank account, gold, sum of money, will be transferred for the benefit of any person living in enemy or enemy-occupied territory.' Without signing this 'Non-Enemy Declaration', Columbia in London could release no royalty payments.

In typically waspish manner, critic and composer Virgil Thomson reviewed Feuermann's performance with the NOA and Leon Barzin on 10 November 1941 in Carnegie Hall: 'No great variety of colour is his; but his universal, all purpose tone is noble and neat, like Kreisler's fiddle tone. His musicianship, too, is serious, dependable, solid. It comforts; it sustains; it leaves no bad taste in the mouth. He was graceful in the Dvořák restaurant music, architectural and eloquent in Bloch's fine old Jewish Rhapsody.'[42] The Dvořák 'restaurant music' was *Waldesruhe* (which Feuermann discovered in the Edwin A. Fleischer Collection in Philadelphia) and the Rondo. Feuermann's student Suzette Forgues, who covered some of the rehearsals for Feuermann of Bloch's *Schelomo*, remembers the dress rehearsal. Feuermann was tense and missed a high note, but far from being perturbed he got off his chair, stared under it, and merrily remarked: 'Where did it go?' But that was not all:

> Still in *Schelomo*, Barzin was not pleased with the brass section. He got off the podium while we were still playing and went to the back to conduct them. Feuermann all of a sudden sees no conductor. So he gets up and with the cello hanging from his shoulder he gets on the conductor's podium and he's playing and conducting with his bow – well, there was pandemonium. But we had a great rehearsal – he made us all laugh – and he played like a god the next day.'[43]

The concert was recorded live for the NOA.

In December, Feuermann was once again with Désiré Defauw in Montreal. A review reads: 'What may be counted as one of the greatest single performances of music in recent years here took place during the program given by the Orchestra of Les Concerts Symphoniques . . . You thought only of this music, its stark reality, its mighty pathos. That is what a great performance can do.'[44] Again, Feuermann was playing Bloch's *Schelomo*. The resonance that this piece held for Feuermann at this time one can scarcely imagine, what with the catastrophic events facing Jews in Europe and the difficulties facing those immigrating to the United States.

A review a few days later of Haydn's D major Concerto and Strauss's *Don Quixote* with the Indianapolis Symphony Orchestra and Fabien Sevitzky adopts a view similar to that of the critic in Montreal. 'Emanuel Feuermann . . . has so perfected his art that the music he performs takes on a searching and profound quality. . . . Feuermann's integrity as an artist, combined with his genius, enabled him to translate the honesty, the beauty and the power to the full.'[45] The writer, however, reserved some fairly harsh words for the orchestra, noting 'technical inadequacies' and that Sevitzky was 'more aware of a great many trees than a solid "forest"'. However, despite any inadequacies, the Indianapolis Symphony Orchestra attracted artists of the highest distinction: Nathan Milstein, Lotte Lehmann, Ezio Pinza and Artur Rubinstein all appeared in the 1941/2 season.

Reviews of Feuermann's performances are generally so remarkable throughout his life that it is difficult to get a sense of progress in relation to his playing. In some sense he sprang fully formed into the world. Critics at this stage in his life, however, did seem to acknowledge a new maturity in his playing. Aged 39, Feuermann had so far lived his life at a tremendous pace. Now, exiled in the United States and with so many personal responsibilities, he may finally have been slowing down. Publicly, especially in the company of musicians, he may have continued to appear jovial and mischievous, but a remarkable letter to Eva from Indianapolis in December 1941 reveals something very different: a confused, burdened, unhappy man in a state of personal crisis. The Toch fiasco with Ormandy, the pressure of the recordings with Heifetz and Rubinstein, and the turbulent changes of the time may have provided an immediate backdrop, but for the normally controlled and rational Feuermann this letter marks something of a watershed:

To excuse myself I can only say that everything together these last weeks and months confused me so much that I couldn't pull myself together for anything. Towards you, too, I must have been pretty odious. Of course, other people have greater worries than I. But so many worries, one on top of the other from different areas, makes me quite sick. As childish as it might sound, my birthday also gave me a shock, and a severe one at that. I cannot get it into my head that I will soon be 40. Such an age doesn't fit me at all, and as I can't change the age, so I will have to change, *have to adjust myself,* and that isn't so easy.[46]

He was also worried that his marriage might be falling apart. His student Marion Davies recalled that in California that summer she had not felt that Feuermann and Eva were altogether happy. Now, in this letter to Eva, he put on paper thoughts that he had not expressed to her before:

You are surely of the same opinion as I am that things between us aren't as they should be. . . . We must both be aware that we have entered a cul de sac and we must both try to get ourselves out of it. It would doubtless not be right for our future to continue to muddle along in this kind of living together. Horrible to think where this could lead.

They had been married for just over six years.

This letter recalls those that Feuermann wrote to Eva before their marriage, in which, sometimes in an authoritarian way, he outlined his views on topics such as marriage, Judaism and values in order to 'teach' Eva and perhaps to enable him to reveal his own needs and insecurities. Feuermann's views on marriage were traditional and remained so:

The old fashioned way of living together is where the husband carries the responsibility, confronts the world and as a counter balance finds at home serenity and satisfaction. On the other hand, the intellectual approach is where husband and wife are either together or separately active and find their satisfaction mainly in success. In my opinion we are both for the *old fashioned way.* We should at least take the time *to find out whether we do live up to this kind of 'ensemble'.*

The tone of the letter is clear; Feuermann, in this completely changed climate, no doubt overwhelmed by events, was finally recognizing the immense gulf in age, background and maturity between himself and Eva. However successful he had become, his background had been one of struggle; hers of blind privilege:

These times are hard for he who has to *struggle*; in our case, me. Have you thought about whether you have really tried to create a certain balance for me? Some people naturally emanate an atmosphere of comfort, give the feeling that they are there for their fellow men. I suppose they are mostly a bit older. Then there are, of course, people *who don't care a bit for doing that,* and then again, there are those who easily have this aura around them but who educate themselves when they recognize that it is necessary. You, I believe, belong to the latter. You are surely not egoistic, but perhaps egotistical. You can't separate your thoughts from your Ego, are always occupied with yourself and thus there remains not much room for others in your thoughts and feelings. Sporadically the awareness breaks through that this is so, but only so weakly that you have a kind of guilty conscience; in any case not strong and permanent enough to give you the impetus to fight against your nature.

These were harsh words to his young wife. Whereas letters written before the marriage, if forthright, always contain some softening, there is little here:

Your anxiety, your constant wanting to become more stupid, your passion for learning, what more is it than revolving around your own self? . . . Of course, everything would be much simpler if I were more sure of everything and, indeed, pompous. It would then be easier for you to look up to me, to trust me, and as it were, give yourself to my care. Your characteristic need to idolize would find full satisfaction in a marriage with such a person. But I am not like that, thank God, and besides, I find devotion coupled with the extinction of your own personality rather unworthy. Stay as you are but become a human being with a mission, responsibility and aim. . . . I don't believe there is much new in what I have said until now. But believe me, Eva, you must become more clear about so much. If you are convinced that I mean well, and I believe you don't think me stupid or bad, it should be possible for you, without difficulty, to do your part so that we can finally really build up a life together. You know that in my view there is never a single cause. I am doubtless at fault in many things but certainly not on purpose. I wish that you have as good a life as <u>possible.</u> You will have to accept me as I am. I am sure that I can be nicer, if you are calmer and don't occupy yourself solely with yourself.[47]

This is Feuermann's last known letter to Eva.

Another of his problems was Sophie, who was causing him considerable unhappiness, as he wrote later in December to Kux: 'Her newest proof of love for me is that she is telling people that I didn't want my parents to come to America and that I now am letting them starve. I try sometimes successfully to find understanding for the most unbelievable things. But in this case I declare myself beaten.'[48]

Whatever his personal turmoil, Feuermann did have work, and December 1941 was a busy month. Katya Aschaffenburg, now also a refugee in America, met him two days after he had written to Eva. She found him tired and changed: 'I told him "what is wrong with you?" And he said "Never mind. None of your business!" And I knew there was something wrong.'[49] Quite what was wrong she didn't know. She felt he was ill, believing that he was suffering from cancer, the illness she believes killed him. No evidence exists to suggest that she was right. Doubtless Feuermann did not disclose his unhappiness with Eva, his difficulties with Sophie, his worries with the new house and his uncertainty towards the future.

Feuermann and Katya had reconnected in Detroit, where Feuermann was performing at the Jewish Community Centre: 'I met him at the hotel and we had lunch together and the evening concert was very exciting because in the intermission instead of Feuermann entering the stage, the manager came and turned on the radio. Roosevelt declared war.'[50] However dramatic this moment was, a local paper noted the uniqueness of the event not so much for the President's speech but for a single flaw in the concert – its brevity: 'It was suggested to Mr Feuermann that he play straight through without inter-mission, cutting if necessary, that the assemblage might hear the President. He replied: "Of course. After all I am only a cellist."' The critic remarked: 'He may be "only a cellist" but as one sat enthralled by his tremendous gifts last night one could not help thinking that that sort of ability will play an important role in the days that lie ahead.'[51] Bloch's *Prayer* and Dvořák's Rondo were cut, but the programme still included Mendelssohn's D major Sonata, Beethoven variations, on '*Bei Männern*' from Mozart's *Magic Flute*, Frescobaldi's Toccata, Debussy's Sonata and Chopin's Polonaise.

A photograph of a sombre-looking Feuermann graced the cover of *Musical America* of 10 December 1941, an accolade in considerable contrast to the remark 'After all I am only a cellist'.

On 14 December at New York's Town Hall, Feuermann, again playing Mendelssohn's D major Sonata with Albert Hirsch, and the Kolisch Quartet replaced the indisposed Lotte Lehmann in a concert for the New Friends of Music. The following day he appeared in the ballroom of the Waldorf-Astoria with Jarmila Novotna, Erica Morini, Richard Bonelli, Emanuel List and Jan Smeterlin for the Albert Morris Bagby Memorial Concert.

A concert on 22 December received mixed reviews, a couple of critics noting that Feuermann was not on best form. The first performance of the 'Mozart' concerto that Feuermann had promised to Saidenberg's Little Symphony had finally taken place (see Plate 20). At Feuermann's request, George Szell had arranged two movements from the Oboe Concerto K.314 (which Mozart himself subsequently arranged for flute) plus an adagio from the Divertimento K.131. The work was not well received: 'The combination

makes a viable work for the repertory, though there is too much bravura writing for cello.'[52] Virgil Thomson in the *New York Herald Tribune* was particularly scathing about Feuermann: 'The cello sounded ineffectual indeed and frequently off pitch, at rendering this lithe and limber flute music. . . . The whole work did small credit to its transcriber, or to its interpreter, and not much to Mozart.'[53] Nevertheless, as stated in a feature article in the *New York Times*, the work was published by Schirmer with orchestral parts and piano accompaniment and a preface by Alfred Einstein.[54] In the same concert, Britten's *Les Illuminations* had received its first New York performance, with the tenor Peter Pears as soloist. About this Thomson was even more scathing: 'I found the work pretentious, banal and utterly disappointing, coming from so gifted a composer. Mr Pears . . . has neither correct French diction nor a properly trained voice.'[55]

Apart from appearances in Elizabeth, New Jersey, Cleveland and Saginaw, Michigan, Feuermann's main engagement in January 1942 was with the Boston Symphony Orchestra. Boston, the only non-unionized orchestra in the United States, was engaged in a bitter and damaging struggle with the American Federation of Musicians, but this did not prevent Claudio Arrau, Louis Bailly,

Yehudi Menuhin, Ruth Posselt and Feuermann, among others, from being secured as soloists for the season. Feuermann performed in five concerts, including recitals in Providence, Springfield and Brooklyn. Bruno Walter had initially been contracted to conduct Feuermann's performances but was prevented from working with this non-unionized orchestra. (Carlos Chávez was also prevented from appearing with the Boston Symphony Orchestra at this time.) Once again, Feuermann's concerts (on 20, 23 and 24 January and 10 and 12 February) were conducted by Richard Burgin. Koussevitzky's decision not to conduct them suggests a further snub, but possibly there were mitigating personal circumstances: Koussevitzky's wife had recently died. Indeed, a week later Burgin also conducted the following pair of concerts.[56]

Feuermann played the Schumann concerto, announced as a 'new' work by the *Boston Herald*; it had not been performed in a Boston Symphony Orchestra concert since 1931. A local critic covering the concert in Springfield, Massachusetts, noted that a high percentage of men in the audience were dressed in uniform. America was at war, a war that for Feuermann had not come too soon. He wrote to Kux in December 1941: 'The greatest favour the Axis did for the Americans was that through Pearl Harbor they took the decision out of their hands. Slowly even *the most stubborn people* have found out that one will have to fight, that is to say that a decision between two worlds has to be made.'[57]

Patriotic duties as well as concert appearances now figured significantly in Feuermann's schedule. In December 1941 George N. Shuster, president of Hunter College in New York, had invited him to take part in a fund-raising concert to honour Franklin D. Roosevelt on his 60th birthday: 'Only the most prominent artists are being invited to participate in this patriotic and social event. . . . Knowing your patriotism and interest in charity we invite you, dear Mr Feuermann, to take part in this Gala Festival.' Elizabeth Schumann, Erica Morini and three singers from the Metropolitan Opera (including Emanuel List) agreed to take part. The proceeds were to go to 'needy and deserving students of Hunter College'.[58]

A radio programme, *Music You Want When You Want It*, was broadcast from New York on 5 March, with Feuermann as a guest. His contribution is unknown since the broadcast has not been found.[59] The following day, he embarked on four concerts with the Philadelphia Orchestra and Ormandy. These were the concerts over which Feuermann had had so much trouble and in which he had hoped to perform Toch's new work. In something of a *tour de force*, each concert consisted of three cello concertos – the Haydn D major, Strauss's *Don Quixote* and a Vivaldi concerto in A minor. The concerts on 6, 7 and 9 March took place in Philadelphia whereas the final concert on 10 March was given in Carnegie Hall. The performance on 6 March was broadcast, but no part of it has been found. A flyer for these concerts advertised Feuermann's 1940 recording of Strauss's *Don Quixote*: the line-up of section principals, Samuel Lifschey (viola) and Alexander Hilsberg (violin), was the same. In Howard Taubman's summing up of outstanding recordings released in 1941 – 'Industry's Biggest Year' – both the Strauss and the Brahms Double were included.[60] Of the opening concert performance of *Don Quixote*, the local critic of the Philadelphia News pronounced: 'This Straussian creation, written in the dim past when this now completely-Hitlerized musician was in his prime and fettle ... was about as close to perfect as has been offered here in a long time.'[61] It is said that RCA Victor contracted Feuermann to record the Haydn concerto with the Philadelphia and Ormandy some time in 1942.[62] If so, the project was never realized.

Following these performances on the eastern seaboard, Feuermann, with Albert Hirsch, once again travelled west, to Colorado, Kansas and Louisiana. In Denver on 16 March, they played before a large audience of Pro Musica members in the Broadway Theatre. On the 17th they found themselves in very different surroundings: the Cavalry Replacement Training Centre of Fort Riley

---

CARNEGIE HALL

FORTY-SECOND SEASON — 1941-1942

PHILADELPHIA ORCHESTRA

EUGENE ORMANDY, *Music Director*

EIGHTH PROGRAM

Tuesday Evening, March 10th, at 8:45 o'clock

EUGENE ORMANDY Conducting
EMANUEL FEUERMANN, 'Cellist

VIVALDI . . . . Concerto in A minor

HAYDN . . . Concerto in D major, for 'Cello and Orchestra
    I. Allegro moderato
    II. Adagio
    III. Allegro

INTERMISSION

STRAUSS . . . "Don Quixote"; Fantastical Variations on a
    Theme of Knightly Character, Op. 35

Incidental solos: EMANUEL FEUERMANN, 'cello
    SAMUEL LIFSCHEY, *viola*

CALENDAR OF NEW YORK CONCERTS
Ten Tuesday Evenings, Season 1941-1942

Date	Soloist	Conductor
October 14		Ormandy
November 11	Sergei Rachmaninoff, pianist	Ormandy
November 25		Beecham
December 16	Dorothy Maynor, soprano	Ormandy
January 6	Artur Rubinstein, pianist	Ormandy
February 10		Toscanini
February 24	Samuel Sorin, pianist	Ormandy
March 10	Emanuel Feuermann, 'cellist	Ormandy
March 24	Nathan Milstein, violinist	Ormandy
April 7		Ormandy

Subscribers are kindly requested to notify the Association of any change in address

HARL McDONALD, Manager   LOUIS A. MATTSON, Assistant Manager
1910 Girard Trust Company Building, Philadelphia

The STEINWAY is the Official Piano of the Philadelphia Orchestra—Victor Records

in Kansas (see Plate 21). As Hirsch recalled: 'Playing at the army bases was something we thought was very worthwhile doing. We felt impelled to.'[63] Fort Riley was described as 'the only camp in the country where both the old-fashioned horse and modern mechanised units are in use'.[64] Feuermann's keenness to appear at the base related to a pledge he had made to a colleague, Mel Adams, formerly in charge of publicity at RCA, that one day he would give a concert at an army post where Adams was stationed. The concert was free, but the enlisted men and officers of the training centre were obliged to submit their names for the limited number of seats available. Feuermann had regarded this engagement as something of an amusement, but it turned out to be a most sobering experience that he later recalled in a magazine article published after his death:

> *The only knowledge I had of army life came through the traditions of Europe, and to a European, it seemed impossible that an ordinary buck-private could have anything to say about entertainment for the men. . . . My accompanist and I neared the camp towards evening. Ordinary passenger trains make the stop at Fort Riley only by arrangement with the conductor, who must be convinced that the traveller's reason for visiting the camp is a sound one. We had to go through some vivid talk before he felt quite easy in his mind that we two strangers and the bulky 'cello case might possibly do the soldiers more good than harm after dark.*[65]

Feuermann, familiar with the spartan harshness and bareness of European barracks, was amazed at what he found:

> *Everywhere were comfortable, well-kept buildings with beautiful lawns and gardens, and an air of peaceful quiet. I asked my escorts if they were quite certain that this was an army camp and not a university campus . . . I had expected to play in a rough barracks hall, with straggling groups of soldiers peering in at the doors to size up the nature of the entertainment being offered them, and to watch out, perhaps, for any pretty girls among the performers. Instead, I crossed over to a fine, large chapel, where I found hundreds of men, soldiers and officers alike, already seated in orderly fashion, well-groomed, quiet, and waiting with the eager expectancy, that is so quickly communicated, for an evening of music. They were in no sense picked musical men. . . . The audience was made up of men of all ages, classes, creeds and kinds, from every section of the country; their presence there reflected the interest the average American soldier (who is also the average American man) takes in music.*

Feuermann had announced a normal programme of Beethoven, Bach, Schubert, Chopin and Dvořák, rather than something lighter: '*Frankly this question was in my mind when I began. As I played on, however, I felt better and played better, as one always does when he feels the glow of unstinted accord between music and audience.'* At the reception following the concert, he again had a surprise: '*I learned that the comments of the men who gave me the pleasure of shaking their hands were very different from the stupid comments one often has to endure after more fashionable concerts.'* In this random group he came across a cellist who had played in an orchestra when he had been soloist and a boy from Vienna who had known Sophie: '*It just seems inevitable that a cross section of the American army yields up a large proportion of musical enthusiasts!'* At breakfast in the Service Club the following day, more surprises were in store: '*I was thrilled by the wonderful spectacle of officers and men sitting together, eating together, with the greatest friendliness yet with that delicacy of regard for official rank that can be achieved only by men who in their souls are free.'* The congeniality of the camp was far from his expectations: '*If I seem to dwell on this point, it is because it makes an unforgettable impression on a European who knows only the herding of army men into compulsory attitudes of submissive respect.'*

This encounter was extremely positive, with Feuermann mixing easily with the soldiers, as usual not holding his status as a barrier between himself and others. Members of the camp felt this: 'His personal charm and humour showed that he is not only a great artist, but also a great personality.'[66] A delightful photograph survives of 'Corporal Bolo', a Boston puppy, wearing corporal stripes, standing on a keyboard, mesmerized by a smiling Feuermann[67] – 'His Master's Voice' in another form (see Plate 22).

After this memorable moment, Feuermann returned to conventional concert life with a performance in New Orleans of the Dvořák concerto conducted by Eugene Goossens with the Cincinnati Symphony Orchestra. It was almost exactly two years since he had played the same work with Goossens in Cincinnati. As usual, the reviews for this 23 March concert were ecstatic. Four days later, he and Hirsch were in Philadelphia at the Curtis Institute. It had just been announced that Feuermann was to take over chamber music instruction as well as cello tuition. It was a faculty recital, perhaps his first, certainly his last. The programme was a standard one: Handel's Adagio and Allegro, Beethoven's Variations on Mozart's '*Bei Männern*', the Schubert 'Arpeggione' Sonata, Stravinsky's *Suite italienne*, Chopin's 'Introduction and Polonaise, the Dvořák Rondo, and Davidov's *At the Fountain*.

A few days later, plans for the 1942 festival at Ravinia, summer home of the Chicago Symphony Orchestra, were announced. Conductors included Dimitri Mitropoulos, Pierre Monteux, George Szell, Eugene Ormandy and Artur Rodzinski. Schnabel, Szigeti and Feuermann were announced as soloists, with

Szigeti and Feuermann appearing once again in the Brahms Double Concerto on 25 July and Feuermann appearing as soloist with Ormandy and the Chicago Symphony Orchestra on 21 July. This would have been Feuermann's third appearance at the festival; in the summer of 1939 he had given two concerts with Vladimir Golschmann – the Dvořák and Haydn concertos – and in 1940 he had played the Schumann Concerto, Strauss's *Don Quixote* and Tchaikovsky's 'Rococo' Variations in concerts with Ormandy. Claudia Cassidy reflected in the *Chicago Sun*: 'Most of us feel while there is Ravinia, there is hope.'[68]

Despite the unusual times, life appeared to continue as normal. Feuermann had thrown himself fully behind various activities supporting the war, including those of the Loyalty Committee of Victims of Nazi-Fascist Oppression which urged refugees driven from Europe by the Axis to contribute to the purchase of a fully equipped fighter plane to be presented to the US Government. Feuermann, Heinrich Mann, Franz Werfel, Lion Feuchtwanger, Elizabeth Bergner, Jakob Goldschmidt and Hans Koster were all members of this organization's national committee; Eleanor Roosevelt was a sponsor. A formal appeal for contributions read: 'We want to show our gratitude to the country that has rescued us and our children from torture and death.'[69]

While the war encouraged substantial change, certain things remained remarkably stable. Cornell College Conservatory in Mount Vernon, Iowa, on 30 April began its 44th May music festival with a recital by Feuermann and Hirsch, a repeat of the programme they had given at the Curtis Institute. This festival was quite a substantial affair, with concerts by the Chicago Symphony Orchestra, the Hans Lange Little Symphony Orchestra and the Cornell Oratorio Society.

A festival also took place from 6 to 9 May at Ann Arbor in Michigan. Although it was only the second festival to be held at Ann Arbor, an ambitious series of six concerts was planned, to include appearances by Marian Anderson and Rachmaninov. Programming was ambitious to match. On 7 May, Honegger's monumental symphonic psalm *King David* was paired with the Dvořák Cello Concerto and the Philadelphia Orchestra conducted by Thor Johnson. The *Detroit Times* found *King David* unappealing: 'Perhaps because of its very epic pretensions, we find "King David" something of a musical impostor. . . . It is a combination of spoken narrative, solo passages, orchestral incidents, oratorical digressions and everything but boogie-woogie.'[70] As the music editor of the *Detroit News* reported, Feuermann upstaged the Honegger: 'The distinction of Feuermann's contribution rather upset the planned values of the occasion, for Thursday evening traditionally belongs to the University

Choral Union. . . . The sturdy bow-arm of Emanuel Feuermann was the cardinal detail."[71] It was perhaps fitting that in this, his final performance as a soloist in any orchestral concert, the work played was the Dvořák Concerto, a late substitute for the Haydn D major.

On 10 May 1942, Feuermann featured in a radio programme of recorded music entitled *Evening Concert* which included the Adagio and Allegro from Handel's Organ Concerto in G minor and Bloch's *Schelomo*, broadcast from the studios of WQXR in New York. He was also the commentator. This was his last broadcast.[72] Two weeks later, he was dead.

Chapter 15

An Untimely End

Oh, it's nothing at all. We will resume our work very soon again.

Emanuel Feuermann[1]

In the last days of his life, patriotic activities continued to occupy Feuermann. An unattributed clipping reveals that on 16 May 1942 he took part in 'I am an American' Day.[2] In a speech, said to be his first in public,[3] Feuermann stood before a vast gathering of RCA Victor defence workers at Camden, New Jersey, telling them of the possession he valued above all others – his forthcoming American citizenship. And 'On a bare wooden platform under the breeze-swept trees of a city park, he played his chosen instrument – played it divinely – and the mellow, sunny tones of his cello seemed to echo and reinforce the man's indomitable courage, his inspired Americanism.'[4] A photograph shows Feuermann playing before a huge American flag (see Plate 23). Hirsch was his partner. Earlier that day, Feuermann had 'made a series of recordings in Camden'[5] – from which the test pressing (said to have been made with Albert Hirsch) of the slow movement of Victor Herbert's Cello Concerto no.2 may possibly have emerged.

Although no one knew it, this patriotic gesture of performing in front of the flag was to be Feuermann's last public appearance. Little is spelt out, but a letter from his wife in early May indicates that he had a medical problem: 'I wonder how you are? Does it hurt badly? Do you follow all Simon's advices [*sic*]? Specially the different techniques.'[6] He was suffering from haemorrhoids, a condition he was not predisposed to discuss freely. To this day, his widow claims that she was aware of his condition only weeks before he entered hospital for treatment. In the light of his medical history, he, his wife and Mrs Reifenberg should all have been deeply concerned about the prospect of the forthcoming operation: in 1935 in Cologne he had experienced a severe reaction during an operation for a hernia. According to Sophie, he had nearly lost his life. It was thought that that reaction was due either to the anaesthetic or to the administration of morphine. Feuermann regarded his current complaint as trivial and embarrassing, and this is perhaps what caused him to deny its importance. As Rubinstein recalled: 'When he had to take that tragic operation, he laughed it off. He told us: 'Oh, it's nothing at all. We will resume our work very soon again' and we were looking on it as a disagreeable little incident.'[7] Albert Hirsch also remembers Feuermann's nonchalance. Following the 'I am an American' Day, he asked Hirsch to take his cello, as he was going directly from Camden to the hospital. He would pick it up again in three days. Hirsch took the Stradivarius on the New York subway to his home. In passing, as he was leaving for the hospital, Feuermann mentioned to Hirsch that he had just signed a contract with RCA Victor to record all the Beethoven sonatas with him.[8]

That day, Saturday 16 May (not 15 May as communicated in the *New York Times*), Feuermann's haemorrhoidectomy took place at the Park East Hospital, 112 East Eighty-Third Street, New York.[9] Although his name does not appear on the 'Physician's Confidential Medical Report', the operation is said by Eva to have been performed by Siegfried Simon, Eva's gynaecologist. It was, of course, to 'Simon's advices' that she had referred in her letter. Feuermann rarely discussed his health with his wife, but it seems that he was reluctant to have surgery performed by a doctor he did not know. Simon was a family acquaintance who Eva believes may have been distantly related to her mother's family. He had graduated in 1912 in Bonn[10] and was now a German Jewish refugee living in New Rochelle. That a gynaecologist performed Feuermann's operation is not remarkable; surgical proficiency in this area of the body at that time was not confined to one sex or the other. What is remarkable is that the 1941–2 *Medical Directory of New York, New Jersey and Connecticut* lists Simon merely as a general practitioner, and the Park East Hospital is not registered at all. Doctors today rank the Park East Hospital at that time as third-rate; it no longer exists. It is not beyond possibility that Simon may have been a qualified surgeon in Germany but that these qualifications had not yet been recognized in the USA. Nevertheless, that Simon as a GP was able to perform surgery without registration was highly irregular. Even less credible is that Feuermann, a well-known celebrity, did not insist on a first-class surgeon nor on admittance to a first-class hospital. Simon, for his part, was probably able to admit patients only to less than first-class hospitals; Jewish doctors

recently arrived from Europe were not extended such hospital privileges that
allowed their patients to be admitted to the finest medical facilities. What
seems likely is that Feuermann, regarding the matter as trivial and wanting
little attention drawn to it, opted for a doctor he knew, disregarding the possibility that anything could go wrong.

Feuermann's student Suzette Forgues recalls arriving at the new house in
Rye:

> I was the last one to go to the house for my lesson and when I got there that
> day there was little Monica. 'Daddy's not here.' I said 'No? I have a lesson
> today.' 'No, Daddy's in the hospital.' So I walked into the house and there was
> Mrs Reifenberg in tears. Well, I'd never seen her crying and I thought
> something is very serious. At that time, Eva was expecting the second child
> and she was not allowed to move out of bed so I went to her room and there
> I discovered that Feuermann was in the hospital. I didn't know what it was
> but as I sat there comforting her the phone rang. Feuermann was calling
> from the hospital. He was delirious. I could hear his voice telling Eva how
> lovely it was in Switzerland and how he enjoyed his little wild strawberries
> in the mountains. It was very sad to hear because you realized that he was
> not fully conscious of what he was saying.[11]

Something had gone terribly wrong. Two documents, the 'Physician's Confidential Medical Report' and the 'Certificate of Death', shed some light. The
former from the Department of Records, Department of Health, City of New
York, is date-stamped 25 May 1942.[12] It is signed not by Siegfried Simon but by
Rudolf Nissen, surgeon, of 116 East 58th Street, as is the 'Certificate of Death'
no.11161. Simon's name or signature appears on neither document. According to
Eva, Professor Berberich, a distinguished ear, nose and throat surgeon and friend
of the family from Germany, visited Feuermann in hospital and it was he who
called in Nissen to perform the second operation. The medical report lists the
principal cause of death as 'Obstructive Ileus' – date of onset 20 May; 'Contributory causes': pneumonia – date of onset 24 May; 'Other pathological conditions': haemorrhoidectomy – date of onset 16 May; 'Laboratory tests that assisted
diagnosis, if any': X-ray and other tests. Nissen certified that he had attended
Feuermann from 23 to 25 May on the death certificate. If Simon performed the
haemorrhoidectomy on 16 May, no mention is made of his name. An
'Obstructive Ileus' was observed on 20 May but it was not until the 23rd that
Nissen was brought in to perform a second operation, a caecostomy. One day
later Feuermann contracted pneumonia. On 25 May at 4.10 p.m. he died.

What had happened? Anecdotal stories abound, the most persistent that
Feuermann was suffering from cancer. Years later, his daughter Monica visited

Dr Nissen in Switzerland. She saw the medical records, from which there was no indication of cancer.[13] There is no reason to suggest that Nissen falsified the medical records, and judging from photographs taken in the last weeks of his life and from the busy schedule Feuermann was undertaking, cancer seems unlikely. It is more likely that cancer, a taboo subject, was lit on as the cause by those unable to comprehend Feuermann's sudden death, particularly in the light of no autopsy.

Professor Berberich believed that the peritoneum had been punctured, causing death.[14] Elinor Lipper, Feuermann's friend from Berlin who became a trained doctor, believes opium caused Feuermann's collapse – as it was said to have done seven years before in Cologne when a nicotine enema was administered to save his life:

> Perhaps he was not told in advance that they would give him opium because surely he would have remembered. Antibiotics were not yet available but they could have given him something else. It wasn't a matter of life and death, it was just to make it easier to allow for the healing. He thought he was going to be in hospital for five days so the opium would have been used not as an anaesthetic, but as a constipatory drug in order to paralyse the system for a few days so that the intestine had time to heal. Once it was given, and in a rather large dose, it was too late, especially at the time. I suppose there was no way of saving him. I suppose it was in a way like an overdose. But opium was used very frequently at that time.[15]

As no autopsy was carried out, there is no proof of cause of death. The meaning of the 'Physician's Confidential Medical Report', in lay terms, can only be the subject of speculation. Four days after the haemorrhoidectomy performed by Simon on 16 May, an obstruction of the intestines was observed. What this obstruction was and how it was caused can only be surmised. Perhaps there was a tumour; perhaps inflammation developed, paralysing the intestine and causing a blockage; perhaps this inflammation was caused by dirty instruments; perhaps the intestines went into paralysis because of an allergic reaction to the anaesthetic; perhaps the peritoneum was punctured. The caecostomy was performed a week after the original operation to relieve the blockage. Peritonitis, though not mentioned in the report, may have set in as a result of the blockage. Pneumonia was contracted the following day; penicillin, barely discovered, was not generally available. Nothing could save Feuermann.

Questions have to be asked as to why Eva, Mrs Reifenberg and Sophie – all of them aware of the near tragedy in Cologne – could not, or did not, prevail on Feuermann to take this medical condition seriously. Eva, just pregnant, never visited the hospital; she had been ordered to stay in bed for fear of a miscarriage. Sophie had broken off all contact since her row with him in 1938; it was George Szell who informed her of Feuermann's illness. She rushed to the hospital and was appalled: 'I went to the worst hospital in Harlem [*sic*]. The worst hospital you can imagine because this gynaecologist could only operate there.'[16] From her account, Feuermann was being restrained by a straitjacket.

Feuermann's tragic and entirely unnecessary death seems to have been caused by a combination of unlucky factors, including his nonchalance, his embarrassment and the historical misfortune regarding Jewish doctors' privileges at the time. Feuermann was only thirty-nine years, six months and three days old when he died. In the Department of Health's *Medical Records Accession Book* his death was not reported for negligence. If, as Sophie maintains, a contributory cause of death was a reaction to the anaesthetic, such cases were not generally referred for investigation. Nevertheless, the absence of Siegfried Simon's name anywhere on the official documentation suggests a peculiarity, if not a cover-up.

Feuermann's former student George Neikrug was in New York at the time of his death:

I remember the very day he died because one of our colleagues, a fellow student who was studying when we went to California, came to New York. My wife was still studying with Feuermann and Claus Adam was with us. We were all there for a reunion, talking about Feuermann. One of us said: 'Why don't we call him up from here', and I think Claus went to the telephone that was in my apartment. He came back white. 'He just died half an hour ago.' We were in complete shock. I think we couldn't sleep so we went to an all-night movie and wandered around. We couldn't believe it.[17]

News of Feuermann's death was broadcast over the radio. The main newspapers, the *New York Times, New York Herald Tribune, New York Sun*, all carried prominent feature articles. One read:

To those who knew the art of Emanuel Feuermann the announcement of his death from a minor operation in yesterday's newspapers must have brought a deep sense of loss. He cannot be replaced. Had he been no more than a consummate virtuoso upon his instrument, Feuermann would have enjoyed his international fame. But his technical supremacy and his profound knowledge were companioned by the warmth, the versatility and insight of his interpretations. . . . This, in a word, is not merely the disappearance of a famous virtuoso in the prime of his powers, but a loss to the art of music the world over.[18]

Musique

par EDGARD FEDER

EMANUEL FEUERMANN

Le monde musical porte le deuil d'un grand artiste ; le monde tout court, celui d'un brave et honnête homme ; et nous, en plus, nous pleurons la perte d'un ami. Pour ceux qui l'ont connu, il est impossible d'associer l'idée de la mort avec l'image de Munio, comme l'appelaient ses intimes. Plein de jeunesse, éclatant de gaîté et d'entrain, se moquant de tous et de lui-même, avec une gentillesse désarmante, chantant sous ses apparences espiègles un coeur d'or, fidèle et généreux, il était bâti pour enterrer tous ses contemporains. Hélas ! Atropos la cruelle, mystérieuse en ses desseins, a prématurément coupé le fil de cette existence et aujourd'hui le nom de Feuermann n'est plus que le symbole d'un cher souvenir. Emblême ... en quelques jours par un mal ... orable, ... 'âge de

pas la longue touche de son violoncelle comme une patinoire à faire des 'glissandi' douteux, tant de violoncellistes encroûtés dans le conservatisme. Sa construction de la technique du violoncelle était essentiellement moderne. Une fois qu'il avait décidé que la nature et le morceau exigeait certaines ponctuations n'était faite aucune concession n'était faite ... besoins de l'instrument et il n'y avait de problèmes insolubles lorsqu'il s'agissait de servir la mesure où le violon fine. Son goût musical était sûr et raffiné. Dans la mesure où le violoncelle peut concourir avec le violon en légèreté et pureté de l'émission sonore, Feuermann a repoussé les frontières admises du possible et a établi un véritable étalon de la perfection.

Et maintenant, Feuermann est entré dans les grandes ténèbres ; mais son souvenir reste impérissablement ancré dans les coeurs de ses amis ... 'mirateurs, ... veille ... peace, cher ... rons sur ...

E. Feuermann, Cellist, Dies

Emanuel Feuermann, 39, the infant prodigy who became one of the world's greatest 'cellists, died yesterday at the Park East Hospital. Death was due to complications resulting from a minor operation.

Feuermann came to the U. S. after he was exiled from Germany by Hitler. He applied for citizenship in 1938. His wife, ... ne, and his daughter, Monika, ... survive.

FEUERMANN, 39, CELLIST, DEAD

Teacher Was Heard Often in Town Hall Concerts.

A funeral service for Emanuel Feuermann, noted cellist, will be held at ... Lexington avenue, Thursday at ... A. M. Mr. Feuermann, who ... s 39 years old, died yesterday ... Park East Hospital after a ... ill illness.

Mr. Feuermann was a child prodigy in his native Austria, and gave his first public concert at the age of 7. Four years later he appeared with the Vienna Symphony under the Weingartner.

His debut here, in 1935 with the New York Philharmonic-Symphony Orchestra, made him under Bruno Walter, made him as a 'cellist ... as he had been in ... In succeeding years ... came here many ... he gave many ... Hall. ...

Cellist and Teacher

...ERMANN, 39, ...MOUS 'CELLIST

..., Who First Played for ...nce at the Age of 7, ...s After Brief Illness

...HT IN NOTED SCHOOLS

Berlin When Hitler Came ...Power—Debut Here in '35 With Philharmonic

Emanuel Feuermann, one of the ...rld's great 'cellists, died yester-...y afternoon at the Park East ...ospital, 112 East Eighty-third ...treet. Death was due to compli-...ations which developed after a ...minor operation, performed on ...May 15. He was 39 years old.

The 'cellist, who first came to ...fame as a child prodigy in Austria, ...made his American debut here ...seven years ago. An American succeeding ...year his position as a front rank ...virtuoso he became more and more ...sure. He had obtained his first ...papers for American citizenship, ...and earlier this year had settled in ...a unique house overlooking ...Long Island Sound.

He leaves a widow, the former ...Eva Reifenberg, and a 4-year-old ...daughter, Monica.

Played in Public at 7

Mr. Feuermann was born in Ko-...lomea, Galicia, on Nov. 22, 1902. ...His father, a 'cellist, is now in Pales-...tine, was a 'cellist. Emanuel start-...ed appearing in public at the age ...of 7, and made his Vienna debut at ...the age of 11, appearing with the ...Vienna Symphony under Felix ...Weingartner.

...The talented youth was ap-...pointed a teacher at the Cologne ...Conservatory in 1917, remaining ...there for six years. After a rest ...from teaching, he returned to that ...occupation in 1929 at the Berlin ...Hochschule, where he taught until ...Hitler came to power.

Mr. Feuermann then went to ...Vienna, where he continued his ...concert career he had started while ...teaching. When he first came to ...this country, for he had already fa-...mous in Europe, and had appeared as ...soloist with such conductors as ...Arthur Nikisch, Carl Muck, Wil-...helm Furtwaengler, Pierre Mon-...teux, Otto Klemperer, Fritz Busch ...and Sir Thomas Beecha...

EMANUEL FEUERMANN 1938

Feuermann Dies; Concert 'Cellist

Refugee from Nazis Sought Citizenship

Emanuel Feuermann, 39, one of the world's greatest 'cellists, died yesterday afternoon at the Park East Hospital, 112 E. 83rd St. Death was due to complications which developed after an operation May 15.

Mr. Feuermann, an infant prod-...igy who made his debut in Vienna ...at 7, came to the United States ...after he was exiled from Germany ...by the Nazis. He applied for cit-...izenship in 1938 and lived in Fr... ...ermann, and his wife, Mrs. Eve F... ...who survive. He was act... ...to concert and recording wor... ...death.

Many critics conside... ...Feuermann the greatest ... ...the concert stage, a re... ...tal technique, as h... ...as known when he rep... ...hanced by the car... ...given since 1935. Bes... ...his annual concerts at ... Hall.

Feuermann,39, Cellist, Is Dead; German Exile

Renowned Artist Recently Gave Series of Recitals in Army Camps; Ill 6 Days

Emanuel Feuermann, one of the most distinguished cellists on the contemporary concert stage and head of the chamber music depart-...ment of the Curtis Institute of Mu-...sic in Philadelphia, died yesterday ...in the Park East Hospital, 112 East ...Eighty-third Street, after an illness ...of six days. He was ... nine years ... old.

Mr. Feuermann ... ...States after he was ... ...many by the N... ...gime of Adolf ... ...citizenship in ... ...N. Y., with ... ...ermann an... ...who surviv... ...Mr. Fe... ...his illn... ...series ... ...Victor ... ...dress... ...had ... ...ci ...

E. Feuermann, Famed 'Cellist, Dies at 39

...nuel Feuermann

Funeral services for Emanuel ...Feuermann, 39, one of the world's ...greatest 'cellists, will be held at 11 ... m. Thursday, at the Universal ...Chapel, 112 E. 83rd st. of com-...died yesterday at the Park East ...Hospital, 112 E. 83rd st, of com-...plications that followed a minor ...operation.

Before he entered the hospital ...last Friday he had made a series ...of recordings in Camden, where he ...also made his first public speech ...as part of the "I Am an American ...Day" rally in the R. C. A. plant.

Born in Kolomea, Galicia, Mr. ...Feuermann studied music under ...his father, Emanuel Feuermann, ...also a 'cellist. He made his debut ...at the age of 11 under the direc-...tion of Felix Weingartner. He ...became a pro-...fessor of music at the Cologne ...Conservatory of Music.

CAME HERE IN 1938.

Three years later he went to ...Berlin, where he became to 'cello ...department of the Hochschule Fue ...Musik. In protest to Nazism, he ...quit Berlin in 1934 and lived in ...Switzerland until 1938 when he ...came here. He made his debut ...with the New York Philharmonic ...Symphony, under Bruno Walter. ...He also appeared with the New ...York Philharmonic, the N. B. C. ...Symphony, under Artuo Tosc... ...nini, and at Carnegie Hall, Tosc... ...played at several the country and ...He made his home in Rye, Sur-...giving are his wife, Eva, and a ...daughter, Monica, four, ...

the leading cellists of his ...to the United States in ...o make his debut as soloist ...he Philharmonic - Symphony ...estra, under direction of Mr. ...lter.

In 193 he brought his wife and ...daughter from Zurich. ...Mr. Feuermann was the owner of ...the "Last Cello" as described because ...it was said to be the last cello made ...by Stradivarius. It was insured for ...$35,000.

Funeral services for Mr. Fruer-...mann will be held at 11 a. m. Thurs-...day at the Universal Funeral Chapel, ...597 Lexington Avenue.

...several years of ...pe, ...before he was ...ssor at the Berlin ...er Musik, a post he ...934, when he went to ...an exile. ...ermann related in later ...er he had appeared as a ...with the National Broadcast-...ture company orchestra, once ...ture Toscanini, that Mr. Tos-...l had heard him play in 1927 ...d been impressed. ...Then twenty-three years old, Mr. ...euermann was admittedly resting ...on his laurels as an infant prodigy ...and a professor at the famous Ber-...lin school. ...'Everybody told me how wonder-...ful I was and I had a bad effect,' ...Mr. Feuermann once said. 'I played ...worse and worse and at last I was ...pretty awful.'

Three hundred people attended the funeral, which took place on 28 May in the Universal Chapel, 597 Lexington Avenue, New York City. The honorary pallbearers included Toscanini, Ormandy, Szell, Schnabel, Zimbalist, Serkin, Mischa Elman, Barzin, Huberman, Edgar Lustgarten, Charles O'Connell, Fritz Stiedry, Emil Cooper, Al Blume, Siegfried Hearst, Charles H. Bubrich, Leo Hofman, Sacha Jacobson, Nathan W. Levin, Arthur W. Percival and Paul Schiff. George Szell spoke on 'Feuermann, the World's Friend': 'The great artist in him, combined with the qualities of a fine human being, will always make him stand out as one of the unforgettable figures of our lives. We are not likely to encounter his equal in our lifetime, and it may well be [that] the singular blend of qualities that made our friend will never occur again.' The *New York Times* critic Olin Downes in a brief speech recalled that Feuermann 'knew that it was the duty of every great musician to impart the secrets of his art to his disciples. In his teaching of young students he has perpetuated the art so that many others may enjoy its beauty in years to come.'[19] Schnabel played the Marche Funèbre from Beethoven's Piano Sonata op.26. A string quartet of Erica Morini, Edwin Bachman, Lotte Hammerschlag and Frank Miller played Beethoven's 'Harp' Quartet op.74, and Morini played the Arioso by Bach, with Albert Hirsch at the piano. Heifetz was unable to attend the funeral, but Charles O'Connell from RCA Victor, producer of the trio recordings, wrote of the effect on Heifetz of Feuermann's death. 'I do know that the same ensemble cannot be gathered together again, for the untimely death of Feuermann completely destroyed the enthusiasm and the spirit that had made these records possible, and therefore Jascha has flatly refused, despite any and all inducements, to undertake further recordings of this kind.'[20] For seven years Heifetz performed with no other cellist, refusing to replace his deceased colleague. It was not until 1949, when invited to give four concerts at Ravinia, that he performed with Piatigorsky and Rubinstein,[21] with whom he resumed recording trios in 1950.

On account of the war, news of Feuermann's death was slow in reaching Europe. Some people, including Gerald Moore, only heard about it long after it had occurred. In America, memorial tributes soon followed: the New Friends of Music dedicated its following season to his memory. Feuermann, who had performed for the New Friends since its inception in 1936, had been engaged to give a series of concerts that season devoted to Bach's solo suites and viola da gamba sonatas; he had intended playing the gamba sonatas on a viola da gamba. The 1942 Ravinia Festival marked his death with a performance by Piatigorsky of the Adagio from Boccherini's B♭ Cello Concerto; Piatigorsky had taken Feuermann's place at the festival. The NOA mounted a concert in November 1942 in memory of Feuermann in which Szigeti, at his own request, played Beethoven's Violin Concerto.

Some time later, Feuermann's student Suzette Forgues, while playing a summer job, visited Toscanini who was on holiday nearby. She wanted to continue studying the cello but needed advice about who to go to. Toscanini was brief: 'You were fortunate enough to study with the best, but most unfortunate because after Feuermann there is no one.'[22]

Feuermann was cremated. A simple granite headstone remains on a gentle incline at the Kensico Cemetery, Valhalla, New York (see Plate 25). In a deed dated 15 June 1943 the 'De Munck' Stradivarius was sold to an amateur cellist, Russell B. Kingman of Orange, New Jersey, for $33,500. Kingman, president of a textile company and a millionaire friend of the family, had helped Feuermann and the Reifenbergs transfer money from Germany. He obtained the cello for a good price; in February, only four months before, it had been valued by Rudolph Wurlitzer at $45,000. The deed, however, specified that it had to be paid for in cash, an indication, no doubt, of Eva Feuermann's financial worries. The new house in Rye was sold soon after that.

It was not until October 1945 that Eva received the following words:

La perte de votre mari a été un choc pour tous ceux qui le connaissaient, l'aimaient, et l'admiraient – Il m'a laissé le grand regret de l'avoir vu et entendu si peu. Je sais cependant par moi – ment [*sic*] quel grande artiste il était, quelle personne exquise et noble il était. La musique et le violoncelle a perdu un de ses grands représentants.

The letter, handwritten from London, was from Pablo Casals.

Chapter 16

Miracle Worker
Writing, Teaching, Performing

. . . if he takes the trouble to pass it on to young students, his art in some measure survives him more than just in the memory of those who heard him play.

Feuermann[1]

Like all professional musicians, Feuermann spent much time away from his family. It was early days for the telephone, which he used, nevertheless, from time to time, and so writing was his main means of communication. Many of his letters survive but many are also known to have been lost – the combined effect of two world wars and limited appreciation until relatively recently of the importance of archives. The vast majority of existing letters are addressed to family and close friends, with very little professional correspondence surviving, although Feuermann may have written more to colleagues than archives suggest.[2] This imbalance may mask a truth: Feuermann was intensely interested in his family and had little real need to promote himself professionally. The result is that proportionately, there is little in Feuermann's correspondence that gives insight into his musical thinking; however, he did leave a number of substantial interviews and articles, some of which were published.

His earliest published writing appears to date from 1929, when he was newly appointed at the Berlin Hochschule. In that year he collaborated with J. Sakom on a revised and enlarged edition of *Praktische Violoncello-Schule* op.30 by Sebastian Lee, which was published in Leipzig by Anton J. Benjamin. The 105-page text is printed on each page in both German and French, with musical examples and exercises. No distinction is made between Feuermann's contribution and that of Sakom.[3] One of the more remarkable features, however, is the inclusion of a set of photographs showing Feuermann demonstrating the holding of the instrument, the holding of the bow (at the point and the frog), the positioning of the left hand (both closed and in extension), and the left hand in thumb position (see Plates 26, 27, 28).

The bulk of his own writing emanates from another period in his life, his last few years in America. The first published article – 'Feuermann Inveighs Against Mechanical "Methods"' – appeared on 25 February 1940 in *Musical America's Educational Department*. A further two feature-length articles for the music journal *Etude Music Magazine* were published in September 1940 ('The Contralto of the String Family') and after his death in October 1942 ('Music Marches With Uncle Sam'). Although published articles cover much the same ground, his most extensive writings remained unpublished in his lifetime.[4] In June 1941 he wrote from California that he had been asked to write a book; from where the invitation came is unknown.[5] Feuermann doubted his ability to write an extensive work: 'I intend to write neither a theory nor a method. I do not know if this will be a thick book or a small pamphlet. I think that the title "Words of Advice" approximates to what I want to say.'[6] The poorly typed manuscript of 45 pages, written in a mixture of English and German, is divided into five differently numbered sections with few headings. The order in which the manuscript survives is not necessarily that which Feuermann intended. Two sections are numbered consecutively: one cast in the form of a letter to an imaginary student beginning (in English) '*My dear friend*' (pages 1–14); the other entitled 'Koerper' ('The body', pages 15–27). In these sections, page numbers have been put in by hand. Three other sections with no titles are numbered individually (again by hand): one consists of six pages, one of two pages, one of ten pages. The occasional inclusion of the word 'example' suggests that part of the text was perhaps intended as the basis for a lecture with cello 'examples'. The manuscript suggests an early draft. In publishing these writings in his biography, Seymour Itzkoff, for ease of reading, has given them section headings and titles, but generally these are not Feuermann's. The following will refer to the five sections as '*My dear friend*' (1–14), 'Koerper' (15–17), Section A (six-page section), Section B (two-page section) and Section C (ten-page section).

Monica Feuermann has said that Feuermann's writings were gathered from 'bits and pieces' written on concert tours and collected in a number of 'spiral notebooks'.[7] But Eva does not recall these notebooks; nor have they emerged.

Feuermann's 'words of advice' express thoughts on many topics: the history of the instrument and its performers, performance and attitude to performance, the physical demands of the instrument, the approach to a score, the performer's responsibility, talent, technique, interpretation, practising, teaching, the virtuoso and prodigies. On certain aspects there is much duplication. To avoid duplication here, extracts have been selected from both the published texts and those texts unpublished in his lifetime.

If doubts existed about his ability to express his thoughts verbally, these writings roundly confound such a notion. Notwithstanding an abundance of grammatical errors in the English parts of the text, his writing is colourful, intelligent, perceptive and uniquely progressive:

> *Artists owe more to their art than just performing before audiences. No matter how great an artist is, no matter how much pleasure he gives to his audiences, the art which he practices on the concert platform is just a passing thing. But if he takes the trouble to pass it on to young students, his art in some measure survives him more than just in the memory of those who heard him play.*[8]

Here is a writer fearless of expressing blunt opinion:

> *In every profession, the more a man appreciates his responsibility towards his work, the farther he will go. And in music there is just one responsibility: towards the music one plays. Yet the average or less-than-average musician, when asked why (for instance) he used a particular fingering or phrased in a certain way, almost never reveals in his answer that he had the composer in mind. He is usually led either by what he was once taught or by his own wishful thinking. He justifies his musical whims by throwing them back upon the composer in an attempt to conceal his own musical thoughtlessness.*[9]

Feuermann's technical ability and originality of thought in his writings about the cello and cello playing was far ahead of its time:

> I realise that in performing, as in all other things, there must be a scale from best to worst. *Nevertheless, the question arises automatically* why in other professions attempts are made to raise the standard and average, while in our profession there is not even the slightest attempt to recognize existing weaknesses, let alone eliminate them. *Nine times out of ten when I hear cello playing, I cannot but ask myself* does cello playing mean turning off the brain and ear and the connecting muscular system? I shall go so far as to insist that, absurd as it may sound, brain and ear muscles must have been turned off in order for generation after generation of cellists to have been produced whose playing is an insult to music and the ear. *Even worse:* it is not generally perceived that there is an even more shameful reason. One expects nothing good from the average cellist and accepts unquestioningly

that the difference between the few real cellists and the mass of cellists must be so great.[10]

Feuermann believed that this attitude accounted for composers of the 19th century treating the cello 'as a stepchild'.[11] Why had the 'the great masters' composed so little?

> A valid answer to this question is impossible. There are only opinions about this and *in my humble opinion*, there is only one answer: cellists failed to succeed in creating a technique that enabled them to eliminate the specific difficulties of the instrument in order that cello playing could produce pure artistic enjoyment . . . Technique was perfected only insofar as it enabled one to play quickly. The development of cello playing stood still where culture – which means art – begins. . . . *One took it for granted that scratching, lack of clarity, poor phrasing, ugly glissandi, as well as poor intonation belonged to the cello. . . . Altogether, I do not hesitate to say that after the cellists had reached a certain level in the beginning of the development of the instrument, this development came to an early standstill. Neither were the composers inspired from what cello playing they had the chance to hear to write great works for that instrument nor was the public too eager to favourise [sic] cello recitals. . . . In a certain way, cellists were pitied for their unsuccessful efforts to compete with the violin and one expected to be bored by a cello recital. The public was only pleased with some short solos: arrangements of some gavotte, Minuet, or an Adagio, with much 'Schmaltz'. . . . The trouble was that no one had shown up to prove that the weaknesses of the instrument can be overcome and that the cello as a solo instrument* could even be superior to the violin through its wider range.[12]

There was, however, Casals. Although Feuermann expressed reservations about Casals's playing – in particular his Bach and his recording of the Dvořák Concerto with George Szell – he had no doubt about his unique contribution:

> *through him, this one man, the cello was established as the* <u>vollwertige</u> [fully valid] *member of the family of solo instruments. . . . Everyone who has heard him knows that a new period of the cello has come. He has shown that the cello can sing without 'Schmalz', that on no other instrument can* [music] *be better phrased; through clever fingerings the* stoerende [disturbing] *distances have disappeared and so have the ugly noises, up to then taught as an integral part of cello playing. What a Liszt was to the piano, a Viotti or Paganini to the violin, Casals is to the cello. We younger cellists must be most grateful to him who brought a new time for us. He showed* <u>us</u> *what can be done on the cello, showed to the public what an artistic pleasure listening to cello playing can be*

... and inspired most of the contemporary composers to write for our instrument.[13]

By employing the device of structuring some of the text of his manuscript in the form of a letter, Feuermann allowed himself to conduct a virtual lesson:

You are talented, you have studied for many years and you are entitled to say that you have the right to assume that you are a good cellist. Still, it was not difficult for me to convinve [sic] you, intelligent as you are, that you are unaware of most of the things which altogether make a good musician and a good cellist. You asked me in the lessons and again in your letter, how it is possible that nobody had ever told or taught you to look at things the way I suggest. The answer is, we have to take it as fact, that in years of studying with a teacher of good standing you haven't been led to recognize the most simple and obvious principles, or almost any principles. What I criticize you for *is not that you did not grasp the idea in a certain piece or that you perhaps play out of tune. It is your* lack of knowledge *of 1) how to read music, 2) how to look over a piece and to recognise its structure and the moods in it, 3) your* lack of knowledge *of the physics of your arms and the proper use of them, 4) your* lack of knowledge *of the disadvantages of instrument and bow and of the rules and principles to overcome them and 5) absolute lack of knowledge of how to bring those rules and principles into life and how to apply them to the best of the music.*[14]

As far as Feuermann was concerned, poor playing is the result, fundamentally, of poor teaching: 'Wherever *I look, I see lack of guidance, very little information and explanation for students and very little responsibility towards them and music.'*[15]

Students are being trained mostly without being taught to use their brains and ears. Ideas deteriorate in passing from generation to generation, and many teachers are still using principles which they have received at third or fourth generation. What a great master has taught as a living thing loses the greater part of its meaning by the time it has passed through the minds of generations of pupils who have been led by their teachers to take everything they are taught for granted instead of having been shown how to rediscover it for themselves. No 'method' should be taken over and passed on purely mechanically. Schools of musical technique and style become as rigid and meaningless as, for example, political parties. We are apt to forget the facts and vital ideas which gave birth to them.[16]

To Feuermann, certain approaches to teaching were simply silly:

> Another form of teaching, found mostly in Germany, is one in which music
> is considered so holy, so metaphysical, not so much of this earth but of a
> higher order, that it would be sacrilege even to accept that within music there
> is anything resembling technique. During the lessons the student will be
> constantly reminded of the seriousness, the majesty, the nobility of the artistic
> profession, while technique or mechanism will be rejected with contempt.
> The result is that after years of such instruction, the young person who
> believes himself an artist, an exceptional person, is sent out into the world,
> often conceited and arrogant, without being capable in the slightest way of
> expressing with his fingers what he visualizes rightly or wrongly as art.[17]

Although Feuermann's life was short, the number of cellists to pass through
his hands was large. He was constantly in demand as a teacher wherever he
played. The length of time that a student spent with him varied greatly. Some
students, particularly the private ones and those in the schools in which he
taught, entered longer-term arrangements, with lessons fitted around his
concert schedule; others appeared in green rooms to play for him, often for the
first and last time.

A fully comprehensive list of all those who studied with him is impossible
to produce but an incomplete, alphabetical list would include : Claus Adam,
Shoji Asabuki, Helmut Auer, Mathilde Bangert, Murray Bromsen (?), Georg
Ulrich von Bülow, Antonia Butler, Mosa (C)havivi, Peers Coetmore, Rowany
Coomara, Jane Cowan, Marion Davies, Jonel Fotino, Suzette Forgues,
'Goodchild', Bernard Greenhouse, Elisabeth Gros, Gillian Hill, Walter Jäkel,
Hilda Jamieson, 'Jenska', Virginia Katims, Hans-Joachim Kittke, Ray Kramer,
Robert LaMachina, Herbert Lehmann, 'Miss Lewis', Robert Lewis, Edgar
Lustgarten, 'Mary', George Neikrug, Zara Nelsova, Paul Olefsky, Dudley
Powers, Kurt Reher, Helmut Reimann, Bernard Richards, Daniel Saidenberg,
Hideo Saito, Peggy Sampson, Heinrich Schuchner, Theodor Schürgers, Bruno
Sesselberg, Alan Shulman, George Sopkin, David Soyer, John Shinebourne,
Agerhard Stenzel, Richard Sturzenegger, Shirley Trepel, 'Tusa', Jimmy
Whitehead, Maurice Zimbler and Ernst Zimmermann. This list includes well-
known cellists but players of other instruments also came to him.

With the exception of Zara Nelsova, who studied for only six weeks with
him, Feuermann produced no great soloist. Students with the potential to be
great soloists are a rare commodity at any time and no student spent any
extended period of time with him. However, many of his pupils became
orchestral section leaders and some of the finest chamber music players, thus
radiating his influence across the profession.

It is hard to quantify Feuermann's influence as a teacher. Unlike Casals or Piatigorsky, he lived so short a life that there was little time for him properly to develop a group of students who could carry forward his musical and technical ideas. 'The enthusiasm he was able to instil in those of us who heard him and studied with him was enormous', noted Bernard Greenhouse.[18] Claus Adam in a tribute to Feuermann in 1967, 25 years after Feuermann's death, remarked: 'It is hard to predict the impact that he would have had on the musical life of our country had he continued to teach. . . . The loss is especially great today since his style of playing seems almost [*sic*] a legend rather than a remembered fact.'[19] Today, the influence of Casals and Piatigorsky as teachers is more readily acknowledged. There is, however, no similarity of circumstance: both Casals and Piatigorsky lived so much longer, both had recordings in the catalogue so much longer, and both were able to popularize the cello through the medium of film and television. Feuermann died before the era of mass media and television began, a fact of immense significance; only the single seven-minute film of his playing and a small amount of 'home video' survive.[20] His recording career may have begun at a very early age – far earlier than that of Casals – but until recently these recordings have been hard to obtain. In 1967 Claus Adam pointed out: 'It is a tragedy that none of his solo recordings are listed in the record catalogues and only three chamber works are available today. . . . It is pitiful that only the Cello Society here in New York has records made by him that can still be obtained.'[21] Nowadays the bulk of Feuermann's commercial recordings are available, released mainly by small, independent labels.

Despite the neglect, Feuermann's playing constitutes a standard towards which the greatest cellists of today must still aspire. The evidence of his recordings, made without edits, suggests that he remains virtually peerless. Although Bernard Greenhouse believes no 'Feuermann school' became definitively established,[22] a number of Feuermann's students were able to pass his ideas on to others. As Jane Cowan has put it: 'You have to listen to me not because of who I am but because I am standing on the shoulders of giants.'[23] Another student, George Neikrug, believed that Feuermann's gift was so special that he could not pass it on:

He really knew that he couldn't make someone understand what he was doing. Otherwise there would be more people playing like Feuermann, and it didn't happen. People got some of the outer aspects of the style but not the motivation. He could explain like somebody could show you the symptoms of a disease and you duplicate the symptoms, but you did not get at the cause, the motivation. You got the result from your ear but not from what he was doing that produced it.[24]

Zara Nelsova, on the other hand, believed: 'There are not too many performers who are aware how they do things on the instrument and that's why there are very few outstanding teachers who can be both. But he was both.'[25] Indeed, Feuermann had the intellectual capacity to be acutely analytical:

> As soon as a cellist plays faster notes on the lower strings in détaché, you hardly can speak of a sound he produces, you rather call it a scratchy noise. The reason? You can only get out a proper sound of a string when it vibrates. Bring the string to vibration and one of the worst handicaps of the cello disappears. Is it a miracle I am speaking about? Certainly not. A very simple fact, as obvious as anything, very easy to get rid of and still not recognized as the cause of one of the ugliest and most widespread ills of cello playing.[26] ... It is my opinion that the basic ill of poor playing lies in the complete disregard of natural laws.[27]

One of these 'natural laws', perhaps the most fundamental of all laws, is how a cellist should sit:

> The body should be so comfortable and relaxed when playing that the use of the muscles, tendons, wrist and fingers is inhibited in no way. It is not stressed nearly enough that the playing of an instrument is physical work and therefore subject to the same laws as any other activity in which skill is demanded. A certain anxiety leads musicians to fear that they will be considered craftsmen, not artists. But how small-minded this is and how much such a suppression of reality damages the development of the real artist. It is art, music, which ennobles technique and skill and which therefore turns the most talented, intelligent and skilful musician into a true artist.[28]

The teaching process for Feuermann divided into two distinct phases, with a gradual transition in between. The first phase dealt with the physical accommodation of the instrument:

> The pupil must be shown everything that applies to the handling of his instrument, and nothing is too small to be included. ... from the first moment of taking up the violoncello, the teacher's duty is to familiarise the pupil with its ways and means, until he feels himself at home on the instrument, independently. During this first phase of study, the teacher is simply the demonstrator of unchangeable laws, which must be individually adapted to the physique of the pupil – a tall person holds a violoncello and bow differently from a short one. These laws are based on the properties of physical matter. If the strings are touched at a given point, only one definite tone results. All such

details must be clearly explained and well understood. At this stage there can be hardly a question of 'personality'. There are simply facts to be mastered.[29]

The second phase addressed interpretation:

As soon as the initial stage is past [sic], music itself becomes the principal aim, and the instrument, which was the main objective in the beginning, becomes merely the means. Now, the whole attitude of the teacher towards the pupil changes. He no longer has the role of commanding officer giving orders, but an older more experienced human being who supervises the student's development, answers questions and explains what everything is about and why. It should be the student's aim to achieve what he wants himself, as well as he can, and the teacher's aim to enlighten him in his attempts.[30]

As Feuermann succinctly put it: '*The teacher supplies explanation, the pupil, application.*'[31] But, as he found, this was generally far from the case:

Hundreds of cellists have played for me and some have become my students. I almost always ask two questions: why they have come to me and what they feel they are lacking. The answers are usually: a need to examine the repertoire and inadequate technique. The cellists who come to me have all completed their formal training and many of them have positions with orchestras either as front-desk cellists, in a section or in a string quartet. They are all persons one can call mature and experienced in music. What has always amazed and depressed me is that not one [pupil] has ever come close to saying: I am aware that perhaps I do not play too badly but I find it impossible to express <u>that</u> which I have in mind. Or: I have a certain idea of how the cello should sound but I cannot achieve it on my own. This has led me to the conclusion that most instrumentalists when they reach a stage where they leave their teacher, become independent and are therefore supposed to think independently and clearly about the music and their instrument are not at all prepared for such a stage and are therefore hardly capable of developing independently. Sad though it is, I explain the standstill most musicians come to at a certain age and stage by the fact that on leaving the school or teachers they think they have already achieved the summit. Yet should not the development of their own faculties begin at this point?[32]

Instrumental technique for Feuermann meant 'facility, secure intonation and mastery over all the different types of bowing, . . . mastery over the entire mechanism.'[33] What it did not mean was the ability to play: 'Mastery of the mechanism of an instrument constitutes the real artist as little as does the mere comprehension of the music, but I could go further and say that the combination of these two factors is still not enough. It is the link <u>between</u> mechanism and music that counts, the application of the mechanism to the music.'[34] For this 'application of the mechanism to the music' Feuermann used the word <u>Interpretationstechnik</u>, which translates uneasily to 'interpretation technique' or possibly 'the technique of interpretation'. As a concept, this latter wording seems clearer to understand. What Feuermann was insisting on is the responsibility of the performer to the wishes of the composer: 'Is not the composition the property of the composer, which is handed to us, the players, only for the purpose of realization, an alien property that we must look after with the greatest conscientiousness and love and input of all our mental and material powers?'[35] 'Every intentional emphasis of one's own personality is a crime against the composition in which only one personality must intentionally be expressed: that of the composer.'[36]

> The function of the performer consists in entering the world of the composer and the content of the particular composition, adjusting his own personality and ability to it. . . . How often have I heard a 'famous' artist presenting a Bach gavotte as if it was a composition by Offenbach and, on the other hand, a piece by Brahms or a movement by Beethoven in which only the notes are played without any content or meaning as if he were reciting a poem in a language he does not understand.[37]

> Without clinging to such concepts as 'classical', 'romantic', etc. it is surely evident that what is necessary for the interpretation of a Bach Suite must be very different from the demands of a composition by Tchaikovsky. Small slides, ritardandi and crescendi, which match the spirit of the serenade or air without which such a piece would have no meaning, have no place in a composition by Bach or Beethoven.[38]

As Feuermann related to his imaginary student: '*Not long ago, I heard the, perhaps, best living violinist play the first movement of a Viotti concerto so perfectly badly with every possible mistake that closing my eyes I would believe to listen to a performance at a pupils concert in Kalamazoo or New York.*'[39] (A peculiarly illogical comparison!)

Feuermann was among the first to stress that communication of the message could be achieved only through analysis of the musical composition:

> As in a written sentence, the only guidelines are the single words, commas, full stops, question marks etc., so in music notation we have only the bar lines, the bowings, the pitch and length of single notes, and expression marks (accents, crescendi, etc., play quite a special role). What meaning can

there be in a mechanical rendering of the words without declamation, which alone gives meaning and significance? Very little. One can roughly recognize the words but that's all. . . . *For a music listener*, it heightens the enjoyment if the music is heard as clearly as beautiful prose and poetry.[40]

A poor musician reads only the notes. A good musician reads exactly what is printed on the page. But the exceptional musician will read the musical meaning beyond the printed symbols.[41]

A combination of most responsible approach towards the music and complete mastery of the instrument to make possible the realization of the music is the ideal towards which I will always continue to strive and that I would like to pass on to my fellow musicians.[42]

Feuermann may have been demanding but he was not blind to human weakness:

Many teachers, of course, are afraid of losing their authority by changing or even contradicting what they have once said. A teacher's authority is not based upon words, or position, or even consistency, but on what he has to give. A teacher is not a lifeless thing, but a human being who has to grow and change himself, and he should not try to conceal that fact. . . . He may stand on his given authority and silence his pupil, but certainly not to the good of either of them. I, for example, do not hesitate to play old recordings of mine together with new ones for my students, to show how my playing has changed and developed. Not only do I feel unashamed to let them see how differently, and to be frank less well, I may have played a work before; I do not mind opening their eyes, even at my own expense.[43]

What might he have regarded as 'less well'? Certainly the most obvious is his use of the *portamento*, which changed dramatically during the early 1920s; it was no longer the inevitable outcome of a change of position but an expressive device used to underline the harmony, shape and phrase and to produce a melodic line divorced of false accents. But how was this physically achieved?

Violoncellists are handicapped by the great size of their instrument. Thus the change of position becomes of utmost importance. Good finger work results as much from a clear conception of what must be achieved as from purely muscular action. In rapid passages, the mechanics of the change must be concealed. Runs must never be marred by the scooping, gliding sounds that result from an unskilful change of position. The change should be executed so suddenly in attack and so cleanly in fluency (with the single fingers put down so evenly) that the run sounds like one on the piano, where there exists no question of positional changes. On the other hand, however, lyrical passages require just the opposite technique in changing. Here, the change of position must not be hidden. There must be no suddenness of attack. The glissando that is ugly and unskilful in rapid work must now be consciously used for beautifying the singing of the phrase. The mechanics of the change must contribute their possibilities to the musical effect.[44]

David Soyer, when first studying with Feuermann, asked him quite bluntly why he used slides so much: 'Being the way he was, he wasn't offended and responded by saying: "well, it's not a clarinet, you know. You don't just stop the holes. I slide and make slides because it gives the sound fluency and sounds vocal."'[45] Bernard Greenhouse made an analysis of Feuermann's left hand and how he effected shifts and positional changes:

Feuermann's departure from the old left-hand technique relates to teachers 50–75 years ago, perhaps more, who would use extensions to put the finger over the note in order to have proper intonation. So there were always extensions of the fingers which made for a great deal of tension in the left hand. What Feuermann was showing people was the enormous flexibility which could be achieved by raising the finger and striking, simultaneously lifting the departing finger and putting down the new finger with such speed that the open string would not sound. It was a feeling of hopping from one note to another rather than stretching from one note to another. . . . The hand was always rounded, without tension. The technique of playing like this except for the turning of the arm is very similar to violin technique. It was the influence of Ševčík, the difference being that the distances on the violin are so much shorter so that a violinist has to do no more than move his wrist in order to make the distances come close together. The cellist has to use the elbow and the arm but the technique would have been basically the same. The whole point of any technique is to make the movement from one position to another as easy as possible, with no tension and once that is found you have the beginning of a facility. If he wasn't the first to do this, he was the one who did it most efficiently and to the point that his playing was so admired that everybody wanted to change and do it his way.[46]

Unfortunately, most lacked the anatomy of Feuermann's hands – the widest of stretches between the first and fourth fingers – and the immense flexibility. (A plaster cast of Feuermann's hands in repose resides at the Curtis Institute; except for the odd sheet of paper, it is, alas, all that remains as evidence of Feuermann's connection to the Institute.) His student George Sopkin felt that

Feuermann never worked in positions: 'He really didn't think in terms of positions, he just thought in terms of notes. So he would play in between two or three positions all the time, whereas most string players during that period were still old-fashioned enough to slide when they had to shift.'[47]

Feuermann's own music with all fingerings, if found, might tell us much about his playing and teaching. Several works in his own editions had been contracted for publication with Carl Fischer, with Eva Feuermann's permission, in July 1945: the Schumann Cello Concerto, Boccherini's Sonata in A, Tartini's Variations on Corelli, Dvořák's Cello Concerto, the Haydn Concerto in D and Chopin's Polonaise. An earlier letter from Carl Fischer indicates that Feuermann had also edited Brahms's F major Sonata op.99. One of Feuermann's students from the Curtis Institute, Marion Davies, passed the cello parts (including Feuermann's fingerings) to Fischer for the Brahms, Schumann and Boccherini. Fischer was also aware of material in the hands of another student, Edgar Lustgarten, but at this time he felt it desirable to start with a smaller list. Only the Schumann and Boccherini were published (in August 1949 and October 1948).[48]

Bernard Greenhouse studied with both Feuermann and Casals: 'They wanted a beginning to each note, even in the quietest of movements, so it was the finger which came down ever so slightly, without an accent, but it started the vibrations going of the note. Not the sound but the vibrations, and then the bow took over to continue the sound.'[49]

The sound produced by Feuermann's playing is unmistakable – it is focused, with a narrow vibrato, a sound initially influenced no doubt by his brother's violin sound, to which he was exposed as a boy. János Starker, a cellist deeply influenced by Feuermann, has commented that composers tend to write not so much for individual instruments but more for the orchestra or human voice:

> Feuermann was for me the first one who in 1935 impressed me that this is not a cello sound. It is a beautiful sound that can be a voice or anything else. It is not automatically recognizable as a cello sound. Casals always played a cello sound wherever he played; there was no tonal distinction between soprano, baritone, bass. Feuermann was the first one to rise to coloratura soprano because of the violin.[50]

Feuermann's sound, like that of Heifetz, has intensity and bloom. In attempting to analyse how he achieved it, Claus Adam echoed Bernard Greenhouse:

> He always wanted every finger to be balanced and not tied to any other finger while it was playing and therefore he had this uncanny, beautiful

sound on every note no matter how fast the passages were. He always said 'there's always time for technique. There's always time to sound well.' His hand was never tight. Each finger was loose in itself and that gave him that wonderful balanced tone. The singing tone. So much in cello technique is based on large extensions where the hand can easily get tightened up and he never had that. He jumped around. He stretched around without any tension of any kind.[51]

Also commenting on Feuermann's sound, George Szell focused on another quality that he felt influenced Feuermann: 'He was given to understatement. He was dead set against what you would call "schmaltz". Even his sound that he chose to use was not that thick, lush, overly sensuous sound, it was a dignified, aristocratic, slim but beautifully focused sound.'[52] Szymon Goldberg summed up his sound in another way: 'He had a beautiful tone, but not just a beautiful tone – there are many beautiful tones – but a tone that you would recognize after a few seconds of listening only to his recordings. A typically Feuermann tone – a tone that you can call the sum total of what he knew.'[53]

Feuermann's phrasing is also unmistakable. He looked to singers, in particular Chaliapin and Caruso, for examples of phrasing and intensity. Suzette Forgues recalled: 'Whenever I was anywhere I would look into tiny little shops with records. One day I found a Caruso record. It was for him the greatest pleasure and now I know why; he played as a singer sings. He listened to Caruso and the bel canto.'[54]

Another wholly remarkable feature of Feuermann's technique is his facility in the highest registers of the cello, the coloratura, as Janos Starker described it. George Sopkin offered this explanation:

He was greatly influenced by his brother Sigmund. When Feuermann was four or five years old that's all he heard, this fabulous violinist. . . . He would imitate all the things that he heard Sigmund do – in the same register. Which meant that he was way at the top of the cello all the time. He was the most comfortable player up at the top that I have ever heard before or since. . . . He had a way of rotating the hand that was quite revolutionary. Casals did some of that – of using his extensions – but Feuermann had long fingers and a very flexible hand. He would play the same number of notes on the cello that could be played on the violin by rotating his hand. He could skip at least a step and a half between even the second and third fingers.[55]

He was well known for playing violin music on the cello, often at its original pitch. He had done so as a child, competing with Sigmund. He was also known notoriously for 'correcting' other players (as did Heifetz), which he no doubt regarded as a bit of fun but which was not always appreciated that way. At a small gathering in London where Feuermann, Franz Osborn and Max Rostal were playing chamber music, Mosa Havivi was a witness to an uncomfortable moment. Osborn had made a slight mistake in a phrase in Dvořák's 'Dumky' Trio. In the following phrase, in which the cello repeats what the piano has just played, Feuermann imitated Osborn's slip. Rostal was outraged: 'He got up and refused to play. Feuermann said: "If you don't want to play, it's all right." He put away his cello and kept on with his jokes as if nothing happened.'[56]

Another feature stressed by Feuermann was coordination. His student Daniel Saidenberg remembered: 'It's something that is as important in sports technique as with musical instruments: timing. He was the first person who made me conscious of the necessity for timing – being conscious of the timing between the two hands. . . . They were never separated. You never worked on a bowing problem without the left hand and vice versa.'[57]

A quite different facet of Feuermann's instruction was his emphasis on self-analysis:

> *Each player, of course has his own special difficulties – the trill, a weak finger, and so on. How to get rid of them? An important and helpful way is to cultivate the trick of listening to oneself. The ear, after all, is as important as the hands in violoncello work. Map out in your mind the tonal and musical goal to be achieved. The nearer the instrumental execution comes to it, the better you will play. . . . Though your teacher can guide, you must depend on yourself to accomplish the balance between ideal and execution.*

Although he recommended that students listen to performances of great masters, he was only too aware of the dangers in such an approach:

> *The benefit to be had from such listening depends . . . on the awareness of the listener as much as on the art of the performer. Unfortunately, the usual process is either for the listener to lose all critical perception in enthusiasm for the artist or to criticise matters which, on the whole, are unimportant. Never mind how the performer sits or holds his hands; these things are individual. Try to penetrate into what he is doing, why he does it that way, how he does it at all. One need not agree with all a performer does; but there is always something to be learned by aware listening, and the word to stress is aware. One learns only when one is aware of what needs correction, when one discovers weaknesses by comparing what one hears with what he can do himself. The secret lies in self-criticism.*[58]

According to Neikrug, Feuermann was 'listening to violinists the whole time. He wasn't listening to cellists.' Hearing Feuermann for the first time was a daunting experience:

We were all so amazed – using violin technique on a cello. I guess I was about 14 or 15, [when] I went to his first New York recital. I was so stunned at this because I had always imagined the cello could be played with the same glamour as a great violinist, like Heifetz, and here was somebody doing it. I was so completely shaken by this that I put my cello in a corner and I couldn't touch it for a month.[59]

This was not an uncharacteristic reaction from a student to Feuermann's dazzling playing. How a lay public reacted, in Starker's view, was more problematic: 'When they heard the kind of playing of Feuermann and Heifetz, they were so fascinated that technical problems were not displayed that the fascination prevented them from hearing the message.'[60] One of the most tellingly intelligent sections in Feuermann's writings is one that discusses the question of musicality versus technique:

A player is characterized as a mere technician but not musical, or else a good musician but without technique. Usually, the latter is said in praise – as if musicality alone makes the artist, while in the expression technician there is a certain condescension. . . . Well-intentioned people believe that through such an underestimation of technique, of basic skills, they can give to the spiritual in music the rank that it deserves, whereas in reality they open wide doors and gates for those who cannot play. . . . How many good artists would one find among dilettantes and among the public if it was merely a matter of recognizing and understanding the spiritual, the metaphysical, and the theory of composition. I, myself, know hundreds of non-musicians all over the world who as dilettantes are completely at home with an orchestra or in chamber and instrumental music and about whom one could maintain that they have grasped the music and understood it. Nothing is easier to answer than the question why they are not capable of also interpreting the pieces. Because they do not have the ability to direct a symphony or present a concerto on some instrument. It is therefore useless to praise the musician above the technician; the juxtaposition in itself brings about confusion from which only fakers and bluffers profit.'[61]

Feuermann's early death caused so many ideas to pass away with him. One can only guess how he would have continued to address the conventional system of one-hour lessons, something he considered to be of dubious value to students:

How often it happens that at the beginning of a lesson a question arises that entails others. I try to explain, to show how it should be done, while other students attending add their problems – and before you can turn round, the hour is passed without the pupil having had the opportunity to show what he has prepared during the week. I always find it very sympathetic to have a pupil who has not just obediently prepared his homework but concerned himself with many problems. He has the right to present his teacher with questions. What a shame that this 'one hour a week' system hardly allows the teacher the time to teach a student, let alone influence or enlighten him.'[62]

His teaching was often painstakingly thorough. Claus Adam recalled: 'I remember a lesson once where one full hour was spent on four measures of this piece, but any intelligent pupil could have learned more about cello technique and more about music in those four measures than fifty lessons with somebody else on a lot of repertoire.' Adam remembered working with Feuermann on the Haydn D major Concerto:

I had two lessons just on the opening phrase. . . . First he would talk about the fingering he used, and then he would start talking about the phrasing. His phrasing was not what one would call natural phrasing. He understood exactly the ebb and flow on every note because he knew exactly what was happening harmonically underneath. The suspension had to be expressed in a certain way. Flowing line had to come out of the harmonic background of the music and he would decide ahead of time where the peak of the melody was so he could reach up to that. Then of course came all the detailed work – how to shift, how to connect well, how to make it sound elegant and easy and how to vibrate on every note so that it was under control, every note one was playing. . . . He taught you an approach. A lesson in good taste.'[63]

Feuermann's demands were exacting and not all his students could cope. Monica Feuermann recalled that most of his female students came out in tears after lessons. One of his 'victims' was Suzette Forgues:

I was very much afraid of him and sometimes it would take me five or six minutes to be able to press the doorbell because I wanted to calm myself. I had practised five hours a day. . . . I don't remember when exactly the bow started to jump on the string. But do you know what he said? 'Go home and practise.' I got home and I thought 'I'm going to the Empire State and I'm going to throw the cello down and I'm going to jump on top of it. This is the end of my life.'[64]

Virginia Katims, wife of Milton, was another:

I had three lessons with this master <u>before I was ready</u> to play for him – I had some nerve to even demand the personal time he gave me. He criticised every note I played, every bow I drew. In the middle of the third lesson, the tears rolled down my cheeks. He walked over to me, observed what was happening and said: 'and you will someday be the mother of future children?' At this moment, I packed up my cello and walked out. (I thought of stabbing him with the endpin.)[65]

The stories of Feuermann's sarcasm with his students are legion:

His way wasn't the screaming and throwing of wastebaskets and inkwells and stuff like this. He didn't do things like that. He would just laugh at you. He used to hit me on the head with his bow once in a while and smile when he did it. And he'd whack me as hard as he could with his bow saying 'no, no!' Whack![66]

Neikrug, Greenhouse and Adam sometimes travelled together to Scarsdale for lessons:

We shared a ride and we'd stand around. Now it's not so bad when you're criticized alone but when he criticised you in front of your colleagues it was something. I remember one time when he praised me, it was worse than when he criticized me because I did some little thing with a trill and he said 'So! Gifted!' I felt like an idiot learning to speak.'[67]

Greenhouse recalled receiving a very sarcastic card:

'Was your last lesson the beginning of better playing or the last? [*sic*]' He used to say to me: 'If you practise five or six hours a day for five years or so you might play as well as Frank Miller. . . . He was always jabbing with the tongue, like a rapier. . . . I know that he admired my talent not because he ever encouraged me, quite the contrary, but people would come back and tell me that Feuermann had such nice things to say about me. But he never spoke one word of encouragement in all the times I was with him.[68]

Daniel Saidenberg was also 'flattered' by him:

I remember once after playing for him for two hours and being stopped it seemed like every 30 seconds because there was something he didn't like or something I was doing wrong. In disgust, I put the cello down and said: 'Don't I do anything right?' It sort of stopped him for a moment and he said 'Oh yes, you do more things right than any of the young cellists I've met in America.'[69]

Neikrug observed:

In a nutshell, in terms of his lessons, you were hopeless and he was great. But he didn't mean it that way. He was trying to be helpful. The only thing was that he applied the same standard of criticism that he applied to himself. He was very self-critical and as you played for him, whatever you played, he would suck his cheeks in and would start vibrating his hand. He was playing along with you actually and he was listening as if he was listening to himself.[70]

Sometimes, to shield themselves from humiliation in front of others, students adopted the ploy of switching languages. Suzette Forgues would suddenly 'switch to French, so Feuermann switched to French. Nobody knew I was getting into trouble. But I remember Jenska noticed what I did, so when she played she turned to Dutch. He could speak Dutch to her! We were both very comfortable that way.' But Feuermann's manner could be cruel:

> I remember one morning I came early for my lesson. I was a little ahead of time and he had another pupil and I could tell from his voice that things were not going too well. I didn't want to embarrass this young man who was there so I stayed in the antechamber. Then I heard 'Suzette, come in!' So I sneak in and sit down. He continued shouting at him and then he ends this way. 'All you know is schmaltz, schmaltz, schmaltz. That's all you know.' He said 'if you come in the morning, you ruin my whole day. If you come in the evening I cannot sleep, you ruin my whole night. Get out of here! Get out, go back to San Francisco, it's good enough for you! Out! Out! Out!' I thought 'Oh, my goodness!' He turns around and says 'Suzette, play!' I was really worried. I thought after this, 'I am finished.' So he looks at me and says: 'Well, can you schmaltz?' And I said 'Mr Feuermann, if you want me to, I can.' That broke the ice. But you saw these things happening. You saw a young boy coming out in tears. I wouldn't give him that satisfaction. I didn't care if I bit my tongue to blood, I would not give him the satisfaction. But I was pretty close [to tears] many times because the sarcasm once in a while would really dig deep but then I kept saying 'if you want to study with him . . .'[71]

Daniel Saidenberg, however, observed:

> What many students don't realize . . . is that when you're concerned and when you criticize a great deal you're giving your all to the student. And the student who has a weak ego feels that you're trying to destroy him. Those with a strong ego realize that you're doing it for him. You're not trying to destroy the student, you're trying to help him. And this was Feuermann's great quality. He took his teaching very seriously.[72]

Claus Adam remembered Feuermann saying that he enjoyed teaching the untalented ones even more than the talented ones because of the challenge it gave him.[73]

Neikrug has suggested that Feuermann's tough approach was perhaps related to his lack of confidence in his ability to teach:

> He had a trick of playing two notes back and forth – bouncing two notes – and I remember a few of us watching him. I was always the class doctor. I was always analysing and telling everybody else what he did. I was always the chief disciple. So I got underneath and watched him and he got put off. 'What's the matter with you? Do you think I'm afraid to teach this to you? Do you think I'm afraid you'll be better than me?' He blew his top. I really had touched a nerve.

Neikrug also remembered how differently Feuermann behaved after a lesson: 'He was a regular guy and talked to you like an equal. There was nothing of the big shot about him. I've never seen anybody so absolutely himself and joking.'[74] And if any student had a car . . . 'I had just bought a car, my first car, and I went up to Scarsdale in my Hudson Convertible. I got up to Feuermann's place and he said: "Go upstairs and practise. Give me the keys to your car." I understand that when he drove, he drove at 75 to 100 miles an hour. He was really a wild character.'[75] But for all his wildness and sarcasm, he was fun to be with, indeed he radiated fun: 'Feuermann was very proud and happy about having a Buick Convertible. He was like a child. "I'll run you down the hill. I'll run you to the railroad station." There was a big curve in the hill and he would take it so fast I really was happy to get out.'[76] His sense of fun may have acted as a counterbalance to the demands he made and expectations he had of his students, and he was not, in his own writings, insensitive to their struggles:

> *You came to me, an established cellist, playing all the concertos and chamber music and feeling that just a few things had to be brushed up. You had the idea that could be done in a few lessons. Up to then you had felt quite confident; of course you had some difficulty with the intonation and the staccato did not seem very good. But that was about all you knew was not quite to your satisfaction. You expected from me help in those respects and besides some inspiration for the interpretation of the bigger works of our literature. When your time was over and you had to leave for home, I felt great pity for you. You seemed quite broken and didn't know any more what was right and what wrong. Your condition can be compared with that of a patient who goes to a doctor complaining about a slight headache and the doctor has to tell him that his whole system is upset. All that did not happen without warning. When you first came to me, I told you you were not the first to come to me, expecting to be helped in a short time and instead given the miserable feeling of never more being able to play.*

Not content with the medical metaphor, he threw in the following:

[It was] *As if you had been out for a new varnish and perhaps two new spark plugs while I had to try to prove that the whole motor has to be taken apart, a new electrical system has to be put in the car not only just to make the car run a little better than before but to give her for the first time her full strength and comfort.*[77]

If Feuermann believed bad playing was the result of bad teaching, bad practising was equally at fault. His 'solutions' were strikingly original:

How are the visual arts taught? A master lets his pupils work in his studio and therefore they are always under his supervision. No time is thus lost, as often happens with us – for example, a pupil who misunderstands the teacher and works incorrectly on one specific thing for a week. He must then go home and unlearn what he has practised. . . . My ideal would be for the teacher to watch his pupils practising.[78]

He went even further with this idea: 'The teacher should work with his students in the same building; in this way the students would always have their teachers as "ears" and the teacher would wander from room to room, and correct pupils while they were practising. A Utopia!' However, he knew that this was improbable: 'Frankly, teachers are not always inclined to lend their ear to pupils for longer than exactly 30, 40 or 60 minutes. A significant question would arise, the answer to which is hardly positive: how intensively or meaningfully do teachers themselves practise?'[79] That Feuermann posed this question begs comment on his own attitude to practising. Many of his students were astounded by how little practice he appeared to do. One of his Berlin students, Georg Ulrich von Bülow, once heard him from outside a window playing very slowly without vibrato and found him simultaneously reading Nietzsche.[80] Feuermann said that this type of playing was very necessary but very boring so he read at the same time. In his letters he constantly congratulated himself on the number of hours worked. Eva Feuermann recalled: 'He had a hard time to make himself practise. He had this inborn facility to learn music very quickly, by reading through once. But in America he said you have to practise because the next year has to be better than the last year or they drop you. It's the most unfaithful audience.'[81] The fact was that Feuermann wasted no time, as observed by Saidenberg:

I spent a summer with him when he was learning a new concerto that was being sent to him piecemeal in manuscript and I had the opportunity to listen to him work, learn the concerto, memorize it and prepare it for a performance

– it was coming quite soon. I've never heard or seen anyone work that intelligently and concentrated, never a second wasted and hour after hour until it was memorized. He had a way of immediately preparing the work for performance from the minute he started to play this new work. It wasn't just playing it through and getting the hang of it. He studied it from score first and he applied everything to the instrument for hours and hours on end.[82]

Sophie Feuermann remembered another occasion when Feuermann was ill in Germany and unable to work on a new concerto. He learnt the entire work flat on his back. When the composer came to congratulate him, full of praise after the concert, Feuermann disclosed, perhaps mischievously, that until the performance he had not put bow to string. The (unnamed) composer was deeply insulted.[83]

Claus Adam visited Feuermann backstage at Carnegie Hall to make a date for a lesson. He found him preparing for the concert:

As I came back he was sitting in an easy chair with the cello sprawled in front of him. He was playing the Mendelssohn *Song Without Words*, which wasn't in the programme. He was playing at about one third the speed, very slowly, making a beautiful vibrato on every note and making perfect coordination with the right hand just to warm up. He was interested in getting this perfect balance, this perfect listening to what he was doing. It gave his playing a certain thrust because he knew every second what was happening.[84]

Apparently he was not on this occasion reading a book, but Sophie also recalled his teaching: 'I heard him say "Prepare. Relax. Prepare. Relax." When he practised . . . he did the same thing. He was sometimes reading a book, the left hand was mute.'[85]

While Feuermann could be harsh and sarcastic with his students, he could also be exceedingly generous. Over payment for lessons, his ideas were typically utopian:

Ideally artists should teach without financial return. Few artists give their best when they are paid for teaching. If they receive high fees they are tempted to take less gifted pupils who can pay, rather than those with greater promise who may be financially handicapped. Naturally they are not inspired to give their best to mediocre talent. They soon find themselves in the position of selling their illustrious names, rather than their knowledge. They take many pupils who merely want to be able to say: 'I studied with so-and-so.' If an artist must supplement his income by teaching, he should at least make it a practice to take as many non-paying pupils as paying ones. He owes it to himself to do so to escape becoming commercialised.[86]

Two of his students who did not pay for lessons were Adam and Sopkin. The British cellist Bernard Richards, who studied with him in Zürich in 1937, did pay: 'He charged me what I believe was the going rate for a first-class teacher of the time, but perhaps not as much as he could have charged.'[87]

There are many stories of Feuermann's generosity. In America he was extremely industrious in his search for work for colleagues, particularly those escaping Europe. And even as early as 1931 in Berlin he was appealing to his friends to help his young Palestinian student Mosa Havivi. Saidenberg recalled: 'He was always intent on finding solo cello positions for his students in different cities and corresponding with them and doing things that most people don't have time to do.'[88] Richards told the following story:

> Before the war, I used to get work playing on the back desk of Sir Thomas Beecham's orchestra, the LPO, and at rehearsal one day Sir Thomas caught me talking to my desk partner when I should have been listening to Sir Thomas himself, which was very foolish of me. I rather think I had a black mark against my name because of this incident. Some months later Sir Thomas got Lionel Tertis to audition all the string players, and to my utter dismay I found that I'd lost my job. This was an absolute disaster for me and I was furious. I wrote to Feuermann to ask if he could help me. He wrote to Sir Thomas. What he wrote I do not know, but it worked like magic and I got my job back! I was immensely grateful to him.[89]

Many of Feuermann's students were very fond of him. There is a touching letter from a British student, Peers Coetmore, written at the height of the war in London. She had joined the ambulance service:

> I thought you might be interested to have a letter from the 'front line' and also from (however humbly) a cellist. You would be surprised how often in the brief hours I can get for work you are at my elbow asking 'is that a note?' Believe me I learnt a very big lesson in the short time I was with you . . . We all live from hour to hour. In the days the sirens wail often seven and eight times a day but daylight seems to dispel their mournful horror. Guns may pound and high up we may hear the zoom of planes with occasional crump of bombs near or far or sometime watch an exciting dog fight amongst the clouds & see a descending parachute . . . Everything that needs to be done away from home must be crushed in before dusk. The awful hour always comes too soon and gives one the same shivery sick sensation that one gets before a big concert. And with the dusk, wail from near and far, the mournful sirens and almost at once the batteries open up. Anything like the noise is indescribable – the house shakes, windows rattle and the shrapnel

tinkles on the roofs or whizzes down on to the pavements. The shells pass over like the rustling of many taffeta petticoats . . . We know all the different sounds of their engines and they can be heard through the loudest cello playing! I usually, as it is better to stay indoors and of course most theatres and cinemas etc. are closed at night, practise in the evenings. Actually the piano is better for drowning the sounds without, and I work my way through the Beethoven and Mozart sonatas of which I have complete editions because I find having to concentrate on reading takes the mind off better than practising something one knows by heart when half one's mind listens for the next bomb. . . . Four gardens away a 500lb bomb fell completely wrecking 5 large six storey houses. Another further down wrecked four . . . Franz Osborn was interned for six weeks and as these wrecked houses are opposite his rooms he has had a narrow escape. He was away that night . . . Did you know Harold Craxton? His house is wrecked. . . . I have had various chances to leave all this for healthier spots but I feel I'd like to see it through. It just makes me furiously angry to see the terrible and widespread havoc of the war, the lives ruined, people maimed. Surely the time has come when ordinary common folk of the world who are the ones who suffer most, rise up and say we must have an end to all this barbarism.

As a postscript to her long letter, Coetmore added: 'I forgot one of the most important things I wished to ask you. I know you admired my Testore cello. If I am killed and it has managed to survive, would you be able to find a purchaser in America for me? I have very little to leave my sister and I doubt if it could be sold easily in this country now.'[90]

Chapter 17

Feuermann's Recordings
Europe and Japan

A powerful image of Feuermann's career is projected through contemporary reviews and criticism, but recordings bring him to life. That a legacy of recordings remains is of inestimable value. These records will astonish musicians and music lovers hitherto unaware of Feuermann's artistry. The freshness, the contemporary cleanness of technique, the sound and, above all, the musicianship of this extraordinary player signal an artist far ahead of his time. He lived before the age of mass media; had he lived to be filmed more extensively, allowing later generations to see his extraordinary physical capability, how different his place in the public memory might be. It is significant that throughout his life he attracted substantial attention from the music press worldwide, bringing glamour and stardom to the cello of a kind very different from that brought by Pablo Casals. Here was a virtuoso cellist with a facility and freedom hitherto unknown on the instrument. Had he lived longer, he would surely be remembered as vividly as Casals. As it is, Casals, born 30 years before Feuermann, enjoyed a further 30 years of performing after Feuermann's death. It was a quirk of fate that during the main period of Feuermann's career Casals for political reasons had virtually ceased performing.

Comparisons between the two players are tempting to make but somewhat treacherous: they were so different in temperament and so different in age. As performers, both were unique. Nevertheless, Irving Kolodin, distinguished music editor of *Saturday Review*, recalled a conversation with a musician he encountered at Perpignan in 1951, when the Casals festivals began bringing young musicians from around the world 'to worship at the shrine'. Expressing some doubt that they were really hearing the greatest of cellists, Kolodin was challenged to name another. 'Feuermann', he replied. 'Oh', said Erica Morini, 'he was in a class by himself.'[1] It is worth noting how the recordings of Feuermann relate in time to those of Casals. Casals made his first recordings in 1915 at the age of 39. Six years later, Feuermann made his first recording aged 19. Feuermann's last recording dates from 1942, the year he died; he was 39. Feuermann had completed all his recordings by the age of 39, whereas Casals did not begin recording until that age.

It is baffling that until the early 1990s so few Feuermann recordings were available on CD. Since then, it has been possible to obtain the bulk of them, released on a number of labels.[2] And his recordings continue to be released. After a period in recording history dominated by the tyranny of technical perfection, the pendulum has swung back, the market for archive recordings made under very different circumstances and with very different artistic values proving to be unexpectedly buoyant. Those unfamiliar with Feuermann's playing will be astounded. Those familiar, merely amazed.

When Feuermann began to record, the industry was in its infancy. Most of his known recordings, both commercial and non-commercial (the private recordings and broadcasts), have been transferred from 78rpm to CD, but there are some crucially problematic aspects to some of these transfers concerning speed and pitch. Some present him playing astonishingly fast, while some transfers are at the 'wrong' pitch. Before the 1930s, $a' = 440$ was almost certainly not the pitch at the time or place of any recording in continental Europe. Indeed a' could vary from 425 to 445.[3] Even today pitch remains far from absolute, despite industry agreements on standardization. Speed also was variable. From the late 1920s, when electrical recording began, speeds of 78s could vary wildly, from 65rpm to 90rpm, with significant implications for both pitch and tempi.[4] (It is worth noting that a difference in speed of 5rpm is equivalent in pitch to a difference of a semitone.) As an industry standard, 78 to 78.26rpm was fixed only in the 1930s and 40s. Before that time, 78rpm was a goal; various factors conspired against achieving that goal, not least unreliable power mains – many electrically driven turntables were on direct current. An alternative method of drive was achieved by weights, but this too produced erratic results: if the weights were not properly adjusted, the speed of the turntable would be inaccurate. Pitch could fluctuate wildly throughout a side; even if an entire side ran steadily at one pitch or speed, all sides in a set or all sides in a session might well not do so. The record companies, too, conspired to complicate the issue: RCA was known to record at 76rpm, with the advice that discs should be played at 78rpm, so creating a more brilliant sound. And artists might play faster in order to accommodate as much music as possible on one side.

Engineers today can 'correct' pitch, with subsequent implications for speed. But given the variables at Feuermann's time, it is not possible to determine the exact speed and pitch at which his recordings were made. So where does this leave us? There is no doubt that Feuermann could play at tremendous speed. He himself referred to playing fast, even too fast, and reviews comment frequently on his virtuoso technique which, alongside other attributes, certainly suggests speed.

Despite dying so young, Feuermann left many recordings in a recording career that spanned 20 years. These fall into three categories: commercial recordings, non-commercial (private) recordings and broadcasts. In general, most commercial recordings survive; most known broadcasts, particularly in Europe, are lost. Test pressings from recording sessions and acetates from broadcasts continue to emerge, but the war and a general ignorance of the importance of his broadcasts may well have robbed us of invaluable perform-ances. Of the private recordings, those made in America of NOA concerts in 1940 and 1941 are particularly precious, as they present not only unusual reper-toire but also Feuermann on top form in a number of solo appearances with orchestra at the end of his life. In this and the next chapter the recordings are considered chronologically rather than by category.[5]

Considering the time when Feuermann lived and the brevity of his life, the number of his known commercial recordings, including those of chamber music, is substantial: there are about 100. They were made in three distinct phases: 1921–32 in Germany for Parlophon and Telefunken; 1934–9 in Japan and England for Nipponophone and the Columbia Graphophone Company (Nippon, Columbia, had a licensing arrangement with Columbia, UK, but could also initiate their own recordings); and 1939–42 in the United States for RCA Victor. No correspondence relating to his earliest recordings in Germany has survived and little has survived from his final period of recording for RCA. (There is no archive at RCA covering the period during which Feuermann was contracted to the company.) But substantial papers survive from the period when he recorded for Nipponophone and Columbia.

Almost all Feuermann's known commercial recordings made in Germany were for Parlophon. All recordings before 1927 used the acoustic process, while those made in or after 1927 used the electrical method with microphones. The acoustic process was primitive and noisy: a horn was used, into which the player or singer performed, a cutting stylus transferring the mechanical vibra-tions on to wax. The cello, with its low frequencies, was not well suited to this medium, and since the instrument was less popular with the public than the voice, the violin and the piano, which recorded comparatively well, few cello recordings were made. We can deduce the esteem in which Feuermann was held from the wholly remarkable fact that when he was aged only 19 a record company was willing not only to invest in him but in orchestral forces (albeit reduced) to record a work by a composer (Haydn) who was far from well appreciated. (In fact it was only in 1913 that the first orchestral record by an orchestra and conductor of international reputation was made – a performance of Beethoven's Fifth Symphony with the Berlin Philharmonic under Artur Nikisch.) Indeed, up until 1933, with the exception of Alexander Barjansky, Feuermann was the only solo cellist to record for Parlophon.[6] Paul Grümmer, Mauritz Frank, Edmund Kurtz, Armin Liebermann, Piatigorsky, Hans Schrader and Ewel Stegmann recorded chamber music only.[7] And Piatigorsky did not record with full orchestra until 1934.

All Feuermann recordings were made at 78 rpm, and every recording is, in effect, a live performance, as each was taken as a single run through. During his entire recording career, there was no concept of cutting and splicing from multiple takes. The only editing tool available was the repetition of complete takes, but it was still not possible for artists to hear the playback of a wax. It is remarkable that each recording that Feuermann made in Germany between December 1921 and September 1932, with the exception of the Dvořák Concerto, was accomplished in a single take.[8] But some qualification may be required: wax was expensive; was he allowed any more than a single wax blank? As there are many instances in these early recordings where an additional take might have been desirable, this seems a plausible explanation. Later in life, he refused release of recordings with which he was not entirely satisfied. Early in his career, he doubtless had less control.

A single recording, in September 1932 of Popper's *Hungarian Rhapsody* with the Berlin Philharmonic conducted by Paul Kletzki, was made for Telefunken. A test pressing – a 10-inch, two-sided white-label shellac, dated 27 October 1932 – of Popper's *Papillon* in two different takes, found recently in a German flea market and never before released, was also made for Telefunken, suggesting possibly that other recordings were made. Feuermann's *spiccato* indeed resembles the fluttering of a butterfly. The pianist on this test pressing was Arpad Sandor, who 18 months later was to record with Heifetz.

Quite why Feuermann left Parlophon for Telefunken is unclear. The economic crisis of 1929 in Germany damaged the smaller recording companies, but Parlophon survived – it was owned by the Carl Lindström Gesellschaft, which in 1926 was bought by the Columbia Graphophone Company Limited. Frieder S. Weissmann, 'house' conductor for Parlophon, claimed in an interview that there were plans in 1933 for Feuermann to make more orchestral recordings with him, presumably for Parlophon. These plans came to nothing when the Nazis came to power and Feuermann, dismissed from his position at the Hochschule, left Berlin.[9] Feuermann's final complete recording for Parlophon, Bruch's *Kol Nidrei*, took place in January 1930.

From 1933 until he left Germany for good in 1937, Feuermann seems to have made no recordings for any German record company. Economic conditions and a slump in the market – in 1932 America sold approximately 6 per cent of its 1927 total sales[10] – may well have accounted for this; in 1931 HMV and Columbia merged to form Electric and Musical Industries Ltd (EMI) because of plunging profits. And as a Jew, Feuermann, in principle, would have been banned from making recordings. However, some Jews continued to record during the 1930s; the Reichsmusikkammer, established by the National Socialists, was unable to enforce many consistent policies, not least those that denied Jews the right to work with commercial recording companies.

Feuermann's first commercial recording session outside Germany took place in January 1934 in London for the Columbia Graphophone Company. Despite the merger between HMV and Columbia, each company maintained its labels and artists, behaving, in effect, like rivals more than partners. Feuermann remained courteous with Columbia but the relationship was not easy. He complained about his royalties, lack of publicity, and the repertoire he was 'allowed' to record. More significantly, Feuermann questioned how seriously the company viewed him as an artist.[11]

Columbia's response in Europe to Feuermann was, by and large, short-sighted and complacent. Greater knowledge and awareness was shown in Japan by Hans Straus of Nipponophone. It was he who believed Feuermann more exceptional than Casals. It was he who recognized the importance of keeping Feuermann on Columbia-Nipponophone's books. No doubt Straus felt particularly frustrated by Columbia's failure to stop Feuermann's move to a rival company. On 13 January 1939 Feuermann recorded for RCA Victor in New York with Hulda Lashanska, Mischa Elman and Rudolf Serkin. While presenting no breach of contract (Nipponophone's contract ran to 31 December 1938), this act came as a surprise to Columbia, who believed that Feuermann would not want to and perhaps would not be able to transfer to another record company. Feuermann signed a contract with the Victor Company to begin on 1 April 1939. Yet the relationship with Columbia-Nipponophone was not entirely severed: negotiations continued over the Schnabel-Huberman-Feuermann trios until autumn 1939, when war in Europe finally ditched the project. Also still-born was a tentative proposal to record Beethoven's Triple Concerto and even Brahms's Double.

With the benefit of hindsight, it seems inconceivable that Columbia failed to anticipate Feuermann's actions. The worsening political situation in Europe in 1938 and the *Anschluss* in Austria forced Feuermann to see that his future could lie only in the United States, where he was enjoying huge success. Having taken out American citizenship papers in November 1938, his decision to sign with an American record company must have been a foregone conclusion.

Early Recordings: Germany 1921–32

Between 1921 and 1932 Feuermann was involved in 11 commercial recording sessions, all of which took place in Berlin. With the exception of 1923 and 1925, he recorded every year. There were also various broadcasts in Germany in 1931 and 1932 taken from shellacs, but these shellacs appear not to have survived.

His first known commercial recording comprises the second and third movements of Haydn's D major Concerto. It was made in a morning session on 15 December 1921 with Frieder S. Weissmann and members of the Berlin State Opera Orchestra.[12] The two movements occupy a single side each of a 12-inch 78 rpm. disc. Feuermann played from the François-Auguste Gevaert edition, the standard version. A feature of much recorded repertoire at this time is the cuts, imposed through the fixed duration of 78s. The tempo of the second movement is excessively slow;[13] out of a total of 68 bars in this movement, 30 bars are cut, including the entire central section.[14] (In the following year, Columbia was much criticized for its recording of an abridged 'Eroica'; the tide was soon to turn.) Given the fact that this is an acoustic recording, Feuermann's sound is remarkably focused, with impeccable intonation. But his hesitant approach makes it hard to believe that this is the playing of a young man. Slides are prominent; the influence of Klengel is clear. The trill at the end of Gevaert's cadenza in the slow movement, however, is unmistakably Feuermann's in its speed. The third movement, in moments of tearaway brilliance, shows astonishing clarity of articulation at dizzy heights, the ending of the concerto an outrageous display of young enthusiasm. Here was a very young man – one foot in the past, one foot in the future.

That same day Feuermann also recorded several works with piano – David Popper's arrangements of Schumann's *Träumerei* op.15 no.7 and *Abendlied* op.85 no.12 and Chopin's Nocturne in E♭ op.9 no.2, plus Popper's own *Elfentanz*. No discs appear to have been released from this session as no issue and side numbers are assigned.[15]

Feuermann's next session took place in April 1922, again with Frieder Weissmann at the piano and conducting an unnamed orchestra.[16] Salon pieces were recorded, including Feuermann's arrangement of Sarasate's *Zigeuner-weisen*, and Chopin's E♭ Nocturne again.

The survival of Feuermann's early recordings is invaluable for evidence of a distinct change in his style of playing between 1922 and 1927. Recordings from the first two sessions in 1921 and 1922 reveal the young cellist heavily influenced by an older generation of playing, harbouring many features of the 'old style', including lugubrious slides and slow vibrato. By 1924 a change is already evident. Chopin's E♭ Nocturne is of particular interest, as he recorded it three times: in 1922 with a very inadequate Frieder Weissmann at the piano; in 1927 with Michael Taube (as with the Frieder Weissmann recording, the version is in truncated form); and in 1936 in Japan with Wolfgang Rebner. Each recording points to an advance in Feuermann's playing. In the 1922 recording, from the opening 6th, the slides are prominent, heavy and laboured, the rhythmic structure of the piece destroyed by incessant *rubato*. At bar 11 Feuermann indulged his youthful daredevilry, trans-posing Popper's arrangement up two octaves and agonizingly missing the top B♭. He stays up in the stratosphere, descending in bar 14 with a bump only to hurl back up again a couple of notes later.

The 1927 recording of the same work bears little resemblance to the earlier recording. The sound is now finely focused, the articulation clean, the intonation almost perfect, the slides gone except for their use as expressive *portamenti*. Here is a vocalist rather than a cellist struggling with distances. Exaggerated *rubato* remains, albeit less than in 1922, but the dexterity is extraordinary. Feuermann's delight in showing off is still evident – he plays at moments in a register far higher than that written in Popper's arrangement – but now the playing has greater safety. Certainly here is a cello being played like a violin.

In 1922 and 1927 Feuermann also recorded his own arrangement of Sarasate's *Zigeunerweisen*. He appears however, only to have recorded the first of the piece's two sections. *Zigeunerweisen* is a show-stopper for violin, which, with its virtuoso flashes of arpeggios, scales, and left-hand pizzicato in the highest registers, benefits from a free, improvisatory feel. The 1922 recording displays thin tone, some high notes spectacularly missed, and prominent *portamenti* in the *Più lento* section. (The *portamento* appears always more exaggerated in a slow tempo.) Nevertheless, given how high Feuermann was playing, the intonation is astonishingly accurate and even the liberties he took with pitch are acceptable. The 1927 *Zigeunerweisen*, like the Chopin Nocturne of the same year, reveals the same advances: a finely focused sound, almost impeccable intonation and great vigour.

Within the five years between the April 1922 and April 1927 sessions, a session in November 1922 with Max Saal (harp) led to no releases,[17] and it was not until June 1924 that Feuermann next recorded.[18] At this session, his partner was Fritz Ohrmann, who in eight works played not only the piano but also the Dominator harmonium. This session is particularly remarkable for the very different ways in which Feuermann played, suggesting that he was experimenting with various different approaches. His playing of Schumann's *Abendlied* is soupy, the slides positively inducing queasiness, with a sound as if through some dense fog, accompanied eerily by the Dominator harmonium. Although attributed to the same session, Dvořák's Rondo and Popper's *Serenade Espagnol* op.54 no.2 (where, in place of cuts, the music is expanded into a repeat of the first 20 bars) sound puzzlingly different. None of the queasiness of the Schumann is displayed, indeed Feuermann appears to have sloughed off the 'old style' almost completely.

Two years later, in March 1926, Feuermann again recorded works by Dvořák and Popper, with members of the Berlin State Opera Orchestra conducted by Michael Taube. In Popper's *Hungarian Rhapsody*, the clarity and vigour of 1924 is maintained. The slow movement of Dvořák's Concerto (the first time Feuermann tackled any part of this piece, but it was released only in England) features a focused sound, warmth and a graceful lyricism – all without slides. Presumably to accommodate the music to disc-length, there is a brutal cut of 42 bars before the '*quasi cadenza*'. Three sides of Haydn's D major Concerto (presumably the first movement, which had not been recorded in 1921), the Adagio from Boccherini's Concerto in B♭ and Popper's Concert Polonaise in D minor op.54 (with Taube at the piano) were recorded at the same session, but appear never to have been released.

With the introduction of the electrical process of recording, the sound-quality of Feuermann's 1927 recordings improved, but sound alone cannot account for the giant strides Feuermann made technically and musically between 1921 and 1927. If the earliest recordings ring with a certain brashness – he could play as high and as fast as his brother, Sigmund – Feuermann's articulation and focused sound in such high registers is quite extraordinary for its time and indeed remains so to this day.

It was during this period that Feuermann established a palpable difference between the expressive slide and the delayed shift. In the upward slide, Feuermann often used a crescendo, which emphasizes and intensifies the arrival note, never shrinking from it, whatever the tessitura. In the downward slide, he frequently used a decrescendo, emphasizing the uppermost note so that the arrival note is met cleanly with the subtlest of *glissando*. The delayed shift is associated with an upward change of position; he never used it with a change of position downwards. The 'delay' relates to the arrival point of an incidental *glissando* produced as a result of a change of position, which, if audible at all, takes place on the beat rather than, in a laggardly fashion, before it. By rapidly shifting on the beat, the sound is buoyant and electric. It was Pablo de Sarasate, the virtuoso violinist, who first adopted this technique as a string device, but essentially the technique belongs to the voice. In Feuermann's playing, the delayed shift – a highly expressive device – is one of his most recognizable characteristics. It is also a device used by Heifetz. Whether Feuermann was aware that Sarasate and Heifetz adopted this method of shifting before he adopted it is not known. What is known is that Feuermann greatly admired the singing of Caruso.

This was a transitional period for the use of slides by musicians in general. A 1927 recording by Klengel of a Bach sarabande reveals lugubrious sliding; recordings of others at about the same time – Antoni Sala (in 1927), Adolphe Frézin (1926) – reveal very little sliding. Casals, in his two earliest recordings of the slow movement of the Haydn D major Concerto (1916 and 1924), demonstrated notable differences in his use of *portamenti*.

It remains generally unknown and thus unacknowledged by the larger public (indeed the profession) that Feuermann was the first cellist commercially to record the entire Dvořák Concerto in B minor. A recording was completed eight years before the Casals–Szell recording of 1937. As well as this complete recording, two further performances by him of the Dvořák concerto survive – a private recording with the National Orchestra Association and a broadcast with the Chicago Symphony Orchestra.

This first recording of the Dvořák reads like a mystery story, so complicated is the sequence of takes and retakes and release at different times in different countries of different takes. On 30 April 1928, again with Taube and with members of the Berlin State Opera Orchestra, Feuermann began to record the concerto, completing the first and second movements only. Parlophon released these two movements in England. On 27 September 1929, 17 months later, a second session was held with Taube and the third movement was recorded. This was separately released in England in 1930. But on 27 January 1930 Feuermann returned to the studio to re-record two sides: the third part of the first movement (from bar 240) and the first part of the second movement. This session, however, was not conducted by Michael Taube, but by Frieder Weissmann. To confuse matters further, Taube's name appears on the disc, but not Weissmann's; presumably Parlophon did not want to release a recording with the names of two conductors attached. In the 27 January 1930 session, Feuermann and Weissmann also recorded Bruch's *Kol Nidrei*, and Weissmann was credited.

There are significant differences between the first-movement takes of 1928 and 1930: the timpani, so alarmingly out of tune in the 1928 take, are marginally improved in the 1930 take; a point of very poor ensemble between soloist and orchestra at bar 283 is also improved: in the earlier take, Taube introduced a molto rit. a bar earlier than called for by the score (and by Feuermann), with consequent ragged effect; in 1928 Feuermann played bars 304–5 an octave higher than written but the 1930 take restores Dvořák's pitch. Doubtless cost prevented the whole of the first movement from being re-recorded, since no attempt was made to 'correct' Feuermann's pitch in the second subject at bar 154 (played an octave higher than indicated by Dvořák) or the moments of appalling ensemble that beggar belief that the orchestra was professional.

On first listening, the most astonishing aspect of the 1928 first movement of the Dvořák is the speed. That Feuermann could play at this breakneck pace at all is remarkable. (There are a number of transfers to CD, but Pearl's transfer is very sharp in pitch.[19]) On Pearl's transfer, the duration of the first movement is 11'55". Even if the pitch is 'corrected', Feuermann's first movement still lasts only 12'03" whereas Casals's in 1937 lasts 13'22" and Fournier's in 1962 lasts 14'38".[20] At each of Feuermann's three sessions for the Dvořák, the turntable ran at a different speed. At the pitch of B minor (in relation to $a' = 440$), the speeds for these three sessions were:

> first and second movements recorded 30 April 1928: 76.1rpm
> third movement recorded 27 September 1929: 77.4rpm
> retakes of first movement and beginning of second movement recorded 27 January 1930: 77.6rpm[21]

To add to the issues of pitch and speed, between the 1928 session and those in 1929 and 1930 there is a notable difference in sound; Parlophon had changed its proprietary recording process.

Claus Adam summed up Feuermann's musical intelligence in two simple words: 'good taste'. A particular example of this can be found in the 1928 first movement of the Dvořák: in the second subject (from bar 139), a long lyrical tune with intervals of a 6th, 4th and octave cries out for slides. Feuermann resisted. Time and again, a high note is approached cleanly but left with a glancing downward slide (bars 145–6, d' to a; bar 154, a' to $f'\#$). Throughout this concerto Feuermann prepared the slide for maximum musical effect by not using it too early nor using it when might be expected in the repetition of a phrase. Not using a slide is as important as using one.

In the slow movement, slides again heighten and release tension in the phrase, Feuermann varying the repetition of musical figures by not repeating the pattern of slide (bars 22, 23 and 24), so giving the phrase architectural shape and freshness without predictability. His full, focused sound and its evenness seems allied to his vibrato, which is maintained from the beginning through to the end of a note without trailing off. He never allowed notes to be left 'exposed' through lack of vibrato, which might change the shape of the phrase and disrupt the flow of sound. Even with a slower vibrato than he eventually adopted, there is a vibrancy and tension to the sound in this movement, a sound instantly recognizable as Feuermann's. The delayed shift is now completely characteristic.

In the 17 months that elapsed between the first and second sessions in which the Dvořák was recorded, Feuermann may have changed instruments[22] (from the Josef Guarneri to the Tecchler), but the orchestra improved little. As with the next concerto Feuermann was to record commercially – Haydn's D major – his playing in its beauty and brilliance far exceeds any orchestral support. The opening orchestral tutti to the third movement of the Dvořák is particularly poor, contrasting acutely with Feuermann's *risoluto* entrance of bite and rhythmic tension. As in the later Haydn recording, there seems to have been no recognition of the way that Feuermann shaped his phrases: the orchestra at the beginning of this movement – with some appalling ensemble – merely repeated passages but with neither the shape nor the intensity of Feuermann's phrasing. The movement improves as it goes on, something of Feuermann's excitement finally arousing the orchestra as the opening theme returns (bar 254). Feuermann's accuracy of intonation is astounding. His sense of purpose, driving the music on, never allowing tension to sag, is notable even if there are moments where he appears to rush (bar 39). However, when space is needed, in the Andante at the end of the movement, there is a wonderful lazy quality to his playing as he allows the music to wind down, his use of downward slides so touchingly effective. The speed of this movement is, once again, hectic and an intriguing liberty is taken in the penultimate bar. While not faultless, this recording in its time must have been completely astounding. It remains so today.

Apart from the recently discovered test pressing of Popper's *Papillon* made in October 1932, Feuermann's last known complete recording made in Germany was for Telefunken, in September 1932. It comprised Popper's *Hungarian Rhapsody* in D for cello and orchestra op.68 with Paul Kletzki and the Berlin Philharmonic. Feuermann had previously recorded this work in 1926, but the 1932 recording has a much clearer and fuller sound, helped, no doubt, by the electrical recording process. Also, Feuermann was playing a different cello; in April 1932 he had acquired the Montagnana. The playing in the 1932 recording is more poised and deliberate, better controlled than in 1926, the tone beautifully burnished, delayed shifts replacing fast slides. His *spiccato* towards the end of the piece is simply staggering in its clarity. These recordings of the *Hungarian Rhapsody* also exhibit Feuermann's ability to turn a piece of no great compositional pretence into a work of arguably greater substance. Heifetz too had this ability. No wonder the public so loved salon music as played by them both.

What emerges clearly from Feuermann's earliest recordings is his readiness to take risks; he displayed an exuberance of a youthful kind. Throughout his life he never lost this confidence, which lent his playing such vitality and freshness.

Middle Period Recordings: England and Japan 1934–9

After it became virtually impossible for Feuermann to record in Germany, he recorded in England for the Columbia Graphophone Company. All these recording sessions, with one exception, took place in Studio 3, Abbey Road. The first session was in January 1934, when Feuermann, Goldberg and Hindemith recorded Hindemith's Second Trio (written for them in 1933) and Beethoven's Serenade in D op.8. The Hindemith trio appeared on three 12-inch discs and was reviewed in the August 1934 *Gramophone*. C.M.C. (Compton Mackenzie), the reviewer, although not able to obtain a score, remarked: 'It is probably the most valuable set of records we could have for the study of contemporary music. . . . I imagine that Hindemith must regard this as an almost perfect performance, as a whole, even though he can doubtless criticise some details. The recording is of that wonderful reproduction to which Columbia are accustoming us in chamber music.' Just a hint of Feuermann cheekiness is manifest: a rather exaggerated pizzicato in the final bar. It was in these sessions that the fiendish little Scherzo that Hindemith wrote overnight was recorded in a mere two takes. Four days later, Feuermann was back to record Hindemith's Solo Sonata, in a single take.

Feuermann recorded only the first of Brahms's two cello sonatas, the E minor. The Dutch pianist Theo van der Pas was his partner in this July 1934 recording, which was again made at the Abbey Road Studios, for Nipponophone. Two movements were completed on 10 July, the third movement on the following day. Pearl's transfer of the sonata to CD is almost a semitone higher than the original, giving the playing more of a rushed quality than may have been the case. As it happens, in the first movement Feuermann did rush the bridge passage to the second subject. This is a tendency in Feuermann's playing; whereas most cellists slow down in technically demanding passages, he speeds up, often taking astonishing risks while creating an atmosphere of tremendous excitement. There is no expositional repeat, as is common in many 78s of this time. The intonation is not always impeccable but there are

moments of very great playing: the return of the second subject in the recapitulation is ecstatic as Feuermann builds to the high *e''* climax, hitting it so truly,
never relaxing the tension. The Trio section has no repeats, but Feuermann
brings back that marvellous, lazy quality brought to the Dvořák Concerto
where the music just courses out. Thanks to good engineering, Feuermann's
notes in the fugal finale cut through the pianist's notes, which too easily cover
the cello in this movement. Feuermann added a double-stopped octave in bars
29 and 30 and also at the equivalent place later in the movement, to give added
weight and brilliance against the accompaniment. And there are other small
alterations to the original score, which are all effective. The final *Più presto* is
thrilling.

It was not until October 1935 that Feuermann's Brahms Sonata was reviewed
in *Gramophone*, by an unattributed author: 'Feuermann is in the front rank of
cellists and it goes without saying that his playing is magnificent.' The reviewer
liked the last movement best, the Allegretto *quasi menuetto* least: 'For this [the
second] movement I prefer Beatrice Harrison's recording.'

Following the Brahms third movement, Feuermann recorded works of a
more 'occasional' kind: Beethoven's Variations on '*Bei Männern*' from Mozart's
Magic Flute, Mélodie from Gluck's opera *Orphée* (arr. Grünfeld), Chopin's
Waltz in A minor op.34 no.2 (arr. Feuermann; originally for piano), and
Sgambati's *Serenata napoletana* op.24 no.2. All these works were recorded in
two takes per side.

Beethoven's Variations on '*Bei Männern*' received a plain, almost businesslike performance, the first variation suffering moments of poor ensemble with
the piano.

Chopin's Waltz in A minor clearly demonstrates Feuermann's slightly
drawn-out downwards slide, fast trill and fast fingerwork. (Pearl's transfer
plays in E♭ minor but Feuermann himself may have played it in another key,
possibly in C minor.) The (unattributed) review in the March 1935 *Gramophone* was scathing: 'The cello playing such music as Chopin's A minor waltz
reminds me of nothing so much as an aged ballerina balancing herself precar-
iously upon her points [*sic*]. Nor do all the liberties Feuermann takes with time
and pitch render this arrangement acceptable. Very much the reverse.' This
would not be the first time Feuermann 'doctored' a piece by Chopin. He was
later to introduce enormous added difficulties to Chopin's Introduction and
Polonaise, making an otherwise playable work for cello and piano into a piece
of monstrous complication. But Feuermann's insistence on adhering to the
wishes of the composer should not be confused with great performance, that
can (and in Feuermann's case does) so often become the improvisatory end of
composition.

Sgambati's *Serenata napoletana* was played to perfection, Feuermann making light of high-lying passages, some of which he played as harmonics. Once again the reviewer in *Gramophone* was unimpressed: 'I am sorry that a cellist of Feuermann's attainments wastes his time this way.'[23] Admirers of Feuermann regard this recording as one of his finest in this genre. In its 78 form it was much sought after by collectors, changing hands at a considerable price. This recording in some sense encapsulates so many of the unique qualities in Feuermann's playing. Feuermann, unlike Casals, had the temperament and gaiety to bring out the best in these slighter works.

Despite another caustic review in *Gramophone*, it was out of this July 1934 session that one of Feuermann's greatest recordings came: Gluck's *Mélodie*. It fills the empty side of the third disc of the Brahms Sonata. The music in B minor is described in *Gramophone* as 'a transcription of the moving tune marked "a troubled spirit crosses the scene" from the "Pantomime" in Act III, the scene in the Elysian fields, of Gluck's Orpheus'. The reviewer had ears only for the transposition of pitch, which he disliked, pointing out that it did not follow 'the exquisitely peaceful F major melody which precedes and follows it'.[24] The reviewer entirely missed the simple greatness of Feuermann's playing. For Feuermann, this was a piece of no technical difficulty; his burnished sound, singing tone and smooth lyricism captures the melancholic spirit of this short work to heartbreaking effect.

Feuermann toured twice to Japan – in autumn 1934 and spring 1936. The record market there was probably larger than in any single European country, so great was the enthusiasm for Western classical music, particularly instrumental music. On each visit to Japan, Feuermann recorded for Nipponophone. In 1934 the works were Japanese: three short pieces by Kōsaku Yamada (one of Japan's most prolific composers) which were arrangements of songs for cello and piano – *Karatachi no hana*, *Nobara* and *Oshoro Takashima*; and an arrangement by Yamada of a song by Rentarō Taki, *Kōjō no tsuki*, which was particularly popular at the time.[25] Yamada's music is a sentimental mix of Western boudoir music and occidental harmonic references. Feuermann's sound is intense and focused, the slides incorporated touchingly into the somewhat cloying tunes. For *Karatachi no hana* there were six takes, more than for any other recording Feuermann made. Perhaps there was some technical difficulty with the recording equipment, or perhaps the composer was present, because it seems unlikely that awkward double stops would have derailed Feuermann. This is salon music of a certain hybrid quality, and once again Feuermann appears to have had an intuitive response to it, projecting it with warmth and commitment, superbly supported by his pianist, Fritz Kitzinger.

Feuermann's next commercial recording took place in London on behalf of Nipponophone in 1935. This recording of Haydn's D major Cello Concerto, while notorious for the circumstances in which it took place, is one of the greatest examples of Feuermann's playing and is of undoubted musicological importance (see Chapter 7). In his 1921 recording of two movements from the Haydn, Feuermann had used the Gevaert edition, standard at that time. For his 1935 recording he used music he had photographed from a copyist's copy of the manuscript he found in the Preussische Staatsbibliothek, Berlin. It was a full score that Feuermann supplied to Dr Malcolm Sargent and the unnamed orchestra, presumably with the parts made for his Vienna performance. Columbia wrote to Feuermann: 'We understand that you have your own orchestral parts of the work and that you will go through these with Dr Sargent before the date of the session.'[26] It was the first time the original version was recorded.

The Gevaert edition varies substantially from Haydn's original. Gevaert changed not only the orchestration (Haydn includes no flute) but also on occasion the harmonies. Notes (sometimes jarringly chromatic) and ornaments were added to the solo part, while the work was substantially cut. In short, Gevaert produced a Romantic travesty of the original.

In his 1935 recording, as can be heard, within five bars of the soloist's first entry, Feuermann excluded Gevaert's chromatic notes. Interestingly, he intuitively played the piece almost as Haydn wrote it: he played a tied note that is in the Haydn (bar 36) but not in the André first edition (1804); he took out a passing note that appears in André, substituting a repeated note as did Haydn (bar 153). Feuermann added slurs over most semiquaver figurations in relation to bowing (in 18th-century notation a slur suggests phrasing rather than bowing). Within the first movement as a whole, brutal cuts in the Gevaert – 43 bars out of 189 – were restored by Feuermann, although he did retain one small cut (bars 65–70].[27] Most importantly, the recapitulation of the first subject is restored.

Feuermann played a 'plain' score, as the manuscript copy instructs, but did add the occasional note and passing note: he completed the rising arpeggio in the perilously high *flautino* bar by adding *b''* (bar 175), which makes better musical sense (although cellists may be relieved to know that it is not what Haydn wrote). He also thinned out arpeggiated figures (bar 178). Gone is the fussy, unstylistic detail introduced by Gevaert. Feuermann's sound is refined, elegant, burnished, noble, too much pressure never applied to his relatively light Voirin bow. Rhythmically his control in difficult, rapid passage-work is remarkable. In the highest registers he showed no fear – a particular characteristic in all his playing. How different it is from Casals's 1945 recording (using Gevaert), in which phrases in the first movement are often distorted by inappropriate *rubato* and dynamic changes that mask technical difficulties. (Casals, however, was twice Feuermann's age when this recording was made.[28])

Except for a single wolf note, Feuermann never tripped up in this recording, whatever the register, allowing the music to sing in long, beautifully shaped phrases. In the first movement he supplied his own astonishing cadenza. It is of considerable length and differs entirely from the cadenzas by Gevaert, Klengel and Casals. Technically perilous, it is most skilfully written and, although well beyond the reach of most eighteenth-century cellists, does not jar musically – but the listener is left gasping. As *Gramophone* remarked: 'the work is obviously designed to give him as good a show as possible.'[29] The 1960 International Music Company edition edited by Leonard Rose printed two cadenzas; an asterisk leads not to authorship but to the statement 'Editor offers a choice of 2 Cadenzas'. Cadenza I is by Casals and cadenza II is by Feuermann; however, neither author is credited.

The orchestral accompaniment in the first movement in no way lives up to the soloist. A sense of instability, a tendency to rush and then pull back, as though Sargent was out of control, are features of the opening orchestral *tutti*. The violin sound is thin, exposed, with often poor ensemble. When Feuermann entered at a palpably slower tempo (described in the *Gramophone* review as 'a pull-up')[30], the accompanying strings were completely thrown.

In contrast to Feuermann's 1921 recording, the slow movement is mature and fully developed. The dated slides of the earlier period are gone and so are the cuts. Feuermann played the André version until just before the end of the movement at bar 62, where he adapted Gevaert's two-bar cadenza. Feuermann's tempo in the 1935 recording is faster than that in the 1921 recording, though slower than Casals's in 1945 (Casals used Gevaert's cuts). Feuermann's sweetness of tone, particularly in the high-lying repeat of the opening tune, is ravishingly beautiful, more so than in the rather businesslike Casals performance of 1945.

In the final movement, Feuermann's lilting phrasing of the rondo tune was entirely ignored by the orchestral strings, their playing dull and rhythmically imprecise. He added the occasional tasteful *appoggiatura*, generally similar to Gevaert though not in André, and adopted the first 15 bars of Gevaert's cadenza, adding his own arpeggio that whoops into the stratosphere, played at tremendous speed and impeccably tuned. He kept a version of Gevaert's scampering arpeggios and scales over the final orchestral *tutti*, which, although not in André (or Haydn), provides a brilliant finish. Perhaps this was standard practice; nowadays cellists often adopt it, since it allows the soloist to finish with the orchestra without being confined to the simple notes of the orchestral bass.

The review in *Gramophone* concentrated on the piece rather than the performance, beginning: 'I should like to know who, after a century of neglect, rediscovered the work'; and ending: 'Any friends you may have . . . might be good subjects on which to try this music. If it does not make them purr, they are pretty sure to be merely beasts of prey.'[31] Any notes that went with the recording clearly omitted Feuermann's name. His efforts went unrecognized. Casals used the Gevaert edition in 1945; and Leonard Rose's edition of 1960 retained many features of the Gevaert, including the cuts and, as already mentioned, used Feuermann's first-movement cadenza, unacknowledged. Whether wittingly or unwittingly, this was not the sole instance of Rose claiming credit for work done by Feuermann, as will be shown.

A letter from Eva Feuermann to Casals dated 4 September 1945 confirms that Feuermann had prepared a performing edition of the Haydn for publication. Eva was seeking permission from Casals: 'les dernières douze mesures ont été pris de votre cadence du même concerto.' This is puzzling. She did not state from which movement this cadenza came; as Casals in his 1945 recording played a modified version of Gevaert in the first movement and pure Gevaert in the second, it seems unlikely that any third movement cadenza would have been specifically Casals's original. Casals granted permission; but did he know what he was granting? In the event, the Haydn remained unpublished.[32]

Feuermann's next commercial recordings were made in Japan in 1936, during his second tour there. On 4 June he agreed a contract with Nipponophone to make a minimum of 15 double-sided records within the period to 31 December 1938. It was intended that six or seven of these should be made in Tokyo, the rest in London 'in approximately December 1936'.[33]

The royalty arrangement was tiered: a) 7½% of retail price for cello solos with piano accompaniment and for sonatas made with the artist's usual accompanist (in which case Feuermann was to bear the cost of the accompanist); b) 5% of retail price for cello solos with piano accompaniment of titles Feuermann had previously recorded for Parlophon; c) 6% of retail price in the case of recordings with orchestra, or in the case that Feuermann made duo sonatas with an artist other than his usual accompanist; d) 3⅓% for trio recordings in which Feuermann took part. Sales figures were calculated on 75% of the total manufactured. This represented about the same rate as agreed the previous year for the Haydn Concerto (5% on the retail price, payable on 85% of the sales[34]), there being a higher royalty (6%) for orchestral recordings on a smaller percentage of the discs actually manufactured (75%).

Nipponophone and Feuermann, keen to have sales in England and Europe, were disappointed that London refused to guarantee release of at least ten recordings within a period of three years. London merely confirmed that they would give them 'preferential consideration'.[35] It is tempting to speculate why. Was it that the repertoire proposed by Nipponophone was too light? Was it that London failed to recognize the quality of Feuermann's playing in the Haydn Concerto? Was it the usual prejudice against cellists? Whatever the explanation, Feuermann's next recordings were all of short pieces, suitable for a single side, and well suited presumably to the Japanese market.

He recorded ten 10-inch sides and five 12-inch sides. The pieces on the 10-inch sides were: Tchaikovsky's *Valse sentimentale* op.51 no.6; Mendelssohn's *Spring Song* op.62 no.6; the Prayer from Bloch's *From Jewish Life* no.1; Godard's 'Berceuse' from *Jocelyne*; Schumann's *Zigeunerleben* op.29 no.3; Schubert's *Ständchen* from book 1 of *Schwanengesang*; Wrighton's 'Her Bright Smile Haunts Me Still'; the Gavotta and Allegro from Piatti's arrangement of Valentini's Sonata in E op.8; Saint-Saëns's *The Swan*; and the Popper Melody in F op.3 no.1. (arr. Rubinstein). The pieces on the 12-inch sides were: Handel's Largo from *Xerxes*; J.S. Bach's Air BWV 1068; Chopin's Nocturne in E♭ op.9 no.2; Schumann's *Träumerei* op.15 no.7; and the Bach/Gounod *Ave Maria*. With the exception of the Handel and the Bach Air, all the pieces were recorded with Feuermann's tour pianist, Wolfgang Rebner. The strings of the New Symphony Orchestra, Tokyo, conducted by Viscount Konoye, accompanied the Handel and Bach.

The issuing of these recordings was sporadic: the Handel and Bach with strings were never issued;[36] some of the 10-inch discs were issued only in Japan; the Chopin Nocturne in E♭ was issued in Japan, France and Britain in 1938;[37] Schumann's *Träumerei* and the *Ave Maria*, while not issued in Japan, were issued in 1938 in Australia and the UK; Mendelssohn's *Spring Song* was issued in Japan on a release entitled *Musical Triumphs*, coupled with Maurice Maréchal playing 'a Japanese melody' (most probably *Kōjō no tsuki*, which Feuermann had recorded in 1934).[38] Until recently, many of these Japanese recordings were particularly rare.[39]

What is striking about the works on 10-inch recorded in Japan is that with the exception of Schumann's *Zigeunerleben* and the Allegro from the Valentini sonata, all the pieces are slow and sentimental. Feuermann, however, never sentimentalized and indeed showed the opposite tendency, preferring to keep the music moving. In the Bloch he eschewed melancholic wailing; in the Saint-Saëns his approach was fast and unsugary, more businesslike than in his 1928 recording, which is, perhaps, the more touching. As usual, the high notes have a distinct ringing quality of great beauty. Of the two faster works,

Zigeunerleben, an arrangement (by Feuermann?) of Schumann's song, shows Feuermann's effortlessness in double stopping, while the Valentini Allegro contains an astonishing display of rapid, clean bowing across the strings, with absolute clarity of articulation – eighteenth century 'noodling'. Feuermann's playing of Baroque music, in its sensitivity to style, pre-dates today's interest in authentic performance practice by decades. He no doubt intuitively regarded it as simply the right musical interpretation. On the whole, all these works were played as demanded in the score (or arrangement), excepting the odd moment when Feuermann succumbed to temptation and played higher than indicated.

The recording of the Chopin Nocturne was Feuermann's third; all of them are based on Popper's arrangement but with additional flamboyant decoration. While the youthful 1922 version displaying old-style vices was supplanted in 1927 by a very much cleaner performance, the 1936 recording (without cuts) retains much rubato and the flamboyant decoration of bars 14 to 16. Interestingly, with the cut restored, Feuermann was not tempted to follow Popper's extravagances in bar 22, although he made up for it in bar 25. In bar 30 in the 1927 and 1936 recordings, Feuermann dropped an octave, making much better dramatic sense of the following bar and its build-up to technical fireworks. In all three recordings the Nocturne ends perilously high on a spread arpeggio, unlike Popper's pizzicato chords.

Quite why Feuermann recorded a single side only for Nipponophone of the Andantino and Variations from Weber's *Konzertstück* op.20 on 22 December 1936 in London is not clear. This was his first recording with the pianist Gerald Moore and was released with Beethoven's A major Sonata op.69, a recording made six months later with Myra Hess. For A.R. (Alec Robertson) in *Gramophone* (October 1937), this coupling (he wrongly attributed Hess to the Weber as well as the Beethoven) tipped the balance in deciding which of two Beethoven recordings the buyer might choose – the Feuermann recording, or a recording by Paul Grümmer and Wilhelm Kempff that had recently appeared. Robertson found the Weber 'delightful and gracious music and very well played by both artists', but this is not, in any sense, an important Feuermann recording.

It is regrettable that Feuermann's only recording of a Beethoven sonata should not rank as one of his finest. Eva remembers that the first session with Myra Hess on 28 June did not go well; only the first movement was recorded. The most successful movement is the third, which was recorded with the second movement on the following day. Feuermann's sound is uncharacteristically thin – perhaps an engineering fault? – and the ensemble with Hess is sometimes rocky, particularly in the Scherzo, where Feuermann has his familiar tendency to rush. The sonata itself was grievously cut: not only are the first movement expositional repeat and the first repeat in the finale gone but also the whole of the second return of the Trio and Scherzo in the second movement.

On that same day, 29 June 1937, when Feuermann finished recording the Beethoven with Hess, he continued with Gerald Moore to record Schubert's A minor 'Arpeggione' Sonata. As one of Feuermann's greatest recordings, it leads one to speculate that any problems in the Beethoven were not so much to do with him but with Hess, a pianist with whom he had not previously worked. With Moore he had already recorded Weber's *Konzertstück* and given a recital. Nipponophone had agreed only grudgingly to Moore, since it implied paying a fee; they had hoped that Feuermann might record 'with his usual accompanist', at this point Wolfgang Rebner. Moore was paid ten guineas.

Schubert's 'Arpeggione' Sonata is a work written for the obscure instrument, the arpeggione. The work is played most usually in arrangement for cello or viola (although flautists, clarinettists and double bass players have also indulged). As there is no agreed version of the piece, it is fair game for players to adopt their own octave transpositions. Feuermann was one of the first cellists regularly to perform this work in his concerts, a work that up until his time was generally regarded as technically too demanding. It has suffered on the one hand from being technically daunting and on the other from critical opinion that frequently lays sentimentality at its door. Feuermann's performance defies both.

It is hard to believe that within one recording session Feuermann's playing could be so transformed. Whereas in the Beethoven Sonata with Hess a certain tightness and constraint is evident, Feuermann responded to Schubert's wistful opening movement with warmth and dignity, without hint of indulgence but astounding clarity of articulation and impeccable intonation in this highly exposed music. It is as if there are no bow changes, the line long and seamless. In the soulful slow movement he produced the most limpid sound, so tenderly shaping the phrases with the merest hint of a slide; his Stradivarius cello seems to issue liquid gold. The third movement, *Allegretto*, despite a small cut, is masterly, Feuermann never straining but capturing its contradictory spirit of joy and melancholy to perfection, revealing so clearly his own Viennese background. (This close identification with Schubert's music will be seen again in the B♭ Trio with Heifetz and Rubinstein.) Feuermann's performance of the 'Arpeggione' remains great to this day, concealing, as it does, the immense technical challenge within music of touching frailty. Great as this performance is, George Neikrug commented: 'I always felt that the recordings didn't do him justice. I always found his playing much better in concert than on recordings. And I think he felt so too. I heard him play the 'Arpeggione' so much better than on this recording.'[40] This is hard to believe.

Feuermann completed recording the 'Arpeggione' on 30 June 1937. A year later, the *Gramophone* review (unattributed) was moderately damning: 'Feuermann's tone, though beautiful and truly lyrical, is rather too consistently luscious and lacking in light and shade; but his phrasing is most musicianly and his florid passages are very delicately negotiated.'[41]

His next commercial recording was not made for Columbia but for the RCA Victor Company in America. In February 1938, while in the midst of his NOA marathon, he had been invited by the singer Hulda Lashanska[42] to a tea in honour of Heifetz. In January 1939, she organized a benefit concert for European émigrés in Carnegie Hall where in two works she was joined by Rudolf Serkin, Mischa Elman and Feuermann. It was these works – an aria by Siegfried Ochs (1858–1929), '*Dank sei dir, Herr*' (usually attributed mistakenly to Handel), and Schubert's *Litanei* – that were taken into the recording studio on 13 January.[43]

Lashanska's performance is not distinguished, her voice heavy, with an inclination to hoot. The novelty of this recording relates to the opportunity of hearing, albeit briefly, a trio of Elman, Feuermann and Serkin. The tonal match between Elman and Feuermann is good, with all three musicians sensitive as accompanists to Lashanska.

Feuermann's contract with Columbia-Nipponophone came to an end on 31 December 1938. Feuermann, however, had not completed the required number of sides; seven more were needed. He suggested recording Reger's unaccompanied Suite in G major, which he believed would take three sides, coupled with two movements from Bach's E♭ Suite for the fourth side. The Reger in fact took four sides and 'dirty little pieces'[44] filled the remaining sides, so there were eight sides in all. The 'dirty little pieces' were by Drigo, Cui, Rimsky-Korsakov and Albéniz.

Reger wrote his Three Suites for unaccompanied cello op.131c in 1914. Each one was dedicated to a cellist: Suite no.1 to Julius Klengel; Suite no.2 to Hugo Becker; Suite no.3 to Paul Grümmer. They were probably first performed in 1916. The earliest evidence of Feuermann playing the First Suite dates from March 1921, and in the following few years it occurred quite frequently in his programmes. The piece was included in his second New York Town Hall recital in February 1935, which was hastily arranged after his phenomenally successful debut recital. The suites are something of a homage to J.S. Bach, whose first two suites are in the same keys as Reger's first two: G major and D minor. However, there are fewer movements than in the Bach: in the case of Reger's First Suite there are only three movements – Präludium, Adagio and Fuge.

Feuermann recorded the Reger on 7 February 1939 at the Abbey Road Studios in London. This was its first commercial recording and Columbia was none too enthusiastic about its appeal. The opening of the Präludium, with its regular semiquavers, strongly recalls Bach's First Suite, but the end of the same movement recalls Bach's C major Suite. Feuermann played with admirable simplicity, with Reger's 'hat-doffing' to the Baroque finely and evenly executed, and double-stops effortlessly in tune. The double stops in the Adagio, mainly in 6ths, are again remarkable, not only for their impeccable intonation but also for the vibrato applied by Feuermann, bringing the sound so tenderly to life. This movement is a study in legato playing. In the final movement, Feuermann's playing wisely makes light of Reger's potentially heavy double-stopping and gruff counterpoint. Again the double stops are impeccable, Feuermann bringing such sensitive musicianship to this work. This was the nearest Feuermann was to get to recording Bach. Alas, not Bach, but a Bach 'sound-alike'.

The 'dirty little pieces' recorded with Gerald Moore were the last salon works that Feuermann recorded for Columbia. Once again, an unerring sense of good taste is displayed. Where these four pieces could so easily be overwhelmed by sentimentality, Feuermann never sentimentalized, merely raising each work to a level well above its content. Great playing of great music is one thing; great playing of less significant music quite another.

Chapter 18

American Recordings

From 1 April 1939, Feuermann was signed to Columbia's rival, the RCA Victor Company in America.[1] Even so, Columbia continued certain negotiations: the trios with Schnabel and Huberman, a recording of Beethoven's Triple Concerto and even a Brahms Double Concerto. None of these projects was realized.

In November 1938, NBC Artists had assigned the pianist Franz Rupp to Feuermann and, with the exception of a single test pressing, all Feuermann's last commercial duo recordings were made with Rupp in the space of six months – 31 July to 14 December 1939. There were seven sessions, all of which took place in 'Studio 2, New York City'.[2] The length of these sessions varied considerably: some were as short as two hours, suggesting that for some reason they may have been curtailed. Unusually, Feuermann kept returning to re-record most of the works. Only Beethoven's 'Ein Mädchen oder Weibchen' Variations were recorded in a single session. It is significant that Feuermann requested that certain works from these sessions should not be issued, including the Beethoven Variations (initially released in 1940 but withdrawn), Mendelssohn's D major Sonata (to which he returned in three separate sessions), J.S. Bach's Adagio BWV 564 (to which he returned twice) and Fauré's *Après un rêve* (to which he returned three times). The only works that he allowed to be released from this six-month period (although still subject to multiple takes) were his arrangement of the Adagio and Allegro from Handel's Organ Concerto op.4 no.3, Chopin's Introduction and Polonaise op.3, Canteloube's *Bourrée auvergnate* and Davidov's *At the Fountain*. After Feuermann's death, the works suppressed all became available.

Sophie Feuermann has said that Feuermann disliked recording (most artists do), but in his letters he did not specifically complain. It was not until the American recordings that he appears actively to have intervened in their release. However, his approach could also be typically casual: 'He did those recordings at 9 o'clock in the morning. He would drive in from Scarsdale. He would put a cigarette in his mouth and start to play.'[3]

The two movements from Handel's Organ Concerto op.4 no.3 were recorded in Feuermann's own arrangement. However, the parts on manuscript paper (Carl Fischer, Monarch Brand), although attributed to Feuermann, are in a hand that is not his.[4] Stylistically the Handel movements, taken with a light bow, are played utterly convincingly. The Adagio is played nobly, free of trills and decoration, Feuermann's sound clean, burnished and focused. Rupp's accompaniment in the Allegro is occasionally over-pedalled and heavy. Perhaps it was this difference of approach that caused Feuermann to return to the work over the course of so many sessions?

Given the beauty of the performance, it says much that Feuermann wanted to suppress his recording of the Beethoven Variations op.66. In his writings, Feuermann repeatedly espoused the view that it is the performer's primary duty to respect the wishes of the composer. But by this he did not mean complete inflexibility; it is abundantly clear from the scores of many works that Feuermann made frequent 'adjustments'. He believed that since the nineteenth century, when composers ceased necessarily being performers, a certain improvisatory feel in performance had probably been lost. His 'fidelity' towards the composer's intentions was more in the sense of spirit than to the letter. For example, in Beethoven's 'Ein Mädchen oder Weibchen' Variations, after the first eight bars of the opening theme Feuermann introduced a repeat. The repeat is wholly logical – the piano has introduced the theme with the cello accompanying; a repeat allows the instruments to change places. It sounds entirely authentic but is not what Beethoven wrote. To the cello part of Chopin's Polonaise, however, he made wholesale additions, adding decorative passages of extreme difficulty. He worked from an edition published by G. Schirmer Inc., New York (1928), initially edited by Joseph Adamowski ('Head of the Faculty of the Ensemble, String Quartet and Violoncello classes of the New England Conservatory of Music in Boston'). The piano part of the Chopin bearing Albert Hirsch's name survives in the possession of Sophie Feuermann. Pieces of manuscript paper are glued into it with the various changes Feuermann introduced; these are written in Feuermann's hand.

This work was subject to some controversy when it was published by International Music Company in 1960. The cellist Leonard Rose, although credited as the editor, used much of Feuermann's arrangement without acknowledgement. According to Bernard Greenhouse, it is not clear that Rose knowingly gave his name to the arrangement. Rose came across Feuermann's cello part through a student who was studying both with him and with Greenhouse. Eva Feuermann had given Greenhouse Feuermann's arrangement of the Chopin, and Greenhouse's student showed it to Rose. Rose liked the Feuermann edition and started to play it. Whether there was any real threat of legal action is unclear, but the publisher did change the inscription on the 1960 printing.[5] The pre-1970 IMC catalogue lists Chopin's op.3 Polonaise as arranged by Emanuel Feuermann and edited by Leonard Rose.[6] The current printing, however, once again makes no mention of Feuermann's name.

Feuermann's recording of Chopin's Introduction leaves it largely unchanged except for a cadential flourish of 6th chords before the *Alla polacca* (which Rose adopted wholesale in his edition). Feuermann's Allegro, as can be heard on the recording, begins by following Chopin's original version, but at bar 30 Feuermann takes off: not only did he add difficult passage-work but he played it at top speed, at the top of the cello, with awesome accuracy. The result is utterly amazing. Feuermann began this recording on 1 August 1939. He took it up again on 13 December, but it was not until the following day that the takes that were finally issued were recorded.

Of the salon works recorded with Rupp, Davidov's *At the Fountain* is again an amazing example of Feuermann's coordination, with rock-solid rhythmic control in this virtual *spiccato perpetuum mobile*. George Neikrug described the sound as 'like a riveting machine'.[7] Another salon work requiring similar virtuosity that survives from around this time, although not a commercial recording, is Pablo de Sarasate's op.23 no.2 *Zapateado* in an arrangement for cello, no doubt by Feuermann. *Zapateado* is a showpiece for violin, a flashy party piece in every virtuoso violinist's arsenal. It is a work that Feuermann frequently performed as a show-stopping *bonne bouche* to end his programmes. This recording probably dates from the broadcast of the *Kraft Music Hall* on 3 August 1939, when Feuermann was accompanied by Theodore Saidenberg.[8]

Zapateado, if performed by cellists at all, is usually transcribed down an octave and a half to D major from its original key of A. In this recording Feuermann played it in A major, at times down an octave but sometimes at violin pitch, making an already notoriously difficult piece even more difficult. His virtuosity is breathtaking – the accuracy of the harmonics, the vigour of the left-hand pizzicato, the flamboyance, the ease in playing so perilously high, and the impeccable rhythm. No wonder Feuermann's 'ha' is heard at the end of the piece.

Another important surviving fragment also comes from a broadcast at this time. On 16 August 1939 Feuermann was the only soloist in a concert from the

Lewisohn Stadium in New York. The concert with the Philharmonic-Symphony Orchestra conducted by Alexander Smallens was broadcast over WABC, New York, and the CBS Network from 9.00 p.m. until 10.30 p.m., suggesting that the first two works in the programme – Mendelssohn's overture *Ruy Blas* op.95 and the Polka and Fugue from Weinberger's *Schwanda the Bagpiper* – were not broadcast. The next piece, Bloch's *Schelomo*, was followed by Chabrier's *España*, Saint-Saëns's A minor Cello Concerto and excerpts from Berlioz's *The Damnation of Faust*. Almost complete performances of the Bloch and the Saint-Saëns have survived, recorded off-air.[9]

The practice of recording off-air by amateur enthusiasts began around 1936, and was an expensive hobby – few had the means to invest in the audio equipment required. Nevertheless there were a number of 'professional amateurs' with some expertise who produced quite good results. On the night of 16 August an unknown enthusiast used 16-inch lacquers playing at 33⅓rpm to record the concert. But he had only one disc-cutter. When space ran out he was obliged to turn over, so losing some of the music; both the Bloch and the Saint-Saëns suffer a fade-out of a few bars. The sound-quality of the Bloch is very poor (there is considerable radio interference), and levels at one point were changed dramatically, bringing the cello prominently forward in the sound spectrum. Nevertheless, there are moments of extraordinary intensity, excitement and expressiveness, with passionate playing of this Hebrew rhapsody from the orchestra – an orchestra no doubt full of Jews.

Of far better sound-quality from this concert is the Saint-Saëns Concerto. Once again, Feuermann sounds very close, but it is another remarkable performance. Feuermann's opening is immediately urgent, intense, clarion-like, the contrasting second subject (bar 178) played with such richness of sound, downward slides caressed and rubato applied so sensitively but never sentimentally. A moment of catastrophic ensemble in the orchestra (from bar 111) led the donor of my tape to suggest that the orchestra was obviously a poor European one! (The New York Philhamonic-Symphony was not identified on the cassette.) Why had the conductor, Alexander Smallens, lost control? The recording of the Saint-Saëns fades out in the middle of bar 550 but is restored from the middle of bar 557. A cut from the *Più allegro* at bar 576 to the *Molto allegro* at bar 588 was made in this performance. Throughout the concerto, Feuermann's phrasing is long and purposeful, with a sense of forward movement, technical difficulties never distorting the line. He held the final note over the orchestral tutti, ending with a double-stopped flourish – another example of a Feuermann 'improvement'. The audience roared its approval and Feuermann obliged with an encore: 'Sarabande and Bourrées by Bach', he announced with his slight German accent. As discussed later, this is the only

surviving recorded evidence of Feuermann playing any of Bach's unaccompanied suites.

Mendelssohn's D major Sonata did not appear in Feuermann's recitals
before 1939, but at his session on 11 September 1939 he began to record it. This
session, which lasted from 10.00 a.m. to 6.15 p.m., was devoted entirely to the
Mendelssohn, and the whole work was laid down.[10] It was a long session, but
relatively few takes were recorded. In November, Feuermann included this
sonata in his annual Carnegie Hall recital. In December he returned to the
studio, devoting more time to the Mendelssohn on the 12th and 13th. The
sonata, however, was never issued on 78s. A letter from RCA to Feuermann's
widow in 1948 gives some explanation:

> I investigated your last suggestion regarding the Mendelssohn Sonata No. 2
> and the 'Après un Rêve'. I find that unfortunately, all the shells were
> destroyed at the artist's request for 'Après un Rêve' and that the
> Mendelssohn Sonata was not only not approved by your husband but was
> also not approved technically by our factory, and so there is no possibility of
> releasing either of these two recordings as performed by your husband.[11]

However, by 1957 the shells miraculously reappeared and both works were
released on LP.

Just what concerned Feuermann in blocking the issue of the Mendelssohn
is open to speculation. Like Heifetz, unless he was entirely satisfied with a
recording he would not authorize its issue. In Europe he may not have had this
authority, and in America, perhaps influenced by Heifetz, his notion of
perfection may have changed. The sound balance is generally not good; the
microphone is too close to Feuermann while Rupp's sound is distant.
Feuermann's playing in the outer movements is brisk and powerful, with some
open strings hit more forcefully than he might have wished. On the other
hand, in the Mendelssohn first movement, as in Davidov's *At the Fountain*,
there is some astonishing *spiccato* bowing. The *Allegretto scherzando* shows the
fullness of sound and vitality of Feuermann's *pizzicato*, while in the Adagio he
poured out his powerful sound as called for in this '*Quasi recit. appassionato ed
animato*'.

The session on 14 December 1939 was to be Feuermann's last with Franz
Rupp. From 21 December 1939 to the end of his life, his commercial recordings
(notwithstanding one test pressing) comprised music for cello with orchestra
or chamber music. It is from this short period that the majority of surviving
private recordings date. In terms of commercial recordings, it is when
Feuermann began working with an orchestra of the highest rank; and to
record with Heifetz.

Feuermann made three commercial recordings with the Philadelphia Orchestra: Brahms's A minor Concerto for violin and cello op.102 in December 1939, Strauss's *Don Quixote* in February 1940 and Bloch's *Schelomo* in March 1940. There were no public concerts to run in the Brahms and Strauss works before the recordings. (Indeed, it was not until March 1942 that Feuermann played Strauss's *Don Quixote* with the Philadelphia Orchestra in public.) Only *Schelomo* was performed in public a week before the recording took place.

The recording of the Brahms Double Concerto with Jascha Heifetz conducted by Eugene Ormandy is not only one of Feuermann's greatest recordings but also one of the most outstanding recordings ever to have been made of this work. As Yo-Yo Ma has commented: 'Feuermann was the only cellist who played really well with Heifetz, who could match him blow for blow.'[12] This recording of the Brahms was the second complete recording to be made following that of Casals and Thibaud in 1929.[13]

Feuermann appears to have first met Heifetz in February 1938 when Feuermann was in the middle of his 'marathon' series for the NOA in New York. Heifetz had wanted to play quartets but their free time had not coincided. Although this may have been their first meeting, a letter from Fred Gaisberg to Rubinstein in September 1935 suggests that Feuermann was actively being considered by Heifetz for a trio with Rubinstein: 'Also there is another idea which Heifetz favours, that is trios, preferably Tchaikovsky or the Schubert Op.100 with Feuerman[n], who will be in London, and yourself. I hope you will give this serious attention.'[14]

Feuermann had played the Brahms Double Concerto from an early age, first with his brother Sigmund. Playing with Heifetz must psychologically have recalled his concerts with Sigmund. Sophie, however, maintains that there was no similarity in the playing of Sigmund and Heifetz.[15]

Between his meeting Heifetz in February 1938 and recording the concerto in December 1939, Feuermann's known concert performances of the Brahms include a BBC Promenade concert at the end of August 1938 with Antonio Brosa conducted by Sir Henry Wood, and a performance in November 1938 with Erica Morini and the Philadelphia Orchestra conducted by Eugene Ormandy. Despite the recording's enormous success, Heifetz and Feuermann never performed the concerto together in public.

The concerto was recorded on 21 December in the Academy of Music – the Philadelphia Orchestra's performing 'home', an acoustically perfect auditorium – in one session that lasted from 2.00 p.m. to 4.40 p.m. But it is little known that a major technical hitch occurred in the first movement. In order to record without making long breaks between the four sides, pre-arranged points were notified to Ormandy and the players: a few extra seconds' break were to be taken between pre-arranged phrases in order for the engineer to start the new side. Unfortunately, the engineer mistook the first break, and side two began, followed almost immediately by a long pause. This matrix and the subsequent matrices for the first movement could not be used. But recalling Heifetz, Feuermann and the entire orchestra to re-record the first movement was not possible either. There was only one course of action: to redub the movement from the faulty takes on to a second wax. This resulted in the sound becoming markedly degraded, but it was this version that was issued and re-released by RCA. It is only on recent transfers – Biddulph, Pearl and Naxos – that the original test pressings made for the producer, Charles O'Connell, have been used, restoring the far better original sound.[16]

The first movement of the Brahms is fast (14′32″), substantially faster than in the Casals–Thibaud recording (15′05″). Feuermann's opening solo generates long phrases and a marvellous feeling of spacious lyricism. Heifetz's entry has a driven quality, at times showing little feeling for, or attention to, Feuermann's shaping of phrases. But the players' clarity of articulation, intensity of sound, energy, ensemble and match is extraordinary. The pick-ups between the two players are so seamless that at times it is difficult to distinguish one from the other. The orchestral strings seemed fired by the electricity between the two soloists, occasionally unable even to keep up.

The slow movement unison theme between the two soloists reveals Feuermann with his arsenal of colours, initially the more expressive and expansive player. Heifetz becomes more expansive as the movement progresses, with the ending octave slide (bar 112) of soaring melodic beauty. The tempo of this movement is about the same as that in the Casals–Thibaud recording.

The final movement begins fast, with Feuermann crisply articulating the repeated notes of the theme while the orchestra is somewhat ragged behind him. Heifetz, repeating the same theme, sounds less at ease, giving slightly less bounce to the notes than Feuermann. At bar 30 Feuermann, a third above Heifetz, vibrates so sweetly that 'blind' listening could confuse the cello for the violin. After initial raggedness from the orchestra, it now picks up in a triumphant *tutti*, answered back by the two soloists in immensely powerful double stops, the balance of attack completely equal between the two players, the intonation impeccable (bars 54–65). Feuermann never labours the double stops, his passage-work is astonishingly clear, indeed as clear and as flexible as Heifetz's despite the greater distances on the instrument. The power and energy of this movement is palpable. It is, once again, substantially faster (7′44″) than the Casals–Thibaud recording (8′30″), and considerably livelier.

The Brahms was not released until September 1941, almost two years after its recording. The press went wild. Reviews were syndicated from coast to coast; 'It is a "Four Star" release in every sense.'[17] 'As performance, it is a breath-taking demonstration of virtuosity by the two soloists.'[18] ' . . . the concerto equals any conceivable performance ever given.'[19] Irving Kolodin in the *New York Sun* was also unequivocal: 'There are very few works, indeed, of the standard repertory which have had no more than a single recording, and that one a classic, unapproachable achievement. However, a distinguished veteran in that group – Pablo Casals's and Jacques Thibaud's playing of the Brahms Double Concerto – must yield its place at last.'[20] 'Platterbug' in another paper wrote:

Brahms Double Concerto in A minor Op.102 takes the place in the literature that has long been waiting for it. These sentences might truthfully be captioned 'rumour becomes reality', for rumours of the recording of this wonderful work by Heifetz, Feuermann and the Philadelphia Orchestra have been flying about the country for months, and music lovers have been asking about it and even getting impatient when told it would be 'released soon'. It is now on the market – a brand new recording by the finest combination of artists available in the world today, from Heifetz down to the last fiddler in the orchestra.[21]

Perhaps the most poetic review came from H.T. Baron in the *N.Y. Times* of Yonkers:

That wonderful performance by Jacques Thibaud, Pablo Casals and the Casals Orchestra under Alfred Cortot of the Brahms Double Concerto in A minor Op.102 has always been the object of this reviewer's particular affection. It was an interpretation of the greatest warmth, power and nobility, and at the time of release it represented a milestone in the history of the modern phonograph. It was, indeed, among the finest and most significant recordings ever released – a monument to man's creative genius. Thus, it is with the sense of losing an old and cherished friend that this reviewer acknowledges the superiority of this month's new version . . . For that this new set is superior is, your reviewer feels, an irrefutable fact.[22]

Victor had a best-seller on its hands. For weeks it was listed. In the week of 18 October at Bloomingdales and in the Terminal Radio Shop it competed with Tchaikovsky's B♭ minor Piano Concerto (Rubinstein, Barbirolli and the London Symphony Orchestra), while at the Lehman Radio Salon it was in competition with 'I guess I'll have to Dream the Rest', by Tommy Dorsey. By the week of 8 November it was competing with 'Chattanooga Choo Choo',

Prokofiev's *Peter and the Wolf* (Stokowski and the All-American Orchestra with Basil Rathbone as narrator) and Tchaikovsky's B♭ minor Piano Concerto performed by Horowitz with the NBC Symphony Orchestra conducted by Toscanini.

The Brahms Double recording was not reviewed by *Gramophone* in Britain until August 1942. It began: 'It was saddening to read, just before beginning this notice, of the death of Feuermann, one of the most satisfying of artists.' The unattributed reviewer wrote his notice with war all around: 'While I've been listening to it [the Brahms], I find that the heaviest (practice) firing guns has been going on, and I heard nothing of it. If it had been heaven's artillery, it would have benefited these lightnings of Brahms; as it is only ours, I'm rather glad he drowned it.'

Several performances by Feuermann in New York were broadcast at around the time of the Brahms recording, including a Carnegie Hall appearance with the New York Philharmonic-Symphony Orchestra conducted by Barbirolli on 17 December (Haydn D major Concerto); and part of a concert on 21 January 1940 with Adolf Busch and Rudolf Serkin for a programme called *New Friends of Music*, from which Mozart's Piano Trio no.7 in C K.548 and Brahms's Piano Trio no.2 in C op.87 survive in the vaults of BMG. (The Brahms Trio is interrupted by a station identification).

A few days after his Town Hall concert with Busch and Serkin, Feuermann was back on stage in Carnegie Hall with Leon Barzin and the NOA. This concert on 27 January is the first from which discs survive, recorded privately, probably by the Carnegie Hall Recording Corporation, for the NOA. The recordings, according to Barzin, were made on 16-inch glass discs (an acetate coating would have been applied). Despite a single microphone being used, the sound and balance are surprisingly good.[23] Both concertos – the Dvořák and Josef Reicha's Concerto in A – have survived. These live recordings attest to Feuermann's brilliance in front of an audience.

Apart from Feuermann's early commercial recording of the Dvořák Concerto in Berlin, two other complete recordings made in America survive: the performance on 27 January 1940 for the NOA, and a broadcast performance with the Chicago Symphony Orchestra conducted by Hans Lange that took place on 9 January 1941. In the absence of a mature commercially recorded version of the Dvořák, these two non-commercial recordings are invaluable. It is most fortunate that the NOA concert was captured on disc, for of the three recorded performances it is the finest. The rushed quality of the 1920s Berlin recording is gone. The total duration of the Berlin recording at 32′4″ (on Pearl) is almost ten minutes faster than Yo-Yo Ma's 1986 recording with Lorin Maazel and the Berlin Philharmonic at 42′08″, and more than ten minutes faster than Mischa Maisky's 1989 recording with Bernstein and the Israel Philharmonic at 43′28″[24]. The first movement of Feuermann's NOA performance at 13′09″ is over two minutes longer than his Berlin first movement but still shorter than Casals's 1937 version at 13′27″. The duration of the first movement with the Chicago Symphony Orchestra is very slightly shorter (13′06″) than the NOA performance, but there are faster moments that contribute to poor ensemble with the orchestra (for example, the lead into figure 4 at bar 110). Feuermann's sound as captured by the engineers in Chicago is distant and much coarser than that of the NOA performance.

The Chicago sound is opulent, but the opening orchestral tutti of the NOA belies its status as a training orchestra, even if 'retirees' from the orchestra were present. The NOA strings are full and strong, inspired no doubt by Feuermann's presence. In this performance there is an almost palpable sense of musical sharing; Feuermann had performed many times with the NOA and Barzin, and Barzin, unlike Hans Lange, knew Feuermann's playing well. In the NOA performance there are moments of luminous beauty: the A♭ minor episode – the 'still centre' of the development section (*Molto espressivo e sostenuto*, bar 224); the fast cross-string bowing of the Animato (bar 240), 'rolled' without overexcitement as Feuermann tenderly accompanied the theme in the wind; the masterly handling of the difficult descending, chromatically-decorated scale (bar 257); the flamboyant octaves into the start of the recapitulation, effortlessly executed. Applause at the end of this first movement was richly deserved.

One of Feuermann's greatest attributes, heard so clearly in Dvořák's lyrical slow movement, is the freedom from false accents in his playing. False accents are a result of incorrect emphasis, which distorts the phrase. They can occur through technical limitations or misunderstanding of the harmonic structure. Feuermann's freedom from false accents accounts profoundly for the 'rightness' of feel in the music he played. In such a lyrical movement as the Dvořák slow movement, Feuermann allowed the music to breathe in long phrases, never disrupted by a misunderstood harmony or a technical challenge. To the accompanying wind players of the NOA, Feuermann, the chamber musician, was infinitely sensitive, his tone limpid, tender, focused, the intensity ratchetted up in a single note by a change of vibrato or bow speed. The passion is strong but the playing never sentimental.

Feuermann and Heifetz both liked fast tempi, but, unlike Heifetz, Feuermann in his playing rarely sounds driven. The last movement in the NOA performance of the Dvořák Concerto is fast and intense, but Feuermann's playing has absolute clarity. The Chicago performance, however, is very much faster, even faster than the early Berlin recording, in fact much too fast. Feuermann, very uncharacteristically, sounds distinctly driven, almost falling over his fingers.

There is a point of unusual interest at the end of the concerto in Feuermann's playing of the Dvořák with the NOA. After the long descent from a high trill on *b''* (bars 475–80) and the repetition three times of a bar beginning on *d#*, instead of playing the customary (and haunting) *d♮* at bar 492, Feuermann continued to repeat the *d#*. This is no 'mistake', for in the 1941 Chicago performance he played exactly the same notes. Why he was convinced that *d#* was the accurate note is unknown. In the piano reduction made by Dvořák in 1895 (published at the same time as the orchestral score and parts in 1896 by Simrock) the last semiquaver in the bar is expressly marked *d#*. Since the key demands *d#* already, this is an emphatic direction. At the same time, the solo cello has just played a *d♮*, so creating a false relation. Perhaps this is the reason Feuermann chose to play a *d#* even though Dvořák's direction clearly suggests the contrary. Interestingly, in his early Berlin recording Feuermann played the customary *d♮*.

In the concert of 27 January 1940 Feuermann also played the A major Concerto by Josef Reicha, a work that he found in the Edwin A. Fleischer Collection at the Free Library of Philadelphia.[25] Reicha was not only a composer and conductor, but a cellist of some distinction: from 1785 he was first cellist in the Electoral Court orchestra of Maximilian Franz in Bonn, becoming director of instrumental music and opera in 1790. Reicha's Concerto, like Haydn's D major Concerto, is scored for two oboes, two horns and strings, and is in three movements – *Allegro Moderato*, *Largo* and *Rondo Allegretto*. Feuermann played virtually verbatim from the manuscript, although he made one cut of 17 bars in the last movement that makes musically good sense.[26] The first movement contains much exposed passage-work with rapid cross-string bowing, often ascending to great heights. Feuermann played with delicacy and elegance, adding his own flamboyant cadenza. The second movement is a graceful *Largo maestoso* with a passionate central episode in the minor key, a vehicle for Feuermann's ravishingly beautiful sound and tenderly shaped phrases. The delightful *Rondo Allegretto* is highly reminiscent of Haydn's D major final movement and like the Haydn is also in 6/8. Feuermann's playing has a pleasing lilt, to which the orchestra responds in kind. Uncharacteristically, at the beginning of the cruelly high and exposed first episode, Feuermann for a moment plays markedly sharp, although recovering himself quickly after only four bars. A clearly audible page turn shows that it was not totally committed to memory, but within the performance there is a tremendous sense of fun and vitality, Feuermann risking all sorts of accidents. Despite Feuermann's championing, the Reicha has remained a neglected work; it deserves far wider recognition. Feuermann was 37 at the time of these NOA performances; his playing was peerless.

Three Feuermann recordings of Strauss's *Don Quixote* (a work written for his predecessor at the Cologne Conservatory, Friedrich Grützmacher) survive: two pirate recordings of both broadcasts in 1938 with Toscanini,[27] and a commercial recording made in February 1940 with Eugene Ormandy and the Philadelphia Orchestra. Although Strauss never cast the work as a cello concerto, it is regarded as one, the cello representing the key character in Cervantes's tale. It was this characterization by Feuermann in a performance with the Philadelphia and Ormandy that so captivated Artur Rubinstein:

> This work was previously played by some other players – I heard it three or four times but I was always rather indifferent. I thought it was a very cleverly written work with all the tremendous mastery of Richard Strauss's orchestration and the cello was rather fine in it but a little bit interfering too much. I thought it was not very important for the cello. This performance in Philadelphia changed wholly my point of view about the work because I had tears in my eyes. . . . The solo cello of Feuermann was something which led me on to what music really means, what it has to say. It was the most masterly, most fine performance I have ever heard and I don't want to ever hear it again by anybody else.[28]

The differences between Feuermann's two Toscanini broadcasts are marked. Where the NBC broadcast (October 1938) sounds rushed, the BBC performance (May 1938) is expansive. Both suffer from poor sound: the sound spectrum of the BBC Symphony Orchestra particularly compressed, the NBC sound thin and brittle, with the orchestra at times sounding out of tune. It is a pity that the BBC broadcast is marred by short-wave interference and breakup, because this is a remarkable performance, with the BBC Symphony Orchestra on top form. Of these two broadcasts, the BBC's is the finer. Feuermann projects the moods of the Don – defiance, despair, resignation – with such intelligence. Although the score calls for a large orchestra, it must be played with the sensitivity of chamber musicians: there are fabulous pick-ups between soloist and orchestra. The viola principal, Bernard Shore, contributed remarkable playing. It is no wonder that the London critics were thrilled. By contrast, in the NBC performance orchestral accidents occur and, more seriously, Feuermann is often inaudible, his playing at times uncharacteristically harsh, unvaried and hurried. But there are wonderful moments: the cello's main entrance (bar 123), in duet with the solo violin (Mischa Mischakoff); the fifth variation, which Feuermann plays so freely and poignantly; and the finale, where Feuermann's imagination and sound so touchingly combine.

The commercial RCA recording was made at the Academy of Music in Philadelphia with the leader Alexander Hilsberg and principal viola Samuel Lifschey as additional soloists. This properly engineered Ormandy recording gives great clarity of sound for this complex score. The performance is relaxed and playful. As in the BBC recording, Feuermann, in chamber music attitude, listening and sharing with the 'official' soloists and the various orchestral soloists, contributed greatly to the beauty of this recording. Amid many moments of formidable playing, the expansive finale and Death of Don Quixote is particularly heart-rending.

The sheer consistency of Feuermann's playing heard in recordings and recorded performances remains extraordinary. Several years after Feuermann's death, Irving Kolodin recalled: 'It is not enough to say that one never knew him to play badly: whether it was chamber music, solo recital, or as assisting artist with orchestra, I cannot recall an occasion on which he was less than superb.'[29] An obituary in the *American Music Lover*, however, singled out one work: 'Feuermann has left a number of recordings which will always be highly valued, but none in which his complete authority and virtuosity is more superbly set forth than in his recording of Bloch's "Schelomo" with Stokowski and the Philadelphia Orchestra.'[30]

Schelomo, Hebrew rhapsody for cello and orchestra, was written in 1916. Bloch had intended writing a vocal work based on the Book of Ecclesiastes, but unable to decide in which language to cast it, he decided to use a cello in place of a voice. Although the work has no programme, it is avowedly programme music:

> It is the Jewish soul that interests me, the complex, glowing, agitated soul that I feel vibrating in the Bible ... the freshness and naiveté of the Patriachs, the violence of the Prophetic Books, the Jew's savage love of justice, the despair of Ecclesiastes, the sorrow and the immensity of the Book of Job, the sensuality of the Song of Songs. All this is in us, all this is in me, and it is the better part of me.[31]

The date of Feuermann's first performance of *Schelomo* is uncertain although he was already enquiring about the work in 1922. But from a letter of 1935 we learn that he had considerable difficulty in memorizing the piece. In a climate of overt or covert anti-Semitism, its quintessentially Jewish character may well have radiated complex and contradictory feelings in Feuermann. Nevertheless, despite his misgivings about the work, Feuermann performed it quite frequently; there are known performances with Sir Henry Wood, Leon Barzin, Ansermet and Alexander Smallens. Three recorded performances survive: the poor-quality radio broadcast from the Lewisohn Stadium concert in August

1939 discussed earlier; a private recording of Feuermann's 10 November 1941 Carnegie Hall performance with the NOA and Barzin; and a commercial recording.

Feuermann's commercial recording for RCA of *Schelomo* with Stokowski and the Philadelphia Orchestra was made on 27 March 1940, a few days after he had performed it at a benefit concert for the China Aid Council. This may account for the speed with which it was recorded: the session began at 5.10 p.m. and was finished by 6.05 p.m. These two performances were Feuermann's first and last with Stokowski, and this was to be his last commercial recording with the Philadelphia Orchestra. After the crazed antics of the Don, Feuermann was now Solomon.

However uneasy he may have felt about the piece, his playing in this recording of *Schelomo* is arguably his finest. While never sentimentalizing a score that risks the depths of sentimentalization, Feuermann brought to the piece 'the sum total of what he knew and what he felt'.[32] Much of the work is a musical conversation, Feuermann responding with the widest variety of colours, powerfully masculine, breathtakingly limpid, so sensitive to the orchestral palette, his line never losing its vitality and focus. The sound engineers captured it all. Stokowski, who rarely praised or criticized, said of this recording to his biographer Abram Chasins: 'He had the warmest colours and purest phrasing I ever heard on that instrument.' Chasins remembered Stokowski visibly moved by the recollection.[33]

The sound-quality of the NOA performance of *Schelomo* does not compare to that of recordings of the orchestra's January 1940 concert. The 1941 spectrum is narrow and in parts suffers from distortion and overloading.[34] Nevertheless, at 23 seconds faster, a tautness and excitement in Feuermann's playing distinguishes this recording from the Philadelphia studio recording. It is worth noting that in both performances Feuermann frequently varied his bowing from that indicated in the G. Schirmer Inc. printed edition (1918), presumably the first edition.

From this November 1941 concert, recordings of two more works survive, with better sound-quality than *Schelomo*: Dvořák's *Silent Woods* and Rondo. *Silent Woods* is notable for the extraordinary beauty and seamless nature of Feuermann's legato. In the Rondo, a fuller version than that performed on film by Feuermann, he added the occasional embellishment or chord, but, unlike in the film (probably pre-recorded) he badly missed a high note in bar 281 – a rare occurrence.

One more important private NOA concert recording survives – that of the Concerto in C by Eugen d'Albert. Once again, it was recorded live in Carnegie Hall, on 22 April 1940. Some New York critics were distinctly critical of the piece, but Irving Kolodin justified the opportunity it provided for Feuermann 'to display his invincible virtuosity, his potent and selfless musicianship'.[35] The work is sectional, but is played without any breaks. It begins and ends with the same arpeggiated material for the solo cello – an accompaniment to a theme on oboe and clarinet that is almost inaudible, the sound-balance very much in favour of the cello. There are moments of striking resemblance to Dvořák's B minor Concerto, a work written less than five years before. A central Molto tranquillo section contains some of the sweetest and most tender moments in all Feuermann's recorded work.

Recordings of Chamber Music

Great soloists are rarely great chamber musicians: the qualities associated with dominance as a soloist are at odds with the needs of accommodation as a chamber musician. Feuermann was an exception. From his childhood, chamber music was of equal importance; his first position at the Cologne Conservatory required his participation in the Gürzenich Quartet; his last position at the Curtis Institute gave him charge of chamber music; and throughout his career Feuermann played in numerous combinations both formally and informally.

Feuermann recorded as a member of three trios: in his Berlin and post-Berlin days in a string trio with Szymon Goldberg and Hindemith that made commercial recordings and also broadcast; and at the end of his life in America in a string trio with Heifetz and William Primrose and in a piano trio with Heifetz and Rubinstein. Despite making commercial recordings, no public concerts or broadcasts with the various Heifetz combinations took place, but comments by Goldberg and Rubinstein on Feuermann the chamber music player are uncannily similar. According to both, Feuermann led while appearing to follow.

RCA Victor was clearly delighted with the signing of Feuermann. On the cover of its January 1942 house magazine, *Victor Record Review*, it printed one of the most famous pictures of Feuermann, squatting on the floor with his cello and four-year-old daughter, gazing into the firelight.[36] The April edition trumpets: 'A few pages of phonographic history were turned late last summer in VICTOR'S Hollywood studios when Jascha Heifetz, Emanuel Feuermann and Arthur Rubinstein made a series of trio recordings . . . Not since the days of Jacques Thibaud, Pablo Casals and Alfred Cortot has such a dazzling violin, cello and piano trio been assembled.' In the summer of 1940 chamber music sessions had taken place in various houses, including Heifetz's in Newport

Beach and Rubinstein's in Brentwood. As Rubinstein recalled, the Victor
Record Company got wind of this: 'After it was apparent that Heifetz,
Feuermann and Rubinstein not only enjoyed playing together but were willing
to spend considerable time rehearsing the great works of the trio repertoire,
the main problem was to get these musicians in the same room, between
concert schedules, so practice could begin.'[37] For once, the war that prevented
extensive concert tours outside the United States proved an unlikely blessing.
In the summer of 1941 the 'Dream Trio' became a reality.

The first recordings were not of piano trios but of string chamber music,
with William Primrose, the Scottish viola player, an inspired additional partner.
Primrose and Heifetz had begun recording a Mozart duo in May, to which they
again returned at the end of August. On that same day, 29 August, Feuermann
and Primrose recorded the Allegro of Beethoven's Duet in E♭ 'with two
obbligato eyeglasses' WoO 32. Beethoven wrote this piece at about the same time
as the string Serenade in D op.8 for himself (playing viola) and his cellist friend
Nikolaus Zmeskall; they were both short-sighted. The work is tricky, with
moments of perilous ensemble and, like the later Triple Concerto, has difficult
high-lying passages for the cello. Feuermann's bowing is again astonishing, the
ensemble and match between the two players extraordinary. It is interesting to
compare this duo of Feuermann and Primrose with the earlier duo eight years
before of Feuermann and Hindemith. No doubt Beethoven's duet was too long
for the blank side that Hindemith's Scherzo was required to fill, but Primrose's
playing is in quite a different class. As a review in 1944 puts it: 'Primrose and
Feuermann romp through it in great style. Their performance can't help
putting one in the proper spirit to enjoy Beethoven's little joke, even if one has
no idea for whom the joke was intended.'[38] Nowadays, the recording is available,
but this is another release that Feuermann would not allow.

Primrose was shattered by Feuermann's death the following year:

> I had seen him in New York only a week or so before, and my parting had
> been 'Mounyo [*sic*], I'll see you in California in about three weeks and we'll
> get started on those Beethoven Trios with Jascha.' I arrived in Hollywood,
> checked into my hotel, and called Heifetz to ask when we would start
> rehearsing and he exclaimed, 'Haven't you heard? Don't you know about the
> Feuermann tragedy?' I thought immediately that perhaps his mother-in-law
> or even his wife had died. I certainly never associated Emanuel with the
> impersonality of death. He was so full of life and vigour, and so vivid. When
> Heifetz conveyed the news, I was shocked and bewildered.[39]

Recalling Feuermann's playing, Primrose wrote: 'the impact was prodigious.
He had a stupendous technique and a bow of infinite facility. The end of the

fourth movement of the Dohnányi Serenade, where he has but a few simple phrases to play, is almost unbearably heartrending.'[40]

This reference to Dohnányi concerns the recording made a few days after the Beethoven Duet, on 8 September, when Heifetz joined Primrose and Feuermann in the Serenade in C op.10, another piece of whimsical humour. Tempi are always a sensitive matter in chamber music, but in the Dohnányi there are obvious moments where Heifetz pushed the pace. Rubinstein spoke illuminatingly about Feuermann's sense of tempo in relation to Heifetz's: 'Heifetz always rushed! He [was] an inveterate rusher, [you know]. His landmark [*sic*]. Whatever existed in music, he played it a little quick. Might be because he had that fantastic, uncanny ability on the violin. But Feuermann stuck to the music absolutely through thick and thin. You couldn't move him at all. He was iron clad.'[41] But Feuermann could rush too, sometimes as a means of increasing tension. However, in his recordings with Heifetz he would leave Heifetz to do the rushing; it is very noticeable that Feuermann took more time in passages where they played the same material.

Brief as Feuermann's life was, he did record some of the finest works of the repertoire, in particular the greatest string trio of the Classical period, Mozart's Divertimento K.563. This is a substantial work in six movements with many repeats (most of which are not recorded): the third, fifth and sixth movements each occupy one side of a 12-inch disc. Mozart's writing in this work is of equal demand for all three performers, but if the technical, tonal and musical match between these three players is scarcely believable, the recording balance is less well matched. Heifetz sounds inappropriately brilliant and brittle in the first *forte* scales of the first movement, at the beginning of the third movement Menuetto and in the Maggiore of the fourth movement. The balance, which brings his playing to the fore, does him no favours. The second movement (Adagio) is warmer, Feuermann adding a palpable sense of mystery and wonder in the chromatic second section, his resonant bass firmly anchoring the music, his phrasing so tender. Primrose in the fifth movement (Trio) is an absolute delight.

The Dohnányi and Mozart were each recorded in a single day, 8 and 9 September. Two days later, Heifetz and Feuermann began to record with Rubinstein. The whole of the 11th – from 10.30 a.m. to 7.00 p.m. – was devoted to Brahms's Piano Trio op.8, but it was not completed. The following day, retakes of the second, third and fourth movements were made and they began recording Beethoven's 'Archduke' Trio. All four movements of the Beethoven were recorded, but on the 13th retakes of movements 3 and 4 took place. Schubert's great B♭ Piano Trio occupied the rest of that day and was completed in a single session.

In a period of little more than two weeks, some of the greatest chamber music was recorded by the greatest of musicians. It was an orgy of recording, as if they knew that these first sessions might be their last. The Brahms trio was the first of the promised 'long and matchless' series of trio recordings that the Victor Record Company released in April 1942 performed by its new, all-star team. The music press received it rapturously: 'Rubinstein! Heifetz! Feuermann! One alone of these names spells distinction but the three on one label, combined as a trio, is really something of an event.'[42] Another predicted that the release 'is likely to lead to the sin of covetousness among record collectors'.[43]

This work had been recorded once before, not by the Thibaud–Casals–Cortot trio, but by the Elly Ney Trio. Peter Hugh Reed, a critic not fond of the Brahms ('I have never been able to develop any real enthusiasm for this work'), commented: 'In the spontaneity, tonal splendour and expression of the performance one obtains the impression that the group has been together for a period of years rather than months.'[44]

In the recording of this trio Heifetz and Feuermann recall the extraordinary cohesion of their Brahms Double. They may not have played long together but they knew each other's playing instinctively. Feuermann's long, lucid opening phrase that includes points of relaxation with the subtlest of slides is exquisitely shaped. In the many passages where violin and cello are in octave unison, the match of tone and vibrato is quite astonishing. But if the first movement is warm and expansive, the second movement Scherzo flashes by like quicksilver, the playing electrical. Has this movement ever been bettered? Throughout the work, the music never sags. Rubinstein, charged with thick, heavy chords, octaves and notes to muddy the texture, holds a somewhat distant position in the sound picture, while the two string players are very much closer.

Whereas the Brahms piano trio demonstrates a substantial measure of agreement between the three players, the Beethoven trio is less cohesive. A longer period of 'settling in' via public performance might have been beneficial; the classicism of the Beethoven trio, with its more transparent texture, demands greater emotional warmth than was given in this recording.

In Schubert's B♭ Piano Trio, the youthfulness of RCA's Heifetz–Feuermann–Rubinstein team is noticeable in relation to HMV's Thibaud–Casals–Cortot trio, who had recorded the piece some 15 years earlier. The first two movements are taken at a faster tempo, and rubato – a particular feature of the Casals slow movement – is mainly avoided. Once again, Heifetz's tendency towards brittle brilliance is offset by the gentler, warmer sound and phrasing of Feuermann. Feuermann's fastidious attention to Schubert's markings is most noticeable. As Peter Hugh Reed noted: 'It is the playing of Feuermann which chiefly engages our attention and admiration';[45] and never more so than in the slow movement where Feuermann, in Schubert's long, luscious opening melody, so subtly 'points' Schubert's accents by a mere quickening of vibrato. Unlike HMV, RCA Victor allowed all the repeats in the Scherzo, achieving a better sense of structure than in the Casals recording. The rhythmic crispness of the Heifetz–Feuermann–Rubinstein recording is a notable feature, the many dotted rhythms so cleanly articulated. The final movement adopts approximately the same speed as the Thibaud–Casals–Cortot recording until the final Presto; the Heifetz recording simply bolts for the end. This was Feuermann's last complete chamber music recording. None of these three trio recordings was issued in his lifetime[46].

The last known recording of Feuermann is something of a curio: the slow movement of Victor Herbert's Second Cello Concerto played with piano accompaniment only. It is a test pressing dating from 1942. Quite why it was made is not known; the Herbert was not a work in Feuermann's repertoire. No correspondence relating to it has come to light. The pianist is said to be Albert Hirsch.[47] Although it is not faultless – there is a moment of uncertain intonation in the central section and a misplaced *pizzicato* – the recording again demonstrates Feuermann's ability to give life to an otherwise slushy Romantic piece. Herbert's work greatly influenced Dvořák's B minor Concerto, but the romance of Herbert is a world away from Dvořák.

There are large gaps in Feuermann's recorded repertoire. Numerous standard and lesser-known concertos were never recorded, and there are serious omissions in the duo repertoire: only one Brahms sonata and a single Beethoven sonata were recorded. But the most serious gap is undoubtedly that left by Bach's Cello Suites. That Feuermann made no commercial recording of Bach's unaccompanied suites is significant but, given that his life was so short, not entirely surprising. Throughout his career, he included them in his programmes, and, according to fellow student Albert Catell, as a boy studying with Klengel, Feuermann learnt all six suites by heart in a week. A reviewer in a Cologne paper in 1920 noted: 'His Bach playing is full of life, phrased with very musical sentiment, full of subtle charm.'[48] From existing programmes it appears that the only suite rarely played by him was the G major, the least challenging technically. Between 1923 and 1925 the C major and flamboyant D major suites occur frequently, and the C minor Suite was added in the years up to 1930. His sensational first recital in New York's Town Hall in 1935 included the C major Suite. On his tour in South America in 1936 the C minor Suite was programmed. In October 1937 in Switzerland it was the Sixth Suite that was most performed. Until 1938 he appears rarely to have played the Fourth Suite in E♭, and when he came to play it at the 1938 Promenade concerts in London, his comments in a letter suggest, somewhat surprisingly, that this was the first time he was really satisfied with his playing of Bach. Two months later, he played the E♭ suite in Carnegie Hall, and reviews confirm his particular ease in this piece. A few months after this recital, he suggested to Nipponophone that the Fourth Suite be recorded at the same time as the Reger – instead, 'dirty little pieces' were recorded. Feuermann told David Soyer of an 'unaccompanied muddle': 'He was playing the Bach D major Suite and he started the Saraband and he played the C major chord and immediately found himself in the slow movement of the Reger G major Suite and he was stuck. He couldn't get out of it. He had to play the whole slow movement of Reger.'[49]

Feuermann was in the habit of playing a movement from one of the Bach suites as an encore, and a single example exists from the concert broadcast live in the Lewisohn Stadium in August 1939. 'Sarabande and Bourrées by Bach', he announced. It was the Sarabande and two Bourrées from the C major Suite that he played. Notwithstanding the outdoor acoustic, the playing is not Feuermann at his best. Perhaps it was an encore that he felt obliged to give; perhaps it was hot and humid; he played little more than efficiently. Although his tuning can be heard beforehand, the intonation in some double stoppings is not perfect. Uncharacteristically, there is an uneven feel to the rhythm. Overall, the playing is stiff.

If this snippet is at all representative, it does seem that Feuermann was less at ease in the performance of Bach than in other work. In December 1937 his wife had written ferociously about his inability to play Bach, even recommending that he should not play it at all. Her comments relate to a broadcast in which Feuermann again had played Bach as an encore. 'I paid good attention, and I think that your left hand fails you when you play Bach. After all you have pretty stiff wrists.'[50] She maintains, remorsefully, that he was influenced by these letters. And it does appear from the surviving material that he may have heeded her advice; Bach's suites do not turn up in Feuermann's programmes for 1938. George Neikrug recalled:

He had a complex about Bach. I remember him saying so. He would sometimes go out and play a Bach suite and play it as if he was cut off and try just to be correct and just go through it. He said 'I really don't know how to play that stuff.' I know he played a magnificent performance of the Sixth Suite but the Sixth Suite was a technical challenge to him. In general he kind of felt he had to do Bach, but he didn't have that great affinity for it and he wasn't secure in the fact that he knew exactly what to do with it and sometimes it was a little bit dry and the Germanic part of his character would come out. . . . I felt that there was this play between his adherence to German discipline and being a good boy and doing what he wanted to and that's why when he had a piece of junk he would play wonderfully, beautifully. He felt not restrained and not to be a 'good musician'. The same thing happened to me with him once. I used to imitate – there were some Rumanian Gypsies that used to play in New York and I played some of their stuff by ear and once at a lesson somebody else said 'ask him to play that.' I didn't want to, but I started to play for Feuermann. I thought he would pounce on me. He said 'Why don't you play like that all the time? Now you're free! All those phrasings.' I thought he was going to kill me! But you see there was this funny conflict there and if you think of his background, and where he came from you can understand it. It's a Viennese background, but he lived a lot in Germany.[51]

It is said that Feuermann regarded the Bach Suites as Casals's territory. Since Casals had recorded them during the period 1936–9 it seems reasonable to speculate that Feuermann was in no hurry to record them himself.[52] Feuermann's attitude to recording may also have been a significant factor. Like so many artists, he disliked the permanent statement it made. At the time of his death, aged only 39, he was probably still experimenting with the suites. No doubt he believed that in due course he would record them, time being of no issue. Days before his death, he signed a contract to record all the Beethoven sonatas. The Bach Suites were to wait.

Appendix I

Feuermann's Fees

From his earliest days, Feuermann's letters reveal a determination never to be undervalued artistically or financially. His Jewish ghetto background, his experience of Germany's hyper-inflation in the 1920s, the economic depression of the 1930s and the persecution of the Jews make this attitude of little surprise. But even for Huberman, whose venture in establishing the Palestine Symphony Orchestra he admired so much, Feuermann would not waive his fee. He was, however, quite prepared to spend large sums on motor cars, no doubt a reflection of the influence of Reifenberg and Mayer wealth, something with which he had come into contact as a very young man.

All artists complain about their fees, but Feuermann railed against something more specific: the injustice of paying solo cellists less than solo violinists, singers and pianists. But how justified were his complaints? Extracting detailed information about artists' fees is never an easy task (this information, except among artists, is customarily confidential), and given the length of time since Feuermann was performing, the obstacles are even greater. All that can be offered here is evidence of some of Feuermann's fees in relation to some other artists' fees.

The bulk of surviving information concerning Feuermann's fees relates to his American performances and is contained in documents from agents and contracts from orchestras with whom he performed. A snapshot of a short period is contained in a list of engagements from October 1938 to January 1939, issued by NBC Artists, which includes fees for Feuermann's recitals, appearances with orchestras and radio broadcasts. These fees are quoted gross – before deductions for travel, accommodation, fees and expenses for pianists, and agents' commissions. They range widely: $1500 for two recitals in Puerto Rico; $250 for a single concert for the New Friends of Music; $350 for a broadcast concert with Toscanini and the NBC; $750 for a Kraft broadcast from Hollywood. For two concerts (repeated programmes) with the orchestras in Philadelphia and Pittsburgh, he was paid $600 and $650 respectively.

As we can see from Feuermann's letters to his record companies, his complaints about recording fees usually centre on comparisons with the level of fees or royalties paid to colleagues. So how do his concert fees compare to those of colleagues? Comparisons of fees between artists is never straightforward; certain artists achieve certain conditions under certain circumstances. In addition, little documentary evidence has survived from the presenting organizations of the time. Those with no documentation at all from the period during which Feuermann was active in America include the New York Philharmonic-Symphony and Los Angeles Symphony orchestras, while the Pittsburgh, Cincinnati and Indianapolis symphony orchestras are unable to provide specific information on fees. The Chicago, Cleveland and Boston symphony orchestras are able to provide figures, but the Chicago Symphony Orchestra is reluctant to reveal information about specific fees.[1] The bulk of Feuermann's papers at NBC Artists has also disappeared.

Feuermann first played with the Chicago Symphony Orchestra in December 1934. Fees paid to artists in that season (1934/5) ranged from $200 to $750 per concert. The average fee was $360. Feuermann was paid $200 – well below the average. It was, however, his first visit to the United States.

In the next season, the Cleveland paid Feuermann $550 for two concerts – some improvement over Chicago, but when compared to the fees paid to Heifetz and the singer Emanuel List (who each received $1500 for two appearances), Feuermann's fee was low. The pianist Mischa Levitzki, however, received the same amount as Feuermann.

Four years later (1939/40 season) Cleveland paid Feuermann $750 for a pair of concerts, but Heifetz was paid $2000, Myra Hess $1000, Josef Hofmann $1250, Rubinstein $1000 and Rachmaninov a princely $2250, also for pairs of concerts. And for a single afternoon concert, Fritz Kreisler took 50 per cent of the takings on the understanding that it should not exceed $4500.

In the same season (1939/40) Boston paid Feuermann $750 for a pair of concerts; Heifetz received $2000, Josef Hofmann $1200, Rudolph Serkin $1000 and Szigeti $900 (all for pairs of concerts). Piatigorsky received less: $500, and when the orchestra played in New York, only $300.

In the following season (1940/1), with fees ranging from $300 to $1250 paid to artists including Rachmaninov, Hofmann, Kreisler, Milstein, Serkin, Menuhin and Horowitz, Chicago paid Feuermann (and Piatigorsky) $330 per night; the average fee that season was $586. This represents a reduction on the level of fee Feuermann received from Cleveland and Boston the season before, though Chicago's fees generally appear low.

In Feuermann's last season (1941/2), Boston paid him $500 for two concerts – $250 less than for his first appearance with them in the 1939/40 season and barely an improvement on his $200 per night from Chicago in December 1934. Claudio Arrau received the same fee as Feuermann and Antonio Brosa slightly less. It is tempting to suggest that Boston's fees were low because the orchestra's six-figure deficit and its long-standing feud with the American Federation of Musicians prevented higher payments.[2] But, by stark comparison, Boston in this season was able to pay Menuhin $2250 (also for two concerts).

Feuermann's fees were low (and got lower) by comparison to the three violinists Kreisler, Heifetz and Menuhin, but these artists were exceptional. But in relation to the fees of almost all pianists, Feuermann's was substantially low. Moreover, his critical success, particularly in his 1938 'marathon' with the NOA, did not translate into higher fees. Only in comparison with Piatigorsky was he doing somewhat better. (It is worth noting that Adolf Busch, in a letter to his brother Hermann in January 1940, reported that NBC Artists had said his quartet could hope for an average fee of $500.[3])

In a tax schedule for 1940, one particular item of expenditure stands out: 'Advertising & Publicity', on which Feuermann spent just over $1400. In relation to the highest item of expenditure, travel expenses, which totalled $2435, this was a considerable sum. Feuermann's total income in that calendar year (1940) is given as $3809.16 (after tax of $137.50), while 'other expenses' total $6951.06. Expenditure far outstripped income.

It was rare for concert promoters or orchestras in America to present a solo cellist more than once per season. In theory, therefore, competition between cellists was fierce. But Feuermann had little competition. In a letter to Kux of March 1940, he summed up his position:

> One thing seems certain: that I stand as the first in my line. The overpowering shadow of Casals is non-existent here[4] and as Cassadó has pretty much come down in the world there only remains Piatigorsky, who, talented as he is, in many respects is lacking in quality. By the way, he already has a second child, a boy, and in that respect at least he has one on me.[5]

Before Feuermann arrived in the USA, Piatigorsky had had a huge career, but this was to change: 'When Feuermann came here and created a tremendous sensation, Piatigorsky sort of retreated from the scene. He got out of it. And I think he lost a lot of concerts to Feuermann. Concerts for solo cello were few and far between, and he took about anything there was.'[6]

In terms of a regular income, if Feuermann had taken a position as principal cellist in an orchestra, he might well have earned more. As Bernard Greenhouse recalled: 'He knew that I was making much more money than he was as first cellist of the CBS Symphony and I was doing commercial recording and doing very well. So there was a little bit of resentment for the fact that here was this young kid who was first cellist of the orchestra and doing so well financially.'[7]

Nevertheless, Feuermann's lifestyle was always comfortable. Despite the horrors of Nazi control in Germany, substantial amounts of Reifenberg money had been transferred to the United States,[8] and Feuermann and his family benefited from it. They employed a couple, Stella and Herman, to cook and look after them, and, as he wrote to his old friend Lily, Feuermann continued to indulge his passion for cars: 'I have the '40 Buick; I've exchanged the other one. I'm a little embarrassed about this but the trade-in is so excellent here that I would have had even less for the car next year.'[9] Since his Berlin days, he had bought only top-of-the-range Buicks.

Feuermann's attitude to money appears schizophrenic. On the one hand, he frequently complained about having too little; on the other, he indulged expensive tastes. His wife no doubt contributed greatly to his feelings of insecurity about money. She had come from a wealthy family with all the trappings this implied and he could not appear financially inferior to her. On some level, however misguidedly, he probably measured his success against the prosperity of the multinational Reifenberg & Cie. Although Feuermann, like all artists of great distinction, was able to jump class and racial barriers, his background of poverty and persecution, together with his new life as an immigrant, must also have contributed to his feelings of financial insecurity.

Feuermann's Cellos, Bows, Strings

During his lifetime Feuermann played several instruments. The instruments may have changed but Feuermann was Feuermann on any instrument: 'He just took the cello and played it in any position, even side-saddle. It didn't matter because he'd produce this sound.'[1]

Feuermann's first cellos

Sophie Feuermann maintains that Feuermann's first instrument was ⅞-size, half French and half Italian.[2] What was this instrument? In 1996 I received some correspondence from Gordon H. Bobbett MD from Florence, South Carolina, with a photograph of a cello. This instrument was bought from Rembert Wurlitzer Inc. in New York. A letter to Dr Bobbett from Ken Jacobs of Wurlitzer, dated 21 August 1974, gives a:

> short supplementary note concerning the serial #S-699 Shop of Paquotte Frères cello we sold you in October 1973. . . . We acquired it on consignment from a close personal friend of Sophie Feuermann who assures us that the instrument was the property, and indeed, had been used by her late brother, the celebrated, Emanuel Feuermann, as a youngster when he had begun study of the cello.

This instrument has been attributed different sizes: Sophie Feuermann believes it was a ⅞-size; Bobbett in February 1996 described it as ¾-size, in March 1996 revising it to ½-size, with a body length measuring 25 inches (63.5 cm). For reference, J. & A. Beare give the following back length sizes for cellos:

Full-size	74.9 cm
⅞-size	72.1 cm

¾-size	69.2 cm
Half-size	65.4 cm

Caution, however, must be observed. Sizes of early Italian instruments varied greatly in different areas according to varying pitch standards. Instruments cannot be described with any accuracy as being ⅞-, ¾- or ½-size (as indeed they cannot today). What seems clear is that Feuermann played on a small cello suitable for a 7-year-old.

Whether the instrument was 'half French and half Italian' is another matter. According to the luthier Ed Smith, who worked on restoring the instrument in the early 1990s, the cello had a false label: 'Paquotte Frères Luthiers, 99 Boulevard St-Germain, Paris année 1900.' The label (which is hard to read) had been cut from a book of labels – on the other side there is the name of another violin maker, J. Hermann Prell. According to Bobbett, in February 1996 the highly respected authority Dario D'Attili examined the instrument and diagnosed it to be 'a "one of a kind", fine Mirecourt cello'.

Feuermann's next instrument, probably loaned to him by Wilhelm Kux, is said to have been a **Nicolo Amati** (1596–1684), a much larger instrument (see above, Chapter 2). Just how long Feuermann played this instrument is uncertain. From a photograph of him playing with the Gürzenich Quartet (taken some time between 1919 and possibly 1923), Ed Smith thinks that Feuermann was not playing the Amati. The varnish is too dark. The 'scuff' marks on the bottom rib suggests that it was an instrument used without an endpin, the knee rubbing at the varnish; later photographs display the same areas of wear. Smith believes that this instrument was the **Josef** [Giuseppe] **Guarneri** (1666–1739) that in 1923 (his final year of employment at the Cologne Conservatory) Feuermann may have been trying out before buying it in 1924. This instrument was subsequently sold in 1931 to Joseph Schuster (see Chapter 3)

David Tecchler: Rome 1741

Back length	75.2 cm
Upper bouts	33.8 cm
Lower bouts	43.6 cm
Middle bouts	23.5 cm

Feuermann appears to have acquired this cello in 1929. In a certificate (no.9238) from The Rudolph Wurlitzer Co. dated 19 March 1948, Wurlitzer wrote that the cello was made by 'David Tecchler in Rome in about 1740 as indicated by the original label it bears'. (The label is obscured by a blotch, but Martha Babcock, the present owner of this instrument, insists the date is 1741.)

> The back is cut from two pieces of maple with handsome flame ascending sharply from the centre joint. The added wings on the lower flanks are original. The wood of the sides matches the back with the exception of the middle bouts which are of a later date. The top is cut from two pieces of spruce unmatched, of excellent quality, the grain being narrow at the centre – very broad on the bass side and medium wide on the treble. The scroll is original – also the varnish which is deep golden both characteristic of the maker.[3]

Feuermann sold this instrument in May 1932 to Thelma Yellin, the distinguished music pioneer in Palestine, later Israel. In her care, the Tecchler was almost destroyed. Following a car accident in Palestine, it was sent in very small pieces to the violin maker and dealer Pauli Merling in Copenhagen for repair. In a letter dated 6 December 1937 to Merling, Yellin congratulated him on mending the instrument: 'The sound is even stronger than before . . . your name will be ringing in Palestine for your quality, for your expertise.' Since Thelma Yellin, the cello has been owned by Erling Blöndal Bengtsson,[4] Mrs T. Newton Stewart, Lazlo Varga, David Miller (son of Frank Miller) and William Valleau.

Domenico Montagnana: Venice 1735

Back length	74.5 cm
Upper bouts	36.3 cm
Lower bouts	44.8 cm
Middle bouts	26.3 cm

Feuermann acquired a Montagnana cello in 1932, playing on it until 1935. After a lengthy period, it was sold in part-exchange for the 'De Munck' Stradivarius.

> Feuermann's cello had not been played on for more than one hundred years before he acquired it. In 1815 it was bought by an English country gentleman who treasured it as a rare antique to be exhibited to honoured guests but not played upon. The cello was passed down in the family to succeeding generations. Eventually financial misfortune overtook them and they were obliged to sell the instrument to Hill's, from whom it was bought by Feuermann.[5]

Between 1935 and 1945 the cello remained unsold, it appears, with William E. Hill and Sons in London. In 1945, the dealer Henry Werro bought the

Montagnana. A certificate dated 26 October, signed by Hill, states that it was:

> made by Domenico Montagnana and bears a label dated 1735. The back is in two pieces, is of wood marked by a faint curl of medium width rising slightly upwards from the joint; the wings on the bottom flanks being original; the wood of the sides and head is marked by a broader curl; the table is of pine of open grain and the varnish with which the entire instrument is well covered, is of a red-brown colour. This violoncello, which is in a singular pure and fresh condition, is one of the finest existing examples of the maker's work.[6]

In an accompanying letter dated 25 October 1945 to Werro in Berne, Switzerland, Alfred Phillips Hill described the instrument as 'one of the most perfect examples of the master's work in existence, being practically in new condition, its dimensions are original and it has never been seriously played upon or subjected to any serious repairs since it was made'. Astonishingly, Hill adds: 'The last owner of this cello was Emanuel Feuermann, who used it for some years for his solo work'. Hill first came across the cello in 1882 when invited to value for probate a quartet of Stradivari instruments belonging to Edward Tyrrell, an amateur musician; the cello was not a Stradivarius but a Montagnana. Tyrrell had purchased the cello and the Stradivari instruments from R. & W. Davis in Coventry Street, London. The Montagnana was sold by the Tyrrell family to a Mr Ellison, who in turn sold it 'to a lady' who brought it to Hill. Hill wrote of it: 'The cello was brought here from Italy, possibly, direct from Venice, at the beginning of the XIX century. When it became our property, we took it to pieces and, removing the fictitious label of Stradivari, inserted in its place an excellent reproduction of an authentic Montagnana label, thus confirming its rightful authorship.'[7] Werro sold the cello in 1953 but apparently got it back because in 1961 he sold it again, this time to the dealer Jacques Français, who sold it to Mihaly Virizlay. The current owner is Guy Fallot.

'De Munck' Stradivarius

Back length	74.5 cm
Upper bouts	32.25cm
Lower bouts	41.6 cm
Middle bouts	21.3 cm
Depth of ribs	11.6 cm – 12.3 cm

(Measurements taken with callipers)

Feuermann seems to have first seen this instrument in November 1935. It was not until February 1939 that he completed its purchase. Its price was £4500, which Feuermann paid by trading in his Montagnana for £3500 and paying a further £1000. At the time he bought the Montagnana from Hill in 1932, Hill was already in possession of the 'De Munck' Stradivarius, which for some unexplained reason was not shown to Feuermann. Feuermann clearly had doubts over the authenticity of the instrument, which may have been a contributory factor to the inordinate length of time he took to pay for it. A letter from Alfred Hill dated 16 March 1939 implies that Feuermann had raised concerns: 'In the meantime, you may accept my word for the authenticity of the instrument, it is mentioned in our 'Life of Stradivari' either under the name De Munck, or that of Gardner, his pupil to whom he sold it.' There is some confusion. In Hill's letter of 5 April 1939 he does not mention Gardner but does mention C.H. Heriot, a pupil of De Munck, as purchaser. On the same date Hill and Sons issued a signed certificate:

> Made by Antonio Stradivari and bears a label dated 1710.
> Description: The back, in two pieces being similar, the head plainer; the table, in three pieces, is of pine of fairly even grain, the top left flank being marked by a small knot; the varnish, of thick texture, is of light chestnut-red colour. This instrument is in excellent state of preservation.

In the accompanying letter, Hill gave the date of the cello as 1730. (In 1943, Wurlitzer gave the date as 'the period 1730–1731'.[8]) The cello is exceptionally narrow. In the last period of his life, Stradivari was still experimenting with size, still trying to improve the instrument. The 'De Munck' pattern first emerged around 1726, when Stradivari was in his 82nd year. On the only surviving paper template it is named the 'B Piccola'. Instruments made before these are known as 'Model B'. Charles Beare has indicated that there are very few instruments, perhaps six, of 'B Piccola' dimensions; these include the 'Pawle' and the 'Braga' cellos. Hill believed these instruments were made for 'lady players'. Feuermann's instrument was probably not Stradivari's last cello and it seems likely that his son, Francesco, was involved in its making. Despite its narrowness, Stradivari maintained the stop length of the model B on the 'B Piccola'. Feuermann wrote about the instrument to Kux in July 1940: 'My cello is marvellous. I have had occasion to play other Stradivarius but none of them has this immediate tenor-like sound of mine.'[9]

Before Feuermann, the cello is known to have been owned by de Barrau (Parisian amateur), Franchomme, Ernest De Munck (a pupil of Adrien-François Servais), and a pupil of De Munck (either a Gardner, or C.H. Heriot), who bought the cello around 1915 and from whom Hill acquired it. Since

Feuermann's death, it has been owned by Russell B. Kingman and Aldo Parisot, and is now owned by the Nippon Foundation. The instrument is today known as the 'Feuermann' Stradivarius and is on loan to Steven Isserlis.

Comparisons between the Tecchler, Montagnana and Stradivarius

As can be seen from the measurements, the Montagnana, apart from its back length, was considerably larger – particularly in width – than the Tecchler. The Montagnana was a significant step up from the Tecchler and would have provided a wider palate of colours. The Stradivarius, the length of which is the same as the Montagnana, is very narrow by comparison to the Montagnana, narrower even than the Tecchler. Getting round the wide shoulders of the Montagnana would make the instrument tiring to play, whereas the reduced size of the upper and lower bouts of the Stradivarius would make it a far more comfortable instrument to play. Nevertheless, it is often said that Stradivari cellos are hard to play. Whereas significant bow pressure can be put on a Montagnana to produce a large tone, the Stradivarius under similar conditions may close up. The Stradivarius suited Feuermann's elegant, refined sound. With his huge hand, stretch and long fingers he could get around it with ease.

Feuermann's bows

Far less has been said about Feuermann's bows, apart from remarks made by many that he would play with practically no hair and borrow a bow if needed from a cellist in the orchestra. Like the instruments he played, it mattered little what bow he used; his gift was so great that, bow or instrument, they sounded well in his hands. One indication of how he used the bow comes from a recollection by Sophie Feuermann. On arrival in the USA, she tried to interest her husband, jealous of her enthusiasm for music, in taking up the cello so that he could play simple chamber music with her. Feuermann lent him a bow. Sophie maintains that due to pressure exerted by Feuermann through his index finger, the stick was entirely bent. This bow has disappeared; Harry, without Sophie's knowledge, sold it almost immediately on receiving it from Feuermann to a dealer in Chicago.

Another bow is remembered by Mosa Havivi, who claims (possibly incorrectly) that Feuermann used it all his life. Havivi's earliest memories of Feuermann date from around 1932 when he went to study with him in Berlin, which suggests that Feuermann must have acquired the bow before then. The maker of the bow was François Nicolas Voirin. Born in Mirecourt in 1833,

Voirin served an apprenticeship in the workshop of Jean-Baptiste Vuillaume. The sticks are described by Etienne Vatelot in *Les Archets Français* as of rare elegance and models of perfection and finish: 'The head, which is light and pleasing to look at, is slightly rounded and terminates in a point which can only be described as perfect. The curve starts just behind the head, which was at this time quite an innovation.'[10] Voirin bows were light, but Havivi believes Feuermann's Voirin weighed in the region of 75–6 gm, quite heavy for a Voirin. When Feuermann moved to a steel A string he continued to use this bow. The sound produced with a Voirin bow has elegance and refinement, no doubt a perfect match for the narrow Stradivarius. The bow was with the Stradivarius when sold to Russell Kingman but when Aldo Parisot bought the instrument from Kingman the bow was not included.

Mention of two other bows has been made. Mosa Havivi met a dealer in Hollywood who said that Feuermann had seen a bow in his shop made by Alfred Joseph Lamy (1850–1919), assistant to Voirin. Feuermann had wanted to buy the bow but the dealer had not wanted to sell it. Laurence Lessor believes that Feuermann used, but never owned, a bow made by Eugène Sartory (1871–1946), a maker from Mirecourt who first worked for Charles Peccatte and later for Alfred Lamy. Sartory bows were heavier – in the region of 82–4 gm.

Strings

From his earliest years Feuermann would have used covered gut for the C and G strings and plain gut for the two upper strings. Photographs show that during his tour to the Far East in 1934 he was still using a plain gut A and D. Mosa Havivi reported that when Feuermann came back to Europe from America, he had started to use a steel A string. Havivi was not specific about which year, but most probably it was 1936, after Feuermann's return from his second trip to the Far East via the United States. A recording of Weber's *Konzertstück* in December 1936 appears to use a metal A whereas recordings made in Japan that summer sound as if Feuermann was still using gut. In a letter of November 1938 Feuermann reported that Sacconi's heart bled when he saw that Feuermann was using a metal A string. Metal strings were not new. They had been in existence for over 300 years, used particularly on keyboard instruments rather than the violin family; they became standard for the violin family only from the middle of the 20th century. On his Far Easten tours, Feuermann was bothered by the hot, humid climate, and such weather might certainly have caused a gut A string to break within as little as a day. Strings need to be adjusted as much to the player as to the instrument. In terms of sound production, however, it probably made little difference what strings Feuermann used, but he may well have preferred a metal string. Apart from holding its pitch, a steel A would have been easier to articulate and more incisive. Havivi recalls that Feuermann's steel A string was a 'Super-Sensitive', made in Chicago. His recollection was that when Feuermann started to use a steel A he stopped using a gut D, preferring an aluminium-on-gut D with silver-covered G and C. As can be seen from photographs, in order to balance the sound of the brighter A with the duller D, Feuermann tied a piece of rubber band once or twice around the A string at the bridge.[11]

Chronological List of Known Recording Sessions and Broadcasts[1]

Although at the time of writing no plan for a complete release of Feuermann's recordings is known, individual releases on individual labels frequently occur (and are as frequently deleted) in many countries of the world. Rather than attempting to give reference numbers for these releases (which are quickly out of date), this appendix endeavours simply to list the known broadcasts and recordings Feuermann made. Matrix numbers (given on the left) and issue numbers (given on the right) for the recordings are listed where known. At the beginning of his recording career, several sessions for Parlophon resulted in no releases although matrix numbers were allocated, suggesting that test discs may have existed. It seems highly unlikely, given the devastation of Berlin during the Second World War, that any of these discs have survived, but for the purpose of providing a trail, the matrix number is given. All Feuermann's German recordings were made in Berlin.

Entries wholly in italics are radio broadcasts and the single commercial film.

1921

15 December, Berlin, Parlophon
Frieder S. Weissmann (conductor) with members of the Berlin State Opera Orchestra

5653	Haydn Cello Concerto in D (Hob.VIIb:2): Adagio	P-1298 I
5654	Haydn Cello Concerto in D (Hob.VIIb:2): Allegro	P-1298 II
5655	Schumann *Träumerei* op.15 no.7 (arr. Popper) no pianist named (unreleased)	

5656   Schumann *Abendlied* op.85 no.12 (arr. Popper) no pianist named (unreleased)

5657   Chopin Nocturne in E♭ op.9 no.2 (arr. Popper) cello part only (unreleased)

5658   Popper *Elfentanz* cello part only (unreleased)

1922

8 April, Berlin, Parlophon

5835   Chopin Nocturne in E♭ op.9 no.2 Frieder Weissmann (piano)

                                                                              P-1342-I

5836   Sarasate *Zigeunerweisen* (1st part; arr. Feuermann)
        Frieder Weissmann (piano)   P-1342-II

5837   Schumann *Träumerei* op.15 no.7 (arr. Popper) with unnamed orchestra, conductor Frieder S. Weissmann (unreleased)

5838   Schumann *Abendlied* op.85 no.12 (arr. Popper) with unnamed orchestra, conductor Frieder S. Weissmann (unreleased)

11 November, Berlin, Parlophon

Max Saal (harp)

6077   Goltermann Cello Concerto in A minor: Andante (unreleased)

6078   Handel Sarabande in G minor (unreleased)

6079   Schubert *Ave Maria* (arr. Wilhelmj) (unreleased)

6080   Pergolesi Siciliana (unreleased)

6081   Schubert *Litanei* (unreleased)

6082   J. Danbé Menuett (unreleased)

1924

4 June, Berlin, Parlophon

Fritz Ohrmann (piano and Dominator harmonium)

6953	Anonymous *Alt-italienisches Liebeslied*	P-2037-I
6954	Schumann *Abendlied* op.85 no.12 (arr. Popper)	P-1395-I
6955	Schumann *Träumerei* op.15 no.7 (arr. Popper)	P-1395-II
6956	Bach Suite no.3 in D for orchestra BWV 1068: 2nd movt (Air)	P-1762-I
6957	Bach/Gounod *Ave Maria*	P-1762-II
6958	Dvořák Rondo in G minor op.94	P-1792-I
6958	Popper *Serenade espagnol* op.54 no.2	P-1792-II
6960	Cui *Cantabile* op.36. no.2	P-2037-II

1926
25 March, Berlin, Parlophon
Michael Taube (conductor and pianist) with members of the Berlin State Opera Orchestra

8759	Dvořák Cello Concerto in B minor op.104: 2nd movt	E 10482
8760	Dvořák Cello Concerto in B minor op.104: 2nd movt	E 10482
8761	Popper *Hungarian Rhapsody* op.68	P-2233-I
8762	Popper *Hungarian Rhapsody* op.68	P-2233-II
8763	Haydn Cello Concerto in D (Hob.VIIb:2): part 1 (movt not specified) (unreleased)	
8764	Haydn Cello Concerto in D (Hob.VIIb:2): part 2 (movt not specified) (unreleased)	
8765	Haydn Cello Concerto in D (Hob.VIIb:2): part 3 (movt not specified) (unreleased)	
8766	Boccherini Cello Concerto in B♭: Adagio (unreleased)	
8767	Popper *Concert Polonaise* in D minor op.54 Taube (piano) (unreleased)	
8768	Popper *Concert Polonaise* in D minor op.54 Taube (piano) (unreleased)	

1927
8 April, Berlin, Parlophon
Michael Taube (piano)

20213	Schumann *Träumerei* op.15 no.7 (arr. Popper)	P-9109-I/0-7542
20214	Schumann *Abendlied* op.85 no.12 (arr. Popper)	P-9109-II/0-7542
20215	Popper *Serenade espagnol* op.54 no.2	P-9123-I
20216	Chopin Nocturne in E♭ op.9 no.2 (arr. Popper)	P-9110-I/0-7543
20217	Sarasate *Zigeunerweisen* (1st part; arr. Feuermann)	P-9110-II/0-7543
20218	Saint-Saëns *Allegro appassionato* op.43	P-9112-II
20219	Bach Suite no.3 in D for orchestra BWV 1068: 2nd movt (Air)	P-9123-II
20220	Valensin Symphony no.1 in G: Menuett (arr. J. Danbé)	P-9671-II /0-7541

1928
30 April, Berlin, Parlophon
Michael Taube (conductor) with members of the Berlin State Opera Orchestra

20748	Dvořák Cello Concerto op.104: 1st movt, part 1	P-9667-I/0-7537
20749	Dvořák Cello Concerto op.104: 1st movt, part 2	P-9667-II/0-7537
20750	Dvořák Cello Concerto op.104: 1st movt, part 3	
20750-2	Dvořák Cello Concerto op.104: 1st movt, part 3	
20751	Dvořák Cello Concerto op.104: 2nd movt, part 1	
20752	Dvořák Cello Concerto op.104: 2nd movt, part 2	
20752-2	Dvořák Cello Concerto op.104: 2nd movt, part 2	P-9669-I/0-7539
20753	Dvořák Cello Concerto op.104: 3rd movt, part 3	P-9669-II/0-7539

Michael Taube (piano)

20754	Giordani *Caro mio ben* (arr. Popper)	P-9270-I
20755	Bach/Gounod *Ave Maria*	P-9270-II
20756	Saint-Saëns *The Swan*	P-9291-I
20757	Granados *Danse espagnol* 'Andalusia' op.37	P-9291-II

1929

27 September, Berlin, Parlophon

Michael Taube (conductor) with members of the Berlin State Opera Orchestra

21582	Dvořák Cello Concerto op.104: 3rd movt, part 1	P-9670-I/0-7540
21583	Dvořák Cello Concerto op.104: 3rd movt, part 2	P-9670-II/0-7540
21584	Dvořák Cello Concerto op.104: 3rd movt, part 3	P-9671-I/0-7541

1930

27 January, Berlin, Parlophon

Frieder S. Weissmann (conductor) with members of the Berlin State Opera Orchestra

20750-3	Dvořák Cello Concerto op.104: 1st movt, part 3	P-99668-I/0-7538
20751-2	Dvořák Cello Concerto op.104: 2nd movt, part 1	P-99668-II/0-7538
21649	Bruch *Kol Nidrei* op.47	P-9500-I
21650	Bruch *Kol Nidrei* op.47	P-9500-II

1931

11 October (radio broadcast), Berlin Gruppe (716 kHz, 419 m, 1,7 kW)[2] 6.30 p.m.–7.25 p.m.

Reger String Trio in D minor op.141b *with Hindemith and Goldberg. End of 2nd movt and 3rd movt Vivace recorded on shellac. No copy found.*

1932

20 April (radio broadcast), Berlin (716 kHz, 419 m, 1,7 kW)[3] 9.20 p.m.–10.10 p.m. **Schubert String Trio in B♭, D.581** *with Hindemith and Goldberg and* **Beethoven String Trio in C minor op.9 no.3** **Beethoven** *3rd movt Scherzo recorded on shellac. No copy found.*

26 April (radio broadcast), Berlin, (716 kHz, 419 m, 1,7 kW)[4] 8.30 p.m.–10.10 p.m.

Brahms Concerto in A minor for violin and cello op.102 *Georg Kulenkampff (violin), Max Fiedler conducting Berlin Radio Orchestra. 2nd movt Andante recorded on shellac. No copy found.*

5 July (radio broadcast), Berlin (716 kHz, 419 m, 1,7 kW)[5] 8.00 p.m.–8.40 p.m. **Tessarini Sonata in F major, Hindemith Sonata for cello and piano op.11**

no.3 (1922), Granados Spanish Dance, Frescobaldi Toccata (arr. Cassadó).
Richard Laugs, piano.
Hindemith 2nd movt *recorded on shellac. No copy found.*

2 September, Berlin, Telefunken
Paul Kletzki (conductor) with members of the Berlin Philharmonic Orchestra

018642	Popper *Hungarian Rhapsody* op.68	B 1235-1
018643	Popper *Hungarian Rhapsody* op.68	B 1235-2

27 October, Berlin, Telefunken, test pressing
Arpad Sander (piano)
18762   Popper *Papillon*
18762I   Popper *Papillon*

3 December (radio broadcast), Südfunk Stuttgart (Mühlacker)
(832 kHz, 360,6 m, 60 kW)[6] 12.45 a.m.–1.15 a.m.
Dvořák Cello Concerto *with Michael Taube [on discs]*

6 December (radio broadcast), 'Virtuosen' Mitteldeutscher Rundfunk (Leipzig)
(770 kHz, 389,6 m, 120 kW)[7] 12.00 a.m.–1.00 p.m. Record programme included
Casals playing Bach Andante and Popper 'Vito' and Feuermann playing **Sarasate**
'Zigeunerweisen'.

7 December (live radio broadcast) Berlin (716 kHz, 419 m, 1,5 kW)[8] 8.00 p.m.
–10.00 p.m.
Haydn Cello Concerto in D *Eugen Jochum conducting Berlin Philharmonic*
Orchestra
1934
19 January, London. Concert and live radio broadcast 9.10 p.m.–10.15 p.m. on
London and Midland Regional. Concert Hall, BBC Broadcasting House,
Goldberg–Hindemith–Feuermann Trio. **Hindemith Trio (1933).** *Mozart Duo in*
B♭, for violin and viola K.424, **Schubert Trio in B♭ op.99**

21 January, London, Columbia, Abbey Road Studio 3
Szymon Goldberg (violin) and Paul Hindemith (viola)
AX 7061–7066   Hindemith String Trio no.2 (1933)   LX 311,312,313

22 January, London, Columbia, Abbey Road Studio 3
Szymon Goldberg (violin) and Paul Hindemith (viola)
AX 7067–7072 Beethoven Serenade in D for violin, viola, cello op.8
                                        LX 354, LX 355, LX 356

23 January, London, Columbia, Abbey Road Studio 3
Paul Hindemith (viola)
A 14295   Hindemith Scherzo   D.B. 1789

27 January, London, Columbia, Abbey Road Studio 3
AX 7076   Hindemith Solo Sonata op.25 no.3   69001-D-I
AX 7077   Hindemith Solo Sonata op.25 no.3   69001-D-II

10 July, London, Columbia (for Nipponophone Co. Ltd, Kawasaki, Japan
[Japanese Columbia]), Abbey Road Studio 3
Theo van der Pas (piano)
AX 7211–7215   Brahms Sonata no.1 in E minor op.38: 1st & 2nd movts
                                         J 8317(A&B), J 8318 (A)

11 July, London, Columbia (for Nipponophone Co. Ltd, Kawasaki, Japan
[Japanese Columbia]), Abbey Road Studio 3
Theo van der Pas (piano)
AX 7214–7215   Brahms Sonata no.1 in E minor op.38: 3rd movt
                                         J 8318-B, J 8319-A
AX 7216–7217   Beethoven '*Bei Männern*' Variations WoO 46   LX 331
AX 7218   Gluck Mélodie from *Orphée* (arr. Grünfeld)   J 8219-B
A 14597   Chopin Waltz in A minor op.34 no.2
                 (arr. Feuermann)   L.B. 18
A 14598   Sgambati *Serenata napoletana* op.24 no.2.   L.B. 18

13 October (radio broadcast),[9] *Japan. Broadcast included* **Beethoven/Mozart
Variations 'Bei Männern' WoO 46**

15 October, Tokyo, Nipponophone Co. Ltd, Kawasaki, Japan [Japanese
Columbia], exact location unknown.
Fritz Kitzinger (piano)
M39476   Taki *Kōjō no tsuki* (arr. Yamada)   35450-1
M39477   Yamada *Karatachi no hana*   35456-1
M39478   Yamada *Nobara*   35450-2
M39479   Yamada *Oshoro Takashima*   35456-2

*17 October (live radio broadcast), Hibiya Public Hall, Tokyo (broadcast by Japan
Broadcasting Corporation, NHK)*
New Symphony Orchestra conducted by Viscount Hidemaro Konoye
Dvořák Cello Concerto
Sarasate 'Zapateado' (encore?)

1935
25 November, London Columbia (for Nipponophone Co. Ltd, Kawasaki, Japan [Japanese Columbia]), Abbey Road Studio 1.
Malcolm Sargent (conductor) with unnamed symphony orchestra
AX 7676–7683   Haydn Cello Concerto in D (Hob.VIIb: 2)
LX 472, LX 473, LX 474, LX 475

1936
9 February (radio broadcast), Studio 8-H Radio City Music Hall, New York, General Motors Symphony Concerts. Programme called 'General Motors Concert Hour'.
GM Symphony Orchestra conducted by Erno Rapée
Programme included **Popper 'Hungarian Rhapsody' in D op.68, Dvořák Rondo and Granados Intermezzo from 'Goyescas' (arr. Cassadó), Saint-Saëns 'The Swan'** *with Edwin MacArthur (piano). No copy found.*

13 May (radio broadcast),[10] *Japan. Programme of* **Beethoven/Mozart Variations** *including 'Bei Männern' WoO 46.*

1 June(?), Tokyo, Nipponophone Co. Ltd, Kawasaki, Japan (Japanese Columbia) Viscount Hidemaro Konoye (conductor) with members of the New Symphony Orchestra
M55140   Handel Largo from Xerxes (unreleased)
M55141   Bach Air BWV 1068 (unreleased)

3 June (radio broadcast), Hibiya Public Hall, Tokyo, Japan
New Symphony Orchestra conducted by Wolfgang Rebner
C.P.E. Bach Cello Concerto no.3
Dvořák Cello Concerto

2(?) June, Tokyo, Nipponophone Co. Ltd, Kawasaki, Japan (Japanese Columbia)
Wolfgang Rebner (piano)

M55142	Chopin Nocturne in E♭ op.9 no.2	LX 719
M55143	Schumann *Träumerei* (arr. Popper)	DX 855
M55144	Bach/Gounod *Ave Maria*	DX 855
M201721	Tchaikovsky *Valse sentimentale* op.51 no.6	J 5515-B
M201722	Mendelssohn *Spring Song* op.62 no.6	J 5511-A
M201723	Bloch *Prayer* from *From Jewish Life*	J 5511-B
M201724	Godard *Berceuse* from *Jocelyn*	J 5515-A

DM201731	Schumann *Zigeunerleben* op.29 no.3	J 5528-A
M201732	Schubert *Ständchen* from *Schwanengesang* book 1	J 5578-B
M201733	Wrighton 'Her Bright Smile Haunts Me Still'	J 5534-B
M201734	Valentini Sonata in E: Gavotta and Allegro (arr. Piatti)	J 5534-A
M201739	Saint-Saëns 'The Swan'	J5578-A
DM201740	Rubinstein Melody in F op.3 no.1 (arr. Popper)	J 5528-B

29 October (radio broadcast), Hollywood, Kraft-Phoenix Cheese Corporation. Programme called 'Kraft-Phoenix Cheese Corporation' with hosts Bing Crosby and Bob Burns, Jimmy Dorsey's orchestra and guests Elissa Landi and Cary Grant. Broadcast over WEAF, New York, and the NBC Red Network 10.00 p.m.–11.00 p.m. (EDST). No copy found.
Theodore Saidenberg (?) (piano)
Feuermann's repertoire is not known.

22 December, London, Columbia (for Nipponophone Co. Ltd, Kawasaki, Japan [Japanese Columbia]) Abbey Road Studio 3
Gerald Moore (piano)
AX 7905   Weber *Konzerstück* op.20: Andantino & Variations   LX 643

1937
28 and 29 June, London, Columbia, Abbey Road Studio 3
Myra Hess (piano)
AX 8004–8008   Beethoven Sonata no.3 in A op.69   LX 641, LX 642, LX 643

29 and 30 June, London, Columbia, Abbey Road Studio 3
Gerald Moore (piano)
AX 8009–8011   Schubert 'Arpeggione' Sonata (1st & 2nd movts)
              (3rd movt)   LX 717, LX 718, LX 719
1938

19 March (live radio broadcast), programme called 'Indianapolis Symphony'. Live concert broadcast over WOR, New York, and the Mutual Network 9.15pm–11.00pm (EST). No copy found.
Indianapolis Symphony Orchestra conducted by Fabian Sevitsky
Weber 'Konzertstück'
Tchaikovsky 'Rococo' Variations

26 March (live radio broadcast), Carnegie Hall, New York. Programme called 'National Orchestral Concert'. Live concert broadcast over WNYC, New York from 2.30pm–5.00pm (EST). No copy found.

National Orchestral Association conducted by Leon Barzin
Tartini Concerto in D
Toch Cello Concerto
Strauss 'Don Quixote' [NOA leader (violin) and Milton Katims (viola)]

23 May (live radio broadcast), Queen's Hall, London. Programme called 'London Music Festival 1938: Second Concert'. Live concert broadcast over the regional BBC station (877 kc, 342.1 m) 8.15 p.m.–9.15 p.m. and 9.35 p.m.–10.10 p.m. Also broadcast short wave to America. [Copy held at National Sound Archive, British Library.]
BBC Symphony Orchestra conducted by Arturo Toscanini
Strauss 'Don Quixote' [Bernard Shore (viola) and Paul Beard (violin)]

22 October (radio broadcast), NBC Studio 8-H, Radio City Music Hall, New York. Programme called 'N.B.C. Symphony Orchestra' hosted by Gene Hamilton. Broadcast over WJZ, New York, and the NBC Blue Network 10.00pm–11.30pm. (EST). Broadcast copy found and issued.
NBC Symphony Orchestra conducted by Arturo Toscanini
Strauss 'Don Quixote' [Mischa Mischakoff (violin) and Carleton Cooley (viola)]

20 November (radio broadcast), (Radio City Music Hall, New York?) Programme called 'Magic Key of RCA' hosted by Milton Cross (with Ben Grauer) and Clifton Fadiman as master of ceremonies. Broadcast over WJZ, New York, and the NBC Blue Network 2.00pm–3.00pm (EST). Broadcast copy found and issued.
Magic Key Orchestra conducted by Frank Black
Dvořák Cello Concerto: 2nd movt

1939
8 January (live radio broadcast), Town Hall, New York City. Programme called 'New Friends of Music'. Part of live concert with Budapest Quartet broadcast over WJZ, New York, and the NBC Blue Network 6.00–7.00pm (EST). No copy found.
Bach Cello Suite no.6 BWV 1012

13 January, New York, RCA Victor, Studio no. 2
Hulda Lashanska (soprano), Misha Elman (violin) and Rudolf Serkin (piano)
CS-031473   Ochs *Dank sei dir, Herr*   15365-A
CS-031474   Schubert *Litanei* D.343   15365-B

19 January (radio broadcast), NBC 'new building', Hollywood, California. Programme called 'Kraft Music Hall' with hosts Bing Crosby and Bob Burns and guests Anita Louise and Colonel Lemuel Q. Stoopnagle. Broadcast over WEAF,

New York, and the NBC Red Network 10.00pm–11.00pm. No copy found.
Wolfgang Rebner? (piano)
Feuermann's repertoire is not known.

7 February, London, Columbia (for Nipponophone Co. Ltd, Kawasaki, Japan
[Japanese Columbia]), Abbey Road Studio 3
AX 8439–8442   Reger Suite in G major op.131c no. 1   LX 817
                                                                        LX 818

8 February, London, Columbia (for Nipponophone Co. Ltd, Kawasaki, Japan
[Japanese Columbia]), Abbey Road Studio 3
Gerald Moore (piano)
A 17337 Drigo Serenade *Les Millions d'Arlequin*   DB 1866
A 17338 Cui *Orientale* op.50.no.9   DB 1860
A 17339 Rimsky-Korsakov *Chant Hindou* from *Sadko* (arr. Klengel)   DB 1866
A 17340 Albéniz Tango in D op.165 no.2 (arr. Kreisler/Feuermann)   DB 1860

Summer, Hollywood, California. Film.
Director Ernst Matray
Cameraman Jackson Rose
Theodore Saidenberg (piano)
Dvořák Rondo in G minor op.94
Popper 'Spinning Song' op.55
Soundtrack probably recorded first, pictures added in 1940(?)
Copyright 1941

31 July, New York, RCA Victor, Studio no.2
Franz Rupp (piano)
CS-038164   Handel Organ Concerto op.4 no.3: 1st movt (arr. Feuermann)
CS-038165   Handel Organ Concerto op.4 no.3: 2nd movt (arr. Feuermann)
CS-038166   Beethoven 'Ein Mädchen oder Weibchen' Variations op.66
CS-038167   Beethoven 'Ein Mädchen oder Weibchen' Variations op.66

1 August, New York, RCA Victor, Studio no.2
Franz Rupp (piano)
CS-038164   Handel Organ Concerto op.4 no.3: 1st movt (arr. Feuermann)
CS-038165   Handel Organ Concerto op.4 no.3: 2nd movt (arr. Feuermann)
CS-038168   Chopin Introduction and Polonaise op.3 (arr. Feuermann)

3 August (radio broadcast), Hollywood, California. Programme called 'Kraft
Music Hall' hosted by Bob Burns with guests Melvyn Douglas, Fay Holm, Pat
Friday and the Music Maids. Broadcast over WEAF, New York, and the NBC Red

Network 10.00pm–11.00pm. A broadcast with this repertoire has been found.
Theodore Saidenberg (piano)
The repertoire played may have been:
Sarasate 'Zapateado' op.23 no.2 (arr. Feuermann)
Fauré 'Après un rêve' (arr. Casals)

8 August, New York, RCA Victor, Studio no.2
Franz Rupp (piano)
BS-041514   Canteloube *Bourée auvergnate* in A (arr. Silva)
BS-041515   Davidov *At the Fountain* op.20 no.2
BS-041516   Bach Toccata, Adagio and Fugue in C for organ BWV 564: Adagio
            (arr. Casals and Siloti)
BS-041517   Fauré *Après un rêve* (arr. Casals)   CAL 292-1

16 August (live radio broadcast), Lewisohn Stadium, New York. Programme
called 'New York Philharmonic-Symphony Summer Series–Stadium Concerts'
hosted by John Daly. Part of live concert broadcast over WABC, New York, and the
CBS Network 9.00 p.m.–10.30 p.m. (EDST) Copy of part of broadcast found.
New York Philharmonic-Symphony Orchestra conducted by Alexander Smallens
Saint-Saëns Concerto in A minor op.33
Bloch 'Schelomo'
Bach Cello Suite no.3 BWV 1009: Sarabande and Bourrées I and II (encore)

11 September, New York, RCA Victor, Studio no.2
Franz Rupp (piano)
CS-042656–042661   Mendelssohn Sonata in D op.58 no.2

12 December, New York, RCA Victor, Studio no.2
Franz Rupp (piano)
BS-041517   Fauré *Après un rêve* (arr. Casals)
CS-042656   Mendelssohn Sonata in D op.58 no.2: 1st movt   CAL 292-1
CS-042657   Mendelssohn Sonata in D op.58 no.2: 1st movt   CAL 292-1
CS-042658   Mendelssohn Sonata in D op.58 no.2: 2nd movt
CS-042659   Mendelssohn Sonata in D op.58 no.2: 3rd movt, part 1
BS 041514   Canteloube *Bourée Auvergnate* in A   2166-B
BS-041515   Davidov *At the Fountain* op.20 no.2   2166-A
CS-038164   Handel Organ Concerto op.4 no.3: 1st movt
            (arr. Feuermann)   18154-A

13 December, New York, RCA Victor, Studio no.2
Franz Rupp (piano)

CS-042659	Mendelssohn Sonata in D op.58 no.2: 3rd movt, part 1	
		CAL 292-1
CS-042658	Mendelssohn Sonata in D op.58 no.2: 2nd movt	CAL 292-1
CS-042660	Mendelssohn Sonata in D op.58 no.2:	
	3rd movt, part 1 & 4th movt, part 1	CAL 292-1
CS-038165	Handel Organ Concerto op.4 no.3: 2nd movt (arr. Feuermann)	
CS-038168	Chopin Introduction and Polonaise op.3 (arr. Feuermann)	

The Mendelssohn sonata was never issued on 78s
CAL 292 is an RCA Camden LP

14 December, New York, RCA Victor, Studio no.2
Franz Rupp (piano)

CS-038169	Chopin Introduction and Polonaise op.3 (arr. Feuermann)	
		17610-B
CS-038165	Handel Organ Concerto op.4 no.3: 2nd movt	
	(arr. Feuermann)	18154-B
CS-038168	Chopin Introduction and Polonaise op.3	
	(arr. Feuermann)	17610-A
BS-041516	Bach Toccata, Adagio and Fugue in C for organ BWV 564:	
	Adagio (arr. Casals and Siloti)	
BS-041517	Fauré *Après un rêve* (arr. Casals)	

*17 December (live radio broadcast), Carnegie Hall, New York. Programme called
'New York Philharmonic-Symphony' hosted by Deems Taylor. Live concert
broadcast over WABC, New York and the CBS network 3.00pm–4.30pm (EST).
Copy not found.*
New York Philharmonic-Symphony Orchestra conducted by John Barbirolli
Haydn Cello Concerto in D (Hob.VIIb:2)

21 December, Philadelphia, RCA Victor, Academy of Music
Philadelphia Orchestra, conductor Eugene Ormandy
Jascha Heifetz (violin)

CS-045645–045652	Brahms Concerto in A minor for violin and	
	cello op.102	18132-A & B
		18133-A & B
		18134-A & B
		18135-A & B

1940

21 January (live radio broadcast), Town Hall, New York City. Programme called 'New Friends of Music'. Part of live concert broadcast over WJZ, New York, and the NBC Blue Network 6.00pm–6.56pm (EST). Broadcast copy found. (Brahms 1st movt is interrupted by a station identification).
Adolf Busch (violin) and Rudolf Serkin (piano)
Mozart Piano Trio no.7 in C K.548
Brahms Piano Trio no.2 in C op.87

27 January, Carnegie Hall, New York
Private recording for National Orchestral Association
Leon Barzin (conductor) with the National Orchestral Association
Dvořák Cello Concerto op.104
Reicha Cello Concerto in A op.4 no.1

24 February, Philadelphia, RCA Victor, Academy of Music
Eugene Ormandy (conductor) with the Philadelphia Orchestra
CS-048027–048036   Strauss *Don Quixote* [Samuel Lifschey (viola)
                    and Alexander Hilsberg (violin)]   17529-A&B
                                                               17530-A&B
                                                               17531-A&B
                                                               17532-A&B
                                                               17533-A&B

25 February (radio broadcast), Studio 8-H, Radio City Music Hall, New York. Programme called 'NBC Civic Concert' – 'Special hour program presented by NBC saluting America's Civic Music Association from coast to coast, in commemoration of NBC's ten years affiliation with the Civic Concert Service' hosted by Milton Cross. Broadcast over WJZ, New York, and the NBC Blue Network 3.00pm–4.00pm (EST). Feuermann's performance has been found and released on disc.
NBC Symphony Orchestra, conductor Frank Black
Dvořák Cello Concerto: 2nd movt

27 March, Philadelphia, RCA Victor, Academy of Music
Leopold Stokowski (conductor) with the Philadelphia Orchestra
CS-047816–047820 Bloch *Schelomo*   17336-A&B
                                                               17337-A&B
                                                               17338-S

22 April, Carnegie Hall, New York
Private recording of live concert for National Orchestral Association
Leon Barzin (conductor) with the National Orchestral Association
D'Albert Cello Concerto in C

22 August (radio broadcast), Hollywood, California. Programme called 'Kraft Music Hall' hosted by Bob Burns with guests Marie Green and her Merry Men. Broadcast over WEAF, New York, and the NBC Red Network 9.00pm–10.00pm. A portion of the broadcast has been found.
Theodore Saidenberg (piano)
Chopin Nocturne in E♭, op.9 no.2
Falla 'Siete Canciones Populares Españolas': no.4, 'Jota' (arr. Maréchal)

22 December (radio broadcast), Carnegie Hall, New York. Programme called 'New Friends of Music'. Part of live concert broadcast over WJZ, New York, and the NBC Blue Network 6.30pm–7.00pm (EST).
Orchestra of the New Friends of Music, conductor Fritz Stiedry
Ibert Concerto for cello and ten wind instruments
Tchaikovsky 'Rococo' Variations
Part of Tchaikovsky's 'Rococo' Variations has been found but the broadcast began mid-performance.

1941
9 January (live radio broadcast), Orchestra Hall, Chicago. Live broadcast over WGN. Copy found.
Chicago Symphony Orchestra, conductor Hans Lange
Dvořák Cello Concerto op.104

9 February (live radio broadcast), Town Hall, New York City. Programme called 'New Friends of Music' hosted by Gene Hamilton. Part of live concert broadcast over WJZ, New York, and the NBC Blue Network 6.05pm–6.56pm (EST).
Albert Hirsch (piano)
Beethoven 'Ein Mädchen oder Weibchen' Variations op.66
Beethoven 'Bei Männern' Variations WoO 46
Beethoven Sonata no.5 in D op.102 no.2
Beethoven Sonata no.1 in F op.5 no.1 *(not broadcast)*
Part of the Beethoven D major sonata has been found.

16 February (live radio broadcast), Town Hall, New York City. Programme called 'New Friends of Music' hosted by Gene Hamilton. Part of live concert broadcast

over WJZ, New York, and the NBC Blue Network 6.09pm–6.57pm (EST). No copy found.
Albert Hirsch (piano)
Beethoven Sonata no.4 in C op.102 no.1
Beethoven 'Judas Maccabaeus' Variations WoO 45
Beethoven Sonata no.3 in A op.69
Beethoven Sonata no.2 in G minor op.5 no.2 (not broadcast)

29 August, RCA Victor, Hollywood Recording Studios
William Primrose (viola)

PCS-061569–061570	Beethoven Duet in E♭ for viola and cello 'with two obbligato eyeglasses' WoO 32	11-8620 A&B

8 September, RCA Victor, Hollywood Recording Studios
Jascha Heifetz (violin) and William Primrose (viola)

PCS-061590–061595	Dohnányi Serenade in C for violin, viola and cello op.10	11-8176 A&B
		11-8177 A&B
		11-8178 A&B

9 September, RCA Victor, Hollywood Recording Studios
Jascha Heifetz (violin) and William Primrose (viola)

PCS-061605–061612	Mozart Divertimento in E♭ K.563	11-8546 A&B
		11-8547 A&B
		11-8548 A&B
		11-8549 A&B

11 September, RCA Victor, Hollywood Recording Studios
Jascha Heifetz (violin) and Artur Rubinstein (piano)

PCS-061622–061629	Brahms Piano Trio no.1 in B op.8 (revised version)	18513 A&B
		18514 A&B
		18515 A
		18516 A

12 September, RCA Victor, Hollywood Recording Studios
Jascha Heifetz (violin) and Artur Rubinstein (piano)

PCS-061624–061629	Brahms Piano Trio no.1 in B op.8 (revised version)	18514 A
		18515 B
		18516 B

PCS-061634–061643   Beethoven 'Archduke' Piano Trio in B♭,
                        op.97   11-8477 A&B

                                                                                11-8478 A&B

                                                                                11-8479 A

13 September, RCA Victor, Hollywood Recording Studios
Jascha Heifetz (violin) and Artur Rubinstein (piano)
PCS-061639–061643   Beethoven 'Archduke' Piano Trio in B♭,
                        op.97   11-8479 B

                                                                                11-8480 A&B

                                                                                11-8481 A&B

PCS-061644–061651 Schubert Piano Trio in B♭, op.99   11-8274 A&B

                                                                                11-8275 A&B

                                                                                11-8276 A&B

                                                                                11-8277 A&B

6 November (radio broadcast), WOR Studios, New York. Programme called
'America Preferred' hosted by Deems Taylor. Broadcast over WOR, New York, and
the Mutual Network 9.30 p.m.–10.00 p.m. (EST). No copy found.
WOR Sinfonietta. Conductor Alfred Wallenstein.
Tchaikovsky 'Rococo' Variations

10 November, Carnegie Hall, New York
Private recording of live concert for National Orchestral Association
Leon Barzin (conductor) with the National Orchestral Association
Dvořák *Waldesruhe* op.68 no.5
Dvořák Rondo in G minor op.94
Bloch *Schelomo*

14 December (live radio broadcast), Town Hall, New York. Programme called
'New Friends of Music'. Part of live concert with Kolisch Quartet broadcast over
the NBC Blue Network 6.06 p.m.–6.30 p.m. (EST). Not broadcast in New York
because of a speech by Mayor Fiorello La Guardia. No copy found.
Albert Hirsch (piano)
Mendelssohn Sonata in D op.58 no.2

1942
5 March (radio broadcast), New York City. Programme called 'Music You Want
When You Want It: Sounding Board'. Broadcast over WEAF 11.15pm–11.30pm
(EST). No copy found.
Feuermann's repertoire is not known.

6 March (live radio broadcast), Academy of Music, Philadelphia. Programme called 'Philadelphia Orchestra'. Live concert broadcast over WOR, New York, and the Mutual Network 2.30pm–4.15pm. The broadcast has not been found.
Philadelphia Orchestra, conductor Eugene Ormandy
Vivaldi A minor cello concerto
Haydn Cello Concerto in D (Hob.VIIb:2)
Strauss 'Don Quixote' *[Samuel Lifschey (viola) and Alexander Hilsberg (violin)]*

? May, Camden, New Jersey (?)
RCA Victor test pressing
Albert Hirsch (?) (piano)
Herbert Cello Concerto no.2: 2nd movt

10 May (radio broadcast), WQXR Studios, New York City. Programme called 'Evening Concert', with recorded music and Feuermann as presenter. Broadcast over WQXR 9.00pm–9.55pm (EDST). No copy found.
Programme included Feuermann's RCA recordings of **Handel Organ Concerto op.4 no.3 (1st & 2nd movts with Franz Rupp)** *and* **Bloch 'Schelomo' (with Philadelphia Orchestra/Stokowski)**

Appendix IV

2002 *Currency Value: US Dollar**

	$250	$500	$750	$1000
1934	3345	6690	10,035	13,380
1935	3272	6544	9816	13,088
1936	3225	6450	9674	12,899
1937	3113	6226	9338	12,451
1938	3180	6358	9537	12,716
1939	3225	6450	9674	12,899
1940	3202	6403	9605	12,807
1941	3049	6098	9148	12,197
1942	2750	5500	8250	16,500

* 'What is a dollar worth?', Woodrow Federal Reserve Bank of Minneapolis

Notes

CHAPTER 1: THE BEGINNING: 1902–17

1 Edmund Kurtz interview with the author, April 1996, London.

2 Sophie Feuermann interview with the author, April 1994, New York.

3 A letter dated 19 January 1939 from Columbia Graphophone Company, Romana S.A., testifies to ten years of recording this orchestra. (Personal papers of Eric Hönigsberg.)

4 Itzak Golan of Israel Broadcasting confirmed this view to the author in April 2001. As a child in Palestine, in exchange for teaching Hebrew to Meier Feuermann, Golan received completely inadequate violin lessons.

5 Sophie Feuermann interview with the author, April 1994, New York.

6 *Lehman Wohnungs Anzeiger, Wien.*

7 Sophie Feuermann interview with the author, April 1994, New York.

8 *Jahresbericht der K.K. Akademie für Musik und Darstellende Kunst über das Schuljahr 1909–1910*, Vienna, 1910 [AWmk].

9 'Schüler Index', 1917, Matrikel no.311 [AWmk].

10 Sophie Feuermann interview with the author, April 1994, New York.

11 AWmk.

12 Sophie Feuermann interview with the author, April 1994, New York.

13 Sophie Feuermann interview with the author, May 1995, New York.

14 See Appendix II.

15 Seymour Itzkoff (while giving no indication of source) suggests that Meier Feuermann bought the instrument cheaply as a result of a 'hardship sale'. See Seymour Itzkoff, *Emanuel Feuermann, Virtuoso: A Biography*, University of Alabama Press, 1979, p.48.

16 Sophie Feuermann interview with the author, April 1994, New York.

17 According to the instrument dealer Charles Beare, Emile Hermann bought the Kux collection of instruments after the Second World War.

18 It has been suggested in a number of sources – Itzkoff, *Biography*, p.34, and Margaret Campbell, *The Great Cellists*, London, Gollancz, 1988, p.160 – that his first teacher was Friederich Buxbaum, principal cellist of the Vienna Philharmonic Orchestra and cellist of the Rosé Quartet. According to Sophie Feuermann this information is incorrect. In *Famous Musicians of a Wandering Race*, New York, Bloch Publishing Company, 1927,

p.271, Gdal Saleski confirms S. Feuermann's view. Buxbaum is not mentioned as Feuermann's teacher. The confusion seems likely to have arisen because Feuermann was known to have been taught by the cellist of the Rosé Quartet. Both Walter and Buxbaum were cellists of the Rosé Quartet.

19 Eva Feuermann interview, WFCR [FA].
20 *Die Musik*, 11/9 (1912), p.187.
21 Artur Weschler-Vered, *Jascha Heifetz*, New York, Schirmer Books, 1986, p.56.
22 Emil Liepe, *Die Musik*, 12/3 (1912), p.186.
23 Sophie Feuermann interview with the author, October 1997, New York.
24 Itzkoff, *Biography*, p.43.
25 Campbell, *Great Cellists*, p.160.
26 Archive of the Gesellschaft der Musikfreunde, Vienna.
27 Itzkoff, *Biography*, p.46.
28 'Notes and some Anecdotes about Feuermann written by himself' [FA].
29 J.K., *Neue Freie Presse* (22 March 1914).
30 Itzkoff, *Biography*, p.49.
31 Campbell, *Great Cellists*, p.160.
32 *Neue Freie Presse* (13 December 1914).
33 Dr Theodore Helm, *Neue Zeitschrift für Musik* (February 1914), p.122.
34 Sophie Feuermann interview with the author, April 1994, New York.
35 Hans Traebert, *Die Musik*, 13/20 (1914).
36 Sophie Feuermann interview with the author, May 1995, New York.
37 *Neue Zeitschrift für Musik* (November 1916), p.360.
38 Years earlier Sigmund Freud had attended the same school situated at Kleine Sperlgasse 2c in the 2nd district of Vienna.
39 Sophie Feuermann interview with the author, April 1994, New York.
40 Eva Feuermann interview with the author, April 1994, Millbrook, New York.

CHAPTER 2: PRODIGY: 1917–23

1 EF's MS, Section C, p.8 [see Chapter 16].
2 William Pleeth interview with the author, May 1994, London.
3 Ibid.
4 Feuermann's name does not appear in the list of students attending the conservatory between 1893 and 1918. A publication in 1993, however, marking its 150th anniversary, claims Feuermann as a student (*Hochschule für Musik und Theater 'Felix Mendelssohn Bartholdy' Leipzig: 150 Jahre Musikhochschule 1843–1993*, Leipzig, Verlag Kunst und Touristik, 1993).
5 EF to Lilli Reifenberg, 2 June 1926 [N].
6 Gregor Piatigorsky, *Cellist*, New York, Doubleday & Company Inc., 1965, p.65
7 William Pleeth interview with the author, May 1994, London.
8 Campbell, *Great Cellists*, p.118.
9 Sophie Feuermann interview with the author, April 1994, New York.
10 Joseph Schuster, *New York Times* (31 May 1942).
11 I have seen no documentary evidence. See Itzkoff, *Biography*, p.48.
12 Itzkoff, *Biography*, p.77.
13 Ibid., p. 81.
14 EF, N&A, p.2

15 Itzkoff, *Biography*, p.81.

16 EF, N&A, p.2

17 Wolfgang (Z'ev) Steinberg interview with the author, April 1997, Israel.

18 EF to Klengel, 8 October 1919 [LEu].

19 William Steinberg (1899–1978).

20 EF to Klengel, 8 October 1919 [LEu].

21 EF, *Musical America* (25 February 1940).

22 EF to Klengel, 8 October 1919 [LEu].

23 *Kölner Zeitung* (22 October 1919).

24 *Kölner Zeitung* (29 October 1919).

25 EF, N&A, p.2.

26 Janna (Marianne) Pentmann interview with the author, June 1996, Lugano.

27 Wolfgang (Z'ev) Steinberg interview with the author, April 1997, Israel.

28 The signatures include Wilhelm Furtwängler (four times), Berta Gaissmar (Furt-wängler's secretary), Otto and Johanna Klemperer, Hermann Abendroth, Pierre Monteux, Bronisław Huberman, Bram Eldering, Erica Morini, Josef Wolfsthal, Joseph Szigeti, Georg Kulenkampff, Szymon Goldberg, Pablo Casals, Paul Grümmer, Gregor Piatigorsky, Edwin Fischer, the Edgar Wollgandt Quartet (with Julius Klengel), the Rosé, Klingler, Wendling, Pro Arte, Kolisch and Budapest quartets, Hans Pfitzner, Emil Bohnke, Egon Wellesz, Paul Hindemith, Carl Ebert, the singer Maria Ivogün, music critic Oscar Bie, Heinrich Simon of the *Frankfurter Zeitung*, Minister of Culture Edwin Redslob, the painter Emil Orlik and the architect Paul Bonatz. Arnold Rosé on 28 October 1920 wrote into the Reifenberg guest book the opening bars of the first violin part of Schönberg's first quartet. In June 1921 Feuermann added his own signature to the Rosé Quartet; a couple of bars of music indicate that Schubert's Quintet was played.

29 Katya Aschaffenburg interview with the author, April 1994, New York.

30 When Katya Aschaffenburg fled Germany in the 1930s and settled in America, she changed her name to Katya Andy.

31 M. Feuermann to Casals, 6 July 1912 (in French), written from II, Obere Augarten-strasse 46, II Stock Tür 20, Vienne [Casals Archive Barcelona].

32 Sigmund Feuermann to Mahler-Kalilstein, 18 June 1949 (in English) [IPO Archive].

33 Hans (b.1900), Carl (b.1902), Kurt (b.1904), Lilli (b.1907) and Eva (b.1914).

34 In some of his letters, however, particularly to Lily Hofmann, he occasionally used Yiddish expressions typical of fairly assimilated Jews talking to one another as a kind of joke.

35 Wolfgang (Z'ev) Steinberg interview with the author, April 1997, Israel.

36 Wolfgang (Z'ev) Steinberg interview with Daniela Cohn-Hofmann, June 1996, Israel.

37 Wolfgang (Z'ev) Steinberg interview with the author, April 1997, Israel.

38 Marianne Pentmann interview with the author, June 1996, Lugano.

39 *Kölner Zeitung* (5 February 1920).

40 *Bösen-Courier* (2 March 1921).

41 This suggests an earlier involvement with Wolff & Sachs than proposed by Itzkoff, *Biography*, p.91.

42 *Führer durch die Konzertsäle Berlins* (1–12 November 1920).

43 A fuller discussion of the recordings can be found in chapters 17 and 18.

44 Dr W. Jacobs, *Kölner Zeitung* (15 March 1922).

45 Ernst Smigelski, *Neue Leipziger Zeitung* on Feuermann's first performance of the Dvořák Concerto on 23 February 1922 in Leipzig with the Gewandhaus Orchestra

conducted by Fritz Busch.
46 Paul Schwers, *Allegemeine Muzik-Zeitung* (October 1922).
47 George Szell interview with Monica Feuermann, 1967.
48 *Musical America* (25 February 1940).
49 Note by Klemperer on a record sleeve of Feuermann recordings [HMV HQM 1079]. See also Peter Heyworth, *Otto Klemperer: His Life and Times, vol. 1: 1885–1933*, Cambridge University Press, 1983, p.156n.
50 *Enzbote Amtsblatt Vaihingen* (January 1923).
51 Karl Hesse, cellist.
52 Feuermann to Klengel, 2 March 1923, from Cologne [LEu] .

CHAPTER 3: NOMAD: 1923–8

1 EF to Klengel's wife, 7 November 1922.
2 Dr Walter Krone. *Allgemeine Musik-Zeitung* (16 March 1923).
3 *Daily Telegraph* (23 June 1923).
4 Maurice Zimbler, a student and distant cousin of Feuermann, has shown the author a printed flyer for two concerts at the Aeolian Hall on Wednesday 17 October and Thursday 28 October 1923.
5 Karl Wolff, *Kölner Tageblatt* (2 July 1923).
6 *Allgemeine Musik-Zeitunug* (28 March 1924).
7 Sophie Feuermann interview with the author, April 1994, New York.
8 Dr Heinz Pringshelm, *Allgemeine Musik-Zeitunug* (24 October 1924) p.781.
9 Paul Schwers, *Allgemeine Musik-Zeitunug* (5 December 1924).
10 EF to Lilli Reifenberg, 27 December 1923 [N].
11 Elinor Lipper interview with the author, June 1996, Lugano.
12 EF to Lilli Reifenberg, 22 December 1924 [N].
13 As quoted by Paul Reifenberg to EF, 23 December 1924 [FA].
14 See Itzkoff, *Biography*, p.96.
15 Letter from EF, 1 August 1935 [J. & A. Beare Archive].
16 Hamma & Co. to Josef Schuster [J. & A. Beare Archive].
17 EF to Lilli Reifenberg, 22 December 1924 [N].
18 Martin Friedland, *Allgemeine Musik-Zeitunug* (13 February 1925).
19 Postcard from EF to Lilli Reifenberg, 13 March 1925 (in French).
20 R. Bertoldy, *Die Musik*, 17/10 (1925), p.793.
21 *Istvestia* review (6 March 1925), quoted in Saleski, *Famous Musicians* p.272.
22 R. Bertoldy, *Die Musik*, 17/10 (1925), p.793.
23 See Campbell, *Great Cellists*, pp.161–2.
24 See Robert Baldock, *Pablo Casals*, London, Gollancz, 1992, p.69.
25 EF to Lilli Reifenberg, 31 May 1925, from Santander [N].
26 *Die Musik*, 17/11 (1925).
27 Toch's Concerto for Cello op.35 on Contemporary Records S8014.
28 A concert on 26 March 1938 with the NOA at Carnegie Hall that included the Toch Concerto was broadcast over WNYC but no part of this broadcast has been found. See Jon Samuels, 'A Complete Discography of the Recordings of Emanuel Feuermann', *Association for Recorded Sound Collections: Journal* XII, 1–2 (1980).
29 N&A, p.3.
30 EF to Lily Hofmann, 22 May 1927 [DC-H].

31 *New York Times* (31 May 1942).
32 EF to Lilli Reifenberg 2 June 1926 [N].
33 *New York Times* (31 May 1942).
34 Feuermann's name does not appear in the Berlin concert guide *Führer durch die Konzertsäle Berlins.*
35 Emma Reifenberg to EF, 10 September 1927 [FA].
36 EF to Lilli Reifenberg, 25 February 1925 [N].
37 Piatigorsky, *Cellist*, pp.117–18.
38 In Edith Stargradt-Wolff's *Wegbereiter grosser Musiker*, Berlin, Bote & Bock, 1954 no mention is made of Feuermann, but the book does suffer mistakes and omissions.
39 EF to Bernhard and Lily Mayer, 17 February 1928 [DC-H]. A 'Kaik' is a pejorative name for an Eastern Jew.
40 EF to Lily Hofmann, 23 December 1927 [DC-H].
41 Sophie Feuermann interview with the author, May 1995, New York.
42 Cesar Saerchinger, *Arthur Schnabel: A Biography*, New York, Dodd, Mead & Co., 1957, p.194.
43 EM to Lilli Refenberg, 27 December 1923 [N].
44 Wolfgang (Z'ev) Steinberg interview with Daniela Cohn-Hofmann, June 1996, Israel.
45 EF to Lily Hofmann, 29th September 1931 [DC-H].
46 Elinor Lipper interview with the author, June 1996, Lugano.
47 Edmund Kurtz interview with the author, April 1996, London.
48 EF to Lilli Reifenberg, 29 November 1924 [N].
49 Eva Feuermann interview with the author, November 1997, Millbrook, New York.
50 EF to Lilli Reifenberg, 7 September 1925 [N].
51 Elinor Lipper interview with the author, June 1996, Lugano.
52 Daniela Cohn-Hofmann interview with the author, May 1996, Israel.
53 Bernhard Mayer, *Memoirs of a Jewish Merchant and Cosmopolitan 1866–1946*, Konstanz, Hartung-Gorre Verlag, 1998, p.188.
54 EF to Lily Mayer, 10 August 1926 [DC-H].
55 Ibid.
56 EF to Lilli Reifenberg, 29 November 1924 [N].
57 EF to Lilli Reifenberg, 25 February 1925 [N]
58 The opening sentence of this letter is a quotation from Goethe's *Egmont*: 'Himmelhochjauchzend, zu Tode betrübt'; here the, author has provided a non-literary translation.
59 EF to Lily Mayer, 4 May 1927 [DC-H].
60 Daniela Cohn-Hofmann interview with the author, May 1996, Israel.
61 Elinor Lipper interview with the author, June 1996, Lugano.
62 EF to Lily Hofmann, 23 December 1927 [DC-H].

CHAPTER 4: BERLIN: 1928–30

1 Kurt Singer, 'Die Hochschule für Musik', *Anbruch*, 3/19–20 (1921), p.350 [see Christopher Hailey, *Franz Schreker 1878–1934: A Cultural Biography*, Cambridge, 1993, p.121].
2 Schünemann to Schreker, 18 July 1925 [Bhm, Doc.103].
3 Eva Feuermann interview with the author, April 1994, Millbrook, New York.
4 EF is referring to Lily Hofmann's car.

5   EF to Lily Hofmann, 12 July 1928 [DC-H].

6   EF to Lily Hofmann, 23 July 1928 [DC-H].

7   EF to Lily Hofmann, 4 October 1928 [DC-H].

8   EF to Carl Flesch, 21 July 1928. See Carl Flesch, *And Do You Also Play the Violin?*, Toccata Press, 1990, p.316.

9   *Hamburgischer Correspondent* (9 October 1928).

10 Itzkoff, *Biography*, p.101.

11 Flesch, *Violin*, p.315.

12 Ibid.

13 Schünemann to EF, 10 April 1929 [Bhm].

14 Ministerial-Kanzleiobersekretar, Prussian Ministry for Science, Art and Public Education, to Städliche akademische Hochschule für Musik, 8 April 1929 [Bhm, Doc. 58].

15 The title of professor could only be offered for longer period contracts and after proof of ability.

16 Feuermann was very young, but it is worth noting that Schnabel was permitted to give private lessons in the Hochschule studios at a fee of 100RM per hour. See Albrecht Dümling, 'On the Road to the "Peoples' Community": The Forced Conformity of the Berlin Academy of Music Under Fascism', *Musical Quarterly*, 77/3 (1993) pp.459–83.

17 Ministerial-Kanzleiobersekretar to Städliche akademische Hochschule für Musik, 13 May 1929 [Bhm, Doc. 76].

18 Schünemann to EF, 10 April 1929 [Bhm].

19 Prussian State Government.

20 Schünemann to Becker, 2 May 1929 [Bhm, Doc. 171].

21 EF to Lily Hofmann, 24 April 1929 [DC-H].

22 22 April 1929, Beethovensaal?

23 EF to Lily Hoffmann, 24 April 1929 [DC-H].

24 The original spelling of the name is 'Chavivi', which he later changed to Havivi.

25 Mosa Havivi interview with the author, April 1994, New York.

26 Ibid.

27 Sophie Feuermann interview with the author, May 1995, New York.

28 Joseph Schuster, *New York Times* (31 May 1942).

29 Artur Rubinstein interview with Monica Feuermann, February 1966.

30 EF to Lily Hofmann, 24 April 1929 [DC-H].

31 EF to Schünemann, 12 September 1929 [Staatsbibliothek Preussischer Kulturbesitz, Berlin].

32 See Norman Lebrecht, *When the Music Stops*, London, Simon & Schuster, 1996 p.73.

33 EF to Schünemann, 12 September 1929 [Staatsbibliothek Preussischer Kulturbesitz, Berlin].

34 EF to Lily Hofmann, 7 December 1929 [DC-H].

35 EF to Lily Hofmann, 11 May 1931 [DC-H].

36 Elinor Lipper interview with the author, 27 June 1996, Lugano.

37 Marianne Pentmann interview with the author, June 1996, Lugano.

38 Meta Cordy interview with the author, April 1994, New York.

39 Undated interview with Franz Rupp by Jon Samuels.

40 The earliest letter from 27 Hohenzollerdamm dates from 19 June 1930 to Lily Hofmann.

41 Kurfürstendamm 56, Pension Louise.

42 EF to Lily Hofmann, 11 May 1931 [DC-H].

43 EF to Lily Hofmann, 20 July 1931 [DC-H].

44 EF to Lily Hofmann, 29 September 1931 [DC-H].

45 Postcard from EF to Lily Hofmann, 10 May 1929 [DC-H].

46 Paul Reifenberg to EF, 5 June 1929 [FA].

47 EF to Lily Hofmann, 16 September 1929 [DC-H].

48 EF to Lily Hofmann, 12 May 1930 [DC-H].

49 EF to Lily Hofmann, 23 June 1930 [DC-H].

50 See Appendix II.

51 EF 1 August 1935 (see above, p.33). There is a notable difference in the sound of the cello between the 1928 and 1930 takes of the Dvořák slow movement suggesting that the Guarneri was used in 1928 and the Tecchler in 1930.

52 EF to Lily Hofmann, 12 May 1930 [DC-H].

53 Schünemann to Becker, 16 July 1929 [Bhm, Doc. 181].

54 EF to Lily Hofmann, 7 December 1929 [DC-H].

55 EF to Frau Klengel, 2 December 1929 [LEu].

56 *Berliner Tageblatt* (6 December 1929).

57 See above, p.31.

58 Letter from Carl Flesch dated 27 November 1916. See Flesch, *Violin*, p.308.

59 Tully Potter, sleeve-notes to *History of the Violin on Record* (Pearl).

60 Carl Flesch, *The Memoirs of Carl Flesch*, Bois de Boulogne, 1973, Harlow, Essex, p.317.

61 Interview with Monica Feuermann, 1966.

62 EF to Lily Hoffmann, 19 June 1930 [DC-H].

63 See below, p.215.

64 EF to Lily Hofmann, 30 September 1930 [DC-H].

CHAPTER 5: 'INTOLERABLE JEW': 1931–4

1 Quoted in Bruno Walter, *Theme and Variations*, New York, Alfred A. Knopf, 1946, p.293.

2 EF to Lily Hofmann, 20 July 1931 [DC-H].

3 EF to Lily Hofmann, 5–6 November, 1931 [DC-H].

4 Eva Feuermann interview with the author, November 1997.

5 EF to Huberman, 12 May 1925, [HA, 1567 SA5].

6 EF to Lily Hofmann, 11 August 1931 [DC-H].

7 Quoted in letter from Siegfried Hearst to EF, 14 July 1932.

8 Siegfried Hearst to EF, 14 July 1932.

9 NBC Music Research Files [NYp].

10 EF to Lily Hofmann, 15 July 1932 [DC-H].

11 EF to Lily Hofmann, 12 December 1932, from Hotel Europeiski, Leningrad. [DC-H].

12 Round-up review from Dortmund by E.A. Schneider, *Die Musik*, 15/4 (1933), p.294. Round-up review of concerts in Bonn also mentions Feuermann playing the Glazunov Concerto on 13 October, *Zeitschrift für Musik* (1933), February, p.164.

13 Berlin Philharmonie, 7 December 1932. Feuermann had previously performed with Jochum, in a concert in 1929 in Lübeck where he had played the Schumann Concerto.

14 Walter, *Theme and Variations*, p.293.

15 Schünemann in a letter dated 28 April 1931 to various professors including Havemann, Daniel, Kreutzer, Hindemith. [Bhm, Doc. 186].

16 Hochschule to the Ministry, 9 September 1930 [Bhm, Doc. 119].

17 Erik Levi, *Music in the Third Reich*, London, Macmillan, 1994, p.11.

18 Artur Schnabel, *My Life and Music*, New York, St Martins Press, 1963.

19 Published by Ries & Erler.

20 Gustav Havemann, 'Offener Brief an Professor Carl Flesch', *Allgemeine Musik-Zeitung* (4 December 1931).

21 See Appendix III.

22 Ministry to Hochschule, 25 February 1932, [Bhm, Doc. 209].

23 Receipt from Eduard Winter A.G. Berlin, 23 April 1932 [FA].

24 EF to Lily Hofmann, 30 April 1932.

25 Thelma Yellin to her husband, Eliezer Yellin, 18 April 1932 [Bentwich-Yellin, *Letters written between 1911–1959*, assembled and edited by Viola Hacohen-Yellin (2001)].

26 Alfred Hill to EF, 13 June 1932 [FA].

27 EF to Lily Hofmann, 15 July 1932 [DC-H].

28 Schünemann to EF, 27 March 1933. [FA].

29 See Dümling, 'On the Road'.

30 Christine Fischer-Defoy, *Kunst Macht Politik: Die Nazifizierung der Kunst – und Musikhochschulen in Berlin*, Berlin, Elefanten Press, 1987, pp.70–1.

31 *Jahresbericht Nr 54: Berlin Hochschule Year Book* (1 October 1932–30 September 1933).

32 Peter Diamand interview with the author, April 1996, London.

33 EF to Huberman, 17 April 1933 [HA].

34 Ibid.

35 Huberman to EF, 20 April 1933 [HA].

36 Huberman to EF, 25 April 1933 [HA].

37 EF to Lily Hofmann, 16 May 1933 [DC-H].

38 EF to Eva Reifenberg, 22 May 1933 [FA].

39 Eva Feuermann interview with the author, April 1994, Millbrook, New York.

40 Emma Reifenberg chose unconventional wording in a sophisticated request for Feuermann not to protest against her feelings.

41 Emma Reifenberg to EF, 2 September 1927 [FA].

42 Emma Reifenberg to EF, 8 April 1928, from Cologne [FA].

43 EF to Lily Hofmann, 11 May 1931 [DC-H].

44 EF to Eva Reifenberg, 22 May 1933 [FA].

45 EF to Eva Reifenberg, 17 June 1933 [FA].

46 EF to Huberman, 11 June 1933 [HA].

47 Letter from Casals to Schönberg, 22 July 1933. See Egbert M. Ennulat, *Arnold Schönberg Correspondence*, Metuchen, NJ, Scarecrow Press, 1991, p.173.

48 Ennulat, *Schönberg Correspondence*, p.187.

49 Schönberg to Joseph Malkin 10 October 1933. See Ennulat, *Schönberg Correspondence*, p.205.

50 *New York Tribune* (13 January 1935).

51 Letter to EF, 5 October 1933 [FA].

52 Eva Reifenberg to EF, 20 November 1933 [FA].

53 Eva Reifenberg to EF, 3 November 1933 [FA].

54 Szymon Goldberg interview with Monica Feuermann, 1966.

55 Hindemith to Willy Strecker, 5 February 1934. See Geoffrey Skelton, *Selected Letters of Paul Hindemith*, London, Yale University Press, 1995.

56 EF to Lily Hofmann, 1 March 1934 [DC-H].

57 Huberman to Mr and Mrs Sieff, 30 April 1934, from Budapest. See Ida Ibbeken and Tzvi Avni, eds., *An Orchestra is Born: A Monument To B. Huberman*, Tel Aviv, 'Yachdav' United Publishers Co. Ltd, 1969, p.17.

58 EF to Huberman, 10 March 1934 [HA, 1574 SA5].

59 EF to Eva Reifenberg, 21 March 1934 [FA].

60 Mosa Havivi interview with the author, April 1994, New York.

61 Wolfgang (Z'ev) Steinberg interview with the author, April 1997, Israel.

62 Sophie Feuermann interview with the author, May 1995, New York.

63 EF to Bernhard Mayer, 3 May 1934 [DC-H].

64 The original spelling of the name is 'Chavivi', which he later changed to Havivi.

65 EF to Bernhard Mayer, 3 May 1934 [DC-H].

66 F.B., *Musical Times* (June 1934).

67 *The Times* (28 May 1934).

68 F.T. [Francis Toye], *Morning Post* (28 May 1934).

69 Samuels, 'Discography', p.44.

70 Mosa Havivi interview with the author, November 1997, New York.

71 EF to Eva Reifenberg, 19 August 1934 [FA].

72 EF to Eva Reifenberg, 19 October 1934 [FA].

73 His repertoire included the d'Albert and Boccherini concertos, Tchaikovsky 'Rococo' Variations, Beethoven A major Sonata op.69, Schubert 'Arpeggione', Bach C major Suite, Reger's G major Suite, Richard Strauss Sonata op.6, Valentini E major Sonata and Bréval Sonata. Salon works: a Mozart Andante, Tartini Variations, Sgambati *Serenata Napoletana*, David Popper *Hungarian Rhapsody* and *Spinning Song*, Kreisler *Liebeslied*, Dvořák *Slavonic Dance* and Rondo, Mussorgsky *Gopak*, Bloch *Baal Shem*, Chopin Waltz, Lalo Intermezzo, Danbé Menuet, Granados *Danse espagnol*, Saint-Saëns *Allegro appassionato*, Piatti Tarantella and Sarasate *Zapateado*.

74 B. Goldschmidt, London 1995, preface to Cello Concerto. The sonata was subsequently lost. In the 1950s Goldschmidt reworked the memory of his sonata into a fully fledged concerto.

75 EF to Lily Hofmann, 14 September 1934 [DC-H].

76 Ibid.

77 EF to Gertrud Hindemith, 22 September 1934 [HI].

78 EF to Eva Reifenberg, 19 October 1934, from Kyoto, Japan [FA].

79 Sophie Feuermann interview with the author, May 1995, New York.

80 Otakuro Hiro, *Tokyo Asahi Shimbun* (6 October 1934).

81 Sophie Feuermann interview with the author, May 1995, New York.

82 *Japan Advertiser* [Tokyo] (20 October 1934).

83 Seiji Osawa interview with the author, August 1998, Tanglewood.

84 *Japan Advertiser*, [Tokyo] (20 October 1934).

85 EF to Eva Reifenberg, 19 October 1934. [FA].

86 *North China Star* (30 October 1934).

87 EF to Eva Reifenberg, 5 November 1934, from Kathy Hotel, Shanghai [FA].

88 Sophie Feuermann interview with the author, May 1995, New York.

89 EF to Lily Hofmann, 22 November 1934 [DC-H].

90 EF to Eva Reifenberg, 21 November 1934, from on board American mail line [FA].

91 Ibid.

CHAPTER 6: NORTH AMERICA AND EUROPE: NOVEMBER 1934 TO JUNE 1935

1 *Winnipeg Free Press* (4 December 1934).

2 Edward Moore, *Chicago Daily Tribune* (7 December 1934).

3 *Chicago Daily News* (12 December 1934).

4 EF to Eva Reifenberg, 19 December 1934 [FA].
5 EF to Eva Reifenberg, 21 December 1934, on the New Haven and Hartford Railroad [FA].
6 *Washington Herald* (28 December 1934).
7 Alice Eversman, *Washington Star* (28 December 1934).
8 Ray C.B. Brown, *Washington Post* (December 1934).
9 Newspaper, untitled, NBC Music Research Files, [NYp].
10 Patricia Coffin in an unnamed newspaper (25 September 1940), [NYp].
11 Patricia Coffin in an unnamed newspaper (21 October 1938) [NYp].
12 Unnamed newspaper [NYp].
13 Julian Seaman, *New York Daily Mirror* (26 December).
14 Francis D. Perkins, *New York Herald Tribune* (3 January 1935).
15 George Sopkin interview with the author, December 1997, Boston.
16 Pitts Sanborn, *New York World-Telegram*, (3 January 1935).
17 *New York Post* (3 January 1935.)
18 *New York Times* (3 January 1935).
19 Francis D. Perkins, *New York Herald Tribune* (3 January 1935).
20 *New York American* (3 January 1935).
21 EF to Eva Reifenberg, 4 January 1935 [FA].
22 EF to Eva Reifenberg, 7 January 1935 [FA].
23 EF to Eva Reifenberg, 9 January 1935 [FA].
24 J.D.B., *New York Herald Tribune* (14 January 1935).
25 Olin Downes, *New York Times* (14 January 1935).
26 Winthrop Sargeant, *Brooklyn Daily Eagle* (14 January 1935).
27 Samuel Chotzinoff, *New York Post* (14 January 1935).
28 Olin Downes, *New York Times* (14 January 1935).
29 Ibid.
30 Ibid.
31 *New York Post* (14 January 1935).
32 *Washington Times* (27 December 1934).
33 *Chicago News* (7 December 1934).
34 *Montreal Star* (13 December 1934).
35 EF to Eva Reifenberg, 15 January 1935 [FA].
36 EF to Eva Reifenberg, 7 January 1935 [FA].
37 EF to Sergey Koussevitzky, 3 February 1935, New York [FA].
38 N&A, p.5.
39 EF to Eva Reifenberg, 15 January 1935 [FA].
40 EF to Eva Reifenberg, 11 March 1935 [FA].
41 Ibid.
42 Eva Reifenberg to EF, 17 May 1933 [FA].
43 Feuermann uses 'Oma', the familiar German term for grandmother. Emma Reifenberg now had three grandchildren from her eldest son, Hans.
44 EF to Eva Reifenberg, 11 March 1935 [FA].
45 EF to Eva Reifenberg, 12 March 1935 [FA].
46 EF to Eva Reifenberg, 18 March 1935 [FA].
47 EF to Eva Reifenberg, 13 March 1935 [FA].
48 Postcard from EF to Herr Tischer, 1 September 1922 [Keith Harvey].
49 George Neikrug interview with the author, April 1994, Concord, Massachusetts.
50 EF to Eva Reifenberg, 14 March 1935 [FA].

51 EF to Eva Reifenberg, 18 March 1935 [FA].
52 *The Times* (19 March 1935).
53 A small provincial town of no cultural importance.
54 EF to Eva Reifenberg, 14 March 1935 [FA].
55 Ibid.
56 EF to Eva Reifenberg, 20 March 1935 [FA].
57 Eva Feuermann interview with the author, April 1994, Millbrook, New York.
58 Janos Starker interview with the author, April 1994, Manchester.
59 EF to Eva Reifenberg, 2 April 1935 [FA].
60 Ibid.
61 EF to Eva Reifenberg, 5 April 1935 [FA].
62 EF to Eva Reifenberg, 7 April 1935 [FA].
63 Ibid.
64 Eva Feuermann interview with the author, April 1994 Millbrook, New York.

CHAPTER 7: COMMITMENTS: JUNE 1935 TO APRIL 1936

1 EF to Lily Hofmann, 8 June 1935 [DC-H].
2 Ibid.
3 Elinor Lipper interview with the author, June 1996, Lugano.
4 Schnabel to EF, 11 June 1935 [FA].
5 EF to Eva Reifenberg, 19 June 1935 [FA].
6 Ibid.
7 EF to Eva Reifenberg, 23 June 1935 [FA].
8 Eleanor Saidenberg interview with the author, May 1995, New York.
9 EF to Eva Reifenberg, 26 June 1935 [FA].
10 Eva Reifenberg to EF, 27 June 1935 [FA].
11 EF to Eva Reifenberg, 29 June 1935 [FA].
12 EF to Eva Reifenberg, 28 July 1935 [FA].
13 EF to Eva Reifenberg, 3 August 1935 [FA].
14 EF to Eva Reifenberg, 21 August 1935, from St Gilgen [FA].
15 EF to Eva Reifenberg, 22 August 1935, from St Gilgen [FA].
16 EF to Eva Reifenberg, 5 August 1935 [FA].
17 *Wiener Tag* (8 October 1935).
18 *Joseph Haydn: Concerto for Violoncello and Orchestra 1783 Hob.VIIb:2*, ed. H.C. Robbins Landon (University College Cardiff Press, 1984).
19 Staatsbibliothek Preussischer Kulturbesitz, Berlin, Mus.ms.9980.H15.
20 EF to Harold Spivacke, 7 February 1940 [FA].
21 Klaus Burmeister, preface to 1995 edition (C.F. Peters, Frankfurt am Main).
22 Palmer to Straus, 7 October 1935 [EMI Music Archives, 4085].
23 H.R. Francis to Mr Duncan at the Columbia Graphophone Company, 3 July 1935 [EMI Music Archives, 29567].
24 Eva Feuermann interview with the author, April 1994, Millbrook, New York.
25 EF to Eva Reifenberg, 19 June 1935 [FA].
26 Paul Bonatz (1877–1956) from 1935 was consultant to the inspector-general of German Highway Construction, building Autobahn bridges (1935–41). Bonatz was responsible for the design of the main railway station in Munich (1939–42), the Naval High Command in Berlin (1939–43) and suspension bridges in Cologne and Hamburg

(1941). In August 1930 Feuermann had planned to travel with Mrs Reifenberg and Paul Bonatz to the south of France.

27 Eva Feuermann in conversation with the author, May 1998, Millbrook, New York.

28 EF to Huberman, 28 October 1935 [HA, 1575 SA5].

29 Gaisberg was responsible for artistic policy at Electric and Musical Industries Ltd. In view of the devastating effects of the Depression, the two rival British record companies, the Columbia Graphophone Company and the Gramophone Company, merged in 1931. Electric and Musical Industries (EMI) was the name of the holding company. Their respective principal labels, Columbia and HMV, continued to operate side by side but rivalries remained.

30 EF to Gaisberg, 28 October 1935 [FA].

31 Gaisberg to EF, 4 November 1935 [EMI Music Archies, 58872].

32 Palmer to EF, 11 November 1935 [EMI Music Archives, 58487].

33 See above, Chapter 5.

34 Interview with Julian Seaman, *Daily Mirror* [US] (26 December 1934).

35 *Wiener Tag* (8 October 1935).

36 See Casals to Schönberg, 15 March 1933, in Ennulat, *Schönberg Correspondence*, p.167.

37 See Casals to Schönberg, 1 October 1933, in Ennulat, *Schönberg Correspondence*, p.179.

38 J.M. Corredor, *Conversations avec Casals: souvenirs et opinions d'un musicien*, Paris, Albin Michel, 1955, p.170. .

39 See Schönberg to Feuermann, 23 February 1934, in Ennulat, *Schönberg Correspondence*, p.199.

40 Piatigorsky, *Cellist*, p.206.

41 See Schönberg to Feuermann, 23 February 1934, in Ennulat, *Schönberg Correspondence*, p.199.

42 Francis Toye, *Morning Post* (November 1935).

43 *Sunday Times* (10 November 1935).

44 EF to Eva Feuermann (née Reifenberg), 14 November 1935 [FA].

45 EF to Eva Feuermann, 17 November 1935 [FA].

46 EF to Lily Hofmann, 19 November 1935 [DC-H].

47 EF to Gaisberg, 14 November 1935, from London [EMI Music Archives].

48 International Artistes' Department, Columbia (Gaisberg?) to EF, 16 November 1935 [EMI Music Archives].

49 Bicknell to Miss Gibbs, 20 November 1935 [EMI Music Archives, 16744].

50 EF to Gaisberg, 22 November 1935, from London [EMI Music Archives].

51 Max Salpeter interview with the author, September 1999, London. Salpeter was joint leader with Manoug Parikian of the Philharmonia Orchestra for several years from 1941.

52 Sibelius Violin Concerto, Heifetz/Beecham and the London Symphony Orchestra November 1935. Discography compiled by Julian Futter and Artur Weschler-Vered, in Weschler-Vered, *Heifetz*, p.224.

53 Rex Palmer to EF, 13 December 1935 [EMI Music Archives].

54 EF to Palmer, 17 December 1935 [EMI Music Archives].

55 Hans A. Straus to Duncan, 21 January 1936 [EMI Music Archives, 15656].

56 Straus to Duncan, 3 July 1936 [EMI Music Archives, 75387].

57 Alfred Hill to EF, 9 December 1935 [FA].

58 Alfred Hill to EF, 15 February 1937 [FA].

59 Alfred Hill to EF, 9 December 1935 [FA].

60 *Variety* (18 December 1935).

61 Olin Downes, *New York Times* (27 December 1935).
62 Ibid.
63 EF to the Hindemiths, 5 July 1936 [HI].
64 EF to Eva Feuermann, 6 January 1936 [FA].
65 *St Louis Globe Democrat* (15 January 1936).
66 Unnamed and undated clipping [FA].
67 *New York Times* (20 January 1936).
68 *New York Post* (20 January 1936).
69 EF to Eva Feuermann, 11 January 1936 [FA].
70 Denoe Leedy, *Cleveland Press* (31 January 1936).
71 Cleveland Orchestra Archives.
72 'M.S.' in an unnamed and undated clipping [FA].
73 *New York Evening Post* (8 February 1936).
74 EF to the Hindemiths, 5 July 1936, [HI].
75 F.D.P., *New York Herald Tribune* (10 February 1936).
76 Samuels, 'Discography', p.61.
77 Programme book, General Motors Concert (9 February 1936).
78 H.T., *New York Times* (11 February 1936).
79 EF to Eva Feuermann, 18 February 1936 [FA].
80 EF to the Hindemiths, 5 July 1936 [HI].
81 Ibid.
82 Dorothy Crawford, *Evenings On and Off the Roof* (University of California Press, 1995). pp.4–5.
83 Isabel Morse Jones, *Los Angeles Times* (undated clipping).
84 Klemperer to Schnabel, 2 April 1936 [SE].
85 EF to the Hindemiths, 5 July 1936 [HI].
86 Here he used the Yiddish word '*Gintschler*' for 'artist'.
87 EF to Lily Hofmann, 17 April 1936 [DC-H].

CHAPTER 8: FULL SAIL: APRIL TO DECEMBER 1936

1 Motoo Ohtaguro in an unnamed newspaper clipping (*Asahi Shimbun*?). Review of 23 April 1936 concert.
2 Josephine Arland in the *Japan Advertiser* (19 April 1936).
3 Repertoire for the recitals: Handel Adagio and Allegro, Locatelli Sonata, Brahms F major Sonata, Beethoven 'Bei Männern' Variations, Bach G minor Viola da Gamba Sonata, Stravinsky *Suite Italienne*, Beethoven G minor Sonata, Schubert 'Arpeggione', and Falla *Suite Populaire espagnol*. Each concert ended with a selection of occasional works: Bloch Prayer, Saint-Saëns *Allegro appassionato*, Debussy Menuet, Schumann *Mit Humor*, Mozart Andante and Rondo, Tartini-Feuermann Variations, Nardini Andante, Fauré *Fileuse*, Klengel Scherzo, Brahms *Hungarian Dance* and Mussorgsky *Gopak*.
4 In his two orchestral concerts he played Haydn, Saint-Saëns, Boccherini, Tchaikovsky 'Rococo' Variations and Glazunov's *Chant du Ménéstrel*, plus salon works (presumably with piano accompaniment, though no pianist's name is given): Bach's Adagio, Tchaikovsky's *Valse sentimentale*, Sarasate–Feuermann *Zapateado* and *Zigeunerweisen*.
5 Feuermann is probably referring to the New Symphony Orchestra.
6 Probably the Chûô Orchestra.

7   EF to the Hindemiths, 5 July 1936 [HI].

8   Motoo Ohtaguro in an unnamed newspaper clipping (*Asahi Shimbun?*). Review of recital on 23 April 1936.

9   Article received by the author from Sumio Okahashi.

10 EF to the Hindemiths, 5 July 1936 [HI].

11 Cable from Kawasaki to Colgraph with date stamps 1 May 1934 and 14 May 1936 [EMI Music Archives, 68258].

12 Cable to Nippolona from Columbia, London, 14 May 1936. [EMI Music Archives, 68827].

13 H.A. Straus, Nipponophone, to F.B. Duncan, Columbia, London, 9 June 1936, in English [EMI Music Archives, 78593].

14 General letter from the export department, Columbia Graphophone Company Ltd., 11 June 1936 [EMI Music Archives 75724, 75667, 75797, 75639, 75622].

15 Columbia Graphophone Company export department to Columbia Phonograph Co. Inc., 10 June 1936 [EMI Music Archives, 73960].

16 H.A.Straus, Nipponophone, to F.B. Duncan, Columbia, London, 9 June 1936, in English [EMI Music Archives, 78593].

17 Columbia accounts department to Passadoro, Milan, 25 June 1936 [EMI Music Archives, 82537].

18 International Artistes' Department, Columbia to EF, 16 November 1935 [EMI Music Archives].

19 H.A. Straus to F.B. Duncan, 9 June 1936, in English [EMI Music Archives, 78593].

20 Information received by the author from C. Nozawa, June 1996.

21 EF to the Hindemiths, 5 July 1936 [HI].

22 EF to Huberman, 4 July 1936 [HA, 1576 SA5].

23 See Itzkoff, *Biography* p.205.

24 EF to Huberman, 4 July 1936 [HA, 1576 SA5].

25 H.A. Straus to Duncan at Columbia, 11 September 1936 [EMI Music Archives, 78592].

26 Columbia to Straus, 15 September 1936 [EMI Music Archives, 98856].

27 Sophie Feuermann interview with the author, 7 May 1995, New York.

28 EF to Schnabel, 12 August 1936 [Schnabel Archive, Akademie der Künste, Berlin].

29 EF to Lily Hofmann, 30 September 1936 [DC-H].

30 EF to Eva Feuermann, 26 October 1936 [FA].

31 EF to Eva Feuermann, 27 October 1936 [FA].

32 EF to Eva Feuermann, 28 October 1936 [FA].

33 Feuermann frequently addressed his wife, Eva, as 'Oeff' (stove) or 'Oefchen' (little stove).

34 EF to Eva Feuermann, 30 October 1936. [FA].

35 EF to Eva Feuermann, 31 October 1936 [FA].

36 Ibid.

37 Daughter of the pianist Leopold Godowsky and a close friend of Feuermann.

38 EF to Eva Feuermann, 31 October 1936 [FA].

39 *Evening Citizen* [Ottawa, Ontario] (Saturday 7 November 1936).

40 Fernando Sacconi (born in Rome in 1895) went in 1931 to work for the instrument dealer Emil Herrmann at 130 West 57th Street in New York. In the field of repair and restoration of string instruments, he had no equal. In 1941, after Herrmann retired, Sacconi (with his pupil D'Attili) went to work for Rembert Wurlitzer.

41 Mosa Havivi interview with the author, April 1994, New York.

42 EF to Eva Feuermann, 13 November 1936 [FA].

43 Ibid.
44 Ibid.
45 Hirschmann interview with Jon Samuels, 1978, New York.
46 'Re-Statement of Aims' by Ira Hirschmann [NYp].
47 Kux to EF, from Sudbahn Hotel, Semmering, 1936 [FA].
48 Huberman to EF, 18 October 1936 [HA, 1577 SA5].
49 Here Feuermann is vague; he could be referring to the Jews or the trio.
50 'Das Licht dieser Welt erblicken' is a phrase about being born, but EF adds the poignant word 'dunkel' (darkness) in view of the times.
51 EF to Huberman, 16 November 1936 [FA].
52 EF to Eva Feuermann, 18 November 1936 [FA].
53 EF to Eva Feuermann, 20 November 1936. [FA].
54 Ibid.
55 EF to Eva Feuermann, 23 November 1936 [FA].
56 Elinor Lipper interview with the author, June 1996, Lugano.
57 EF to Eva Feuermann, 27 November 1936 [FA].
58 George Szell interview with Monica Feuermann, 1967.
59 EF to Eva Feuermann, 30 November 1936 [FA].
60 The two horn players in the Beethoven Sextet were Domenico Caputo and John Barrows.
61 EF to Eva Feuermann, 30 November 1936 [FA].
62 EF to Eva Feuermann, 3 December 1936 [FA].
63 A topical quip alluding to the King Edward and Mrs Simpson scandal.
64 EF to Lily Hofmann, 9 December 1936 [DC-H].
65 Gama Gilbert, *New York Evening Post* (12 December 1936).
66 At his Carnegie recital debut, as well as Hindemith and Chopin, Feuermann played Beethoven Variations in E♭ and Sonata op.102 no.1, Schubert's 'Arpeggione' and salon pieces: Fauré *Après un Rêve*, Brahms *Hungarian Dance* and Sarasate *Zapateado*.
67 Telegram sent to Feuermann, Alteburgerstr. 376, Cologne. Received 12 December 1936 [FA].
68 *New York Times* (12 December 1936).

CHAPTER 9: EUROPE: 1937

1 Letter of Contract between Columbia and EF, 17 February 1937 [FA].
2 Gerald Moore interview with Monica Feuermann, 1967.
3 Ibid.
4 *Observer* (14 February 1937).
5 EF to Eva Feuermann, 14 February 1937 [FA].
6 EF to Eva Feuermann, 12 February 1937 [FA].
7 Humphrey Procter-Gregg, *Beecham Remembered*, London, Duckworth, 1976, p.98.
8 EF to Eva Feuermann, 12 February 1937 [FA].
9 EF to Eva Feuermann, 14 February 1937 [FA].
10 Ibid.
11 EF to Eva Feuermanan, 7 February 1937 [FA].
12 Eva Feuermann interview with the author, 12 April 1994, Millbrook, New York.
13 EF to 'My dear women', 26 February 1937 [FA].
14 Straus to Duncan at Columbia, 22 December 1936 [EMI Music Archives, 33776].

15 Rex Palmer to EF, 11 February 1937 [EMI Music Archives, 9866].
16 EF to Palmer. 15 February 1937 [EMI Music Archives, 11123].
17 H.A. Straus to Duncan, 16 March 1937 [EMI Music Archives, 78590].
18 EF to Palmer, 21 April 1937, [EMI Music Archives, 9081].
19 Ibid.
20 Palmer to EF, 26 April 1937 [EMI Music Archives].
21 EF to Palmer, 5 May 1937, [EMI Music Archives, 81282].
22 Palmer to EF, 7 May 1937 [EMI Music Archives, 53971].
23 H.A. Straus to F.B. Duncan, 16 March 1937 [EMI Music Archives, 78590].
24 EF to Palmer, 22 July 1937 [EMI Music Archives, 12520].
25 Palmer to H.A. Straus, 14 September 1937 [EMI Music Archives, 89973].
26 Straus to Duncan, 7 October 1937 [EMI Music Archives, 37516].
27 Palmer to Straus, 14 September 1937 [EMI Music Archives, 89973].
28 Straus to Duncan, 7 October 1937 [EMI Music Archives, 37516].
29 N&A, p.5.
30 Eva Feuermann interview with the author, April 1994, Millbrook, New York.
31 See Hans Mayer, *Gelebte Musik Erinnerungen*, Frankfurt am Main, Suhrkamp Verlag, 1999, p.65.
32 Bernard Richards interview with the author, May 1994, London.
33 Kramer and Kolscher to EF, 3 August 1937 [FA].
34 EF to H. Simon, 6 September 1937 [IPO].
35 Palmer to Herrn Rona, Österreichische Columbia Graphophon Agentur, 10 September 1937 [EMI Music Archives, 88621].
36 EF to Eva Feuermann, 13 October 1937 [FA].
37 Heinrich Funk was appointed organist of the Zürich Minster in 1943.
38 EF to Eva Feuermann, 24 November 1937 [FA].
39 EF to Eva Feuermann, 1 December 1937 [FA].
40 EF to Eva Feuermann, 6 December 1937 [FA].
41 EF to Lilli Lucas (née Reifenberg), 4 December 1937 [N].
42 EF to Eva Feuermann, 6 December 1937 [FA].
43 EF to Eva Feuermann, 3 December 1937 [FA].
44 Eva Feuermann to EF, 14 December 1937 [FA].
45 EF to Eva Feuermann, 16 December 1937 [FA].
46 Sophie Feuermann and Katya Aschaffenburg in conversation with the author, September 2001, New York.
47 Nickname for the unborn child.
48 EF to Eva Feuermann, evening of 16 December 1937 [FA].
49 EF to Eva Feuermann, 17 December 1937 [FA].
50 EF to Eva Feuermann, evening of 16 December 1937 [FA].
51 EF to Eva Feuermann, 17 December 1937 [FA].
52 Eva Feuermann to EF, 17 December 1937 [FA].
53 EF to Eva Feuermann, 20 December 1937 [FA].
54 Ibid.

CHAPTER 10: MOMENTOUS YEAR: 1938

1 EF to Eva Feuermann, 11 January 1938 [FA].
2 EF to Eva Feuermann, 12 January 1938 [FA].

3   EF to Eva Feuermann, 16 January 1938 [FA].
4   EF to Eva Feuermann, 13 January 1938 [FA].
5   Here he used the word 'pover', Yiddish for 'poor' or 'paltry'.
6   EF to Eva Feuermann, 21 January 1938 [FA].
7   EF to Eva Feuermann, 22 January 1938 [FA].
8   EF to Eva Feuermann, 25 January 1938 [FA].
9   EF to Eva Feuermann, 22 January 1938 [FA].
10 Mosa Havivi interview with the author, April 1994, New York.
11 EF to Eva Feuermann, 22 January 1938 [FA].
12 EF to Eva Feuermann, 25 January 1938 [FA].
13 Ibid.
14 Mary Kurtz, sister of Efrem and Edmund, wife of Julius Rosenwald, an early partner with Sears Roebuck.
15 EF to Eva Feuermann, 22 January 1938 [FA].
16 EF to Eva Feuermann, 5 February 1938 [FA].
17 EF to Eva Feuermann, 25 January 1938 [FA].
18 Käthe is Katya Aschaffenburg, Meta her cousin. EF to Eva Feuermann, 27 January 1938 [FA].
19 Sophie Feuermann interview with the author, May 1995, New York.
20 Eva Feuermann interview with the author, November 1997, Millbrook, New York.
21 David Soyer interview with the author, April 1994, New York.
22 EF to Eva Feuermann, 5 February 1938 [FA].
23 EF to Eva Feuermann, 1 February 1938 [FA].
24 Ibid.
25 EF to Eva Feuermann, 22 January 1938 [FA].
26 NOA publicity material [NOA Archive].
27 Mstislav Rostropovich gave nine concerts in London with the London Symphony Orchestra in 1965.
28 NOA publicity material [NOA Archive].
29 G.G., *Sunday New York Times* (6 February 1938).
30 EF to Eva Feuermann, 8 February 1938 [FA].
31 EF to Eva Feuermann, 1 February 1938 [FA].
32 The four members of the Budapest String Quartet shared between $200 and $300 per concert at this time.
33 *New York Sun* (21 February 1938).
34 EF to Eva Feuermann, 20/21 February 1938 [FA].
35 Ibid.
36 Ibid.
37 Ibid.
38 EF to Eva Feuermann, 27 February – 1 March 1938 [FA].
39 EF to Eva Feuermann, 20/21 February 1938 [FA].
40 EF to Eva Feuermann, 27 February – 1 March 1938 [FA].
41 *New York Times,* (21 February 1938).
42 EF to Eva Feuermann, 20/21 February 1938 [FA].
43 Ibid.
44 EF to Eva Feuermann, 27 February – 1 March 1938 [FA].
45 EF to Eva Feuermann, 7 March 1938 [FA].
46 *Philadelphia, P.A. Record* (1 March 1942).
47 Al Blume was a family friend and lawyer.

48 EF to Eva Feuermann, 7 March 1938 [FA].
49 EF to Eva Feuermann, 15 March 1938 [FA].
50 Feuermann's own censoring.
51 EF to Mrs Reifenberg, 15 March 1938 [FA].
52 EF to Eva Feuermann, 15 March 1938 [FA].
53 EF to Sashinska, 13 March 1938 [FA].
54 EF to Eva Feuermann, 15 March 1938 [FA].
55 EF to Mrs Reifenberg, 15 March 1938 [FA].
56 Ibid.
57 EF to Eva Feuermann, 19 March 1938 [FA].
58 EF to Mrs Reifenberg, 15 March 1938 [FA].
59 Sophie Feuermann interview with the author, April 1994, New York.
60 EF to Eva Feuermann, 1 April 1938 [FA].
61 From 1936, Casals had stopped performing in countries that recognized General Franco.
62 EF to Eva Feuermann, 19 March 1938 [FA].
63 George Neikrug interview with the author, April 1994, Concord, Massachusetts.
64 The concert was broadcast but no trace remains.
65 EF to Eva Feuermann, 1 April 1938 [FA].
66 Mosa Havivi interview with the author, April 1994. New York.
67 EF to Eva Feuermann, 1 April 1938 [FA].
68 *Time* magazine (4 April 1938).
69 EF to Eva Feuermann, 1 April 1938 [FA].
70 EF to Eva Feuermann, 22 March 1938 [FA].
71 Signed Marks Levine, NBC Artists, 25 March 1938 [FA].
72 EF to Eva Feuermann, 22 March 1938 [FA].
73 The eminent soprano Ria Ginster.
74 EF to Eva Feuermann, 1 April 1938 [FA].
75 EF to Lilli Reifenberg, 15 April 1938 [N].
76 Rex Palmer, Columbia, to EF, 14 April 1938 [EMI Music Archives, 55007].
77 EF to Rex Palmer, 17 April 1938 [EMI Music Archives, 79307].
78 'Emanuel Feuermann', an appreciation presented on the radio with gramophone records, by Gerald Moore, *Home Programme*, Tuesday 2 June 1942 [FA].
79 Reid Stewart, *The Strad* (July 1938).
80 Eva Feuermann interview with the author, April 1994, Millbrook, New York.
81 Mosa Havivi interview with the author, April 1994, New York.
82 Sophie Feuermann interview with the author, May 1995, New York.
83 AT to Ada Mainardi, 24 May 1938. See Harvey Sachs, *The Letters of Arturo Toscanini*. London, Faber and Faber, 2002, p. 333.
84 EF to Heinrich Simon, 29 June 1938 [IPO].
85 EF to Huberman, 25 July 1938 [HA, 1580 SA5].
86 EF to Huberman, 3 August 1938 [HA, 1581 SA5].
87 Ibid.
88 Harvey Sachs, *Toscanini*, Weidenfeld & Nicholson, 1978, p.268.
89 Itzkoff, *Biography*, p.140.
90 Sophie Feuermann interview with the author, May 1995, New York.
91 EF to Eva Feuermann, 1 September 1938 [FA].
92 *The Times* (4 September 1938).
93 EF to Eva Feuermann, 1 September 1938 [FA].
94 *The Strad* (October 1938).

CHAPTER 11: BREAKS: OCTOBER 1938 TO FEBRUARY 1939

1   *New York Post* (21 October 1938).
2   Eva Feuermann to EF, 30 August 1938 [FA].
3   Eva Feuermann interview with the author, April 1994, Millbrook, New York.
4   Eva Feuermann to EF, 30 August 1938 [FA].
5   Eva Feuermann to EF, 1 September 1938 [FA].
6   Carl Flesch, son of the violinist.
7   EF to Eva Feuermann, 2 September 1938 [FA].
8   EF to Schnabel, 22 August 1938 [SE].
9   EF to Schnabel, 14 September 1938 [SE].
10 EF to Schnabel, 22 August 1938 [SE].
11 EF to Schnabel, 14 September 1938 [SE].
12 Ibid.
13 EF to Schnabel, 27 September 1938 [SE].
14 *New York Herald Tribune* (19 October 1938).
15 *New York Evening Post* (24 October 1938).
16 *New York Post* (21 October 1938).
17 *Brooklyn Eagle* (Sunday 6 November 1938).
18 *Cincinnati Enquirer* (14 January 1940).
19 Eva Feuermann to EF, 17 December 1938 [FA].
20 Eva Feuermann to EF, 9 November 1938 [FA].
21 EF to Eva Feuermann, 9 November 1938 [FA].
22 EF to Eva Feuermann, 10 November 1938 [FA].
23 Franz Rupp, sleeve note to 'The 1939 Victor recordings of Feuermann', LAB 048 1991.
24 Samuels, 'Discography', p.66.
25 *Philadelphia Bulletin* [evening] (26 November 1938).
26 Samuel L. Laciar, *Evening Public Ledger* (26 November 1938).
27 *Cue Magazine* (26 November 1938).
28 *New York Sun* (29 November 1938).
29 J.D.B., *New York Herald Tribune* (29 November 1938).
30 H.T., *New York Times* (29 November 1938).
31 *New York Times* (30 November 1938).
32 Emma Reifenberg to EF, 10 December 1938 [FA].
33 EF to Eva Feuermann, 19 December 1938 [FA].
34 Sophie Feuermann interview with the author, April 1994, New York.
35 Serkin to his children, 22 December 1938, quoted in Adolf Busch, *Letters-Pictures-Memories*, Walpole, NH, Arts & Letters Press, 1991, vol. 2, p.388.
36 Although attributed to Handel, the composition is thought to be by Siegfried Ochs (1858–1929), who published it as an 'arioso' from a cantata.
37 H.A. Straus to Rex Palmer, 24 December 1938 [EMI Music Archives].
38 EF to Rex Palmer, 1 January 1939 [EMI Music Archives].
39 Rex Palmer to EF, 1 February 1939 [EMI Music Archives].
40 Rex Palmer to H.A. Straus, 13 February 1939 [EMI Music Archives, 17840].
41 Unnamed paper dated 1 December 1938, NBC Music Research Files [NYp].
42 EF to Eva Feuermann, 18 January 1939 [FA].
43 Eva Feuermann to EF, 11 January 1938 [FA].

44 EF to Eva Feuermann, 18 January 1939 [FA].
45 Ibid.
46 Schönberg to EF, 19 December 1938. See Ennulat, *Schönberg Correspondence*, p.203.
47 EF to Schönberg, 1 January 1939. See Ennulat, *Schönberg Correspondence*, p.205.
48 Mrs Reifenberg to EF, 10 January 1939 [FA].
49 Mrs Reifenberg to EF, 1 January 1939 [FA].
50 Artur Schnabel, *My Life and Music*, New York, St Martins Press, 1963, p.93.
51 Douglas Cameron to Keith Harvey.
52 *Sunday Times* (12 February 1939).
53 Eva Feuermann to EF, 10 February 1939 [FA].
54 Eva Feuermann to EF, 16 February 1939 [FA].
55 *Liverpool Daily Post* (22 February 1939).
56 *Manchester Guardian* (24 February 1939).

CHAPTER 12: *TRIOS: MARCH TO NOVEMBER 1939*

1 EF to Schnabel, 14 July 1938 [SE].
2 Ibid.
3 EF to Rex Palmer, 10 March 1939 [EMI Music Archives, 29858].
4 Huberman to EF, 17 March 1939 [HA, 1584 SA5].
5 EF to Huberman, 18 March 1939 [HA, 1585 SA5].
6 EF to Huberman, 16 March 1939 [HA, 1583 SA5].
7 EF to Huberman, 18 March 1939 [HA, 1585 SA5].
8 EF to Huberman, 19 March 1939 [HA, 1586 SA5].
9 Huberman to EF, 5 April 1939 [HA, 1588 SA5].
10 EF to Kestenberg, 17 March 1939 [IPO].
11 Ibid.
12 EF to Huberman, 3 April 1939 [HA, 1587 SA5].
13 Huberman to EF, 5 April 1939 [HA, 1588 SA5].
14 EF to Kestenberg, 12 April 1939 [IPO].
15 EF to Huberman, 12 April 1939 [HA, 1590 SA5].
16 EF to Hulda Lashanska, 26 April 1939 [FA].
17 Paul Schiff to EF, 30 May 1939 [FA].
18 Paul Schiff, OAI, to EF, 7 June 1939 [FA].
19 F. Horwitz, OAI, to EF, 7 July 1939 [FA].
20 Paul Schiff, OAI, to EF, 30 May 1939 [FA].
21 F. Horwitz, OAI, to EF, 22 July 1939 [FA].
22 EF to Miss Bass, 22 July 1939 [Ibbs and Tillett Archive].
23 EF to 'Herr Doktor' (possibly Felix Kuhner of the Kolisch Quartet), 20 August 1939 [FA].
24 *New York Sun* (21 June 1939).
25 15, 16 July 1939, playing Dvořák and Haydn.
26 *New York Times* (3 August 1939).
27 Samuels, 'Discography', p.67. Samuels records Saidenberg's doubts about the exact *Kraft* programme in which these two works were played.
28 EF to Miss Bass (Emmie Tillett), 15 August 1939 [Ibbs and Tillett Archive].
29 W.L. Streeton, BBC, to EF, c/o Ibbs and Tillett, 13 September 1939. [FA].
30 International Artists Department, the Gramophone Co., to Charles O'Connell,

15 October 1939 [EMI Music Archives, 66875].

31 *Dallas Texas News* (11 October 1939).

32 Michel Mok, *New York Post* (26 October 1939).

33 *Brooklyn Eagle* (5 November 1939), and *New York World-Telegram, N.Y.* (28 October 1939).

34 Edward Downes, *Boston Evening Transcript* (4 November 1939).

35 Oscar Thompson, *New York Sun* (9 November 1939).

36 *The Standard-Star* [New Rochelle, NY] (16 November 1939).

37 *Cleveland Press* (17 November 1939).

38 EF to Hulda Lashanska, 17 November 1939 [FA].

39 Ibid.

40 EF to Lily Hofmann, 17 November 1939 [DC-H].

41 Ibid.

42 Sophie Feuermann interview with the author, April 1994, New York.

43 EF to Lilli Reifenberg, 2 June 1926 [N].

44 Sigmund Feuermann to Mahler-Kalistein, 18 June 1949 [IPO].

45 Emil Hauser to Heinrich Simon, 17 July 1938 [IPO].

46 EF to Mrs Reifenberg, 18–19 April 1940, from Scarsdale [FA].

47 Erez Israel Orchestra to Sigmund Feuermann, 25 August 1946 [IPO].

48 Sigmund Feuermann to Mahler-Kalistein, 18 June 1949 [IPO].

49 Erna Catak to 'Sir', 20 June 1950 [IPO].

CHAPTER 13: CELLIST AT LARGE: NOVEMBER 1939 TO FEBRUARY 1941

1 Howard Taubman, *New York Times* (23 November 1939).

2 Howard Taubman, *New York Times* (23 November 1939).

3 Gama Gilbert, *New York Times* (18 December 1939).

4 EF to Eva Feuermann, 20/21 February 1938 [FA].

5 Gaisberg to Rubinstein, 24 September 1935. See Harvey Sachs, *Arthur Rubinstein. A Life*, New York, Grove Press, 1995, p.275.

6 Katya Aschaffenburg interview with the author, April 1994, New York.

7 N&A, p.4.

8 *New York Sun*, 10 October 1941.

9 See Weschler-Vered, *Heifetz*, p.89.

10 Ibid., p.91.

11 Laurence Tibbett (1896–1960), baritone, was a matinée idol and popular on film. He made his debut at the Metropolitan in 1923.

12 Walfredo Toscanini to the author, November 1997.

13 *Jackonsville Courier* (10 January 1940).

14 *Cincinnati Times-Star* (12 January 1940). Howard Hess notes that in this programme Beethoven op.70 no.2 was substituted for the announced 'Ghost' Trio.

15 Busch, *Letters*, vol. 2. p.398.

16 Wrongly described in the press – *New York Herald Tribune*, *New York Sun*, etc. – as the Fleischmann Collection.

17 *New York Times* (21 January 1940).

18 G.G., *New York Times* (28 January 1940).

19 *Musical America* (1940), 27 January 1940.

20 Leon Barzin interview with the author, June 1994, Paris.
21 Samuels, 'Discography', p.51.
22 Henry Pleasants, *Philadelphia Evening Bulletin* (22 March 1940).
23 Samuels, 'Discography', p.70.
24 *New York Times* (21 January 1940).
25 Feuermann to Spivacke, 5 March 1940, [FA].
26 EF to Mrs Reifenberg, 9 April 1940 [FA].
27 EF to Mrs Reifenberg, 13 April 1940 [FA].
28 EF to Eva Feuermann, 3 December 1937 [FA].
29 EF to Mrs Reifenberg, 18/19 April 1940 [FA].
30 *New York Times* (23 April 1940).
31 EF to Toch, 21 March 1941 [ET].
32 Hindemith to Gertrud, 28 July 1940. See Paul Hindemith, *Das private Logbuch, 'Briefe an seine Frau Gertrud'.* Serie Musik Piper-Schott. Band 8355, Schott, Mainz, *c.* 1995, p.475.
33 It is not clear which 'Walter' this is. It seems likely that it should be Bruno Walter if he was attempting to get Huberman a position, but it is odd that Feuermann later in the same letter refers to 'Bruno Walter'. Eva Feuermann had a cousin called Walter Albersheim.
34 Bruno Walter's daughter who committed suicide.
35 EF to Kux, 24 July 1940 [FA].
36 EF to Mrs Reifenberg, 18/19 April 1940 [FA].
37 EF to Kux, 24 July 1940 [FA].
38 Ibid.
39 Ibid.
40 A proverb: people who are close, quarrel.
41 Kux to EF, 16 September 1940 [FA].
42 Aria from Verdi's *Rigoletto*.
43 Radio programme called *Kraft Music Hall*, Hollywood, 22 August 1940 [FA].
44 Coolidge to Adolf Busch, 28 September 1940. See Busch, *Letters*, vol. 2, p.411.
45 Coolidge to Adolf Busch, 6 October 1940. See Busch, *Letters*, vol. 2, p.412.
46 *New York Times* (20 November 1940).
47 Ross Parmenter in the *New York Times* (23 December 1940).
48 In the possession of Bertelsmann Music Group.
49 Ross Parmenter in the *New York City Paper* [FA].
50 Mildred Hirsch in conversation with the author, April 1998.
51 Albert Hirsch in conversation with the author, April 1998.
52 Mildred Hirsch in conversation with the author, April 1998.
53 Albert Hirsch in conversation with the author, April 1998.
54 Suzette Forgues interview with the author, April 1994, Long Island. .
55 Noel Strauss, *New York Times* (17 February 1941).
56 F.D.P., *New York Herald Tribune* (17 February 1941).

CHAPTER 14: DIFFICULT TIMES: FEBRUARY 1941 TO 10 MAY 1942

1 Quoted by Cecil Betron, *Michigan News* [Detroit] (10 December 1941).
2 *Dartmouth* (26 February 1941).
3 Doris Reno in the *Miami Herald*, 6 April 1941.
4 Suzette Forgues interview with the author, April 1994, Long Island.

5 *Herald-American* [Syracuse, NY] (5 October 1941).

6 Ernst Toch to Eva Feuermann, 5 April 1941 [ET].

7 EF to Lily Hofmann, 2 June 1941 [DC-H].

8 EF to Kux, 31 December 1941 [FA].

9 Claus Adam interview with Monica Feuermann, 1966 [FA].

10 Artur Rubinstein interview with Monica Feuermann, 1966 [FA].

11 Daniel Saidenberg interview with Monica Feuermann, 1966 [FA].

12 EF to Kux, 31 December 1941 [FA].

13 Weschler-Vered, *Heifetz*, p.110.

14 Artur Rubinstein interview with Monica Feuermann, February 1966 [FA] .

15 Charles O'Connell, *The Other Side of the Record*, New York, 1947, p.247–8.

16 EF to Kux, 31 December 1941 [FA].

17 O'Connell, *Other Side of the Record*, pp.212–13 .

18 EF to Rubinstein, 24 October 1941 [Harvey Sachs].

19 EF to Rubinstein, 18 November 1941 [Harvey Sachs].

20 EF to Rubinstein, 24 November 1941 [Harvey Sachs].

21 Sachs, *Rubinstein*, p.277.

22 EF to Rubinstein, 15 December 1941 [Harvey Sachs].

23 Jon Samuels ('Discography') suggests that the soundtrack was made in the summer of 1939 in Hollywood but Feuermann indicates in letters that most of that summer, a particularly hectic period, was spent in New York. .

24 According to a Maryland newspaper, it was shown in January 1942 as a benefit for the Red Cross (*Hagerstown Herald*, 8 January 1942). Samuels ('Discography') suggests that the film was originally made for Music Appreciation in High Schools and Colleges and that there were other sections with Vronsky and Babin and the Coolidge Quartet. The producers, in order to recoup their investment, combined the sections to produce a feature film called *Adventure in Music*, which received its premiere in New York at the Little Carnegie around 1943–4.

25 EF to Kux, 31 December 1941 [FA].

26 EF to Lily Hofmann, 2 June 1941 [DC-H].

27 *Musical America* (25 March 1942).

28 Marion Davies telephone interview with the author, March 1998.

29 Eva Feuermann interview with the author, April 1994, Millbrook, New York.

30 Suzette Forgues interview with the author, April 1994, Long Island.

31 Marion Davies telephone interview with the author, March 1998.

32 EF to Lily Hofmann, 2 June 1941 [DC-H].

33 EF to Kux, 31 December 1941 [FA].

34 *New York Times* (25 January 1942).

35 EF to Ernst Toch, 21 March 1941 [ET].

36 Ernst Toch to EF, 6 October 1941 [ET].

37 EF to Ernst Toch, 26 October 1941 [ET].

38 EF to Ernst Toch, 14 December 1941 [ET].

39 Ira Hirschmann interview with Jon Samuels, New York, 1978.

40 EF to Ernst Toch, 14 December 1941 [ET].

41 Ernst Toch to EF, 3 January 1942 [ET].

42 *New York Herald Tribune* (12 November 1941).

43 Suzette Forgues interview with the author, April 1994, Long Island.

44 Thomas Archer, *Montreal Gazette* (3 December 1941).

45 Unattributed newspaper review.

46 EF to Eva Feuermann, 6 December 1941 [FA].
47 Ibid.
48 EF to Kux, 31 December 1941 [FA].
49 Katya Aschaffenburg interview with the author, April 1994, New York.
50 Ibid.
51 Cecil Betron, *Michigan News* [Detroit] (10 December 1941).
52 *New York Times* (23 December 1941).
53 *New York Herald Tribune* (23 December 1941).
54 *New York Times* (21 December 1941).
55 *New York Herald Tribune* (23 December 1941).
56 In January 1942, on the occasion of the New York Philharmonic-Symphony Orchestra's centennial celebrations, Koussevitzky had been granted permission to conduct by the American Federation of Musicians. He also withdrew from this engagement.
57 EF to Kux, 31 December 1941 [FA].
58 George Shuster to EF, 31 December 1941 [FA].
59 Samuels, 'Discography', p.74.
60 *Sunday New York Times* (28 December 1941).
61 Philip Klein, *Philadelphia News* (7 March 1942).
62 Information from Jon Samuels.
63 Phone interview with Albert Hirsch, 10 April 1998.
64 *Jewish Express* [Philadelphia] (3 April 1942).
65 *Etude Music Magazine* (October 1942). Feuermann in conversation with Rose Helbut.
66 C.R.T.C. News-Notes Junction City March 1942.
67 *Savannah Evening Press* (11 April 1942).
68 *Chicago Sun* (4 April 1942).
69 *New York Post* (7 April 1942).
70 Charles Gentry, *Detroit Times* (8 May 1942).
71 Russell McLauchlin, *Detroit News* (8 May 1942).
72 Samuels, 'Discography', p.75.

CHAPTER 15: AN UNTIMELY END

1   As recalled by Rubinstein in an interview with Monica Feuermann, February 1966.
2   Unattributed cutting (26 May 1942) [FA]. Senate Bill 358 Session of 1939 of the General Assembly of Pennsylvania designated the first Sunday in October as 'I am an American Day' to recognize publicly those who by birth or naturalization had become citizens of the United States of America.
3   *New York Journal-American* obituary, May 1942.
4   Unattributed cutting (26 May 1942) [FA]
5   *New York Journal-American* obituary, May 1942.
6   Eva Feuermann to EF, 2 May 1942 [FA].
7   Rubinstein interview with Monica Feuermann, February 1966.
8   Albert Hirsch interview with the author, April 1998. No contract has been found.
9   'Physician's Confidential Medical Report', Municipal Archives, Department of Records and Information Services, City of New York.
10 *Medical Directory of New York, New Jersey and Connecticut* (1941–2).
11 Suzette Forgues interview with the author, April 1994, Long Island.

12 Municipal Archives, Department of Records and Information Services, City of New York.
13 Meta Cordy interview with the author, April 1994, New York.
14 Berberich made a rough pencil sketch of the abdomen [Feuermann's file. Library of Congress].
15 Elinor Lipper interview with the author, June 1996, Lugano.
16 Sophie Feuermann interview with the author, May 1995, New York.
17 George Neikrug interview with the author, April 1994, Concord, Massachusetts.
18 Editorial, *New York Times* (27 May 1942).
19 Unattributed, *New York Herald Tribune* (29 May 1942).
20 O'Connell, *Other Side of the Record*, pp.212–13.
21 Sachs, *Rubinstein*, p. 278. Weschler-Vered omits mention of the 1949 Ravinia concerts when referring to Heifetz not performing with another cellist for nine years. See Weschler-Vered, *Heifetz*, p.111.
22 Suzette Forgues interview with the author, April 1994, Long Island.

CHAPTER 16: *MIRACLE WORKER: WRITING, TEACHING, PERFORMING*

1 NBC publicity material, 1940/1 season. In English.
2 There are no letters from Feuermann in the archives of Bruno Walter, Thomas Beecham, Toscanini, Stokowski, Ormandy, Heifetz or Szymon Goldberg.
3 Musikabteilung mit Mendelssohn-Archiv, Staatsbibliothek Preussischer Kulturbesitz, Berlin.
4 These writings are included in translation by Seymour Itzkoff in his 1979 *Biography*.
5 EF to Lily Hofmann, 2 June 1941 [DC-H].
6 EF's Manuscript: Section C, p.8.
7 Itzkoff, *Biography*, Appendix, 1. p.215.
8 Feuermann in NBC's publicity material for the 1940/1 season.
9 *Musical America* (25 February 1940).
10 EF's MS, '*My dear friend*', p.3.
11 EF's MS, Section A, p.3.
12 EF's MS, Section A, pp.3–4.
13 EF's MS, Section A, pp.4–5.
14 EF's MS, '*My dear friend*', pp 4–5.
15 EF's MS, '*My dear friend*', p.11.
16 *Musical America* (25 February 1940), p.31.
17 EF's MS, 'Koerper', p.23.
18 Bernard Greenhouse interview with the author, May 1996, Manchester.
19 Claus Adam, 'Emanual Feuermann: A Tribute 25 Years Later', unpublished typescript, NYp Music Section.
20 Silent, black-and-white archive footage of Feuermann in Zürich and Ascona survives [DC-H] as well as limited footage of the Chatham Square Music School benefit concert.
21 Located in NYp. [See note 19].
22 Bernard Greenhouse interview with the author, May 1996, Manchester.
23 Article by Caroline Heslop, *The Strad* (March 1999), p.263.
24 George Neikrug interview with the author, April 1994, Concord, Massachusetts.

25 Zara Nelsova interview with the author, April 1994, Manchester.
26 EF's MS, '*My dear friend*'.
27 EF's MS, '*My dear friend*', p.12–13.
28 EF's MS, 'Koerper', p.15.
29 EF, 'The Contralto of the String Family', *Etude Music Magazine* (September 1940), p.584.
30 *Musical America* (25 February 1940).
31 EF, 'The Contralto of the String Family', *Etude Music Magazine* (September 1940), p.584.
32 EF's MS, Section C, p.7.
33 EF's MS, 'Koerper', p.20.
34 EF's MS, 'Koerper', p.21.
35 EF's MS, 'Koerper', p.17.
36 EF's MS, Section C, p.6.
37 EF's MS, 'Koerper', pp.17–18.
38 EF's MS, 'Koerper', p.17.
39 EF's MS, '*My dear friend*', p.3.
40 EF's MS, '*My dear friend*', p.8.
41 EF, 'The Contralto of the String Family', *Etude Music Magazine* (September 1940), p.630.
42 EF's MS, '*My dear friend*', p.8.
43 EF, 'Feuermann inveighs against mechanical "methods"', *Musical America* (25 February 1940), p.31.
44 EF, 'The Contralto of the String Family', *Etude Music Magazine* (September 1940), pp.584 and 630.
45 David Soyer interview with the author, April 1994, New York.
46 Bernard Greenhouse interview with the author, May 1996, Manchester.
47 George Sopkin interview with the author, December 1997, Boston, Massachusetts.
48 Gustave Reese for Carl Fischer to Eva Feuermann, 29 June 1945 [FA].
49 Bernard Greenhouse interview with the author, May 1996, Manchester.
50 Janos Starker interview with the author, June 1998, Bloomington, Indiana.
51 Claus Adam interview with Monica Feuermann, 1966 [FA].
52 George Szell interview with Monica Feuermann, 1967 [FA].
53 Szymon Goldberg interview with Monica Feuermann, 1967 [FA].
54 Suzette Forgues interview with the author, April 1994, Long Island.
55 George Sopkin interview with the author, December 1997, Boston, Massachusetts.
56 Mosa Havivi interview with the author, April 1994, New York. Franz Osborn (b.1905) studied at the Berlin Hochschule with Leonid Kreutzer and Schnabel. Feuermann helped the Osborns escape from Germany by securing them affidavits. Max Rostal (b.1905) studied with Carl Flesch at the Berlin Hochschule. Both Osborn and Rostal settled in England in 1934.
57 Daniel Saidenberg interview with Monica Feuermann, 1966 [FA].
58 EF, 'The Contralto of the String Family', *Etude Music Magazine* (September 1940), p.630.
59 George Neikrug interview with the author, April 1994, Concord, Massachusetts.
60 Janos Starker interview with the author, April 1994, Manchester.
61 EF's MS, 'Koerper', p.20.
62 EF's MS, 'Koerper', p.25.
63 Claus Adam interview with Monica Feuermann, 1966 [FA].
64 Suzette Forgues interview with the author, April 1994,. Long Island.

65 *Seattle Violoncello Society Newsletter,* republished in *Violoncello Society, Inc. Newsletter,* Autumn 1996, p.3.

66 David Soyer interview with the author, April 1994, New York.

67 George Neikrug interview with the author, April 1994, Concord, Massachusetts.

68 Bernard Greenhouse interview with the author, May 1996. Manchester. Frank Miller was principal cello of the Chicago Symphony Orchestra and occasionally soloist.

69 Daniel Saidenberg interview with Monica Feuermann, 1966 [FA].

70 George Neikrug interview with the author, April 1994, Concord, Massachusetts.

71 Suzette Forgues interview with the author, April 1994, Long Island.

72 Daniel Saidenberg interview with Monica Feuermann, 1966 [FA].

73 Claus Adam interview with Monica Feuermann, 1966 [FA].

74 George Neikrug interview with the author, April 1994, Concord, Massachusetts.

75 Alan Shulman, 'Music from the Heart', *Violoncello Society Inc. Newsletter* (Autumn, 1995).

76 Suzette Forgues interview with the author, April 1994, Long Island.

77 EF's MS, 'My dear Friend', p.1.

78 EF's MS, 'Koerper', p.25.

79 Ibid, p.26.

80 Georg Ulrich von Bülow telephone interview with the author, 1996, Berlin.

81 Eva Feuermann interview with the author, April 1994, Millbrook, New York.

82 Daniel Saidenberg interview with Monica Feuermann, 1966 [FA].

83 Sophie Feuermann interview with the author, April 1994, New York.

84 Claus Adam interview with Monica Feuermann, 1966 [FA].

85 Sophie Feuermann interview with the author, April 1994, New York.

86 NBC publicity material for 1940/1 season.

87 Bernard Richards interview with the author, May 1994, London.

88 Daniel Saidenberg interview with Monica Feuermann, 1966 [FA].

89 Bernard Richards interview with the author, May 1994, London.

90 Handwritten letter from Peers Coetmore, 55 Belsize Lane, London NW3, to EF, 13 October [no year]. In 1945 Coetmore married the composer E.J. Moeran.

CHAPTER 17: FEUERMANN'S RECORDINGS: EUROPE AND JAPAN

1 Record sleeve notes, 'The Art of Emanuel Feuermann', Mono VIC 1476, 1969 (Mendelssohn, Handel, Beethoven Variations).

2 Chanterelle, Pearl, Biddulph, EMI, RCA, Philips, Naxos.

3 Roger Beardsley, *The Strad* (April 2000). 'From 78 to CD', p.464

4 Ibid.

5 A complete list of recordings and their source is given in Appendix I.

6 Barjansky recorded Bruch's *Kol Nidrei* and Handel Concerto in G minor with Frieder Weissmann on 4 May 1925. Hansfried Sieben, *Parlophon: Matrizen-Nummern der akustischen Aufnahmen 30 cm,* vol. 1: *1910–1926,* Düsseldorf, Herbst, 1990, p.129.

7 Ibid.

8 Samuels, 'Discography', pp.38–42.

9 Samuels, 'Discography', 13/1, p.57.

10 Roland Gelatt, *The Fabulous Phonograph: The Story of the Gramophone from Tin Foil to High Fidelity,* Philadelphia, PA, and New York, 1954.

11 See above, Chapter 9.

12 Sieben, *Parlophon (Band I)*, p.89.

13 The transfer to CD by Pearl (GEMM CDS 9077) is a semitone sharp, implying that the original tempo might have been even slower.

14 Both Feuermann in this 1921 recording and Casals played from the Gevaert edition, but Feuermann introduced more cuts in the slow movement than Casals in his 1916 recording – perhaps because of his slow tempo.

15 Sieben, *Parlophon (Band I)*, p.89.

16 Jon Samuels believes the orchestra were members of the Berlin State Opera. Deutschesmusikarchiv, Berlin lists no orchestra nor does Hansfried Sieben (p.93).

17 Sieben, *Parlophon (Band I)*, p.97.

18 Ibid., p.117.

19 Tests at the National Sound Archive on the English set of 78s of the first movement reveal that it plays in A minor – a 3rd lower in pitch than Pearl's release (GEMM CDS 9077).

20 Jan Smaczny, *Dvořák Cello Concerto*, Cambridge University Press, 1999, p.94.

21 Measurements taken by Mark Obert-Thorn, who has sound-engineered the most accurate release of the first recording complete with additional takes (Naxos 8.110908).

22 See above, p.55.

23 *Gramophone* (March 1935).

24 *Gramophone* (October 1935).

25 Kōsaku Yamada (1886–1965) studied at the Berlin Hochschule with Max Bruch and Karl Leopold Wolf. He was a guest conductor in 1918 of the New York Philharmonic Orchestra, conducting a concert of his own compositions in Carnegie Hall. He was well known for his symphonic music and operas (including one entitled *The Depraved Heavenly Maiden*).

26 Letter from Palmer (or Gaisberg) to EF at the Hyde Park Hotel, 13 November 1935 [EMI Archives].

27 See H.C. Robbins Landon (University College Cardiff Press, 1984).

28 Casals never completed a recording of the Haydn D major. Two acoustic recordings of the slow movement date from 1916 and 1924. A 1945 recording of the first and second movements only was released in 1997 by Biddulph Recordings (LAB 144).

29 *Gramophone* (April 1936).

30 Ibid., p.462.

31 Ibid.

32 The whereabouts of Feuermann's music following his death remains unknown to the author. Sophie Feuermann maintains that much of it was in the hands of Edgar Lustgarten, who died on 25 August 1979.

33 Contract between Feuermann and Mikitaro Miho, president of Nipponophone Co. Ltd. Tokyo, dated 4 June 1936 [FA].

34 International Artistes' Department, Columbia (Gaisberg?) to EF. 16 November 1935 [EMI Music Archives].

35 Palmer telegram to Nippolona, Kawasaki, 14 May 1936 [EMI Music Archives. 68827].

36 Samuels, 'Discography', p.45.

37 In a release on CD by Pearl in 1990, 'Feuermann: The English Columbias', vol. 1, GEMM 9442, it is incorrectly labelled as recorded in 1937.

38 Both performances by Feuermann and Maréchal can be heard on 'Kosçak Yamada Works', CD COCA-13181.

39 I am grateful to Christopher Nozawa for sending in 1996 a cassette tape from his library of these Japanese recordings. Since 1996, two CDs of these works have been

released: 'Lost Feuermann', Music & Arts 2000 (CD 1075); and Cello Classics: 'Emanuel Feuermann' (CC1003).

40 George Neikrug interview with the author, April 1994, Concord, Massachusetts.

41 *Gramophone* (June 1938).

42 Hulda Lashanska (1893–1974) was a soprano of Russian-Jewish descent, notably a student of Marcella Sembrich. Her career was mainly in the USA, where she was known for *Lieder*. She recorded extensively for Victor and Columbia.

43 Letter of contract between RCA Manufacturing Company Inc. and the artists, dated 13 January 1939.

44 EF to Palmer, 1 January 1939 [EMI Archives].

CHAPTER 18: AMERICAN RECORDINGS

1 The contract has not been found but the date is noted in correspondence between Columbia and Nipponophone.

2 Samuels, 'Discography', pp.48–51.

3 George Neikrug interview with the author, April 1994, Concord, Massachusetts.

4 The manuscript is with the Feuermann papers [FA].

5 Sophie Feuermann interview with author, May 1995, New York.

6 Bernard Greenhouse interview with the author, May 1996, Manchester.

7 George Neikrug interview with the author, April 1994, Concord, Masachusetts.

8 A tape of Sarasate's *Zapateado* was given to the author by Sophie Feuermann, who was unable to identify its origin.

9 These performances are housed at the Rogers & Hammerstein Archives of Recorded Sound, New York Public Library for the Performing Arts, Lincoln Center.

10 Samuels, 'Discography', p.49.

11 Constance Hope, director of Red Seal Artist Relations Record Department, to Eva Feuermann, 16 November 1948 [FA].

12 Yo-Yo Ma interview with the author, April 1994, Manchester.

13 In 1932 Feuermann, with Kulenkampff, broadcast the Brahms concerto from Berlin. A shellac from the slow movement was made but has since disappeared (see Appendix III).

14 Gaisberg to Rubinstein, 24 September 1935. See Sachs, *Rubinstein*, p.275.

15 Sophie Feuermann interview with the author, May 1995, New York.

16 Information from Mark Obert-Thorn, transfer engineer of the Brahms Double Concerto for Pearl (GEMM CD 9293) and Naxos (8.110940). These transfers use unpublished alternative takes for the second and third movements of the Brahms.

17 Robert Humphreys, *International News Service* (2 October 1941).

18 *New Leader* [New York City] (25 October 1941).

19 Eugenia Bridges Harty, *Constitution* [Atlanta, Georgia] (5 October 1941).

20 *New York Sun* (26 September 1941).

21 C.A. CAL. Westward. HS NS-Press (10 October 1941).

22 H.T. Baron, *N.Y. Times* [Yonkers] (6 October 1941).

23 Leon Barzin interview with the author, 4 June 1994, Paris. In the 1930s it was not uncommon for orchestral recordings to be made using a single microphone. See Timothy Day, *A Century of Recorded Music*, Yale University Press, 2000, p.24.

24 For a detailed analysis of timings in recordings of the Dvořák Concerto, see Brinton Averil Smith, 'The Physical and Interpretive Technique of Emanuel Feuermann' (Doctoral thesis, Juilliard School of Music, New York 1997).

25 J. Reicha, Concerto in A major, Edwin A. Fleischer Collection, 708c.

26 A Russian edition (1960) and an edition by Rudolf Lojda and Jaroslav Mastalir for Panton (Edice Hudebni Mládeze: Edition Jeunesses Musicales, Prague, 1985) are severely cut in relation to the Simrock edition in the Fleischer Collection.

27 The National Sound Archive at the British Library holds a copy of the London performance on 23 May 1938 dubbed on to 16-inch transcriptions from the short-wave broadcast to New York, which was recorded at the NBC short-wave receiving station.

28 Artur Rubinstein interview with Monica Feuermann, February 1966.

29 *Saturday Review* (24 September 1949).

30 *American Music Lover* (June 1942).

31 Quotation in *Gramophone* (July 1941) taken from M. Tibaldi-Chiesa, *Ernest Bloch*, Turin, 1933.

32 Szymon Goldberg interview with Monica Feuermann, 1966.

33 Abram Chasins, *Leopold Stokowski*, London, Da Capo, 1979, p.118.

34 Connoisseur Society In Synch transfer 1986.

35 *New York Sun* (23 April 1940).

36 *Victor Record Review*, 4/9 (January 1942).

37 Richard Gilbert, 'The Art of the Trio', *Victor Record Review* 4/12 (April 1942), p.6.

38 *New Records*, 12/8 (October 1944), p.5. In 1948 a further movement came to light. See British Museum's Kafka Sketchbook.

39 William Primrose, *Walk on the North Side: William Primrose Memoirs of a Violist*, Brigham Young University, 1978, p.83.

40 Ibid., p.83.

41 Artur Rubinstein interview with Monica Feuermann, 1966.

42 E.W. Rowland, *Artists and Records on Parade* [Commerce, Texas] (28 April 1942).

43 Charles Hoofnagle and Clarence Walton, *Records of the Week: Ledger-Dispatch* [Norfolk, Virginia] (17 April 1942).

44 *American Music Lover* (May 1942).

45 *American Music Lover* (November 1942).

46 See above, Chapter 14 for further extended commentary on the trio recordings.

47 At the age of 86, Hirsch denied he was the pianist, but Jon Samuels insists that he was.

48 *Kölner Zeitung* (12 November 1920).

49 David Soyer interview with the author, April 1994, New York.

50 Eva Feuermann to EF, 17 December 1937 [FA].

51 George Neikrug interview with the author, April 1994, Concord, Massachusetts.

52 It is worth noting that Piatigorsky also never issued the complete suites. The various movements he recorded were either not to his liking or incompatible for release with other repertoire [Terry King].

Appendix I: Feuermann's Fees

1 Information received from the archives of the Cleveland, Chicago and Boston symphony orchestras.

2 The American Federation of Musicians successfully blocked the orchestra from radio appearances and, threatening the record companies with a strike if non-unionized musicians were allowed to record, effectively removed the BSO from RCA Victor.

3 Adolf Busch, *Letters*, vol. 2, p.398.

4 Casals's last concert appearance in the United States took place in 1928 and he did not set foot there again for 30 years.

5 EF to Kux, 2 March 1940 [FA].

6 David Soyer interview with the author, April 1994, New York.

7 Bernard Greenhouse interview with the author, May 1996, Manchester.

8 EF to Emma Reifenberg, 3 May 1940 [FA]. In May 1940, Feuermann indicated in a letter that Mrs Reifenberg would enjoy an annual income of $15,000, just over $192,000 today.

9 EF to Lily Hofmann, 17 November 1939 [DC-H].

APPENDIX II: FEUERMANN'S CELLOS, BOWS, STRINGS

1 Havivi interview with the author, April 1994, New York.

2 Sophie Feuermann interview with the author, May 1995, New York.

3 Certificate 9238 dated 19 March 1948. The Rudolph Wurlitzer Co. I am indebted to Martha Babcock for supplying this information.

4 I am indebted to Erling Blöndal Bengtsson for supplying information about the cello's repair in Copenhagen.

5 *Winnipeg Free Press* (1 December 1934).

6 Copy of Hill certificate supplied by Guy Fallot.

7 Copy of Hill letter supplied by William Moennig & Son Ltd, Philadelphia, Pennsylvania.

8 Rudolph Wurlitzer to C.H. Huberich, 11 February 1943 [FA].

9 EF to Wilhelm Kux, 24 July 1940 [FA].

10 Vatelot, *Les Archets français*, vol.2, Paris, Sernor-Dufour, 1977, p.984.

11 Suzette Forgues interview with the author, April 1994, Long Island, USA.

APPENDIX III: CHRONOLOGICAL LIST OF KNOWN RECORDING SESSIONS AND BROADCASTS

1 Sources: Hansfried Sieben, *Parlophon: Die Matrizen-Nummern der akustischen (und elektrischen) Aufnahmen 30cm*, Düsseldorf, Herbst, 1990, vols 1–3; Radio programmes: Deutsches Rundfunkarchiv, Frankfurt; Deutschesmusik Archiv, Berlin; Christopher Nozawa, Japan; Jon Samuels, 'A Complete Discography of the Recordings of Emanuel Feuermann', *Association for Recorded Sound Collections: Journal*, 12/1–3 (1980).

2 Also broadcast over Berliner Gleichwelle Berlin II, Stettin, Magdeburg on 1058 kHz, 283,6 m, 0,5 kw.

3 Ibid.

4 Ibid.

5 Ibid.

6 Also broadcast over Freiberg i. BR 527 kHz, 569,3 m, 0,25 kW.

7 Also broadcast over Dresden 941 kHz, 318,8 m, 0,25 kW.

8 Also broadcast over Berliner Gleichwelle Berlin II, Stettin, Magdeburg on 1058 kHz, 283,6 m, 0,5 kw.

9 Source: Christopher Nozawa, Japan.

10 Source: Christopher Nozawa, Japan.

Select Bibliography

Principal unpublished sources

Letters of Emanuel Feuermann in the possession of his widow, Eva Feuermann Lehnsen [FA]; letters of Emanuel Feuermann to Lily Hofmann (née Mayer) in the possession of her daughter, Daniela Cohn-Hofmann [DC-H]; letters of Emanuel Feuermann to Lilli Reifenberg in the possession of her daughter, Eva Nizan [N]; letters to Emanuel Feuermann from Emma and Paul Reifenberg and Eva Reifenberg in the possession of Eva Feuermann Lehnsen [FA]; correspondence between Emanuel Feuermann and Bronisław Huberman (Felicija Blumental Music Centre and Library, Tel Aviv) [HA]; correspondence between Emanuel Feuermann and Columbia Graphophone Company, Nipponophone (EMI Music Archives) and RCA Manufacturing Company, Inc.[FA].

Unpublished writings of Emanuel Feuermann: '*Notes and some anecdotes about Feuermann written by himself*' [FA]; '*My dear friend*' [FA]; 'Koerper' [FA]; A (6 page section) [FA]; B (2 page section) [FA]; C (10 page section) [FA].

Printed sources

Axelrod, Herbert. *Heifetz*, Neptune, NJ, Paganiniana Publications, 1976.

Baldock, Robert. *Pablo Casals*, London, Gollancz, 1992.

Beller, Steven. *Vienna and the Jews: 1867–1938*, Cambridge University Press 1989.

Bickel, Sh., ed. *Pinkes Kolomey* [Memorial book of [P.] Kolomey], New York, 1957. [Yiddish]

Brandt, Nat. *Con Brio*, Oxford University Press, 1993.

Busch, Adolf. *Letters–Pictures–Memories*, vols.1 and 2, Walpole, NH, Arts & Letters Press, 1991.

Campbell, Margaret. *The Great Cellists*, London, Gollancz, 1988.

Cardus, Neville. *Sir Thomas Beecham*, London, Collins, 1961.

Chasins, Abram. *Leopold Stokowski*, London, Da Capo, 1979.

Chernow, Ron. *The Warburgs*, New York, Random House, 1993.

Chotzinoff, Samuel. *A Lost Paradise*, New York, Alfred A. Knopf, 1955.

Corredor, José María. *Conversations avec Casals: souvenirs et opinions d'un musicien*, Paris, Albin Michel, 1955.

Crawford, Dorothy. *Evenings On and Off the Roof*, University of California Press, 1995.

Dawidowicz, Lucy. *The War Against the Jews*, London, Weidenfeld & Nicolson, 1975.

Day, Timothy. *A Century of Recorded Music*, Yale University Press, 2000.

Dümling, Albrecht. 'On the Road to the "People's Community": The Forced Conformity of the Berlin Academy of Music Under Fascism', *The Musical Quarterly*, 77/3 (1993), pp.459–83.

Ennulat, Egbert M. *Arnold Schönberg Correspondence*, Metuchen, NJ, Scarecrow Press, 1991.

Farrer, David. *The Warburgs*, London, Joseph, 1975.

Feuermann, E. 'Feuermann inveighs against Mechanical "Methods"', *Musical America*, 25 February 1940.

Feuermann, E. 'The Contralto of the String family', *Etude Music Magazine*, September 1940.

Feuermann, E. ed. Rose Heylbut, 'Music Marches With Uncle Sam', *Etude Music Magazine*, October 1942.

Fischer-Defoy, Christine. *Kunst Macht Politik: Die Nazifizierung der Kunst und Musikhochschulen in Berlin*, Berlin, Elefanten Press, 1987.

Flesch, Carl. *And Do You Also Play the Violin?*, London, Toccata Press, 1990.

Flesch, Carl. *The Memoirs of Carl Flesch*, trs. Hans Keller, Bois de Boulogne, Centenary Edition, Harlow, 1973.

Forner, Johannes, ed. *Hochschule für Musik und Theater 'Felix Mendelssohn Bartholdy' Leipzig: 150 Jahre Musikhochschule 1843–1993*, Leipzig, Verlag Kunst und Touristik, 1993.

Gaisberg, Fred. *The Music Goes Round*, New York, Macmillan, 1942.

Gay, Peter. *Freud, Jews and Other Germans: Masters and Victims in Modernist Culture*, Oxford University Press, 1979.

Gay, Peter. *Weimar Culture: The Outsider as Insider*, London, Secker and Warburg, 1969.

Geissmar, Berta. *The Baton and the Jackboot*, London, Hamish Hamilton, 1944.

Gelatt, Roland. *The Fabulous Phonograph: The Story of the Gramophone from Tin Foil to High Fidelity*, Philadelphia, PA, and New York, J.B. Lippincott, 1955.

Gillies, Malcolm, ed. *The Bartók Companion*, London, Faber and Faber, 1994.

The Gramophone Shop Encyclopaedia of Recorded Music, supervising editor: Robert H. Reid, New York, Crown Publishers, 1948.

Grünberger, Richard. *A Social History of the Third Reich*, London, Weidenfeld & Nicolson, 1971.

Hacohen-Yellin, Viola, ed. *Thelma Yellin-Bentwich. Letters written between 1911–1959*, 2001 (unpublished).

Haggin, B.H. *Conversations with Toscanini*, New York, Doubleday, 1959.

Hailey, Christopher. *Franz Schreker 1878–1934. A Cultural Biography*, Cambridge University Press, 1993.

Helter, M., ed. *Sefer Kolo* [Memorial book of [P.] Kolo], Tel Aviv, 1958. [Hebrew, Yiddish]

Heyworth, Peter. *Otto Klemperer: His Life and Times, vol.1: 1885–1933*, Cambridge University Press, 1983.

Heyworth, Peter. *Otto Klemperer: His Life and Times, vol.2: 1933–1973*, Cambridge University Press, 1996.

Hindemith, Paul. The collection. Yale University Music Library Archival Collection MSS 47. New Haven, CT, 1994.

Hindemith. *Das private Logbuch, 'Briefe an seine Frau Gertrud'*. Serie Musik, Piper-Schott. Band 8355, Mainz, Schott, *c.* 1995.

Hirschberg, Jehoash. *Music in the Jewish Community of Palestine 1880–1948*, Oxford, Clarendon Paperbacks, 1995.

Hurok, Salomon. *Impresario*, London, Macdonald & Co., 1947.

Ibbeken, Ida, ed. *The Listener Speaks: 55 Years of Letters from the Audience to Bronisław Huberman*, Ramoth Hashawin, 1961.

Ibbeken, Ida and Avni, Tzvi, eds. *An Orchestra is Born: A Monument to B. Huberman*, Tel Aviv, 'Yachdav' United Publishers Co. Ltd, 1969. [The founding of the Palestinian Orchestra as reflected in Bronisław Huberman's letters, speeches and articles, compiled from the Huberman Archives in the Central Music Library in Israel.]

Itzkoff, Seymour. *Emanuel Feuermann, Virtuoso: A Biography*, University of Alabama Press, 1979.

Jezic, Diane Peacock. *The Musical Migration and Ernst Toch*, Iowa State University Press, 1989.

Katz, Jacob. *From Prejudice to Destruction*, Harvard University Press, 1980.

Kennedy, Michael. *Barbirolli: Conductor Laureate*, London, MacGibbon and Kee, 1971.

Lebrecht, Norman. *When the Music Stops*, London, Simon & Schuster, 1996.

Lee, Sebastian, revised and enlarged by E. Feuermann and J. Sakom. *Praktische Violoncello-Schule (Op.30)*, Leipzig, Anton J. Benjamin 1929.

Levi, Erik. *Music in the Third Reich*, London, Macmillan, 1994.

Lowe, Jaques. *The Incredible Music Machine*, London, Quartet/Visual Arts, 1982.

Mayer, Bernhard. *Memoirs of a Jewish Merchant and Cosmopolitan 1866–1946*, Konstanz, Hartung-Gorre Verlag, 1998.

Mayer, Hans. *Gelebte Musik Erinnerungen*, Frankfurt am Main, Suhrkamp Verlag, 1999.

Menuhin, Yehudi. *Unfinished Journey*, London, Macdonald & Jane's, 1977.

Merrill-Mirsky, Carol. *Exiles in Paradise*, Exhibition catalogue, Hollywood Bowl Museum, 1991.

Milstein, Nathan and Volkov, Solomon. *From Russia to the West*, New York, Henry Holt, 1990.

Moore, Gerald. *Am I too loud?: Memoirs of an Accompanist*, London, Hamish Hamilton, 1962.

Muck, Peter. *Einhundert Jahre Berliner Philharmonisches Orchester*, vol.3: Hans Schneider, Tutzing, 1982.

Noy, D. and Schutzman, M., eds. *Sefer zikaron le-kehilat Kolomey ve-ha-seviva* [Kolomeyer memorial book], Tel Aviv, 1972. [Hebrew]

O'Connell, Charles. *The Other Side of the Record*, New York, Knopf, 1947.

Owen, Laurinel. *Bowed Arts – Reflections of Bernard Greenhouse on his Life and Music*, Kronberg im Taunus, Kronberg Academy Verlag, 2001.

Philip, Robert. *Early Recording and Musical Style*, Cambridge University Press, 1992.

Piatigorsky, Gregor. *Cellist*, New York, Doubleday & Company Inc., 1965.

Prieberg, Fred. *Trial of Strength: Furtwängler and the Third Reich*, London, Quartet Books, 1991.

Primrose, William. *Walk on the North Side: William Primrose Memoirs of a Violist*, Provo, Utah, Brigham Young University, 1978.

Procter-Gregg, Humphrey, ed. *Beecham Remembered*, London, Duckworth, 1976.

Ringer, Alexander L. *Arnold Schönberg*, Oxford, Clarendon, 1990.

Rubinstein, Arthur. *My Many Years*, London, Cape, 1980.

Rubinstein, Arthur. *My Young Years*, New York, Alfred A. Knopf, 1973.

Sachs, Harvey. *Arthur Rubinstein: A Life*, New York, Grove Press, 1995.

Sachs, Harvey. *Reflections on Toscanini*, London, Robson Books, 1992.

Sachs, Harvey. *Toscanini*, London, Weidenfeld & Nicholson, 1978.

Sachs, Harvey. *The Letters of Arturo Toscanini*, London, Faber and Faber, 2002.

Saerchinger, Cesar. *Artur Schnabel: A Biography*, New York, Dodd, Mead & Co., 1957.

Saleski, Gdal. *Famous Musicians of a Wandering Race*, New York, Bloch Publishing Company, 1927.

Samuels, Jon. 'A Complete Discography of the Recordings of Emanuel Feuermann', *Association for Recorded Sound Collections: Journal*, XII, 1–2; 1980.

Schnabel, Artur. *My Life and Music*, New York, St Martins Press, 1963.

Schoenfeld, Joachim. *Shtetl Memoirs: Jewish Life in Galicia Under the Austro-Hungarian Empire and in Reborn Poland 1898–1939*, Hoboken, NJ, Ktav Publishing House, Inc., 1985.

Schorske, Carl E. *Fin de Siècle Vienna: Politics and Culture*, New York, Knopf, 1980.

Shanet, Howard. *Philharmonic: A History of New York's Orchestra*, New York, Doubleday, 1975.

Sieben, Hansfried. *Parlophon: Die Matrizen-Nummern der akustischen Aufnahmen 30 cm*, vol.1: *1910–1926*, Düsseldorf, Herbst, 1990.

Sieben, Hansfried. *Parlophon: Die Matrizen-Nummern der elektrischen Aufnahmen 30 cm*, vol.2: *1926–1933*, Düsseldorf, Herbst, 1990.

Skelton, Geoffrey. *Paul Hindemith: The Man Behind the Music*, London, Gollancz, 1975.

Skelton, Geoffrey. *Selected Letters of Paul Hindemith*, London, Yale University Press, 1995.

Smaczny, Jan. *Dvořák Cello Concerto*, Cambridge University Press, 1999.

Smith, Brinton Averil. 'The Physical and Interpretive Technique of Emanuel Feuermann' (Doctoral thesis, Juilliard School of Music, New York, 1997).

Stargardt-Wolff, Edith. *Wegbereiter grosser Musiker*, Berlin, Bote & Bock, 1954.

Stuckenschmidt, Hans Heinz. *Arnold Schönberg*, London, John Calder, 1959.

Taylor, Fred. *The Goebbels Diaries 1939–1941*, London, Hamish Hamilton, 1982.

Temianka, Henri. *Facing the Music*, New York, David McKay, 1973.

Vatelot, Etienne. *Les Archets français*, vol.2, Paris, Sernor-Dufour, 1977.

Walter, Bruno. *Theme and Variations*, London, Hamish Hamilton, 1947.

Weschler-Vered, Artur. *Jascha Heifetz*, New York, Schirmer Books, 1986.

Willett, John. *Art & Politics in the Weimar Period: The New Sobriety 1917–1933*, New York, Pantheon Books, 1978.

Index

Accompanying CD: Track Listing

Words will never replace the sound of Feuermann's playing. The selection of excerpts on this CD aims to give the reader an indelible impression of Feuermann's artistry. Special thanks are due to Jon Samuels, Julian Futter, Keith Harvey and Peter Mann for supplying the rarest of records and to Sebastian Comberti for producing the CD. This selection of tracks presents Feuermann as concerto soloist, duo partner, chamber musician and solo player over a recording career of 20 years.

Re-mastering by Morgan Roberts at The Classical Recording Company

Track 1 (pp. 24, 297)
1921 Haydn, Cello Concerto in D (Hob. VIIb:2): third movement. 3.36
Frieder S. Weissmann (conductor) with members of the Berlin State Opera Orchestra.

Track 2 (p. 298)
1922 Sarasate, '*Zigeunerweisen*' (first part) (arr. Feuermann) 3.46
Frieder S. Weissmann, piano.

Track 3 (pp. 37, 298)
1927 Sarasate, '*Zigeunerweisen*' (first part) (arr. Feuermann) 3.44
Michael Taube, piano.

Track 4 (pp. 38, 300–2)
April 1928 Dvořák, Cello Concerto in B minor op.104: first movement
(excerpt)   9.33
Michael Taube (conductor) with members of the Berlin State Opera
Orchestra.

Track 5 (p. 295)
1932 Popper, 'Papillon'   1.27
Arpad Sandor, piano.

Track 6 (pp. 76, 305)
1934 Gluck, Mélodie from *Orphée* (arr. Grünfeld)   3.15
Theo van der Pas, piano.

Track 7 (pp. 118–21, 306–8)
1935 Haydn, Cello Concerto in D (Hob. VIIb:2): first movement   14.23
Malcolm Sargent (conductor) with unnamed symphony orchestra.

Track 8 (p. 310)
1936 Chopin, Nocturne in E♭, op.9 no.2 (arr. Feuermann)   4.12
Wolfgang Rebner, piano.

Track 9 (pp. 156, 311–12)
1937 Schubert, 'Arpeggione' Sonata: first movement   7.03
Gerald Moore, piano.

Track 10 (pp. 239, 331)
1941 Brahms, Piano Trio no.1 in B op.8: Scherzo (revised version)   5.44
Jascha Heifetz, violin and Artur Rubinstein, piano.

Track 11 (pp. 223, 322–4)
1940 Dvořák, Cello Concerto in B minor op.104: third movement   10.38
Leon Barzin (conductor) with the National Orchestral Association.

Track 12 (pp. 211, 333)
1939 Bach, Cello Suite no.3 BWV 1009: Sarabande and Bourées I and II 6.43
(announced by Feuermann).

Total running time   74.52